TROPICAL AFRICA

VOLUME I LAND AND LIVELIHOOD

PARTICIPANTS IN THE STUDY

CONSULTANTS: Sir Philip Mitchell, G.C.M.G., *Chief Consultant*; Stanley G. Browne, M.D., B. J. Garnier, J. H. G. Lebon, J. Gus Liebenow, Leo Silberman.

CONTRIBUTORS OF WORKING PAPERS: David E. Apter, Nancy Gouinlock Berg, Kenneth Bradley, George W. Carpenter, R. J. Harrison Church, James S. Coleman, L. Gray Cowan, Frank Debenham, Hubert Deschamps, Walter Deshler, St. Clair and Elizabeth Drake, Eugene P. Dvorin, F. Grévisse, Alfred and Grace G. Harris, George R. Horner, D. Hobart Houghton, Sir Bernard A. Keen, Hibberd V. B. Kline, Jr., Gaston Leduc, Jacques Lefebvre, Jacques J. Maquet, Jacques M. May, M.D., Peveril Meigs, Paul Mercier, N. C. Mitchel, Eduardo C. Mondlane, William Dawson Moreland, Jr., W. B. Morgan, Thomas G. Murdock, Margaret Nairn, B. S. Platt, R. M. Prothero, Tor Fr. Rasmussen, Rebecca Reyher, Kurt Roselius, Cecil W. Scott, Ruth C. Sloan, Helmer Smeds, Hugh Tracey, Glenn T. Trewartha, Kimani Waiyaki, A. T. de B. Wilmot, Alvin D. Zalinger, Wilbur Zelinsky.

MAPS: Robert C. Kingsbury, *Cartographic Editor*; Patricia R. Kingsbury and Jean Paul Tremblay, *Cartographers*.

PHOTOGRAPHS: Omar Marcus, *Photographer*; Anita Ventura, *Picture Editor*.

TROPICAL AFRICA

VOLUME ONE

LAND AND LIVELIHOOD

BY GEORGE H. T. KIMBLE

THE TWENTIETH CENTURY FUND

NEW YORK · 1960

The following firms in Germany generously presented the study's photographer with photographic equipment: Albert Schacht G.m.b.H., Optical Equipment, Ulm, Donau; Multiblitz, Mannesmann Electronic Equipment, Porz-Westhoven, Cologne; Agfacolor, AGFA A.G., Leverkusen.

FOREWORD

To EMBARK upon a major study of tropical Africa seemed to the Trustees of the Fund a challenging undertaking when it was first considered. The years during which this book has been written have certainly not made the task any easier, or any less important.

These years have seen swift and profound changes in the political structure of tropical Africa. The flood of independent nations beginning in the fall of 1958 has advanced by a schedule which foreshortened history and radically compressed time itself. To keep up with such a situation means, necessarily, to go below the surface. That is what the author has aimed to do, projecting the basic conditions which set the framework within which change occurs.

The Twentieth Century Fund considers itself fortunate in having secured George H. T. Kimble, now of Indiana University, as director of the study. A geographer by profession, Dr. Kimble interprets geography to involve not merely physical facts but the whole mysterious relationship between man and the environment of which he is a part. A scholar, Dr. Kimble does not assume that scholarship precludes good writing. The number of people who helped in gathering and weighing the information is indicated by the Acknowledgments; yet the whole massive body of fact has been shaped by the mind of one man and bears the unmistakable imprint of his style.

It is a particular pleasure to record here the help provided the project at a critical stage by President Herman B Wells of Indiana University. He cooperated with the Fund in making possible Dr. Kimble's freedom to complete the work, though it meant postponing teaching and administrative services which the University was anxious to draw upon. As a result the large undertaking has been brought to conclusion in the happiest of circumstances.

For Americans to know what they should do about the problem of African development is important. But it is important, first of all, that they know the full facts about Africa itself. The danger, from the point of view of a sound policy and approach, is that the complete ignorance which formerly prevailed should be replaced by incomplete knowledge.

FOREWORD

The issues in this part of the world are of an importance which calls for the fullest possible understanding.

The Fund hopes that this study will make a contribution to knowledge about Africa — the startling kind of knowledge which may let Americans see what is really there and not merely what their imagination and unanalyzed assumptions have told them is there.

AUGUST HECKSCHER
Director, The Twentieth Century Fund

41 East 70th Street, New York
August 1960

ACKNOWLEDGMENTS

N<small>O BOOK</small> is entirely the author's own, and probably few books are less so than this one. It might even be contended that the main reason for having a single name on the title page is that somebody had to take responsibility for the mistakes! Certainly, to have listed all those who had a hand in this book would have set the printer a ticklish problem, and heaven knows he has had his share of problems. From start (all too long ago) to finish (if, indeed, such a theme is ever finished), *Tropical Africa* has been nourished by many minds and groomed by many more.

The idea for the book came from Evans Clark, before his retirement as Executive Director of the Twentieth Century Fund. The material for it was derived in large measure from the working papers of the forty-six contributors listed opposite the title page. Material was also provided, along with much excellent criticism, by those — likewise listed opposite the title page — who served as consultants, and by those who did the map-making and photography. No less substantial was the help, administrative and editorial, supplied by colleagues in the Fund. Individually smaller but indispensable contributions were made by persons (on a conservative count, more than a thousand) in Africa, Europe and the United States who uncomplainingly endured the author's questioning, and greatly facilitated his field work and that of his associates. The study's photographer, in particular, received courtesies and help from innumerable sources on his travels in Africa. The author owes hardly less to people he never met — newspapermen, novelists, Africanists and others whose insights into what has been happening in tropical Africa during the time of its travail have been a constant source of illumination. To all of these he tenders his sincere thanks.

Inevitably, an author senses a deeper indebtedness to some than to others. Special thanks are due to Sir Philip Mitchell, who read and reported on each working paper, on the draft of each chapter and on several hundred galleys, and who was at once an uncompromising critic, a wise counselor and an elegant host. Similar thanks are due to Dr. Herman B Wells, President of Indiana University, for providing office space and granting released time during the later stages of the study; to Robert

ACKNOWLEDGMENTS

Lemaignen and Emmanuel Mayolle for their sustained interest and memorable Gallic hospitality; and to August Heckscher, Director of the Twentieth Century Fund, for his energetic support and encouragement. Also gratefully acknowledged is the invaluable assistance of Paul M. Henry, Ian Hess, Phyllis M. Horwitz, Lilly Kay (Lesin), André Némo, Esther I. Persson, Anne C. de Nanteuil, Anna Rapaport (Paul), Hugo Fosco, Ian B. Thompson, Roger Vaurs and Richard E. Webb. Most of all, the author wishes to pay tribute to his editor, Elizabeth Blackert, Assistant to the Director of the Fund. Her understanding of what a book should be is matched only by her ability to delude an author into thinking he can write that kind of book, and to make any book better than it would otherwise have been. Her exertions to this end will long be remembered with appreciation — and awe.

GEORGE H. T. KIMBLE

Solsberry, Indiana

Information obtainable in the summer of 1960 is included in Selected Territorial Data (Vol. II, p. 445). Elsewhere the record is brought up to the end of 1959 or early 1960, within the limits of the data available at that time.

CONTENTS

CONTENTS

TABLES

VOLUME I

TABLES

TABLES

ILLUSTRATIONS

VOLUME I

ILLUSTRATIONS

LAND AND LIVELIHOOD

Wʜᴇɴ David Livingstone "discovered" tropical Africa a century or so ago, most Americans were too busy discovering their own country to pay much heed to his despatches. Of those who went there in his footsteps, few came back. Those who did had no great opinion of the place. It was a white man's grave, and, what with its slave raiding, its tribal warfare, its hungry seasons and its climate of fear, no health resort for the African either. There were, seemingly, no prairies to plow; no uniform stands of timber to cut; and no minerals worth talking about. Nobody had anything to sell or any great need to buy. It was, they said, little more than a Stone Age museum; and no American was then greatly interested in the Stone Age. Accordingly, it was ignored as far as possible.

Many people still think of tropical Africa as a kind of museum, but the day when it could be ignored has gone, for several reasons.

First, the "exhibits," as we took them to be, are very much alive. True, the signs of life are not always to the taste of the attendants or, for that matter, the spectators, but like those of a lusty-lunged infant, they succeed in attracting the attention of everybody within earshot. In these days it is only a matter of hours before a cry uttered in secret in the Congo is heard on the rooftops of Manhattan. Therefore, even if we wish to do so, we cannot remain ignorant of the region.

Second, tropical Africa is no longer, so to speak, an island "intire of itselfe." Rather is it a pivotal part of "the main." It has a foot in all four hemispheres. Its western borders are no farther from the Americas than its northern borders are from Europe or its eastern borders from Soviet Asia. Its heartland is handier to Moscow than Texas is, and more tempting strategically. Economically, no area in the world is more dependent upon external demand. The involvement of tropical Africa "in mankinde" is no less great politically. How Ghana resolves its governmental problems, whether in favor of democracy or authoritarianism, is a matter of concern for the friends — and the enemies — of freedom everywhere. So, too, is the manner in which the Federation of Rhodesia and Nyasaland resolves its racial problems.

Third, its peoples plainly do not intend to be ignored. The Nkrumahs, Tourés and Mboyas of tropical Africa are among the most articulate of men and among the most successful in making themselves heard, whether in the United Nations, the Afro-Asian conferences or elsewhere. Tropical African students are fanning out all over the Western and non-Western worlds in search of new knowledge, skills and friends. Tropical African artists and men of letters are busy creating (or re-creating) an "African personality" and selling their images of it on the overseas intellectual market.

Fourth, and related, the peoples of tropical Africa are no longer ignorant of us. Eighth graders in the schools of Nigeria know more about the American way of life than the average American sophomore knows about the Canadian. Decisions reached on Capitol Hill yesterday are being discussed today in the hills of Ethiopia and Uganda. The ripples made by our "Little Rocks" have a habit of penetrating almost overnight into the backwaters of the Zambezi.

And, fifth, the region almost certainly has the world's largest untapped reservoir of natural resources. It has workable deposits of almost every important mineral; enough falling water to supply the world with hydro-electric power; and enough hardwoods to keep it in such things as veneers, cellulose, plastics and industrial alcohol. A dozen nations have already beaten a path to the African's door for the purpose of helping him develop these resources, in his interest as in their own. And each year the path is getting busier.

Self-interest — to invoke no higher motive — demands that we take cognizance of these facts. It also demands that we try to see the significance of what is happening to the land and its people, to their livelihood, welfare and development.

What is the land of tropical Africa? Areally, it is that part of the mainland and those offshore islands lying between the Sahara and the Limpopo River — the region, roughly, between the Tropics of Cancer and Capricorn. Environmentally, it is a mosaic. Large parts of it conform to the Hollywood stereotypes of dank, gloomy forest where bread and boots go moldy in a night, and baked, shimmering veld where shade is precious and water the greatest wealth. But parts of it are neither very African nor very tropical. Some look and are like the hills of Idaho and Wyoming, where a man can see a hundred and fifty miles and be glad of a blanket on the bed almost any night in the year. Others are as bare as the Painted Desert and every bit as beautiful. The region presents as many different types of landscape as do all the fifty states. And the environmental variety goes deeper. Differences arising from sunshine and soil, height and slope, moisture and drainage are compounded by differences in the distribution of cultivable and edible plants, noxious insects and useful animals, malleable metal and clay, workable wood and reed, and harnessable power. The land is more than mineral, vegetable and animal. For most of its indigenous inhabitants it is the begetter of the unborn, the upholder of the living, the custodian of the dead; it is, in fact, "mother earth."

The people are as various as the land. They consist, on the most conservative basis of reckoning, of not less than 600 groups — African,[1] European and Asian — that do enough things differently from their neighbors to be recognizably different. Most of these 600 groups talk differently from their neighbors, sometimes so differently that villagers living on opposite banks of a river are unable to communicate with each other. Many of them have different ways of raising food and family, of settling disputes, of dealing with illnesses and emergencies, and even of burying the dead.

Superimposed on these cultural differences, but in no sense obliterating them, are the differences resulting from the "opening up" of Africa by European powers in the nineteenth and early twentieth centuries. Largely as a result of their exertions, the people today live under 41 different managements, none of which is entirely of their own devising, or entirely of their wanting. It is true that the Republic of Guinea, Liberia, Ghana, the Republic of Sudan and Ethiopia are now (as of December 1959) self-managing. But in none of these are the territorial boundaries coincident with cultural boundaries, and in no case are all the included peoples well pleased with the arrangements. The other 36 units still owe varying degrees of allegiance to their European founders. Six of them — (French) Togo, the British Cameroons, the French Cameroons, (Belgian) Ruanda-Urundi, (Italian) Somalia and (British) Tanganyika — are administered as United Nations Trust Territories. Four are administered as "overseas provinces" of Portugal: Portuguese Guinea, São Tomé and Príncipe Islands, Angola and Mozambique. One is administered as a colony of Spain, namely, Spanish Guinea (including Fernando Po and neighboring islands). One, the Belgian Congo, is administered as a colony of Belgium. Five are British protectorates: Bechuanaland, British Somaliland, Northern Rhodesia, Nyasaland and Uganda. Four — Gambia, Sierra Leone, Nigeria and Kenya — have the status of British "colony and protectorate." One, Zanzibar (including Pemba), has the status of a British-protected sultanate. And one, Southern Rhodesia, is a self-governing British colony.[2] Twelve are administered as "autonomous republics" of the French Community, namely, the Malagasy Republic (formerly Madagascar), the Islamic Republic of Mauritania (formerly Mauritania), the Sudanese Republic (formerly French Sudan, and not to be confused with the Republic of Sudan), the Republic of Senegal, the Republic of Chad, the Gabon Republic, the Republic of the Congo (formerly Middle Congo), the Central African Republic (formerly Ubangi-Shari), the Republic of Dahomey, the Republic of the Ivory Coast, the

---

[1] An "African," in the customary sense of the term, is a person whose forebears were domiciled in Africa before the coming of the European and Asian. The term is so used throughout this study except where otherwise indicated.

[2] The federating of the two Rhodesias and Nyasaland in 1953, to form the Federation of Rhodesia and Nyasaland, while it added yet another management, did not alter the existing constitutional relationships.

Republic of the Upper Volta (also called the Voltaic Republic) and the Republic of the Niger. One, French Somaliland, is administered as part of overseas France.

The most populous of the 41, Nigeria, has by now nearly 35 million inhabitants, or twice as many as New York State and more than half as many again as the next most populous territory, Ethiopia (including Eritrea). The least populous territory, São Tomé and Príncipe, has about 62,000 inhabitants; this is less than one eighth the population of the Nigerian city of Ibadan.

All told, the 41 territories have a population of probably not less than 167 million and occupy an area well over twice the size of the United States. They constitute the largest understudied and underdeveloped area in the world and, in the opinion of many, the most underrated.

CHAPTER 1

Economic Life at the Turn of the Century

THE LABORER

CHARACTERISTIC LIVELIHOODS

STANDARDS OF LIVING

SYSTEMS OF LAND TENURE

Before we can begin to appreciate the magnitude, to say nothing of the meaning, of the changes that are taking place in the land and life of tropical Africa, we need to remind ourselves of the kind of place it was before these changes came about.

Not that it was ever unchanging. Long before the technician arrived with his bag of tricks, other agents of change had been at work. There were the slave traders. On the east coast, Africans had been carried off by Arabs to the slave markets of the Middle East for hundreds of years, perhaps for more than a millennium. On the west coast, the slave trade began only in the fifteenth century, but quickly gathered momentum with the establishment of plantation agriculture in the New World. On both sides of the continent it had resulted in the depopulation of great tracts of land, the breakdown of the economic and social life of a great many more, the removal of the young and virile to the detriment of the breeding lines, and the spread of old diseases and the introduction of new ones. It also engendered new fears and hatreds, and forms of violence that did nothing to ease the task of those who followed in its wake. The slave traders were responsible for other changes, too. It was they, along with those in search of more legitimate business, who introduced into Africa maize (corn), manioc (cassava), tobacco, the potato, peanut, papaya, cayenne pepper and tomato. By the end of the nineteenth century most of these crops had penetrated deep into the heart of Africa, becoming an integral part of the daily diet in some cases.

From still earlier times there had been peaceful infiltrations of the Sudanese grasslands and the highlands of east Africa by peoples of Arabian origin, resulting in intermarriage with Bantu, Negro and Hamite, and the widespread acceptance of many foreign things. Among these were the Islamic religion, some useful crops including, it seems, the greater yam, banana and taro, some equally useful animals including the pig, the sheep, the camel, the chicken and the goat, and a *lingua franca*, Swahili, based largely on Arabic words. There had also been invasions of Bantu by Hamite and of Negro and negroid pygmy by Bantu that led in some places to cultural collapse, but in others to the creation of new cultures far outstripping their predecessors. And in many "untouched" tribal areas there had been prophets who, as the spokesmen for the dead custodians of their tradition, had succeeded in getting many innovations enshrined in the law and custom of the land.

In a sense, then, the surging flood of economic, social and political change of the past half century has been merely "an extension into the present of a continuing characteristic of African life," made apparent by the study of pre-European African history and "reinforced by the logic of the differences discernible in the distribution of physical types, languages and cultures over this great land mass." [1]

At the same time, until the end of the nineteenth century, there were features of the life and livelihood of many groups that, so far as anyone can see, had not altered significantly for hundreds of years. Sir Philip Mitchell's now classical description of the people of British East Africa as the British found them round about 1890 would appear to apply just as well to most east African people of about 1500, or earlier:

Inland of the narrow coastal strip they had no units of government of any size or stability; indeed with a few exceptions such as Buganda, nothing beyond local chiefs or patriarchs. They had no wheeled transport and (apart from the camels and donkeys of the pastoral nomads) no animal transport either; they had no roads nor towns; no tools except small hand hoes, axes, wooden digging sticks and the like; no manufactures, and no industrial products except the simplest domestic handiwork; no commerce as we understand it and no currency, although in some places barter of produce was facilitated by the use of small shells; they had never heard of working for wages. They went stark naked or clad in the bark of trees or the skins of animals, and they had no means of writing, even by hieroglyphics, nor of numbering except by their fingers or making notches on a stick or knots in a piece of grass or fibre; they had no weights and measures of general use. Perhaps most astonishing of all to the modern European mind they had no calendar nor notation of time, and reckoned by the moons and seasons and the rising and setting of the sun. Before European occupation there was no way of saying "1st January, 1890" or "2:30 p.m." or their equivalents in any language spoken from Abyssinia to the Transvaal, except Swahili on the coast . . . They were pagan spirit or ancestor propitiators, in the grip of magic and witchcraft, their minds

---

[1] M. J. Herskovits, "Peoples and Cultures of Sub-Saharan Africa," *Annals of the American Academy of Political and Social Science*, March 1955, p. 11.

cribbed and confined by superstition . . . [and] in 1890 were in a more primitive condition than anything of which there is any record in pre-Roman Britain.[2]

This description could be made to serve most parts of central Africa at the close of the nineteenth century. With a little redrawing to accommodate the interregional commerce, specialized labor and centralized governments that characterized some of their societies, it could also serve for most of west and west central Africa.

Although primitive, however, the pristine cultures of tropical Africa were neither simple nor inept. On the social side, they were (as will be seen in Volume II) often highly evolved and frequently elaborate to the point of being unintelligible to all but the initiated. On the economic side, they commonly showed a regard for the limitations of the earth, and a degree of ingenuity in putting it to work, that has not always been shown by more recent comers. And the men and women who labored to produce these cultures knew what labor was.

THE LABORER

In this Africa almost everybody worked — not only men and boys but women, girls and little children. There were hierarchies of work as in all other societies, and there were many kinds of workers. By modern standards the tempo of work was slow and the output slim, but that was less the fault of the workers than of the food most of them ate and the diseases they harbored. Few, though, except the incapacitated and the aged, were excused from the obligation to work. If a person did not work, he would be unlikely to eat, and in a hungry world there was always pleasure in eating. This is not to say that everybody worked all the time. If the women appear to have done so, and the majority of them did, the men certainly did not.

One of the most notable features of the workaday life of this Africa was, in fact, the contrast in the kinds and amounts of work done by the man and the woman. Among most tribes it was customary for the woman not only to do the fetching of fuel and water, the grinding and pounding of food, and the making of pots and baskets but also to do the sowing, weeding, hoeing and harvesting of the main food crop, or crops.[3] In other

---

[2] Sir Philip Mitchell, *The Agrarian Problem in Kenya*, Government Printer, Nairobi, 1948, pp. 2-3.

[3] It seems that the men (or perhaps the women themselves?) had devised an iron-clad argument in favor of woman-run farming. "Can a man born a *pickin'*? No more can he grow rice. Woman is the life-keeper. Seed dropped from a man's hand would only rot and be waste." So speaks a woman in Esther Warner's *Seven Days to Lomaland* (p. 144). The locale is the Liberian hinterland; it could just as well have been a hundred other places and the crop banana, yam, maize, manioc or millet instead of rice.

words, she did most of the continuous, repetitive work necessary to maintain the family. She usually had a large family; at least she usually bore a large number of children, and though not all of them lived long they needed to be fed and cared for while they lived.

The African woman's work therefore admitted of no respite. She was astir before dawn, about her business in the fields, at the well, or on the path from sunrise to dusk, and usually she was the last to retire. She worked hard as well as long. Where water and fuel were scarce, as they are in many parts of Africa, it was nothing for one woman in the family to spend from three to six hours each day making the trip to the nearest well and back, and another two to three hours gathering dried dung for the evening fire. Where wood provided the fuel, as was more customary, it was likewise nothing for a woman to cut a load of wood and then carry as much as one hundred pounds on her back over a rough bush path for half a dozen miles. On the days when she was not doing this, she would be carrying as heavy burdens of water, or animal feed, or bunches of bananas and other foodstuffs. For many millions of African women this is still the daily round and the uncommonly hard task.

By contrast, the lot of the African man seemed easy — and it frequently was. Ordinarily, the man was more concerned with intermittent tasks, such as the clearing of bush, the making of fences, the cutting of tracks, hunting and trapping, the holding of palavers and the repelling of aggressive neighbors. Such work was strenuous while it lasted but, except for the repelling of neighbors, it could be done more or less when the mood was on him. What is more, it yielded the peaceable fruits of leisure — often weeks of it on end; and leisure was one of the most highly esteemed blessings of manhood. When it could be shared with those with whom one had worked on a common project, the possessors of it were twice blessed.

Work often yielded prestige also. The singlehanded killing of a lion, elephant or buffalo could confer a lifetime of honor on a man, as could a successful hand-to-hand encounter with a gorilla or a close-quartered spear fight with a cattle stealer or slave raider. Prestige could also be had for prowess in much more conventional pursuits. Among the Bemba of Northern Rhodesia the climbing of trees to cut brushwood is still regarded as one of the more prestigious male activities. The men dare each other to incredible feats and call out taunts as they climb. They liken themselves to high-climbing squirrels and fierce chiefs who are lopping off the limbs of their enemies.[4]

While most men thought of themselves as self-employed, or employed in the interests of their kin or the people in their age group, nearly all of them spent a number of days each year working for their local chief or

---

[4] Audrey I. Richards, *Land, Labour and Diet in Northern Rhodesia*, Oxford University Press, London, 1939, p. 291.

more distant rulers. Normally a chief had the right to demand unpaid labor from his people as service to the community or as a contribution to the support of himself and his court. His people had to keep up the roads, work his fields and maintain his house and public buildings. It was a species of direct taxation that nobody seems to have greatly minded. On the contrary, everybody had an interest in seeing that such work was done. The reputation of the community would have suffered had it not been done, for it was a matter of honor that the chief should be so amply supplied with foodstuffs that he could maintain a liberal table for himself and his guests and thus stand well in the eyes of his peers — a point of view not very different from that prevailing in the twentieth century among some trade unionists.

The typical attitude of Africans toward their performance as workers, on the other hand, was rather different from that of the modern trade unionist. While work well done brought its own satisfaction, as it does the world over, work poorly done could always be explained away. If a man broke an axe, or if his spear failed of its mark, the customary explanation was that it "died." If he was asked why it died, he would be likely to reply, "Because it was a bad day." If the inquiry was pursued still further by asking why was it a bad day, he might say that somebody, perhaps his neighbor, had put a spell on him. The possibility that the "badness" may have resided not in his stars but in himself was seldom entertained.

CHARACTERISTIC LIVELIHOODS

Before the present century, almost every sub-Saharan African earned his living by gathering food (including hunting and fishing), by cultivating crops or by herding, or by a combination of these activities. We have no means of knowing exactly how many Africans followed a given livelihood, but it is clear that some livelihoods were more common than others.

FOOD GATHERING

Contrary to the still popular belief, almost no tribal groups lived exclusively by hunting. Possibly the Bushmen of the Kalahari Desert and bordering areas, the Banyambo of the Ruanda-Urundi–Tanganyika borderlands, the Bwamba of Ruwenzori, and the Dorobo of the Kenya Highlands came as near to doing so as any, but their womenfolk spent a good deal of time grubbing for insects and their eggs and for honeycombs, and collecting edible roots, berries, nuts and other plant foods. Similarly, not many groups lived entirely by collecting foodstuffs. Thus, the Babinga and other food gatherers of the deep forests of equatorial Africa seem to have divided their attention between catching elephants, monkeys and fish, and seeking out wild honey and edible roots.

By far the great majority of the aboriginal peoples were either cultivators or pastoralists, or partly one and partly the other. Indeed, they still are. And, though times are changing, many African peoples still work their land and keep their animals the way their pre-European forefathers did. Much of what follows could as well speak for the present as for the 1890s.

CROP CULTIVATION

All told there are more than 4 million square miles of tropical Africa where crop cultivation, if not the sole economic activity, has long been the main one, and where the role of the food gatherer, hunter and herder has been secondary at best. Significantly, in a number of African tongues spoken within this area the same expression is used for "to work" and "to cultivate the field." The boundaries of the area coincide roughly with those of the distribution of sleeping sickness and tsetse fly infestation.

The cultivation was of two main types, permanent and bush-fallowing. The first of these, bush-fallowing — more usually though not always correctly called shifting cultivation — was the more common of the two, largely because the areas which lent themselves to it were more numerous.[5] The forgotten generations who pioneered agriculture in tropical Africa were faced with a situation in which land was plentiful and the soils, with few exceptions, difficult. Left to his own devices, the African cultivator's response to these conditions was basically the same whether it was worked out in the steaming rain forest of Liberia, the open parklands of Northern Rhodesia or the grassy slopes of Ruwenzori.

He would first mark out a piece of forest or bush, often by tying knots in the grass. So far as possible, he would choose the piece for its presumed fertility. In this he was often helped by indicator plants: in the French Cameroons the Bulu favored soils on which they found the ringworm bush growing. In other areas, as in Dahomey, the quality of the soil was sometimes established by tasting it.

Next he felled the trees and piled the brushwood in heaps, or distributed it evenly over the cleared area. Big trees were usually left in place, both because of the labor involved in felling them and because their root systems served to keep the soil anchored against the forces of erosion. Smaller trees were customarily cut off about four feet above the ground. The cleared land had anything but a tamed and tidy look, but in a

[5] Shifting cultivation involves the deliberate destruction of new areas of forest or bush for the purpose of farming with the intention, not of returning to them, but of moving on to repeat the process. It implies shifting habitation as well as shifting farming. It does not appear to have been nearly so widespread a practice as bush-fallowing. What is commonly stigmatized as "shifting cultivation" is the process of re-clearing land that was formerly under cultivation but has been held under a bush or forest fallow to refresh the soil.

virtually plowless world this mattered little.[6] The aim of the tree feller was to collect the maximum amount of readily inflammable material, not to remove every obstruction from the path of the sowers and hoers who came after him.

In the forest zones the disposing of this brushwood was normally done toward the end of the dry season. At any other time of the year, the ground would have been too wet to set fire easily. Even in the dry season the relative humidity of the duff layer remained so high that fire did less damage to the animal and vegetable life of the subsurface layers of the soil than would be the case with a forest fire in, say, the western Sierras. Forest wind velocities being typically low, the risk of a fire getting out of control was not very great. In the drier, better-ventilated bush and parkland zones, it was different. On the plateaus of east Africa, for instance, it is still not uncommon to see bush fires that started innocently enough in a two-to-three-acre clearing eating up land the size of a Texas county. In his *African Afterthoughts* Sir Philip Mitchell recalls having seen "hundreds of square miles of pasture and light forest reduced to a blackened, smoking ruin, as the first step on the part of three or four men and their wives in the cultivation of maybe an acre each." The aim of the savanna burner was not just to get wood ash for fertilizer, but also to obtain a finely powdered seedbed for the ensuing crop. He might get a meal or two of small game and vermin as well, a much appreciated bonus in a predominantly vegetarian society.

As a rule, sowing amounted to nothing more than the placing of seeds or tubers in holes made by a digging stick, the holes then being filled in with a kick of the foot. In some areas, as in the Bemba country of Northern Rhodesia, only one crop was planted in a given clearing at a time, but it was more customary to sow a mixture of seeds and tubers. In this way the cultivator was able to safeguard himself to some extent against the vagaries of the weather and the ever-present threat of erosion, the combination of crops providing a protective mantle of vegetation. In this way, too, it was generally possible to obtain from a single clearing a main crop, such as yam, millet, manioc or maize, and one or more subsidiary crops, such as beans, peppers or squash. In these subsidiary crops the woman took a special interest. Her success as a wife and housekeeper could well hinge on her ability to garnish the staple dish with them, and with the foodstuffs she could find in the surrounding bush.

The combination of crops intertilled in this way was legion. It still is. In the Cross River district of southern Nigeria, Daryll Forde has found that the inhabitants of a typical village, whose staple was the yam,

[6] The plow, in a rudimentary form, spread from the east and north of Africa to the Sudanese fringe of the Sahara and the Ethiopian-Somaliland "horn" early in the Christian era, if not before. It does not appear to have reached negro country, even in those regions where the presence of cattle would have made its use attractive.

also grew squash, maize, peanuts, peppers, one or more varieties of beans, manioc and, less frequently, other food plants as well.

As with every other phase of the cultivator's work, the sowing was commonly preceded, accompanied and followed by prayers and sacrifices. And for compelling reasons, some of which a modern-day Mossi peasant expressed when he prayed: "My God, I give you this fowl; in exchange, help me to get millet. Making the millet grow, harvesting and eating it are the three things which keep the world going. God, I give you this fowl so that you may help me in these three things." [7]

The time devoted to the tending of the patch varied according to its original condition, its age, the kinds of crops grown on it, and the need for protection from intruders. In forest clearings hoeing was not usually necessary during the first year, for the fire was likely to have killed the seedlings of weeds and trees. From the second year onward it was necessary because on exposure to sun and rain the topsoil soon lost its friability and began to cake. In savanna clearings it was necessary even in the first season, for there the fire, having less fuel to work on, was seldom fierce enough to destroy the rhizomes of the big grasses; these the cultivator had to take out with his hoe if they were not to stifle the growth of his crops. Hoeing played a particularly important agronomic role where tubers and cereals were grown in ridges or on mounds.

Often it was the intruders that made most work for the cultivator. The primeval bush abounded in herbivorous animals that had either to be frightened away or kept outside the palings laboriously erected season by season. Herbivorous birds, not so amenable to discipline, had to be kept at bay with stones, verbal volleys or hand-operated clappers. As the harvest approached, it was sometimes necessary to take up temporary residence at the crop patch. None of these stratagems availed anything against hungry elephants.

The harvesting of the crops was highly responsible work, since an error of judgment could have serious consequences for the family. Unripe grain is wasteful. Overripe grain blows too much dust into the eyes and is partially lost in the gathering. Damp heads of grain hang down and are hard to cut. An educated Bemba once told Audrey Richards [8] that a field sufficient to fill three fourths of a granary would fill only half of it if the grain (millet in this case) were reaped at the wrong time.

The productive life of a clearing depended on several factors. Where the land was fertile, as around the flanks of volcanic mountains, it might be as much as fifteen to twenty years, the same staple being grown year after year. Over most of the not so fertile forested and savanna-covered lowlands, three to four sowings of the same crop in quick succession

[7] Quoted by R. Delavignette in *Freedom and Authority in French West Africa*, Oxford University Press, London, 1950, p. 112.

[8] *Op. cit.*, p. 299.

could easily reduce a field to impotence. And there were places, as, for example, in the Ilorin Province of Nigeria, where it was imprudent to use a field for more than one year at a time.

Practically the only staple crop that did not have to be kept "on the move" was the banana (plantain). Provided the ground was heavily composted with decaying leaves and other handy vegetable matter, and the cultivator regularly replaced the worn-out stems with new suckers, his banana patch could be maintained almost in perpetuity.

The permanent farming of a tract of land is nowhere the easiest of undertakings. In tropical Africa it must be reckoned among the hardest. Seasonally flooded alluvial plains, valleys capable of irrigation by simple lifting devices, and rock outcrops that weather into rich, easily worked and durable soils are scarce. Even scarcer in pre-European times was knowledge of the agronomic virtues of crop rotation, which, in the absence of rich soils and fertilizing floods, alone can keep cultivated land in good heart. Most cultivators believe it is simpler, and better, to keep planting a patch of ground with their favorite food until the soil is exhausted than to grow a succession of fertility-renewing crops, some of which they do not like or cannot eat, and others of which they have trouble in storing because of mildew, fermentation, and depredations by animals and insects.

However, there have been some superior cultivators who have refused to be overwhelmed by the difficulties of keeping African land productive. Among them are the Kara people living on the island of Ukara in Lake Victoria. They have developed a remarkably intensive mixed-farming system which maintains the fertility of the inherently poor land under almost continuous cropping, and they have done so without European guidance. They stall feed their cattle on crop refuse, eked out by the loppings of trees and fodder, consisting mainly of water grasses planted by the edge of the lake. Vegetable wastes are used as bedding, and in this way enough farmyard manure is obtained for the arable land to receive at least four tons per acre annually.

The cropping system developed by the Kara is elaborate and at the present time supports a population of over 600 to the square mile, one of the heaviest concentrations to be found anywhere in Africa. It could scarcely have been less than 300 to the square mile at the turn of the century.

The Kara were unusual in two other respects. They believed in the individual ownership of land; and they regarded cattle as an integral part of a mixed-farming system, and, accordingly, limited their numbers to fit the size of the holding and the fodder supply. It is tempting to connect these two circumstances with the success of their system.

In west Africa the Kabrè, hill dwellers of northern (French) Togo, long ago learned how to live continuously off a piece of land. This they did, and do still, by dint of feeding it with manure from their cattle kraals and water from their irrigation ditches, and following a set pattern of crop rotation. In spite of its rugged character, practically the whole of their small territory today gives the impression of being a carefully tended and terraced garden. Similar pre-European examples of a practically self-perpetuating agriculture are to be seen in other highland areas, from the Cameroons to Ruanda, and from the Tigre-Amhara region of Ethiopia to Kilimanjaro and Meru.

The peoples of the low tropics, on the other hand, had made very little progress toward stabilizing their cultivation before the European era. Why this should have been so is not fully known. One of the contributing reasons no doubt is the tendency of soils to leach and so to become exhausted faster under conditions of constantly high humidity and high temperature, conditions which are more characteristic of the lower than the higher tropics.

PASTORALISM

How and where cattle keeping got its first foothold and how it spread until it embraced no less than one third of tropical Africa is beyond the scope of this inquiry. For that matter, it is probably beyond the scope of present knowledge. What is fairly certain is that the chief pastoral peoples came from the Nile valley and brought with them a derivative of the giant-horned wild ox found in upper Egypt, similar to the present-day long-horned cattle of the Ankole and other east African pastoralists. And it is clear that the chief cattle-raising peoples, such as the Fulani of west Africa and the Tusi, Masai, Suk, Samburu, Turkana and Kamasia of east Africa, are quite distinct in physical as well as in other ways from the main crop-raising peoples.

The major ends served by the cattle were social rather than economic. A man was known by the company of cattle he kept. If he had a large herd, he was a wealthy man. The physical condition of the individual animals was not very important; generally it did not affect the reckoning of a man's wealth any more than the physical condition of dollar bills affects their purchasing power.[9] In a sense, cattle were currency. In another sense, they were also "invested capital at a high rate of interest."[10] With the "interest" a man could make friends and influence people. Without it he was a nonentity. With cattle he could get wives and keep his kraal swarming with children who would work for him, and, if need be, fight for him and so enhance his social standing. Without cattle a man

[9] A common equivalent of "How do you do?" among the Tusi and other cattle keepers was "I hope your cattle are well," but presumably all that mattered was that they were alive.

[10] D. W. Malcolm, *Sukumaland: An African People and Their Country*, Oxford University Press, London, 1953, p. 133.

might well find himself childless, servantless and statusless, unworthy to rank as an elder among his own people. If, through misfortune, a Tusi was forced to abandon stock raising and become a crop raiser instead, he ceased to regard himself as a Tusi.

Above all else, cattle signified "bride wealth." If a man had four sons, he must take care to acquire enough cows and bulls to enable his sons to marry four wives, or more. If he had four daughters, it was his hope that they would bring him a corresponding number of cattle when they married. On no account must his "capital" become depleted. It had been entrusted to him by his ancestors, and he must pass it to his descendants intact — better still, augmented.

For a pastoralist, there was no pleasanter occupation than to be among his animals, admiring them, grooming them, and inventing pet names for those he liked best. Almost from the time they could walk, a cattle keeper's sons "grew up" with the herds, and all their lives they lived in a world where the everyday talk turned on the number, kind, color and horns of their animals. Among the Shilluk and some other pastoral groups, the size and form of the horns were of such moment that a man was set aside for the purpose of shaping the horns of young oxen to their owners' desires. To men reared in this world, separation from a favorite animal was a hardship scarcely more tolerable than separation from a wife.

Not all the pastoralists were cattle keepers, however. In the more arid parts of the Republic of Sudan, the Republic of Chad and west Africa, the horse and the camel occupied important roles, frequently superseding cattle as the basis of the economy. Scattered all over east and central Africa were societies that made substantial use of smaller animals, such as sheep, goats and donkeys. This was especially true of the areas infested by the cattle-killing tsetse fly. Among the Masai, for instance, sheep, notwithstanding their lower social significance, were almost as numerous as cattle.

For the most part, these pastoral societies were self-sufficing, usually of necessity, but sometimes from choice, for surpluses were not unknown. The Masai often had more animals than they could conceivably use, or maintain on the grass and water available, but it does not seem to have occurred to them that they might have traded the surplus off to their crop-raising neighbors. If it did occur to them, they must either have decided that there was nothing they wanted in exchange, or that anything they could have obtained would have been a poor exchange for the pleasure and prestige they derived from owning a large herd.

Like the Bedouin, and for the same reasons, the herdsmen of eastern Africa were wanderers. To keep animals within reach of grass and water was a clever trick in the best of seasons; in bad seasons it was genius. To do so, the herder must be able to smell water and scent grass without seeing it; to outwit wild animals with the same needs but not with the same scruples about what is edible; and to shake off the attention of other herders, not all of whom were accustomed to settling their grazing disputes as peacefully as Abraham and Lot. Tribes living on the arid fringe of east Africa thought nothing of spending eight months out of every twelve traveling to and fro with their herds, in the wake of the solstitial rains. In periods of subnormal rains they might be kept "on the hoof" the year around and walk twenty-five hundred miles in the course of it.

To such men there was but one great commandment: to maintain the herd. To keep it they could covet their neighbors' animals, steal them, kill them. They could kill their neighbors, if need be. Indeed, they could do almost anything, except deny their birthright.

STANDARDS OF LIVING

Ingenious as the aboriginal African undoubtedly was at making a living, he rarely succeeded in making a good living. For most people life was hard most of the time. Jungle cultivators faced the periodic threat of too much rain and too little sun, and of crop destruction by elephant, monkey, grain-eating bird, termites and mildew. Pastoralists on the velds and savannas faced the threat of too little rain and too much sun; their herds were constantly exposed to the attentions of lion, leopard and hyena, and to the ravages of pests and disease. Food collectors lived from hand to mouth; they had few means of keeping surpluses and none of protecting their food sources against foraging animals, or other humans. Food hunters often had the hardest time of all; game is where you find it, and it was not always to be found when it was wanted. And seldom could the surpluses of one week be stored away to supply the deficiencies of another.

DIET

All the same, it does not follow that those who had the hardest life had the poorest diet. It is arguable, for instance, that the hunters and collectors on the whole did better than the cultivators, since their diet was more varied and more nutritious. Frequently they did not have enough food to satisfy their hunger (neither did the cultivators for that matter), but what they had was rich in protein and fats. And in bad times they could more easily resort to cannibalism, which, after all, was only another kind of hunting. Because their diet was more nutritious, they seem to have suffered less than the cultivators from enforced fasting, and to have recovered more quickly from its effects. W. J. Burchell, in his *Travels in the Interior of Southern Africa* (published in 1822), was particularly struck by the "proof of the good effects" of four days' hospitality given to an elderly starving hunter. When the man arrived at Burchell's camp along with three younger men, the skin on his body hung in large wrinkles and his "meagre emaciated state" excited great pity. When they left, the wrinkles had gone, the skin seemed to have a flow of blood beneath it and his body was smooth and "ridiculously plump." And, says Burchell, "I found that I had been mistaken, at least ten years, in his age: . . . he was but a middle-aged man."

On balance, it would seem that the not so hard-working pastoralists did as well as anybody, and better than most. Unlike the collectors and hunters they were never without the possibility of food, satisfactory food at that. Further, cattle-owning tribes often went in for the growing of rainy-season catch-crops of grain and vegetables. Even so, most herders knew what it was to be periodically hungry, if not to starve. Milk yields throughout most of the cattle belt are very low to this day, and there is no reason to suppose they were any higher fifty years ago. During the rainy season in some of the more arid areas of east Africa, two pints, morning and evening, after the calf is fed, are about all that can be expected. Walter Deshler, in a paper prepared for this study, says: "During the dry season the milk supply decreases and often fails. A cow does well to feed her own calf, and a yield of half a pint after calf at this time is considered good." B. S. Platt points out, also in a paper prepared for this study, that the milk itself tended to be "unbalanced, very fatty, rich in casein, low in lactose, and poor in chloride in relation to potassium." Although nursing mothers cannot have known this, it was — as it still is — customary for many of them to put off as long as possible the critical moment of the child's graduation to animal milk. Curds, cheese and butter, favorite foods with most herding peoples, shared the shortcomings of the milk they were made from.

Blood, obtained from the necks of bullocks and cows and drunk fresh, clotted, or mixed with milk, was a widely esteemed food, but the amount that could be drawn off a small, underfed, "bloodless" animal at any one time, without jeopardy to its health, was quite limited. Writing of the Dodose of northern Uganda, Deshler tells us that "the prudent man bleeds his animals no more often than once a month and then only during the wet season. Up to two pints may be taken from cows and about half a pint from sheep and goats," so that blood can only be a frequent item of diet during four to five months of each year at the most.

As for meat, it was not eaten at all by some cattle people, and where it was eaten, it was seldom eaten regularly. Most pastoralists ate it only when an animal died — which was quite often in the drought season, when meat became a sort of famine ration — or on the occasion of a marriage, a funeral or an age group initiation. Others did so when it was desirable to condition themselves for the rigors of cattle raiding. Thus, when the Masai *moruak*, or warriors, planned to make an especially large or dangerous raid they would go into a meat-eating camp, where they would gorge themselves for four or five days or longer.

The average daily diet of the Masai warriors has been given, on somewhat slender evidence according to Platt, as consisting of 1,135 grams of meat, 2,000 cc. of milk and 50 cc. of blood. The average daily diet of most pastoralists was much less impressive. The diet of the west African Fulani consisted largely of milk curd, about 500 to 600 grams of it, representing between 2,000 and 2,200 calories. But even at that, it was almost certainly superior to the diet of most of the cultivators.

While the luckiest of the cultivators — those who practiced permanent crop-and-cattle farming — may have eaten as well as the pastoralists, the average run of them, that is, the bush-fallowers, fared considerably worse, worse even than the hunters and collectors. Most of their staple crops, including the banana, yam, millet, maize, and various oil-bearing seeds, such as palm oil and benniseed, were poor in protein, and, except for the oilseeds, poor in fat. Then, they seldom knew what it was to have a steady supply of food. Hungry months, preceding the harvest of the main crop, alternated with months of plenty over large parts of their domain. Manioc, which has the useful property of not going bad if left in the ground until it is needed, was grown by many tribes as a reserve hungry-season food, but it is a poor substitute for, say, maize or millet. The Bemba farmer who likened a meal of manioc to "a long drink of water" was nearer the nutritional truth than he knew. Then, too, the system failed to provide regular and marketable surpluses with which a man could obtain the missing ingredients of a healthy diet.

Many cultivators, like many pastoralists, fortified their diet with foods they did not grow. Some forest-dwelling cultivators were in the habit of catching fish, small game and other sources of fats and protein. Some of the peoples living in drier and open country were, by turns, food collectors, hunters and cultivators. Some, like the Dodose and Karamojong of northern Uganda, occasionally combined all three pursuits with those of pastoralist.

MATERIAL GOODS

In material goods there were comparable differences between the hunter, collector, cultivator and pastoralist. Almost all of them had to make do with the things they could contrive out of the raw materials that were handy. And there were considerable variations in the availability of such materials.

At the lower end of the scale stood the hunters and collectors. No peoples were ever less bothered by "the abundance of things." The home of the Bushman, for instance, was a half-open beehive hut rudely constructed of bits of wood, reed and grass. His weapons and tools were few — a bow, a throwing stick, a spear, a drill to produce fire, each made of wood; a water-sucking tube made of reeds; bowstrings made of animal sinew; arrows made of reed and bone; wood and hide scrapers made of flint, or occasionally of iron; and bags made of skin. His minimal clothing was also made of skin. The food gatherers of the rain forests had even fewer possessions. Thus, the Babinga lived — as most of them still do — in small huts, about eight feet long and five feet high, made of leaves, sticks and lianas, and furnished only with a bed of bark and some cushions of leaves, which were left behind with each shift of location. For covering the men used a loincloth of bark, and the women two tufts of leaves tied to a string. For tools they had a "tinderbox" made of two kinds of wood (one hard and the other soft) which when rubbed together produced a flame, an iron spear for hunting, and little else.

Being more or less mobile, the pastoralists also lived a streamlined existence. About the only materials most of them had to work with were the hides, sinews and bones of their dead animals. With these they made clothes, household equipment, weapons and ornaments. Their huts were usually built of long, pliant wood stakes strengthened with ropes of osier, and covered with hide. Where a tribe or family was under no compulsion to keep moving, it was in the habit of giving its dwellings a more elaborate finish, walling and roofing them with long grass, and plastering them with a layer of fresh dung mixed with mud. Whether the huts were temporary or permanent, the furnishings were meager. They consisted of raised couches of close-set poles or pads of straw on which hides were laid, milking gourds, and a simple wooden stool or two. Some cattle tribes also knew how to fashion iron ore into a variety of articles. Among the Masai, almost every clan had its family of smiths, who, in addition to spearheads, made cowbells, hatchets and iron wire for use by their women in the manufacture of coiled leg, arm and neck ornaments.

The cultivators tended to be more acquisitive. This is to be expected, for their homes were more permanent, and in the course of a year or so they were called upon to perform a wide variety of tasks, each requiring its own tools. Their houses were generally simple one- or two-roomed affairs, constructed of whatever materials lay closest to hand. The commonest of these were wood, osier, reed, grass, leaves, clay and dung. Inside there would be a plain sleeping couch or bench covered with straw or skins or, more rarely, a homespun blanket. The floors would, most likely, be without covering and the walls without ornament other than weapons. A pestle and mortar, some pots for storing water and food as well as for cooking, some sticks and hoes for digging and weeding, and a paring knife or two comprised the bulk of equipment in day-to-day use. Tribes that combined other activities, such as fishing, cattle keeping, hunting and crafts, with their crop raising would have a little additional gear, appropriate to their specialty. Even so, it would not have taken the average cultivator more than five minutes to make an inventory of all his goods.

How very little in the way of durable goods most Africans had can be seen from an inspection of their burial grounds and kitchen middens. Whereas in other parts of the world these are rich in artifacts, in sub-Saharan Africa they yield next to nothing. Here and there the spade of the archaeologist has unearthed the skeleton of a man a million years old, bone and stone implements in use between three thousand and thirty thousand years ago and, dating from much more recent times, a selection of metal objects, both ornamental and useful; but he has had to work hard to find them. The great majority of settlements yield "nothing at all before the rubbish dumps of modern colonial towns." [11]

ARTS AND CRAFTS

Most people, then, more often kept company with drudgery and dearth than with ease and abundance. Some groups, of course, managed to do better for themselves than others. This was particularly true of those who produced surpluses. The surpluses were often too small to matter, but in a good year or on a good soil they could be considerable. And where there were surpluses, there came to be specialization, not only of "unskilled" labor such as weeding and hoeing, but of skilled manufacture. For once a person is freed from the necessity of working solely to appease his hunger, he can begin to think of other things, including the making good of the deficiencies he senses in his local environment.

This specialization, though rarely carried to great lengths in pre-European times, was a noticeable feature of the economy of several agricultural societies. In some areas, for example west central Africa including the Congo basin, the specialization was by tribe. Elsewhere, as, for example, along the Guinea coast and inland, it was by craft. As Melville Herskovits points out in a recent paper, this tradition of specialization was responsible for a very remarkable flowering of culture hundreds of years before the coming of the colonizers. It produced "such recognized art forms as the Ife and Benin bronzes, the Agni-Ashanti gold weights, the Dahomeyan and Cameroons brass figures, and the intricately designed Congo throwing knives." [12] It also made possible "the embellishment of houses and temples with carvings and paintings of a high order, and the development of sculpture that from Guinea and Sierra Leone to the Congo has given the world the masks, statuettes, and other carved figures that today have world-wide renown." [13]

And, not least, specialization was responsible for the development of more utilitarian skills. Outstanding among these was the skill acquired by many African groups in the making of those iron tools and weapons

[11] Sir Philip Mitchell, *Africa Today*, edited by C. Grove Haines, Johns Hopkins Press, Baltimore, 1955, p. 12.
[12] Herskovits, *loc. cit.*, p. 18.
[13] *Ibid.*

upon which hung the success of their farm work, fishing, hunting and warfare, and their ability to build a house and furnish it. The careful routine of the smelter, working generally in isolation — for the art of extracting iron from stones was not one to be lightly shared — and guided only by the transmitted experience of countless generations of ancestors, has often been described.

The physical prerequisites of a simple metallurgical industry are widespread in tropical Africa. It is well that they should be, for where would the African have been without the smith? In a very real sense he was the upholder of the African's primeval universe. "Are not those hundreds of miles of smiling African tillage," asked Daniel Crawford, "all traceable to this man who digs the ore from the hillside and manufactures hoes, spears and axes?" [14] It was he who opened the earth that yielded the ore that made the axe that broke the forest, and the hoe that made the field of grain that made strong the boat builder, the weaver, the dyer, the potter, the brewer and the other African men of skill.

TRADE

Equally, specialization made for trade. All the time men were jacks-of-all-trades, there was little call for their services. The moment they became masters of one and their mastery was acknowledged, the seeds of a more effective demand were sown. But the supply of specialized goods available for exchange remained small, because the techniques of producing them were time-consuming, tiring and wasteful.

Trade, too, was generated by the external demand early developed by the Arabs and later expanded by the Europeans, for slaves and ivory. But this was largely a one-way trade. The return trickle of beads, cloth and muzzle-loading guns did little to modify the basic self-sufficiency of the recipients' lives. Contacts between buyers and sellers were spasmodic, slight and lacking in cordiality. The buyers had no desire to jeopardize a paying business; the sellers were given little opportunity of developing one of their own. Neither group built roads or developed facilities that would have aided the expansion of regional and foreign trade. The only ways of transporting anything were by foot (slaves, of course, transported themselves, and often the ivory as well, down to the coast), by canoe (in areas having navigable waters), and, in the open savanna country to the south of the Sahara and in northeast Africa, by pack animal. Further, there was no money and little capital accumulation. "[Such] capital equipment as existed was mostly as perishable as man, while skill and knowledge — which also have a capital value — had only the narrow channels of oral tradition and personal example in which to flow." [15]

[14] D. Crawford, *Thinking Black,* Morgan & Scott, London, 1912, p. 276.
[15] Godfrey and Monica Wilson, *The Analysis of Social Change: Based on Observations in Central Africa,* Cambridge University Press, Cambridge, 1954, p. 4.

WEALTH

Where trade, no matter how small, was based on specialization, no matter how limited, wealth and its corollary, power, accrued nonetheless. West and west central Africa, where specialization was carried to its farthest precolonial extent, saw the rise of many highly developed kingdoms, priesthoods and theological systems. These were maintained by specialists that only economies capable of producing substantial surpluses could carry. Among the best known of these were Mali, Tekrur, Ghana, Bornu, Songhai and Hausa — empires of the marchlands between the Sahara and the forest — the Guinea coast kingdoms of Ashanti-Dahomey, Yoruba and Benin, and those of Kongo, Lunda and Bushongo in the Congo. Many smaller principalities "with simpler but comparable political forms, were interspersed among these more powerful, more numerous, and more widely spread entities." [16]

With the ability to support a larger population came the beginning of town life. And it came early, for in the Arabic travel literature of the tenth and following centuries, we are told of the existence of many cities in "the Land of the Blacks." While most of them were small and mean, a few were large and rich, having their own armies, running a big trans-Saharan business in gold, ivory, salt, fabrics and slaves, and having their own centers of higher learning. Kano, in northern Nigeria, is estimated to have had a population of many thousands when it was first visited by Europeans.

SYSTEMS OF LAND TENURE

The ideas men hold about the land they live on depend largely on how much there is of it and the uses to which it can be put. There being in the tropical Africa of pre-European days plenty of land but few ways of using it, the basic ideas concerning the ownership and use of land were everywhere much the same.

The most widespread of these ideas was that of communal ownership. Land was not thought of as belonging to persons, but to people; and the people could be the members of a clan, a village, a tribe or a kingdom. One Nigerian chief spoke for many millions of his fellow Africans when he said, "I conceive that land belongs to a vast family of which many are dead, few are living, and countless members are still unborn." Although a person could have the use of a particular piece of land, his rights over it and what he could do with it were limited by other rights over the same piece of land held by the other members of his "family." These rights were limited both as to the period of effective occupation and as to transfer and succession. So long as a man worked a piece of land or

[16] Herskovits, *loc. cit.*, p. 19.

members of his community worked it for him, it remained in his possession and no one might encroach on it. Should he leave it temporarily, he could, as a rule, take possession of it again on his return. If he did not wish to retain the use of it he might negotiate its transfer to another, receiving in exchange goods or services of some kind. But usually he could not treat it as either a salable or a rentable commodity. There was, accordingly, no opportunity for land speculation and no incentive to acquire large holdings from which a return might be derived in the form of purchase money or rent. There were no rentiers, and no tenants in the American sense of the term; but a landowner always had plenty of relatives and friends to whom he could loan land in return for help given him in cultivating and reaping crops on his "home farm."

In many areas, customary law limited the extent of land that anyone might hold to the amount he required for the support of himself and his family. The absentee owner was therefore a rarity. So, too, was the compact lot, since in most areas either bush-fallowing or shifting cultivation was the rule and, by the laws of inheritance, good and bad land had to be divided equitably. This almost always meant that a man's holdings consisted of a series of patches scattered over a wide area.

The ideas entertained about useful trees were in several respects similar to those entertained about the land on which they stood. Thus, the fruit of a wild palm tree was generally anybody's, but the moment the tree was tapped for wine it became the tapper's. He retained possession of it even though he neglected the land on which it stood — even though he did not own the land on which it stood. Similarly, if a person planted a palm tree, or any other tree of economic importance, the tree belonged to him no matter on whose ground it was planted. To make sure that its ownership was accepted, the planter would be likely to summon the village elders to witness the planting, more particularly if the ground did not belong to him.[17] In a sense, a tree was more of a property than land, for if a man who owned both a tree and the land on which it stood should leave his village, he would not automatically lose his rights over the tree. If he wished, he could even rent out his tree.

Land and trees, then, were regarded in the same light as sunshine and air: as plentiful and necessary, and as things to be enjoyed by all members of the community according to their requirements. In themselves they had little or no value; it was the work which a man, a family or a community put into a piece of land or a tree that gave it value. Consequently, when a piece of land was transferred from one owner to another, its value was adjudged to be the value of the standing crop, if

---

[17] The importance of establishing ownership of a tree was not unconnected, in the minds of many Africans, with the widespread belief that the man who plants a tree will die before it bears, and so be unable to defend, in person, his family's right to its fruit.

any, and of the work which had gone into clearing and breaking the ground for the crop.

Departures from this generalized pattern of land tenure were frequent, especially among pastoral societies. Where cattle keepers were accustomed to range freely in search of grass and water, as in the semi-arid country of the northern savannas, close delimitation of land rights was impracticable. For one thing, there were few landmarks; for another, there were not enough people to guard them; and, for a third, hungry animals do not bother about the laws of trespass. Where pastoralists were restricted in their movements, more definite rights arose, though they were seldom as definite as cultivators' rights. Thus, in the Sukuma country of western Tanganyika individuals were able to establish rights over grazing areas and demand rents from cattle owners for their use. This was reasonable enough since the conversion of bush lands into well-demarcated grazing grounds involved much labor. Rights of ownership arose in many areas in respect of salt licks, water holes and the like. But the granting of such rights was attended by all manner of possibilities for the litigious possessor of them and his less fortunate neighbor, particularly where individuals sought to reserve areas with a view to producing short, sweet herbage. Even today wherever personal rights in grazing grounds are recognized law suits are frequent, since the grounds often form a patchwork lacking easily distinguished boundaries.

Among agricultural peoples, too, important differences of land law and custom existed. Where the population was sparse and given to changing its base, as in some of the more forested parts of the Congo basin, allocation to families of specific areas was less definite than in more thickly populated places. Where village sites were permanent, land allocations were generally made with some precision and, once made, seldom altered. In parts of Uganda, for instance, land had been "in the family" for unnumbered generations, and even though the area held by a given family might be greater in some cases than the needs of a shifting or bush-fallowing system of cultivation required, none of it could be occupied except by the family's consent. More often the chiefs or councils of elders, acting for the community, retained the right of allocating "unimproved" lands, and of reallocating land that had been distributed but was no longer used. However, though family rights over specific pieces of land were in almost all cases well defined, there was no doubt about the existence of other rights, equally well defined.

Some of the most interesting departures from the standard land-tenure system were those which developed in areas where pastoralists and cultivators had come to occupy the same territory. The Bunyoro region of western Uganda is an example. Here the governing classes have long claimed descent from an immigrant pastoral people known as the Hima. The king, or Mukama, who was regarded as a divine being, was the "owner" of the country, and the sole distributor of grazing rights — the only kind of rights that mattered to a cattle-keeping aristocracy. Where these rights obviously conflicted with the pre-existing rights of the aboriginal cultivators of the country, they were not absolute. The cultivators were left free to occupy such alienated lands as they required, on the understanding that they supplied the Mukama and his local liege lords, on whose lands they farmed, with annual gifts of grain and performed certain state services such as keeping the royal enclosure in repair. That is, they were "free" as long as they were willing to live as serfs in a feudal relationship with their masters.

Although not always produced from the same stock, feudal forms of tenure have flourished at one time or other in several areas of Africa, including Ruanda-Urundi, the Belgian Congo and Nigeria as well as parts of Uganda. Usually they came into being through the granting of fiefs or estates to members of ruling families, high government officials, and other notables. More usual still has been the tendency for chiefs to become landlords, and landlords, chiefs.[18]

Clearly, then, there was nothing immutable about indigenous land-tenure systems. Nor was it only conquest of one group by a more powerful one that could bring changes about. Sometimes they were brought about by the development of strong governments ruling over large areas, as in the case of the emirates of northern Nigeria and the kingdoms of Ashanti-Dahomey and Benin. In each of these cases the central authority became strong enough to take over from smaller groups their traditional land-allocating functions.

Sometimes changes were brought about by force of economic circumstances. This was especially true of areas where the population pressed hard upon the capacity of the land to support it, and where, as a result, men sometimes found themselves greatly straitened. Thus, in the Ibo country of eastern Nigeria and in Kikuyuland, to name only two populous areas, the practice had arisen, well before the arrival of the European, of pledging land and so parting with the use of it, at least until the creditors had been paid off. In point of fact, pledged land was often lost for good, which helps to explain how some landowners got bigger in spite of safeguards to the contrary, while others became landless. Further, persons from tribes that had outgrown the lands traditionally available to them were sometimes allowed to hold land in other tribal areas on presentation of suitable gifts to the local authorities. These gifts were not regarded as payment for the land, but rather as a thank offering for admittance into a new community, and as an evidence that the authority of the local chief or elders was recognized. Membership in a community, not the payment of a price, was the basis of land ownership.

[18] To this day, the feudal relationship can still be found. Thus, many of the Babinga of the Sangha region of the Republic of the Congo continue to live in a servile relationship to *les grands noirs* who inhabit the lands bordering their rain forest domain.

Sometimes these migrations were not only allowed but encouraged. This was the case, for instance, with the quite recent settlement of the hill peoples of Sierra Leone in the rice-growing coastal districts of that territory. To quote Sir Keith Hancock: ". . . the strangers who have come down from the uplands to cultivate the swamps have easily and quickly achieved full security of occupation . . . ; there were large and empty chiefdoms which were glad to receive on any terms reinforcements to the tribute-paying population." [19]

Such conceptions of land-holding were very different from those the Europeans brought with them. To Europeans land was property which a person could buy, sell, rent or mortgage, use or abuse, in much the same way as he could a house or a bicycle. In the circumstances there need be no surprise that over the years a great many misunderstandings have arisen between Africans and Europeans as to the precise meaning of land transfer agreements made at the beginning of the century, or that problems of land tenure continue to be numbered among the most acute of the many that confront the governments of tropical Africa.

[19] Sir K. Hancock, *Survey of British Commonwealth Affairs*, Book II, Part 2, Oxford University Press, London, 1942, p. 247.

CHAPTER 2

The Physical Frame

THE RELIEF MAP

THE CLIMATE AND WEATHER

THE VEGETATION

THE SOILS

THE physical personality of tropical Africa is not readily caught in a web of words, and most of the things that are true about it take long to say. It could hardly be otherwise when we consider the kind of place tropical Africa is.

Consider, to begin with, its dimensions. More than 3,200 miles in width and 4,600 miles across at its longest, it has an area of about 8.5 million square miles. True, size does not necessarily spell diversity, but the greater the size, the greater the chances that it will. When a place is big enough, it "breeds" differences. For instance, a large land mass tends to make for "continentality," that is, increasing range of temperature with increasing distance from the ocean — a thermal phenomenon commonly observed over continents. This in turn makes for seasonality of rainfall, that is, the division of the year into wet seasons and dry seasons; which, in its turn, makes for marked differences in plant and animal responses between the coast and the interior, and also in the processes of mechanical and chemical weathering by which the surface of the land becomes differentiated.

In the second place, consider its location. Although it lies astride the equator, it is not all "equatorial" for it runs more than 1,600 miles northward and southward, and by the time the tropics are reached, it is not always "tropical" in the conventional palm-tree sense of the term. Indeed, along parts of the Atlantic seaboard of tropical Africa palm trees are more likely to die of cold than of heat, and in many sections, again at sea level, the cool-season conditions are more reminiscent of San Francisco than of Panama. For an explanation of this rather surprising state of affairs we need go no further than the ocean current map in our atlases. The western seaboard of tropical Africa is being invaded continuously by water which has its origin in higher latitudes, reinforced, in the offshore trade winds zones, by water that upwells from the colder subsurface levels of the ocean. Because water is conservative of its properties, the inshore waters of the Canary current and the Benguela current are anything up to 15°F cooler than the waters of the open ocean, and cooler still than the air which originates over the adjacent mainland. By contrast, off the eastern shores of tropical Africa there are only warm waters. Frequently these are warmer at their tropical margins than at their equatorial middle. Where they flank a desert shore, notably in the case of the almost land-locked waters of the Red Sea, it is an understatement to call the resulting hot-season conditions either tropical or equatorial.

Whether Nature is fashioning climates, physical landscapes or living things, sameness is seldom one of her long suits. In tropical Africa it certainly is not. In addition to the diversity the region has acquired by virtue of its size, it has, so to speak, a long inheritance of diversity. This inheritance is etched deeply on the face of every watershed, and in the lineaments of every horizon and shore. It is the inheritance of an unresting geological past during which, time and again, valleys were exalted and mountains laid low, plains and plateaus were fractured, coastlines gnawed away, and cycles of erosion arrested before they had half run their modulated course. It is an inheritance that compounds the diversities born of size, location, and distance from sea. And it is one that does nothing to simplify the task of description, since of very few things in the make-up of tropical Africa can it be said that they are thus and so. The most that can be said of the great majority is that they are partly thus and only sometimes so.

THE RELIEF MAP

A glance at the ordinary map of Africa may seem to give the lie to this talk of diversity, for if it suggests one thing more than another it is simplicity. Who can look at a physical map of the continent without agreeing with Laurens van der Post that "Africa has the neatest and most composed shape on the globe, quite unaffected by the spread which affects the waistlines of some other ageing continents" or that "like a good house, it was built on a foundation . . . of rock raised well above the levels of the militant seas"? [1] But maps are in their nature gross simplifiers of facts, and the bigger the area to be put on the page, the grosser the simplification. Since Africa is very big, most maps of it are able to do no more than hint at the true character of its relief. Some cannot even do that. Tropical Africa's neat and composed shapes are full of concealed articulations.

[1] "Africa," *Holiday*, March 1954, p. 38.

At the same time, the smaller articulations, like the bigger features which survive translation from three dimensions to two, are not haphazard in their occurrence. They are where they are for perfectly good geological reasons. And because geological processes frequently operate on a big rather than a small scale, there is frequently some recognizable grouping and patterning of their occurrence. Let us look, then, at the larger features of the relief map.

TYPES OF SURFACE

Though the ordinary observer would never guess it from just traveling up and down, the roughly 8.5 million square miles of tropical Africa contain only three major kinds of surface. One is the kind that bears the stamp of what geologists call "the fundamental complex"; another is the kind that has developed on horizontal or slightly inclined continental sedimentary beds and volcanic lavas; and the third the kind that has been formed out of accumulated beds of sand and alluvium.

The fundamental complex is largely made up of very old sedimentary rocks into which rocks of volcanic origin, such as granites and gneisses, have been widely intruded. Where these intrusions have taken place, the sedimentary beds have been much folded (i.e., bent) and metamorphosed into quartzites, ironstones, slates and other resistant rocks. Consequently, surfaces formed on the "complex" tend to be very uneven, for the granitic rocks erode rapidly, leaving the harder metamorphosed rocks upstanding as rugged and irregular ridges. Where this erosion has taken place under arid or semi-arid conditions, the harder rock cores frequently survive as *inselbergs* (literally, island mountains). This type of topography is particularly common in the Republic of Sudan (Darfur Province), Tanganyika and the Rhodesias.

The continental sedimentaries consist mainly of sandstones and shales with associated lava flows, but they, too, include some ancient quartzites. The surfaces which have developed on this kind of rock have a tabular look about them, being the product of dissection, by wind or water or both, of beds which are disposed horizontally or nearly so. In the drier regions where wind is erosion's chief tool, these surfaces are commonly so little accented that the rains, when they come, tend to lie about on the surface, at least until they have been lost by evaporation to the air. In the wetter regions with their more intense erosion "the surface generally takes on the character of plains interrupted by table mountains and koppies [literally, little heads] of varying extent but of nearly equal height." [2] The former type of surface is very well represented in Southwest Africa; the latter in the southern margins of the Congo basin.

The third major kind of surface is the product of accumulation by water

[2] John H. Wellington in *Africa South of the Sahara*, edited by Anne Welsh, Oxford University Press, London, 1954, p. 26.

or wind. The basin of the Congo with its generous mantle of sands and clays — the floor of former lakes — provides perhaps the best inland examples of water-induced accumulation, and the lower Niger valley and delta perhaps the best coastal examples. The Kalahari Desert undoubtedly provides the best examples of wind-induced accumulation. According to Professor John Wellington of Witwatersrand University, it has "the most extensive continuous surface of sand accumulation in the world."[3] There is also a large amount of "accumulative" relief in the Sahara and some in the semi-arid lands of northeast Africa (mainly in Somalia) and along the coast of Mozambique.

PHYSIOGRAPHIC REGIONS

The fashioning over long periods of time, at different elevations and under a variety of climatic circumstances, of these three major kinds of surface has produced a richly patterned landscape capable of many kinds of areal subdivision.

At the physiographic, or distinctive land-form, level, it will probably be enough for our purpose if we recognize the following seven divisions: east Africa, central Africa, Madagascar, the Congo basin, west Africa, the middle Nile basin and the Sahara.

East Africa

This region comprises the roof of Africa, the adjacent supporting plateau walls, and the land at the base of them. As if the uplift and arching of this part of Africa had been excessive, the land has been rent by deep, double faults that have riven the surface as no other place on earth has ever been riven. The main fault system trends southward from the Red Sea through Ethiopia, Kenya and Tanganyika to Nyasaland. A secondary system runs to the west of it and takes in Lakes Tanganyika and Albert, and part of the upper Nile valley. Because of their dimensions these systems are best comprehended from the air. Then — in the evocative if ungeological language of an artist —

it appears as if the earth . . . is in the grip of unimaginable and unendurable conflict. One sees the central plateau of Africa pushed up into a great wrinkled dome as if squeezed between two opposite and irresistible forces into long chasms, valleys and gorges under such pressure that it cracks and snaps the skin of the imprisoned earth like a ripped drum.[4]

There can be no mistaking the ripping. At many points these rifts are between 30 and 50 miles across, and anything from a few hundred feet to several thousand in depth. At its deepest, Lake Tanganyika goes down nearly 5,000 feet and at their highest the flanking walls rise more than

[3] *Ibid.*
[4] Van der Post, *loc. cit.,* p. 40.

5,000 feet above the water level. From end to end the main rift system is more than 3,000 miles long.

The Ethiopian Highlands form the highest part of the plateau, or dome. At their maximum they exceed 14,000 feet in elevation, but their mean elevation is less, between 8,000 and 9,000 feet. Their abrupt south-eastern face overlooks the floor of the rift, the Danakil Desert, "a sea of sad yellow sand." Beyond the rift rises that part of the Highlands known as the Harar Plateau; its faulted eastern edge hems in the narrow coastal plain of British Somaliland. The not quite so abrupt, but still impressive, western face of the Highlands overlooks the burnished savannas of the Sudan. While it is customary to speak of the Highlands as a plateau, it is not an altogether satisfactory term. There are, it is true, large expanses of table-flat land composed of horizontally disposed sandstones and lavas, but they are so deeply dissected by chasms and gorges that their plateau character is often more apparent than real. They are, accordingly, more readily crossed by air than by any form of surface transportation.

In Kenya and northern Tanganyika large lava-based plateaus also occur, at elevations between 5,000 and 9,000 feet above sea level. In the section of these known as the European Highlands the elevation, the structure and the climate have combined "to create a landscape that [has] not its like in all the world. There [is] no fat on it, and no luxuriance anywhere: it [is] Africa distilled up through 6,000 feet, like the strong and refined essence of a continent . . ." [5] These factors have also combined to create, for settlers from higher latitudes, opportunities the like of which can be found in but very few other places. It is here that the European came fifty to sixty years ago, and it is here that he has stayed to prosper — economically at any rate. Here, too, are Africa's highest mountains, Kilimanjaro, Kenya and Ruwenzori, "their feet planted firmly on hot equatorial rock and their heads capped with snow," each one of them, along with their second- and third-magnitude neighbors, a memorial to the ancient days of fire and earthquake.

To the south of the latitude of Lake Victoria in central Tanganyika the plateau assumes a more homely appearance: it has, so the geologists tell us, "the typical aspect of a surface formed by the fundamental complex." Though its even granitic surface is frequently punctuated with "island mountains," it lacks the vitality and drama of the plateaus to the north. It also lacks most of their fertility, for its soils are sandy and acid, and its rainfall light. But toward the south of the territory, the plateau gains some height — and so some rainfall — until in the rolling grasslands of the Iringa uplands it comes to resemble strikingly the high veld of the better-watered parts of the Union of South Africa.

Toward the Indian Ocean the central and southern portions of the plateau fall away in a series of broad steps, or terraces. The lowest of

[5] Karen Blixen, *Out of Africa*, G. P. Putnam's Sons, London, 1936, p. 3.

these, the coastal plain, is formed of fairly recent marine sediments. Wide in Somalia, narrow elsewhere, it is low-lying and often marshy in the wet season, and comes as near to being physically unadorned as any part of tropical Africa. Toward their western margins, formed by the Lakes Albert-Tanganyika-Nyasa arm of the great Rift Valley, the plateaus rise irregularly, reaching their greatest heights in the region of Ruwenzori and in Ruanda-Urundi. Ruanda-Urundi itself averages between 5,000 and 6,000 feet in elevation and is more mountain than plateau. The steep gradients of its valleys and their often alp-like grassy shoulders, when seen against the stark backdrop of the mountains, have more than a suggestion of Switzerland about them, a comparison which the Belgians have not been slow to make in the interest of the territory's developing tourist business.

Central Africa

This region is really only the truncated portion of a much larger physiographic region occupying most of southern Africa. The divide between the central African part of it and its northern physiographic neighbors is nowhere sharp. Very approximately, it follows the height of land between the waters of the Congo-Cuanza and those of the Zambezi-Cunene systems. We say "very approximately" because hydrographic divides do not necessarily have anything in common with physiographic divides. In the Lake Nyasa region they have nothing in common, for while the lake is structurally part of the great African rift system that belongs to east Africa, hydrographically it falls within the Zambezi basin, which belongs to central Africa. What identifies this region physiographically is its "hollow-ground" plateaus, set at different levels and linked (when they are linked) by rivers which have bitten deep into the bedrock to form some of the world's most spectacular gorges, falls and cataracts, the most spectacular of all being the Victoria Falls. The lower plateaus have great difficulty in attracting rainfall and husbanding it. Parts of the sand-covered Kalahari plateau, or basin, have no surface drainage at all, while other parts have only a system of swamps, playas [6] and streams that contract, sometimes almost to the vanishing point, in the long dry season. The biggest of these swamplands is formed by the Okavango, Linyanti and Zambezi rivers. The higher plateaus are better watered, have integrated drainage systems and deeply gouged surfaces. In the Eastern Highlands of Southern Rhodesia they rise to over 8,000 feet. Most of these plateaus, high or low, have residual table-like hills (or mesas), bizarre-shaped bosses of granite and other hard-wearing rock, and, less frequently, long, low ragged hills. These seldom bear any

[6] Shallow depressions which are temporarily covered by water after heavy rain or flooding.

relation to the river systems, most of which have such inconspicuous water partings that they can be detected only by careful leveling.

However, it is not the sentinel hills, the sunken valleys and the many waters of this region that alone capture the eye of the traveler; its unmatched expanses of earth and sky can work a seduction no less powerful. What Alan Paton has said of the plateaus of his native Union of South Africa is as true of many lying north of the Limpopo: "South African scenery is wide and sweeping, set under a wide and sweeping sky. Its beauty is vast, a matter of light and color and distance, not of field and stream and tree." [7]

Where these plateaus come down to the coast, they frequently do so with a flourish. Indeed, some of the grandest scenery in the whole of Africa is located along the line of the Great Escarpment, the name by which the dissected plateau wall of southern and southeast Africa commonly goes. Fortunately there are many breaks in this wall to ease the problem of getting roads and railways from the coast onto the high ground. At its base there is usually a pediment zone, a zone composed of the products of the wall's wastage by erosion; this is followed seaward by a coastal plain of rather limited width. The plain reaches its maximum width, about 250 miles, on the low-lying marine sediments located between the Save and Limpopo rivers. The western wall of the plateau is neither as continuous nor as high as the southeastern and southern walls. It is seen at its best in the highlands of Southwest Africa, which culminate in the Auas Mountains to the south of Windhoek. The western coastal belt, most of it forming part of the Namib Desert, varies from 30 to 50 miles in width.

Madagascar

The "un-Africanness" of Madagascar — the continent of the Indian Ocean, as it has been called — is a favorite theme with scholarly writers. Valid as this characterization may be in many respects, it scarcely applies to the relief. The eastern two thirds of the island continually call to mind the country of the Great Escarpment, for their narrow coastal plains are backed by high, broken walls that give access through the breaches to the central plateau beyond. The central plateau — better, central highland, for the country is less on the level than on the up and up — likewise has many suggestions in it of the neighboring continent, especially of the highlands of Ruanda-Urundi.

The western third of the country consists of a series of gently seaward-sloping plains and low plateaus, 60 to 120 miles across. While no mirror-image of the lands that face it across the Mozambique Channel, it is generally comparable to them in height and articulation.

[7] Alan Paton, "The Tragic, Lovely Land of South Africa," *Holiday*, February 1957, p. 36.

The island's coastline likewise carries more than a hint of Africa in it, for it is remarkably compact, badly off for deep sheltered water and navigable inlets, and therefore most inhospitable to shipping. Its only sheltered anchorages of any size are in the north, at Diego-Suarez and in Antongil Bay.

The Congo Basin

This basin is a mammoth shallow saucer let into the table top of tropical Africa. From an elevation of approximately 1,000 feet at its center, the land rises slowly and often imperceptibly to between 3,000 and 4,000 feet at the saucer's rim.

The alluvial floor of the basin is almost dead flat. Between Stanley Falls (above Stanleyville), where the mainstream reaches the floor of the basin, and Stanley Pool (below Léopoldville), where it cuts through its western rim, the average gradient of the river is only about six inches a mile, or less than 1:10,000. The rivers which flow over the floor of the basin are of varying but generally great width, and much given to inundation. Marshes, swamps and lakes — all of them permanent — form an extravagant proportion of the total drainage area.

The highlands forming the rim of the saucer vary in character according to their structure and rainfall. The southern and eastern segments of the rim (the Malanje-Katanga and Kivu uplands) are formed mainly of crystalline and ancient metamorphosed sediments and, at their lower levels, of comparatively soft and horizontally set sandstones. The former have a rather more rugged, weatherbeaten look about them than the latter with their clean-cut tabular lines, reminiscent of the South African high plateaus or karoos. The Banda uplands to the north of the basin are almost entirely granitic in origin; here the products of subequatorial weathering provide "a comparatively even watershed area which passes into a deeply dissected surface with increasing distance from the divide." [8] The western segment of the rim, separating the basin from the coastal plain, is likewise largely composed of granites, associated with quartzites and schists. Its dissection has been intense, accelerated by the unending action of equatorial rain-fed streams. To reach the sea, the Congo River has cut a tortuous channel through the impeding Crystal Mountains.

Beyond these mountains — which are really no more than hills, being at their highest only about 3,400 feet above sea level — lies the lower Guinea coastal plain stretching from Benguela in Angola northward to Douala near the foot of Cameroons Mountain. The seaward side is floored by marine (Cretaceous) deposits which, though they have been uplifted, still preserve their level alignment. The landward margin has a granitic surface and an appropriately rougher topography.

[8] Wellington, *loc. cit.*, p. 32.

West Africa

As with the other divisions, west Africa can lay no claim to physiographic unity. It is rather the aggregate of several physiographic regions whose margins are as "melded" as their middles are distinctive. The Cameroon Highlands, the upper Guinea coast zone, and its flanking plateaus, comprise the chief of these regions.

The Cameroon Highlands stretch, apron-fashion, around the northern flank of the lofty pile of Cameroons Mountain (approximately 13,350 feet) toward the valleys of the Chari and the Benue. Their largely granitic surface has been much disturbed by volcanic activity, and masked by lava flows. These have produced a landscape of more than usual topographic complexity and altitudinal range. Their height — for the most part between 5,000 feet and 10,000 feet — makes them one of the most climatically desirable parts of tropical Africa; their volcanic soils, one of the most fertile.

Approached from the sea, the most conspicuous feature of the upper Guinea coast is its vagueness. Except in a few places, it is low-lying. Frequently it is so low-lying that a mariner's only landmark is a tree, and so festooned with sandbanks, interlacing channels, lagoons and creeks that it is difficult to tell where the domain of the sea ends and that of the land begins. The usual run of coastal hills is, to quote from the first book of sailing directions ever compiled for the Guinea coast, "not as high as the ignorant may imagine . . . However, because the rest of the country is very low these hills seem quite high." [9] Though the observation is four hundred and fifty years old and applies to a part of Ghana, it is as fair a one as any we could make, and is of wide applicability. Behind the sand bars, lagoons and creeks, lies a largely featureless sedimentary plain variously composed of sands, clays, shales, limestones and even lignites. Usually it is not more than 10 to 20 miles across, but in a few places it is vastly bigger. Along the Niger-Benue valley, for instance, it extends upstream for some 700 miles, all the time remaining below the 600-foot contour. Only here and there, as in Sierra Leone behind Freetown and near Cape Palmas, that is, on the Liberian–Ivory Coast border, does the plateau wall abut directly onto the ocean.

The plateau zone of west Africa lies at a much lower mean elevation than the corresponding zones of east and central Africa. Most of it is less than 1,500 feet above sea level; in two areas only, the Fouta Djallon highlands of the Republic of Guinea and the Jos Plateau of northern Nigeria, does it rise above 4,000 feet. It is also, with these two major exceptions and some smaller ones, much less well articulated than the plateau zones previously described. Frequently, where the escarpment is missing or buried, the transition from coastal plain to plateau and from plateau

[9] Duarte Pacheco Pereira, *Esmeraldo de Situ Orbis,* translated and edited by George H. T. Kimble, Hakluyt Society, London, 1937, p. 117.

to highlands is imperceptible to the traveler's eye; and frequently, too, the plateau provides no immediate clues to its structural identity. What gives character to much of the plateau is the unusual behavior of its rivers, especially the Niger. Most rivers are steeply graded in their upper courses and gently graded in their middle and lower. The Niger does things differently. In its upper course, above Timbuktu and for some little way below that city, it moves sluggishly and maturely like the lower Mississippi, whose flooding propensities it follows, to the extent at least of inundating the so-called "dead delta" above Timbuktu every summer with its excess waters. At Tosaye, it changes character completely, becoming fast-flowing, strewn with rapids, and an avid eater of its own bedrock. To the geomorphologists this spells "river capture" in the not too distant past; by this they mean that the upper Niger was once a Saharan stream that had its waters tapped by a faster-flowing Atlantic stream — a forerunner of the present lower and middle Niger — able to cut farther and farther back into the plateau until it had invaded the upper Niger's watershed. It seems that the upper Benue is bent on the same business and that before long it will draw off a major part of the Chari River water supply that at present feeds Lake Chad. When this happens, the southern margin of the Sahara will lose what little supply of water it now has, with consequent further encroachment of the vegetated land — already serious — by the desert sand.

The Middle Nile Basin

As the name suggests, it is water rather than rock that gives this region its physical identity. For this is the meeting place of the great waters. Through the shallow basin lying between the Darfur plateau and the Ethiopian Highlands meander three of Africa's greatest rivers, the Bahr-el-Ghazal, the Bahr-el-Jebel or Mountain Nile, and the lower Bahr-el-Azraq or Blue Nile. At the center of the basin, the gradient is so gentle and the volume of converging waters so great that frequently more water than land is to be seen, and much of the "land" is in reality only floating vegetation, or *sudd*. In the flood season some of this vegetation finds its way into the main channels, where it is liable to cause further flooding from the blockages it creates. Most of the seasonally, and perennially, dry land is formed of fine alluvial silts, often of great depth and high fertility and blessed with a high water table. One of the greatest expanses of such soils is located in the Gezira, or island between the converging White and Blue Niles, south of Khartoum. On the drier margins of the basin, the monotony of the landscape is attenuated here and there by the presence of hills and, toward the desert, by dunes; the soils become sandier and less rewarding, and the water table sinks lower and lower. By the time the highland rim of the basin is reached, we are back in the land of granite and sands, island mountain and mesa, plateau and playa.

The Sahara

Structurally the Sahara is part of the great African tableland and is thus indistinguishable from the plateau-and-basin territories just described. Physiographically it is a world apart, "a world tawny from dust, dusty from dryness," and dry from the prohibitions of high atmospheric pressure. Because maritime air is repelled at almost every possible point of entry, there is scarcely any rain; wind, sun and frost are therefore the chief instruments of erosion, and wind the chief agency of transport and accumulation. So the characteristic land forms of the true desert are the wind-worked sand and gravel plain, typical of the Tanezrouft, or "the land of thirst"; the sand-blasted and often grotesquely eroded outcrop of bedrock; and the steep-sided dune, always beautiful and almost always changing. Only along the semi-arid margins of the desert and around the bases of the higher cloud-catching hills, where seasonally flowing streams are to be found, does water play a sculptor's role comparable in importance to that of wind.

THE CLIMATE AND WEATHER

GENERAL CIRCULATION

Tropical Africa has such a great range of altitudes and exposures that, its name notwithstanding, it is comparable in climatic diversity with any other region of equal size. Most of its climates, however, have two traits in common — sustained heat and marked seasonality of rainfall — traits in sharp contrast to those marking the climates to which the majority of Europeans and North Americans are accustomed. Many of the qualities and problems of human life, economic, social and, perhaps, political, are related to these two facts. The high temperatures obviate the need for heated shelter and heavy clothes over most of the inhabited territory and provide an abundant source of energy for the year-round growth of crops. On the debit side, they create, especially when combined with high humidity, a physiologically uncomfortable situation for man, African, Asian and European alike; and, on that account, they put a premium on the cooler uplands. The unevenly spread rains tend to divide the year into times of plant activity and plant dormancy, abounding food and hunger, work and unemployment.

The explanation of these fundamental traits is to be looked for in the circulation of the atmosphere, and in the character of the individual elements that make up the climatic whole. In his study of the climates of tropical Africa, prepared for this book, Peveril Meigs points out that:

The conventional notion of belts of easterly trade winds circling the globe in the tropics finds little support in tropical Africa . . . The centers of action most significant to tropical Africa are undoubtedly the high-pressure cell over the South Atlantic west of the Kalahari and the high-pressure cells existing over the Sahara and the Atlantic in the vicinity of the twentieth parallel. Apparently the subsidence and adiabatic [10] warming and drying of these masses are a basic cause of the great desert region that sharply delimits the humid tropical climates to the north, and of the lesser Kalahari and Namib Desert lobe that forms the southern limit.

Along the eastern margins of these "highs," the mean movement of air is toward the equator. The line or zone of convergence between these moving streams is known variously as the intertropical front and the intertropical convergence zone. It is the air to the south of this convergence zone which gives most of tropical Africa its rain, the seasonal distribution of which is controlled by the northward and southward movements of the convergence zone in rhythm with the seasonal shift of the overhead sun. From the accompanying maps it will be seen that the latitudinal sweep of this convergence zone is more than twice as great on the east coast of Africa as it is on the west, ranging on the average between 2°N and 18°N on the Atlantic side and between 24°S and 18°N on the opposite side of Africa, though the extreme positions may vary two or three degrees from year to year. Thus the zone reaches nearly to the southern end of Mozambique and the Malagasy Republic in January, following the southern solstice, but not even to the mouth of the Congo River on the Atlantic coast.

One reason for the striking difference between the rainfall of the west and east coasts is the existence of a belt of upwelling cold water along the inner margin of the Benguela current which flows northward past Southwest Africa and Angola. Being cold, it cools and so increases the density and stability of the air in contact with it. Because the air is dense, it resists displacement by the unstable, lighter air of the migrating convergence zone; because it is stable, it resists convection, the main rain-making process of the tropics. Another factor that contributes to the dryness of this section of the coast is the presence there, or nearby, of the "Kalahari" high-pressure cell. The air in the cell is constantly subsiding in the manner of all high-pressure systems. And subsiding air is, of course, warming and drying air. All of this helps to explain why desert and near-desert conditions prevail along the Atlantic coast to within about 9° south of the equator. Since there is a discernible, though by no means perfect, inverse relationship between the monthly rate of displacement of the convergence zone and the monthly amount of rainfall, it is not difficult to see why the Atlantic side of the continent, north of the equator at least, should be on the whole better watered than the "Indian" side. There are exceptions, needless to say.

[10] In the atmosphere "adiabatic" changes of temperature are said to occur when air is warmed by compression, that is, by increasing its pressure, or cooled by expansion, that is, by decreasing its pressure. Thus rising air tends to be adiabatically cooled, descending air adiabatically warmed.

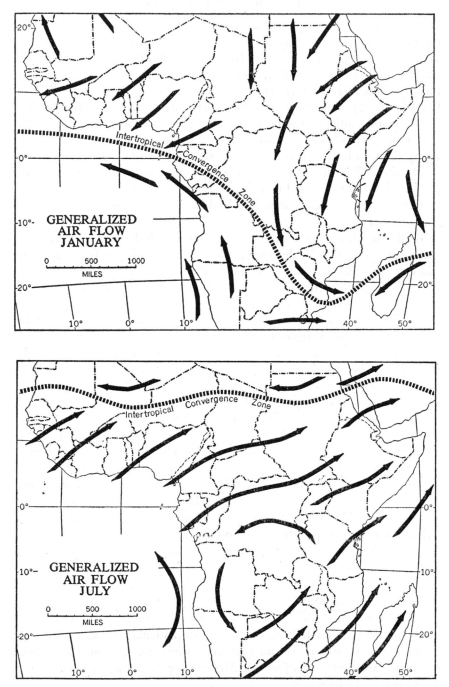

FIGURE 1 (After Maurice A. Garbell, *Tropical and Equatorial Meteorology*, Pitman Publishing Company, New York, 1947)

As the convergence zone moves northward from its January position in
the Gulf of Guinea, it brings in its wake (that is, on its southern side) a
stream of moist air that provides the moisture for the rainy season. This
air, originating in the South Atlantic "high," swings to the right (in conformity with Ferrel's law, or, as it is more commonly put, with the
Coriolis effect), becoming a southwesterly rather than a southerly wind.
During the months of the northern summer it frequently maintains this
direction overland to the Republic of Sudan, Ethiopia and the Rift Valley.
Being the rain bearer, it is sometimes referred to as the monsoon. Most
of its rains fall in one of two ways: in quasi-frontal situations which can
produce fierce east-to-west traveling squalls known as tornadoes, or in the
convectional thunderstorms which build up on the equatorward side of
the convergence zone.

To the north of the convergence zone are winds of a very different
character, since their birthplace is in the Sahara and the Arabian Desert.
They are, on this account, exceedingly dry and dust-laden. As the zone
moves southward at the end of the northern summer, these northeasterly
winds follow in close pursuit until, by January, they are frequently in
possession of the Guinea coast, less frequently the eastern part of the
Belgian Congo, and, upon occasion, even parts of Northern Rhodesia.
They are steadiest in west Africa. The movement of the zone, being
largely governed by the fluctuating strength of these winds, is made up of
a series of erratic advances and retreats. Thus, in January, places like
Accra and Abidjan are quite likely to find themselves having alternating
spells of heavy rains and desiccating drought.

For the lands lying to the east of the Rift Valley, the Indian Ocean–
Arabian Desert region is, on balance, a much more important weather
source than the North Atlantic Ocean–Sahara region. It is true that in the
northern summer the trend of the wind over most of east Africa is southwesterly, and some of the weather it receives, including some of the rain,
is unquestionably Atlantic in origin. However, by the time winds of
Atlantic origin have penetrated inland as far as the "horn" of Africa, they
have usually been "rained out," or are only capable of further precipitation as a result of forced ascent (as against the sides of lofty mountains),
which may help to explain why the Ethiopian Highlands get rain in summer from southwesterly winds and the lowlands around them get very
little. It is also true that in the northern winter some of the dry air occasionally found over the high east African plateaus is Saharan in origin.
At the same time it is certain that most south-going winter air masses
originate outside the continent of Africa in or near the source region of
Asia's northerly monsoon.

In both hemispheres, summer and winter alike, the bulk of the rains of
east Africa come from air which, if it did not originate over the Indian
Ocean, had a long trajectory over it before striking inland. Even in the

northern summer it seems likely that most of the rainy spells which occur from time to time north of the equator are associated with incursions of moist tropical air from the Indian Ocean. In the southern summer, the Indian Ocean is without rival as the rain maker for eastern Africa. By the time the prevailing northeasterlies have traveled, mostly over water, to the southern hemisphere, they are heavy with moisture and easily induced to shed some of it at the promptings of convection, or convergence. Then, again, in late summer and early fall the Capricorn section of the east coast is liable to hurricane (cyclone) rains, likewise long in the making over the Indian Ocean.

THE MAJOR CLIMATIC ELEMENTS

Solar Radiation

The fierceness of the sun's rays is a favorite topic with both travelers and residents in the tropics. There is no denying that the rays can be fierce, especially during the middle hours of the day. At the same time, in most parts of tropical Africa so much of the incoming radiation is cut off, even in cloudless weather, by the atmospheric screen of dust and smoke (in the dry season) and invisible moisture particles (especially in the rainy season) that the danger from exposure to sun is seldom very great. At its greatest, the danger is probably no greater than it is in middle latitudes. The daily duration of sunlight is much less within the tropics than at mid-summer in middle and high latitudes as a consequence of the tilting of the earth's axis at an angle to the plane of its path around the sun. In contrast to the more than 15 hours of possible sunlight at New York and 16¾ hours at London at the summer solstice, places on the equator can never get more than 12 hours, 7 minutes of sunlight a day, and even at the tropics (Cancer and Capricorn) the longest days can have no more than 13½ hours of sunshine.

In cloudy weather the amount of solar radiation is still further reduced, and over a large part of tropical Africa a high percentage of days are cloudy. The average daily amount of sunshine received by the coast of the Cameroons is less than four hours, making it one of the most sunless. Many inland places in the Congo basin receive less than 2,000 hours of sunshine a year, or less than any lowland area in the United States. Only the most cloudy, foggy margins of the far northern and southern oceans have less sunshine than equatorial Africa. Northward and southward from the equator the mean expectation of sunshine increases, amounting to between 3,000 and 4,000 hours a year along the twentieth parallel of north latitude and between 2,400 and 3,400 hours a year along the twentieth parallel of south latitude.

But this is not to belittle the *climatic* role of the tropical sun. Its two equinoctial crossings of the equator and its solstitial swings to the northern and southern tropics set both the pace and the range of all major seasonal changes of temperature, wind, storm and rainfall.

Temperature

Lowlands

The amount of solar radiation received is large enough to produce high mean annual temperatures in the lowlands everywhere, the year around. Within 10° of the equator, they run between 77° and 81°F, much on a par with the mean July temperatures along the eastern coastal plain of the United States south of Washington, D. C. Between the tenth parallel and the tropics they may run 3°–4°F lower. Differences between the mean temperatures of the warmest and coldest months are small near the equator, amounting, as a rule, to between 2° and 6°F. Near the poleward margins of the region the annual range increases, but rarely exceeds 15°F, and only infrequently exceeds 10°F.

This striking uniformity or, as many would prefer to call it, monotony of mean temperature can be attributed partly to the fact that the sun rises high in the heavens at all times of the year, and partly to the fact that the time of highest sun is, with few exceptions, the time of greatest cloudiness, the time when the atmospheric screen against the sun's rays is most effective. This screen is so effective that the season of greatest heat often occurs either well before or well after the sun reaches its vertical noonday position. When this happens, "summer," using the word in its astronomical sense, is cooler than "winter."

The diurnal temperature range over most of the lowlands is greater than the annual range, a state of affairs that gives more than a degree of truth to the saying that "the night is the winter of the tropics." This seldom averages less than 5°F, and often it is more than 15°F. In cloudless weather it is commonly twice as large as it is in cloudy weather. Then the night minimum can go as low as 60°F. In west Africa when the harmattan is blowing, the diurnal range may be as much as 45°F, and the minimum as low as 50°F. For the African lacking heated shelter and warm bedding, such temperatures spell real discomfort.

But it is the hot days, rather than the cool nights, that cause most of the climatic discomfort of the low tropics, and practically no part of them is altogether immune to it. Of course, what is discomfort to one African, or European, is not necessarily discomfort to another, and what is discomfort to a man at work or play is quite unlikely to be discomfort to the same man at rest. Scientists have almost as much difficulty in drawing the line between comfort and discomfort as most ordinary people. What is certain is that the "line" is not any given isotherm. The moisture content of the air certainly enters into the reckoning, as also does ventilation, or air movement. According to a recent study by W. S. S. Ladell,[11] "an effective temperature" of 80°F and 100 per cent relative humidity with still air may be taken as the threshold between comfort and discomfort, above which the slightest activity results in sweating for the average individual lightly dressed. The same "average individual" will probably be just as comfortable — or no more uncomfortable — at considerably higher temperatures provided the air is drier. Thus, at 65 per cent relative humidity, the threshold temperature can be increased to 86°F; at 40 per cent it can be raised to 90°F. If a light breeze of, say, six miles an hour is blowing, each of these threshold temperatures can be increased by about 5°F.

By these criteria, most parts of the lowlands are comfortable the greater part of the twenty-four hours the greater part of the year, provided the air is in gentle motion, which is not unusual. At Lagos, Nigeria, for example, when there is a breeze blowing, only the very hottest days (in February or March) are likely to be considered uncomfortably hot by the average person, and then only during the hottest time of the day. However, on still days, or in wooded or otherwise enclosed areas, it is probable that the average person would feel uncomfortable in any of the hot-season months (December through May), and that he would be comfortable most of the time in July and August only. Farther away from the equator the seasonal contrasts are greater. At Kano in northern Nigeria, for example, the period from early November to mid-March practically never experiences uncomfortably hot weather. In fact, most of the time during this period the weather could be called invigoratingly cool, with night temperatures dropping below 60°F and relative humidities averaging about 25 per cent.

Highlands

Although the schoolboy's rule of thumb that temperature drops roughly 1°F with every 300-foot rise in elevation is far from unexceptionable, it works well enough in the African tropics for us to be able to say that places located within 10° or so of the equator about 6,000 feet above sea level are likely to have a mean annual temperature of between 57° and 61°F. In other words, such places are more temperate than equatorial. And because low-latitude places tend to have a small annual temperature range whether they are at sea level or snow level, places 6,000 feet up, and over, tend to be temperate in the strictest sense of the word — which is more than can be said for most places in the so-called "temperate latitudes" of the earth. The illusion of eternal spring created by such a thermal regime is fortified in some highland areas by the sight of an

[11] "Physiological Classification of Climate, Illustrated by reference to Nigeria," reprinted from "Proceedings of the International West African Congress, Ibadan, 1949," by the Department of Antiquities, Jos, 1955.

occasional ground frost, rarely below the 8,000-foot contour on the equator but occurring down to the 4,000-foot line in Southern Rhodesia; by the more common sight of morning mists in the low valleys and snow on the high mountains; and, not least, by that most unwelcome phenomenon of spring, capricious rainfall.

Rainfall

Nobody can be long in tropical Africa before coming to realize that it is rain, or its lack, that is the big conversation-opener. Heat and, where it applies, high humidity are taken for granted, but rain, practically never. Nor is it difficult to see why. While every day is hot, not every day is rainy, not even in the rainiest regions. Again, while there is unlikely to be more than a fractional difference between the mean temperature of a given day, month or season and the next, the order of magnitude of rainfall differences between two consecutive days, months or seasons may be 50, 500, even 5,000 per cent. Then, too, while the thermometer seldom springs a surprise, the rain gauge frequently does. Days that promise to be very rainy do not always live up to their promise. Months that should be wet turn out to be dry. A run of abnormally rainy seasons can be followed by a run of subnormal rainy seasons, to the undoing of many a farming community. And conversely.

The most striking features of tropical African rains are, in fact, the sharpness of their average seasonal differences, their uncertainty, and their range of intensity and amount.

Let us consider, first, the characteristic division of the tropical African year into dry and wet seasons. Even in the wettest areas, most rainfall graphs show a clearly marked tendency to fluctuate from month to month. However, while the maxima on these graphs leave us in no doubt about the timing, length and intensity of the wet season (or seasons), the minima are seldom low enough or long enough in duration to enable us to speak with conviction of a dry season. In the less wet areas the amplitude of the monthly fluctuations tends to increase. The peak or peaks of the graph may be as high as those on the rainfall graphs of the wettest areas, but the troughs tend to be lower and flat enough to warrant their being identified as a dry season, or seasons. As can be plainly seen from the map (Figure 2), most parts of Africa have a dry season of ample proportions. Only the equatorial core of the Congo basin, the highlands around Lake Victoria, parts of the Guinea coast, and the east coast of Madagascar have a dry season of as little as or less than three months. With very few exceptions the duration of the dry season increases with distance from the equator. At the tropics themselves it is, with one exception (Mozambique), everywhere more than eight months long, and at many points it is virtually perpetual.

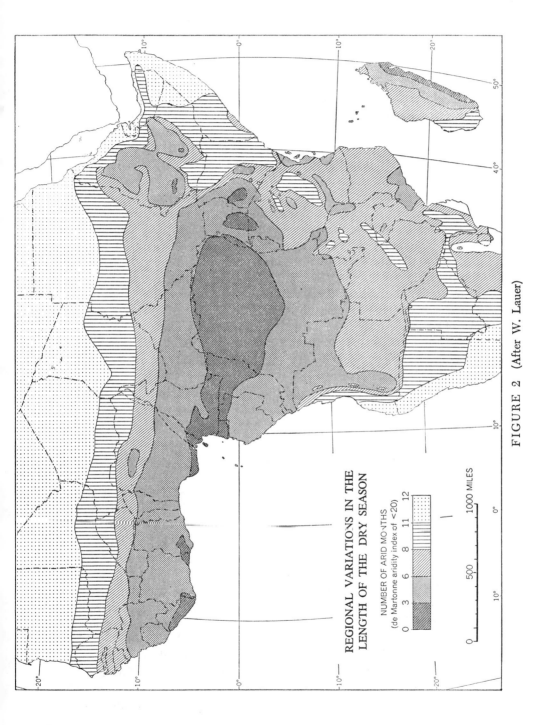

REGIONAL VARIATIONS IN THE
LENGTH OF THE DRY SEASON

NUMBER OF ARID MONTHS
(de Martonne aridity index of <20)

0   3   6   8   11 12

0   500   1000 MILES

FIGURE 2   (After W. Lauer)

47

The significance of this phenomenon of seasonality is fundamental. It governs, as will be seen, the responses of plants and animals and it confronts almost every man, woman and child with problems of food and water supply, problems which are not made any easier by the frequent failure of the seasons to observe the practice of seasonality!

For the fact is that the map showing regional variations in the length of the dry season (Figure 2) suggests a precision and permanence which the data scarcely warrant. Indeed, we can take it that, in any given year, not less than one place in three has a dry season that differs in duration from that indicated in the map, and that most of the others have a dry season which is somewhat "off-beat" — one that either starts and finishes early, or starts and finishes late. This is true not only of the regions with a very long dry season, but also of those with a short dry season. Even in the Belgian Congo the start of the rainy season may vary from the norm by as much as five to seven weeks. At one equatorial locality — Karawa — the mean date for the end of the dry season, or, if you will, the beginning of the rainy season, is February 9, but over a recent three-year period the actual dates differed by nine weeks (January 9 and March 14). Fluctuations in the mean date of the end of the rainy season are of the same order. As the magnitude of both tends to increase with the duration of the dry season, the hazard of crop and cattle loss by drought is often greatest where the farmer's ability to cushion himself against it is least.

Nor is it only the duration and timing of the wet and dry seasons that vary in this way. The amount of rainfall is subject to very considerable seasonal variation, and here again the magnitude of the variation tends to increase with the length of the dry season, which compounds still further the difficulties of those people who, in the absence of wells, rivers and storage waters, must live off the rainfall.

In places where the rainfall is marginal for "dry" farming, it is really more important to know the scale of these seasonal variations than it is to know exactly how much can be expected in a given season. For the British East African region, the degree of variability is now known fairly accurately. Maps expressing this — or rather the complementary aspect of it, namely, reliability — were published in the historic *East Africa Royal Commission 1953-1955 Report*.[12] What they show are the percentage chances of places receiving (a) 20 inches and (b) 30 inches of rain in a twelve-month period. These specific amounts were chosen since they correspond, respectively, to the quantity of rain needed in east African conditions of subsistence farming to give a reasonable yield of a fairly drought-resistant crop such as sorghum and, at a higher farming level, to the quantity needed to give a reasonable yield of maize. These maps show that, except for the forest areas, the European Highlands and those

[12] H.M.S.O., London, 1955.

parts of Uganda adjacent to Lake Victoria, east Africa falls in the 30 per cent zone of the 30-inch map, and that a very considerable proportion of it also falls in the 30 per cent zone of the 20-inch map. In other words, they show that a very large proportion of the marginal land can reckon to live up to its rainfall expectation only about once in every three years. This is not a good enough risk for most "dry" farmers.

Even when rainy seasons arrive and depart on schedule and their yield is up to par, they are still capable of posing a problem or two. For tropical rains often come in the form of short concentrated showers and thunderstorms. And the concentration can be ferocious. It is not uncommon for three to four inches of rain to fall in a single shower, or for a month's rainfall of 10 to 15 inches to fall in half a dozen showers on as many different days. Such falls cannot easily be accommodated by the African earth. All too often more rain is lost in run-off than is saved in seepage. And the run-off is frequently the cause of other losses, such as removal of precious topsoil from unprotected surfaces, siltation and flooding of low-lying areas, which in turn is likely to ruin standing crops even as it is likely to redeem the life of every stagnant-water-loving insect.

If only the average fall in such areas were divided between twice as many days, how much more serviceable it would be! But then, the African tropics are no place for half measures, as a glance at the annual rainfall map clearly shows (Figure 3). Primarily, this map is a study in contrasts — often startling in their magnitude and proximity — between prodigality and scarcity, between the equatorial forest zones which can measure their rain in feet and the deserts which have difficulty in measuring it at all. At Debundja, on the windward side of Cameroons Mountain, the average annual fall is over 33 feet, and in many lowland stations thereabouts it is over seven feet. At many Saharan oases, and at points in the Kalahari, Namib and Somaliland deserts, the only precipitation is dew. All told, at least a million square miles of tropical Africa have a mean annual rainfall of 60 inches or more; at least a million square miles have a mean annual rainfall of six inches or less; and a million square miles are so arid that even if they were given double their average fall, they would still not have enough. Even twice twenty is not enough in a land where the evaporation is of the order of 60 inches a year. Bushmen, it is true, know how to live with low rainfall and high evaporation, but who wants to live like Bushmen? Not even Bushmen, it seems.

Evapotranspiration

While a knowledge of the seasonal amounts and variations of temperature and rainfall helps us to form a good idea of what a place is like for people to live in, it does not always tell us very much about what it is like for plants to live in. For plants are more concerned with "moistness" and "dryness" than with actual quantities of moisture, and it is impossible

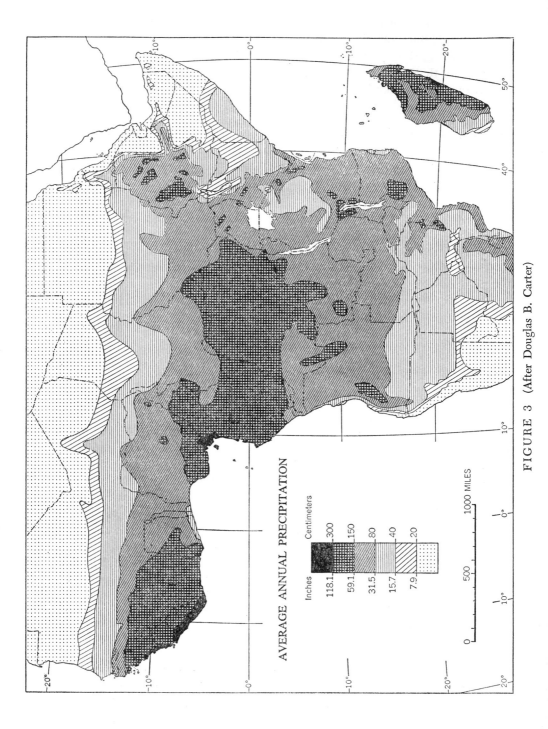

AVERAGE ANNUAL PRECIPITATION

Inches   Centimeters

118.1 — 300

59.1 — 150

31.5 — 80

15.7 — 40

7.9 — 20

0   500   1000 MILES

FIGURE 3 (After Douglas B. Carter)

to determine whether a climate is moist enough or dry enough for a particular plant simply by knowing the temperature and rainfall. The only way to tell this is by comparing the rainfall, or available water supply, with what is known as the potential evapotranspiration of the plant. This concept of potential evapotranspiration was developed by C. Warren Thornthwaite, and may be defined as the water need of a plant, or, more technically, as the quantity of water that is evaporated and transpired from a given vegetation-covered area when the soil enjoys a constant optimum moisture condition.

Unfortunately, data on measured rates of evapotranspiration are scanty. The Thornthwaite system, which assumes a direct relationship between potential evapotranspiration and temperature, has been applied to Africa by Douglas B. Carter. The results of his investigation show that the only place of any size where the rainfall exceeds the potential evapotranspiration is in the rain forest, that is, in the wettest zones of equatorial Africa. Over most of the rest of tropical Africa, the annual potential evapotranspiration exceeds the annual rainfall; in other words, even if the whole of the year's rainfall were conserved and utilized by the plant cover, still more could be used if it were available. Estimates of evapotranspiration made on the basis of the difference between rainfall and run-off in the Belgian Congo agree well with the values arrived at by using the Thornthwaite formula. In Nigeria, however, B. J. Garnier has found that the Thornthwaite formula underestimates the rate of evapotranspiration in the dry season, because it relies solely on temperature and makes no allowance for the relatively low moisture content of the air during the dry season. He has also found that over more than half of that country the mean annual rainfall is less than the mean annual water need.[13] In South Africa, too, it has been found that high temperatures are not in themselves enough to bring about a high rate of evapotranspiration: what is needed also is dry air or high winds.

On the basis of the relations between rainfall and computed potential evapotranspiration, Carter has produced a map of moisture regions (Figure 4). Although differing in detail from climatic maps of other authorities, it is in broad agreement with them, after allowance has been made for differences in terminology; and it has the merit of rigid mathematical consistency. It is used to furnish part of the basis for our subdivision of tropical Africa into climatic regions.

Other Moisture Elements

All over tropical Africa both the rainy seasons and the dry seasons tend to be associated with certain conditions of cloudiness, humidity and evaporation.

[13] See *Natural Resources, Food and Population in Inter-Tropical Africa,* edited by L. Dudley Stamp, Geographical Publications Ltd., London, 1956, p. 31.

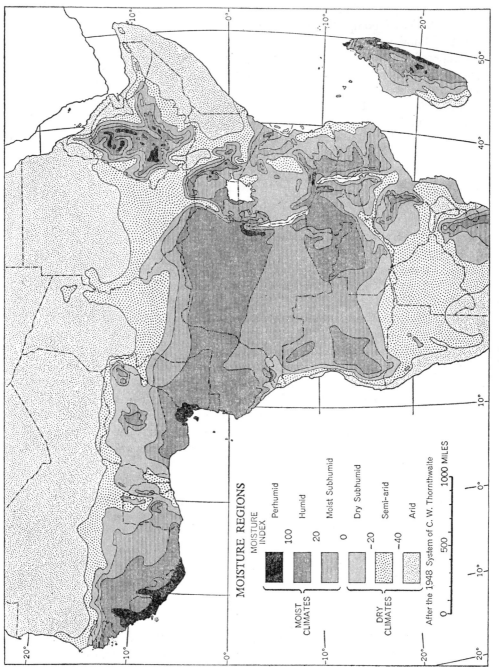

MOISTURE REGIONS

MOISTURE INDEX

MOIST CLIMATES
- 100 — Perhumid
- 20 — Humid
- 0 — Moist Subhumid

DRY CLIMATES
- −20 — Dry Subhumid
- −40 — Semi-arid
- Arid

After the 1948 System of C. W. Thornthwaite

0 ⊢——————⊣ 500 ⊢——————⊣ 1000 MILES

FIGURE 4   (After Douglas B. Carter)

For example, during the rainiest months of the wettest (rain forest) areas the sky is not characteristically overcast, but between half and three-quarters cloud-covered. During the dry months of the intermediate (savanna) areas, the sky is usually about 20 to 30 per cent cloud-covered; at the margins of the desert, it is seldom more than 10 per cent covered. In many parts of the rain forest zone the amount of cloud changes less between the seasons than between early morning and afternoon. Thus, at Eala in the Belgian Congo the cloud cover averaged close to 65 per cent throughout the year during a ten-year period, but at 6 A.M. it averaged 72 per cent and at 6 P.M. 58 per cent. Even when there are no clouds, the sky is frequently more white than blue on account of the moisture contained in the air, or the dust and smoke carried aloft from drier areas.

Although as a general rule cloud amount and rainfall are directly related, there are exceptions. One of the most interesting of these is found in the desert coastal zones of Southwest Africa and southern Angola. Walvis Bay, for instance, has cloudy skies (70 to 90 per cent covered) most mornings of the year, yet it hardly ever gets rain. Here the cloudiness is caused by the constant cooling and moistening of the air in contact with the upwelling inshore waters of the Benguela current.

The invisible moisture content of the air likewise tends to vary with the rainfall. In the rainy season the relative humidity rises on most nights to the high 90s, if not 100 per cent. On clear, still nights, the invisible frequently becomes visible in the form of mist or dew. During the daytime in the rainy season, the relative humidity may get down to 65 per cent, but seldom below 60 per cent. In the dry season it falls much lower — sometimes below 10 per cent during the reign of the west African harmattan. However, to say that the relative humidity of a sample of air is 65 per cent, or 100 per cent, tells us very little about the moisture content of that sample, since the relative humidity of a given sample of air varies with its temperature. Thus, a 65 per cent relative humidity in 80°F air becomes a 100 per cent relative humidity when that same air has been cooled to 68°F. A much more useful, if less widely available, measure of atmospheric moisture is vapor pressure, which expresses the absolute amount of moisture in the air. Another value highly regarded by plant physiologists, though subject to large daily temperature-induced variations, is the saturation deficit, or the difference between the maximum vapor pressure possible at a given temperature and the actual vapor pressure present. This gives us a measure of the evaporative power of the atmosphere. As might be expected, vapor pressures tend to be high and saturation deficits small in the wetter (rain forest) climates, and in the rainy season of the drier climates, and conversely in the drier climates and the dry season of the wetter climates. Two of the most notable exceptions to this rule are provided by the Namib coast, where a high vapor pressure is coupled with a small saturation deficit, and the Eritrean coast of the Red Sea, where a high vapor pressure is coupled with a large saturation deficit.

Wind

Most of the winds of tropical Africa are little better than light breezes. In the open, a wind of over eight to ten miles an hour is something to talk about. In the rain forest it is something to be anxious about, since it almost certainly means that a gale is raging overhead. And most winds die away at sundown, a fact that adds to the discomfort of tropical nights. The best-served areas are the coasts, for on most of them comparatively cool onshore (sea) breezes spring up during the morning and last until late afternoon. But their range is short. Along some desert coasts they can be felt up to 25 miles inland, if anybody happens to live there; but usually they do not penetrate inland more than ten to twelve miles.

Of the few prevailing — seasonal — winds, the most talked about is the harmattan, a very dry and dusty wind that comes down from the Sahara to the Guinea coast, and often beyond, during the northern hemisphere winter. By day it is hot, sometimes unbearably so; by night it is usually cool, even to the point of discomfort. But in a land of great heat and moisture it is on the whole a welcome visitor deserving the alias of "The Doctor" by which it is widely known in west Africa.

Almost the only winds that reach or exceed gale force are the tornadoes of the intertropical convergence zone, the squalls that herald the rain-bringing thunderstorm, and the much bigger and often very destructive cyclones (hurricanes) that occur along the coasts of the Malagasy Republic and Mozambique during the late summer and fall.

CLIMATIC REGIONS

Important as these individual elements are, it is their occurrence in combinations that gives them their great human importance. For what the people of tropical Africa know are not, so to speak, the easy-to-label laboratory specimens, but the hard-to-live-with syntheses produced from these specimens. And where there are so many "specimens" of rainfall, temperature, wind and the like, the possibilities for synthesis are almost endless. André Aubréville, to whose scholarship we shall have many occasions to refer gratefully, has identified not less than 73 different syntheses, or climatic regions, in tropical Africa. For the present purpose it will be enough to follow the much simpler synthesis suggested by Peveril Meigs. It recognizes eight basic types of climatic region, three of them belonging to the humid lowlands, two to the areas of aridity, two to the humid uplands, and one to the truly mountainous, or alpine, area. Seven of these divisions appear in Figure 5.

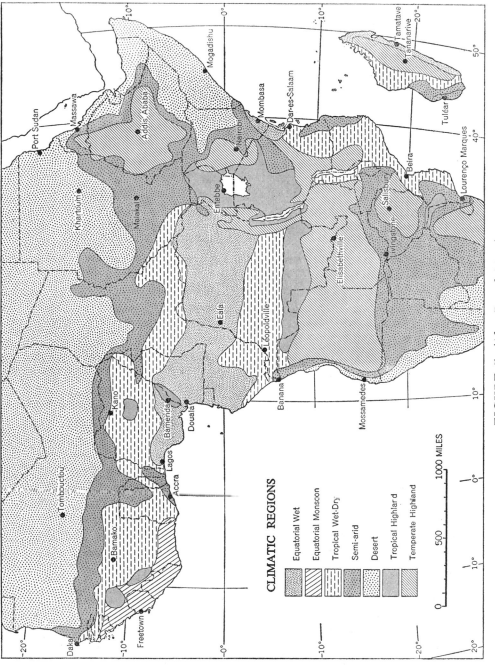

CLIMATIC REGIONS

	Equatorial Wet
	Equatorial Monsoon
	Tropical Wet-Dry
	Semi-arid
	Desert
	Tropical Highland
	Temperate Highland

0   500   1000 MILES

FIGURE 5 (After Peveril Meigs)

1. The *equatorial wet region* is characterized by high mean temperatures, a small annual temperature range, heavy rainfall, and the absence of a marked dry season. It comprises the heart of the Congo basin, Spanish Guinea, most of the Gabon Republic and the Republic of the Congo, southern Nigeria and the southern Cameroons (in their lower levels). Small "outliers" of this region are found along the coast of east Africa and the Malagasy Republic.

At Eala, a typical station (except for its 1,100-foot elevation, which is responsible for a 3°–4°F lowering of the mean temperature), there is a difference of only 6°F between the means of the warmest (February) and the coolest (July and August) months. The daily range is from about 66° to 86°F. Temperatures of more than 95°F and less than 60°F are rare. Rain falls, on the average, twelve days a month, the range being from six (in July) to seventeen (in October). High relative humidities and cloudy skies are customary the year around.

This is the so-called "evergreen" region of the rain forest (see p. 65).

2. The *equatorial monsoon region* also has high mean temperatures, a small annual temperature range, and a heavy rainfall. What chiefly distinguishes it from the first region is the existence of a three to four months' dry season — a circumstance which favors the development of deciduous rather than evergreen species in its rain forest flora. As the map shows, this region — roughly coincident with the lowlands of the Ivory Coast, Liberia, Sierra Leone, the Republic of Guinea, and Portuguese Guinea — is much smaller than the equatorial wet region and is territorially distinct from it.

Freetown, Sierra Leone, is representative of its thermal quality, for it has a mean temperature of 81°F and a mean annual temperature range of 3°F. Its 150-inch rainfall is higher than that reported by most other coastal stations in the region, but its concentration into eight of the twelve months of the year is quite typical. During the height of the season of onshore monsoon winds, in July and August, the fall averages about 35 inches a month, as against the nine-inch monthly maximum at Eala. The dry season (December through March) brings a welcome respite from lowering skies and hissing rains, but not from the daytime heat, which, in fact, reaches its peak just before the onset of the rainy season. As trying as the heat on some days is the dust of the harmattan.

3. The *tropical wet-dry regions* lie on the poleward sides of the equatorial wet and the equatorial monsoon regions. They have a high mean temperature, a moderate annual temperature range (more than 10°F except in coastal areas) and a mean rainfall, of between 30 and 50 inches as a rule, that is strictly seasonal. Indeed, seasonal duality is the keynote to the climate. During the rainy season wet equatorial conditions prevail, with cloudy, hot, humid days and nights, swollen streams, and luxuriant plant growth. During the dry season, which lasts, according to the locality, anywhere from four to seven months, the skies are often

cloudless, relative humidities are low (so low in parts of west Africa that lips become parched and skin cracks), the days are hot and the nights cool. And, whether from desert dust or bush fire, the air is hazy and the visibility consequently poor. The seasonal temperature peak usually occurs, as in the monsoon region, just before the onset of the rains. In parts of the French Cameroons this is called, expressively, "the season of burning feet, when even the calloused soles of the African hate to tread the parched red earth." [14]

The largest of the tropical wet-dry regions is located in west Africa (in Nigeria, the Republic of Dahomey, and the hinterlands of the Ivory Coast and the Republic of Guinea), whence it extends in a sinuous belt eastward to the Equatoria Province of the Republic of Sudan. Smaller regions are located in the lower Congo and Kasai valleys, in the coastal lowlands of Mozambique and Tanganyika, and in the lowland western third of the Malagasy Republic.

Where it has not been altered by cultivation, cattle keeping or fire, the vegetation of these wet-dry regions is of the type commonly referred to as savanna — a word that is almost as much abused as the various associations of grasses and trees it stands for.

4. The *semi-arid regions* are those which fall into the −20 to −40 moisture index zones of the Thornthwaite classification. Less precisely, they are the regions where the dry season lasts eight to nine months of the year and the rainy season is anything but dependable. The only thermal characteristic they have in common is a high daily range. Their mean temperatures vary from the equatorial 80s to the "temperate" 60s, depending upon their elevation and, to a lesser extent, their latitude.

The main region of semi-aridity, thus defined, extends in a belt of variable width almost completely across Africa from the Atlantic at Dakar to the Red Sea at or near Massawa. A second, more sinuous and shapeless transcontinental region runs from near Banana in the Belgian Congo southward through Angola to Southwest Africa, thence across Bechuanaland and the southernmost part of Southern Rhodesia to the coast of Mozambique at Lourenço Marques. Other, smaller regions of semi-aridity are located along the coast of northern Mozambique and southern Tanganyika, back from the coast in central Tanganyika and southern Kenya, and in the southwestern corner of the Malagasy Republic.

The natural vegetation of these regions consists of coarse grasses, shrubs and low trees (often thorny), in varying ratios.

5. The *desert regions* lie on the poleward margins of the semi-arid regions. The greatest of these regions is of course the Sahara, large parts of which lie outside the field of this study. It, too, runs from coast to coast. Virtually continuous with it are the much smaller deserts of the Somali-

[14] L. K. Anderson and W. S. Skinner, *Bridge to Africa,* Board of Foreign Missions of the Presbyterian Church in the United States of America, New York, 1952, p. 131.

lands, Ethiopia and northeastern Kenya. South of the equator only the Namib of Southwest Africa and its northward extension into southern Angola rank as true desert. But the aggregate is big enough, and bigger by far than the aggregate for either the American or Asiatic-Australian tropics.

Topographically and thermally these deserts range all the way from featureless plains seared by temperatures that almost daily run well up in the 100s and even at night seldom drop below 80°F (such a desert is the Danakil of eastern Ethiopia) to rocky plateaus where the daily range may be as much as 40° to 50°F (as in many parts of the Sahara), and coastal dune-covered deserts where the mean temperatures are more temperate than tropical and the daily range only a very little more than in the rain forests (for example, the Namib Desert and its northward extension into Angola). But they are all alike in two things: they are rainless almost all of the time, and the rain they do get is too capricious, too small and generally too torrential to support a permanent economy, whether plant, animal or human. What life they do support is more dependent on the existence of adventitious supplies of water (from springs, wells and exotic rivers) than on the rains, though these may be ample enough from time to time to produce a flush of herbaceous growths.

6. The *tropical highland regions* are those which are high enough to pull down the mean temperature for the coolest month to between 64° and 70°F, and moist enough to escape classification as semi-arid or desert. Apart from the many "islands" of such climate too small to appear on a small-scale map, there are five such regions in tropical Africa. These are the Guinea Highlands, the Jos Plateau (Nigeria), the Cameroon Highlands, the plateaus of Uganda and northern and central Tanganyika, and the highlands of southern Kasai (Belgian Congo). Except for their common coolness, it could be argued that these regions have closer affinities with the areas immediately around them than with each other. Thus, the Guinea Highlands share the eight-to-nine-month rains of the monsoonal coast of Sierra Leone and Liberia; the Kasai Highlands share the four-to-five-month dry season of the tropical wet-dry region of the central Congo, and the southern Cameroon Highlands, with their ten-month rains and more than 100-inch annual fall (104 inches at Bamenda), are much closer to the adjacent equatorial wet region of the Gabon Republic than they are to the six-month rainy season and average annual fall of between 50 and 60 inches of the Jos Plateau. Much the same line of argument could be taken with regard to relative humidities and other moisture elements, and the annual and daily ranges of temperature.

Even so, the lowering of the mean temperatures induced by elevation, which in these regions is almost everywhere over 3,000 feet above sea level and frequently exceeds 4,000 feet, is enough to warrant their separation from their lowland neighbors. For these are the areas where a man lives in considerably greater physiological comfort than is generally possible in the lowlands and where, for a part of the year, at any rate, he often finds it necessary to bestir himself in order to keep warm.

7. The *temperate highland regions* are those which are high enough to pull down the mean temperature of the coolest month to between approximately 64° and 50°F, and, like the tropical highlands, wet enough to rank as humid rather than arid areas. Such areas lie for the most part between 5,000 and 8,000 feet above the level of the sea. The Ethiopian Highlands, the Kenya (European) Highlands, the mountains and plateaus bordering the Rift Valley, the plateaus of southern Tanganyika and northern Mozambique, the Angola-Katanga–Northern Rhodesia plateaus, the Midlands and Eastern Highlands of Southern Rhodesia, and the highlands in the center of the Malagasy Republic constitute the chief of them.

Other thermal characteristics of these regions are the large daily range of temperature (up to 20°F in the rainy season and 30°F in the dry season) and the small annual range (at Nairobi, for instance, there is only 7°F difference between the mean temperatures of the warmest and the coolest months).

Like the tropical highland regions, the temperate highland regions exhibit a wide range of rainfall characteristics — from heavy, well-distributed equatorial-type rainfall (as in the Kivu region) and heavy double-maximum-type rainfall (as in Ruanda-Urundi) to heavy monsoonal-type rainfall in the Ethiopian Highlands and moderate monsoonal or summer-maximum-type rainfall in the Eastern Highlands and Midlands of Southern Rhodesia. Where the terrain is more mountain than plateau, aspect plays a big role in determining the amount of the rainfall. Thus, the windward slopes of mountains like the Ruwenzoris, Kilimanjaro and Kenya are much better watered than the leeward. They also tend to be cooler, level for level, because of their cloudiness and the frequency of the precipitation.

8. The *alpine regions* are confined to those beclouded mountains that lie above about 8,000 feet. We say "about" because their lower limit lies higher (by 1,000 feet or more) at the equator than at the tropics. As such localities are not extensive — usually being little more than mountain summits — they are not shown on the generalized map. The most notable of them are Mt. Kilimanjaro (which rises to more than 19,300 feet above the level of the sea), Mt. Kenya (17,000 feet), the Ruwenzoris (16,750 feet) and Mt. Elgon (14,150 feet). Others are found in the Ethiopian Highlands and one (Cameroons Mountain) is found in west Africa. In each the mean temperature of the coldest month ranges from about 50°F at intermediate levels to 32°F or less at the summit. The presence of glaciers at the summits of Mt. Kilimanjaro, Mt. Kenya and the Ruwenzoris is proof enough of their "alpine" quality.

THE VEGETATION

Since nothing is so sensitive to its physical environment as a plant, it is not surprising to find that the vegetation map of tropical Africa (Figure 6) at once reflects the circumstances of relief and climate and compounds their differences. The main elements of the map are simple enough, namely, forest, grassland and desert, but it is full of fussy detail. For there are several different kinds of forests, grassland and deserts. And the reality is much more complicated than the map. In any patch of forest, grassland or desert, represented uniformly on the map, the eye of the botanist will detect local variations in the membership, virility and size of plant communities that are significant to the African inhabitant (who spotted them long before the botanist did) because they tell of variations in soil quality, underground water supplies and the availability of food and forage.

There are other complications, too. Thus, there are natural forests, grasslands and deserts and "semi-natural" forests, grasslands and deserts; and, of the two kinds, it is arguable that the semi-natural is the more important, or at any rate the more extensive. For, unlike some other parts of the world, tropical Africa has been subject to so long and intensive a colonization by man that what we mostly see today is not "such as creation's dawn beheld" but such as Dame Nature has contrived to keep going in face of the inhabitants' never-ending campaign of pilfering, larceny, arson and abuse. And the scale of this campaign has been well-nigh continental. It is now widely supposed that almost all the savannas are what the botanist calls a "fire climax"; that, if the lands on which they are presently found could be completely protected from fire, there would be no savannas, but only a continuous graded cover of woody plants all the way from the equatorial forests to the desert. In other words, there are probably not many natural grasslands in tropical Africa.

As for the desert, there seems to be reason to suppose that it, too, in part, is not natural, but the end product of long-continued seasonal burning of marginal bush by cultivators in need of new ground and herders seeking to encourage new and more succulent growths for their animals. Cultivators have not always stopped to consider the propriety of breaking marginal bush, even though they have known that they were likely to be scourged for their pains by dust and sandstorms. Herders have not always been careful to keep a nice balance between the size of their herds and the size, and quality, of their pastures. And hooves are often as quick as hoes to set soil in motion. Once set in motion, either by wind or water, semi-arid soil is always difficult, and generally impossible, to replace.

Even many of the forests are not natural. What with the ageless needs of the forest cultivator for crop land and of the newly developed needs of the lumberman for their prized timbers, most of the more accessible forests are but a shadow of their former selves, as glimpsed in the "relict" forests that still remain.

The state of affairs is further complicated also by the fact that, since man lives largely on vegetation, either directly or indirectly, he is perennially modifying the vegetation, natural and semi-natural, to provide himself with the kinds he wants. Over large parts of east and west Africa these modifications have been so radical that in places even the botanist is hard put to tell what the natural or semi-natural vegetation used to be.[15] And because the African's need of food and vegetable raw materials is growing every year, these modifications are increasing both in scale and in kind. In many places the landscape has ceased to be African in almost everything but location. The trees that grow there are natives of Brazil, Mexico, the Caribbean, India and Australia; the grasses, natives of the United Kingdom, Western Europe and the Mediterranean; the bush and field crops, natives of the Americas, Europe and Asia.

With these considerations in mind, let us now look at the major vegetation zones of the region.

THE FORESTS

There are a great many forests in tropical Africa — more than anyone has ever bothered to count. While some of them live up to the impressive things travelers are in the habit of saying about them, most do not. Many are forests only by courtesy, and many that are forests in fact are not recognizably "tropical." However, most of them fall conveniently into two categories. These have been given different names by different botanists, the commonest and least equivocal of which are "rain forests" and "dry forests." Of the two, the former occupy a much smaller area than the latter, but their economic value is much greater.

The Rain Forests

Characteristics

Rain forests have been variously defined. The definition given by the famous German plant geographer, A. F. W. Schimper, as long ago as 1898 is still widely accepted. It runs as follows: "Evergreen, hygrophilous [i.e., moisture-loving] in character, at least 30 meters [nearly 100 feet] high, but usually much taller, rich in thick-stemmed lianes and in woody as well as herbaceous epiphytes [i.e., parasitic growths]."[16] But a definition, however accurate or useful, does not take us very far along the road to reality. In dealing with the African rain forests, a definition

---

[15] See K. M. Buchanan and J. C. Pugh, *Land and People in Nigeria*, University of London Press, London, 1955, p. 36.

[16] *Plant Geography upon a Physiological Basis*, translated by W. R. Fisher, Oxford University Press, London, 1903, p. 260.

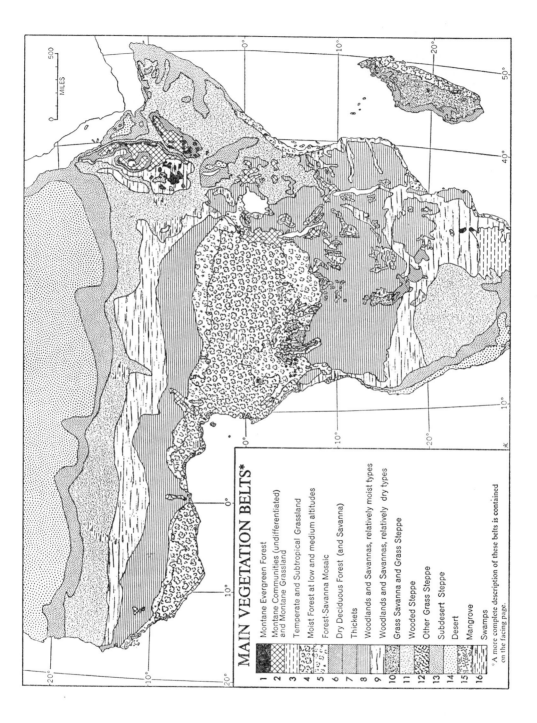

MAIN VEGETATION BELTS*

1 Montane Evergreen Forest
2 Montane Communities (undifferentiated)
   and Montane Grassland
3 Temperate and Subtropical Grassland
4 Moist Forest at low and medium altitudes
5 Forest-Savanna Mosaic
6 Dry Deciduous Forest (and Savanna)
7 Thickets
8 Woodlands and Savannas, relatively moist types
9 Woodlands and Savannas, relatively dry types
10 Grass Savanna and Grass Steppe
11 Wooded Steppe
12 Other Grass Steppe
13 Subdesert Steppe
14 Desert
15 Mangrove
16 Swamps

*A more complete description of these belts is contained
on the facing page.

MILES
0   500

FIGURE 6 (After *Vegetation Map of Africa South of the Tropic of Cancer*, prepared by A. Aubréville, P. Duvigneaud, A. C. Hoyle, R. W. J. Keay, F. A. Mendonça and R. E. G. Pichi-Sermolli under the auspices of the Association pour l'Etude Taxonomique de la Flore d'Afrique Tropicale and published with the assistance of UNESCO; Clarendon Press, Oxford, 1959)

Detailed description of vegetation belts

Explanations of the vegetation belts have been abbreviated in some instances for reasons of space. The full description of each belt is as follows:

1 Montane Evergreen Forest

2 Montane Communities — undifferentiated; Montane Communities with afro-alpine communities; Montane Grassland

3 Temperate and Subtropical Grassland

4 Moist Forest at low and medium altitudes

5 Forest-Savanna Mosaic; Coastal Forest-Savanna Mosaic

6 Dry Deciduous Forest (and Savanna) — with abundant *Baikiaea plurijuga*; Dry Deciduous Forest (and Savanna) — Madagascar types

7 Thickets — Itigi type; Thickets — Madagascar types; Thickets — Ethiopian evergreen types

8 Woodlands and Savannas: Undifferentiated — relatively moist types, Northern areas — with abundant *Isoberlinia doka* and *I. dalzielii*, Southeastern areas — with abundant *Brachystegia* and *Julbernardia*,

Southwestern areas (principally on Kalahari Sand) — with abundant *Brachystegia, Julbernardia, Cryptosepalum pseudotaxus, Marquesia, Guibourtia coleosperma* and areas of steppe (type no. 10)

9 Woodlands and Savannas: Undifferentiated — relatively dry types, Ethiopian types, Type with abundant *Colophospermum mopane*

10 Madagascar Grass Savanna and Grass Steppe; Grass Steppe on Kalahari Sand

11 Wooded Steppe with abundant *Acacia* and *Commiphora*

12 Grass Steppe with Thicket Clumps — W. Uganda type; Grass Steppe — Luanda type

13 Subdesert Steppe: Karoo shrub and grass, transitional and mixed Karoo, tropical types

14 Desert

15 Mangrove

16 Swamps

takes us almost nowhere. Practically every statement we can make about them needs to be qualified by a further, and sometimes contrary, statement.

When seen from a river, the rain forest (the "moist forest" of Figure 6) appears fully to justify Peter Abrahams' poetic description of it:

> Damp earth and no grass
> Dank heat and no air
> Giant trees and dark waters
> Rustle and whisper, hiss and silence
> Stealth and menace . . . [17]

In their competition for light, air and moisture, every herbaceous plant, bush, liana, epiphyte and tree within reaching distance struggles for a riverside frontage, with a resulting congestion that is unparalleled in nature. Horizontal visibility is down to a few feet, and every step is an adventure. But when viewed from within, a rain forest is rather different. "[If] one's hands are free to bend back a twig here and there, it is not difficult to walk in any direction . . . [and] it is usually possible to see another person at least 20 [meters] away." [18] Nor is it sunless, for the overhead canopy is seldom continuous. And it is only the trees in the top story of growth, forming perhaps less than 10 per cent of the total, that are very tall, say more than a hundred feet. The rest are smaller, averaging about 60 feet for the middle story, where it exists, and 30 feet for the lower story.

Seen from the surface, whether within or without, a rain forest is likely to give the impression of being dressed in monotonous and rather dowdy greens. Seen from above, it is splashed with all the colors of a painter's palette. To the unskilled eye, there is an apparent uniformity of tree type. Most of the trees are slender and straight and only branch out near their crowns. Their bases are commonly provided with buttress-like outgrowths. Their barks are smooth and thin; and their leaves are large and leathery, reminiscent, in shape, size and texture, of the cherry laurel of more temperate climates. Yet the fact is that a mature tropical rain forest exhibits more heterogeneity to the acre than any other forest on earth. "There are seldom less than 40 species of trees over 4 inch diameter per hectare [2.47 acres] and sometimes over a hundred species." [19] The Malagasy rain forest usually scores 30 to 40 different species in every count of a hundred plants. The Ivory Coast forest contains at least 500 species of tree belonging to 248 different genera and 55 different families.

Not all rain forests are alike. In the closed rain forest, or high forest, the canopy formed by the tree crowns is practically continuous and the

[17] A Wreath for Udomo, Alfred A. Knopf, New York, 1956, p. 251.
[18] P. W. Richards, The Tropical Rain Forest, Cambridge University Press, Cambridge, 1952, p. 5.
[19] Ibid., p. 3.

floor practically clear of growth. Here the dominant species are ever-greens. On the wetter and marshier margins of this type of forest, as, for instance, along the coast of Nigeria, the trees do not grow to the same large diameter and are usually of different species. Many of them have stilt-like roots, a growth habit that enables them to breathe more freely in waterlogged soil. Raffia and climbing palms abound. Some of the larger species of tree grow to be 150 feet tall, but for the most part the forest is lower. In places it is little more than a low-growing tangle of mangrove shrubs and lianas beneath a very open canopy.

Toward its drier margins the closed forest undergoes a striking floristic change. The number of species decreases, the canopy becomes more open with consequent increase in the amount of undergrowth, and many trees shed their leaves during part of the dry season. This type of forest is often referred to as the mixed deciduous rain forest. In between the two a third type going by the name of dry evergreen forest is sometimes to be discerned.

There are other variations. Where the virgin, or primary, forest has disappeared for one cause or another, its place has been taken by a secondary growth. Depending on the length of time it has been left alone, this land will be occupied by plant associations ranging from low brush to jungle 60 feet tall. If it is left alone long enough, it may revert to true forest, but seldom to "primeval" forest. Instead it is likely to be composed of the more common and widely distributed species, sometimes found in pure stands, such as the aptly named parasol tree.

In some rain forest regions no primary rain forest remains. In well-populated rain forest country it is possible to drive all day without passing through, or seeing, a single stretch of primary forest. Even in sparsely populated country, it is rare nowadays to find primary forest standing by the roadside, unless it forms part of a state reserve.

Distribution

The still considerable limitations of most maps and surveys coupled with the uncertainty, hardly less considerable, as to what constitutes a rain forest insure that any estimates of the area under rain forest are no more than first approximations. Those given in Tables 1 and 2 for the western and eastern rain forests are the work of Aubréville, who has made a lifetime study of tropical African forests. To use his own words, they suggest "relative orders of magnitude." Of the total area of 218 million hectares (nearly 540 million acres) in the western rain forests, Aubréville thinks that perhaps 139 million hectares, or about 64 per cent, are in actual forest and that the rest forms part of the domain of the bush-fallowing cultivator. The rain forest areas of eastern Africa are much less extensive, as the territorial breakdown in Table 2 clearly shows.

Although the rain forests on the Atlantic side of Africa are almost continuous, longitudinally, for 3,000 miles, they are much better represented in some areas than in others. These areas are situated along the Guinea coast, around the Bight of Benin and in the Congo basin. In Aubréville's nomenclature they are designated the Guinea, Nigerian and Equatorial forests.

The Guinea forest borders the coast from Sierra Leone eastward to the Black Volta River in Ghana. It covers only a small part of Sierra Leone and the Republic of Guinea, almost all of Liberia, the greater part of the Ivory Coast and a good part of Ghana. It often begins at the seashore, within a few yards of the high-water mark, and stretches in

Table 1

APPROXIMATE AREAS OF
WESTERN RAIN FORESTS, AROUND 1950

(Million Hectares)

AREA	FOREST ZONE	FORESTS
Total	218	139
Guinea Forest	33	17
Nigerian Forest	16	4
Equatorial Forest	169	118
Cameroons-Congo	63	43
Central Congo	105	74
Eastern Mountains	1	1

Table 2

APPROXIMATE AREAS OF
EASTERN RAIN FORESTS, AROUND 1950

(Thousand Hectares)

Uganda	654
Ethiopia	6,000 [a]
Kenya	1,400 [b]
Tanganyika	1,500 [b]
Mozambique	600 [b]
Nyasaland	50
Malagasy Republic (Madagascar)	6,000 [c]

[a] Very roughly.   [b] Includes dry closed forests of the coastal zone.
[c] Includes the dry forests of the western part of the island and the rain forests of the eastern part.
1 hectare = 2.471 acres

Source of Tables 1 and 2: André Aubréville, "Tropical Africa" in *A World Geography of Forest Resources,* edited for the American Geographical Society by Stephen Haden-Guest, John K. Wright and Eileen M. Teclaff, Ronald Press Company, New York, 1956, pp. 359 and 376-83.

places more than 260 miles into the interior. Its maximum length is about 800 miles.

The Nigerian forest is separated from the Guinea forest by a wide tongue of savanna country that has been largely transformed into oil palm groves and crop land. It begins almost on the Dahomey-Nigerian border and casts its coarse-meshed mantle [20] over a coastal belt some 100 to 150 miles wide. Near the French Cameroons border the belt narrows, because of the approach of the mountains to the sea, to 75 miles or so.

The Equatorial forest is the biggest and least disturbed of the three. For convenience Aubréville divides it into three parts: the Cameroons-Congo forest covering the southern part of the French Cameroons, Spanish Guinea, most of the Republics of Gabon and the Congo, and the Central African Republic, Mayumbé (Belgian Congo), Cabinda, a small part of northern Angola; the Central Congo forest, covering most of the Equateur and Orientale provinces of the Belgian Congo; and the Eastern Mountains forest, covering the Kivu-Ituri and Ruanda-Urundi areas.

The eastern rain forests are not only much smaller, they are much less compact. They occur in patches along the Indian Ocean and at many well-exposed points, mostly mountainous, inland. The coastal forests begin to the south of Tanga in Tanganyika and continue southward sporadically, and often unconvincingly, to southern Mozambique and beyond into northern Natal. Even at their best and highest they are less spectacular than the Equatorial forest. At their poorest, they are not easily distinguished from the east African dry forest.[21] Their moisture comes chiefly (exclusively in the case of the coastal forests) from the slow-moving air masses that originate over the Indian Ocean; only the inland forests receive significant amounts of rainfall from air masses moving in from the Atlantic and Congo regions. The coastal forests resemble those of the western side of the continent, for they are well endowed floristically, perennially green, and multistoried. Many of their species are identical with those of the Atlantic forests. Much the same is true of the lower-level forests of the interior. But toward the 5,500–6,000-foot level they begin to undergo a transformation. Tree dimensions decline, species decrease in number, most of the usual rain forest ones disappearing altogether, and there is a marked shift from mixed to pure stands. At the higher levels, above about 7,500 feet, conifers are frequently well represented. In every territory between Eritrea and Nyasaland stands of African juniper and other softwoods are found. Kenya alone has an estimated 2 million acres of coniferous forest. At still higher elevations pure stands of bamboo are common.

[20] Not less than three quarters of the original rain forest of Nigeria is now honeycombed with farms and villages.

[21] See pp. 69-70.

The Malagasy rain forest, an evergreen forest of extraordinary floristic richness, forms a band that extends almost unbroken along the eastern coast of the island for a distance of 900 miles or so and inland for a distance, at its widest, of between 70 and 80 miles. At one time it stretched continuously from the coast to the eastern edge of the central highlands occupying the backbone of the island.

The Dry Forests

Characteristics

From the true rain forest to the arid thorn lands that border the deserts, many types of vegetation succeed one another. The transitions between them are seldom sharp; at times they are subtle enough to defy exact delimitation and make the classification of a specific landscape difficult.

The classifier's difficulties are frequently increased by the existence of ambiguous terms and the absence of an agreed terminology. What is dry forest to one is savanna forest to another; what is savanna forest to a third is often plain savanna to a fourth — which, to say the least, is unfortunate since the name savanna is derived from the term applied by early Spanish settlers to the great plains of *treeless* grassland they found in the New World. In tropical Africa almost the only treeless grassland is man-induced and is seldom called savanna! The present discussion will steer clear of the term savanna so far as possible and use a plain-language classification which, though it ignores most of the botanical subtleties, suffices to distinguish the main types of forest, other than rain forest, which are of economic interest. It contains the following categories: dry dense forest, dry open forest, wooded tall grassland, bush and scrub, and thorn land. Very roughly these correspond to categories 5 through 11 in Figure 6.

The features which, above all others, distinguish these forests from the rain forests are the length of their rest (or "drought-dormant") season, and their degradation by fire. The drought season is almost nowhere less than three months long. Toward the drier margins it is nearer nine months long. During this generally hot season the vegetation becomes dormant. To avoid excessive loss of moisture by transpiration most trees shed their leaves. Almost all herbaceous growth stops. Grasses become as dry as tinder and burn at a touch. As Aubréville explains:

Nearly all dry Africa burns during the dry season; few parcels of soil are exempt from the fires which sweep through the savannas [i.e., tall grasslands] and dry open forests, attack the edges of the dry dense forests, and make them retreat year after year. . . . The brush fires burn for the most part in the herbaceous vegetation. Fanned by the parching winds of the dry season, they pass rapidly over the soil, leaving it littered with ashes and carbonized fragments.[22]

[22] "Tropical Africa," Chapter 16 of *A World Geography of Forest Resources*, edited for the American Geographical Society by Stephen Haden-Guest, John K. Wright and Eileen M. Tetclaff, Ronald Press Company, New York, 1956, p. 379.

However, the fires seldom at once destroy the trees in their path, which is just as well. Were they able to do so, they would long ago have deforested the drier lands. "The persistence of the forest vegetation, despite the annual fires, is due to the protection afforded by thick and often corklike barks which are bad heat conductors, and to the ability of the woody species to regenerate by stump shoots and suckers." [23] Even so, the fires destroy millions of seedlings, shoots and young branches that lack the protection of a thick bark, and mutilate millions of immature trees.

The disastrous effect of the periodic brush fires is easily demonstrated where parcels of wooded savanna are protected against fire for a number of years. The forest cover slowly re-forms and then closes completely, killing the herbaceous plants beneath its shade. Unhappily, however, it is very difficult to control the brush fires. The custom of burning the savannas is deeply rooted in the native tradition, and surveillance of these vast areas is practically impossible except in a few special places.[24]

It seems, then, that the dry lands of tropical Africa are condemned to go on living, at least for many years to come, below their botanical par; or, to put it more technically, below their climax level. Meanwhile, the forest services of the regions chiefly concerned are doing what they can to secure the future of the commercially most valuable stands of "dry" timber by placing them out of bounds to cultivators and cattle grazers, at any rate during the burning season.

Distribution

Dry dense forest. Forest of this type, whether evergreen or deciduous or mixed, no longer occupies much of tropical Africa. The west African forest zone has been almost entirely stripped of it. A few small remnants remain, as, for example, in the Casamance basin in Guinea, and in the Central African Republic. The only regions where it occurs on any scale are (a) along and near the best-watered parts of the British and Portuguese East African coasts, merging here and there into rain forest; (b) on the western side of the Malagasy Republic in isolated tracts, some large, some small; and (c) on the better-favored and still lightly populated plateaus of the central area, as, for example, in the south of the Belgian Congo and adjacent sections of northeastern Angola and northwestern Northern Rhodesia. But in most of these regions it is likewise retreating, the victim of attrition by fire and cultivation. The rainfall requirements of this forest vary somewhat from place to place, but generally they are a mean annual fall of between 35 and 55 inches and a dry season of not more than four to five months.

Dry open forest. Forest of this type is found chiefly on high ground where the mean annual rainfall is between 25 and 50 inches and the dry

[23] *Ibid.*
[24] *Ibid.*

season lasts from five to seven months. It is found most widely on the plateaus of Angola, Tanganyika, the two Rhodesias, Nyasaland, Mozambique, Bechuanaland and the Katanga region of the Belgian Congo, and along the northern flanks of the Guinea-Equatorial forest belt.

When well-developed, this forest has a canopy close enough to suppress herbaceous growth. More usually the canopy is not continuous and grasses and other herbaceous plants carpet the ground. Toward the forest's arid margin, both trees and undergrowth thin out and become dwarfed. Where brush fires occur regularly, as they do over large parts of the zone, there is little if any undergrowth, but only a short tussocky grass, the burning of which fortunately does not do serious damage to the trees.

The most extensive dry open forests at the present time are the miombo forests of the eastern and central African plateaus. These are marked by the predominance of a few leguminous species. The finest stands average between 45 and 60 feet in height and between 25 and 50 trees of more than 12-inch diameter to the acre. It is more usual, however, for the miombo to average between 30 and 45 feet in height and between 10 and 35 trees to the acre. At its poorest it averages 10 to 15 feet in height and 5 to 10 trees to the acre. Depending on the tree density and other factors such as soil and drainage, the number of species to the acre varies from about 5 to 15, of which perhaps three or four at the most will be well represented. More often than not these will belong to one species or another of *Brachystegia* and *Isoberlinia*.

The dry open forests of west Africa are much less extensive than those of east and central Africa and much poorer in species. Degradation of the plant cover by fire, grazing animals and other agents has been carried to greater lengths in this section than elsewhere, largely because the population is heavier. Around most settlements the natural vegetation has been completely suppressed as a result of long-continued cultivation. Beyond this zone comes one of secondary dry open forest which is cultivated, grazed and bush-fallowed by turns. And beyond this comes a third zone which is either exploited only for its fuel or left relatively undisturbed.

Wooded tall grassland. This tends to occur where the mean annual rainfall is less than 25 to 30 inches and the rainy season lasts less than four to five months. It reaches its greatest extension on the poleward sides of the dry open forests of west and central Africa and in the more arid sectors of the east African plateaus. Where the soil is deep and the water table high, the trees may reach a height of 50 feet and form dense stands. Characteristically the trees are much smaller, more widely dispersed, and occupy less territory than the grasses. Some of the most thickly wooded areas are found along the river valleys of the Limpopo and Zambezi and in the termite-mound country of Uganda and Tanganyika. Most of the west African areas have been too greatly modified by man to retain more than the isolated patch of mature woodland.

As in the dry open forest, there is considerable areal variation of the dominant species of tree. Thus, much of the central African sector is dominated by mopane, one of the Leguminosae; much of the east African and Malagasy sectors by palms; and much of the Sudanese sector by acacias.

Bush and scrub. This type of "forest" is well represented in east Africa, especially in central Tanganyika. Aubréville describes it as follows:

. . . thickets from two to six meters [say, 6 to 20 feet] high, usually dense but sometimes open, composed of bushes and small trees that tend to be spiny, twisted and exceedingly branchy, and that have deciduous leaves. A few taller trees, irregularly spaced, may dominate these thickets, and the ground may be covered with a herbaceous carpet of Acanthaceae. Lianes are common.[25]

The mean annual rainfall in the central Tanganyika sector, where it covers well over 3 million acres, is between 25 and 30 inches and the rainy season lasts three to four months. In the south of the Malagasy Republic this type of bush is remarkable for its multitude of extraordinary octopus-like trees belonging to the Didieraceae family, with bottle- or spindle-shaped trunks, and its big euphorbias.

Thorn land. Where the rainfall is less than 25 inches, and the dry season lasts more than six to seven months, it becomes exceedingly hard for trees to survive the fight for life. Only a comparatively few species (mostly acacias) do survive, and these by dint of possessing heat-shunning and water-conserving devices such as thin, spindly leaves (which present their minimum surface to the sun), spines, thorns, deep tap roots and thick bark. Under the least unfavorable circumstances, these trees may either form very open forests about 50 feet in height above a grassy floor or they may crowd together in jungle-like thickets of about the same height. More usually they are stunted, gnarled and misshapen, and rise from an uncompromisingly thorny ground. They are nothing if not hardy: some of them manage to survive on the desert's very edge.

THE GRASSLANDS

Most of the grassland of tropical Africa occurs in association with bush, shrub and tree growth and is not grassland in the sense that the prairies and the pampas are, or were. The extent of the natural grasslands is not known (largely because we have as yet no scientific means of dividing the line between a "semi-natural" and a "natural" grassland), but the indications point to its being quite small. For instance, where tree-grass associations, like the dry open forest and the tall wooded grasslands, have been rigorously protected from fire and heavy grazing for a period

[25] *Loc. cit.*, p. 381.

of years, there has almost always been a marked tendency for the tree communities to increase at the expense of the grass communities, and for areas of unbroken grass cover to give place to scattered patches.

The only African grasslands that are not mixed with trees and other woody growths and that, at the same time, are unlikely to be fire-climax grasslands are the following (corresponding roughly to categories 3, 16 and 2 in Figure 6):

1. The tall-grass region of the high veld of southern Africa, none of which falls within the limits of this study. The most important element in this herbaceous association is the rooi grass, which, when fully grown, reaches about three feet in height. On these grasslands there are winter frosts. The rainfall — between 30 and 40 inches — comes in the summer.

2. The marsh grass regions of central and east Africa, notably those in the ill-drained upper and middle basins of the Nile valley. By far the commonest member of this association is *Cyperus papyrus*, the papyrus of Egypt, which can flourish in a wide climatic range provided it keeps its roots in water or mud.

3. The alpine grasslands found on the Ethiopian Highlands, and in the mountains of Kenya, Uganda, Tanganyika, Nyasaland and Southern Rhodesia. None of these grasslands is very extensive, but in the aggregate they probably occupy between 350,000 and 375,000 square miles. In appearance they are not always as "alpine" as their name suggests, but certainly they are the least "African" of all African landscapes. The unwary traveler is more likely to get lost in their "Scotch mists" than in their ravines and more likely to suffer from cold than from heat. Most of their grasses are rather coarse and not especially attractive to native game or domesticated animals.

The grasses characteristic of most dry forest zones are also coarse. In the lusher areas, as, for instance, on the edges of the closed rain forest, they frequently grow 12 feet high. Toward the drier — bush and scrub — margins they may attain a height of only a few inches. Unlike temperate grasses, they tend to grow in tufts or tussocks, each plant being distinct at its base. Turf development is not common. At the end of the rains, they dry out rapidly. The taller the dried grass, the less attractive, seemingly, its merits as forage, for most ruminating animals avoid eating it whenever there is anything else to work on. Even many of the poorer "bush" grasses are sufficiently unpalatable to have earned the name, in their southern African habitat, of "sour veld."

THE DESERTS

Deserts occupy more than one third of the whole of Africa and not much less than one quarter of tropical Africa, say 2 million square miles. Of this area true desert probably occupies not less than 10 per cent. The rest carries vegetation of sorts, in some places (such as oases and wadis) the year around, but in most places for only short spells following rain or flash floods. Because such places offer at best marginal conditions for plant survival and no two of them offer identical conditions, the floras and floristic communities they support are inclined to be localized. To generalize about them, except in the broadest of terms, is consequently impossible.

Take the Sahara, for instance. Parts of it, such as the Tanezrouft, are so bare of vegetation that a camel can walk day after day without finding a speck of pasture. Other parts, though equally short of rain water, are perennially vegetated with palms, grasses and succulent shrubs. Oases, whether fed by river, well, *foggara* [26] or spring, belong to this category. Some parts, like the Ahaggar Mountains, rise high enough above the cloudless plateaus around them to be able to cover their nakedness in winter with cloud and dew, and so with greenery. Some sporadically receive enough rain to induce a growth of short-lived grasses and weeds. In parts of Spanish Sahara, these rains, though never reliable, are continually being sought out by the nomad camel and sheep herder, for rain today means green pastures tomorrow. The Regibat tribe, whose home is on the inner margins of Spanish Sahara, sometimes migrates 400 miles in pursuit of such fugitive pastures.

Most tropical African desert vegetation falls into three broad categories: scrub and grass; scrub; and salt scrub. The Sahara provides examples of all three types, but especially of the first. The deserts of northeast Africa — of the Somalilands and adjacent areas — offer many examples of scrub floras, in which acacias are conspicuous. The Kalahari and Namib deserts, with their numerous salt pans and larger areas of inland drainage, have extensive areas of salt scrub.

THE SOILS

If there is one physical generalization for which a strong case can be made in tropical Africa, it is that good soils are the exception. Most of the soils are no better than the poorest mid-latitude soils; some are poorer, and all are more easily impoverished than enriched. At first sight this would seem to be an unlikely generalization, for where do the rain forests get their almost incredible luxuriance from, if not from the soil? And what are the 12-foot-tall pastures of the dry forests, if not an evidence of uncommon strength at the grass roots? But the fact is that the luxuriance and strength of tropical plant life come not so much from the "capital account" of the soil, as from the "current account" of the air,

[26] A *foggara* is a tunnel, sometimes as much as six miles long and big enough for a man to negotiate, dug not quite horizontally to tap underground water and conduct it to an oasis by gravity.

the rainfall and the nutrients made available by the process of plant decomposition. In many parts the capital account is so low that if it is
drawn on for more than two or three years in succession by cultivators
who have destroyed the ecological equilibrium, its funds are exhausted; in
other words, crop yields decline to the vanishing point. Almost nowhere
is it big enough to stand for long the old-time fertility-robbing tactics of
the prairie farmer.

On analysis most tropical soils prove to be poor in assimilable bases
(such as lime, magnesia and potash) and therefore acid in reaction; poor
in phosphorus — what there is is frequently precipitated before it becomes accessible to the roots of plants; poor in humus, or organic material; and given to compaction.

Why should most tropical soils have these qualities, all of which make
for infertility or difficulty, or both? There are several reasons, most
of them having to do directly or indirectly with the climatic environment.

Because the air temperatures are prevailingly high, the soil temperatures are high. Since most chemical reactions occur more rapidly in a
warm environment than in a cold one, processes such as the oxidation of
organic compounds are speeded up in the tropics. Instead of dead
vegetable matter being converted slowly into valuable humus, as in
middle latitudes, it customarily combines with the oxygen of the atmosphere to form carbon dioxide, which is driven out of the soil by the water
before it can be replaced by air. Thus the oxygen is continually being
renewed, a state of affairs favorable to combustion, that is, the chemical
breakdown of the humus. Then, because the soil is warm, bacterial activity is much faster. This means that dead vegetable matter is not only
oxidized faster, it is "digested" faster than in middle latitudes. Frequently
the micro-organisms working on the fallen leaves, twigs, lianas, etc., in a
rain forest can transform the organic nitrogen in them into soluble nitrates
as fast as they become available and much faster than they are needed
by the living plants. In such forests the soil contains on the average less
than 2 per cent of humus, as against more than 10 per cent in ordinarily
fertile middle latitude soils. And humus is the stuff of which soil stamina
and fertility are made.

The rainfall regime of the tropics is no less an enemy of soil fertility.
Because warm water can hold more of a given compound in solution than
cold water, the loss of chemical plant nutrients from the soil by percolation tends to be greater than in middle and high latitudes. And because
warm water can carry a heavier chemical load than cold water, rock
weathering, or decomposition, takes place faster and goes deeper than
in middle and high latitudes. In many tropical areas the bedrock has
been weathered to a depth of several dozen feet. The deeper it
goes, the farther down are plant nutrients carried, and the greater the
percentage of such nutrients that is washed clear of the feeding system
of the vegetation, since not many species of plant draw on more than the

first few feet of soil for their food supply. The characteristically torrential nature of tropical rains merely serves to make a more thorough job of this soil-wasting, or leaching, process. Nor is the damage done in the wet season retrieved in the dry. Sometimes it is aggravated, for in the dry season highly mineralized waters are drawn above the zone of permanent soil saturation by capillary action, leaving behind chemical compounds when the water evaporates. Given the right conditions, these compounds, which consist mainly of iron and aluminum salts, will in time form a crust, or hardpan, that provides no plant food worth speaking of and forms an effective obstacle to plants seeking to reach any food and moisture that may lie below it.

Two things follow. First, most tropical soils tend to get poorer rather than richer with age; the older they become, the deeper the weathered layer becomes, and the greater the loss of inorganic and organic compounds from the soil levels at which they can be serviceable.

Second, most tropical soils tend to get less rather than more tractable with age. The rock residues remaining after the soluble materials, bases and nitrates have been carried away by percolating waters usually consist of coarse sand or heavy clay particles. Both make for serious soil compaction and difficult working conditions.

The sand, for the most part, is composed of hard, angular quartz grains of different sizes. It is derived from metamorphic rock, the kind of rock that yields diamonds. As John Loudon McAdam, the road maker, discovered a long time ago, nothing makes for compaction better than sharply angular material of different sizes. Where this type of sand is found in tropical Africa, it almost invariably develops a macadam-like surface. In some places it would seem that the pounding of a bare quartz sand surface by raindrops in a downpour, or the constant padding of barefooted cultivators, has been enough to bring about its consolidation. And there can be no doubt that in more and more places it is being brought about by the ill-advised use of the caterpillar tractor and other heavy mechanical gear.

The heavy clay frequently builds down to a depth of many scores of feet. When freshly exposed to the air, it is soft, unbelievably sticky and uniform in character, and usually mottled gray, yellow and red in color. It makes for slow going, for men and machines alike. After being exposed for a time, the yellowish parts become dark red or brown-red and hard. The grayish parts remain soft and may be washed out by rain, leaving a mass which often looks something like badly fused gunshot and is just about as hard. At any rate, it is hard enough to be widely used for building purposes and for road surfacing. Among the people who have to live with it, this material is given many names, the most polite of which is laterite (from the latin *later*, meaning a brick).

Large areas, however, are underlain neither by sandy, packing soils nor by laterite, even where the predisposing conditions exist. Soil scientists have, in fact, already identified a great many soil types, and are busy identifying more. The soil map which is emerging from their studies (see Figure 7) has a closer affinity, it seems, to the climate map than to the geology map. This, in the light of the foregoing argument, is reasonable enough. The most significant departures from the climate map are those where the chemical cycle has been halted or otherwise disturbed by a geological cycle, such as mountain building and its accompaniment of igneous activity, alluviation (the deposit of river-borne materials) and erosion.

The chief areas of igneous soil are located along the flanks of the Rift Valley and its nearby mountains, and on the slopes of the Cameroon Highlands. The soils in these localities are mostly of above-average fertility, partly because of their comparative newness — they haven't had as much time to become sterile — and partly because igneous rocks are, as a rule, richer in mineral nutrients than other kinds of rocks.

The chief areas of alluvial soil are found along the valleys of the great rivers, notably those of the Nile, the Congo, the Niger and its delta, and the lower Senegal, Zambezi, Limpopo and Incomati. The soils in these valleys are a composite of almost every kind of soil found in their watersheds. On the whole, this is to their advantage. As we have seen, it is the good properties of most African soils that get removed. But what is one soil's loss can be another soil's gain. Indeed, it often is, for the plant nutrients that are leached out of the upland soils get washed into the subsurface waters that feed the streams that feed the rivers that feed the lakes, marshes and deltas in which alluvial soils are deposited. Although the solid particles that form the substance of these soils may sometimes be as sterile as the angular sands of the uplands, the waters that flood them and help maintain their high saturation level have lost little of their load of nutrients in the course of their long descent, to the evident advantage of the natural vegetation and the cultivator's crops.

At their best these alluvial soils are equaled in fertility only by the best soils developed on igneous rock. By European and North American standards neither group is outstanding, but in the general context of African infertility, they are invaluable.

As L. Dudley Stamp reminds us,[27] erosion is as much a natural process as, say, alluviation. Immediately dry land appears above the waters of a river, lake or sea, it is attacked by the atmosphere. In time, the combined effect of heating and cooling, frost, ice, snow, rain and wind is to reduce all land surfaces everywhere to peneplains (literally, almost-plains). Since the greater part of tropical Africa lies high above the level of the sea, it follows that the forces of erosion have had plenty of opportunity to work their will upon its surface. One result of this is that over

[27] *Africa: A Study in Tropical Development,* John Wiley & Sons, New York, 1953, pp. 99ff.

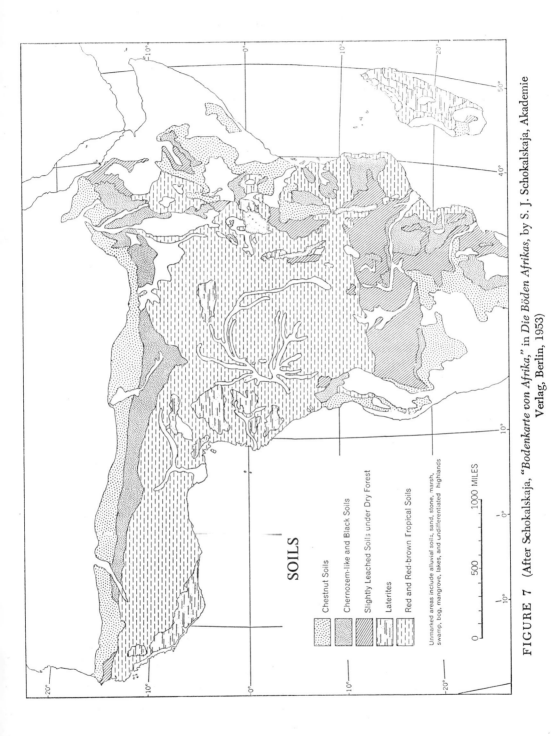

SOILS

Chestnut Soils

Chernozem-like and Black Soils

Slightly Leached Soils under Dry Forest

Laterites

Red and Red-brown Tropical Soils

Unmarked areas include alluvial soils, sand, stone, marsh, swamp, bog, mangrove, lakes, and undifferentiated highlands

0   500   1000 MILES

FIGURE 7   (After Schokalskaja, "Bodenkarte von Afrika," in *Die Böden Afrikas*, by S. J. Schokalskaja, Akademie Verlag, Berlin, 1953)

extensive areas the soils are derived from "foreign" rather than local materials. Another result is that over extensive areas the soil particles get
removed, either by wind or water, as soon as they form on the surface.

When erosion is simply a natural phenomenon, it is subject to checks
and balances that prevent it from getting out of hand. Sooner or later
(and it is sooner in most cases) all moving soil particles are immobilized
by firm-footed grasses, shrubs and trees, or by lakes, ponds and swamps
that block their further advance. But once erosion becomes a "cultural,"
man-made phenomenon, it ceases to be as readily amenable to control. Instead of being, so to speak, a manifestation of youthful exuberance, it
becomes a manifestation of youthful delinquency.

The basic cause of cultural erosion is, in Stamp's words, "the exposure
of the naked soil by the removal of its vegetation cover which both pro-
tects it and, by the development of root systems, binds it together." [28]
This exposure may be brought about in a number of ways: by clearing
land for cultivation; by allowing animals to crop herbage so closely that
they prevent its natural regeneration; by stripping forests for their lumber
and fuel; and by simply neglecting to protect the weak spots produced by
miners, quarrymen, road and house builders, and the millions who,
season by season, set light to the African bush. Once started, erosion is
extremely hard to control, particularly in the tropics. It is almost as hard
to have a little erosion as it is to have a little corruption — a species of
which it can well be said to be. What is simply a gash today can be a ten-
foot gulley tomorrow, and a gorge in ten years' time. What is good
average topsoil this morning — soil that took ten thousand years to evolve
— may disappear in tonight's torrential rain. And the longer erosion lasts,
the harder it is to control, let alone cure; for as land is lost or rendered
unusable by its ravages, the pressure of man and beast on what remains
becomes greater. In other words, the predisposing causes of erosion increase with increase in the work load of the land.

Fortunately all this is very well known to the governments of tropical
Africa, and, as will be shown in later chapters, some strenuous attempts
are being made to contain, and remove, the menace which erosion poses.
For the moment we are simply concerned to draw attention to the fact
that, while erosion is nothing new in tropical Africa, the scale on which it
operates has increased vastly in the past generation, until it can now be
said almost to span the region. No single territory is immune to it, and
although there are in each territory large areas which have not yet been
corrupted by it, there are few where it is not a potential danger. It is an
ever-present threat to every hillside and a present fact on every hillside
that is not either densely forested or carefully "bunded," or terraced. It is
scarcely less of a threat to every plateau where desiccating heat alternates
seasonally with torrential rain; the one can lift the topsoil high into the

[28] *Ibid.*, p. 101.

atmosphere, while the other can hurry it into the nearest valley. It is a threat, also, to the valleys, since they become the dumping ground for the ever-growing loads of silt and sand brought down by rivers from their eroded watersheds. And, not least, it is a threat whenever modern man introduces his ecologically disturbing technologies. For in tropical Africa it seems easier to inflict a wound with a bulldozer than to heal one, and to start a dust storm with a multiple-disc plow than to stop it.

CHAPTER 3

The Pattern of

Population

RACIAL CONSTITUTION

GEOGRAPHICAL DISTRIBUTION

DEMOGRAPHIC CHARACTERISTICS

POPULATION TRENDS

THE student of modern tropical Africa soon discovers that he must work with makeshift tools. In some respects, no doubt, his task is simpler than that of the historian who seeks to reconstruct the tropical Africa of fifty years ago. At least he has plenty of tools to work with: maps, monographs, bluebooks, yearbooks, handbooks, textbooks and learned journals by the thousand; and automobiles and airplanes to speed the process of gathering them and making more. But the maps are uneven, the statistics are mostly approximate, not all the monographs are up to date, and automobiles and airplanes are expensive. And everywhere there are gaps. These gaps are frequently serious, and always frustrating.

In the field of population studies the gaps are unquestionably serious. Some of them are nearly as large as they were when Jonathan Swift claimed that

> . . . geographers, in Afric maps,
> With savage pictures fill their gaps,
> And, o'er unhabitable downs
> Place elephants for want of towns.

Many Ethiopian maps, for instance, are still rather casual in their portrayal of the towns. Some towns are up to ten miles from where the maps show them to be. Others, according to the same maps, are non-existent. Small wonder that nobody yet knows precisely where all the people of Ethiopia live or how many of them there are. Nor is this a

81

unique situation. Several territories in tropical Africa do not know their population within a million or so, because they have been unable as yet to devise, or afford, a census that compares with those regularly taken in Western Europe and North America. However, since World War II most territories have compiled enough data to enable us to discern, perhaps for the first time, the general pattern of population for the territory as a whole. That is to say, enough is now known to enable us to tell broadly how many people there are in tropical Africa, where most of them live and in what densities, and how their distribution is altering; and to relate these things to a wide range of variables, such as climate, vegetation, elevation, insect pests, agriculture, mining and manufacturing, all of which bear directly or indirectly on them.

In this chapter we attempt to unravel the main strands of the population pattern and establish their more important relationships. We shall have occasion to deal more specifically with some of these relationships in later chapters. If some topics, and some territories, receive less notice than others, it is not because they are necessarily of less importance. As a rule it is simply because much less is known about them.

RACIAL CONSTITUTION

There are many kinds of African. Exactly how many depends largely on one's definition of "kind." If we mean a group of related intermarrying individuals possessed of one or more distinctive cultural traits (such as language, religion, nationality, historical tradition and social organization), we can safely say that in the entire continent there are over 750 kinds of Africans, and probably as many as a thousand. If we interpret "kind" to mean a group of related intermarrying individuals possessing "well developed and primarily heritable physical differences from other groups,"[1] then the number is very much smaller — nearer ten than a thousand. It is with these racial groups of African peoples that we are immediately concerned.

Tropical Africa is thought of traditionally as a black man's country, and the French still speak of it as *Afrique noire*. It is true that about 95 per cent of its inhabitants are dark-skinned. But skin color is so fickle — some negroes have lighter skins than some Europeans, and many Europeans can change color merely by exposing their bodies to a strong sun — that no anthropologist worth his skull would dream of making it the critical measure of a man's race. Some anthropologists are no longer sure that it is either possible or necessary to talk of "races," or, in other words, to classify the species *homo sapiens* by subspecies. Those who do continue to recognize the existence of subspecies of the human race generally

[1] UNESCO, *The Race Concept: Results of an Inquiry,* Paris, 1952, p. 11.

do so on the basis of combinations of such measurable characters as stature, head form, blood group, hair texture, iris color, skin color and proneness to specific diseases. While these characters vary in genetic value, and are susceptible to change with change of environment, the variations are believed to keep within as yet undefined, gene-determined limits.[2] On the basis of these characters, ten "kinds" of Africans may be said to exist. From this enumeration Europeans and Asians, other than Arabs, are excluded as being "un-African" in the usual anthropological sense of the word. They are, of course, kinds of Africans, and their cultural role, if not their racial role, in contemporary Africa is second to none. Their geographical distribution and demographic characteristics are discussed later in the chapter.

The Bushman

Small-boned, and with a correspondingly small cranium, with yellowish-brown skin that wrinkles easily, with flat face and nose, bulging forehead and prominent cheek bones, eyes narrow and slightly oblique, "pepper-corn" head hair and sparse body hair, the Bushman is just about as "un-African" as the European. His womenfolk have a tendency — highly prized, if unprepossessing to Western eyes — to run to fat on the buttocks. His habitat is the waterholes of the Kalahari Desert and bordering regions of Bechuanaland, Southwest Africa and southern Angola. Once comparatively prolific, he has fared ill in his fight for survival against the European; miscegenation, disease and "liquidation" have taken a heavy toll of his numbers and resistance. According to the most recent estimate the number of relatively pure-blooded Bushmen is now about 55,000.[3] Some students put the number much lower — below 10,000. But almost all agree that it is declining.

The Pygmy

The pygmy is one of the shortest men in the world. He averages about 54 inches in height, as against about 60 inches for the Bushman. His skin is more brown than black, and covered with light downy hair. His nose is broad and flat; his face squat and usually prognathous. There is no general agreement about his racial affinities. By some anthropologists he has been grouped with the Bushman, and by others he is regarded as quite distinct. His home is in the rain forests of the Belgian Congo (Kibali-Ituri and Aruwimi districts), the Ouesso district of the Republic of the Congo, the Gabon Republic, the Cameroons and

[2] "Stature is highly plastic and iris-color very fixed, and most of the other characters lie between these two extremes." J. C. Carothers, *The African Mind in Health and Disease* (Monograph Series, No. 17), World Health Organization, Geneva, 1953, p. 15.
[3] See P. V. Tobias, "On the Survival of the Bushmen," *Africa*, April 1956, pp. 174ff.

Angola. Possibly related to him are the few remaining (less than 1,000) hunters and collectors who live around the forested shores of Lake Tana in Ethiopia. The pygmy's ability to play "hide and seek" successfully with all comers probably helps to explain why he has so far managed to keep his identity. Pierre Rolland, who has lived for many years as a French administrator and anthropologist among the pygmies of the Ouesso district, believes that there may be as many as 250,000 pygmies in tropical Africa. The more usual estimate is between 100,000 and 150,000.

The Hottentot

The Hottentot [4] is slightly taller than the Bushman. By different anthropologists he is regarded as a cross between Bushman and Hamite, as a cross between Bushman and Negro and as the last pure remnant of the ancient Boskop race. Like the Bushman, he has a brown rather than black skin and a "peppercorn" head of hair, but his cranium is larger and his prognathism more marked. Like the Bushman, too, he has found it difficult to keep his blood lines pure; many of the Cape Colored people have a strong Hottentot strain. Today there are probably not more than 15,000 or so persons who would rank as relatively pure or predominantly Hottentot.

The Negro [5]

The typical Negro is a man of medium stature, say 68 inches. His skin is dark brown to black and he has little body hair. His head hair tends to be dull black and woolly; his forehead upright and narrow; his nose flat and broad; his lips thick and often everted, and his jaw prognathous. The shape of his head varies from mesocephalic to dolichocephalic, or, in plain language, it may be either as broad as it is long, or longer than it is broad. Most of the estimated 55 million to 60 million true Negroes live in the rain and dry-forest belts of west Africa from the Senegal River eastward to the Cameroons. Representative of them are the Kru (Liberia), Fanti (Ghana), Wolof (Senegal) and the Yoruba (Nigeria).

The Hamite

The characteristic physical features of the "pure" Hamite are as different from those of the "pure" or true Negro as both are from the "pure" Bushman. Many of them are more European than African, which perhaps is not so surprising seeing that in prehistoric times Hamites and Caucasians, from whom most Europeans are descended, were one. The general run of present-day Hamites are of medium height, light brown

[4] The name is said to be derived onomatopoetically, for the Hottentot's speech, like that of the Bushman, abounds in "click" sounds.

[5] Sometimes spoken of as the "true," or Sudanese, Negro.

in color, dolichocephalic, with wavy or fuzzy hair, straight nose and narrow face, non-receding chin, and thin rather than full (but if full, not everted) lips. They are very well represented in the highlands of Ethiopia and Eritrea, notably in the Keren, Tana, southern Habesh and western Galla regions, in the Somaliland "horn," and in the Sahara, mainly among the Tuareg. They have intermarried freely with the peoples living around and among them. The Hausa and Fulani owe their origin to such intermarriage. Until we have a better idea of the population of Ethiopia and the various Somalilands, their numbers within the limits of tropical Africa can be only roughly surmised: they are unlikely to exceed 35 million.

The Half-Hamite

It seems that anthropologists are no more keen to invent names than they are to invent races. Anything less calculated to feed the self-esteem of a fine upstanding person like a Masai than to call him a half-Hamite can hardly be imagined. It suggests nothing so much as half-caste or half-breed, which he certainly isn't, if by this we imply that he is a straight cross between, say, pureblood Hamite and pureblood Negro. The typical Masai, for instance, is, in fact, far more of a Hamite than a Negro. He is tall and slender, with long, small limb bones, narrow feet and hands, and long fingers. His skin color varies from light chocolate to very dark brown. His head is high and narrow; his face rather thin with fine-cut features; and his lips, though often full, less thick and everted than those found among more negroid peoples. His language is related to the Hamitic speech of the still more markedly Hamitic peoples of the Republic of Sudan and neighboring parts of Ethiopia. Nor is the blending as recent or as simple as the term half-Hamite might suggest; "the modifications have more probably passed through a number of stages over a long period of time."[6] There may be as many as one million half-Hamites in the entire region. Most of them live near the border of Uganda and the Republic of Sudan, in northern Tanganyika and in the drier parts of Kenya.

The Nilote, or Nilotic Negro

The Nilote is less equivocally a crossbred Negro than his neighbor the Bantu. Hamite and Negro have mingled to produce a population with still predominantly negroid features, but with more than a tincture of the Hamite's poise and elegance. Most of the inhabitants, including the very tall Shilluk, of the upper Nile valley are Nilotic. Together with their kin living to the westward in the Republic of Chad, they probably number less than 10 million.

[6] C. Daryll Forde, *Habitat, Economy and Society*, Methuen & Co., London, 1953, p. 288.

The Bantu Negro

Because the negroes who inhabit the greater part of central and southern Africa speak variants of a common language, they are usually referred to by the name of that language — Bantu, or more properly Aba-ntu.[7] While many Bantu people show evidences of admixture of Hamitic and other blood, it is doubtful if this racial group as a whole is more "mixed" than the true Negroes, who have also been extensively infiltrated by the Hamites in their time. Some anthropologists see no basic difference between the two, and rather deprecate on that account their separation, since the *raison d'être* of it is more linguistic, that is, ethnic, than racial. Very considerable physical differences do exist between individuals and, for that matter, between tribes coming from the various parts of the negro domain, but it is probable that no broad separation of Africans into Negro and Bantu is likely to prove justifiable on other than linguistic grounds. The Kikuyu constitute one of the more notable elements of this group. Excluding those groups living in the Union of South Africa, the Bantu Negro population of central and southern Africa is of the order of 55 million.

The Semite

The Semite is a comparative newcomer to tropical Africa and has played little part in its racial evolution, though his cultural influence has been great. He is closely related to the Hamite, and usually goes by the name of Arab. Many so-called Semites have more than a trace of Hamitic and Negro blood. This is especially true of those living in the caravan country of the northern part of the Republic of Sudan, and in parts of the Ethiopian Highlands. At the most there may be 2 million Semites in the region as a whole. Nowhere are they numerically strong, except on the island of Zanzibar, and in some of the larger cities and seaports of east and northeast Africa.

The Malgache

For many years it was supposed that the bulk of the indigenous population of the island of Madagascar were "descended from immigrants from the East who crossed the Indian Ocean in the early centuries of the Christian era, bringing with them the language which later developed into Malgache, rice and many culture traits which are still common to Madagascar and Indonesia."[8] This is still the majority view. However, there is growing anthropological support for the belief that most of the in-

[7] Signifying "human beings."

[8] Robert F. Gray, *Anthropological Problems of Madagascar: A Bibliographical Introduction,* mimeographed, Department of Anthropology, University of Chicago, 1954, p. 7.

habitants (other than the Merina people, who almost unquestionably arrived, Kon-Tiki fashion, from Indonesia) are racially akin to the Bantu Negro, and that they arrived from east Africa, perhaps using the Comores Archipelago as stepping stones. Louis Michel in a recent defense of this belief cites the fact, among others, that the physical characteristics of the Malgache negroes are "entirely unlike" those of Melanesian negroes.[9] Even the Merina, it seems, have "a strong African element, for a study made in 1913 revealed that of the 850,000 claiming to be Merina only 300,000 really belonged to the Merina race, the others being more or less mixed with other tribes."[10] According to Hance, only about one fifth of the total indigenous population of some 4.75 million (1956) is of "relatively pure descent from the earlier eastern migrants." The rest display varying degrees of Bantu negroness.

GEOGRAPHICAL DISTRIBUTION

PROBLEMS OF ENUMERATION

The census taker in tropical Africa faces a task of prodigious difficulties. First, there is the difficulty of getting about. Away from the towns motorable roads are scarce, and all-weather roads scarcer. And not all Africans live by a road; to find many of them a man must still walk, or take a camel, a horse, a boat or a bicycle. Second, because of the prevailing illiteracy it is extremely difficult for a census taker to communicate the meaning and purpose of a census. Third, most Africans are still reluctant to stand up and be counted, lest, by doing so, they may later find themselves paying heavier taxes, and rounded up for civil or military service. Fourth, many of them still live under a tribal taboo against the disclosure of numerical facts. Of the people living in the "hungry country" to the north of the Congo basin, Louise A. Stinetorf has written that

it is an unforgivable insult, an injury even demanding redress, to ask a man to number his possessions. The jealous, malicious spirits are always listening, and the man will tell any lie to escape arousing their envy and greed and spite. Also, the generous, friendly spirits are disgusted with and flee from a man who boasts, taking their favors with them. Even the government census-taker only estimates.[11]

This taboo is very common among the cattle keepers. Fifth, in a world that has more than its share of rough terrain, trackless swamps and dense forests, it is no great feat for a man to elude the census taker. Sixth, the semi-nomadic way of life of many pastoral peoples and the migrations,

[9] Louis Michel, "L'Origine des Malgaches," *Revue de Madagascar,* No. 25, 1955, pp. 8-18.
[10] William A. Hance, *African Economic Development,* published for the Council on Foreign Relations by Harper & Brothers, New York, 1958, pp. 249-50.
[11] *Beyond the Hungry Country,* J. B. Lippincott Co., Philadelphia, 1954, p. 232.

seasonal and otherwise, of many agricultural peoples to and from the mines and cities pose tricky questions for those who must plan an enumeration. For instance, shall a migrant be counted as a member of his home community or as an inhabitant of the place of his temporary sojourn? As census practice differs from territory to territory, many migrants no doubt succeed in missing the count, while others are double-counted. Seventh, over much of the region the arm of the law is neither long nor strong. Administrative staffs are small and frequently so encumbered with regular duties that their attitude toward special tasks like a census is apt to be less dutiful than philosophical. It has been claimed by more than one French commandant that the gathering of the census data required by headquarters would consume more than their entire time, which is fully occupied as it is. So, in the interests of amity, if not of verity, they are reduced to conjuring up figures that will satisfy their superiors, who, they know from long acquaintance, are never likely to be in a position to check them! Possibly, French commandants are not the only ones to resort from time to time to this kind of stratagem.

Even where the European administrator is able to give himself wholeheartedly to census work, results can still fall far short of his expectations, for it frequently happens that his subordinates who must do the actual counting or estimating are motivated more by the wish to please their superiors than by any desire to further the cause of population science. The situation in a district in the northern part of the British Cameroons where, for a while, the satisfactory yearly increase of taxpayers turned out to be a fiction of the minds of some African treasury clerks eager to keep up the revenue may well point a moral of wide application.[12]

It follows that, with the possible exception of certain small entities, such as the Portuguese islands of São Tomé and Príncipe, the Spanish island of Fernando Po, and perhaps the island of Zanzibar, for all of which satisfactory data exist, population figures should generally be treated with reserve, if not outright skepticism. It also follows that the figure of 167 million given in Table 3 as the total number of people in the region of this survey is no more than a very rough estimate. That the actual figure is likely to be higher than this is the conclusion drawn by Glenn T. Trewartha and Wilbur Zelinsky in their population study of tropical Africa prepared for this book. "Most independent checks," they point out, "reveal that official figures generally underestimate actual population."

It needs but a glance at the accompanying tables and maps to realize that the estimated population of 167 million is dispersed across the approximately 8.5 million square miles of tropical Africa with little regard for territorial boundaries, and none for tidiness. Enormous tracts are

---

[12] D. A. Percival, "Notes on the Count of a Pagan Tribe in West Africa," *Journal of the Royal Statistical Society*, Vol. I (1938), p. 616.

Table 3

AREA AND ESTIMATED POPULATION AND POPULATION DENSITY, BY TERRITORY, AROUND 1957-1958

TERRITORY	POPULATION	AREA	INHABITANTS PER SQ. KM.
	(*Thousands*)	(*Thousand Sq. Km.*)	
Tropical Africa	167,447	22,207	7.5
Angola	4,392	1,247	3
Bechuanaland	334	712	a
Belgian Congo	13,124	2,345	6
British Cameroons	1,591	88	18
British Somaliland	650	176	4
Ethiopia (inc. Eritrea)	20,000	1,184	17
French Cameroons	3,187	432	7
French Equatorial Africa	4,891	2,523	2
French Somaliland	68	22	3
(French) Togo	1,093	57	19
French West Africa [b]	16,793	4,388	4
Gambia	290	10	29
Ghana	4,836	238	20
Republic of Guinea (French Guinea)	2,498	246	10
Kenya	6,351	583	11
Liberia	1,250	111	11
Malagasy Republic (Madagascar)	4,930	590	8
Mozambique	6,234	783	8
Nigeria	32,433	878	37
Northern Rhodesia	2,300	746	3
Nyasaland	2,710	117	23
Portuguese Guinea	559	36	16
Ruanda-Urundi	4,568	54	85
São Tomé & Príncipe	62	1	62
Sierra Leone	2,120	72	29
Somalia (Italian Somaliland)	1,310	462	3
Southern Rhodesia	2,640	389	7
Spanish Guinea & Fernando Po	214	28	8
Republic of Sudan	11,037	2,506	4
Tanganyika	8,916	937	10
Uganda	5,767	243	24
Zanzibar & Pemba	299	3	100

Source: United Nations, *Demographic Yearbook, 1958*, New York, 1958. Based on latest census or official estimates.

[a] Less than 1.   1 square kilometer = 0.386 square mile
[b] Excluding French Guinea, which became an independent republic on October 2, 1958.

virtually empty; others are crowded to the point of embarrassment and acute distress. Some of these highly contrasted areas lie cheek by jowl; others are separated by almost half a continent of patchily populated territory. But quite clearly the low-density areas outnumber the high-density ones. In fact, the region as a whole is, by Western standards, and even more so by Oriental standards, one of very low density — less than 20 to the square mile (7.5 to the square kilometer). More than 75 per cent of the total area is occupied by countries with population densities of less than 26 persons to the square mile (10 to the square kilometer), and containing in the aggregate less than half of the total population. At the other end of the scale, the most thickly settled 5 per cent of the region has nearly 25 per cent of the population.

The chances are that in a given density zone, the actual location of the units of population, be they houses, hamlets, villages or cities, is anything but "normal" in the statistical sense of the word. In most cases, the distribution will not even follow a discernible pattern, though demographers are inveterate seekers after signs of form and rhythm. And it is anything but static. Traditionally, most Africans are wanderers. Range lands occupied in a given year may be deserted in the following. Much of the land under cultivation at the time of one census will have reverted to uninhabited bush by the time of the next. Today the migrant laborer is adding new momentum to the forces of mobility, for the roads are full of travelers moving to and from mines, plantations, factories and cities.

Consequently no African population map can be considered as anything more than a first approximation. This should be borne in mind in the following discussion of the main components of the population picture.

AFRICAN POPULATION

Of the estimated population of 167 million, all but one million or so are Africans, and the residential classification of over 90 per cent of them is rural. The accompanying map (Figure 8) shows the salient facts of their distribution and suggests that the region can be subdivided into three clearly differentiated population zones: (1) a west African–Sudanese zone of moderately to densely settled country; (2) a much more thinly populated central African zone; and (3) an east African zone characterized by a seemingly random scattering of quite dense population clusters through an area that is on the whole thinly settled and in places virtually empty.

1. The *west African–Sudanese zone* covers all the territories south of the Sahara as far east as, but not including, the Republic of Chad and the French Cameroons. It contains about 28 per cent of the entire land area of tropical Africa, and probably not less than 40 per cent of its

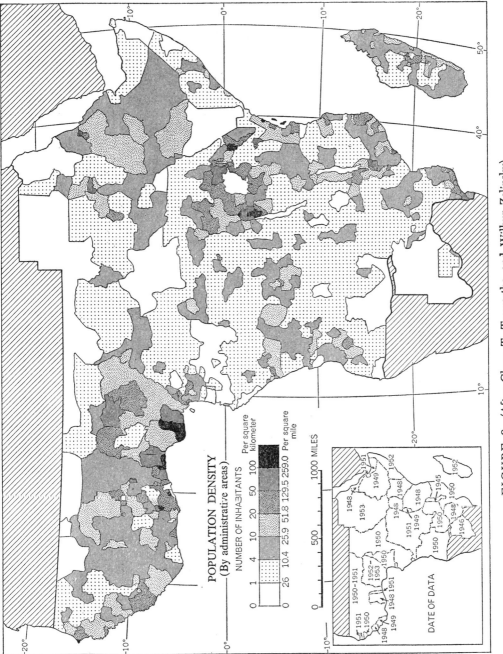

FIGURE 8 (After Glenn T. Trewartha and Wilbur Zelinsky)

population — say 67 million. Most of this population is concentrated in two belts. The first is found in the wooded tall grassland country, the second in the rain forest. In some portions of these two belts, as, for instance, in the upper and eastern portions of the large Niger delta and in the vicinity of the larger towns, densities greatly in excess of 250 to the square mile are to be found. Conspicuously absent are sizable tracts of land carrying little or no population. Such small enclaves of unoccupied land as are found are located mostly in the "middle belt" of relatively low-density settlement separating the heavy-density belts of the wooded grassland and forest country.

2. The *central African zone* is, on the whole, much more thinly peopled than the west African–Sudanese zone. Though roughly the same in size, it supports less than 20 per cent of the indigenous rural people of tropical Africa. Here again the population is disposed far from evenly. The most thickly settled area runs roughly east-west between 4°S and 8°S from the Atlantic coast as far east as the Kasai Province of the Belgian Congo. A second above-average-density area is located near the northern perimeter of the Belgian Congo. The only other important rural groupings are located in the Benguela Highlands of west central Angola and in the southeastern half of Southern Rhodesia. But in none of these areas are the rural densities comparable to those characteristic of the well-populated areas of west Africa, and in none of them is it possible ever to be far from unoccupied territory. More conspicuous than the well-populated areas are those much larger areas inhabited only by small, scattered communities, namely, the central Congo basin, the Gabon Republic and the central and southeastern parts of the French Cameroons, eastern and southern Angola, all of Bechuanaland except for its southeastern fringes and a few districts in the northwest, and the greater part of the region extending from the Katanga Province of the Belgian Congo southward across Northern Rhodesia into the northwestern portion of Southern Rhodesia. The density of population in these areas seldom exceeds 60 to the square mile; more often it is less than 25.

3. The *east African zone* is the largest of the three zones. With over 40 per cent of the entire region's area and about 40 per cent of its population, it approaches the average population density for the whole of tropical Africa.

In this zone, there are a larger number of sharply defined population regions than in either of the other zones. Conspicuous among the high-density regions are western Eritrea, the "Mesopotamian" area above the confluence of the White and Blue Niles, central Ruanda-Urundi, the country to the northeast of Lake Victoria and around Kilimanjaro, south central Kenya, the islands of Zanzibar and Pemba and the adjacent mainland coast, the Shire Highlands district of southern Nyasaland, and the coastal districts of southern Mozambique. In each of these regions the population density exceeds 125 to the square mile, and in some cases it exceeds 250. At the other end of the scale, northeastern Kenya, the eastern reaches of Ethiopia and Eritrea, northern Somalia, the Saharan and equatorial portions of the Republic of Sudan, northern Uganda, the middle third of the Kenya-Tanganyika border country, eastern and southern Tanganyika, central Mozambique and the west central portion of the Malagasy Republic carry rural populations averaging less than ten to the square mile and falling here and there below one to the square mile. At the same time, in some of these human deserts it is not uncommon to come upon "oases" of dense population. Thus, the five small Laki Islands of Lake Zwai, to the south of Addis Ababa in Ethiopia, were estimated by Helmer Smeds and Kurt Roselius in their report for this study to have in excess of 1,700 people to the square mile. The adjacent shores of the Rift Valley in which the lake is situated have only a sparse population of nomadic Galla cattle herders. In Lake Victoria, Ukara Island, situated off the sparsely peopled Kibara peninsula, is a similar "oasis," with a population density of over 600 to the square mile.

EUROPEAN POPULATION

The approximately 750,000 Europeans presently living in tropical Africa [13] are dispersed irregularly within the area — far more irregularly than the indigenous population. Over half are to be found in four territories: Southern Rhodesia, Angola, the Belgian Congo and the Republic of Senegal. This marked unevenness of distribution is illustrated in Figure 9, where the absolute size of the European population is shown by means of graduated circles within the smallest statistical units for which recent data are available. This spatial "unbalance" would be seen to be more striking still were it possible to pinpoint the geographical location of each European. Europeans are a negligible factor in the population of vast areas, especially in the Republic of Chad, the Republic of Sudan, the northeastern "horn" of Africa (with the exception of Eritrea, which still has a considerable Italian population), Bechuanaland, northwestern Mozambique and southwestern Tanganyika. Even in Southern Rhodesia, Angola, the Belgian Congo and the west African members of the French Community the European population is highly localized. Only in the following districts do Europeans form more than one per cent of the total population: Senegal, the Republic of the Congo, the Léopoldville and Katanga provinces of the Belgian Congo, the Copperbelt region of Northern Rhodesia, the extreme south of Mozambique, the Luanda region of Angola, and the central part of Southern Rhodesia, in all of which they are predominantly town dwellers; the Benguela Highlands of Angola,

[13] According to census data published in the various territories between 1931 and 1952, the European population (including Americans, Canadians and other peoples of European origin who do not hail directly from Europe) was 620,340. There is reason to believe that it had increased to 750,000 by 1958.

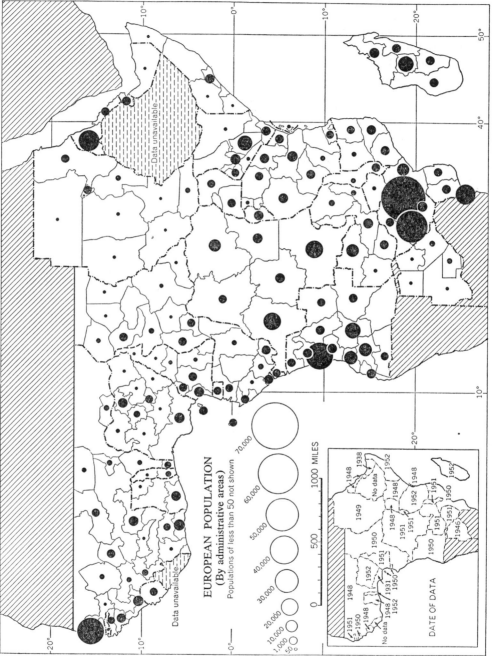

EUROPEAN POPULATION
(By administrative areas)
Populations of less than 50 not shown

FIGURE 9 (After Glenn T. Trewartha and Wilbur Zelinsky)

94

Eritrea, the Rift Valley Province of Kenya, and the central plateau of the Malagasy Republic, where they are characteristically country dwellers. Taking the territories as a whole, in only two of those for which data on rural-urban distribution are available is the European population officially regarded as being more rural than urban. These are Uganda, where 45 per cent of the Europeans are classified as urban, and Tanganyika, where the urban percentage is put as low as 18. In the rest, the urban percentages range from 53 in Kenya to 77 in the western members (other than the Republic of the Ivory Coast) of the French Community.

The country with the largest European population is Southern Rhodesia, with 193,000 (in 1957). Angola comes second,[14] with 110,000 (1955); the Belgian Congo third, with 108,000 (1957); Senegal fourth, with over 80,000 (1957); and Northern Rhodesia fifth, with 72,000 (1957). The countries with the smallest European populations are British Somaliland, with about 250 (1948); Gambia, with about 500 (1951); Zanzibar and Pemba, with about 300 (1948); and Sierra Leone, with about 1,000 (1956). So far as can be gathered, the relative standing of these countries has not altered appreciably since these counts were made.

As is to be expected, by far the greater part of the European population is made up of the nationals of the colonial powers. Between 80 and 90 per cent are of British, Portuguese, French, Belgian and Italian origin; only Spain among the colonial powers is poorly represented, presumably because of the very small size of its holdings. In 1950 no non-colonial nation had more than about 5,000 nationals in the region. United States citizens, or former citizens, living there at that time numbered 2,600. Today the number is undoubtedly much higher, particularly in such countries as Ethiopia and Liberia where extensive American technical assistance programs are under way.

ASIAN POPULATION

The Asian (including Arab) population is much smaller than the European, and still more localized. Of the approximately 400,000 Asians in tropical Africa, about 300,000 are domiciled in the territories of British East Africa. Of the remainder, only one fifth are to be found in countries not contiguous to either the Indian Ocean or the Red Sea. (See Figure 10.) Even more than the Europeans, the Asians are town dwellers, most of them showing a strong preference for the larger centers. In Tanganyika over 60 per cent of the Asian population live in cities and towns; in Kenya over 80 per cent; and in Southern Rhodesia over 90 per cent — all well above the corresponding percentages for Europeans.

---

[14] In dealing with Portuguese and French data it must be remembered that there is usually no way of distinguishing between individuals of full European ancestry, those of mixed ancestry, and those Africans who have acquired full citizenship rights. All are equally entitled to register themselves as Portuguese and French.

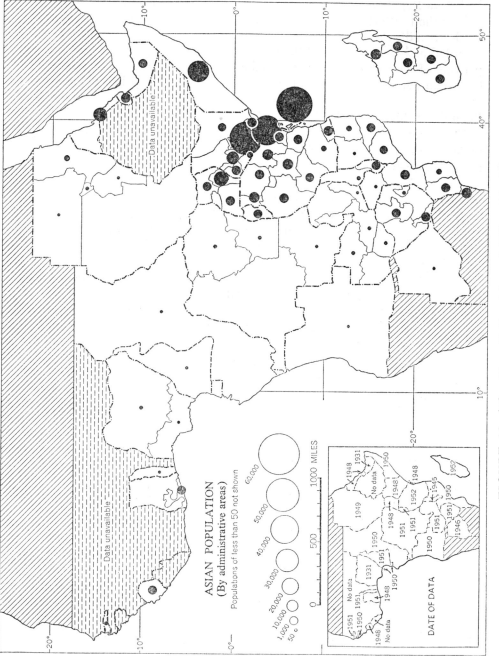

ASIAN POPULATION
(By administrative areas)

Populations of less than 50 not shown

60,000
50,000
40,000
30,000
20,000
10,000
1,000
50

1000 MILES

0   500

DATE OF DATA

FIGURE 10 (After Glenn T. Trewartha and Wilbur Zelinsky)

Though the Arabs at one time had trading posts (mainly for slaves) as far west as the Congo valley, today they are seldom found in any numbers away from the Indian Ocean, and on the coast they are out-numbered, about two to one, by Indians and Pakistanis. Goans, or Portuguese Indians, constitute the third largest group of Asians, with approximately 20,000; Chinese the fourth, with some 7,000. The former are widely scattered and are especially well represented in almost all east African territories. The latter are confined almost entirely to the Malagasy Republic (about 6,000 in 1952) and Mozambique (about 750 in 1950). The Syrians and Lebanese,[15] who come next in numerical importance, are mostly found on the west side of the continent. According to the latest count there are only about 3,500 of them — a figure that is hard to believe, because they have a way of turning up almost everywhere, including the most uncomfortable and otherwise unpromising places.

URBAN POPULATION

It is common in these days to make much of the urbanizing of African life, and it is indeed important — as we shall have many occasions to point out when we come to deal with the changing economy and society of the region. At the same time, it is as well to realize that tropical Africa is still the most unurbanized part of the earth. Less than 10 per cent of its people live in communities that have a population of 5,000 or more, and a great many of these communities are more rural than urban in form and function.[16] The territories where the percentage of urban population, as thus defined, exceeds 10 are Eritrea, French Somaliland, Ghana, the two Rhodesias, Zanzibar and, possibly, Ethiopia. By way of comparison, in the Philippines the corresponding percentage is about 25, and in Brazil, also a tropical country, about 33. In the United States it is about 60, and in the United Kingdom about 80.

Not only is the urban population small, the bulk of it is found in small cities. According to figures compiled by Trewartha and Zelinsky in 1955, out of an estimated total of 455 places with a population of 5,000 or more, only 41 had more than 50,000, 16 more than 100,000 and five more than 200,000 (Table 4).

The spatial distribution of these towns is shown in Figure 11. Approximately two thirds of them are located in west Africa — a quarter in Nigeria alone. The remainder are scattered, almost at random it might

15 This Levantine population is classified as Asian for the purposes of this study; it could just as well be termed European.

16 It is often very difficult to know where to draw the line between towns and villages in tropical Africa. To take an extreme example, in Bechuanaland there is at least one purely rural village of 20,000 inhabitants, and several posts of a strictly urban character with no more than 100 inhabitants. In the absence of detailed knowledge of the social and occupational structure of all the communities involved, about the only kind of line that can be drawn is an arbitrary numerical one.

Table 4

DISTRIBUTION OF URBAN POPULATION, BY SIZE OF CITY, AROUND 1955

SIZE OF CITY	NUMBER OF CITIES	TOTAL POPULATION	PER CENT OF TOTAL URBAN POPULATION
		(*Thousands*)	
Total	455	10,115	100
5,000-10,000	227	1,656	16.4
10,000-20,000	110	1,474	14.6
20,000-30,000	42	1,057	10.4
30,000-50,000	35	1,388	13.7
50,000-75,000	12	715	7.0
75,000-100,000	13	1,129	11.2
100,000-200,000	11	1,397	13.8
More than 200,000	5	1,299	12.8

Source: Census data.

seem, across the east and central African territories. The least urbanized areas are inland Angola and Mozambique, the Gabon Republic and the Republics of Chad and the Congo, the French Cameroons, the southern part of the Republic of Sudan, Northern Rhodesia (with the exception of the Copperbelt) and Bechuanaland.

Most of the larger towns and many of the smaller ones are European creations and therefore comparatively new. Conspicuous among these are Dakar, with a population today of approximately 230,000 (including more than 30,000 Europeans); Léopoldville, with about 18,000 Europeans and nearly 300,000 Africans; Salisbury, with over 60,000 Europeans and almost 150,000 Africans and other ethnic groups; Bulawayo, with over 40,000 Europeans and 100,000 Africans and others; and Nairobi, with approximately 20,000 Europeans, 65,000 Asians and over 100,000 Africans.

But a few of the largest towns are African in origin. The most important of these is Ibadan, capital of the Western Region of Nigeria. Although founded only one hundred or so years ago, it has grown rapidly until today it has a population estimated to be between 400,000 and 500,000. In spite of the fact that a good deal of its Yoruba architecture has in recent years disappeared beneath the rising tide of corrugated tin and cement, Ibadan is still a recognizably African town with an overwhelmingly African population and a way of life that is a very far cry from that, say, of Léopoldville, or even that of its near neighbor, Lagos. Noon or midnight, the streets are never empty, the women never far from their stalls, and the men never done with padding to and fro, greeting, smoking and gossiping.

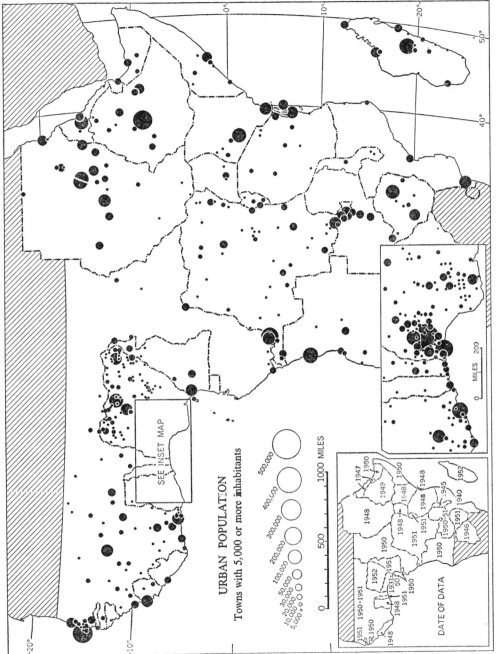

URBAN POPULATION

Towns with 5,000 or more inhabitants

FIGURE 11 (After Glenn T. Trewartha and Wilbur Zelinsky)

99

Farther north, lying near the steppe-like margins of the Sahara, are other African towns of greater antiquity and considerably greater historical, if not greater contemporary, significance. Timbuktu, Gao and Kano were flourishing caravan centers between 750 and a thousand years ago, and were known in Europe long before Prince Henry the Navigator's men had begun to push southward beyond Cape Bojador.

The urban tradition of northeast and east Africa goes back even further, at least on the coast from the Mozambique Channel northward. Sofala, Kilwa, Zanzibar, Mombasa and Malindi were already gray with age when Vasco da Gama "discovered" them in 1498. It is true that these towns were not built by Africans but by Arab traders from Oman; even so, in a very real sense they were more African than Arab, since it was upon the African slaves that the Arabs depended for most of their labor and their profit. How old the oldest of the east African towns is nobody seems willing to hazard. There was certainly trade between the island of Zanzibar and Arabia before the Christian era, and there were towns in the Nile valley below the confluence of the White and Blue Niles in what is now the Republic of Sudan in the second millennium B.C. One of these towns, Kawa, located three miles from Dongola, was already a large town in the New Empire period (1550-1100 B.C.).[17] And near Merowe there are the skeletal remains — pyramids, temples and other stately buildings — of a city which, if not quite so ancient, appears to have been occupied from about the seventh century B.C. onward.

At the present time Addis Ababa, the capital of Ethiopia, is the largest city in east Africa. Its exact population is not known, but including some 10,000 Europeans and other non-Ethiopian peoples, it is undoubtedly over 300,000 and is, by some, considered to exceed that of Ibadan. Though founded in quite recent times, it was until the coming of the Italians essentially an indigenous city, without plumbing, sanitation, hard-surfaced roads or distinction save for its Coptic churches. Today it is more European than Ethiopian in appearance, though still rather short on European facilities. In its streets you may hear more non-African languages spoken than in any other African city; the Bank of Ethiopia alone employed nationals of no less than 19 countries in the middle 1950s.

After Addis Ababa comes the triple city of Omdurman-Khartoum-Khartoum North, with a population of approximately 250,000 (1955) including about 5,000 Europeans; and Asmara, with approximately 150,000. The only other east African city of comparable size is Tananarive in the Malagasy Republic, with a population of around 200,000 including some 20,000 Europeans. Strictly speaking, however, Tananarive should not be classed as an "African" city, for it was founded, along with a number of other Malagasy cities, by people who migrated to the

<hr />

[17] J. A. de C. Hamilton (ed.), *The Anglo-Egyptian Sudan from Within*, Faber & Faber, London, 1935, p. 24.

island from southeastern Asia centuries ago and established a powerful hegemony over the local inhabitants, based on sizable capital cities.

LOCALIZING FACTORS

The thing that most readily strikes the reader about the gross population map of tropical Africa (Figure 8) is that, taken in its entirety, it is not strictly comparable with any other distribution map for the region. No doubt parts of it will remind him of parts of other maps. The areas of dense coastal settlement in Sierra Leone and Nigeria, for example, correspond broadly with the areas having 80 inches of rainfall and over. Again, the areas of very sparse settlement in Bechuanaland and along the northern borders of tropical west Africa, the Republic of Chad and the Republic of Sudan correspond broadly with those areas having less than 10 to 15 inches of rainfall. Or again, in Ruanda-Urundi and adjacent parts of the Belgian Congo, the rural population densities are, with few exceptions, conspicuously higher on the high ground than on the low. In the semi-arid parts of east Africa the distribution of rural population is no less clearly related to the availability of ground water in the dry season from springs, wells, gulleys and streams, which is determined by such physical factors as rainfall, surface relief, plant cover, subsurface geology and the character of the soil. In his report for this study Deshler has shown how close this relationship can be in the so-called pedimented [18] landscapes of northern Karamoja in Uganda. Where the pedimentation process is still in its early stages, and the layer of soil is still thin and intermittent, the country supports hardly any permanent settlers. Where it is well advanced, and the layer of soil is sufficiently thick and continuous to be retentive of rain and flood waters, the country supports up to 86 persons to the square mile. The climatic differences between the two types of country are scarcely measurable.

But any attempt to relate the rainfall map, the relief map, the vegetation map or the drainage map of the whole of tropical Africa to the population map of the whole region will quickly prove fruitless. Thus, whereas the mean annual rainfall in Nigeria decreases northward from the Bight of Benin to the Sahara, the population density first decreases and then increases with distance from the coast, so that by the time the northern emirates are reached, where the annual rainfall is less than half what it is at the coast, the mean density is as high as, if not higher than, it is at the coast. Similar "anomalies" can be cited from the southern part of the Republic of Sudan, where the population tends to decrease rather than increase with increase in rainfall; from Mozambique, where the population tends to decrease rather than increase with elevation; from the French

[18] A pediment is the apron-like soil-covered surface which develops at and near the base of steep, usually rocky hill slopes that are undergoing physical and chemical weathering.

Cameroons, where some of the heaviest concentrations of population occur in the forest zone and some of the lightest in the savanna zone; and from the Androy district of the Malagasy Republic, where a large population manages to subsist under near-desert conditions.

Attempts to show close connections between population density and soil quality have likewise been a little disappointing, even where we have reasonably precise information to go on. Generally speaking, the full discriminatory influence which soil fertility can have on the distribution of population is felt only where permanent agriculture of the European type has been developed. The African cultivator's ability to tell the fertility, whether directly by inspection of the soil or indirectly by study of the vegetation, is often quite uncanny. All the same, when left to himself, he seldom exploits this ability as the cultivators of India or Indonesia do, by making the more fertile soil carry a heavier population load than the less fertile. The Africans who farm the alluvial valleys of the Guinea coast, the volcanic soils of Kilimanjaro and the plain of Zanzibar are perhaps the most notable exceptions to this general rule.

The case for linking population density with the incidence of sleeping sickness or other disease is likewise far from proved, as Trewartha and Zelinsky point out:

Thus, although it is true that the tsetse fly is widely distributed in central Africa, there is little evidence of any strong correlation between its occurrence, or the endemicity of trypanosomiasis, and low population densities within the area. The prevalence of this disease, or others, may have been responsible for small-scale local dislocations of population, but no one has yet established any effect of disease upon the grosser patterns of population distribution.

Nor is such a connection thought to be very likely, since the tsetse fly has no chance of surviving against an extending or stationary human population dense enough to keep down the harboring vegetation. (It is probable that most parts of tropical Africa presently infested by tsetse, but otherwise fit for habitation, can be successfully colonized by means of compact group settlement.)

In short, the population map makes it rather hard to credit explanations of human distributions in tropical Africa couched exclusively in physical terms, let alone the certitude of those who claim that primitive peoples live in bondage to a set of iso-lines. African man may be cabined and confined by his earth, but seldom is he compelled by it. Indeed, it is arguable that over large sections man's presence, or absence, is more readily accounted for in cultural and historical terms than in physical ones. Thus, again to quote Trewartha and Zelinsky:

. . . the evolution of a large population in the northern border areas of Nigeria and other sections of the savanna belt may be explained in large part by the fact that this area is the middle ground between the arid and humid portions of west Africa and as such has seen the development of a series of cities and states thriving upon the proceeds of local markets and the many caravans passing through the belt along north-south routes. The development during the past several centuries of a group of powerful states or empires, such as the Hausa or Fulani, has provided the basis for an intensive development of agriculture and grazing.

As for the nodular clustering of population in the wooded grassland (savanna) belt, especially in northern Nigeria, this is probably related to the fact that "civil strife in the nineteenth century depopulated large areas in the marcher zone between the emirates of Katsina and Sokoto and, east of Kano, in the old shatter zone between the Fulani and Bornu empires." [19]

The more it is studied, the more important this military factor is seen to be in west Africa with its troubled pre-European history. More than any other single factor it helps to explain the important agglomerations of population in the relatively stable kingdoms of Ashanti-Dahomey and southern Nigeria, and the relative emptiness of the "middle belt" separating the densely populated coastal and interior zones. The lesser nodes of population, such as those of Fouta Djallon in Guinea and the difficult hill country of northern Togo and those of central Dahomey, may also owe their existence to the need in earlier times for a place of refuge from the military invader and the no less bloody slave raider. During the three centuries and more that the American slave trade lasted, raiders repeatedly swept over the area, and if they did not always succeed in carrying off the local population, they forced it to retreat to the sanctuary of the densest bush or most difficult terrain. It can be argued that the population of the middle belt has not yet recovered from the havoc wrought in those times.

The upper (southern Sudan) section of the White Nile valley was similarly harried in the nineteenth century by slavers from Mongalla and southern Darfur, with equally serious losses of population among such tribes as the Moru and the Bongo.[20]

Of more modern significance for the population map of tropical Africa are the differing policies followed by the various colonial powers. Thus, the often marked disparities between the population patterns in the British territories of Gambia and Sierra Leone and the neighboring French areas and, to a lesser degree, between Ghana and its territorial neighbors — the common borders of which are endowed with much the same physical qualities — can with some justification be ascribed to migration from French to British territories caused by higher wages and lower prices and the lack of conscription in the latter. The same factor may also have been operative in Portuguese Guinea, which likewise has an appreciably larger population than the onetime French territories surrounding it.

[19] Keith Buchanan, "The Northern Region of Nigeria: The Geographical Background of Its Political Duality," *Geographical Review*, Vol. 43 (1953), pp. 457-59.
[20] But not among the Dinka, who apparently were more than a match for the slavers, both in fighting and in evasion.

History and politics, between them, have probably had an even bigger hand in the making of the population map of central Africa. In the centuries preceding the European penetration, most of the peoples living there had been engaged in a series of complex migrations prompted by a variety of needs and desires, and producing a succession of relatively haphazard population distributions determined largely by the accidents of leadership, folk beliefs, oppression and warfare. During the nineteenth century most of these migrations came to an end. In some cases the end came so suddenly that it had the effect of almost "freezing" the existing population distribution. Although the European occupation has brought about many important changes of detail, many of the lineaments of this rather arbitrary pattern appear not to have radically altered. So far as the Belgian Congo is concerned, it can be shown that the areas of currently high and low population density are inherited from the pre-European era and that recent changes have, for the most part, merely accentuated the differences.[21] The fact that many formerly uninhabited areas owed this condition to historical events rather than to any inherent disabilities is further suggested by the recent flow of migrants from Angola eastward into the upper Zambezi valley and the large increases during the present century in the rural population of Katanga Province, areas once emptied by the Arab slave raiders.

Over on the eastern side of central Africa, mass population movements went on longer. For instance, it has been estimated that in the first twenty years of this century alone, 100,000 people entered Nyasaland from Mozambique,[22] mostly in order to escape from the excesses of the *prazo* system under which the administration of Portuguese overseas territories was sold, for stated periods, to the highest bidder. The present heavy concentration of African settlement in the Shire Highlands of southern Nyasaland is the direct outcome of this migration.

Even in east Africa, where the physical environment sometimes seems to wield an imperious authority over the rural settler, cultural and historical forces have been far from negligible. Indeed, it is probably fair to say that east Africa has suffered more from warfare and its disruptive effects than either of the other major sections. Throughout its history this region has been furrowed with paths along which tribes and nations have migrated almost without pause, and not always peacefully. The last of these major migrations was halted by the European occupation at the end of the nineteenth century, so that the present pattern of rural population, which is not basically different from what it was about 1900, has

[21] See G. T. Trewartha and W. Zelinsky, "The Population Geography of Belgian Africa," *Annals of the Association of American Geographers,* Vol. 44 (1954), pp. 187-92.
[22] See Sir Philip Mitchell, *African Afterthoughts,* Hutchinson & Co., London, 1954, p. 27.

in it elements both of improvisation born of tactical necessity and of slowly matured adaptation to environmental circumstances.

Some of the closest correspondences between such circumstances and settlement are to be found in Uganda and Ruanda-Urundi, where relatively powerful, stable states ruled by a caste of alien Hamitic warriors have been in possession of the land long enough, and securely enough, to realize more of the population potential of their habitat than their less stable, less powerful and shorter-established neighbors could readily do. As for the high population densities of the Ethiopian Highlands and the central part of the Malagasy highlands, it may be argued that these, too, are related to the rise of strong political entities following on major invasions. Likewise it may be argued that the cause of the emptiness of many physically well-endowed territories is to be looked for in the fact that they once were the battlegrounds of contending tribal powers, which, for political and other reasons, continue to be avoided. The series of gaps between the core areas of major tribes and kingdoms in pre-French Madagascar have been only partially filled in during the current century in spite of massive migrations. Even today in northwest Tanganyika the people of crowded Sukumaland, remembering their long and costly battles with the Masai, are reluctant to move eastward into good, unoccupied land for fear of inciting their warlike neighbors.[23] Throughout east Africa there are tribes for whom security from attack is still the primary goal of settlement. The hilltop (*amba*) villages of Eritrea and the Tigre Province of Ethiopia are among the world's most spectacular examples of "security-conscious" settlement. The monastery of Debra Damo can be approached only by the aid of fifty feet of stout rope.

It would, however, be wrong to conclude that the African population of east Africa or, for that matter, of central and west Africa is a demographic anachronism, and that its distribution is out of tune with the times. While many areas undoubtedly have much the same distribution pattern as they did fifty years ago, others have had theirs transformed. Not only have the European administrations allowed the filling in of previously empty areas by preserving civil order, but they have sometimes actively encouraged it by disease control measures and improvements in transportation. This has been especially true of the alienated sections of Kenya, Tanganyika, Mozambique, Angola, the two Rhodesias, the Belgian Congo and the territories that until recently constituted French West Africa and French Equatorial Africa. Though not empty, and certainly not unowned, at the beginning of the twentieth century, these areas carried a much smaller *African* population than they do today. Then, too, there has been an increase in the African population of those areas, such as southern Uganda, southern Nigeria and Ghana, where the Africans themselves

[23] D. W. Malcolm, *Sukumaland: An African People and Their Country*, Oxford University Press, London, 1953, pp. 11-12.

have developed cash crop economies requiring more labor than the locality can provide.

Since the things which brought Europeans and Asians to tropical Africa, and which keep them there, are different from those which actuate the bulk of the African population, it follows that they tend to distribute themselves differently. Most Europeans and Asians are engaged in one or other of seven main groups of activities: government administration; mining; manufacturing; commerce; transportation; agriculture; and what, for want of a better word, we may call tutelage — secular and spiritual. Of the seven, the first four are essentially urban occupations, or become such as their scope and significance increase. Transportation is nine parts urban or interurban; and nowadays even much of the tutelage is done in, or from, urban hospitals, schools, colleges and mission stations. Agriculture alone remains distinctively rural.

In the light of these circumstances it is not difficult to see why at least 50 per cent of the European population and not less than 75 per cent of the Asian population is urban, as against less than 10 per cent in the case of the African; or why the degree of urbanization of both groups is everywhere greater than that of the African population. Nor is it difficult to see why it is only where Europeans are engaged predominantly in agricultural pursuits [24] that the population patterns of the two groups tend to take on common characteristics, or why a very large proportion of the rural Europeans have gravitated to areas resembling as closely as possible those from which they or their forebears came. These areas are the uplands of Angola, the central Malagasy highlands and the two Rhodesias, and the highlands of Kenya, Nyasaland and the Belgian Congo. By the same token, it is not difficult to see why most of the Europeans who live in the equatorial lowlands with their uncomfortable heat and unaccommodating ecology belong to one or other of the nonagricultural categories. It is possible, though, that the rating of the agriculturists in such areas would have been somewhat higher had land-holding by Europeans not been officially discouraged, almost from the start, by the colonial governments.

DEMOGRAPHIC CHARACTERISTICS

What was said about the unreliability of gross population statistics applies with still greater force to statistics relating to the demographic characteristics of the population. Opportunities, and reasons, for the concealment or misrepresentation of such facts are plentiful. The head of a household may be able to overcome his reluctance to reveal the total number of people under his care, but if he lives in a territory where there

[24] With the exception of the clove growers of Zanzibar and some sisal and sugar planters on the mainland, the Asians incline more toward commerce, industry and administration than toward agriculture.

is conscription or where contract labor is obligatory, he may find it tempting to discount the number of eligible males. Where family allowances are provided by the government, as in the Belgian Congo, he may feel that a margin of error should be provided for. Where he is under no such constraints, the chances are that any information he supplies regarding the age distribution of his family will be approximate. He has probably never seen a birth certificate and is unlikely to have registered the birth of any member of his family. Some governments require such registration, but what are a thousand registrars among more than 60 million children? And throughout his life the African is less likely to reckon time by the calendar than by age groups which may have a span of anything from a few years to a generation. Even adulthood is less a matter of the calendar than of custom. Frequently unmarried males of 18 are reported as children while married females of 13 are reported as adults. Since females normally reach puberty at an earlier age than males and are married shortly after, while marriage and full recognition as adults are often delayed for males until well past the onset of puberty, it is especially difficult to get reliable figures of child population and child: adult ratios.

SEX RATIO

In any community the balance of the sexes is a matter of great demographic significance because of its bearing on the rate of population growth and also on the social order. In tropical Africa the sex ratio (that is, the number of African males per 100 African females) varies strikingly from one territory to another. At one extreme stands the island of Fernando Po with 227.4; at the other stands Nyasaland with 86.1. The mean for the territories publishing such data is 95.6.

That this figure is low by world standards can be seen in Table 5. Only Europe among the major regions of the world has a lower sex ratio. Since tropical Africa has enjoyed a half century of comparative peace, the cause of this low ratio cannot be attributed, as in the case of Europe, to heavy war casualties. Nor is it likely to be fully explained on the ground of male labor migrations, since, with the exception of the comparatively recent movement to the Union of South Africa, most of these migrations are *intra*tropical. The most plausible explanation seems to be that a greater number of the constitutionally weaker males succumb to the rigors of existence under a difficult physical environment, an extremely low standard of living, and a highly inadequate system of hygiene and medical care. The demonstrably greater "toughness" of the womenfolk extends even to their ability to survive the hazards of childbirth under unhygienic conditions and without medical attendance. While infant mortality rates among Africans are almost everywhere high — up to 60 per cent of live births in some areas — maternal mortality for the two or three territories

Table 5

SEX RATIO AMONG TOTAL POPULATION IN MAJOR WORLD REGIONS, AROUND 1950

(Males per 100 Females)

Tropical Africa (African population only)	95.6
Non-tropical Africa	107.2
India	106.4
Southeast Asia	103.0
South America	100.9
Middle America	99.7
Anglo-America	98.6
Southwest Asia	97.3
Japan	96.2
Europe (exc. U.S.S.R.) Prewar	95.2
Postwar	91.8

Source: Calculated from United Nations, *Demographic Yearbook*, 1952, 1956 editions, New York, 1952, 1956.

for which partial data are available is less than 2 per cent of live and still births. In Uganda it is thought to be below 0.5 per cent.

In general, the regions of high sex ratio are either those with sizable urban populations, such as southern Nigeria, or those rural areas, such as Fernando Po and the Ghana cocoa belt, which have attracted migrants from economically less-developed areas. Conversely, the regions of lowest sex ratio tend to be those that serve as exporters of labor. Examples are the Gabon Republic, the Republics of the Congo and Dahomey, and Nyasaland. Very roughly, therefore, the sex ratio is an index of the source, destination and volume of African migration.

But it is difficult to explain all the areal variations of sex ratio in terms of migration. Thus, Bechuanaland, the Republic of Chad, the Central African Republic and the northeastern part of the Belgian Congo — all of them regions of high sex ratio — are not important sources of labor for the mines or the plantations of equatorial Africa; and they are among the least urbanized regions of the continent. So far no adequate explanation of such anomalies has been given. Whatever it is, it is unlikely to lie within the realm of the physical, since these are environments that make the going tough for the physically "softer" sex. Possibly the anomalies are only apparent. A demographic study undertaken in the Republic of Chad comments on the general tendency of the menfolk to conceal their wives from the census taker, for one reason or another. Such concealment may occur elsewhere.

When children are omitted from sex ratio calculations, the deficit of males would appear to be even greater. Thus, in Nyasaland in 1945 there were only 68.4 adult males for every 100 adult women. In Portuguese

Guinea in 1950, there were 87.9; in Angola in 1950, 90.9; in the French Cameroons in 1955, 91.3; in Madagascar in the same year, 92.3. Of the territories reporting these data to the United Nations, only Zanzibar and Togo showed a surplus of adult males, the figures being 117.7 and 104.7 respectively. The mean figure for the territories reporting to the United Nations between 1945 and 1955 was 89.9. In Trewartha and Zelinsky's view this represents a far greater deficit of males than occurs in most other underdeveloped areas, or, indeed, in any other region of the world, with the possible exception of one or two of the worst-hit belligerent countries of Europe. (See Table 6.)

That the areal differences between the adult sex ratio and the total sex ratio patterns are considerable should not surprise us when we bear in mind, first, that the general deficit of males among the tropical African population can only increase with age, since the mortality differential between males and females favors the latter throughout their entire life span; and, second, that it is mainly the adult who migrates to city, mine or plantation. While the first factor operates uniformly, or nearly so, throughout the region, the second factor operates differentially, being much more weighty in the labor reservoir areas than elsewhere; it therefore tends to heighten the areal contrasts already apparent in the total sex ratio. How sharp some of these contrasts are is evident from the fact that many administrative districts in central Africa

Table 6

SEX RATIO AMONG ADULT POPULATION,
TROPICAL AFRICA AND SELECTED UNDERDEVELOPED COUNTRIES

(Males per 100 Females)

COUNTRY	DATE	SEX RATIO
Tropical Africa *	1945-55	89.9
Algeria (Moslems)	1046	112.4
Burma	1931	110.2
India	1931	106.9
Union of South Africa	1946	105.0
Formosa	1940	100.3
El Salvador	1944	98.9
Brazil	1940	98.9
Philippines	1948	98.4
Korea	1944	97.8
Egypt	1947	97.5
Mexico	1940	95.1

Source: Calculated from United Nations, *Demographic Yearbook*, 1952 and 1958 editions, New York, 1952, 1958.

* Figures available for only Nyasaland, Malagasy Republic, French Cameroons, (French) Togo, Portuguese Guinea, Angola and Zanzibar. African population only.

with adult sex ratios of 100 or higher lie alongside districts with ratios below 70 — even below 50 in parts of the Belgian Congo, Northern Rhodesia and Nyasaland.

AGE COMPOSITION

For almost all of the territories, age data are limited. They are also unreliable, for reasons already apparent. Angola and Portuguese Guinea attempted an enumeration of Africans by precise age in 1940 and 1950 respectively, but a close scrutiny of the results shows them to harbor grave discrepancies. Efforts to gather information by five-year age groups in Bechuanaland, Ghana, Mozambique and Nigeria have had only modest success. In all the other countries, the only age group data available are for "children" and "adults" — categories for which it is difficult to find agreed age equivalents. For purposes of discussion, it will be assumed arbitrarily that those below 15 are children, and those 15 and over are adults.

What is known and surmised of the division of the African population into these two categories is set forth in Table 7. The most striking fact to emerge from the figures is the youthfulness of the population. Taking the region as a whole, over 43 per cent of the inhabitants would appear to be less than 15 years of age. This compares with 27 per cent in the United States in 1950. The main reasons for this high figure are the high fertility rate prevailing over much of the continent,[25] and the still distressingly high mortality rates. The age pyramid, if it were possible to construct one for the region, would probably be very much the same as the pyramid for tropical American and other primitive areas: wide at the base and tapering rapidly through the middle years to an extremely narrow peak by the 50s. That the young rather than the old dependents constitute the major burden on the resources of the adult population is evident.

Although the population of the region as a whole can be classified as youthful, there are large and interesting variations from territory to territory in the percentage of children among the population, the extremes being 53.2 per cent in Nyasaland and 32.8 per cent in Sierra Leone. It is possible that the high percentages in Nyasaland and such other territories as Southern Rhodesia and Ruanda-Urundi are the result, in part at least, of a higher-than-average fertility, and conversely with the relatively low percentages in Sierra Leone, the French Cameroons, the territories formerly constituting French Equatorial Africa, and Portuguese Guinea. Another factor of considerable significance in determining the relative size of the child and adult population is the interterritorial migration of adults, mostly male. This no doubt helps to account for the above-average child: adult ratios in Mozambique, Nyasaland and Ruanda-Urundi, all three of

25 See p. 114.

Table 7

AGE COMPOSITION OF
AFRICAN POPULATION, BY TERRITORY

(Per Cent of Total Population)

TERRITORY	DATE	CHILDREN (0-14 YEARS)	ADULTS (15 YEARS AND OVER)	
			MALE	FEMALE
Average for territories listed		43.2	26.5	30.1
Nyasaland	1945	53.2	18.9	28.9
Southern Rhodesia	1948	51.4	22.8	25.8
Ruanda-Urundi	1949	50.5	22.8	26.7
Mozambique	1940	49.7	22.0	28.3
Angola	1950	47.5	23.4	29.1
Tanganyika	1948	46.2	24.4	29.4
(French) Togo	1951	44.2	26.6	29.2
Kenya	1948	44.0	24.9	31.1
Northern Rhodesia	1950	43.6	24.9	31.5
Ghana (Gold Coast)	1948	43.0	28.5	28.5
Nigeria: Northern Region	1952	42.4	26.9	30.7
Uganda	1948	42.4	28.1	29.5
Belgian Congo	1951	41.1	28.3	30.6
Bechuanaland	1946	40.7	27.7	31.6
Malagasy Republic (Madagascar)	1952	39.8	28.5	31.7
Zanzibar	1948	39.8	33.3	26.9
Portuguese Guinea	1950	38.4	28.9	32.7
French Equatorial Africa	1950	37.8	29.3	32.9
French Cameroons	1945	35.3	29.0	35.7
Sierra Leone	1948	32.8	31.3	35.9

Source: Estimates based on census data.

which are large exporters of labor, and for the below-average ratios in Portuguese Guinea, Sierra Leone and Zanzibar, which are among the larger importers. As is to be expected, the bigger cities tend to show a rather close affinity in this respect with the labor-importing territories. The question of the effect of regional variations in mortality on the age composition cannot be satisfactorily resolved with the data at present existing.

MARITAL STATUS

While much is known about African marriage institutions, particularly from the standpoints of ethnology, sociology and law, reliable statistics concerning any aspect of the subject are at a premium. What statistics there are have been assembled in Table 8; this lists the incidence of unmarried persons among Africans of approximately 20 years and over in

Table 8

UNMARRIED PERSONS OF 20 YEARS AND OVER,
SELECTED COUNTRIES

(Per Cent of Total Population 20 Years and Over)

COUNTRY	DATE	TOTAL	MALE	FEMALE
Bechuanaland	1946	32.3	36.0	28.4
Mozambique	1950	11.0	17.1	6.2
Portuguese Guinea	1950	11.2	23.0	1.6
Nyasaland [a]	1945	8.9	8.8	9.0
(French) Togo	1951	—	18.3	—
Switzerland	1941	30.2	31.9	29.5
Brazil	1940	29.4	32.1	26.8
England and Wales	1931	28.4	27.9	28.9
Australia	1947	21.4	25.1	19.0
France	1946	19.0	21.4	16.9
Egypt	1947	11.9	19.4	4.6
Formosa	1930	10.6	16.6	4.3
India	1931	7.1	11.9	1.9
Korea	1930	5.4	10.4	0.5

Source: Calculated from United Nations, *Demographic Yearbook,* 1952–1958 editions, New York, 1952–1958. For countries of tropical Africa, African population only.

[a] Figures refer to persons 18 years of age and over.

four tropical African countries and, for comparative purposes, in certain other countries. We see immediately that there are important differences either in age at marriage or in the prevalence of celibacy between the countries in question. Since marriage rates have to do partly with social values and traditions which, for all the dislocation of African life, still manifest extraordinary vitality, the wide territorial variations revealed in this table can no doubt be explained in some measure as a by-product of tropical Africa's great cultural diversity. But marriage also has to do with economic opportunities, and there can be equally no doubt that the massive temporary exodus of adult males, married as well as unmarried, from labor surplus countries and their entry into labor deficit countries is another reason for these wide variations.

On the whole, it would seem that most Africans continue to marry at an early age by Western standards, and that there are relatively few bachelors and spinsters. In their study Trewartha and Zelinsky argue that perhaps only 15 to 20 per cent of the adult male population of tropical Africa and about 10 per cent of the female are unmarried at the present time. Even these figures may be too high, for where detailed local studies have been made, the investigators have almost always reported the virtual absence of unmarried women.[26]

---

[26] See Jean Croqueville, "Etude démographique de quelques villages Likouala (Moyen-Congo)," *Population,* Vol. 8 (1953); and Frère Lamal, S.J., "Essai d'étude

It will also be seen from the table that, despite the prevailingly low adult sex ratio, there are more unmarried men than women in three of the territories for which figures are available. As these are fairly representative territories, it is possible that this demographic feature is widely shared. The reason for it is to be looked for, more than likely, in the continuing vogue of polygyny and of bride wealth, or marriage settlement. Though polygyny is in disrepute in many areas, notably the more Westernized, it is still highly regarded among pagan and Moslem groups. Even in the strongholds of polygyny, however, the average number of wives per married male is thought to be decreasing, because the compensation demanded of a suitor by his prospective wife's family for the loss of the woman's services has been steadily increasing over almost the whole of tropical Africa in the past generation. To raise the sum for one wife may now necessitate a four- or five-year stint at the mines, and a correspondingly long postponement of marriage by the male.

Statistics relating to plural marriages are scantier than most. In Bechuanaland, one of the few territories where the number of wives per husband has been tabulated, 14.3 per cent of all married men had two or more wives in 1946. In the Belgian Congo in 1950 a 3 per cent sample survey showed that about 30 per cent of all husbands living under tribal conditions (*en milieu coutumier*) were polygynous.

Reliable data concerning the occurrence of divorce, widowhood and separation are the scantiest of all, so that it is impossible to make any general statement of their significance except to note that the demand for wives is such throughout most of tropical Africa that few eligible females need go unclaimed for long.

VITAL STATISTICS

Here again the student of demography soon finds himself in difficulty. "There are for the majority of the territories no comprehensive systems of vital registration and in such territories where registration has been carried out it is incomplete so that the official data in general grossly underestimate birth and death rates." [27]

It may be assumed that deaths are recorded more accurately on the whole than births, for they are usually accompanied by ceremonies and public rites that make concealment difficult. Also, in most of the towns a permit must be obtained for burial, and the issuing of such permits is dependent on registration. But the wide disparities of census practice make it hard to arrive at a reliable crude death rate. And the crude death

démographique d'une population du Kwango, les Basuku du Territoire de Feshi," Institut Royal Colonial Belge, Section des Sciences Morales et Politiques, *Memoires*, Tome 15, Fasc. 4, 1949.

[27] Arne Barkhuus, "Non-European Mortality and Infant Mortality in the Non-self-governing Territories in Africa South of the Sahara," paper presented at the United Nations Conference on Population, Rome, September 1954.

rate (number of deaths per 1,000 persons) is not by itself sufficient for any detailed investigation of mortality matters. Where, as is customary, deaths are reported for only certain specific groups of the population, the size of these groups is seldom known with exactness.

As for infant mortality data, these are available only for a few territories and, in those, for rather limited areas. Much the same is true of birth and fertility data. Child:woman ratios frequently provide the nearest substitute.

The position is improving, however. Each year sees an increase in the number of sample surveys undertaken and in the accuracy of the methods followed. While individual samples have little or no indicative value beyond the borders of the areas concerned, it is probable that the conclusions to be drawn from the sum of them are of more than academic interest. An analysis of 40 such surveys made at different times during the past twenty-five years elicits, among others, the following facts:

1. Birth rates and death rates generally exceed those found in Europe and North America. Except that the range of fertility tends to be less than that recorded for certain parts of Central America and Southeast Asia, these rates are similar to those found in most other tropical areas. The median crude birth rate (number of births per 1,000 persons) is between 30 and 40 and the median crude death rate is only slightly less. Some of the birth rates are among the highest in the world. The death rates, though high, are exceeded by a number of countries, including Egypt, Mexico and India.

2. There are very considerable areal differences in both birth and death rates. Crude birth rates run all the way from 12 per 1,000, in parts of the Gabon Republic, to 59 in Northern Rhodesia. Crude death rates range from 14 per 1,000 in the Malagasy Republic to 39 in parts of the Belgian Congo. Infant mortality rates (deaths under one year per 1,000 live births) range from well below 100 in some parts of the Belgian Congo and of the Rhodesias to well above 400 in parts of Sierra Leone and Tanganyika. Often neighboring places show differences as striking as those between places a thousand miles apart.

3. There are no less considerable temporal differences in the two rates. A study made in the Unyamwezi district of Tanganyika covering the twelve-year period 1941-1952 revealed annual variations in the infant mortality rate from a low of 145 to a high of 462.[28] In the Bas-Congo district of the Belgian Congo the crude death rate fluctuated between 34.8 and 22.7 during a recent eleven-year period. Over the same period the crude birth rate fluctuated between 33.8 and 43.3.

4. Urban populations tend to have both higher birth rates and lower death rates than rural populations. In many company towns, for example

---

[28] A. M. M. Nhonoli, "An Enquiry into the Infant Mortality Rate in Rural Areas of Unyamwezi," *East African Medical Journal*, Vol. 31, No. 1, 1954, pp. 1-12.

those of the Union Minière du Haut-Katanga, African birth and death rates can now hold their own with those of most European countries.

POPULATION TRENDS

Such facts are instructive, but they tell nothing about the rate at which the population as a whole is changing, nor do they tell whether it is increasing or decreasing, let alone how the areal pattern is changing. There is no satisfactory way of finding out such things, or even of knowing what the population in any one territory is doing, since no two successive censuses are sufficiently accurate to afford a reliable notion of recent rates of increase. Writing in 1947, Kuczynski had to admit that "practically nothing is known of the population trend in . . . the whole of British East Africa." [29] With equal truth he might have said the same of British West Africa, or of any part of tropical Africa. Most trends are little better than extrapolated guesses.

The following statements, though widely supported in the demographic literature of Africa, have therefore a rather low confidence rating.

1. The period immediately following the European occupation of the late nineteenth century was one of arrested population growth, if not of absolute decline. Not only did considerable loss of life occur in the military campaigns, but the exploitation of African labor on plantations and public works and the consequent disruption of family life, the increased opportunity for exposure to European disease, the spread of locally endemic diseases through the stimulation of migration, and the serious social malaise that grew out of the demoralizing impact of a materially superior culture, all contributed to depress the rate of population increase. In general it may be said that the inauguration of European rule was harmful demographically in inverse proportion to the cultural development of the indigenous folk. Thus, it is likely that, initially, west Africa suffered least, east Africa considerably more, and central Africa most seriously from Europeanization.

2. Since about 1930 the population as a whole has been increasing relatively fast. It is possible that over most of the region the present total is greater than that reached either in the pre-European period or during the early decades of European rule. Even some of the areas, such as Ruanda-Urundi and the Nyanza Province of Kenya, from which there has been a large permanent migration appear to have shared this trend.

3. Taking the best of the figures available, the current rate of increase for the region as a whole is between 1.0 per cent and 1.6 per cent, giving an annual increment of between about 1.7 and 2.7 million.

[29] R. R. Kuczynski, "Demographic Survey of the British Colonial Empire," Oxford University Press, London, 1949, Vol. II, p. 125.

4. With minor exceptions, the greatest gains are being registered in areas which either were characterized previously by dense indigenous settlement or are currently being developed by European mining, industrial and commercial enterprise, and the least gains and absolute losses, where they occur, are being registered in areas of traditionally sparse settlement. From this it follows that, given a continuation of the assumed trends, the distribution of population over much of the region will become more, rather than less, uneven in the course of the next few decades.

In the absence of more refined statistics of uniform scope and quality, perhaps one of the most helpful clues to the direction and rate of population change in the constituent territories of tropical Africa is that provided by the child:woman ratio, for this provides at least a rough measure of fertility and so of population growth potential.[30] The highest recorded child:woman ratios and hence, by hypothesis, the highest fertility and the highest population growth potential occur in east central Africa, with Southern Rhodesia, Nyasaland and Ruanda-Urundi well ahead of their neighbors. In west and west central Africa the areas with high ratios are smaller and more scattered, the chief being located in the Bas-Congo region, the Léopoldville, Kasai and Equateur provinces of the Belgian Congo, and in Nigeria, Togo and Ghana. The regions with the lowest child:woman ratios and so, by hypothesis, the lowest fertility and lowest population growth potential are found in the French Cameroons, the Gabon Republic, the Republic of the Congo, central and northeastern Belgian Congo and eastern Angola. (See Table 9 and Figure 12.) At best these areas may be maintaining their numbers of inhabitants at current levels; they may even be losing population.[31]

For certain, usually very limited, areas covered by sample and other types of survey, a considerable amount of information is now available regarding population trends, though just how significant this information is for the region as a whole is, again, debatable. The facts can be summarized as follows:

1. There are more instances of falling than of rising fertility. In spite of the encouraging upturn that has occurred among several groups formerly in demographic distress, declines are still being widely reported. A particularly grave situation exists in the Gabon Republic, where many groups appear to be headed directly toward extinction during the next several decades. Contrary to expectations, it is the towns rather than the country areas that have been reporting most of the increases in fertility. In the company towns of the Union Minière du Haut-Katanga for

---

[30] It can be no more than "rough," since it takes no account of child or adult mortality, or of the ratio between the number of females in the childbearing span of years and the total adult female population.

[31] Some of the sample surveys taken in this general area do in fact show deaths to be outnumbering births.

Table 9

CHILD:WOMAN RATIO
AMONG AFRICAN POPULATION, BY TERRITORY
(*Number of Children 0-14 Years per 100 Women*)

TERRITORY	DATE	RATIO
Average for territories listed		136.5
Southern Rhodesia	1948	199.6
Nyasaland	1945	192.2
Ruanda-Urundi	1950	189.6
Kenya	1948	163.8
(French) Togo	1951	157.1
Ghana (Gold Coast)	1948	151.2
Tanganyika	1948	149.2
Uganda	1948	144.1
Northern Rhodesia	1950	143.1
Mozambique	1940	137.9
Nigeria: Northern Region	1952	136.3
Belgian Congo	1951	134.8
Republic of Chad (Chad)	1950	122.4
Angola	1940	122.0
Republic of the Congo (Middle Congo)	1950	118.3
Central African Republic (Ubangi-Shari)	1950	116.3
Bechuanaland	1946	113.6
Portuguese Guinea	1950	110.4
French Cameroons	1945	98.9
Sierra Leone	1948	91.4
Gabon Republic (Gabon)	1950	74.9

Source: Estimates based on census data.

instance, the number of births per 1,000 inhabitants increased from 46 in 1930 to more than 75 in 1957; between 1930 and 1957 the number of children per 100 adult women increased from 67 to nearly 264.[32] But it is unlikely that the rising urban trend will long continue, since the experience of almost all cities, including those in the Union of South Africa, is that sooner or later urban residence makes for lower fertility. In some urban and plantation areas of the Belgian Congo the European small-family pattern is already in evidence in African urban society.[33] Precisely to what extent this is due to either contraceptive practices or sterility consequent upon the increased incidence of venereal disease, or to both,

[32] M. Parent, "Les Oeuvres médicales organisées à L'Union Minière du Haut-Katanga pour les femmes et les enfants africains," *Problèmes Sociaux Congolais,* March 1959, p. 21.

[33] J. Van Riel and R. Allard, "Contributions à l'étude de la dénatalité dans l'ethnie Mongo," Institut Royal Colonial Belge, Section des Sciences Naturelles et Médicales, *Mémoires,* Tome 23, Fasc. 3, 1953, pp. 25-26.

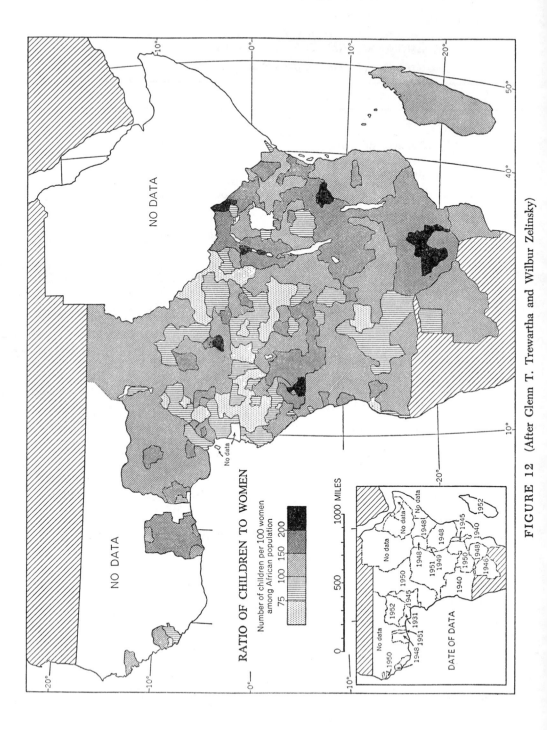

RATIO OF CHILDREN TO WOMEN

Number of children per 100 women
among African population

75 100 150 200

0   500   1000 MILES

DATE OF DATA

FIGURE 12 (After Glenn T. Trewartha and Wilbur Zelinsky)

118

is not yet clear, but among those groups in west and central Africa that have undergone special investigation, the incidence of sterility is known to be increasing.

2. In the same sample areas the mortality trend, including infant mortality, is downward, though as yet the statistical material will not permit any definite conclusions as to the degree of decline. The most conspicuous declines are occurring in those territories with relatively good medical facilities, such as British East Africa, the Malagasy Republic and the Belgian Congo, particularly in the larger towns. On the Katanga copper mines the infant mortality among the families of African employees fell from 360 per 1,000 live births in 1930 to 57 in 1957.[34] But, generally, infant mortality rates continue as high as any known elsewhere.

3. A significant portion of the reported population changes, absolute and relative, must be attributed to causes other than changes in fertility and mortality rates. Migration continues to be the most important of these. Though permanent migrations of the kind and magnitude common down to the nineteenth century no longer occur, the volume of migration has shown little sign of falling off over the years. Indeed, it has unquestionably grown in most parts of the region, but by exactly how much nobody knows. What is clear is that there have been four major migration movements in recent decades. In west Africa and in west central Africa there has been a strong movement of people from the interior to the cities and plantations of the coastal belt. Within east and east central Africa, there has been a fairly steady flow of migrants from the poorer areas to the "wealthy" lands and towns of southern Kenya and Uganda, northeastern Tanganyika, Zanzibar and southern Nyasaland, the mines and plantations of Southern Rhodesia, and the mines of Katanga Province, the eastern Belgian Congo and Northern Rhodesia. In the region of the upper Nile a two-way movement has occurred: an emigration from the poorer areas of Equatoria Province of Sudan into Uganda and the Belgian Congo and from the Northern Province into Egypt, and an immigration of "westerners" (west Africans) along the Mecca pilgrimage route into the Gezira and adjacent areas of economic opportunity. From some of the areas, notably Mozambique, Bechuanaland and Nyasaland, there has been a continuing, if now declining, exodus of laborers in search of employment in the Union of South Africa.

The net effect of these and other migratory movements on the population map is difficult to gauge, except for a very few territories, or parts of territories.

In the Belgian Congo, the main effect of them has been to heighten the existing density contrasts. In the central portion of the Congo basin, where losses of population from this cause are combined with low fertility, all the signs point to a declining population. In Katanga Province, with

[34] Parent, *loc. cit.*

its vast mining and related industrial concerns, and in the vicinity of
Léopoldville, Stanleyville and Luluabourg heavy immigration is combining with above-average fertility and below-average mortality to produce
a sharply rising population curve. There are other areas, in the southeastern portion of Léopoldville Province for instance, which, while ex-
periencing high fertility and rapid rates of natural increase, seem to be
doing no better than holding their own. Some localities, though handy to
large employment centers and not too well endowed with natural resources, have failed to respond to the labor demands of those centers, and
so continue to register more gains than losses. In such localities, it seems
that the critical factor is not job opportunity in the town, but economic
and social stability in the villages. In other words, migration is less likely
to occur in a group when morale and culture are intact than in one where
they are in process of disintegrating.

In Ghana there have been no less substantial changes in the population
map resulting from migration. The place-of-birth material collected for
the 1948 census indicates that sections of the southern half of the country,
particularly the urban districts, have attracted large numbers of migrants,
while the Northern Region and Trans-Volta Togoland have suffered a
large net loss. The general effect of these internal movements has been to
shift the population center of gravity southward. The same material also
reveals the fact that no less than one fourth of the African population of
Ghana, women and children included, were residing in enumeration
districts other than those of their birth, which in many thousands of cases
were outside Ghana, thus indicating a remarkable degree of mobility
for a predominantly peasant people.

Though most of this migration is of an internal nature, much of it is
interterritorial. The fame of countries like the Belgian Congo and Ghana
as lands where the burden is light and the yoke easy has traveled far.
Probably the only territories which have not acquired a significant portion
of their population from "outside" are Mozambique and Angola. The
islands of Fernando Po, Príncipe and São Tomé have perhaps the largest
percentage of immigrants. In each of these a strong influx of plantation
laborers has been accompanied by a steady decline in the indigenous
population.

Most demographers seem to feel that the present trends will continue;
that, short of some continent-engrossing calamity, the mortality rates will
continue to decline, perhaps even at an accelerating rate thanks to the
multiplication of medical and health services, specifics against endemic
diseases, better sanitation and better feeding, and that fertility, while also
declining, will stay well above the mortality rates. If they are right, then
the population of tropical Africa will double itself within the next fifty
years. If the natural rate of increase reaches 2 per cent a year — a figure it
already exceeds in some localities — it will double itself in the next

thirty-five years. Possibly, therefore, about 350 million Africans will be living between the Sahara and the Limpopo by the end of the century. Such a prospect is thought-provoking, to say the least.

To the "bush" African, in so far as he is aware of it, it is no doubt an agreeable prospect. For to him a child is still an asset, not a liability. "Generations of struggle against the forces of Nature to keep the population stable, reinforced by fertility rites which lie at the core of African religion, have produced an outlook, and buttressed an instinct, which cannot be altered as quickly as the environment." [35] A child may be an extra mouth to feed, but it is also an extra pair of hands to be put to work in the field, around the house, hewing wood and drawing water, and, if it is a girl, a most valuable capital asset. Happy indeed is the man who has his quiverful of them!

To the educated African nationalist, the prospect can hardly be less pleasing. For nations need men for the engines of industry, commerce, communications, agriculture, administration, education — and, alas, of war. Most of the fledgling nations of tropical Africa do not as yet have enough men, certainly not enough to carry through their ambitious development programs unaided.

To the businessman, whether African, Asian or European, it is a prospect to strain the imagination. The tropical African market for consumer goods is potentially one of the largest in the world. A doubled population would mean much more than a doubled import of textiles and a doubled production of such basic necessities as sugar, shoes and bicycles. It would mean new industries and services, and possibly higher standards of living, as it has meant in North America. A doubled population would also mean a doubled labor supply to mine the minerals, tend tree crops, cut timber and build dams. Labor, as every employer knows, is the key quantity in the African economic equation at the present time. [36]

To the administrator, African and alien, the prospect is disturbing, even menacing. He is having all his work cut out looking after the present population, giving it a slightly firmer hold on the basic freedoms, a modicum of education, security and economic stability. A doubled population means many more schools, hospitals, dispensaries, law courts — and prisons; twice as many people to encumber the roads, tax the transportation services, crowd the already congested cities, spread disease and disaffection. Most important of all, it means finding at least twice as much food.

The food problem is already grave in some parts of tropical Africa, so much so that many observers doubt the capacity of the region as a whole to support a larger number of people at present, let alone improved, living

[35] Elspeth Huxley, *The Four Guineas: A Journey Through West Africa,* Chatto & Windus, London, 1954, p. 282.
[36] See Chapter 13.

standards. They point to the water-eroded, cutover hillsides of Ethiopia, to the declining productivity of bush clearings in parts of the Rhodesias, the overgrazed pastures of the Sudan, Tanganyika and Somalia, the seemingly interminable struggle of the agronomist and veterinarian for the control of plant and animal disease, and to the fact that even the relatively small and dispersed populations that have occupied tropical Africa for many centuries have been able to subsist only by means of a rotational system wherein vast amounts of land must lie fallow at any given time. In some parts of east Africa and the Cameroons the pressure put upon land to produce food has reached the point of no satisfactory return. In parts of Northern Rhodesia the ratio of present population to the estimated carrying capacity of the land if its fertility is not to be badly depleted exceeds 3:5, suggesting that a 40 per cent increase in population is all that can be contemplated without radically disturbing the existing low-level economy. In Ruanda-Urundi the position is more critical still. There the little land left vacant is now being occupied. Once it has gone — unless meantime there is a very big upturn in productivity of both crops and cattle — the government will again have to reckon with the possibility of famine, such as that of 1943-1944, when an estimated 60,000 lives were lost and many thousands left the country in search of food and work.

But a tremendous amount of agricultural research and development work is being done to save the peoples of tropical Africa from the Malthusian morass. Some of it has already borne fruit.[37] Much more may be expected to do so within the next ten to twenty years, given enough political stability, administrative machinery and money. Even now the outlook is far from hopeless. Lands until recently unpopulated because of tribal warfare or taboo are being settled, often with government assistance and farm supervision, by peoples from more crowded regions.[38] Other lands, hitherto neglected because of lack of population pressure, as in the case of the Malagasy Republic, or because the techniques necessary for their development were not known, as in the case of the swamplands of Bechuanaland, are likewise slowly being added to the African's living space. And there is still much that can be done in the way of irrigating the dry but potentially fruitful lands of the Sudan, Ethiopia, the Somalilands, and east Africa generally.

Nor does tropical Africa's food problem threaten to be merely one of land. It will be equally one of livelihood. The industrial development of Europe and North America, and the vast surge of population that accompanied it, was matched by an agrarian development that greatly increased per capita productivity and so gave those who stayed on the land a standard of living not very different from that of those who went to the

[37] See Chapter 4.
[38] See Chapter 5.

towns. Tropical Africa's economic development has so far been unbalanced. While the economy of the cities has undergone a radical transformation — revolution is scarcely too strong a word — the economy of
the rural areas continues to run, with some very notable exceptions as
will be seen, according to a timeless and inflexible set of rules. It continues to be an economy of drudgery and scarcity. Most of the surpluses
it yields are fortuitous, and provide no steady source of income. The cash
that comes in is soon squandered. The towns, no doubt, are in most cases
a poor exchange for the country, but there is money there, and wine,
women and song on which to spend it. And for those who are so minded,
there is schooling there and opportunity for self-improvement. "Going
to town" is more than a vogue these days; it has become a vocation. "Back
to the land" campaigners have so far found it rather hard to make themselves heard, possibly because it has not always been easy for them to
demonstrate the advantages of rural life. But unless such advantages can
be demonstrated, and quickly, the great promise of Africa's economic
dawn may perish, like Africa's own morning mists, from want of nourish-
ment.

CHAPTER 4

Farming the Land

AFRICAN AGRICULTURE

EUROPEAN AGRICULTURE

THREE people out of every four in tropical Africa are directly dependent on the land for a living.[1] In no territory is the proportion much below 60 per cent; in some it is as high as 90 per cent. Although, taking the region as a whole, there has been a gradual trend away from agriculture in recent years, there is little to suggest that this will seriously weaken the dominant role which the farmer plays in the region's economy. The welfare of its 167 million inhabitants will, in all probability, long continue to be bound up inextricably with the more than 4 million square miles which are either already under some form of cultivation or capable of it.

It need hardly be said that the agricultural uses to which this vast area is being or can be put are many. They cover almost every type of farm organization found in either the Old or the New World, and the raising of every crop in the farmer's book. Even a comparatively small country like Kenya has between 30 and 40 different agricultural commodities on its commercial list. And these commodities are raised on almost as many different types of holding. Some of Kenya's best cattle are raised on 100,000-acre ranches, some of its worst on two-acre *shambas*. Some of the grain is grown on farms as modern, and efficiently run, as any to be found in Iowa; some is grown by methods more primitive and wasteful than those of the bygone generation of Tennessee backwoodsmen. Some crops, like millet and manioc, are grown almost exclusively for local consumption; some, like pyrethrum and coffee, mainly for export. Some are raised on communally owned land; some on land that has been individually acquired by due process of law, occupation of empty lands, and

[1] According to figures quoted by the Food and Agriculture Organization of the United Nations, the proportion engaged in agriculture in 1948, together with their nonworking dependents, was 74 per cent of the total population. This compares with a figure of 70 per cent for Asia, 60 per cent for South America, 40 per cent for Oceania, 33 per cent for Europe and 31 per cent for North and Central America.

conquest; and some on land which until recently was thought of as useless and ownerless.

It was not always so. Before the coming of the white man, agriculture throughout the region was a small-scale enterprise undertaken almost solely for purposes of subsistence. It was characterized by dearth of equipment, by a limited use of fertilizer (particularly in the tsetse fly country), by poor and uncertain yields, and, in some areas, by a distressing ability to exhaust the soil and uproot its followers. At best it sufficed to fill their bellies with starches and sugars once a day; at worst it reduced them to a state of cyclical starvation, with a few fat weeks after each harvest, followed by many lean and hungry months in which more deaths than births were wont to occur. This traditional indigenous type of agriculture still characterizes much of Africa, although it is almost everywhere coming under foreign influences.

Before 1890 or so almost the only foreign thing about the agriculture of tropical Africa was the origin of the great majority of the crops grown. Of some 136 east African food plants, the histories of which have been worked out,[2] only 30 are believed to be of African origin. Of the others, nearly 60 are believed to be of Asiatic origin, and the rest — including most of the present-day staples — of European and American origin.

Around the turn of the century the agricultural position began to change, for several reasons. First, the highlands of east and central Africa were then being opened up for European settlement. This settlement was based on the assumption that plenty of good land was going begging, needing only the plow and African labor to turn its clods into crops of grain, sisal, tobacco, cotton, sugar, tea and coffee. Second, world demand for vegetable oils started to mount beyond the existing productive capacity of mid-latitude lands. In casting about for new sources of supply, Lever Brothers turned to the forests of equatorial Africa, where many species of oil palm are found. Soon plantations of the *Elaeis* palm were burgeoning along the banks of the Congo, the lower Niger and many another Atlantic coast river, and new African communities dependent upon the sale of the palm kernel and its oil were mushrooming among the plantations. Although many of these communities also grew foodstuffs, few, if any, grew enough for their needs. Third, the colonial administrations began requiring tax payments of the African for the services they were rendering, and although the taxes could sometimes be paid in the form of produce or labor, it was generally more convenient for both parties to deal in cash. Fourth, and perhaps most significant of all, traders began arriving with the manufactured wares of Europe and Asia. Soon their stalls of bright calicoes, gleaming bicycles and fancy trash were the cynosure of a million eager-eyed and contriving Africans. Some did not contrive hard enough to become customers, and some turned to the

---

[2] By P. J. Greenway in *East African Agricultural Journal*, Vol. XI (1945).

mines, railroads and ports rather than the fields in search of the needful money. But for many the incentive to farm for money became strong; and the European businessman, eager to increase the export flow of vegetable oils, cotton, tobacco and so on, lost no opportunity of nursing it.

AFRICAN AGRICULTURE

PASTORAL FARMING

On the whole, the African tropics are tough on the pastoralist. In the first place, they are superlative breeders of diseases that plague the life of cattle and their masters. The most noxious cattle disease is the tsetse-fly-borne trypanosomiasis that all but eliminates the practice of pastoralism from the forest belt. Only the indigenous dwarf cattle of west Africa and a few larger breeds such as the N'Dama and White Fulani seem to have a high degree of natural immunity to it. Although a good deal of hopeful research is being done on this disease, much of it by institutions that specialize in the work, so far no satisfactory specific has been discovered.[3] Mass inoculation campaigns are being carried out in the Republic of Sudan and other territories, to the comfort of many cattle keepers and the benefit of many animals, but the only really effective strategy against the fly is still to clear the territory that harbors it. High temperatures and high humidities being indispensable to the tsetse fly's existence, its distribution is confined to areas of thick bush below about 5,000 feet in the vicinity of water. Here it lives and breeds; as soon as it finds itself exposed to the strong rays of the sun, it languishes and dies.

Tick-borne diseases constitute a second major problem, especially in east Africa, where east coast fever is widespread. Although tick control is unanimously held to be desirable, and is, in fact, practiced on every European stock farm, opinions differ on the merits of tick eradication by spraying or dipping. Wherever it has been tried, as it has been in every territory, there is evidence that it has hindered the development of immunity and tended to create highly susceptible cattle populations.

The full list of epizootic diseases that bedevil the life of cattle is depressingly long. The Inter-African Bureau for Epizootic Diseases has published a memorandum listing 11 virus diseases, nine bacterial and four protozoan infections and one fungoid infection;[4] these and the enzootic diseases are said to be responsible for the loss of "several million head of livestock . . . annually . . . in the territory lying between the

---

[3] Horses, camels and dogs, as well as cattle, bitten by the tsetse usually die. At first no effect is seen, but a few days after the animal has been bitten, the eyes and nose begin to run, a swelling appears under the jaw and the muscles become flaccid. The animal begins to stagger and may go mad before it dies.

[4] *Bulletin of Epizootic Diseases of Africa* (Commission for Technical Cooperation in Africa South of the Sahara, London), Vol. I, No. 1, March 1953.

tropic of Cancer and the extreme southern point of the African continent
. . . The losses in cattle alone represent the disappearance of 300,000
tons of meat a year, sufficient to furnish the minimum animal protein
requirements of 10 million people." [5] However, most of these diseases
could be kept under control if adequate staff and facilities were available.

Diseases are only one of a number of obstacles to be overcome or
circumvented by the pastoralist. Over large areas the climate is anything
but helpful. In the lowlands, it works against the preservation of all
forms of pastoral produce. Meat decomposes rapidly; milk turns sour,
butter rancid,[6] and cheese hard, dried up or moldy. In a less direct but
no less potent way, the climate adversely affects both the quality and the
quantity of tropical pastures. The flora of the savannas is very different
from that of the mid-latitude prairies where grasses share the ground
with leguminous plants, for, typically, it consists almost wholly of coarse
grasses. The difference is largely consequent upon the fact that savanna
soils are poor in humus, without which the bacteria necessary for the
development of legumes do not thrive. There are some good tropical
fodder grasses, but they are rare. Most grasses native to tropical savannas,
though quite nutritious when they are young, become fibrous as they
grow older, with consequent decrease in their protein and water content.
Except for a few weeks of their cycle they also tend to be very poor
in phosphorus, which all animals require for healthy development.

Tipping the scales still more heavily against the pastoralist is the highly
seasonal regime of the rainfall over most of the grazing country. Grass
growth on the savannas is rapid during and immediately after the rainy
season, or seasons; but during the rest of the year, which may be up
to eight or nine months, it is negligible, causing the stocking capacity of
the pastures to fall off. On unimproved pastures this stocking capacity
may be less than one head of cattle for 50 acres. Even when seeded
with more nutritious grasses, the pasture lands are seldom able to carry
more than one head of cattle for each four or five acres without supplementary rations of cake or maize.[7]

In the circumstances, it is remarkable that livestock raising should
ever have become established in the African tropics, and even more remarkable that today the domestic animal population of the region is to
be numbered in tens of millions. According to R. Larrat there were in
1953 approximately 55 million cattle, 60 million sheep and goats, and 4
million pigs in the region south of the Sahara; this means that in the
region between the Sahara and the Limpopo there were approximately
41 million cattle, 17 million sheep and goats, and 3.5 million pigs.

[5] R. Larrat, in *ibid.*, p. 2.

[6] Clarified butter, such as the *semn* made by the pastoralists of the Northern
Province of the Republic of Sudan, keeps longer than ordinary butter, but seldom
longer than a few weeks.

[7] On some recently sown pastures in the Kenya Highlands the carrying capacity
has been raised to 1.5 cows per acre, but this is most exceptional.

The most unhelpful feature of African pastoralism, however, continues to be the pastoralist himself. He is, it is true, neither unwitting fool nor witting knave. He has a flair for improvisation — for living off his animals and keeping them alive in time of dearth; for cooperation — for seeing that scarce water and grass are fairly shared among the contending herds. No dowser is more adept at "scenting" water; no veterinarian at telling what kind of vegetation is good for what kind of malady. Yet his herds are among the sorriest in the world. Culling of weak and diseased animals is rarely practiced except under compulsion, and controlled breeding almost never. Some herds are in much better shape than they were twenty years ago, but others have deteriorated badly.

Nor as yet is very much thought given to the capacity of the land to sustain cattle, with the result that there are abounding evidences of land abuse. Once disturbed, the ecological equilibrium is hard to restore in the best of environments, and savannas are not the best of environments. Over much of them the equilibrium can be upset at the touch of a flame. True, the firing of savanna clears the ground of useless straw and woody growths and encourages the growth of tender shoots at the first fall of rain, but the damage done to the stability of the soil, its bacterial life and humus content is out of all proportion to the benefits obtained. And there are parts of the savannas where the equilibrium can be upset by the touch of a hoof. A water hole that is overworked in a dry season all too easily becomes a dust bowl. Overgrazing of pasture quickly leads to the destruction of the perennial forage plants, and encourages the development of annuals with small value as cattle feed. Such rain as falls on the impoverished plant cover is mostly lost to productive uses because of increased evaporation and run-off. Soil erosion by both water and wind is a very potent factor in the dry season. It leads to silting up of streams, flood risk and attendant risk of stagnant water — the breeding place of many harmful insects — and, indirectly, strain on the ground water resources.[8]

The average pastoralist's diet has not changed much with the years. The chief ingredients continue to be milk, butter, blood, meat (mainly of animals that died of natural causes or were killed for ceremonial purposes), and items that can be obtained for the gathering, such as wild honey eaten fresh or fermented into beer. However, few pastoral tribes any longer rely exclusively on animal products for their sustenance; millet and maize for the menfolk, root crops and bananas for the women and children constitute important supplementary foods in many of the better-favored range lands. To these are added an ever-increasing variety of

[8] The water table has fallen sharply over many parts of central and east Africa. Robert Laws has listed twenty important watercourses in the single district of Mombera in Nyasaland which have lost their permanent character since the beginning of the century. (See W. Vogt, *Road to Survival*, William Sloane Associates, New York, 1948, p. 252.)

canned and packaged goods obtainable at the market centers and wherever two roads meet.

It is, of course, extremely easy to exercise the gift of hindsight and to
conclude that pastoralism should never have been introduced into Africa;
that the damage done by it is incalculable, and the economic advantages
insignificant. It is much less easy to devise remedial measures adapted
both to the physical environment and to the capabilities and customs of
the people — and to see that they are applied.

Among the measures being taken by African governments to this end,
four are of particular importance.

1. The imposition of a higher cattle tax. The root of the pastoral problem, it is generally conceded, is that there are too many cattle for the
good of the land and their keepers. What could be more obvious, then,
than to impose a tax heavy enough to discourage cattle hoarding? Alas,
most African pastoralists are not easily discouraged. The cattle taxes already imposed in some areas are more penal than fiscal, but they have not
led to any very noticeable lowering of the livestock population. What
usually happens among the Fulani herders of northern Nigeria, for
instance, is that the cattle that have to be sold to pay the *jangali* (cattle
tax) simply change hands and go from one overstocked pasture to another.
To raise the tax even higher might simply mean that cattle, being still regarded as the soundest form of investment by all the traditionally pastoral
tribes, would pass from one set of owners to another, namely, the newly
moneyed mine workers and the petty traders, for most of whom a herd of
cattle is as much a dream as are "a place in the country" and a nice bank
balance to the average American. (In many parts of Africa there is no surer
way for the migrant laborer to increase his social prestige on returning
home than to buy a few head of cattle.) A higher tax rate would also almost certainly lead to an increase in the already large number of tax
evaders.

2. The development of smaller, better herds. It might well be supposed that this measure would be even more unpopular than the first.
Certainly almost everywhere it has been advocated it has met with great
resistance. However, the fact is that in many areas herds are smaller
than formerly, even though the gross cattle population of the region is
larger. This is due in part to the rinderpest epidemics of fifty years or so
ago, from which in some cases (the Fulani for one) the cattle stocks have
never completely recovered. But in part it is due to the slowly growing
realization of some of the more discerning pastoralists that safety does
not reside in numbers.

There are good reasons why herds should not be as large as formerly.
First, the larger the herd, the greater the hazard and ravages of disease;
the higher the mortality from attack by wild animals; and the poorer its
general quality. Second, the larger the herd, the less susceptible it is to

controlled breeding, which is essential if livestock quality is to be raised. Third, the larger the herd, the greater the difficulty of finding food and water in a dry year, or a series of dry years; and the greater the difficulty, at a time of increasing population like the present, of keeping the pastures in a self-perpetuating condition. Already the Masai, who at the height of their prosperity and power in the nineteenth century are believed to have numbered between 60,000 and 80,000 and today number nearer 150,-000, are hard put to it to maintain themselves in their traditional fashion. Then they had the run of at least a quarter of a million square miles of the highlands of east Africa from about 1° north of the equator to about 5° south, and the power, which they were not slow in exercising, to keep down the population, both animal and human, to the size which the land could safely support. Now they have the run of perhaps 3,000 square miles and are in some danger of losing part of this to their land-hungry agricultural neighbors; they are, of course, no longer free to "control" the surplus population. The arithmetic of such a process is inexorable. Each acre added to the sown means an acre subtracted from the savanna. Each herd multiplied means pasture diminished, if not divided, and each pasture diminished means, sooner or later, a larger remainder of eroded, useless earth.

In the circumstances, it is cause for good cheer that in the Livestock Improvement Areas of Uganda, and elsewhere in east and central Africa, cattle-owning peoples are beginning to think that it is perhaps better to have a score of well-favored animals yielding useful amounts of milk, and calving satisfactorily, than a hundred diseased, dry and unproductive beasts. Such perceptions are still uncommon, but the important fact is that they are found.

Here and there, too, a beginning has been made with selective breeding, in place of promiscuous breeding, of indigenous stock. A wide range of cattle types is to be found in tropical Africa and although some, such as the Chad and the Shuwa, appear to have only a limited environmental range, others, including the Zebu breeds, have greater powers of adaptability. Crossbreeding with imported animals is also being tried, but for several reasons, including cost, climatic intolerance, susceptibility to disease and inability to keep condition on unimproved pasture, European and Indian bulls are a luxury few herders can afford; accordingly most of this crossbreeding has to be underwritten by the governments.

3. The introduction of controlled grazing. This is being pressed throughout the pastoral areas. Where it has been practiced over any length of time, it has yielded encouraging results. In the comparatively sparsely populated region between Timbuktu and Kabara in the Sudanese Republic (formerly French Sudan) the French government for many years reserved an area of 10,000 to 12,000 acres on which to raise the cattle needed to supply the troops stationed there. The temptation to over-

stock the land was resisted and the encroachments of nomadic pastoralists were consistently thwarted. In 1958 the pastures were better than they were sixty to seventy years before, and the troops were better fed. Similar protective measures have been taken in the nearby Goundam region, and in the Yatta plains of south central Kenya, also sparsely populated, with similar results. But controlled grazing becomes a very different proposition in places where the pressure of human and animal population on the land is already heavy, where overstocking is of long standing and alternative range lands are not readily available. There are plenty of such places. As long ago as 1933 the Kamba Land Unit in Kenya had roughly three times its estimated grazing capacity in cattle, goats and sheep. Such situations call for change more than control. A major resettlement program was the answer in the case of the Kamba, as will be seen in Chapter 5. Among more moderate changes being urged upon pastoralists and their governments are alternate grazing, whereby pastures are rested periodically (this has already proved successful in the Zimutu Reserve in Southern Rhodesia and in some other areas), the provision of fire lines to prevent excessive burning in any one season, and of well-distributed water supplies to relieve seasonal overcrowding of the better-favored localities (ponds and wells already form important items in the development budgets of most of the governments), and the fencing of pastures, the advantages of which have long been demonstrated by European ranchers in Kenya and the Rhodesias.

4. The encouragement of supplementary crop raising. Many cattle herders have long made a point of keeping a patch of land cultivated with maize, millet, bananas and other stand-by foodstuffs. In some cases, they do the work themselves. In other cases they are in the habit of employing "lesser breeds" to do it for them. In a few cases the crop raising has proved so successful that it has ceased to be supplementary. With many of the Ganda of Uganda it has become the major activity, and the more prestigious one at that, since it is now customary for those Ganda who do keep cattle to employ Hima herders. But with most of the pastoral peoples crop raising continues to be no more than a secondary activity.

Since the end of World War II many African governments have given thought to ways of making crop raising more attractive to such people. The gains which accrue from a mixed economy of this sort are substantial. In addition to a fuller and richer diet, and increased protection against the impact of cattle epidemics, it gives its practitioners a more responsible attitude toward the care of land and water resources, and a greater purchasing power. The animals also gain from it. Even in a bad season they are likely to find more sustenance among the maize stubble than on the parched ranges. In a good season they can be given supplementary rations of grain and green crops. But the combination of nomadic, or semi-nomadic, herding with cultivation is not easy in the best of circumstances, since the need to work the land at set seasons restricts freedom of movement in search of pasture; in the more arid fringes of the pastoral belt it may not be feasible because of inadequate water supplies.

While the trend toward supplementary crop raising is continuing and will doubtless gather momentum as the pressure of people and animals on the better lands increases, there is little question of stock raising losing its primacy with Africa's pastoralists. They could do nothing else with most of the lands at their disposal. Only a few want to do anything else; for the rest, cattle raising is still a man's meat and drink, his wealth and his world — his highest good. It follows, therefore, that any solution to the pastoralist's problems that envisages the abandonment of cattle herding for more sedentary pursuits is likely to be no solution at all; it would almost certainly create more difficulties than it removed. Fortunately there is no need to advocate such a revolutionary measure, except perhaps in those, still limited, areas where the ecological equilibrium is so badly out of kilter that restoration to their original condition is deemed impractical.

SUBSISTENCE CROP FARMING

Like pastoral farming, subsistence crop farming as engaged in by the ordinary African cultivator has changed little during the past two generations. Its tools are still few and simple — a hoe, a cutlass and a knife of sorts. Its techniques are still more attuned to a philosophy of scarcity than one of abundance. Conformity to custom is still the paramount consideration in most areas. So little has the pattern of this type of farming changed that many nineteenth-century descriptions of it still have a very topical flavor. What has changed most is its areal extent, which has declined; and the terms on which it is practiced, which have generally deteriorated.

Subsistence crop farming is, self-evidently, a system with no future that any ambitious African would feel was worth waiting for. It is unproductive; its customary crops — manioc, banana, maize, millet, sorghum and yams [9] — are generally poor in proteins; it leaves hungry mouths; it provides the cultivator with no incentive to change his ways; and it is prodigal in its wastage of both the organic and inorganic resources of the bush. Yet it was probably the most satisfactory system that could have been devised by "pre-mechanical" peoples living in a wet tropical environment.

In the first place, it requires comparatively little labor. The Bemba of Northern Rhodesia do about four months' agricultural work in the year. Some of the deep forest tribes manage to do even less. Bearing in mind the toll taken by disease of the African's vitality, this is fortunate; the chances are that many tribes, in their pristine condition, could not have

[9] See Figures 13 and 14 for the distribution of manioc and maize.

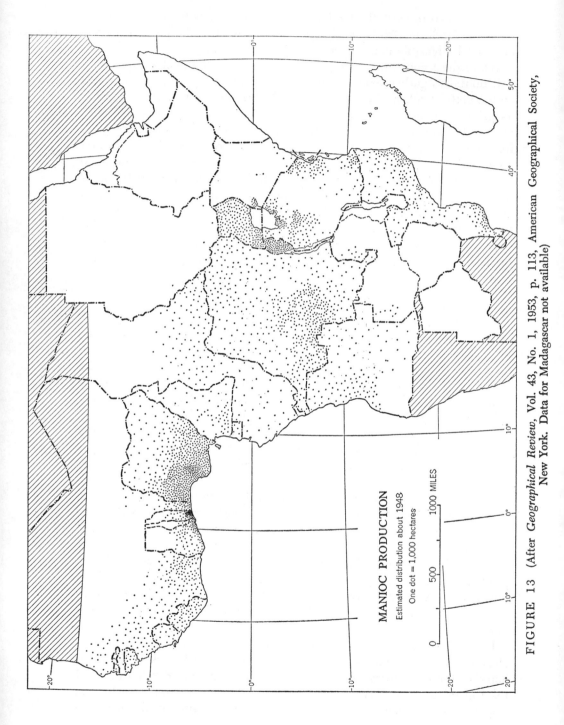

MANIOC PRODUCTION

Estimated distribution about 1948

One dot = 1,000 hectares

0   500   1000 MILES

FIGURE 13 (After *Geographical Review*, Vol. 43, No. 1, 1953, p. 113, American Geographical Society, New York. Data for Madagascar not available)

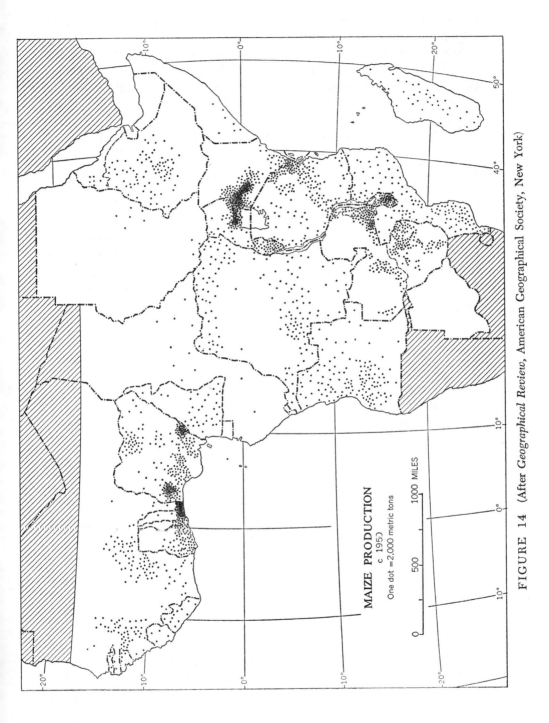

MAIZE PRODUCTION
c 1953
One dot = 2,000 metric tons

1000 MILES

500

0

FIGURE 14 (After *Geographical Review*, American Geographical Society, New York)

coped with more intensive and sustained demands on their time and energies.

Second, given enough acreage, the system provides the cultivator with a supply of fertilizer, for the firing of the bush yields a temporary concentration at the surface of phosphate, potash, calcium and other valuable plant foods. At the same time it turns a slightly acid soil into a slightly alkaline one.

Third, subsistence farming traditionally allows, and indeed assures, that the fertility of the earth will be periodically renewed. However impressive the debit side to forest burning may be, the debit side to forest cultivation is even more impressive. The cultivation of field crops on cutover land is very wasteful of the mineral stores of the soil. Crops such as millet and maize waste up to ten times the mineral substances they consume; the nitrogen loss alone may be as much as 900 pounds per cultivated acre per year. Clearly the simplest way to get this lost mineral balance restored is to allow the cultivated land to revert to forest in the shortest convenient time, which is precisely what the typical shifting cultivator does. As a matter of fact, many Bantu cultivators go so far as to expedite the reversion process by planting trees on the abandoned land.

Fourth, the system carries its own insurance against soil erosion, the menace of which is second only to soil exhaustion over most of tropical Africa. Anyone who has seen, and heard, tropical rainstorms beating out their savage tattoo knows that they can strip a two-inch layer of exposed topsoil in minutes. The forest zone clearings are seldom "clean" enough of trash, stubble, growing crops, tree roots and weeds or large enough to present a rainstorm with this kind of opportunity. This is less true of the savanna clearings, which are open to erosion by wind as well.

Perhaps the greatest merit of the system is the concern it shows for the preservation of the natural equilibrium and the complementary need to interfere as little as possible with the delicate processes by which the soil succeeds in maintaining itself and keeping a certain degree of fertility in the difficult circumstances imposed by the tropical climate. It is a "perfectly rational" agricultural system, as Pierre Gourou points out.[10] Though primitive, the cultivator's techniques are skillful. According to Gourou, "the disasters brought on by agricultural methods which have taken no account of the treasures of wisdom and experience accumulated in the old tropical system are a sufficient proof of the latter's value . . . This agricultural system which is lightly termed primitive and backward was capable of recovering its vigor whenever a favorable opportunity presented itself."

[10] *Les Pays Tropicaux,* Presses Universitaires de France, Paris, 1947, pp. 36-37.

CASH CROP FARMING

It may seem odd that the African subsistence crop cultivator should have responded to the white man's demand for exportable crops, let alone become successful at providing them. He had no notable tradition of crop specialization behind him, and few of the incentives that appeal to the Westerner made much of an appeal to him initially. Very few of the crops he habitually grew were of any commercial interest; those that were, being mostly exotics, often had a hard time getting established and staying strong. That he did respond was due largely to three important facts. There was money to be had in cash crop farming, and money was beginning to assume a place in his life. Cash crop farming required no skills additional to those needed for subsistence crop farming, and it could be practiced within the traditional shifting framework of indigenous agriculture. It called for no extra effort; frequently it called for less, since the successful cultivator might well find himself making enough money to employ some paid labor or to buy his "subsistence" crops with the proceeds of his cash crop.

While a few communities were in the cash-cropping business as far back as the turn of the century (a little cocoa was being shipped from Ghana in the late 1890s), it was not until the 1920s and 1930s that it became big business. But the incidence of cash crop farming remained very patchy, as it still is. The early leaders in the field, besides Ghana, were the territories of the then French West Africa, Sierra Leone, Nigeria, the Belgian Congo and Uganda. The chief cash crops, besides cocoa (grown mainly in Ghana, Nigeria, French West Africa and the Cameroons), were peanuts (French West Africa and Nigeria), cotton (Uganda, the Belgian Congo and French West Africa) and palm products (Nigeria, Sierra Leone and French West Africa).

Some indication of the extent to which the production of African-raised cash crops has expanded in recent years is to be found in a comparison of the production of typical export crops before and after World War II. Partial data collected by the Food and Agriculture Organization of the United Nations on three predominantly African-raised crops, peanuts, cocoa and cotton, show that between prewar and 1957 the production of peanuts increased by more than 50 per cent and of cocoa by nearly 25 per cent, while the production of cotton increased by more than 100 per cent between prewar and the mid-1950s.[11]

Although somewhere or other in tropical Africa almost every tropical crop is nowadays raised for cash, or part-cash and part-subsistence, only a few crops lend themselves to the rather casual habits and traditional systems of the ordinary cultivator, and fewer still are big money-makers. Such figures as are available suggest that out of the 50 and more crops

[11] See United Nations, *Statistical Yearbook, 1958*, New York, 1958.

commercially raised, five, namely, peanuts, coffee, cocoa, cotton and palm oil (and kernels), account for not less than four fifths of the cash received in a given year by African producers. Possibly as much as four fifths of this cash goes to cultivators in the following territories: the western members of the French Community, the Republic of Guinea, Ghana, Nigeria (including the British Cameroons), the Republic of Sudan and Uganda. In recent years Guinea and the western members of the French Community have produced between one third and one half of the total African peanut crop, up to one third of the coffee crop and up to one sixth of the palm kernel and cocoa crops, mostly African-grown and African-owned in each case. Ghana has produced around 45 to 50 per cent of the total cocoa crop, all of it grown and owned by Africans. Nigeria has accounted for more than 60 per cent of the palm kernel crop, about 55 per cent of the palm oil output, 30 per cent of the peanut crop, and more than 20 per cent of the cocoa crop — all grown and owned by Africans.[12] The Sudan has produced between 25 and 30 per cent of the cotton crop, most of it on tenant farms in the Gezira. And Uganda has produced about 20 per cent of the cotton crop (all African-grown) and between 10 and 15 per cent of the coffee crop (mostly African-grown).[13]

Other important cash crops raised by Africans are maize and sorghums (these have become especially important in the vicinity of the bigger towns and mines of the Belgian Congo, the Rhodesias, British East Africa and west Africa generally), tobacco (Nyasaland, Uganda, Tanganyika and the Malagasy Republic), copra (Zanzibar and in many coastal districts of west and east Africa), and sugar cane and citrus fruits.[14]

The cash accruing to the growers from the sale of these crops has been very considerable. It has made many rich. Some growers have become very rich by African standards — indeed, by any standards. Among Ghana cocoa farmers postwar incomes in excess of £1,000 have been common. Several Uganda and Tanganyika coffee growers are known to have had even higher incomes — between £3,000 and £4,000 in some instances (which makes them far better off than most government officials and local college professors). The median incomes have been very much lower. Most growers have only enough land, or grow only enough crops on their land, to pick up incomes of between $75 and $150 — which, after payments have been made for clothes, taxes and sundries, leaves them with very little for the savings bank, or the secret hole in the ground.

[12] The Belgian Congo is a heavy producer, too, of both palm oil (between 130,000 and 140,000 tons a year) and palm kernels (between 70,000 and 90,000 tons a year), but most of these crops are raised on plantations owned and managed by Europeans.

[13] Other large coffee producers are Angola, the Belgian Congo and Kenya, where the business is run mainly by Europeans, and Ethiopia, the Malagasy Republic, the French Cameroons, Ruanda-Urundi and Tanganyika, where it is mainly in indigenous hands.

[14] Because these commodities are generally raised in small garden patches, their cash value to the individual grower is small, but as they are very widely raised, their total value is large.

These incomes have not been earned without cost, and loss. The basic feature of this cash crop economy has so far been its concentration on a single crop. This suited the African; once learned, the agronomic requirements of a single crop were easily remembered and never changed. It also suited the governments, since it facilitated the organization of buying, selling and shipping services, and pest control, and gave them a fairly reliable source of revenue. It did not suit the earth so well. The African earth is much more expendable than the European or North American earth and much less tolerant of abuse. It can take only so much punishment and then it rebels. This it has begun to do in many places and under several guises. Soils yearly exposed to wind, sun and rain by cotton, maize or peanut farmers soon lose more than their fertility; they lose their structure and their stability — their "roots" in fact. Bush that has been stripped of its natural cover and replaced either by a single crop or by two or three crops grown in rotation may survive the surgery only to fall heir to insect pests and virus diseases that hitherto were kept in check by natural mechanisms. Already there is scarcely a crop, or a cash crop locality, that is not plagued in this way.

Just what the total losses to the earth have been we have no means of telling. They are visibly enormous, being etched on the face of a thousand hoed-up hillsides and as many more plowed-up plains and plateaus. The invisible losses of the soil's chemicals, humus and water supplies are almost certainly of the same magnitude.

GROWTH OF RATIONAL FARMING

It is easy to deplore, and almost everybody does, the bankruptcy of such a system; it is difficult to find another that is at one and the same time self-perpetuating, economically rewarding, and feasible. One-crop farming has been rewarding, but is self-destroying rather than self-perpetuating, and certainly not feasible in a rapidly expanding society. Subsistence crop farming was self-perpetuating, but not rewarding, nor is it any longer feasible. The obvious alternative — obvious, that is, to a Westerner — is to get the African to adopt a stabilized form of agriculture based on crop rotations or, where possible, on mixed (crop and cattle) husbandry. But it has yet to be proved whether this is either an acceptable or a feasible alternative to most of those Africans who have been drawn into the money economy. To ask the "successful" cash-in-hand cultivator to mind his agricultural manners and adopt techniques of a more skillful and arduous and, at the same time, less remunerative kind, in the long-term interests of his land, is to ask a great deal, as any prairie farmer would readily concede. To get him to accept the necessity of doing so, and to acquire proficiency in the art of it, is asking a very great deal, not only of the African farmer himself but also of his European tutors and advisers. That both can be done is not in dispute; the question is whether enough farmers can be made to do both quickly enough to save the living earth from death by exposure. The omens are both good and bad.

On the bad side must be reckoned the African cultivator's much lamented inertia, ignorance, poverty and fear. His inertia disinclines him to change his ways; his ignorance makes him slow to "see" and quick to forget; his poverty predisposes him to be impatient for fast results, and often, because of its debilitating consequences, incapable of long-sustained hard work. His fear leads him to doubt the motives of the European who wants him to alter his habits, and to hate those of his neighbor who does.[15]

On the debit side, too, must be placed the land laws and customs of the African. These constitute, without doubt, the greatest obstacle to the general adoption of more rational farming systems. It is customary for a man's lands to be scattered in fragments over a wide area. In parts of Kenya — and this is typical of conditions in much of tropical Africa — a single family may possess from 10 to 20 small fields; there are recorded instances of farmers having as many as 29. While these may be, and probably are, distributed equitably from the standpoint of their intrinsic properties of soil and drainage, they cannot be developed efficiently, either from the standpoint of the farmers' inclinations or from that of the government agricultural officer whose job it is to try to increase the farmers' productivity. As the Swynnerton Report pointed out, "It is impossible under such circumstances to develop sound farming rotations, to cart and apply manure, to establish and manage grass, to improve the management and feeding of livestock or to tend cash crops in any satisfactory manner."[16] Nor is the cause of good husbandry advanced by the general absence of indefeasible titles to land in tropical Africa. So long as a farmer is unable to use his land as security against such financial credits as he may wish to obtain, and unsure that he won't at some time or other find himself litigated out of his land, he is hardly likely to be an enthusiastic supporter of expensive long-term development policies.

What of the good omens? There are several, and their significance is considerable. In the first place, some African communities have already adopted self-perpetuating forms of husbandry, and with excellent results. Thus, the Amharic inhabitants of the small Laki Islands of Lake Zwai in central Ethiopia manage to get two crops a year (cotton and a grain) off their poor hillside soils by dint of terracing and regular manurings. The coffee-growing Chagga manage to maintain themselves around the slopes of Mt. Kilimanjaro on plots averaging not more than three acres in size

[15] In some parts of Africa, arson is the poor man's answer to the challenge of his more successful (African) neighbor.

[16] "A Plan to Intensify the Development of African Agriculture in Kenya," compiled by R. J. M. Swynnerton, Government Printer, Nairobi, 1954, p. 9.

by mulching heavily both their subsistence crops (mainly yams, sweet potatoes and banana) and their main cash crop. By so doing they now have what is probably the nearest thing to continuous agriculture in the world. To do this on such small holdings, and to live as well as they do, is no light accomplishment, even though their lands are, for tropical Africa, exceptionally fertile and well watered.

Other communities are also "catching on." Many African leaders in the more crowded parts of west, central and east Africa now recognize that the present slow death of the land must be stopped, and that they must back the central governments' schemes for stopping it. In Ghana, for instance, the Prime Minister, Dr. Kwame Nkrumah, and his cabinet have given their support to the cutting-out campaign urged by the West African Cacao Research Institute as the only effective means of controlling the swollen-shoot disease — an action that called for a good deal of courage as well as wisdom. No leaders newly come to power willingly adopt policies that hurt the pockets of their electors. In many parts of British East Africa and the Belgian Congo local communities are already so convinced of the need for better farming that they are providing the authorities with free labor to carry out the necessary conservation work. Some local chiefs and councils are paying, voluntarily, for the use of soil-ridging and -contouring equipment. Others have even accepted the ideas — revolutionary for them — of individual ownership and permanent cropping that the government sponsors are anxious to wed to it. One of the most successful developments of this kind has taken place in the Kipsigis country of the Nyanza Province of Kenya. Cattlemen by tradition, the Kipsigis did little cultivating until the idea of enclosed farms took hold. These were sown to the hitherto despised maize and other crops as thousands of Kipsigis switched over to a mixed-farming type of economy. A great part of their country is now fully settled, and the entire Kipsigis Native Land Unit well on the way to being physically and economically reconstituted.

Some African communities are beginning to accept the no less revolutionary idea of consolidation of land holdings. In fact, in some Kenya communities, including one or two in Kikuyu territory, "consolidation" programs have already been carried out; and in more than one instance the initiative for this has come, not from the government, but from the farmers themselves.

The second good omen is a growing realization on the part of the central governments that the African farmer is more readily attracted to a new idea when it can be worked out on his own broken-down acres than when it is demonstrated on a large experimental farm equipped with machinery he cannot afford and staffed by highly qualified scientists and technicians who do not speak his language. Wherever possible, farm improvement schemes are being scaled down and carried out on the lands of cultivators chosen for their good standing, good sense and willingness to serve as "guinea pigs." Instances of such schemes are given in the next chapter. In Southern Rhodesia, where the "guinea pig" method has been widely followed, over 25 per cent of all African farmers are now within the sphere of influence of these schemes. True, only about 2.5 per cent — categorized as master farmers and plot holders — have as yet adopted rational farming systems, but as the word gets around, the number is increasing. The average output per acre on the master farms is between four and five times greater than on the others. In the face of such a persuasive fact, the misrepresentations of the fearful, the jealous and the unbelieving lack much of the attraction they once possessed.

Third, an increasing number of Africans, disillusioned by their experiences of life in the towns and the mining compounds, are turning to the country again for their support, and solace. Many of them may take a poor view of the European's role in their lives, but they are quick to admit that he has the knowledge and resources which are necessary if their lands are ever to yield well enough to supply them with the good things of life. They are therefore more ready to take the advice of the government's district officer and his technical colleagues. And in many cases they have more capital — saved from their urban wages — to put into the recommended farming systems.

This trend is noticeable in many places. It is particularly marked in those areas which serve as labor reservoirs, either for local towns, as in Kenya, the Republic of the Congo and west Africa, or for distant mines and industries, as in Mozambique, Nyasaland and Ruanda-Urundi. Many Kikuyu, shriven by their unwholesome experiences of the past few years, are now more than happy to turn their backs on the towns and to be given the chance of a fresh start on their family lands — particularly where these lands have been "consolidated," cleared, contour plowed or bench terraced, and supplied with access roads and other services. Some are already making more money than they ever made in town, are eating better and living better, and, to boot, thinking better. The Portuguese authorities in Mozambique are also beginning to find that many of those who formerly left the country to work on the mines of South Africa and the Rhodesias require very little inducement to stay on their small holdings. In the Macia district of the lower Limpopo emigration to the Union of South Africa has fallen off sharply since the Inhamissa and other land development schemes have strengthened the rural economy. Around 1950 about 5,000 men went regularly each year to the Union; by the mid-1950s the number was down below 200. All that these men ask is a chance to sell what they grow at a modest profit, or, less still, a chance to grow something that they can sell.

Fourth, there is a deepening conviction that what is needed most to solve Africa's land problems is not techniques, equipment and capital, but understanding, and that it is not only the African who needs the understanding. True, it has generally been assumed that the average

African farmer is an ignorant sort of fellow and must be told what is good for him, and made to do it. It is, however, no less true, though much less generally assumed, that the European is still ignorant of a great many things he ought to know about the earth of Africa and the handling of its resources, to say nothing of understanding the African's viewpoint in such matters. If, for example, the average African pastoralist cannot be made to see the necessity of carrying out government "de-stocking" orders, may it not be that what he objects to is not the de-stocking so much as the manner in which the order is put to him, and carried out? Impatient men clamoring for compulsory de-stocking could create resistance or at least increase it among cattlemen the world over; so, too, could unscrupulous men buying low and selling high. Given patience, a well-organized system of stock auctions in which fair trading is ensured, and reasonable prices (which can always be ensured when an official buyer is present at the auction and authorized, if necessary, to break up middlemen's rings), stock soon begin to be sold freely in many parts of Africa.

It is becoming clear also that what, in the long run, determines the success or failure of a farm improvement plan is not so much its agronomic merits, or its timeliness, or even its financial feasibility, but the personal qualities of the African and European men who are in charge of it. It is perhaps more than a coincidence that some of the most promising farm improvement schemes under way at the present time are shoestring affairs, like St. Faith's Mission Farm at Rusape, Southern Rhodesia, run by people who make up in dedication, insight and willingness to dirty their hands what they lack in paper qualifications.

This is not to belittle the need for agricultural education. On the contrary, there can be no true understanding of the African's lands or the various African governments' plans for them without such education. But we dare to bespeak prior attention to the need for understanding since one of the commonest of our modern self-deceptions is that to "know how" is more important than to "know." The former may make us clever; only the latter can make us wise.

The need for agricultural education is now recognized by public and private agencies alike. In most territories such education has already become part of the curriculum by which it is hoped to raise the sights of the African peasant and so equip him better for self-government. Much of the education is rather thin, for Africa is broad, the peoples scattered and the governments, with few exceptions, poor. In some places it may amount to no more than a yearly visit to a village by the government officer, or a handout of simple illustrated pamphlets written in the local vernacular. In other places it is in the hands of the local African leaders, the younger generation of whom are usually glad enough to cooperate with the central authorities in matters of the plainest self-interest. Here and there it assumes more spectacular forms, as in Ethiopia, where, thanks largely to the personal concern of His Imperial Majesty Haile Selassie, the annual expenditure on agricultural education is one of the largest items in the whole educational budget, and where the U. S. International Cooperation Administration has been conducting very sizable agricultural teaching programs.

Scarcely less urgent than the need for education in agricultural techniques and systems is the need for education in the uses of new foods and better ways of using traditional foods. Soybeans, one of nature's best protein-endowed foods, grow well in many African environments that are short of both animal and vegetable proteins, yet hardly anywhere have they come, as yet, to form a significant element of the diet. They are not liked well enough to oust the existing staples, which is perhaps another way of saying that not enough thought has been given to either the eating habits of African peoples or the possibility of developing new food products that in form and taste are akin to the traditional ones.

The price of better African agriculture is clearly not to be reckoned only in dollars and cents, or even in physical and intellectual effort. Exactly what that price is, is still a matter of debate. But most of the debaters seem to be agreed on one point: the price includes moral as well as mental and material expenditures and, as such, is a function of philosophy as much as of farming. There are also those who say that African farming is never likely to be much better until European farming in tropical Africa is much better.

EUROPEAN AGRICULTURE

BIRTH AND GROWING PAINS

For long Europeans were not very interested in the agricultural uses of tropical Africa. There were many better places in the world in which to make a living off the land, and in tropical Africa there were many better things to bother about than agriculture. Those who did bother with it usually got into difficulties pretty quickly. Often they were opposed by the indigenous population. More often they were hampered by lack of laborers. Not infrequently they were their own worst enemy, being quite unprepared for the living problems that awaited them. And almost everywhere they were hampered by the land — if not its floods, then its droughts; if not its erosion, its exhaustion; if not its plant pests, its animal plunderers.

Their biggest difficulty perhaps was their inability to farm the land on traditionally European lines. As a distinguished French administrator has put it, the African agricultural system was

a complete mystery to us . . . Not only was the system of land tenure unintelligible to us, but their methods of tillage defeated us . . . With our background of European individualism we did not perceive that Africa had succeeded in combining family forms of ownership with communal methods of labour . . . The whole situation was so different from what we had expected that we sometimes even denied to these people the status of peasants: we did not realize how they must have laboured and suffered to make their soil into cultivable land, and we regarded them as merely labourers, only fit to be used on European plantations.[17]

Most of the nineteenth-century and earlier essays in tropical farming had the plantation for their theme, exploitation for their motive, and unskilled (often impressed) labor for their means. But few of them were successful. After being worked a lifetime (in some cases much longer), only a handful of the nineteenth-century plantations in Portuguese and Spanish tropical Africa had more than 250 acres under cultivation; after slavery was abolished, even many of the cocoa and coffee plantations on São Tomé and Fernando Po went out of business. The attempts, around the beginning of the present century, by the Independent State of the Congo to raise rubber aroused such hostility among humanitarians everywhere (including Belgium) that they had to be abandoned. The German attempts, in pre-World War I days, to grow coffee, rubber and oil palm in Tanganyika were likewise no match for the opposition put up, in this instance by the environment. The French had little better luck. Except for western Senegal, which for a time produced good crops of plantation-grown peanuts, and French Guinea, where bananas did well, the land did not take kindly to the planter's assaults upon it. The story of the early British plantations in east and central Africa was similar. Coffee plantations started in southern Nyasaland in the 1880s were wiped out within a decade by the coffee leaf disease. Cotton plantations started in the Rhodesias and Nyasaland about the same time yielded well enough, but had difficulty in competing with American and Egyptian crops on the world market. And while tea (in Nyasaland), tobacco (in the Rhodesias) and maize (in the Rhodesias and Kenya) periodically made money for their growers, in some years during the 1920s and 1930s it did not pay even to harvest the crops.

There was, however, a credit side to these early plantation experiences, for they disclosed the terms on which the land would do business with its suitors and keep them in business, namely, respect for its needs and limitations, and an ample supply of development capital. It is these things, more than any others, that help to explain the steady growth in the interwar years of the Belgian Congo's oil palm plantations. With its great resources, Lever Brothers had by 1939 cleared and planted most of the country's 187,000 acres of oil palm and was shipping most of its 70,000-ton export of palm oil and 88,000-ton export of palm kernels. The same factors played a comparable role in building up, during the interwar

[17] R. Delavignette, *Freedom and Authority in French West Africa*, Oxford University Press, London, 1950, pp. 111-12.

period, the sisal, coffee, tea and pyrethrum plantations of Tanganyika and Kenya, and the mixed-farming economy of Kenya.

But these credit entries apart, the pre-World War II balance sheet of European agriculture made rather poor reading. It contained too much evidence of false moves, misspent energies and meager returns.

WARTIME CHANGES

World War II left its mark on European agriculture as it did on every other facet of life in tropical Africa. Almost from the day the war started the constituent territories found themselves hard put to it to export anything but the most urgently needed military supplies, and largely cut off from outside sources of food, both raw and processed. The consequently increased demand for locally grown foods and industrial crops did not go unheeded by the European planter and farmer.

In Kenya, where to the domestic needs were added, as the war progressed, the needs of prisoners, refugees, and European and African troops stationed in east Africa, the output of cooperatively produced butter increased from 2.8 million pounds in 1938 to 5.7 million in 1946. The production of wheat, of which Kenya had been a net importer before the war, rose from 23,020 tons in 1938-1939 to 75,090 in 1945-1946. In addition, a vastly increased amount of maize was raised for African consumption on the European farms, though not enough in some war years for the country's needs. In Tanganyika, the sisal production almost trebled between 1938 and 1946. Fortunately the Mlingano Sisal Experiment Station had been able to demonstrate that sisal could make serviceable marine cordage before the need for it became imperative with the cutting off of Philippine supplies of Manila hemp in 1942.

By the end of the war the whole of British East Africa was virtually self-supporting in essential foods and producing greatly increased amounts of many non-food crops, thanks in very large measure to the initiative of European growers.

World War II gave a similar stimulus to the farm economy of the Rhodesias and Nyasaland. As in east Africa, there were more mouths to feed — among others, those of the Royal Air Force personnel brought to Southern Rhodesia for training purposes. And more Africans were eating more food, especially those serving in the army and on the mines. To meet this domestic demand, European farmers increased their grain production by nearly 200 per cent during the war years. Because of the curtailment of most overseas supplies, Rhodesian and Nyasaland farmers found themselves called upon to increase greatly their production for export to Great Britain of vegetable oils and those two great morale builders, tea and tobacco. Nyasaland's tea export increased by 3.5 million pounds between 1938 and 1946. Northern Rhodesia's tobacco crop increased by nearly one third between 1943-1944 and 1945-1946, and

Southern Rhodesia's tobacco crop more than doubled, from less than 30 million pounds to over 60 million, between 1939 and 1945.

In the Belgian Congo the European planters had never been greatly concerned with the production of foodstuffs beyond their own needs. Except on the mines and in the towns there was no demand for ordinary field crops. Nor did the war substantially increase the need for such crops, since the Belgian Congo, unlike Kenya, did not have to victual a large defense force or handle large numbers of prisoners and refugees. But it was required to make a no less important agricultural contribution to the war effort, for most of its revenue-earning crops, of which the European *colons* and corporations grew by far the largest part, either could not be as easily obtained elsewhere or could not be readily synthesized. When Malaya fell to the Japanese in 1942, rubber became one of the Western allies' most pressing needs, notwithstanding the expansion of the synthetic rubber industry in North America. Though the Congo was never able to satisfy more than a fraction of the military demand, its rubber output increased by more then 700 per cent between 1939 and 1945.[18] The export of palm oil and palm kernels more than doubled over the same period. During the years 1940-1945, deliveries to the allies amounted to nearly half a million tons. The planters were also able to supply the bulk of the allied quinine requirements, which continued to be heavy notwithstanding the wartime appearance of other anti-malaria drugs. The demand for pyrethrum was likewise heavy. In wartime it was important that everything possible be done to secure food crops against insect attack, and for that purpose there was no more effective treatment than a dusting with pyrethrum powder.

At the war's end, few European planters found themselves any the worse for their exertions. Most of them were, in fact, doing far better than they had been doing in 1939. They may have been a little weary of the unaccustomed pace of life, and the not inconsiderable restrictions on their movements (the annual or biennial trips "home" had been denied to most of them, of course), but they were eating well, had money in the bank, and were hopeful of even better times to come. Meanwhile the colonial governments had given no small thought to the future of white settlement and the possibilities of raising European agriculture to higher levels of efficiency. The standard had never been very high, and, with some notable exceptions, had fallen rather than risen as the war progressed. The majority of the essential agricultural services had been maintained, but research and supervision had languished with the result that many of the hard-won agronomic gains of the late thirties had been lost. Moreover, erosion was stalking the land, and plant and animal diseases were being reported where hitherto they had been absent.

[18] Rubber exports from the Belgian Congo increased from around 1,100 tons in 1939 to nearly 8,000 in 1945. The acreage under rubber trees increased over roughly the same period from about 25,000 acres to about 125,000.

MAIN TYPES OF FARMING

At the present time most of the agricultural production for which Europeans are responsible falls into three categories: cattle raising (dairy and beef ranching), mixed farming and specialty-crop farming.

Cattle Raising

Over most of the highlands occupied by the European settler the tsetse fly is naturally absent; and over most of the same areas the dry season is too long, or the rains are too irregular, for dry-land farming either by Africans or Europeans. It is in such areas, among them the Rift Valley of Kenya and the surrounding countryside, the Southern Highlands and Northern provinces of Tanganyika, the semi-arid veld of eastern Bechuanaland, the Kivu highlands of the Belgian Congo and the *planalto* of Angola, that most of the cattle keeping by Europeans, especially for meat and hides, is done. The dairy herds tend to be located on the better-watered, richer pastures and as close as possible to the main centers of consumption.

Variations in size and caliber of the herds are very great. In Kenya, herds number anywhere from 50 to 10,000, or even more.[19] In Bechuanaland the usual range is from 300 to 500. Some of the best herds can compare in meat and milk yield with the best in Europe. But there are, as yet, few such herds. All too often the herds consist of large numbers of "grade" cattle produced promiscuously with a succession of bulls of different breeds and low standard.

In several territories European dairy and beef breeds have been acclimatized successfully, or crossed with native cattle to increase their tolerance of disease and drought. Although some ranchers continue to hold that what is a good breed in Europe is necessarily a good breed in Africa, more are coming to feel that environment is too big a factor to be ignored, and that pedigree is not as important as performance. On the whole, native and crossbred cattle seem to do better than the purebred exotic types. Thus, in Kenya many of the leading ranchers run carefully bred Boran herds. The Boran — a shorthorn Zebu species native to East Africa — is slow to mature but yields up to 750 pounds of good-quality beef. With careful breeding, it is considered by many farmers to be capable of serving as a dual-purpose animal, producing both meat and milk. In Southern Rhodesia many ranchers have come to favor the Afrikander for the drier bush veld. Some have, in recent years, built up purebred herds of Afrikander cattle 5,000 to 6,000 strong.

In parts of the drier and cooler European settler zones, sheep raising

---

[19] Under the "extensive" type of ranch production of beef cattle in Kenya it is generally assumed that no farm supporting fewer than 1,000 animals is likely to be economic.

compares in importance with cattle raising. Most sheep farmers continue to be especially interested in the wool clip, probably because "the exceptionally high prices for wool have unbalanced sheep husbandry all over the world in recent years." [20] However, a number, notably in Kenya, have had great success with meat-producing breeds, and there is every prospect that the mutton and lamb output will increase, not only on the ranches but also on the mixed farms, where they can graze the grass leys [21] that have already been grazed by cattle.

There is much scope for the sheep breeder. The native sheep are hardy, but generally small and with a low ratio of meat to bone. Exotic breeds, such as Corriedale and Romney Marsh for the wetter reaches and merino and "Down" breeds for the drier reaches, are proving their worth. Some crossing of native and exotic breeds has already been done to the obvious advantage of both.

At the same time several factors work against the rapid expansion of the sheep-raising business. In many European farming communities knowledge of sheep management is sadly lacking both on the part of the farmer and the veterinary surgeon. There is a constant attrition of the flocks by wild animals and thieves, to counter which it is frequently necessary to confine the sheep at night in pens, or *bomas,* with consequent reduction of the grazing period and increase in infection by internal parasites. In the wetter areas a good deal of trouble is caused by foot rot and the too rapid growth of pasture.

Pigs, being less finicky about feed than either sheep or cattle, and having a wider climatic tolerance than both, are widely, if unevenly, distributed over the European farm lands. On large stretches of the tropical highlands environmental conditions for pigs are as good as can be found anywhere in the world. They can live out of doors the year around. They can be taken to their feed instead of having it brought to them. They tend to need less food per pound deadweight than pigs raised in cooler climes, because of the higher temperatures and slower metabolism. The pork products, at their best, can stand comparison with those of Western Europe. With the African pitifully short of animal proteins, it is not difficult to see why the production of pork products is regarded by many people as offering one of the greatest economic, and humanitarian, opportunities open today to the European farmer in the African tropics.

Most of the European cattle farmer's products are destined for the local market. There is some interterritorial movement of high-grade meat and butter, especially from Kenya to Tanganyika, Uganda and the Belgian Congo, but since most of the movement is by air and air freight charges

[20] L. G. Troup, *Report: Inquiry into the General Economy of Farming in the Highlands [of Kenya],* Government Printer, Nairobi, 1953, p. 20.
[21] "Ley" is the old Saxon word for a pasture clearing in a forest. It is now used of land that is temporarily under sown grasses or some other pasture crop.

are heavy, and since the "carriage trade" market is limited, the amounts involved are quite small. Attempts have been made to develop an overseas trade in cattle and sheep products, but they are not likely to meet with any real success until freight charges can be scaled down and the danger of rinderpest infection can be eliminated. The market for whole milk has been growing in recent years with the growth of the European and Asian populations and the practice of big corporations to supply the mothers and children of their African employees with regular milk rations. So far production of whole milk has been confined largely to the vicinity of the bigger towns and mines, because of its perishability and the heavy labor costs. Cheese making has also been developed to satisfy local demand, but surplus whole milk is generally separated and the cream used to make butter.

The rancher's biggest problem, however, is not the improvement of breeds, or the combating of disease, or the disposing of his products. Rather it is the amelioration of his pastures. Because of seasonal fluctuations of rainfall and failure to rotate the pastures regularly, and reluctance to cull surplus stock (the African is not alone in this!), the carrying capacity of most ranges, already naturally low, is getting lower. Here and there it has been increased with the help of irrigated alfalfa, but generally in range country fresh water is scarce and expensive, and has to be conserved for more fundamental purposes.

To make matters worse, bush is colonizing many areas formerly grass-covered; in certain cases it is practically impenetrable. This change of plant association is partly the result of the prohibition of annual burning (where that applies), partly the result of the extermination of wild animals and the control of domestic animals such as goats, and partly a direct consequence of overgrazing. Once under bush the range is lost, for the cost of eradicating it, either by the use of specially designed mechanical equipment or by hand labor, is prohibitive. At the same time, many African pastoralists are finding it increasingly difficult to maintain their herds on their tribal lands and are demanding grazing rights on the European's.

In the face of such uncompromising facts, many are beginning to think that the future of cattle raising belongs to the mixed farmers rather than to the ranchers.

Mixed Farming

Like ranching, mixed farming is confined to the tsetse-fly-free areas, but unlike ranching, it is usually practiced in the better-watered portions of such areas. Also, it is usually run on more intensive lines and therefore on smaller holdings. In most areas it is still in its infancy; for of all the kinds of farming open to a farmer in a new country, mixed farming is generally the last, because the most difficult and demanding, to which he turns his hand. However, there is already ample evidence to show that, though it is harder on the farmer, it is easier on the land than either ranching or one-crop farming, and in the long view more rewarding.

The practice of mixed farming, or alternate husbandry as it is frequently called, involves, as its name suggests, the marriage of crops and cattle. It is therefore an undertaking calling for more knowledge and skill than either ranching or one-crop farming, more capital per unit area of farm land, and a longer time lag between investment and return. Accordingly, it is not the kind of undertaking established grain and cattle farmers readily turn to while they are making money. And it is a little late for them to turn to it when they have stopped making money.

Instead of merely raising a sequence of cash crops on his arable land, the mixed farmer makes great use of leys, sown to grass, clover, etc., in his rotations. These leys, which he may retain for three or more years before plowing under, are the pivot of the mixed-farming system; it is on their productive capacity that the cattle depend, rather than on such permanent pasture as the farm may carry. At their best such leys are capable of carrying one beast or more to the acre with good gains in weight or milk yields and for as much as nine months at a time. In several instances in Kenya an average yield of approximately 700 gallons of milk per cow per year has been maintained on leys carrying three cows to two acres. Leys, too, are a safeguard against soil loss, and a source of nutriment to succeeding tillage crops. On land lately under a grass ley, grain yields are often as much as 200 per cent higher than they are on ordinary arable land. Leys are steadily gaining favor therefore in many places where the settler finds himself faced with soil erosion and soil exhaustion consequent upon his one-crop "mining" activities. In Kenya the total acreage in leys in 1946 was only about 12,500. By the late 1950s it had risen to nearly 100,000.

Given the right altitude, precipitation and ground water regimes, and other environmental requirements, there is practically no limit to the crops that can be rotated with sown leys. In east Africa the crops most favored are wheat, at elevations above 6,500 feet, and maize at lower levels. In addition, most mixed farmers go in for barley (in demand by brewers and pig raisers), oats (often cut as silage), sunflower (a fine source of oil and protein for animal feeding), and a wide range of forage crops (including beans, kale and alfalfa). In the Rhodesias mixed farming has up to now made less progress than in east Africa, largely because the European farmer has not yet begun to run out of virgin land. Where it is practiced, the cash crops most usually associated with it are maize, tobacco, wheat, peanuts, potatoes and other vegetables. In the Belgian Congo and Angola it is only the larger company farms, specializing in the production of meat and dairy products for their employees, that make any considerable use of mixed farming. In the rest of the territories mixed farming is still little more than an idea — though one with a future.

Specialty-Crop Farming

More than 50 cash crops are grown by Europeans in tropical Africa. And they are grown in as many ways and on almost as many different scales. Agronomically, therefore, they do not lend themselves to generalization. But most of their growers have at least this much in common: they are specialists. They spend their lives growing one crop, or perhaps two, and in the course of doing so they come to know pretty well all there is to know about it. Growing it becomes their profession; on its fortunes, or misfortunes, their livelihood hangs. In spite of all its hazards, specialty-crop farming has been, almost from the beginning, the backbone of European agricultural interest in tropical Africa.

The crops grown are of many types and varied environmental requirements. Important among them are (1) field crops such as cereals, tobacco, potato, pyrethrum, sugar cane, cotton and sunflower; (2) bush crops such as sisal, coffee, tea and the rose (cultivated, with other flowering plants, to make scent); and (3) tree crops such as banana, rubber, coconut, oil palm, clove, tung nut, wattle (valuable as a soil stabilizer as well as for tannin) and citrus fruits.

Some of these crops, such as pyrethrum, coffee and the rose, are often grown on small holdings of five to 50 acres; others, such as tobacco, cotton and wheat, are more often grown on estates of 500 to 5,000 acres; while crops like sisal, palm oil and rubber are characteristically grown on plantations of around 10,000 to 50,000 acres. Some of the farms are operated by tenants, some by individual owners and some by corporations. Some have been consistently big money-makers; some have never made much more than expenses; most have made and lost money by turns.

The methods of cultivating these specialty crops are, at their best, exemplary — a tribute to the planners, investors and operators alike. At their worst, they are execrable — a monument to folly and apathy, if not to avarice (though there are those, too, who seem to operate solely on the basis of a "cut down, clean up, clear out" policy). More often, the methods are no better and no worse than those to be encountered in any other part of the world where men are in farming for the sole reason of getting out of it as speedily, and decently, as possible. And we must not forget that a large percentage of the Europeans engaged in tropical farming are not "settlers" in the usual sense of the word. They are prepared to stay only long enough, thirty to forty years at the most, to make a competence and retire to the land of their birth, or to the greater comforts and more congenial society of some nearby urban center. What happens to the land in the course of that sojourn is not, for the general run of them, as important as what happens to their investment in the land. Most of them are short of capital to start with and in need of an early cash return. This often applies to corporations as well as to individuals. Consequently they start by clearing those areas which appear to be easiest to work and the most profitable. On these they experiment with crops which, from prior knowledge, seem well fitted to the environment.

Having found a crop that gives satisfactory yields, what could be more natural, and simple, than to go on growing it on the cleared land until it ceases to show a profit or, what amounts to practically the same thing, until the land gives out? When it does, what could be more natural, and simple, than to move on to another area and repeat the process? Specialty-crop farming is essentially a form of monoculture, with all that that implies in use, and abuse, of the land's resources.

Commendably, most of the large corporation-owned plantations long ago eschewed the more serious evils of abuse. Many of them today have a thirty-to-forty-year record of enlightened development in the social and medical fields as well as in the scientific and technical. The list of such corporations is long, too long to be quoted in a short review of this nature. It covers each of the more largely grown bush and tree crops; rubber, banana, sisal, oil palm, tea, sugar and coffee are especially well represented in it.

One of the most significant of all such enterprises — partly because it helped put the sagging economy of a whole country on its feet, and partly because it has, throughout its history, served as a model of humanitarian concern as well as operational efficiency — is the Firestone Plantations Company, located at Harbel in Liberia.

In 1926 the company was granted the right by the Liberian government to lease for a term of ninety-nine years land to be selected by it from time to time as suitable for rubber planting, up to a total of one million acres. By the early 1950s the company was annually paying over to the Liberian government in income tax more than $3 million, a sum which represented approximately one third of the national revenue. In addition, the 25,000 to 30,000 Liberians and other Africans employed by the company put more than $1 million of cash into circulation, much of which went to the government in the form of import duties on food, clothing and other articles bought by the workers.

This wealth is derived entirely from the approximately 12 million rubber trees growing on the 90,000 acres so far developed by the company. The acres thus used do not appear any the worse for their long years of wear and tear. In the view of the Firestone agronomists, they are probably a great deal better, for the rubber tree, they maintain, has improved the fertility and strengthened the humus content of the soil.

The Liberians who work on the plantations are unquestionably a great deal better, both in health and general well-being. If they want medical care, it is there, and none finer anywhere in Liberia. If they prefer to resort to the medicine man, no objections are raised. If they want education for themselves and their children, there are schools within easy reach of all parts of the plantations. If they want to go back to their tribal lands, as many do, they are free to leave at a moment's notice. If they remain throughout their working life — a few have already completed thirty years' service — they qualify for the company's retirement plan.

This is not to say that all the people are happier than they were thirty years ago, that large plantations are necessarily better than small farms, or that the standard recruitment method (involving money payments to local chiefs, graduated according to the number of men in their chiefdoms working for Firestone at any one time) is ideal; but at least it is difficult to see how else, in that hot, humid and lethargy-inducing climate, a comparable transformation of the fortunes of the people could have been wrought. The history of the Lever Brothers (Unilever) operations, the Sudan Gezira Board, and a dozen other corporate enterprises in other parts of tropical Africa provides similarly impressive examples of economic and social progress.

RECENT DEVELOPMENTS

Three developments in European agriculture during recent years have been particularly noteworthy: (1) a trend toward heavier capitalization and more economically sized units; (2) an increased application of scientific practices, such as rotational cropping and controlled grazing; and (3) a leveling off of the rate of expansion of both farm population and output.

Heavier Capitalization and More Economically Sized Units

The trend toward heavier capitalization and more economic units has been going on for a long time in the older settled farm belts of the world as a means of increasing output (and hence income) per unit of labor, and a way of reducing drudgery. Over large parts of tropical Africa, because of poor soil, difficulties of labor supply, risk of crop failure, and the high cost of experimental work, the type of agricultural enterprise that stands most chance of putting its products onto a highly competitive world market is either the mechanized plantation financed by a corporation or the adequately financed, economically sized and efficiently run private farm.

When the region began to be opened to European farm settlement, nobody had much of an idea of what would constitute an economic unit. Most of the experience available to colonial governments was based on more temperate lands and on more friendly earth. In some parts of British East Africa, immigrant farmers were given "sections," that is, 640 acres or one square mile, or multiples of sections, for no better reason, it seems, than that parts of the Canadian prairies were being broken up on this scale. As things turned out, this was not a sufficient reason. Elsewhere, farmers were allowed to have all they could buy, and since much of the land could then be had very cheaply, they bought thousands of acres —

far more than they could possibly farm. Economic units were the exception rather than the rule. This is not surprising, for how could a man determine the limits of such a unit until he knew what the land was well endowed to grow? What would be an economic unit for a coffee plantation would not necessarily be an economic unit for a wheat farm, or a cattle ranch.

After forty to fifty years' experience — some of it bitter, much of it costly and all of it chastening — both governments and farmers are now in a better position to decide what is, and is not, "economic." Generally, those farmers who elected to go in for bush crops, such as tea and coffee, and, more recently, mixed farming, took on too much land. Labor and other problems which they could hardly have anticipated are now causing many of them to reduce their actively farmed areas. Not many of them have as yet been inclined to dispose of the unusable balance of their land. This is frequently left in bush or given over to squatters. But what is being used is gradually being used more productively and conservatively.

In contrast, many field crop farmers, notably those specializing in grain, took on too little land, not realizing how much less stamina it had than the arable land of France, Belgium, Portugal and Britain. Today, with diminishing yields and rising costs of operation, they are, wherever possible, enlarging their holdings, often to their greater grief. Bigger fields may mean greater mechanical efficiency. They may also mean greater erosion and greater losses from drought and pests. Similarly with the cattle rancher and the planter of industrial crops, though the reasons in the two cases differ. The cattle rancher has overcrowded his pastures and must find new ones while the old recuperate. The industrial crop planter is facing keener competition each year from other parts of the world and from other commodities, and must therefore secure every last advantage offered by the economies of mechanized, heavily capitalized, large-scale production.

Though much of the land was to be had cheaply, and some still is, none of it is very kind or obliging to the undercapitalized farmer. Even before World War II, colonial governments were in the habit of applying a quite rigorous means test to the would-be settler. In Southern Rhodesia, a man needed at least £1,500 to make a decent start. In Kenya he was said to need nearer £5,000. Today £5,000 does not go very far in any British-settled area of Africa. In fact, to begin a sisal plantation in Tanganyika or a banana plantation in the Cameroons that would stand a chance of competing with already established plantations would require nearer £250,000. Ordinary unimproved farm land in the tobacco and dairy belt of Southern Rhodesia costs anywhere from £2 to £20 an acre, and to be on the side of solvency a farmer is reckoned to need at least 1,200 acres, half of which should be plowable. Good coffee land in Kenya and the Belgian Congo costs very much more. Tropical Africa was never "poor white" country. Today it takes a rich man to be a pioneer. But there are no longer many rich men who are willing to be pioneers — indeed, in most parts of Europe there are no longer many rich men. Some governments are willing to make generous loans to a few very carefully selected newcomers, but this is done more for its effect on public opinion outside than for its effect on the economy within the territory.

In the circumstances, it is not difficult to see why corporations, public as well as private, are coming to play a major role in the economic life of the region.

Scientific Practices

While the success of these corporations has been due in part to their financial strength that has enabled them to cushion hard knocks and recover from initial reverses, it is also due to their respect for scientific research and its agronomic and technical by-products, a respect which is now being shared by more and more individuals engaged in tropical agriculture, and by their governments. Creditable as was the prewar record of many corporation- and government-supported research institutions, it has been eclipsed by that of the postwar period.

In the territories belonging to the French Community, research and experiment in the use of soils, crop rotations, mechanical gear and so on were launched on a massive scale after the war with the help of FIDES financing (Fonds d'Investissement pour le Développement Economique et Social). Today at least a dozen institutions are engaged, partly or wholly, in promoting European and African agricultural welfare. At Dakar, under the auspices of the Office de la Recherche Scientifique et Technique d'Outre-Mer, pedologists are studying the mode of formation and evolution of west African soils. Similar studies are being made under the same auspices in each of the other main territories. The Services de l'Agriculture, de l'Elevage et des Forêts of the Ministry of Overseas France (now the General Secretariat of the French Community) have stations that specialize in plant and animal breeding, and, indeed, in the whole gamut of problems involved in raising tropical crops. To these government agencies must be added such private agencies as the Institut de Recherches pour les Huiles de Palme et les Oléagineux, the Institut de Recherches du Coton et des Textiles Exotiques, the Institut des Fruits et Agrumes Coloniaux, and the Compagnie Générale des Oléagineux Tropicaux. The combined annual budget of these organizations runs into several million dollars.

In the Belgian Congo, the research stations of INEAC (Institut National pour l'Etude Agronomique du Congo Belge) have been engaged for many years in developing heavier-yielding and more disease-resistant strains of both tree crops and field crops and in educating European and African farmers in the importance of such things as manures and, where feasible, mixed farming. More recently the work of these stations has been reinforced by the activities of the Mission Anti-Erosive (MAE), with visible benefit to the Kivu countryside, where contoured and terraced slopes contrast sharply with the gullying to be seen in neighboring parts of central Africa. Since 1948 the Institut pour la Recherche Scientifique en Afrique Centrale (IRSAC) has been applying itself to fundamental research in entomology, nutrition, zoology and many other fields of interest to the agriculturist.

In British East Africa, where much of the European agricultural enterprise is concentrated, the East African Agriculture and Forestry Research Organization, with headquarters at Kikuyu, near Nairobi, has since 1948 expanded and intensified the work of its lineal ancestor, the East African Agriculture Research Institute at Amani (near Tanga, Tanganyika), itself the descendant of the institute established by the Germans early in the century. In each of the High Commission territories (Kenya, Uganda and Tanganyika) the government maintains experiment stations and a corps of agricultural officers whose services are available to European, Asian and African farmer alike. In addition, sisal research is undertaken at two stations, one at Thika (high-level) in Kenya, the other at Mlingano (low-level) near Tanga. Both are financed jointly by the Sisal Growers Association.

The contribution of Portuguese areas to better farming through the medium of research and development has so far been more modest than that of their neighbors, but it is substantial for all that. The government, through its Junta das Missões Geográficas e de Investigações do Ultramar, maintains a number of experiment and breeding stations, or *postos zootécnicos*. At these, instruction is provided for the training of colonists' sons in scientific agriculture, supplies of improved seed and stock are made available, and systematic research on crop and animal problems is prosecuted. At these stations, too, proof is provided for the theory that most of the European settlers — to say nothing of the Africans — could, at small expense and some additional effort, treble, or even quadruple, their customary yields of coffee, sugar cane, palm nut, coconut and sisal. There are also several public institutes, or *juntas*, that have been created and are maintained by "autonomous economic organizations." One of the most conspicuously successful of these is the Centro de Investigação Cientifica Algodoeira Lourenço Marques (CICA), which under the direction of Professor A. Quintanilha has been responsible, among other things, for a fourfold increase in the per acre yield of Mozambique cotton.

While it is not always possible, or even necessary, to measure the effect of scientific and technical advances by the yardstick of per acre yield, every farmer is glad when he can do so. Not many farmers, European or African, in any part of tropical Africa can speak of fourfold increases of yield. And perhaps it is just as well, for widespread increases of that magnitude could easily tempt the opportunists to take excessive risks with land which is neither physically nor chemically equipped to stand the strain of heavy production. High yields tend to be equated with "scientific" techniques when, in actual fact, they may be the direct result of misapplying those techniques. The inordinate use of fertilizers may stimulate phenomenal plant growth, for example, only to leave the soil badly fatigued.

What is perhaps even more important in tropical Africa than increased fecundity is increased soil stability and stamina. Without this no form of agriculture can long flourish, least of all European forms with their continuous tapping of the earth's moisture and fertility stores. It has taken the immigrant farmer quite a time to understand the essential differences between the earth of Europe and the earth of Africa. He soon appreciated its areal variation — the fact that some soils were much better, some much worse, than the average — but he was slower to see that tropical soils form and evolve differently from most mid-latitude soils, that they have different physical and chemical properties, and that they respond differently to exposure and cultivation. Nor, at first, were all these differences perceived by the professional agronomist. Today he is quick to concede that the differences are quite real and that, when you come to think about them, they stand to reason. For instance, whereas in Europe the "dead" season for plant growth and micro-biological activity occurs when the soil is cold and saturated, in most of tropical Africa it occurs when the soil is dry and hot. The agronomic importance of this circumstance is considerable. Besides its bearing on the optimum content of organic matter and its rate of renewal, it directly affects the moisture regime of the soil.

The East African Agriculture and Forestry Research Organization and similar organizations in other parts of tropical Africa are concerned with basic soil studies quite as much as with studies directed toward plant improvement and the elimination of plant diseases. But those who work for these agencies would be the first to admit that they are still a long way from making the land "safe" for farming — either European or African. Most of the European farmers would be as ready by now to admit that it can never be made safe without such studies.

Slower Expansion

Perhaps the most important postwar trend in European agriculture is the slowing down of its rate of expansion. Even before the war, the flow of settlement was very slow in some territories. In Southern Rhodesia between 1931 and 1935 there was actually a reduction (from 4,500 to 4,300) in the number of Europeans actively engaged in farming. To be sure, the rate has never been comparable to that which characterized the prairies, or the pampas. Nor have the colonial governments of tropical Africa ever thought of themselves as being in the same league as Canada or Argentina when it came to agricultural settlement. At the most they have settled 250,000 farming folk in the past fifty to sixty years on approximately 50 million acres.[22] Of this population, not less than 200,000 were already domiciled in Africa in 1939; and of this acreage, at least 90 per cent was already being farmed by that date.

In the first postwar decade it is estimated that not more than 500 additional farm holdings were established in the Kenya Highlands, bringing the total number to about 3,000 and the total number of European farmers to about 4,000, or less than 10 per cent of the total European population. In Tanganyika between 750 and 1,000 rights of occupancy of agricultural and pastoral land were granted to non-Africans over the same period, but not all of these rights appear to have been exercised. In the Belgian Congo the postwar figure for new farms and plantations is nearer 250 than 500. In Portuguese Africa it is between 500 and 1,000. In the whole of west Africa, it is not more than 500 at the most. Even in the two Rhodesias the flow of farm immigrants has been anything but strong. Since 1946, less than 5 per cent of the economically active Europeans entering these territories have gone into agriculture. The number of new Rhodesian farms started in this period is almost certainly less than 1,000. In Nyasaland the corresponding number is almost certainly less than 100.

The explanation of this trend no doubt lies partly in the sharply rising costs of financing and operating European holdings and their generally low investment yield compared with, say, the mining and manufacturing enterprises run by Europeans. However, at least two other factors are involved: the growing recognition of the primacy of African land rights and needs; and the growing shortage of African farm labor.

More than forty years ago some of the colonial powers began to entertain scruples about the propriety of opening up the African tropics for large-scale land settlement by immigrant groups. The feeling that the satisfaction of indigenous land requirements should take precedence of all other considerations may not always have been as keenly felt, let alone expressed, in high places as the humanitarians would have wished, but it turns up repeatedly in the government literature of the period. Between the first and second world wars it was further fortified in such memorable declarations as that contained in the White Paper issued by the British government in 1923: [23]

Kenya is an African territory, and His Majesty's Government think it necessary definitely to record their considered opinion that the interests of the African natives must be paramount, and that if, and when, these interests and the interests of the immigrant races should conflict, the former should prevail.

[22] The *alienated* acreage—that which has been appropriated by the government for European use—would be considerably higher.

[23] Generally known as the Devonshire Declaration, after the Duke of Devonshire, who was then the Colonial Secretary.

By 1939 there was scarcely a government in Africa that was unwilling to pay at least lip service to the idea of African paramountcy. Some even used it as a recruiting argument — that Africans were fighting for their own lands; and many promises were made of more land and better agricultural services when they returned. These promises were not always honored, but the postwar surge of nationalist sentiment, much of it having its origin in the experiences African soldiers had while serving abroad, certainly impressed the British and the French governments with the necessity of proceeding cautiously wherever new land alienation schemes are under discussion. In some territories the authorities have decided that the better part of caution is inaction. And in the more progressive territories they are discovering that the African's aversion to the idea of land alienation is becoming so strong that he is opposed even to the use of land by European technicians engaged in building and operating dams, power stations and factories designed to bring the African the benefits of Western technology. The way one intelligent and well-educated group of Ganda put it recently was as follows: "We would rather stick to our kerosene lamps which we know how to operate and repair — and which we own — than have electricity which we can neither own, operate nor repair and which necessitates the settlement of more and more Europeans on our lands."

Of scarcely less importance is the fact that in many of the European-occupied areas the African farm laborer either is already hard to find or is unreceptive to the idea of working permanently on a farm or plantation.

Shortage of labor has, of course, been a feature of African economic life since the first contacts of Europeans with Africans. As early as the seventeenth century the Dutch East India Company introduced laborers from the Far East into Cape Colony. In the latter half of the nineteenth century the Natal sugar estates were developed on the basis of imported Indian labor. Attempts to obtain workers from local sources were rarely successful in the early days of colonization without resort to some form of pressure. The African laborer lacked incentives, beyond the need to provide himself with tax money, to exchange his leisure, which he cherished, for wages, with which he could do little beyond purchasing back the leisure that previously had cost him nothing.

Today there is no lack of incentives, for the bush is full of little stores stocked with goods calculated to appeal to the eye and the ego of the African. Even so, the bush is not full of Africans willing to give the European or Asian employer their services in order to secure these goods. The Firestone Plantations Company continues to have the greatest difficulty in keeping its labor force up to strength. Not more than one in five work longer than one season at a time. The prevailing attitude, even after decades of seductive piping on the theme of the uses of a wage economy, is still "Why should I work for that which satisfies not, when I can eat, drink and be comfortable on my tribal land with no one to boss me around eight hours a day, six days a week?" Fortunately, not all Africans are so slow to respond to the piper. Hundreds of thousands are already the proud possessors of a bicycle. Hundreds of thousands more are by now equally interested in such things as footwear, fine clothes, and musical instruments. But the list of priority purchases for most Africans is still short and subject to cancellation at almost any time by the higher priorities of customary life.

Still more disturbing to the would-be employer of African labor is the growing realization that even if all the Africans were willing to leave their communities and work for him, there would not be enough, in some parts of the tropics, to satisfy the current market for unskilled labor. Liberia is, it seems, one such place. The estimates of total population (up to 1959 there had been no census) run all the way from 500,000 to 3 million. Those who know the country best are inclined to put the population between 1 and 1.5 million. By the time a 50 per cent reduction is made for the women who normally do not go out to work, and allowances are made for old folk and children, this leaves the country with a potential labor force of between 250,000 and 300,000, of which Firestone alone employs about 10 per cent. With the coming of the Free Port of Monrovia, the Liberia Mining Company at Bomi Hills and the B. F. Goodrich Company, and with the granting of various oil palm, cocoa, coffee and timber concessions, the demands made upon this unskilled labor force have been sharply increasing. And with education making large strides throughout the country, more and more laborers are beginning to demand white-collar jobs, instead of tapping rubber trees at a few cents a day.

Even if enough unskilled labor were available to satisfy all the white man's needs, the chances are that, in most areas, it could be had only at the expense of the African's own economy. There are already signs that recruitment of migrant labor for mines and plantations from subsistence agricultural communities is profoundly disturbing the economic balance of their societies,[24] and that the standard of indigenous cultivation is being unfavorably affected by the absence of large numbers of male workers, resulting, as it does, in a decline in the output of basic foods.

It is such facts that have been behind the reluctance of the Belgian Congo government to encourage new European colonization of the Kivu and Katanga highlands, for this would have meant "a further draft on labor now producing food and cotton after 700,000 have gone to rubber and palm plantations and to the mines."[25] A further reason for the government's reluctance, and a wise one, has been its desire "to disturb the fabric of native rural life as little as possible, so that, in the event of an

---

[24] United Nations, Economic and Social Council, *Aspects of Economic Development in Africa,* mimeographed, March 1953, pp. 59-69.

[25] R. L. Pendleton, "The Belgian Congo: Impressions of a Changing Region," *Geographical Review,* Vol. 39, No. 3, 1949, p. 398.

economic crisis, when most of the mines and plantations would almost certainly have to shut down, the laborers could return quickly and easily to their villages and to food production." [26]

Not all the governments as yet share this concern for the maintenance of a balanced economy and for the well-being of their wards, but without it there is unlikely to be very much future for European agriculture in tropical Africa, or, indeed, for any European.

[26] *Loc. cit.* At the same time, where labor shortages occur in tropical Africa they are not so much shortages of men as of skills; that is, they mostly arise from the inability or unwillingness of Africans to increase their output. As the workers become more skilled and more industrious, fewer will be needed to do the available work. So it is possible that before long some governments may become worried more by the shortage of work than of workers. This is already coming about in parts of Kenya.

CHAPTER 5

Settlement on
the Land

THE NEED FOR LAND

THE PROBLEMS OF THE SETTLER

SETTLEMENT SCHEMES

PROSPECTS

IN the hierarchy of African values, there is still little to compare with land. "The restless anxiety to obtain and hold on to the land,"[1] concerning which the authors of the East Africa Royal Commission's *1953-1955 Report* have a good deal to say, has not noticeably abated over the years of European occupation; nor is it peculiar to the territories of British East Africa.

THE NEED FOR LAND

If anything, belief in the worth of land and the need to possess it is stronger and more widespread today than it used to be. The need arises partly from the fact that there are more people to feed. For the ordinary African cultivator the customary answers to such a problem are still either to increase the amount of land under cultivation or to decrease the resting period of exhausted land — which in the end is no answer at all. In addition, today's African cultivator has a greater need to safeguard himself and his dependents against the threat of crop failure from drought and destruction by insects, birds and animals. In the past the victim of such visitations could assuage his hunger by hunting wild game, raiding his neighbors' granaries, cannibalism, and other means no longer endorsed

---

[1] *East Africa Royal Commission 1953-1955 Report*, H.M.S.O., London, 1955, p. 279.

by public opinion. The cultivator also needs land to lessen the risk of soil erosion induced by overcropping, overgrazing and overstocking. He needs it, too, to supply himself with salable surpluses, without which he must continue to face the world of buyers and sellers empty-handed. Finally, land is needed to replace the acreage that is being engrossed by the public and private agencies of that world — industrial, extractive, educational, scientific, civil and military. Every new highway, railroad, airfield, mine, factory, research station, forest or farm concession increases the African's need, actual or potential, of land.

It is difficult to appreciate just what land means to the African. To do so we might try to imagine a United States or, better still, a United Kingdom where there is less land to go around, shorn of its industries, with few exports to pay for its necessary imports, and providing few opportunities of earning a living other than by tilling the soil. America's and Britain's millions would at once start competing for the best-favored lands. Almost overnight the land would become the primary concern of the politician, the preacher and the policeman. Before long, we may take it, many would be holding ideas not very different from those of the Tanganyika African who, in his testimony before the East Africa Royal Commission, spoke of land "flying away" from his people with every gain in numbers, leaving them unhappy, and uncertain where the food was coming from that would enable them and their children to live out their lives in peace.

THE PROBLEMS OF THE SETTLER

Agronomically, there is still a vast amount of "untrodden" ground in Africa. Tropical Africa, especially, is slow to yield up its secrets to those who go to it full of assurance that an all-round mid-latitude experience of life can take a person anywhere. For that matter, it does not readily yield up its secrets to anyone. It took the aboriginal Africans a long time to learn what they know about the business of living in ecological equilibrium with their surroundings, and what they learned was little enough. If there is one fact more than another that has become increasingly plain to students of tropical agriculture during the past two or three decades, it is the inapplicability of most of the lessons learned in non-tropical localities. What is needed is a whole new science and associated technology. But such things take time and money, and most governments are as reluctant to wait for results as they are to spend money getting them. It is not surprising, then, that there is still a shortage of satisfactory data on which to base land settlement schemes, whether they are the schemes of an individual family, a corporation or a government. All too frequently such schemes have to rest on an unsteady tripod of fact, inference and hunch.

The problems faced by settlers on the land — or "resettlers," who form an increasingly important segment of the agricultural society of tropical Africa — are of four main kinds: physical, social, economic and political.

Physical

It is odd to the point of being paradoxical that a place of such prodigal physical riches should make life so difficult for its inhabitants. It is true nonetheless: scarcely a locality or a resource of tropical Africa does not, in some way or other, pose the settler with problems.

Take the matter of water. Where water is abundant, as it is in the forest belt, the settler faces the problem of protecting his crops from waterlogging and flooding, and his health from attack by water-borne diseases. Where it is scarce, as in much of the bush and grassland area, the problem is how to protect his animals from seasonal thirst and starvation, and how to make the most of what water he has with the technical and financial means at his disposal. Even where it is adequate, as on the higher ground of east and central Africa, it must be protected against the uneconomic encroachments of population and stock, for these are attended by the risk of overuse, and so of erosion and loss of fertility. No less than four fifths of the land surface of Tanganyika — approximately 275,000 square miles — is maimed on this account. And altogether in tropical Africa there are not less than 2.5 million square miles of such land.

Or, again, consider the problem presented by the widespread occurrence of the tsetse fly. About 50 per cent of tropical Africa is still tsetse fly country. Since the distribution of infested areas is not unlike that of the areas best suited climatically to carry stock, and since cattle-keeping Africans are most unwilling to be separated from their animals, this as good as precludes the settlement of such areas by the people best equipped culturally to settle them. It is true that the occupation of an infested area by settlers in large numbers may cause the tsetse fly to evacuate it, since the fly does not find plowed land and pasture nearly as hospitable as bush, its natural habitat. But up to now it has more often been the settlers who have done the evacuating. They make easier targets than the flies. Besides, the flies do not get tired so quickly, and bush clearing is tiring work. To be effective of its purpose, it must be followed up immediately by settlement of the right kind, a much more thoroughgoing kind than that customarily undertaken.

The maintenance of health, human and animal, is perhaps the greatest of all the physical problems confronting the African settler, as it probably is of the African who stays at home. And just because disease is such a big factor in the life of the ordinary African, it is not to be wondered at if he sometimes prefers to live with the devil he knows than the one he doesn't know. The knowledge that the area into which he is thinking of going is, on the whole, healthier may not be for him half as important as the conviction that by going there he will lose a partial immunity built up by long residence in his home district. Even if he is not sophisticated enough to argue along these lines, he may ask for proof that the area under consideration has been treated for epidemic diseases. If he is a cattleman, he is likely to insist that he be allowed to keep over-large herds on the new land, as a safeguard against possible loss by animal disease. Otherwise he will almost certainly prefer to stay where he is.

Social

But the African's commonly observed reluctance to move permanently is compounded of more than physical ingredients. Into it frequently go as well a superstitious fear of abandoning the religious, ritualistic and magical associations of his place of origin, a dislike of environmental changes, and an unreadiness to live differently — especially noticeable in the case of herders, who suspect that they may be called upon to live without cattle. As the members of the East Africa Royal Commission remind us, in a "status" society, the individual looks for "a safe livelihood for himself and his posterity not in pioneering originality but in routine conformity to his fellows in the clan."[2] Between the ancestors, the ancestral lands and the posterity of the clan, or tribe, there is a mystical bond, the strengthening of which brings much good to the whole community and the weakening much harm. The welfare of the individual is still thought to be determined very largely by the showing he makes in this field of relationships. In such a context, migrations (other than those of a most temporary kind) pose a major problem. They weaken the family tie; they break the chain of tribal privilege and obligation; and they destroy the sense of security that comes from living in a small, closed world, where, though there are enemies and fears aplenty, there are also friends. So people try to "cling to their land, however emaciated; to their homes, however hungry; and to that special bit of soil that holds the bones of their fathers and so links them with their ancestors, their tribal past, the spirit world."[3]

Economic

For these reasons a migration of permanent settlers is not the easiest thing to bring about in most parts of tropical Africa. Indeed, the disinclination to migrate is seldom overcome except under the most acute pressure, resulting from excessive fragmentation of holdings, falling crop

---

[2] *Ibid.*, p. 285.
[3] Elspeth Huxley, *The Four Guineas: A Journey Through West Africa*, Chatto & Windus, London, 1954, p. 108.

yields, worse than usual undernourishment, prolonged drought, devastation by animal or insect plagues, or, occasionally, oppression.[4]

This disinclination is of considerable economic significance, since it militates against the provision of stable labor forces for the farms, plantations and forestry concessions that are being developed by African and non-African settlers. More than one otherwise promising settlement scheme has been handicapped on this score.

A still bigger economic handicap facing the promoters of many otherwise promising schemes is the shortage of transportation facilities. Access to markets is an obvious and most important factor in the development of any area. In tropical Africa it has long been crucial. Almost all the towns and markets that have sprung up in the past seventy-five years are located in areas which, although not always highly productive initially, have been penetrated by railways and roads. Examples of the stimulus which railroads can give to settlement, and so to economic development, are to be seen in the Djibouti–Addis Ababa railway, the Kenya-Uganda and the Central (Tanganyika) Lines of the East African Railways and Harbours system. Although each of the lines was built for other (including strategic) purposes, in each case the stimulation of settlement has been one of the most conspicuous results.

The days of strategic road and railroad construction are just about over. At the same time, it is even less possible today than formerly to visualize economic development, including organized land settlement, without the prior construction of roads and railroads. But their construction requires large-scale financing, and this is unlikely to be forthcoming unless the agricultural potentialities of the areas to be served are such as to warrant the expectation of a reasonable return over the years. Such assurances are seldom forthcoming.

It is these agricultural uncertainties that constitute the biggest economic problem for the settler and resettler, African and non-African. Most of the crops that could, or can, be grown in the undeveloped lands can also be grown in the developed lands. In most cases it would be cheaper, if not easier, to increase the productivity of the land already under crops than to extend the area of their cultivation into what is, often as not, *terra incognita*. On this point there is wide agreement, especially among those people who have had much to do with the more ambitious postwar settlement schemes. So far as the European settler is concerned, many would go further and say that it has yet to be shown whether the productivity of even some of the developed areas can be raised to the point where it is capable, in good times, of giving him more than a modest return on his investment and, in bad times, of keeping him from

---

[4] The migration of some 100,000 Mozambique Africans into Nyasaland in the early years of the century was largely inspired by the desire to escape the inequities of the Portuguese *prazo* system.

becoming a charge on the resources of his government — and a pawn on the politician's chessboard.

Political

Until recently most settlers did little worrying about political problems. They were usually content to leave these to their governments, while reserving the right to abuse them for incompetence and to oppose more or less anything that was "government" in origin. They had, in fact, comparatively few political problems to worry about. Land disputes between tribe and tribe were regarded as "chiefly" matters, to be taken up between chief and chief, or between chief and district officer, who in turn would take them up with his territorial government. Likewise, land disputes between tribe and occupying power were not regarded as problems on which it was important for the foreign settler to have very definite views. The government had alienated or bought the land. The government needed the settlers' taxes to help in the running of the country. The government, therefore, could do any worrying there was to be done about the Africans' worrying to get the land back.

But that era of complacence is passing — has already passed in most cases. Certainly since 1952 no settler in the European ("White") Highlands of Kenya can have failed to see the political significance of a situation in which less than 10,000 persons occupy more than 10,000 square miles of farm land (some of it divided into farmsteads of over 2,000 acres in size), while nearby more than a million Africans are living on farms averaging less than four acres each, and in concentrations that frequently exceed 1,000 persons to the square mile. Nor is this political awareness confined to the European settlers of Kenya, and their African neighbors. It is now evident in all of the multiracial territories. It is especially evident in the two Rhodesias, and among the *colons* of the Belgian Congo and the French Community. More than a trace of it is to be found in Mozambique and Angola, where the Portuguese government has wisely attempted to forestall "Mau-Mauism" by insisting that settlers from the homeland do all their own farm work and farm only such lands as they can work efficiently.

Here and there Europeans face a political problem of a slightly different sort. Many African settlers need to be persuaded, it seems, that they will be allowed to live in the permanent enjoyment of the betterment schemes being carried out on their lands. They sometimes find it easier to believe that the schemes are just another European laborsaving device, whereby they are made to do the hard work of improving land, prior to its being taken over by the "schemers."

SETTLEMENT SCHEMES

Tropical Africa, wide though it is and obviously made for wandering, is no longer wide enough to accommodate without some semblance of control all those who are willing to do better for themselves. Those who insist on wandering soon find themselves guilty of trespass. It is perhaps inevitable therefore that, as the colonial governments have become more alert to their responsibilities — their *mission civilisatrice* as the French used to call it — they should have become increasingly preoccupied with schemes for the settlement of habitable land that was still unoccupied and for the improved settlement of land that was already occupied.

The schemes that have been put into operation during the past thirty years and more are of many kinds. In scope they range from small-scale pilot projects costing next to nothing beyond the effort of mind and muscle that went into them, to mammoth, multi-million-dollar, TVA-type excursions into "social engineering"; from one-man campaigns for the re-siting of villages to quasi-military operations calling for the making over of whole countrysides into the likeness of blueprints, and using the armory of weapons — financial, technological, political and scientific — available to a Western democracy. Some have been inspired and undertaken by governments, some by private organizations. Some have been directed to the needs of the African, some to the needs of the European, and some to both. Their geographical location has been as varied as their scope, for they have been tried out in forest and veld, swamp and desert, plateau and plain. They have had an equally wide range of fortunes — and misfortunes.

SOME SCHEMES THAT FAILED

There have, alas, been many misfortunes, and several failures. Nothing is to be gained by giving a full recital of them, but the study of some unrewarding settlement schemes is illuminating, not so much for the evidences of folly and unjustifiable optimism it discloses as for the insight it gives us into the nature of tropical Africa — its environments and peoples, and our still lamentable ignorance of both.

Ghana: The Damongo Settlement

In 1949 the Gold Coast government established the Gonja Development Company for the purpose of opening up to African settlement several blocks of practically unused bush at Damongo in the Northern Region. In order to make the scheme attractive to farmers living on the badly overcrowded, eroded and unproductive lands to the north, and to give it a flying start, the company undertook to clear and contour plow the bush with heavy caterpillar tractors, to supply houses for the settlers, along with piped water, roads, a hospital, schools and baby clinics. It also provided expert advice on what to grow (mainly peanut, tobacco, rice and sorghum) and how to grow it.

But it takes more than a Santa Claus to change a people's pattern of living. After nearly four years only 2,560 acres had been cleared, and only 1,130 acres cultivated. Of those Africans who had come down from the north to help get the scheme under way, only a handful had taken up land. Fewer still had settled there with their families, and not all of these were happy about the results of the move. They missed the companionship of their kin, most of whom still lived in the north. Their traditional life disrupted, they had no sense of security. Successful settlement, or resettlement, it would appear, was not merely a matter of material things but equally a matter of mind. The skills of the social anthropologist should have been used as well as those of the engineer and agronomist.

Nigeria: The Mokwa Settlement

The Niger Agricultural Project, one of several postwar settlement schemes in Nigeria, ran into somewhat similar difficulties.[5] In 1949, at Mokwa in the Northern Region of Nigeria, the (central) Nigerian government in partnership with the Colonial Development Corporation took over a large block of tsetse-infested and sparsely settled savanna. Its purpose in doing so was to try out the possibility of large-scale land settlement — and resettlement — on the basis of mechanized cultivation, particularly of peanuts, bambarra nuts and sorghum. In return for clearing the bush, providing farm machinery, fertilizers, roads, houses and other amenities, the sponsors of the project were to take two thirds of the settlers' crops on their 48-acre units. Originally ten settlements, each of about 80 families, were planned. By mid-1952 only 7,500 acres had been cleared, of which only 3,240 acres had been planted; and only 135 families had been settled. By the end of 1954 the project expired. Its obituary appeared in the report of the Colonial Development Corporation for that year. The net loss to the corporation was stated to be £123,494.

The cause of death? The authors of the report hint at one possibility when they state that the "project was well and economically managed, but more experiment is needed to prove crops, methods of cultivation and economics of mechanization." Lack of prior agronomic knowledge was without doubt a contributory cause. Lack of prior climatic knowledge was a further and related cause. Everybody knew the mean rainfall and temperature, but nobody, it seems, knew how much water it would take to grow the planned crops in a region of almost constant high tem-

[5] For a book-length treatment of the project, the interested reader is recommended to consult K. D. S. Baldwin, *The Niger Agricultural Project*, Harvard University Press, Cambridge, 1957.

peratures; that is, nobody knew anything about the all important matter of evapotranspiration.[6] Between them the harsh thirsty earth and the unskilled African took a heavy toll of the corporation's bulldozers, plows and harrows. Some of the crops were disappointing, even to cultivators unaccustomed to the white man's expectations. Some of the prices obtained for them were even more disappointing, because the lack of economic access to wider markets frequently made it necessary to sell crops, especially sorghum, locally. But there was more to it than that. Part of the trouble lay, as Elspeth Huxley observes in her *Four Guineas,* in the fact that most people in that part of the country prefer living in towns and villages, if possible by trade, to working in the heat of the sun. Traditionally, cultivation had been slaves' work.

Tanganyika: The Groundnut Scheme

As all the world knows, for it aroused more enthusiasm and obloquy than any other, the Tanganyika Groundnut Scheme was the biggest of the failures. At the same time it is probably the failure with the biggest future, and deserves on that account alone to be treated in some detail.

To see the scheme in its true perspective, we need to remind ourselves of the serious food situation confronting Western and Central Europe at the close of World War II. With the numbers of breeding animals reduced by killings and undernourishment, and the acreage of arable land reduced by shortage of labor and by military use and abuse, there was urgent need to develop new supplies of proteins and fats. This need was particularly urgent in Great Britain, where by no conceivable rationing or farming system could the needs of the population be met. In the opinion of the experts, disastrous shortages faced the country for at least ten years if it had to rely exclusively on its prewar sources of food. To a country that had already had more than six years of shortages, this was a prospect to dismay even the most stout-hearted. As events turned out, the experts were wrong, but no government, especially one newly come to power, could afford not to base its plans on the assumption that the experts were right. To a Labor government, it was no less a challenge to apply to the waging of peace stratagems as bold and imaginative as those that had been used in the waging of the war. And this it proceeded to do. The Overseas Food Corporation (of which the Tanganyika scheme was a very big part) was to be a kind of crusade for the betterment of African and Briton alike; the vision of swords being turned into plowshares was to become a reality, and at a cost equivalent to that of only two or three days' fighting.

But the scheme was not planned as wars are planned — carefully, logistically and well in advance of operations. With the end of the war,

[6] See Chapter 2.

a host of other pressing needs had to be met, and the promoters of the Groundnut Scheme found themselves in a long line-up. The tractors and tree-clearing equipment required for it were very scarce, and widely scattered; they were mostly secondhand at that. The little port of Dar-es-Salaam was ill-equipped to handle the unloading and servicing of heavy equipment; the single-line meter-gauge railroad upcountry was already badly congested with freight traffic; and the final lap of the journey to Kongwa, the site of the main operation, was over practically roadless country that soon became strewn with casualties — victims of age, inadequate care and the environment.

Nobody was given an opportunity to gain on-the-spot experience and very few Africans were farming the area at the time of the "invasion." The whole agronomy of the scheme had to be based on extrapolated experience, which in Africa has seldom been known for its reliability. Selection of the 30,000-acre units on which Africans were to be settled and peanuts raised was done primarily by aerial surveys of the general nature of the relief and the broad plant associations. But these were inadequate criteria of the suitability of a given locality. After field operations had begun, the need for a ground survey was realized and a reconnaissance team was organized to undertake it. What they found out about the necessity of combating erosion and the cost of doing it bore little relation to the original blueprints and estimates. These had been based on the assumption that the units could be farmed in American style, or possibly in Russian state farm style. Because of the necessity of contouring most of the land, even land with only a 2° to 3° gradient, and the difficulty of training Africans to do this efficiently with the machines at their disposal, the estimated costs of cultivating, seeding, weeding and harvesting were soon greatly exceeded. The cost estimates of clearing the land were also greatly exceeded. In place of the planned figure of £4 an acre, the actual costs ran between £15 and £20 an acre.

The planners' reliance on the ecological characteristics of the countryside, coupled with such scanty rainfall data as were available, led to even greater troubles. On the basis of this evidence they assumed that the average annual rainfall over the area of operations was adequate for the growing of peanuts. What was not taken seriously into account was the variation in the seasonal and annual incidence of the rains. As luck would have it, the planners struck some very un-average rains that began too late, finished too early and yielded too little too quickly. They also struck some very unaccommodating soils — soils that were only for short periods in a condition suitable for cultivation, seeding and harvesting. To take full advantage of these periods would have necessitated keeping an impossibly lavish supply of machines. For the greater part of the year, most soils had an almost rock-like hardness; some of them had it all the time. Their cultivation imposed disastrous strains on tractors and implements, and an almost fantastic rate of abrasion on plowshares and tines. After they had been worked into some sort of shape for seeding, they quickly compacted again, thereby making for serious harvesting problems. Sir Bernard Keen notes in a paper prepared for this study:

Although this difficulty was later reduced by growing the crops on ridges, the basic problem of compaction remained unsolved. Profiles subsequently dug in the undisturbed bush showed this inherent soil property only too clearly. A reconnaissance survey would have disclosed the danger, but this was one of the lengthy preliminaries ruled out by the urgency.

The practical consequences of all this are seen in the divergence between goals and achievements in the Kongwa, Central Province, area of operations.[7] Whereas the original program called for 150,000 acres to be felled, cleared and planted to peanuts in 1947, only 13,750 acres were felled and cleared and only 7,500 planted to crops in that year. By 1949 less than 200,000 acres had been cleared and less than 100,000 planted to crops, though the expectation had been that nearly a million and a half acres would be cleared and nearly a million and a quarter would be producing peanuts.

The consequences are also seen in two further statistics: the average yield of peanuts off the planted acreage was about 200 pounds per acre compared with the planners' estimate of 700 pounds; the cost of the operation to the British government was approximately £26 million — a large sum to pay for so small a crop.

However, that is not the only thing it bought. It also bought experience — expensively no doubt — that is today being put to profit in the area and elsewhere, and that promises good returns in crops, cash and healthy new communities in the years to come. It had at least one good immediate result: it injected a lot of money into an economy that was very short of it. True, not all of the £26 million got to Tanganyika, let alone stayed there, but nobody doubts that at least 40 per cent did.

SOME SCHEMES THAT SHOW PROMISE

Tanganyika: The Farming Settlement Scheme

When the Overseas Food Corporation abandoned the Groundnut Scheme, it retained a technical and managerial task force. With this it set to work not only to salvage what it could of the "wreckage" of the scheme, but also to make a fresh start on what was, after all, still a very pressing problem, namely, what to do with environments with which nobody had been able to do very much.

As is pointed out in a recent report of the Tanganyika Agricultural Corporation (which took over the Tanganyika projects of the Overseas

---

[7] Two other, more humid, areas were in the scheme, namely, Urambo (Western Province) and Nachingwea (Southern Province).

Food Corporation in 1955), what has been done since 1951 falls into two categories, both experimental. The corporation has sought to provide the government of Tanganyika with "a ready instrument through which it would be able to promote its own experiments and schemes of development" and to establish "within the financial provision available a system or systems of agriculture which will enable the land comprised in the said undertaking [the Overseas Food Corporation] to be fully utilised in self-supporting agricultural production." [8] While not all of these experiments and schemes have to do directly with land settlement, some of the more important ones do. Of these, the most promising is the Farming Settlement Scheme. This is designed to enable the African peasant cultivator "to emerge from the trough of subsistence farming and become a self-reliant and prosperous yeoman farmer able to contribute to the economic development of his native land." [9]

On the site of the Nachingwea (Southern Province) peanut operation there are now (1959) 79 tenant farmers on approximately 2,800 acres of land, of which about 1,360, or 17 acres per farm, are under cultivation, much of it to oilseeds. In the Urambo (Western Province) region there are 87 tenant farmers, most of whom are concentrating on tobacco. Where these tenants have shown that they can handle small acreages, they are encouraged to take on larger farms, of up to 200 acres. Down to the present time fewer than 20 such farms have been leased to Africans. However, at least two of the "yeoman" farmers working on them made a net profit of one thousand dollars or more in the 1957-1958 season. In the Kongwa (Central Province) region there are another 90 tenants, most of whom are now turning from cash crop farming to mixed farming in which cattle are coming to play an increasingly important role.

In each area the Tanganyika Agricultural Corporation provides the tenant with advice on all the agricultural problems he meets, brings within his means the benefits of mechanized and partly mechanized farm practices, provides him with credit, training, marketing facilities, housing and, not least, land. Unfortunately, it cannot supply him with a reliable rainfall or stable commodity prices. As luck would have it, most of the early birds have had to make do with rather exiguous worms.

It is still too soon to speak of the success — or, for that matter, the failure — of this settlement scheme. But at least it makes progress. The stickers have made some money, and most of them now have a bicycle and a decent suit of clothes. All eat well and are in better health than most of their "unsettled" compatriots. What is perhaps the best index of all is that the scheme does not lack for joiners.

[8] *Tanganyika Agricultural Corporation,* a memorandum prepared for the World Bank, mimeographed, June 1959, p. 1.
[9] *Ibid.,* p. 6.

THE FACE OF
TROPICAL AFRICA

Photographs by Omar Marcus, from a collection made by him
for the Twentieth Century Fund; arranged by Anita Ventura

THE LAND

Tropical Africa is a fabric woven of many physical threads. Into it go water and soil, heat and aridity, marsh and jungle, mantled hill and naked valley, beaches fringed with palm and coral, "sunny fountains" that sometimes freeze. The threads have been woven by nature and man into many patterns. While some of these recall those of other lands, all are unique and, to the accustomed eye, identifiably African in texture. This is as true of the French Cameroons as of the Belgian Congo, of the east African plateaus as of the Rift Valley that cleaves them, of the Gezira no less than of Zanzibar. The following landscape pictures evoke some of the many images which tropical Africa impresses on the mind.

A watery clearing in the rain forest, used as a fish farm, in the Central African Republic

Rolling savanna country, used for peasant farming (Belgian Congo)

Rough bush country (B. C.)

Coconut palm grove, Zanzibar

The cancer of erosion

The mountains of east Africa — high and wide, and handsome even in dry-season haze

Bouali Falls (C. A. R.)

Grazing country (B. C.)

In the rainy season much of tropical Africa lies under water (Mozambique)

In the dry season much of it is parched and bare (upper Niger valley) ▶

The dry season, and even the desert, can be redeemed by irrigation (Gezira)

The river is the dominant thread in the rain forest fabric (Vouri R., French Cameroons)

Grasslands of a Kenya game park

High above sea level in Ethiopia

By the Gezira's still waters

One of many surf-ridden coasts

THE PEOPLE

A mosaic of tribes and tongues, of cultures, societies and nations, tropical Africa is the home of negro and Bantu, of Hamite and Semite, of European, Asian and Colored. Within its borders live herder and hunter, cultivator and fisherman, miner, manufacturer and trader, and the followers of every other art and calling. While most of these people still belong to an antique world, almost all of them now know there is another world and, from time to time, make excursions into it. Increasing numbers are coming to terms with its ways of eating, drinking and dressing, are coveting its wealth and power. But the grass roots of Africa wither slowly.

The time, the present; the man, Ethiopian; the mien, timeless and universal

Confronted with the new, while still cherishing the old (Luanda, Angola)

The "new": an umbrella (Ethiopia) . . .

. . . or a pair of sneakers (B. C.)

Hatted in Mozambique

Veiled in Khartoum

Shaven in Zanzibar

Wigged in Ethiopia

The old Africa, shy of roads, strides robustly down the byways ▶

To school in Buea (Nigeria)

To work in Khartoum

To prayer in Ft. Lamy

To a party in Nairobi

◀ The new Africa steers for town on surfaced highways

Seeking cover in Mozambique

Translation from the Amharic: "Let's have fewer nursemaids and more freedom!"

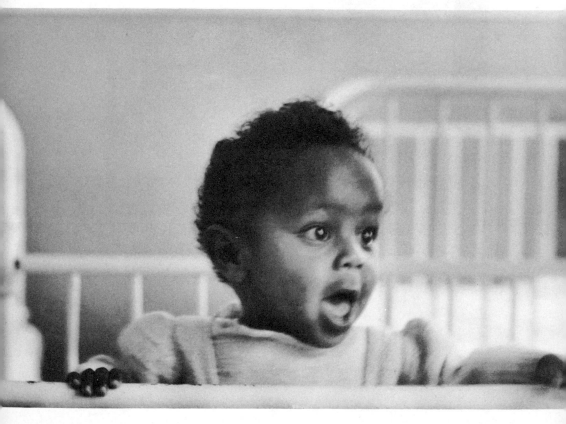

Feeding time, Addis Ababa

Clinic time, Bomi Hills (Liberia)

Bath time, Sansanding (Upper Volta)

Play time, Brazzaville

Factory worker, Tanganyika

Farm worker, Kivu (B. C.)

Social worker, Tamale (Ghana)

Dock worker, Republic of the Congo

High fashion in Ft. Lamy (Chad)

High fashion in Dakar (Senegal)

Settler, European Highlands (Kenya)

Settler, Gezira (Republic of Sudan)

Land surveyor in Kikuyu country (Kenya)

Naval rating, Freetown (Sierra Leone)

Teacher at Community Development
Center, Uganda

◀ Cool clothes for a hot campus
(University College, Ibadan, Nigeria)

Chemistry student at Makerere
College, Uganda

Weekday in Cela colonization center (Angola)

Sunday in Bangui (Central African Republic)

European dress, for church (Sierra Leone)

Mimicry at a cocoa festival (French Cameroons)

European tea, for conversation (Ghana)

European accouterments, for study (University of Khartoum)

TRANSPORT

At the beginning of the twentieth century few Africans had anything to sell or any great need to buy. Few traveled far, except under duress. For the many, life was as poor in things as it was parochial in reach and outlook. Today the roads and rivers are full of travelers. Where two roads or rivers meet there is a village where a traveler may board a bus for the nearest town. In the towns there are markets and factories to buy his goods, offices and mines to buy his services. From the towns autos and trucks, trains and planes will take him wherever his business dictates or his means allow.

The dugout is slow, but companionable and accommodating (near Bangui)

For moving about the bush, the small plane is swift, safe and convenient

Bicycles go by French plane (Chad)

Commuters go by "London" bus (Freetown)

Roads in Africa look better than they are, especially in rain (B. C.)

Taxi service, Brazzaville

"Mammy lorries," Accra

Train travelers in Katanga (B. C.)

Divided highway in Nairobi (Kenya)

The town is Léopoldville; for traffic it could be any one of a score ▶

Lagos: deep-water wharf

Takoradi Harbour: bauxite siding

SHIPPING

Almost all of tropical Africa's roads and railroads lead to the sea, for the region does most of its business with overseas countries. Without ships there would be no large sale for cocoa or copper, palm oil or peanuts, tobacco or timber; without ships there would be no large purchase of machinery and other heavy goods. But getting ships to the goods and the goods to the people who want them has not always been an easy task. Large stretches of the coast are shelterless; some are rocky or strewn with sand bars and reefs; nearly all are surf-ridden. In the more than ten thousand miles of coast there are not more than ten natural deep-water harbors, and few of these are where they could do most good. The problem of the overseas transporter has therefore been formidable.

Lourenço Marques: timber haulers

Dakar: peanut oil ready for loading

mports in crates

Exports on flatcars

Exports in canoes

Exports pickaback: loading Ghanaian cocoa in surf boats

Manpower in Accra

Womanpower in Lobito (Angola)

Machine power at the U. S.-built Free Port of Monrovia ▶

MINERALS

The economic resources of tropical Africa are of many kinds, for it is a region that "has everything." It has climate to grow every crop under the sun; lakes, rivers and seas with more fish in them than ever came out; enough falling water to drive all the turbines in the world. Its forests, large and diverse in species, could supply much of the world's demand for hardwoods and hardwood products. Its soils may not be the richest in the world, but with coaxing and care they can be made to bring forth abundantly and continuously; and beneath them lies what is almost certainly the world's richest storehouse of minerals.

There is high-grade iron ore in the Bomi Hills of Liberia . . .

. . . so much that the easiest way to mine it is to remove the Hills ▶

Copper *(also below)* heads the minerals list in N. Rhodesia and the Belgian Congo

Electrolysis plant, Jadotville

Rotary furnace, Elisabethville

Refined ingot bars, Jadotville

Tank house, Copperbelt

◀ Limestone is plentiful and increasingly in demand for cement (Mozambique)

Seine fishing (Cape Coast region, Ghana)

FISHERIES

Few parts of the world have made so little use of so much fish as tropical Africa. Its waters swarm with palatable varieties, yet only about one in three Africans eats fish in any amount. A climate that hastens decay, customs that discourage or prohibit fish consumption, and the existence of large expanses that lose their surface waters in the dry season are among the causes of this seeming anomaly. But with alternative sources of animal protein scarce and expensive in most of the wooded areas, and with the population almost everywhere increasing faster than the supply of alternative foods, more and more people are becoming interested in fishing, either as a source of food or trade, or both.

Netting pond fish (Bangui)

Mending lake net (Kivu)

Sawfish research (Freetown)

Fishing fleet (Cape Coast)

Fishing gear (near Bangui)

Fish farmer (near Bangui)

Farm headquarters in Ghana

FARMING AND LUMBERING

Tropical Africa, though no Garden of Eden, can grow everything that is "pleas-ant to the sight, and good for food." Kenya alone grows thirty-five of the world's leading crops, including such "untropical" crops as wheat and barley. Quite a few crops can be raised that are neither very pleasant (such as the castor oil plant) nor very palatable (such as pyrethrum). Any kind of tree will grow. The native forests contain some of the most versatile woods known to industry; ex-otics range from Australian eucalyptus to Mexican pine, from Chinese tung to Brazilian rubber. For good measure, any animal can be raised. Although it is true that most of the cattle on tropical Africa's hills are of not much use to their keepers, and distinctly bad for the hills, some can and do enter the show ring.

African field help on a European farm in the Kenya Highlands

Peanut pyramid (Dakar) ▶

The day's chore (Gezira) The morrow's maize (Kenya)

Motive power on an experimental dairy farm (Kivu)   Cattle power (S. Rhodesia)

Manioc for the pot (B. C.)

Piassava for the inspector (Sa. Leone)

Sisal for the rope-maker (Kenya)

Cattle for the market (Mozambique)

◀ Planting a sisal field (near Morogoro, Tanganyika)

Sisal fiber being dried for baling and shipment overseas (Tanganyika)

Liberian rubber tappers returning to the tank station with their take of latex

A tapper making the rounds

A tankman watching the flow

Sheet rubber goes to the smokehouse before baling and shipment (Br. Cameroons) ▶

Log jam in Takoradi Harbour, Ghana's timber port

Haulage by tractor

Haulage by water

Haulage by train

Haulage by crane

◀ Ghanaian timber, stamped, addressed and ready for shipment

Village sheep market, Ethiopian Highlands

Businessmen in Khartoum

Business woman in Accra

THE MARKET PLACE

For long, the people of tropical Africa had few needs that could not be supplied by their own exertions. For long, too, they had few salable surpluses, other than ivory and gold — and slaves. Today, there is hardly a tribe that does not feel the need of things it cannot produce, or that is without the means to buy some of them. There is hardly a village that does not have at least one store or market place, and hardly a family that does not patronize it. For many, the patronage is still occasional, and then only for penny "screws" of tea, sugar, flour, soap and similar luxuries. But for millions it is steady and substantial; and for almost all, the wish to be a buyer is second only to the wish to be a seller.

Slow sales in Sierra Leone

(Overleaf) The curb market, where the business is often better
than the goods, and the goods better than the gossip

Shop talk in Ethiopia

High hats in Ghana

Low counters in Tanganyika

Kenya: Resettlement of the Kamba

In Kenya, the resettlement of large numbers of Kamba — necessitated by their rapid increase under British administration and by the inroads of soil erosion — is already being spoken of by some of its promoters as an assured success. Certainly no visitor to Makueni or Machakos, the chief centers of activity, can fail to see that much has been achieved since the African Land Utilisation and Settlement Board moved in with its trucks, bulldozers, surveyors and agronomists.

At the end of the 1940s most of the 400,000 Kamba were "living in a breadline," to quote the Provincial Agricultural Officer, T. Hughes-Rice. For almost twenty years many of them had been kept alive by the ministrations of famine relief officers. The hillsides were torn with gullies; hardly anything except worthless thornbush and succulents would grow on them. Today the Machakos district is "still no Garden of Eden, but it has a river of life running through it." The people have been persuaded to re-site their homesteads along the line of the machine-built bunds, or contour-ridges, to accept far-reaching measures of livestock control and improvement (including the stall feeding of animals in the dried-out months), and to raise cash crops such as banana, pineapple and coffee. What is more, they now grow all the food they need, even though the population is greater than it was at any time during the past generation.

Uganda: Resettlement of the Kiga

In Uganda a similar resettlement scheme for the farmers of Kigezi — the grossly overpopulated province in the southwest of the territory — has also been hailed as a success by some. Others, especially those who feel that the criterion of success of a resettlement scheme is what happens to the areas providing the settlers quite as much as what happens to those receiving them, prefer to reserve judgment for the time being.

Few Kiga had ever heard of the places picked for them, and fewer still had ever seen them. Even though some of the elders were taken to see them and reported favorably, and the government provided free transportation, staging posts and free overnight accommodation en route, there was no early enthusiasm for the scheme. In time, however, thanks largely to the unpushing, "take it or leave it" tactics of the authorities, and their willingness to let the settlers choose their own sites and fix their own boundaries, the movement gathered impetus. In 1946, the first year of the scheme, 1,500 people made the trek; by 1951, 20,000 had made it; by the mid-1950s the emigration rate was up to more than 7,000 a year.

But the Kigezi picture is still far from bright. The emigration rate is well below the rate of population increase; and those who have stayed behind show little or no sign of mending their wastrel ways. Indeed, in his Annual Report for 1954 the Agricultural Officer for the Western Province of Uganda had to admit that the problem of soil conservation was becoming more rather than less acute, with the population still increasing at about 15,000 a year. Until drastic depopulation and stringent land control measures are in sight, it is open to doubt whether the early promise of the scheme will be realized.

The Sudanese Republic: Irrigation

Some of the most promising settlement schemes in the whole of tropical Africa are to be found outside the British colonial territories. One of the oldest, and boldest, of these has been carried out by the French in the Niger valley under the auspices of the Office du Niger. Although conceived as far back as 1920, and planned in 1932 to provide for 4,000 square miles (more than 2.5 million acres) of irrigated rice and cotton tended by nearly a million people, the scheme did not make a great deal of headway until 1948 when the Sansanding Dam on the Niger River was completed. Even now it is still a long way from the full realization of its founders' hopes. By 1958 only about 35,000 people had been settled on the irrigated land and only about 100,000 acres of land had been put under cultivation. The total cost of the scheme down to 1958 was not far short of $100 million.

The land affected by the scheme is located in the so-called central delta of the Niger that extends from Ségou downstream almost to Timbuktu. Most of it forms part of a prehistoric or "dead" delta that, fortunately, can be irrigated by the gravity flow of the impounded waters. But the flood control provided by the dam and the Macina and Sahel irrigation systems now integrated with it have also improved the agricultural prospects of the present or "live" central delta of the Niger, so that the total area of land capable of being benefited by the scheme is considerably greater than 4,000 square miles. Some estimates place it as high as 30,000 square miles (more than 19 million acres). It is the hope of the Office du Niger to open up more and more of this land as African cultivators in the poorer and overpopulated parts of west Africa become aware of its possibilities. And the news is getting around.

Each successful applicant for a lot receives a house to live in (on which he pays no rent), livestock and tools, seed and fertilizer, a supply of food to tide him over until the first harvest, and 10 acres or more of irrigated land. In some of the rice-growing sectors where mechanized cultivation is possible, he may receive five acres per household member. The houses and villages are a scrubbed, modernized version of the type generally found in the area. What they may lack in atmosphere they make up in tidiness and salubrity. Each village is supplied with well water (not always used, alas, as many villagers find it less tiresome to draw water from a nearby irrigation ditch or canal), a livestock yard kept by a salaried stockman, a medical post visited daily by a nurse, a school, shade and fruit trees, and kitchen gardens. All these services cost the settlers nothing. Further, each village is settled by people of the same cultural origin, thus increasing its appeal and cohesion. So far the settlers have generally come from areas not more than 200 miles distant.

The land is cultivated either by the settler or by the Office du Niger. Where the settler does his own cultivating, he does it mostly by hand, using methods that can best be described as "European-improved African traditional." The Office du Niger uses mechanical methods wherever possible, as they generally are in the rice fields; it also makes extensive use of seasonal labor.

The standard Office du Niger contract with the immigrants provides for a ten-year "period of adaptation." If, at the end of this time, the settler has carried out his obligations to develop his lot and live decently, and is judged to be a good farmer, he may be granted a "lease of permanent establishment." Such a lease includes all the advantages of ownership, including transmission by inheritance but not the right to transfer it outside the family. The contract also provides that the settler becomes a member of the local Association Agricole Indigène. This body provides research, medical and veterinary services, maintains irrigation works, sells consumer goods, and looks after the processing and marketing of crops. It also conducts on-the-job training programs.

In recent seasons the total value of crops (mainly rice and cotton) grown by the settlers has averaged approximately $250 per person. Several households have had gross incomes in excess of $2,000, which have given them net incomes of not less than $750 — incomes that are up to ten times as large as those earned by the farmers in neighboring areas. If such incomes can be maintained, let alone bettered, the Office du Niger will not need to worry much about the outcome of its great enterprise.

Paysannat *Schemes*

In the past few years the French have become interested in other, less spectacular, types of peasant settlement, or *paysannat*, schemes adapted to the circumstances of their hot-and-wet territories. In essentials, these are very similar to the schemes the Belgians have been developing in the Congo over a longer period; indeed, it was the Belgians' performance in this field that inspired the French experiments.

Because of the vast physical differences between one part and another of their Community, the French have not sought to gain their settlement goals by applying a single formula. In the lands formerly constituting French Equatorial Africa, three types of *paysannat* schemes have been undertaken:

1. Mechanized or semi-mechanized — grouped — settlement in flat country susceptible to the techniques of "industrial" farming.

2. Non-mechanized — dispersed — settlement, or rather resettlement, in heavily forested and mountainous country that is not susceptible to industrial techniques.

3. Intensive mixed-farming settlement in the vicinity of the larger towns.

Progress has been made with all three types, but because there are few large towns and because the heavily forested and mountainous country will always have great difficulty in competing economically with flatter and more open country, it is the first type that holds the greatest promise of a raised standard of rural living.

The Madingou (Niari valley) *paysannat* illustrates the kind of thing the French have attempted. Here in the extreme south of the Republic of the Congo (formerly the Middle Congo Province of French Equatorial Africa), a score or so of villages, comprising several hundred families, have been established on good soils, and in close proximity to both the road and railroad linking Brazzaville with Pointe Noire. Each village is surrounded by, or adjacent to, a number of fields that the administering authority has had mechanically cleared and plowed. These fields may be anything up to 100 or 150 acres in size. Each family with two working adults has been given approximately seven acres of arable land. Families with more than two working adults (and there are many such families, for polygamy is common in the Niari region) have been allocated land at the rate of roughly three and a half acres for each worker. This land they sow and cultivate by hand as directed by their supervisors. The crops grown are the peanut (the linchpin of the system), sweet potato, urena (a fiber that has all the uses of hemp and some others besides), manioc, maize, and a variety of green crops for plowing under; they are grown according to a strict four-year rotation. In addition to the arable land, each family has been given a pig and about half an acre of land for coffee.

As the Madingou scheme was begun only in 1955 it is still too early to pass judgment on it. But the prospects of success seem good. The scheme has been very well received by the settlers, and the early crops — which the government has bought at a guaranteed price — impressed even the skeptics. Some of the first settlers were recruited from the ranks of unemployed artisans who had gone to the towns in the boom building period of the late 1940s and early 1950s. They may have known little about agriculture, but since, for the present, the government is doing most of the thinking for them, this limitation is more than outweighed by their workshop skills. They have another qualification, too. Having lived in the towns meanly and, for the most part, insecurely, they are quick to see merit in a life that offers them a competence with stability and decency.

The Belgian Congo *paysannat* campaign has gone much further, and has been conducted on a bigger scale with the aid of very substantial technical and financial resources. But its object has been the same: to

develop a permanent indigenous peasantry that will be content to stay on
the land because the life it offers can be as good and as rewarding as
town or mine life, at its best, can be.

For the campaign to be successful, the Belgian agronomists long ago
realized that increased productivity, without which its economic objectives could not be reached, was not merely a matter of more machinery,
more fertilizer, better cultivation and the use of rotations, but also of
better soils. They realized, too, that the best way to get better soils was
to go out and find them, and that the next best way was to discover what
was wrong with the not so good soils. Accordingly an extensive program
of soil mapping was put into operation. The findings of this survey have
made it possible to delimit fairly accurately those soils which would be
strong enough to take the strain of a stabilized, permanent agricultural
economy.

By the late 1950s, 15 million acres had been systematically surveyed;
approximately 200,000 tracts of land had been divided into plots and
nearly 150,000 farmers settled on them. The occupied tracts totaled
more than 2.5 million acres.

Because of the variety of environmental and cultural conditions encountered in the Congo, the Belgians have found it desirable to adopt an
empirical approach to their *paysannat* program. They have been less concerned about hewing to a particular line of policy, whether in regard to
agronomy or land tenure, than about giving cultivators the best possible
chance of succeeding economically with the least possible chance of
destroying themselves socially. It is not possible, therefore, to speak of a
standard *paysannat*, although most *paysannats* have some things in common. Each farmer is generally told what crops to plant in what locality
and in which sequence. It is usual for the government to buy up the
whole of the cash crop harvest in order to give the farmer a stable
market. It is also usual for the government to make him a part-pay-
ment when his crop is gathered, and to pay him the balance after it has
been processed, shipped out, and all operating costs have been covered.
The government provides most *paysannats* with educational and social,
including medical, services.

To talk in generalities, however, is no way in which to get the measure
of the Belgians' achievements, or the Africans'. These need to be seen,
and sensed (for they are not only material in character), on the spot.
They can be seen, and sensed, wherever *paysannats* have become firmly
established, as, for instance, at Luala, situated about midway between
Léopoldville and Matadi near the border of the Republic of the Congo.
When this *paysannat* was started in 1951 the Luala valley was a sleeping
sickness area. Its few inhabitants were backward, lethargic and undernourished; they produced next to nothing beyond their immediate necessities. Although only a hundred miles distant from Léopoldville, they
were two thousand years from it in time. Four years later some 350

African families were working 10 acres of arable land apiece. Another 350 laborers, approximately, were engaged in doing everything from servicing and repairing harvesters to building homes for their own people and for the eight Europeans who provided the technical and administrative direction of the scheme. The main crops grown on the *paysannat* were peanuts, rice and urena. The bush clearing and plowing, and most of the harvesting,[10] was being done mechanically by Africans, who, when trained, were said to be every bit as good as Europeans. After deducting charges for these services and for the supply of fertilizer, maintenance of roads, land drainage and so on, the better farmers were netting 20,000 Belgian francs, say $400, a year. Formerly they were lucky if they could net ten dollars a year from their home-grown produce; even those who left home to work on palm oil and timber plantations did well to earn $250.

By the late 1950s the Belgians were doing better still for their Luala peasants, for they were giving each settler the chance to go in for such additional money-makers as coffee and cattle. And in the Luala valley there is no lack of land well suited to both and no lack of people willing to make money.

In the beginning, not unnaturally, the Belgian *paysannat* plan was looked upon with some suspicion. Was it a trick to keep the African out of the towns and the higher brackets or, worse, first to open up the African's lands with African labor and then expropriate them? Today this suspicion has gone. Wherever the traveler goes in *paysannat* country he is struck by the evidences of well-being, friendliness and pride (African as much as Belgian) in achievement. It is difficult not to believe, with the engineer-agronomist in charge of the Luala *paysannat,* that the Belgians have the peasants' confidence. They came to effect an economic and social revolution. This the peasants now understand, and they seem grateful for it.

Portuguese Colonization Schemes

The Portuguese are interested in peasant farming schemes for their own people as well as for the African. In this they are unique among the colonizing powers. The reasons for their interest are plain. They have, in Portugal, a large impoverished peasantry for whom another way of life, or a more propitious setting for the existing one, must be found. They have long harbored the conviction that the best way to get the Africans to go in for better farming is to show them what hard-working Portuguese peasants can do with the land. This is what is now being done in both Angola and Mozambique — the Portuguese African provinces best suited to the experiment.

---

[10] There is still no satisfactory way of harvesting urena by machines.

Fortunately, in both territories there is plenty of land that has, until now, remained practically unused by the African cultivator. In some cases it has remained so because it was too marshy and malarial; in others because it was infested with tsetse fly; elsewhere because it was too raw for African comfort. No less fortunately, much of this undeveloped land has rewarding, well-watered soils and a climate that makes it easy for the immigrant from southern Portugal (Algarve) to forget that he is more than 4,000 miles from home.

In Mozambique the main European colonization schemes are aligned along the valleys of the lower Limpopo and Incomati rivers. In Angola most of the colonizing effort is at present being put into the development of the Cela plateau about 200 miles southeast of Luanda. Though the individual schemes differ from each other in matters of size, agronomy and administration, they have common "sights." Prime Minister Salazar has expressed them with befitting simplicity: "For each hand, a hoe. For each family, a home. For each mouth, bread." In Western ears attuned to the beat of the fast "commercial" and to hymns in praise of Utopia, such words have a most uninviting sound. To landless peasants with nothing to look forward to in southern Portugal but continuing servitude to a soil that consumes all their energy without adequately sustaining them, they are sweet music. In the late 1950s the Cela colonization project alone had several hundred families on its waiting list.

The Cela project — it is as representative as any — was begun in 1952. The area set aside for it was approximately 1.25 million acres of grassy plateau situated at an elevation of some 4,000 feet and all but girdled by mountains rich in timber and perennial streams. Across the plateau flow several streams, the control of which is fundamental to the undertaking. In the rainy season such control is effected by drainage canals; in the dry season, by irrigation ditches. Each holding consists of about 15 acres of irrigated land, 30 acres of unirrigated land, five acres for coffee, two acres for orchard and garden, and a hundred acres for grazing — more than 150 acres in all. The main recommended crops, and those giving the best results, are rice, maize, soybean, vegetables (including the Irish potato) and peanut. Most of the land is fertile and, with irrigation and proper rotations, can support two crops a year. So far yields have been good, maize doing especially well — over 60 bushels to the acre in some instances.

In addition to land, each incoming family is given six head of cattle (either cows or oxen), three pigs and some poultry. Selected families also get a few sheep. And every family gets a fine three-to-four-room house, complete with basic furniture, and a food supply to keep it going until harvest. In accordance with the "for each hand a hoe" ideal, all the work — apart from clearing and preparing the ground — is done manually or with the aid of draft oxen. Fortunately most of the farmers have large families: some have nine or ten children. Even so, there is already talk among the more progressive and successful farmers of the possible advantages of investing in cooperatively owned machinery.

At the end of 1955 nine farm villages, each with about 25 houses, had been built and occupied. Two more were in construction. By 1958 more than 20 were complete and over 400 families were in residence.

Each farmer is given free passage for himself and his family from Portugal, and free land. He is lent, on repayment over a maximum period of twenty-five years, his house, cattle, farm equipment, and proportion of the development costs. The total value of all these goods and services is put at somewhat less than $6,000. With gross incomes of the order of $2,400 a year at the present time and outgoings at about $1,000, the average settler should have no difficulty in amortizing his debts well before the end of the twenty-five-year period. Some have already begun to do so, without availing themselves of the three years' initial moratorium. After paying off the total debt settlers acquire title deeds, but they are not allowed to break up their holdings.

So far, overhead costs have been small. In 1955 the director of the Cela settlement, Dr. Francisco Boaventura, had only three European technical assistants; his labor force was largely African, much of it compulsorily recruited and poorly paid by the Public Works Department. But the overhead costs are bound to rise as the social services are extended, and the Portuguese government is determined to make these the talk of the land. Recently a 90-bed hospital for Europeans and Africans and a high school were completed. Each village already has a church that doubles as a primary school during the daytime. Other amenities also recently added include a cinema, swimming pool, sports ground and hotel.

Impressive and inviting as the settlement is, it is not yet, in the view of its Portuguese planners, assured of success. They do not forget that somewhat similar schemes were tried between the two world wars and failed.[11] Much will depend on the quality of the immigrants. So far there has been no lack of immigrants with the necessary flexibility and stamina. So far, too, nearly all the immigrants have readily accepted the condition of self-employment with no recourse to African labor. Of the first 130 families that went to Cela, only eight were failures. These were sent back to Portugal. Since that time the failures have been left to fend for themselves, for the government has no desire to see the scheme become a means of rotational migration at its expense. Not that there would seem to be any real danger of this, to judge by the kind of opinions expressed by those who have stayed. Much, too, will depend on the attitude of the settlers toward the African. Up to the present this has generally been correct, if not cordial — an attitude which the Africans have reciprocated.

[11] More recently still, in 1953, the Benguela Railway Company opened up some good "homesteading" territory close to its main line. Each approved family was granted 125 acres, 50 head of cattle, and credits sufficient to build a house and farm buildings. Of the 21 who came, 12 left within the year.

Paradoxically, it is possible that the more successful the present, avowedly experimental, scheme is, the greater the risk of its ultimate failure. For if the 550-family phase comes up to the planners' expectations, as seems likely, then the government plans to expand it to 1,000-family or even 2,000-family size. And if this should be successful, the government would be willing to think of a mass colonization large enough to ease, perhaps even remove, the population pressure that at present bears so heavily on the mother country. Such an end could not be achieved unless more than one million — possibly two million — Portuguese emigrated. Even if enough families of the right type should be willing to emigrate, it is by no means certain that they would stay. Although large areas of Angola are "empty," they are not so empty that the African would remain unaffected by such an invasion. He would almost certainly be involved in some sizable migrations of his own to enable the Portuguese to settle in cohesive groups, migrations which he would have every reason to oppose. Long before the scheme was consummated, he might have decided to put a stop to it, once and for all. The Portuguese government needs no one to tell it this. It has had dealings with the African for five hundred years and more, and has come to know him very well in that time. We may take it therefore that not the least of the reasons why the Portuguese are careful to promote African settlement schemes alongside their European schemes — sometimes dovetailed into them — is the realization that in so doing lies their best chance of solving an old metropolitan problem without precipitating a new colonial one.

Among the most promising of these Portuguese schemes for African tenant farming are two located in the lower Limpopo valley, in Mozambique. One is near the town of Guijá, almost in sight of the new Lourenço Marques–Bulawayo (Southern Rhodesia) railroad. The other is at Inhamissa. By the late 1950s several hundred African families had taken up land in the Guijá area. Eventually 2,000 families are expected to be settled there, all of them on good soil, much of it already drained and irrigated. Each successful applicant for land is given about five acres of irrigated land and 30 of unirrigated. The European peasant farmers in the same area are given twice as much.

In most respects the conditions imposed on the European farmers, to all intents the same as those for the settlers at Cela, apply to the Africans. The cropping systems for African and European settlers are much alike. Crops are raised according to a prescribed rotation, in which peanut, wheat, cotton, rice, alfalfa and vegetables all play a part. Wherever possible, as, for example, on irrigated land, two crops a year are raised. The settlers must work their own land, peasant fashion. Hired labor is excluded — a restriction that may deter some of the more ambitious spirits, since one of the first things many successful cash crop growers like to do is farm out the rough work. There must be no absentee-landlordism; settlers who go off to the mines for a spell (not that many do) lose their right to farm the land. Nor must there be any "coasting" or non-cooperation. It is intended that the scheme should pay its way, everybody paying part of it.

Because of their diverse social and linguistic backgrounds, the African peasants are not housed, as the Europeans are, in planned and ready-made villages. Most of them live in the bordering bush in their customary fashion. But there is no thought of segregation. On the contrary, Africans and Europeans farm holdings side by side, to the evident advantage of the African and unconcern of the European.

In contrast to the Guijá settlement scheme, on which a large, but undisclosed, sum of money is being spent, the Inhamissa scheme is being run on small change. Not more than $40,000 had been spent on it by 1956. But seldom was $40,000 spent to such good effect, for it was used to drain and irrigate more than 2,000 acres of marshy, malarial and sparsely inhabited flood plain that in the first three years of its development yielded approximately $150,000 worth of maize, rice and beans — and this notwithstanding one serious inundation of the Limpopo during this period. The drained land is farmed exclusively by local African peasants, who, depending on the size of their families, get anything up to six acres. By the late 1950s some 2,000 families were living on the drained lands (as against 115 families at the outset), and most of them were living well by the standard of the country. Some farmers were clearing $275 a year, or more than most of the laborers who go from the neighboring areas to the Rand mines. Not surprisingly, there was a waiting list of several hundred families, some of them living at a distance of more than 70 miles.

Encouraged by the economic results, the government is now turning its attention to other matters. It is building schools, welfare and trading centers, and a number of four- and five-room cement houses for sale to some of the more prosperous settlers. It has also launched an African cooperative buying and selling society; this is being run, not by administrators, but by the local agronomists — a somewhat novel idea in Africa but a sensible one, since it is the agronomists who understand the settlers' problems and who have by far the most to do with them.

The government is also turning its attention to other areas in the lower Limpopo valley and in the adjacent Incomati valley. In time, and given the money for an extensive dyking program, it expects to drain more than 125,000 acres and settle them with African and European farming families. José Firmo de Sousa Monteiro, the chief architect of these schemes, believes that not less than 10,000 African families can eventually be established in the reclaimed lands of the lower Limpopo and between 8,000 and 10,000 in those of the lower Incomati. No firm estimates of the potential European farm population are available. Much will depend on whether or not the government restricts the reclaimed land to peasant-type operations.

Never the most talkative of the colonial powers, the Portuguese are reserving judgment on these schemes until there has been time to assess not only their "dollars and cents" value, but also their impact on the economy of the wider region of southern Mozambique in which they lie. If the government has an anxiety, it is probably lest the schemes should prove too successful. The lower Limpopo and Incomati valleys are already among the most thriving areas in the territory. Because of this, it is difficult even now to get farm folk to go to work in the towns, and, being producers of salable quantities of food, they cannot be compelled to leave their land. Further, because they are thriving it is difficult to get them to sell enough cattle to satisfy the growing urban need of meat: they make enough money by selling field crops and vegetables. As more and more Africans settle on the reclaimed land this meat shortage may disappear, but at what cost? A worse labor shortage in the towns?

SOME SCHEMES THAT HAVE SUCCEEDED

It is seldom easy to draw the line between promise and fulfillment. In appraising land settlement schemes it is often extremely difficult to do so. Many an advertised success has subsequently proved to have no more substance than the "bubble reputation" of the politicians who announced it. Likewise, many a scheme widely characterized as promising can be said to have already attained some of the set goals — albeit at a cost in excess of the set amounts — and so to deserve the label of success. Nor should we forget that, before now, phoenixes have risen from ashes and been made to soar. Not to draw too fastidious a line, it can certainly be said that there have been very few successes, and these mostly small-scale, if we take success to mean the ability of a scheme to become, and continue to be, self-supporting.

Northern Nigeria: The Anchau Scheme

Of the small scale schemes that can be said to belong to this category, one of the most interesting is the Anchau Rural Development and Settlement Scheme of northern Nigeria. This project stands apart from most of the others discussed so far, in a number of respects. It was launched in 1937 and benefited from the more leisurely approach to planning which was characteristic of the prewar years. The program involved the removal of population from several districts in the north of Zaria Province and adjacent parts of Kano Province that were badly infested with tsetse fly. In some places the sleeping sickness rate was 50 per cent, and over the area as a whole it averaged 30 per cent. To eradicate the fly the planners argued that it would be desirable to remove approximately 10 per cent of the population living in the worst-affected areas to more sparsely peopled areas which had been rendered fly-free, but which would not remain so unless there were enough people to keep down the fly-harboring bush.

At the outset it was recognized that such a displacement of population would involve considerable social and economic upheaval. It was also recognized that to reduce this to a minimum it would first be necessary to know much more about the living habits of the peoples involved, and the agricultural potential of the lands to which they were to go. To get this information careful studies were made of the existing distribution of the population, its family composition, its water consumption, its fuel needs, and the vegetation and soils (mostly with the aid of plant indicators) of the receiving areas. After ten years' intermittent work, the "Anchau Corridor," 70 miles long by 10 miles wide, and running parallel to the line of the Zaria-Jos railroad, was established. Along it moved 5,000 people with their goods and chattels. In it was built one new town, and 16 new villages. Most of the existing villages were improved by lowering their dwelling density, by constructing wells and pits for the disposal of refuse, and by planting shade trees. To facilitate the shipping of produce, mainly cotton, to the railroad, 60 miles of dry-season road were constructed.

With some twenty years of experience behind them, both planners and participants can afford to look with satisfaction on their achievements. At a cost of approximately £1 per capita, more than 50,000 people have acquired health, economic security and a sense of well-being, without losing their social cohesion. And those who stayed behind have also gained by the resettlement.

Resettlement in Tanganyika and Ruanda-Urundi

Other successful resettlement schemes have been carried out in recent years in Tanganyika and Ruanda-Urundi. In the Sukuma territory of Tanganyika no fewer than 30,000 people moved, over a five-year period, from the overpopulated areas of the Mwanza district into the relatively underpopulated Geita district — all of them voluntarily and without serious economic or social disturbance. No small part of the credit for this achievement belongs to the administration, which has been successfully moving people away from dangerously crowded areas since about 1934. The recipe for success is apparently quite simple: first observe where people tend to move when under pressure, and then make it easy — by digging wells and clearing bush of tsetse fly — for them to follow their inclination. Fortunately, there is still plenty of uncrowded, if not enormously attractive, land in Tanganyika available for such movements.

The problem facing the Belgian government in Ruanda-Urundi was tougher. There the overcrowded areas are large, the uncrowded ones small and often radically different in climate and opportunities from the overcrowded ones. Most of the overcrowded areas are on high ground that is healthy and free from "fly." Most of the uncrowded areas are in the low-lying, marshy, debilitating, fly-ridden valleys of the middle and lower Ruzizi to the north and northeast of Usumbura, and the Malagarasi valley in the extreme south of the territory. All the same, under its ten-year (1950-1959) plan for the development of Ruanda-Urundi, the Belgian government has carried out an extensive regrouping of the population. Overcrowding still exists, especially in the regions to the north of Kigali and to the south of Astrida; but the newly surveyed, sanitated and crop-tested valleys are carrying a steadily increasing population load, and may in time significantly relieve the pressure on the higher ground. With both *paysannat*- and plantation-type economies offering highly satisfactory returns from rice, cotton, oil palm and other oil-yielding plants, and with social and welfare agencies offering every settler the chance to lead a fuller and more interesting life, the Belgians are hopeful that they will. Meanwhile they can claim to have put parts of their scheme into paying operation, and to have had the ready cooperation of the Africans in doing so.

The Republic of the Congo: "Concession" Farming

European interest in the accessible and well-endowed Niari valley goes back a good many years. It was not until after World War II, however, that the French government did much to promote the region. The promoting was done through an organization — the Comité d'Aménâgement de la Vallée du Niari — which worked on the premise that no *grands colons* or corporations would be likely to invest money in the region until they had been shown cause. This it proceeded to do by conducting careful soil, drainage and erosion studies of all alienated lands; by finding out what could be raised there, and how best it could be raised. The committee also guided the research programs of the various agricultural stations that came to be established in the Niari valley.

Thanks in no small measure to the activities of this committee, some 40 concessions had been taken up in the valley by the mid-1950s. Some of these concessions are small, less than 2,500 acres, but most are large, the total area conceded being well over 250,000 acres. Nearly all of them are heavily capitalized and run on "industrial" lines. Most of the settlers also get good value out of the soil. In a fair season peanuts yield between two and three tons to the acre. On one experimental plantation bananas yield up to 10 tons an acre and pineapples up to 15 tons. Other heavy-yielding crops are cotton, urena, oil palm and sugar cane. So far the peanut has been the big money-maker, and the foundation of the valley's prosperity.

While these postwar developments have not increased the European settler population by more than a few hundred, they have led to a sharp increase in the African population. Some of the larger concessionaires now employ between 500 and 1,000 laborers, many of whom have taken up permanent residence in the valley, often on the concessions themselves.

The British Cameroons: Banana Plantations

In the same postwar decade the British Cameroons has witnessed a development which, although not consciously directed to settling people on the land, has had this as one of its most successful outcomes. In 1946 the Nigerian government took over from the Custodian of Enemy Property the old German plantations, mostly of bananas and mostly moribund, and set up an independent body called the Cameroons Development Corporation to run them "for the use and common benefit of the inhabitants of the territory." Today the plantations cover an area of nearly 300,000 acres, are as productive as any in the world, and are run with a labor force of about 140 Europeans and 19,000 Africans. In place of the old migratory labor system with its high turnover and low productivity, the directors of the corporation are building up a corps of labor that is stabilized, reasonably skilled and productive. They are doing it by establishing modern-style villages in each of the larger plantations, complete with attractive stores, family-size houses and gardens, schools, dispensaries, clinics and community halls and sports grounds. Not by any means all of the estimated 50,000 African men, women and children living on the corporation's lands have as yet come to think of themselves as settlers, but increasing numbers are doing so. And why not, when they can have all these things, and a livable wage in the bargain, for about four hours' work a day?

The Republic of Sudan: Agricultural Redevelopment

Without question, the outstanding instance of a successful resettlement is provided by the Sudan Gezira Board. Unlike the instances previously considered, here the resettlement was not occasioned by overcrowding, or deterioration of the land, or disease; nor did it necessitate migration from one part of the country to another. In a sense it was more of a rearrangement than a resettlement of people, for the purpose of creating a productive asset in very unproductive land, and, at the same time, of associating them as principals in the enterprise. The association took the form of a partnership between the Sudanese government, which raised capital from loans to finance the major irrigation works; the peasant farmers whose lands were incorporated in the scheme; and a private company (nationalized in 1950) which managed the undertaking and paid for the supervisory and technical staff.

As a controlled layout was essential for irrigation, the land was rented by the government from the peasant owners at the rate current before development, and the original crazy quilt of peasant holdings was redesigned to facilitate the digging of canals and the dividing of the land into units of equal size. The original owners were then installed as tenants of the scheme on their own reorganized land, provided they were agreeable to the government's terms. These were restrictive, but logical. A landlord was not allowed to take up as a tenancy more land that he could individually manage. A tenant was prohibited from negotiating the transfer, sale or mortgage of his tenancy, as a safeguard against his own improvident inclinations. Further, he had to agree to follow the rules of good husbandry that had been worked out for the region by the agronomists. He had also to agree to deliver his cash crop — cotton — to the management, which in any case possessed the only ginneries in the region.

Thanks to the readiness of landlords and tenants to accept these terms, the imagination of the engineers who designed the scheme, and the skills of those who have been running it for the past twenty-five years and more, some 29,000 farmers living in more than 950 villages on more than a million irrigated acres today enjoy net incomes unsurpassed by any comparably-sized group of African cultivators. In the 1953-1954 season the average net income was approximately 500 pounds (Egyptian), or nearly $1,500; in the 1950-1951 season, 650 pounds, or about $1,800. The figure has dropped sharply during the past two or three years owing to a combination of adverse factors (which include the loss of a portion of the once all-important British market), but the cotton cultivators are still eating regularly, and many of them still have money in the bank. Also benefiting financially from the scheme are more than 2,000 permanent employees of the Gezira Board and 150,000 migrants who find seasonal employment for themselves and feed for their animals on the irrigated land. Including the families of the settlers and employees, the scheme today supports about 500,000 people.

On the debit side of the ledger are the inability of the peasant to do what he likes with his land, the reliance on corporative rather than individual initiative, and the high cost of running an organization that cannot as yet dispense with its corps of highly trained expatriate specialists. Other debit entries must surely be the heavy dependence on a single cash crop; the alluring ease with which, until recently, the grower has made money from it; and the difficulty of finding any other cropping or mixed-farming system that would be as rewarding to the partners or as well suited to so rigorous an environment and one so remote from the world's markets.[12]

But so long as cotton is king there can be no question of the debits canceling out the credits. And even if the time should come when the

[12] This difficulty is widely admitted. In a recent note in the *Geographical Review* (October 1954), C. W. Beer, formerly Social Development Officer of the Gezira Board, put it as follows: "The Gezira Scheme is a strictly controlled cotton-production factory; and while cotton prices hold, it can give only limited opportunities for mixed farming, which will never be able unaided to carry the high costs of irrigation and agricultural administration."

scheme ceases to balance its books, it could never be written off as a failure. It has already done enough things for the Sudan to deserve ever-lastingly well of its beneficiaries. It could even be argued that without the Gezira Board there would have been no possibility of Sudanese independence. At least there would have been no revenues on which to maintain an effective independence, for the Gezira Board has for many years supplied between 25 and 50 per cent of the country's total revenue.

PROSPECTS

There is clearly much to be said for the periodic scrutiny of man-land relationships and their orderly readjustment through the medium of settlement or resettlement schemes. For such relationships are constantly changing, or being changed.

Europeans have been taking up land in tropical Africa and settling it successfully for two to three generations, but, for the most part, there has not been much "scheme" about it. Generally, the governments concerned have merely delineated areas in which European farm settlement was believed to be feasible, supplied them with essential services and left the settling of them to the initiative of individuals or private corporations. They could hardly have done otherwise in the early days. They did not know enough about the areas they delineated to warrant their assuming responsibility for the settlers. They did not know enough about the settlers to know if they would stay, let alone succeed, in a new and untried environment. Furthermore, they did not have enough money to underwrite expensive settlement schemes.

But the position has changed greatly since the turn of the century. Now most governments have a wealth of agronomic information at their disposal, though still not as much as they would like. They also have more money, and more reason for using it to increase the settler population without which their future revenues — and security — may be jeopardized. Now, too, few individuals in Europe or in Africa have the capital necessary to make pioneer farming pay, or, if they have the capital, are willing to lock it up in farming.

As a result, European agricultural settlement has come to take on a rather more planned and regulated appearance in recent years. It has not been, on that account, conspicuously more successful than the *laissez-faire* settlement of earlier years, but at least it has had some successes.

As we have seen, resettlement of Africans is more easily talked about than implemented. Peasants are loath to change their ways even when the land changes its ways; and as a rule they are even more reluctant to move, or be moved. For pastoralists distant grasses may be greener, but for cultivators the firmest earth is the earth underfoot — no matter how little there may be of it, or how stony and sterile. There are exceptions, to be sure, and their number is growing as understanding increases and crops decline. Then, too, governments and corporations are loath to sink money into schemes which enjoy neither the confidence of the peasants for whom they are intended nor the wholehearted support of such physical and economic facts as can be mustered in their favor.

At the same time, the need for "schemed" settlement, and resettlement, is yearly becoming more urgent. Already there is not enough land left to accommodate, on a catch-as-catch-can basis, the foreseeable increase of farming people in the next generation; and what remains is not always located where it is most needed. Most of the land of tropical Africa, moreover, is problem land — either too hot, or too wet, or too dry, or too rough, or simply too vast to be tamed by haphazard means. Another weight on the scale is the fact that almost every government is committed to advancing the African economically. If the rural African is to advance, he must learn a great many new skills and habits. Most of these, it is arguable, can be learned more readily, and their advantages proved more quickly, under controlled and carefully supervised settlement conditions than on a bush farm which an agricultural officer visits only two or three times a year, and which is not amenable to the use of modern production techniques. Moreover, something has to be done to stop the drift to the towns of ambitious and educated Africans, who up to now have thought of farming — if they have thought of it at all — as unrewarding and unworthy work. For such men, well-conceived settlement schemes with openings for business and farm specialists, and with good housing and living conditions, can offer much that is frequently missing from urban life, including economic security and the chance to keep family and tribal traditions alive.

But what sort of settlement or resettlement schemes are best suited to the African (or, where it applies, the European) settler's background and aptitudes? What sort do the most good — or least havoc — to the soil? And which stand most chance of ultimately paying their way? Just what is the answer to these questions, and whether the answer that is right for one place, people and time is right for any other, are matters on which opinion is still sharply divided. Of the many opinions that are voiced, two are more insistent and persuasive, and more polarized, than the rest. These may be characterized, a little crudely perhaps, as "the bigger the better" school and "the smaller the safer" school.

Members of the first school take the view that because nature operates on a big scale — and certainly there is nothing picayune about African plagues, droughts and floods, or African deserts and forests — it should be tackled on a big scale; that every weapon in the armory of technology, agronomic science, international banking, mass education and social welfare should be brought into play; that to do less is to keep the African chained to his immobilizing past, and so out of reach of the best things in life. They can point to some very convincing pieces of evidence, including, as we have seen, the Gezira Board. But the conditions which have made the Gezira Board a success — such as the presence of a wide, open and easily irrigated plain close to populated areas and lines of transportation and capable of being farmed profitably enough to justify heavy capital and maintenance costs — are not widely found elsewhere in tropical Africa. Some people would say that they are not found anywhere else on the same scale. And scale is of the essence in settlement schemes that are predicated on the employment of industrial methods of production. Unfortunately, the places where there is talk of employing such methods suffer from one or more disabling circumstances.

One such place is the Sabi valley in Southern Rhodesia. Its agricultural potential has been shown, by the American agronomist Charles D. Converse, to be enormous. It has at least 250,000 acres that could be brought under year-round cultivation and be made to surpass in productivity the Imperial Valley of California. But it is off the beaten track of Rhodesian business. It has no large local population accustomed to living in its heat, which is torrid for six months of the year. Most of the crops it can grow, such as cotton, maize, rice, alfalfa and the potato, can be grown more easily in the more populated parts of the territory.

Another example is the Rufiji valley in Tanganyika. Here are not less than 68,000 square miles of poverty-stricken, fly-ridden bush that cry out for development. The valley is only a little over a hundred miles from Dar-es-Salaam, where it would find a ready market for the cattle and crops it could surely produce on the estimated one million acres capable of intensive irrigation agriculture. The valley has the magnificent Stiegler's Gorge, across which any engineer would be happy to build a dam. But the rainfall regime is so irregular and unpredictable that it would take twenty years, according to the hydrologists, to find out how big the dam would need to be to ensure the permanence of its water supply — in other words, merely to find out how much it would cost.

It also needs to be remembered that schemes which were monetarily and politically feasible in the Anglo-Egyptian Sudan in the 1920s may not be feasible today in territories that are yearning to be free from colonial control, or are already free from it. Confidence is a fragile flower; it does not readily bloom in lands with a lopsided economy, or in those that are inexperienced in the art of responsible government and deficit financing.

Members of the second school, while recognizing that small schemes do not stand much chance of competing with big schemes, either in yield per acre or in yield per cultivator, contend that they are frequently productive of greater economic and social stability. For, in the first place, the small scheme will generally be less heavily capitalized and staffed. Its overhead costs will be much lower; hence the visible cost of operating a holding, as measured by the "cut" of each crop taken by the management, will be lower. (Most peasants find some difficulty in seeing why crops which they have grown entirely by their efforts — as they view it — should be used to help keep European supervisory staff living in what to them is unbelievable luxury.) Then, the small scheme tends to be more understandable to the cultivator. It is more "African," and so more rational, in his eyes. He can see how it works. He may even be able to identify the boundaries of his own family holding; and he will almost certainly be known in person to the management — small matters to most Westerners perhaps, but important to almost every African. Again, he is likely to be given somewhat greater freedom of action on a small scheme than on a large one, both in regard to when he works and what he grows. He is also more likely to be given a say, if only a small one, in the running of it — likewise a matter of considerable moment to him and his family. Further, the smaller the scheme, the less the likelihood of his being primarily dependent on the vagaries of world supply and demand; for small schemes tend to have more flexible cropping systems and to serve, in part at least, the domestic market. For all these reasons, the small scheme, according to this school of thought, is more likely to be able to ride out heavy weather. And nobody looking at the agricultural situation in tropical Africa can help noticing the storm warnings.

CHAPTER 6

The Wealth of
the Woods

USES OF THE FORESTS

CHIEF COMMERCIAL TIMBERS

PROBLEMS OF FOREST EXPLOITATION

WOOD FELLINGS AND TRADE

THE FOREST ESTATE

AFFORESTATION

TRENDS

A forest means different things to different people. To one it means raw material; to another food; to a third adventure; to a fourth fertility; and to a fifth firewood. Frequently it means contradictory things. To the pygmy it means shelter; to the pastoralist danger. To the administrator it may be an impediment, standing between him and the taxpayer (or tax non-payer!), the delinquent conscript, even the armed rebel. To the conservationist it is always an aid, as much in the fight against erosion as in the quest for a durable water supply and a self-sustaining wildlife.

USES OF THE FORESTS

Whether the uses to which it is put are direct or indirect, a forest means wealth. The forests of tropical Africa are perhaps its greatest wealth. Consider the moisture-conserving function of a forest — even a

dry forest. André Aubréville, whose knowledge of African forests is unsurpassed, is of the opinion that one of the most important functions of the
dry forests "is to preserve the environment of dry Africa from a deterioration that would aggravate the effects of the severe climate." [1] Certainly
nobody who has seen a dry forest degraded by drought, uncontrolled
cutting, fire and other abuse, is likely to dispute Aubréville's opinion. For,
as he goes on to say, when these forests are destroyed, "they give place
to savannas or steppes; and, after the annual fires have passed over these
in the dry season, the soil lies bare and blackened, exposed to the intense
heat of the day, to desiccation and wind erosion, and to water erosion by
the violent rains of the wet season."

While there may be room to doubt the ability of a forest to increase
rainfall, there is no question whatever of its ability to cause rain to fall
more often and less violently than it does in nearby unforested areas. This
it is able to do partly as a result of the trapping of moisture under the
canopy, partly as a result of the feeding back into the air of moisture from
the evaporating surfaces of the trees, and partly because the convection
set up over a soil-shaded surface is less intense than that over a soil-
exposed surface. And since rain falls more often and less violently, a
larger proportion of it is available for plant use, and the dry spells, when
they come, are generally less than disastrous, either to the forest or the
crops growing within it.

Neither can there be any doubt that forests reduce the run-off of rain
water. Whether bare or in leaf, the trees break the force of the falling
rain, their fallen leaves form a spongy mass capable of holding large
quantities of water, and their roots provide innumerable small channels
along which water can sink deep into the soil. The characteristically
much higher run-off from cultivated fields and from land shorn of its
natural vegetation means not only little carry-over of moisture for growing plants but also less "topping-up" of the well and spring water supplies
on which forest dwellers chiefly depend in the dry season.

According to Sir Bernard Keen, "the minimum forest cover needed in
east Africa to maintain a proper hydrological regime is around 8 per cent
of the total land area." The figure for other dry-forest areas in tropical
Africa is probably not very different. Low as it is, it is a figure far above
that attained in many occupied areas.

The provision of shade and shelter is another important indirect function of the forests, almost as vital for some crops as the assurance of a
stabilized moisture supply. No less than four of the biggest revenue-
earning crops of tropical Africa are plants which cannot flourish if exposed
to the full glare of the vertical sun, or to drying winds. Cocoa needs all
the shade it can get from taller trees. Tea needs almost as much. Coffee

[1] André Aubréville, "Tropical Africa," p. 382, in *A World Geography of Forest
Resources*, edited for the American Geographical Society by Stephen Haden-Guest,
John K. Wright and Eileen M. Teclaff, Ronald Press Company, New York, 1956.

is not quite so fastidious, but it is all the better for some shelter when it grows below about 4,500 feet. So, too, is the banana, though more as protection against strong wind than sunlight. Nor is this need confined to cultivated crops. It is necessary for the maintenance of the forest itself. Few species of forest tree, in or out of the tropics, are so "hardy" that they can survive long exposure to an alien — deforested — environment.

But, needless to say, it is the direct uses of the forest that are the first concern of most Africans and, increasingly, of Europeans. For the forests provide fuel, fodder and wood ash; oils, fruits and nuts; gums, resins, dyes, drugs, fibers and flosses; logs and sawn timber for carpentry, construction, pulp and other commercial uses, and for such domestic wares as pestles, mortars, spoons, dishes, matting and bedding, and dugout canoes.

Without wood fuel, the domestic economy of the region would be paralyzed, for almost every African and most European households cook by wood. Without wood fuel, the industrial economy of many areas would be badly hurt. Stationary power-raising engines frequently burn nothing but wood and many more burn wood when no alternative is available, which is quite often. In 1952 the Northern Rhodesian Copperbelt consumed a million tons of fuel wood, representing the yield of 30,000 acres of dry open forest, and in 1953 the amount consumed was 750,000 tons. Similarly, without wood fuel many of Africa's railroad engines would be immobilized. Exactly how much wood is annually consumed for fuel nobody knows, since much of it is unrecorded, but it can hardly be less than 250 million tons. The consumption of fuel wood in Nigeria alone amounts to "something like 50,000,000 tons . . . a year." [2]

A second major use of the forests is for forage. This is especially true of the dry forests, which, on the whole, are much healthier for cattle than the rain forests. In pastoral areas such as northern Nigeria, the low veld of Southern Rhodesia and the Rift Valley of Kenya, the ordinary herd animal would be unable to survive the drought season were it not for the dried foliage and fruits of bushes and trees.

Moreover, the burning of forests, destructive as it is of timber, provides nine out of ten bush-fallowing cultivators with an otherwise unobtainable source of fertilizer. Without it they could hardly keep going.

Scarcely less important is the direct contribution of both the rain and the dry forests to food resources. From the rain forests come the oil palm from which west and west central Africa nowadays derives so much of its wealth, the "wine" palms and the kola nut. From the dry forests come the fruits of the tamarind, the locust bean, the mango [3] and the shea-butter tree, the last of which provides not only a major source of fat ("karité

---

[2] D. R. Rosevear, "Forestry" in *The Nigeria Handbook*, Government of Nigeria, London and Lagos, 1954, p. 193.

[3] Not a native of Africa, but found growing wild in many places nowadays.

butter") for the people living within its range, but an exportable surplus to boot. From the very dry forests come a number of shrubs such as *Salvadora persica,* from which that most precious of all commodities — salt — can be obtained.

The range of the forests' industrial resources, other than timber, is impressive and becoming more so each year. It includes gum arabic, gum copal, vegetable ivory (from the dum palm), kapok, piassava (a stiff fiber derived from the raffia palms and used for the manufacture of brooms), tannin (from the bark of certain species of mangrove), sandalwood oil, sansevieria fiber, beeswax collected from forest hives, and kola nuts.

The timber resources have been left to the end of this enumeration, not because they are the least important, which is by no means the case, but rather as a safeguard against the assumption that the length of a list necessarily bears any relation to its significance. The list of timber-yielding trees is certainly long. But the fact is that, for the bigger part, it is a list of trees capable of large-scale exploitation rather than of trees being exploited on a large scale. And it is also a fact that the less the forests of tropical Africa are regarded as an exploitable resource and the more they are regarded as the indispensable prerequisite of a durable African economy, the better for cattleman, cultivator, hydrologist, merchant, manufacturer and forester alike.

CHIEF COMMERCIAL TIMBERS

RAIN FORESTS

Although the rain forests contain some softwoods, it is the hardwoods that have given them their commercial importance so far.

In the early days it was the cabinet woods, and among them most notably the mahoganies, that brought European lumbermen to tropical Africa. They still provide a large part of the export business in sawn timber and logs, particularly on the western side of the continent. The distribution of several species is shown in Figure 15.

Mahoganies and Similar Woods

The trees which in the lumber trade go by the name of mahogany belong to two distinct genera, *Khaya* and *Entandrophragma.* Both are represented in the rain forests of the Atlantic, Indian Ocean and Mediterranean (Nile) basins, but it is in the first that they are most widely distributed. *Khaya* yields three main species of mahogany, namely, *K. ivorensis, K. anthotheca* and *K. nyasica. Entandrophragma* yields four: *E. utile, E. cylindricum, E. angolense* and *E. candollei.* The *Khaya* mahoganies and the first two *Entandrophragma* mahoganies make highly

SELECTED FOREST SPECIES

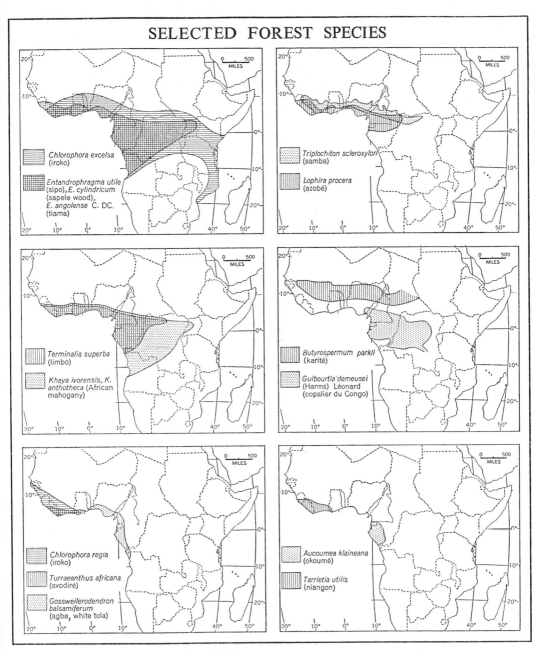

FIGURE 15 (After *A World Geography of Forest Resources*, Copyright 1956 by the Ronald Press Company, New York. Data for Madagascar not available)

desirable cabinet woods; the last two *Entandrophragma* are more suitable for general carpentry.

Scarcely less sought after as cabinet woods and no less beautiful than the mahoganies are the baku, or makoré (*Mimusops heckelii*) — the pride of the Guinea forest — and the bossé, or scented guarea (*Guarea cedrata*), which is found throughout the Atlantic Ocean basin rain forests. Both yield fine-grained, rich-looking woods of great versatility.

Other Cabinet Woods

Of the many other rain forest cabinet woods for which there is a commercial demand, the following are among the more important:

1. Avodiré (*Turraeanthus africana*). This is a native of the Guinea forest, where it is found in small and infrequent patches. Its wood is more workable than most hardwoods and frequently gives a moiréed finish considered pleasing in certain styles of furniture; when not so figured, it is used for general carpentry.

2. Iroko, or mvule (*Chlorophora excelsa*). This is one of the more common varieties of African hardwood and, luckily, one of the best. It occurs all over the west, central and east African rain forests; a related species, *C. regia,* is found in the western part of the Guinea forest. It is especially partial to mature secondary bush. Its dark-brown timber can be employed for the same purposes as Asiatic teak. Indeed, there are very few purposes for which it cannot be satisfactorily employed.

3. Various species of *Guibourtia* (e.g., *G. demeusei, G. tessmannii*) and *Dalbergia* (e.g., *D. melanoxylon*). The former are found in the Equatorial forest, the latter in the east African and Malagasy forests. Both yield richly veined rosewoods.

4. Ebony (*Diospyros* spp.). Small amounts of this wood continue to be taken out of the Equatorial and Malagasy forests.

General Timber

The full list of useful timbers is much longer. However, not many species have as yet been exploited on any scale. Of those that have, most rank either as medium hard or very hard timbers and only a very few as softwoods.

Very Hard Woods

The most important species is azobé, or ekki (*Lophira procera*), which is plentiful all the way from the Ivory Coast to the French Cameroons. In some places in the Cameroons it accounts for 20 per cent of the stands of full-grown trees. Its dark-chocolate-colored wood is used mostly for pit props, heavy construction work, and floors and stairways subject to heavy traffic. It is exported in large quantities from the French Cameroons.

Other durable hardwoods for which there is a market are: kusia, or opepe, or bilinga, or badi (*Sarcocephalus trillesii, S. diderrichii*), which is found widely in the Guinea-Equatorial forests and has much the same range of uses as azobé; douka (*Mimusops africana*) and moabi (*M. Djare*), both of which are found in the Nigerian-Equatorial forests; denya, or oken (*Cylicodiscus gabonensis*), which at present is exported on a small scale from Ghana; tali, or sasswood (*Erythrophleum* spp.), which in the old days provided a favorite west African "ordeal poison," and niové (*Staudtia gabonensis*), also of west Africa. In east Africa *Grevillea robusta* makes excellent flooring material and is being exported in increasing amounts from Tanganyika.

Medium Hard Woods

In this category the most commonly exploited woods are:

1. Niangon, or kola mahogany (*Tarrietia utilis*), a tree that is found, patchily, throughout the rain forests of the Atlantic Ocean basin. Although it resembles mahogany, its high resin content makes it unsuitable for cabinet work. It is, however, very well suited for general construction and carpentry, not least because of its excellent behavior under humid conditions. At the present time it is exported chiefly from the Ivory Coast.

2. Dibétou, or African walnut (*Lovoa trichilioides*), which belongs to the same family as the mahoganies (Meliaceae) and yields a walnut-colored wood that can be used for cabinet work. It is found throughout the African rain forests.

3. Camphor, or east African camphorwood (*Ocotea usambarensis*), which, as its name declares, is a native of the Indian Ocean basin rain forest. It favors the terrain of Mt. Kilimanjaro, Mt. Meru and the Usambara Mountains.

4. Lolyondo (*Olea welwitschii*), which is also an east African mountain dweller and, like camphor, a versatile and much sought-after wood. Both have been exploited beyond the point of prudence in Tanganyika.

5. Various species of *Afzelia* (e.g., *A. pachyloba*), which yield a wood locally known as ape or doussié. It has the same value and uses as the cabinet-class mvule. "At present little known, it is one of the best timbers of the African coast," according to Aubréville.

Other lesser-known woods of medium hardness that are coming onto the market are framiré, or idigbo, or emeri (*Terminalia ivorensis*), a pale-yellow wood that is excellent for carpentry, and bété (*Mansonia altissima*) — both of the Guinea forest; movingui, or ayan, or dahoma, or bonsandua (*Distemonanthus benthamianus*), a yellow wood also, multipurpose and found throughout the African rain forests; and, in the Guinea-Equatorial forests, two species of *Piptadenia* (*P. africana* and *P. leucocarpa*).

"Soft" Woods

With the growth of the plywood and veneer industries there has come a demand for softer woods than those used for cabinetmaking, carpentry and general construction.

The most wanted species so far has been *Aucoumea klaineana,* commonly called okoumé. Though found only in the Gabon Republic and Spanish Guinea, it heads the list of woods exported from the Atlantic coast. Its pale-pink wood is easily peeled and processed into veneers. But the supply of okoumé accessible to the ports from which it is shipped, Libreville and Port Gentil, is diminishing, so that alternative woods have had to be sought. The chief of these is limbo, or limba, or ofram, or afara (*Terminalia superba*). Limbo, like okoumé, favors land that has been bush-fallowed and abandoned; that is, it is found mainly in mature secondary forests. Unlike okoumé, it is found in nearly all parts of the African rain forest, and it has a rather wider range of uses. Some purchasers buy it mainly for cabinet work; others buy it primarily for processing into veneers and plywoods; others as a general utility wood. Up to now the chief exporters of it have been the Belgian Congo and the Republic of the Congo.

Running these two woods close in popularity is obeche, or samba, or ayous, or wawa (*Triplochiton scleroxylon*). Indeed, in some west African territories, among them Nigeria, Ghana, the Ivory Coast and the French Cameroons, it leads the field. Its whitish wood works and peels easily; in addition to veneers and plywood, it is used extensively for crates and boxes.

Other species used, though not as yet on a big scale, for the manufacture of veneers include: agba, or white tola (*Gossweilerodendron balsamiferum*), which is found in small stands between southern Nigeria and Mayumbé in the Republic of the Congo; bahia, or abura, or subaha (*Mitragyne ciliata*), a marsh-loving tree that grows in almost pure stands in parts of the Guinea-Equatorial forest belt; and ilomba (*Pycnanthus kombo*), a useful substitute for okoumé that also favors secondary forests.

Aubréville adds a few others to the list:

Equally suitable . . . are certain leguminous trees — as yet not well identified — with pale pink wood similar in color to okoumé. In Gabon these are known under the name of andoung. Ozigo (*Dacryodes buettneri* . . .), with a medium-hard pink wood, is also suited to the same uses. So is olon (*Fagara heitzii* . . .), with a magnificent straw-yellow wood that is generally moiréed; very soft, it would be splendidly adapted for veneers, and even for cabinet work, were it more common. It seems limited to Gabon and the Lower Cameroons.[4]

Softwoods are also the most important native [5] timbers at present exploited in the rain forests of the Indian Ocean basin. But here they are

---

[4] *Loc. cit.,* p. 370.
[5] A later section on Afforestation deals with the growing commercial interest in exotics.

coniferous, rather than broad-leaved evergreens or deciduous. The chief of them are:

1. Podo (*Podocarpus* spp.), which makes up the bulk of the log output of Kenya and Tanganyika. It resembles European redwood and can be used for many of the same purposes.

2. African pencil cedar, or cedar (*Juniperus procera*), which is exported in some quantity from Kenya in the form of pencil-slats.

3. Mlanje cedar (*Widdringtonia whytei*), which has provided "the bulk of the constructional timber used in Nyasaland ever since the 1890s." [6]

In all some 40 species of wood are being exploited on the Atlantic side, and a dozen or so on the Indian Ocean side, of the rain forest zone. But of these less than half figure importantly as yet in national revenues.

DRY FORESTS

Throughout the dry-forest zones the climate is rather hard on saw timber trees. Most of those that do succeed in circumventing the obstacles to their growth either do not grow to commercial dimensions or do not grow in the right places. With a few exceptions therefore, the saw timber production of the dry forests is quite small and directed to the satisfying of domestic needs — local needs at that. The most notable exceptions are as follows:

1. Umgusu, or Rhodesian teak [7] (*Baikiaea plurijuga*). This grows on the Kalahari sand formations of Barotseland in the west of Northern Rhodesia, and in the northwest of Southern Rhodesia. Because of its durability, attractive grain and deep-red color on exposure to light, it is highly esteemed for flooring; but because of the cost of getting it down to the coast, to say nothing of shipping it overseas, most of the cut gets no farther than the Union of South Africa. Much of it gets no farther than the central African railroad tracks, where it is widely used for ties. A little gets to Great Britain.

2. Mukwa, or mlombwa, or mninga (*Pterocarpus angolensis*). This is an exceptionally fine wood, "the most valuable furniture wood in Central Africa," [8] and amenable to a wide range of purposes. It occurs throughout the dry open forests of central and eastern Africa and is especially important in Tanganyika, Mozambique and the Federation of Rhodesia and Nyasaland. In Tanganyika it has become in recent years the most used timber, providing about 30 per cent of the total output. There is a large export of it, in the form of railroad ties, from Mozambique.

3. African blackwood (*Dalbergia melanoxylon*). This has a very spotty distribution in the dry forests of west and central Africa and here and there forms part of a rain forest association, but it is rarely

[6] *Nyasaland, 1953,* Colonial Reports, H.M.S.O., London, 1954, p. 70.
[7] It is not related to the true teak of Burma, but shares many of its qualities.
[8] *Nyasaland, 1953,* p. 70.

found in sufficient quantity to permit large-scale working by modern methods. It is commonly used for the making of curios and ornaments.

4. Mkora, African mahogany, or mahogany bean (*Afzelia quanzensis, Erythrophleum guineense, Guibourtia coleosperma*). This also occurs widely in east and central Africa, but its commercial importance is still small.

5. Mtundu (*Brachystegia* spp.), one of the dominant members of the miombo forests, is being used increasingly as a second-preference timber in those parts of east and central Africa where first-preference timbers, such as mninga, are running short. It is suitable for building and other types of construction work if carefully seasoned and preserved. In Tanganyika it already occupies a high place on the list of commercially exploited timbers.

PROBLEMS OF FOREST EXPLOITATION

The seeker of tropical timbers soon finds himself up against problems. Unlike the high-latitude lumberman, he can almost never count on finding pure stands of the species he is interested in. As a rule, he will not find more than two or three members of a given species to the acre. The other 20 to 30 trees will, most probably, have no commercial value; if they do have some value, the chances are that the uses to which they could be put are so different from those the lumberman wishes to exploit that he would find it impossible, both technically and commercially, to offer them on the market simultaneously. And the felling of unwanted trees in the hope of developing pure stands rarely achieves its purpose, since it is not the habit of tropical hardwood trees to live with their own kind. Only the conifers do this, and, except where they are being developed in connection with government afforestation schemes, coniferous forests are found in very few areas. It follows, then, that the useful timber potential per unit of area is generally small: ". . . a good average stand of apparently rich [west African rain] forest may yield no more than 300 cubic feet [per acre] of saleable timber and often very much less." [9] But at least it is the giants of the forest — the top-story "emergents" as they are sometimes called — that provide the majority of the trees in demand locally and for export.

Because of the very great floristic variety of the rain forests, the lumberman frequently has trouble in identifying the trees that are of use to him. At ground level it may be impossible to see the distinguishing crowns through the lower- and middle-story growths. The trunks, being characteristically smooth-barked and branchless, often conceal more than they reveal. Trees that look alike and are alike floristically may not be alike in woodworking quality. Age can beget important differences, and

[9] Rosevear, *loc. cit.*, pp. 193-94.

so can habitat; such differences are sometimes not acceptable to the buyer in search of a uniformly high-quality product.

Furthermore, most rain forest species are unevenly distributed. "Abundant in one place, a particular species may be wholly absent a short distance away, then reappear in scattered form, then, farther off, again dominate the stand, only to disappear elsewhere." [10] A species that is abundant in certain localities and scarce in others often totals less over an area of, say, a hundred square miles than a species that is always found scattered. Some species appear to live in such sensitive equilibrium to their habitat — soil, altitude, drainage as well as climate — that it is entirely unrealistic to base estimates of their total density over large areas on spot checks or general geographical considerations.

Paradoxically in view of the fantastically fast rate of growth of much tropical vegetation, most of the indigenous species of trees grow slowly. Accurate figures for tropical African trees are still hard to come by, but measurements of annual growth made in Brazilian and Indian rain forests range between one twentieth and one fifth of a cubic yard an acre.[11] There is reason to suppose that African rates are not radically different, since many of the more desirable indigenous African hardwoods take upward of one hundred years to mature, and some indigenous African softwoods, such as podo, take "about 150 years to reach millable size, that is, about 24 inches in diameter." [12]

The economic difficulties are as serious as the physical ones. Most of the area covered by forest has a low population density, a low standard of living and a high mean temperature. Domestic timber consumption is therefore small. Few Africans who buy timber can afford to buy much, and most Africans do not need to buy any; they have cheaper and more satisfactory materials than wood when it comes to protecting themselves against the heat. Even the demands of the European and Asian populations in the region are small by customary lumbering standards.

The foreign demand is mainly for softwoods, and up to now, production of these has been very small. The demand for hardwoods in the great industrial countries of the world is capable of being met, with some exceptions, by the output of their own deciduous forests. So far the exceptions — provided by woods esteemed for the beauty of their coloring, their strength and durability, and their suitability for veneers — have spelt big business in only two or three territories.

Operating costs are almost everywhere high. They could hardly be otherwise. Most forests are ill-supplied with roads, so the operator must

[10] Aubréville, *loc. cit.*, p. 366.

[11] Comparable figures for European hardwood forests are between one and two cubic yards an acre; and for coniferous forests, between four and five cubic yards an acre.

[12] B. Alwyn Jay, "The World's Supplies of Timber," *The Times British Colonies Review*, Summer 1955.

build his own. The floating of logs by river is possible only in a few localities, as in west and equatorial Africa, and even then not for all logs, since
some of the hardwoods have such a high specific gravity that they either
float low in the water and are grounded, or sink. Road transportation
of unwieldy hardwood timbers calls for motorized equipment that is expensive to buy and difficult to maintain. African wage levels, it is true,
are much lower in most forestry areas than wages in competing areas in
Europe and North America, but over against this must be set the African's
low output and indifferent technical skill, and the high cost of employing
expatriate supervisory staff. Aggravating the operator's troubles still further is his distance from the best markets. According to some lumbermen,
handling and shipping charges from port of origin to port of destination
frequently represent 50 per cent of the total cost of the timber.

Social problems exist as well. The cultivator is accustomed to thinking
of the forest as reserve farm land — to be stripped of whatever it may
yield or burned down according to the day's need. The lumberman, on
the other hand, has a very understandable horror of forest burning, forest
grazing and all other forms of interference with the cycle of forest growth,
decay and regeneration. As the demand for tree products increases, so
must the conflict of interests between forester and settler. In some areas
it is already acute and the source of anxiety to governments and governed
alike. It is not difficult for a zealot to persuade the uninformed that the
forests are being torn down to fatten the purses of the fly-by-night lumbermen, rather than being used to strengthen the status of the permanent
inhabitants of the land. But it is often difficult for a technician concerned
with maintaining water and soil supplies to persuade the same people
that there is any virtue in reserving certain forest areas inviolate from fire,
hoe and grazing animal, especially when those areas form part of their
tribal patrimony and they are no longer free to encroach on territory belonging to other groups. Thus, since 1947 the administration of the French
Cameroons has been trying to classify its forests as a preliminary to establishing a permanent forest domain, without which most of the steeply
graded land will sooner or later fall prey to erosion and become unoccupi-
able. But at almost every turn the classifiers have run into opposition from
Africans who apparently fear that the upshot of the classification will be
loss of freedom to do as they have always done with their tribal lands —
and any lands they have come to consider as their own.[13]

Some technicians also have the problem of persuading their governments that there is often more to be said for keeping forests that give
valuable watershed protection, and a "crop" of timber and fuel in the
bargain, than for replacing them with plantations of coffee, cocoa, tea,
palm oil and bananas, the fortunes of which are subject to the fluctuations

[13] United Nations, Trusteeship Council, *Report on the Cameroons under French
Administration . . .,* New York, 1954, p. 23.

of world supply and demand, the attack of crippling disease and the subtle deterioration of soil content and structure common to almost all one-crop farming enterprises.

WOOD FELLINGS AND TRADE

Table 10 gives point to many of the foregoing observations. In particular it brings out the modest producing role of the forests. Fellings in 1957 amounted to only some 6 per cent of the world's total, and over 90 per cent of them went to keep the home fires burning — the estimated 40 million compound and kitchen fires and the many thousand boilers that still rely either largely or entirely on wood fuel.

The table also shows that in no territory is wood felled primarily for export. The one apparent exception to this rule, the then French Equatorial Africa, is no exception, for (as the rubric indicates) the figures given are for authorized fellings only. The exact amount of unauthorized fellings is unknown, but it is thought to be very considerable — as, indeed, it is in almost all tropical African countries. And in less than half of the territories can the export of wood and wood products be considered a decent-sized business. These territories are Angola, the Belgian Congo, the Federation of Rhodesia and Nyasaland, the French Cameroons, the territories then known as French Equatorial Africa and French West Africa, Ghana, Mozambique, Nigeria, Kenya, Tanganyika and Somalia. Not the least interesting thing about this list is the strong representation of Atlantic coast countries. Primarily this is the result of the largest and best African hardwood forests being located on or near the Atlantic coast. But it is also partly due to the availability of cheap river transportation to the coastal ports, the comparative nearness of these ports to the industrial centers of Europe and North America, the forestry research programs carried on by the French, British and Belgian governments in their respective territories, and the postwar restrictions in Great Britain and other sterling countries on the use of wood from dollar countries.

Western Areas

For many generations Great Britain has been the world's biggest importer of timber, and has looked to west Africa for most of its hardwood requirements. The present-day importance of Ghana and Nigeria as timber exporters is, in large measure, a reflection of Great Britain's continuing demand for this kind of wood. To cope with the wartime and postwar demand, the number of sawmills in both territories was greatly increased, with consequent increase in industrial opportunities for the African worker and in the export of sawn timber as distinct from logs, which

Table 10

WOOD FELLINGS AND EXPORT TRADE, 1957

(Thousand Cubic Meters)

TERRITORY	FELLINGS			EXPORTS			
	TOTAL	INDUSTRIAL WOOD	FUEL WOOD	LOGS	SAWN WOOD	PLY-WOOD, VE-NEERS	OTHER WOOD PRODUCTS (INC. TIES)
Approximate total	97,881	8,155	89,726	2,539	436	87	202
Per cent of world total	6.3	0.9	13.3	28.0	1.3	6.8	0.5
Angola	2,400 [a]	100 [a]	2,300 [a]	44	22	—	7
Bechuanaland	816	—	816	n.a.	n.a.	n.a.	n.a.
Belgian Congo	3,876	950	2,926	120	51	24	4
British Somaliland	6 [b]	3 [b]	3 [b]	n.a.	n.a.	n.a.	n.a.
Ethiopia (inc. Eritrea)	8,062 [c]	62 [c]	8,000 [c]	1	—	—	[d]
Federation of Rhodesia and Nyasaland				[d]	11	[d]	12
Northern Rhodesia	525	156	369	n.a.	n.a.	n.a.	n.a.
Nyasaland	5,814	21	5,793	n.a.	n.a.	n.a.	n.a.
Southern Rhodesia	2,306 [e]	345 [e]	1,961 [e]	n.a.	n.a.	n.a.	n.a.
French Cameroons	2,415 [f]	365 [f]	2,050 [f]	100 [f]	30 [f]	—	20
French Equatorial Africa	1,908 [f, g]	1,832 [f, g]	76 [f, g]	974 [f]	24 [f]	45 [f]	2 [f]
French Somaliland	6 [f]	— [f]	6 [f]	n.a.	n.a.	n.a.	n.a.
(French) Togo	46 [f]	10 [f]	36 [f]	n.a.	n.a.	n.a.	n.a.
French West Africa	9,857 [f]	457 [f]	9,400 [f]	228 [f]	4 [f]	1 [f]	— [f]
Gambia	160 [a]	— [a]	160 [a]	n.a.	n.a.	n.a.	n.a.
Ghana	10,223 [h]	1,699 [h]	8,524 [h]	695	217	4	1
Kenya	491	226	265	—	4	—	15

Table 10 (Continued)

TERRITORY	FELLINGS			EXPORTS			
	TOTAL	INDUSTRIAL WOOD	FUEL WOOD	LOGS	SAWN WOOD	PLY-WOOD, VE-NEERS	OTHER WOOD PRODUCTS (INC. TIES)
Liberia	900	50	850	n.a.	n.a.	n.a.	n.a.
Malagasy Republic (Madagascar)	2,380[b]	240[b]	2,140[b]	—[f]	—[d,f]	—[f]	—[f]
Mozambique	520[a]	120[a]	400[a]	8	—	—	120
Nigeria	1,010[i]	863[i]	147[i]	367	53	13	—
Portuguese Guinea	320[a]	—[a]	320[a]	n.a.	n.a.	n.a.	n.a.
Sierra Leone	2,647[a]	97[a]	2,550[a]	n.a.	n.a.[d]	n.a.	n.a.
Somalia (Italian Somaliland)	559	2	557	—	—	—	17
Spanish Guinea	270[a]	150[a]	120[a]	n.a.	n.a.	n.a.	n.a.
Republic of Sudan	8,886[e]	111[e]	8,775[e]	n.a.	n.a.	n.a.	n.a.
Tanganyika	18,559	219	18,340	2	17	—	3
Uganda	12,851	71	12,780	—[d]	1	—	—
Zanzibar	68	6	62	—[d,f]	—	—	—

Source: All figures are taken from the 1958 Yearbook of Forest Products Statistics published by the Food and Agriculture Organization of the United Nations, Rome, 1958.

[a] 1955.
[b] 1953.
[c] 1956 plus Jan.-Sept. 10, 1957.

[d] Less than 500 cubic meters.
[e] Year ended June 30, 1957.
[g] Authorized fellings only.
[h] Year ended March 31, 1957.
[i] Year ended March 31, 1956 for Western Region and year ended March 31, 1957 for Eastern Region.
n.a.: not available (mostly insignificant)

[f] 1956.

209

comprised practically the whole of the prewar trade. The establishment of these sawmills has also increased the acceptance of the product with importers, for sawn timber is less extravagant of shipping space than round logs and carries a much lower percentage of waste. It is, moreover, easier to grade and gives the importer a better idea of the quality of wood he is buying.

In the Gold Coast (as it then was) the sum total effect of all this was — to quote from the report of a 1951 fact-finding committee — an "unprecedented increase in the importance of timber as a factor in the country's economy." Between 1939 and 1950 the export of sawn timber increased more than 100 times, and log exports 16 times. But, as is not unusual in underdeveloped countries, unprecedented increases brought unprecedented transportation problems in their train. Before 1939 timber shipments seldom if ever got beyond the handling capacity of the railways, roads and ports. By 1950, however, the unsatisfied demand for rail freight space alone was calculated to be 125,000 tons; and soon after their completion in 1951 the extensions to the harbor facilities of Takoradi, the main port, proved inadequate to deal with the mounting traffic. During most of the 1950s fellings have continued at a rate highly gratifying to the producers. It is doubtful, though, whether they can long continue at their 1957 level, owing to the approaching end of supplies in the unreserved forest areas.

The woods mainly responsible for this business, both domestic and export, are "soft" woods such as obeche, or wawa, and agba and various mahoganies; and such medium hard timbers as framiré.

The development of the Nigerian timber industry has proceeded along much the same lines as that of Ghana. Exports of sawn timber to Great Britain increased nearly fivefold between 1938 and 1951, and those of logs elevenfold, from 1.5 to 16.8 million cubic feet. The chief commercial species are similar to those of Ghana; abura and agba are more important export timbers, but, as in Ghana, obeche leads the field. Again Great Britain is easily the chief customer, taking about four fifths of the logs, sawn timber and plywood. And, as in Ghana, the boom brought its problems — almost a disaster. People without knowledge of the timber trade exported whatever was available, often of poorest quality. Timber yards in Britain were filled to overflowing with unsalable inferior stock. This, fortunately, killed the market for the exporters without experience and the trade settled down to the steady exports of those who knew their timber.[14] The timber companies that stayed in business have continued to do pretty well for themselves.

But there is at least one important difference between the two territories. In Nigeria the rivers and creeks form ready-made waterways for floating log rafts down to the coast. In Ghana there are few waterways

[14] See Rosevear, *loc. cit.*, pp. 196-97.

suitable for this purpose, and most of the timber moves overland by much more expensive, if faster, transportation. The economics of the timber business of Ghana are therefore rather different from those of Nigeria, a fact which some Ghanaian companies have recognized by placing sawmills in the center of their timber concessions, many miles from the coast. In this way no waste wood needs to travel farther than the sawmill, where it can be used as fuel for the power plant by which the mill is operated.

The non-British territories of west and west central Africa which have shared in the postwar expansion of the timber trade include the Republic of the Ivory Coast, the French Cameroons, the Gabon Republic, the Central African Republic and the Belgian Congo. They, too, have had their share of growing pains. None of them is blessed with a strong local demand for its timber products. All of them have to compete for a share of a foreign market which is still small, very price-conscious and "choosy," and subject to wide fluctuations of demand. Most of them, to begin with, were short of transportation facilities, capital, manpower and technical knowledge. Many of the pains still remain, but progress has been made, especially in knowledge of the purposes for which various species are best adapted and the processing required to put them on the market in the best possible shape.

The Belgian Congo has been particularly successful in exploiting the uses of one of its commoner veneer woods, namely, *Terminalia superba, alias* limbo, limba, afara, etc. This tree, which grows well in the very accessible Mayumbé region of the lower Congo, yields a straight-grained wood with a blonde finish much in favor among the designers of modern furniture. Not the least of its virtues is that it is a "natural blonde" and requires no bleaching. To speed production, a veneer-cutting mill was set up at Lemba in the Mayumbé region. In the first six years of its development, Korina, the trade name by which this veneer is generally known, had become the leading foreign blonde wood on the American market.

The role of the rain forest in the economy of the neighboring Gabon Republic and Republic of the Congo has likewise grown in recent years. The fellings of industrial wood in these territories increased more than threefold between 1948 and 1957, and the percentage contribution made by wood and wood products to the total exports grew from approximately 22 to 43 over the same period. About 80 per cent of the timber exported (more than 50 per cent of the authorized fellings) is okoumé; most of the remainder is limbo. The Gabon Republic is particularly well supplied with the former, and the Mayumbé district of the Republic of the Congo with the latter. As in the Belgian Congo and the Commonwealth territories of west Africa, the bulk of this export trade continues to be furnished by logs and sawn wood. Most of the okoumé is exported from Libreville and Port Gentil, and most of the limbo from Pointe Noire.

The export of wood has also increased in the French Cameroons and the territories known until 1958 as French West Africa. In the case of the former, more than twice as much wood was exported in 1957 as in 1948; in the case of the latter, more than three times as much. At the same time, the relative contribution of wood to the export trade of these territories has remained small. In 1957 wood and wood products provided less than 5 per cent of the total exports from the French Cameroons and less than 4 per cent of the total exports from French West Africa.

Eastern and Central Areas

The exploitation, for their timber, of the forests lying to the east of the Atlantic watershed has been stimulated more by domestic than by overseas demand. There is some overseas demand, notably in Great Britain, for certain species of wood, such as Rhodesian teak and podo, but the cost of getting this wood onto the market is discouragingly high. Unlike the best timbers of west and west central Africa, those of east and central Africa are remote from the sea; in many cases they are remote from navigable rivers, roads and railroads as well. And the ports to which they are tributary are on the wrong side of the continent for European trade. Fortunately the domestic demand for timber and timber products in most of these countries is already substantial and growing. This is particularly true of Uganda, Kenya, Tanganyika, Ethiopia, the Republic of Sudan and the Federation of Rhodesia and Nyasaland. In the case of the Federation, the present consumption of wood, for all purposes, exceeds the available supply, but, as in British East Africa, efforts are being made to redress the balance by various means. A small but significant part of the timber crop of Kenya, Tanganyika and Nyasaland consists of indigenous softwoods, such as podo and Mlanje cedar. The bulk of the east African crop consists of hard woods: mvule, mninga and mahoganies; that of the Sudan, of mahoganies (in the forest reserves of Equatoria Province) and acacias; and that of central Africa, of Rhodesian teak and mninga.

The countries in east and central Africa with the largest timber export business are Mozambique, the Federation of Rhodesia and Nyasaland, Tanganyika and Kenya. The Mozambique export consists mostly of railroad ties, which are in steady demand in the Rhodesias and the Union of South Africa. In 1957 the timber shipments were valued at roughly $1.5 million. Though sizable, the exports, mainly of Rhodesian teak, from the Federation of Rhodesia and Nyasaland are small in relation to the imports of softwoods from North America and Europe, and hardwoods from the neighboring countries of Mozambique, the Belgian Congo and the Union of South Africa. In 1957 the Federation exported over 400,000 cubic feet of unmanufactured wood and nearly 440,000 cubic feet of manufactured wood. In the same year it imported over 4.3 million cubic feet of unmanufactured coniferous and more than 2.6 million cubic feet of other types of unmanufactured wood, together with over 6,000 tons of wooden casks, boxes, veneers and wood pulp. The Tanganyika export consists mainly of podo, mvule, mninga and *Grevillea robusta*. Most of the increasing Kenya export of native woods consists of podo, pencil cedar and mangrove.

THE FOREST ESTATE

Hardly a territory in tropical Africa does not have a forestry problem. The well-forested territories have the problem of making the most of their rich legacy, while leaving it intact to their successors. The poorly forested territories have the problem of keeping what forests they have and enlarging them where possible, and doing it without serious dislocation of the economic and social systems. The heavily peopled territories have the problem of keeping a working balance between cleared land needed for crops and cattle and forested land needed for fuel, fertility, water supply and so forth. Even some of the lightly peopled territories have a forestry problem, for where there are not enough people to keep the bush at bay, it is often hard, and at times impossible, to wage a winning campaign against disease, such as trypanosomiasis, and the depredations of wild animals.

While no forest problems are solved by legislation alone, few of any magnitude can be solved without it. For wherever there is competition for forest land, whether for its products, its by-products or its soil and waters, there is likely to be conflict of priorities and objectives, if not of ideals. And where there is conflict, there is danger of disorderly use and, indeed, of outright abuse. With the need for land for all purposes growing year by year, and the consequent growth in competition for its use, there are scarcely any forested areas, or areas capable of being forested, in tropical Africa that would not be the better for some legislative control.

Forest Policy

But legislation presupposes a policy. This in turn presupposes a knowledge of forest resources, the needs of those who use forests, and the existence of forestry services able to organize the necessary technical and scientific programs and of educational services able to put them over. All of which presupposes the existence of large amounts of money. We need not be surprised then if the forest policies of tropical African territories frequently look better on paper than on the ground, or if most territories still have a long way to go before they are in sight of the goals they have set themselves. If there is any cause for surprise it is rather that the progress made has been as great as it is. For, while African governments have been talking policy for years, few of them began to do much about it until the interwar years or still more recently.[15]

In their early days most of the governments, and the companies to which they had given forest concessions, seem to have been so impressed by the size of the forests and their prodigal array of flora that scarcely a thought was given to their expendability. In the accessible parts of the region more wood was to be had than any African or European settler could conceivably want for a hundred years, and it was hard to believe that the lumber marts of the world would be wanting much of it when they had, almost on their doorsteps, all the softwoods they could use, and a great variety of versatile hardwoods. Although warnings were voiced from time to time by administrators, economists and foresters, and compulsory-powers ordinances were passed defining the rights of governments over forested domain, they did little good. In Nigeria, for instance, where a compulsory-powers ordinance was introduced as far back as 1916, "the notion prevailed [until roughly 1930] that the only proper way of setting about forest reservation was to talk individual chiefs into the public-spirited action of giving up part of their people's land for a purpose which they did not truly comprehend." [16]

It is true that many other "notions" were entertained regarding forest reservation and management in other territories and, for that matter, in Nigeria itself, but there is no doubt that most governments were, and are, reluctant to resort to compulsion. This has been the case even with lands claimed by colonial governments as their own, such as the Crown lands set aside in some British territories for use only at the behest of the authorities. The upshot of this is that few governments succeeded over the years in securing, or keeping, control of a forest estate adequate for the foreseeable needs of their wards. In this they were perhaps more sinned against than sinning, as their policies were usually unselfish, and often wise, but almost always unpopular. Not many African, or non-African, owners take kindly to the discipline of saving today's trees for tomorrow's woods.

One of the biggest difficulties which governments face when making forestry laws is the delimitation of rights. It is one thing to establish by fiat a forest reserve. It is another thing to get people who invoke customary rights of forest grazing, burning and cutting to stop exercising them on land that has suddenly been reserved. It is another thing again to stop people from squatting on forest land that has been reserved, particularly when they begin to run short of unreserved land and advance claims, which usually can be neither proved nor disproved, to the immemorial use of the reserved land. To oppose all such claims is often the

---

[15] It was not until 1949 that the Forest Service of French Equatorial Africa was given funds that would enable it to do anything.

[16] Rosevear, *loc. cit.*, p. 189.

surest way to produce unrest. On the other hand, to concede all such claims is tantamount to making the forest uneconomic or even unworkable. And at its best the forest is far from easy to work economically.

Forest Management

In the minds of many, the management problems are every bit as difficult to resolve as the legal and administrative problems. Consider, first, some of the management problems of the large forest concessionaire. At the start it was assumed that most of the rain forests were true selection forests, in other words, that they consisted of a well-graded series of trees of all ages and that over a span of years it would be possible to take out of a given piece of forest a succession of the desired commercial species and still leave a mature forest. Consequently, lumber companies were in the habit of cutting out all such species of more than an agreed minimum girth and of doing nothing about replacing them. It is now known that this assumption was seldom correct, for in most primary rain forests the ratio of saplings and poles to the total tree population is too low for satisfactory regeneration.

The standard "clean out, clear out" practice of lumber companies was therefore, to say the least, ill-considered. But because it is easy and fairly profitable, this practice is hard to alter. Large sectors of the Equatorial forest in particular continue to be stripped of their valuable trees, becoming in the matter of a few years worthless jungle that, if left to itself, may take centuries to recover its lost timbers. In some territories, however, this practice is being rigorously curbed. Since 1944 in Nigeria, for instance, all company holdings have been worked conservatively, that is, on the basis of their estimated sustained yield. Under this system, as Rosevear describes it, it is assumed that

the forest takes one hundred years to mature and that consequently only one-hundredth part of the forest may be cut each year, and regenerated. This would result at the end of a century in a forest of equal-sized compartments aged from one to ono hundred years. In actual practice, in order to give latitude to the commercial firms in the matter of marketing, five annual coupes are combined into one which may be worked over for various species, according to demand, during a five-year period. The agreements specify that exploiters must take or pay for all merchantable timber of certain defined species and may, if they wish, take other species as well . . .

The regeneration which must accompany this system of management is brought about by . . . the Tropical Shelterwood System. In essence it consists of gradually admitting more light to the forest floor, and so encouraging the growth of seedlings, by first cutting the climbers and clearing the undergrowth and then poisoning the unwanted trees of the middle storey which slowly die and gradually let in an increasing amount of light. Finally, five years after this treatment has commenced, the main crop of dominants is removed in the course of exploitation, leaving a sturdy crop of saplings.

All these operations . . . are carefully laid down in detail in a working plan which covers a period of twenty-five years and whose prescriptions must be closely adhered to. Although the system of control by equal annual areas is not the highest in the forester's art it is, for many reasons, the only one at present feasible.[17]

Such a system is less difficult to devise than to operate. It calls for increased operating costs, since it takes more labor to sustain and "service" a forest than it does to destroy it. It calls for a steady labor supply and, what is more problematical, steady markets to take the steady output of timber. It also calls for an acceptance of lower revenues per unit of area, and, often, per employee. Most difficult of all, it calls for a willingness to have the scale of one's business determined by the amount of timber that can be cut annually off a very small part of one's holdings rather than by the size of the market at any given time; for, as Rosevear points out in his study of Nigerian forestry, "it must not be overlooked that the first requirement of good forest management is a flourishing and little fluctuating market which will regularly absorb at least the major part of the production." [18] Unfortunately, the domestic demand for sawn timber in most territories is still too small and the foreign market too uncertain to make possible the planned management of more than a small part of the forests.

Furthermore, there is no guarantee that because this system is successful in one place, it would be successful in another. What is good for the rain forest of Nigeria with its mosaic of roughly even-aged patches and its timber woods requiring a great deal of light in their sapling stage would almost certainly not be good for the *Podocarpus* forests of east Africa, which are not especially light-demanding and seem to be best maintained in an uneven-aged condition.

Consider, in the second place, some of the problems attendant on the management of the thousands of small forests, wood lots and plantations that exist throughout the timber belt for the supply of firewood, poles, lumber, canoes and so on. To begin with, there is the problem of getting the African to use them for the designated purposes and not for farm land or village settlement. Then, there is the problem of getting him to provide for the regeneration of the trees he removes. In deforested country there is the problem of getting him to plant trees and of keeping them from premature death at the hands of the improvident. If the trees planted are exotics or all of a kind, there may be the additional problem of keeping them free of disease. The fact is that Africans are not "men of the trees." They are not yet timber-minded; they have little or no understanding of the ecological requirements of trees, or their soil-saving function; and many of them strongly object to planting trees, on the ground that they will die before the trees come to maturity — which in the case of the great timber trees is very likely, since they are not much good until they are seventy to eighty years old. To make matters worse in

[17] *Ibid.*, pp. 198-99.
[18] *Ibid.*, p. 199.

the eyes of most African planters of trees, the land planted is put out of circulation for all of this time. Consequently, instead of the usual fifteen-to-twenty-year cycle, bush-fallowing farmers who go in for tree planting need to adopt a cycle roughly four times as long and requiring roughly four times as much land. Need we wonder, then, that many African tree planters get tired of waiting for results and refuse to have any part in forestry development schemes? Or that some of those who are convinced of the contribution of forestry to the well-being of the land and its people should prefer to plant the quicker-growing exotics that are coming into favor with many lumber companies?

AFFORESTATION

Valuable as the indigenous forests of tropical Africa are, they do not begin to compare with the forests of middle and high latitudes. For the most part, they grow slowly, promiscuously and inconveniently. In any given acreage of forest, there is usually a large amount of trash and wide variations in the quality of a given species. Although every type of timber in the lumberman's book is represented in one or other of the forests, some of those he prizes most highly, such as coniferous softwoods, are either very scarce or nonexistent. It is not difficult, therefore, to make out a case for the planting of exotics that grow rapidly in pure stands of uniform quality, that are commercially acceptable, and that provide the kinds of wood and wood products which up to now have had to be imported.

Fortunately, there are many such exotics. Some of them have already demonstrated their liking for different tropical African environments; others are still in the process of being proved. Among the better performers are eucalyptus, wattle, teak, pine (notably *Pinus patula*, or Mexican pine) and cypress. Most government forestry stations now have plots on which one or more of these exotics are being grown experimentally and several territories have schemes for their commercial exploitation. The territories that are leading the way in this enterprise are the Federation of Rhodesia and Nyasaland, British East Africa and Ruanda-Urundi.

The Federation of Rhodesia and Nyasaland

Southern Rhodesia has long been aware of the inadequacy of its forest resources. As far back as 1922 it began to reserve land and plant it with imported eucalyptus, but it was not until World War II and the resulting curtailment of timber imports that the idea of large-scale afforestation schemes aroused much enthusiasm. Although imports are easy again, and on an unprecedentedly large scale, the enthusiasm has not abated.

On the contrary, the Southern Rhodesian government has gone ahead with a planting program which, it is believed, will ensure the supply, from about 1980 onward, of the softwood needs of the country. A measure of the progress of this program in the early postwar years is contained in Table 11.

Plantings have continued. By 1956 more than 74,000 acres in the Federation of Rhodesia and Nyasaland were under softwoods, mainly conifers — about 60,000 in Southern Rhodesia, over 11,000 in Nyasaland and nearly 2,000 in Northern Rhodesia. In the same year, the Rhodesian Wattle Company, Ltd., started processing plantation-grown wattle in its newly completed tannin extract factory. Ecological conditions in the Inyanga-Melsetter-Chipinga districts of the Eastern Highlands, where most of the acreage is located, could hardly be bettered. Wattle grows at the rate of six to eight feet a year, reaches maturity in eight to ten years, and yields about eight tons of extract per acre of wattle. Mexican pine begins to give a return, in fencing poles and so on, after five to six years, and eucalyptus can be thinned for firewood in its fourth year.

With a large and rapidly increasing population and less than one fifth of its land surface under forest, much of it of low intrinsic worth, Nyasaland likewise has good reason to be interested in afforestation. So far the species that have given the best results under plantation conditions are the native Mlanje cedar and some of the exotic pines and eucalyptus. A number of other exotics are being tried out, as are some indigenous hardwoods. Several plantations have been established in different parts of the territory, nearly all of them postdating World War II. As early as 1954 they were producing useful crops of firewood and poles and, in one or two cases, logs suitable for sawn timber. The government Forestry Department has plantations in all three of the territory's provinces. There are also many small plantations of eucalyptus under private management. The total area planted to trees is still inadequate — in 1957 around 16,000

Table 11

ACREAGE PLANTED TO EXOTIC TREES
BY PUBLIC AND PRIVATE AGENCIES, SOUTHERN RHODESIA, 1946-1952

YEAR	TOTAL	EUCALYPTUS	CYPRESSES, PINES, OTHER CONIFERS	WATTLE	OTHER TYPES
1946-1947	47,219	26,315	14,688	5,758	458
1949-1950	73,943	30,589	20,817	21,581	956
1950-1951	82,839	29,403	24,963	28,081	392
1951-1952	95,701	30,967	28,075	36,244	415

Source: *Agricultural and Pastoral Production of European Farmers, 1952-1953,* Government of Southern Rhodesia, Salisbury.

acres for the government plantations and slightly more for the private ones — but it is growing steadily. Given the increasing demand, it is difficult to see why this acreage should not be increased fiftyfold, or even a hundredfold, in the next twenty years. The climate is good; the favored exotic softwoods grow as fast as, and in some instances faster than, those of Southern Rhodesia. The land is waiting, for very few Africans seem to care for the rawness of the Nyika Plateau or the Zomba and Mlanje Mountains. The water, too, is there, in the rivers and Lake Nyasa, to provide the necessary power and transportation.

Northern Rhodesia has done less than either of its neighbors in the way of afforestation. But it is beginning to plant a number of fast-growing species where they are likely to do most good, as, for instance, near Ndola on the Copperbelt. Here the demand for wood for all purposes is heavy and the domestic supplies have been much depleted by the felling campaigns of the early 1950s. The most promising species are pines native to Mexico and the Far East.

British East Africa

Few, if any, of the territories are as badly off for commercial woods as Kenya. Less than 3 per cent of its total area is under forest, much of it either worthless as timber or unusably remote from where it is needed. A strong local demand for timber coupled with a ready overseas market for its pencil cedar and certain other species has only served to heighten the need for systematic planting. Afforestation and reforestation schemes designed in the 1920s to add 8,000 acres a year to the forest cover have now been stepped up to provide 200,000 acres of new forest by about 1980. In addition, the government has under way a softwood forestry scheme which should in future result in a greatly expanded timber export trade. The chief species being grown under plantation conditions are wattle and exotic conifers.

In Tanganyika there is also "tremendous scope for the afforestation of highland areas with exotic conifers."[19] So far, little has been done with conifers beyond "converting poor types of rain forest to plantations of cypress with the aid of licensed forest cultivators."[20] More has been done with wattle. In late 1949 the Colonial Development Corporation set out to plant with wattle 30,000 acres of open grassland in the Southern Highlands Province. By the end of 1955 it had planted 33,000 acres. Production of the tanning extract began in 1959 with the opening of a factory at Njombe.[21] In the same area the local government authorities, with as-

[19] *Tanganyika: A Review of Its Resources and Their Development*, edited by J. P. Moffett, Government of Tanganyika, Dar-es-Salaam, 1955, p. 659.

[20] *Ibid.*

[21] See Annual Report and Statement of Accounts for Year to 31.12.58, Colonial Development Corporation, H.M.S.O., London, 1959, p. 52.

sistance from CDC, are encouraging Africans to grow a further 20,000 acres of wattle on their own land. This scheme also promises well.

Although Uganda has only about 8 per cent of its land and swamp area under forest, the sustained-yield capacity of much of it is so high that "during the next decade or so potential forest production will exceed internal needs, and export markets may have to be developed." [22] This does not mean that there is no interest in the territory in plantation forestry. As a matter of fact, government-controlled plantations of eucalyptus have for many years supplied the bigger towns with the bulk of their fuel and pole requirements. And there are a number of small softwood plantations in districts remote from railhead which are being added to systematically. But it does mean that no large expansion of the present modest planting program is envisaged. For, in the opinion of the members of the Agricultural Productivity Committee, "future softwood supplies are likely to be met from Kenya more economically than by local production." [23] At the end of 1950 there were some 20,000 acres of afforested land in the entire protectorate. Since then plantings have been at the rate of about 500 acres a year.

Ruanda-Urundi

The Belgian-administered Trust Territory of Ruanda-Urundi has the unenviable distinction of being the most badly deforested tropical African territory. Before the pastoral Tusi (Watusi) made it their home, forests are believed to have covered the greater part of its approximately 21,000 square miles. In 1950 they covered about 600 square miles, or scarcely 3 per cent of the land. The wood yield of these vestigial forests did not begin to meet the local needs, even of fuel.

As a part of its Ten Year Plan (1950-1959) for the development of the country, the Belgian government has been concerning itself since 1950 with three afforestation projects: (1) the enrichment of the existing forests with valuable timber woods; (2) the planting of areas for firewood production; and (3) the restoration of the vegetative mantle in heavily eroded and wasted pastoral areas. The "enrichment" program has been carried out from five centers and covers a forested area of nearly 10,000 acres. The firewood program has consisted in imposing on African communities the responsibility of "afforesting one hectare per 300 taxpayers and encouraging them further to plant trees in the vicinity of their houses." [24] When the plan began, more than 81,000 acres of such afforestation work had already been carried out, for there was nothing novel about

[22] *Report of the Agricultural Productivity Committee,* Uganda Protectorate, Entebbe, 1954, p. 101.

[23] *Ibid.,* p. 103.

[24] *Plan Décennal pour le Développement Economique et Social du Ruanda-Urundi,* Ministère des Colonies, Brussels, 1951, p. 383.

this part of the program. Another 55,000 acres of land were scheduled to be planted to trees for exclusively African use by the termination of the program in 1959.

The last of the three projects has been the biggest by far. It involved the covering of not less than 250,000 acres of land, possibly more, with bushes and shrubs, and the no less arduous task of safeguarding the worst-eroded areas against slippage and washouts. Unlike so many of the best-laid plans of tropical administrators, these have not gone astray. They are already earning useful dividends in increased economic and social stability.

Other Territories

Also worthy of mention are the afforestation programs of the Republic of Sudan and Ethiopia. The introduction of mesquite in the Sudan is proving to be a most satisfactory means of checking dust and wind around the margins of the otherwise almost treeless towns of the semi-arid north. Eucalyptus afforestation — perhaps colonization would be a better word — has been going on for many years in the highlands of Ethiopia. *Eucalyptus globulus* was imported by Emperor Menelik II in 1894 to beautify the newly established capital of Addis Ababa. Today the city and its suburbs, when seen from the air, appear to be mantled in a silver-blue mist. Eucalyptus woods, most of them self-sown, have spread all over the high plateau, reaching in places to well above the 9,000-foot line. Not even the Ethiopians' ceaseless search for kindling, firewood and fodder in an otherwise almost treeless land has succeeded in staying the advance of this hardy intruder.[25] And not even the rigor of the climate, which at 8,000 to 9,000 feet can be as torrid by day as it can be frigid by night, seems able to discourage eucalyptus from growing between six and nine feet a year. If it were as good for timber as it is for fuel, Ethiopia's forest problem would have been solved by now. So far, little attempt has been made to increase, by planting, the limited native stands of the very fine timber-yielding *Podocarpus gracilior*, or to experiment with faster-growing exotic softwoods.

TRENDS

Heterogeneous though the forests of tropical Africa may be in composition, condition, location and use, one trend is clear. During the past generation the forest cover nearly everywhere has begun to acquire a new look, in the eyes of its beholders if not always in physical fact. For

[25] The total forest cover of Ethiopia has been estimated on various occasions, each time differently. But at least all the estimates are low: between about 3 and 8 per cent.

both the governed and the governors have come to realize that well-being rather than revenue is the criterion of success of a forestry program; that the chief end of a forestry policy or forestry service is to maintain, not to destroy; and that in the long run the prevention of erosion and the preservation of satisfactory supplies of ground and river water are every bit as important as the supply of cash and raw material. Young countries, as Sir Bernard Keen reminds us in his paper for this study, are in the habit of "buying" food out of capital rather than out of income:

. . . local catchments are denuded and cultivation eats more and more into the lower margins of the permanent forest. The long-term consequences are overlooked in the pressure of the immediate needs, so that forest departments usually fight a losing battle against encroachment.

Too many parts of tropical Africa have had this kind of experience for it to sit well any longer on the consciences of their rulers. More and more territories, therefore, are bringing in forestry legislation that will promote the following ends:

1. The development, through reservation and planting, of an adequate forest estate for protective and productive purposes.

2. The management of this estate to obtain the best returns consistent with those objectives.

3. The fostering of a real understanding of the value of forests among the peoples concerned.

4. The encouragement of sustained-yield and other sound forestry practices by local authorities and private enterprises.

5. The education of a corps of Africans in modern forestry principles and techniques.

A trend can be seen, too, toward greater emphasis on coordinated research, government control, multiple use and local processing.[26]

Coordinated Research

Trees are more than floristic entities. They are members of associations, or communities, which are continually changing or being changed by stress of competition, disease, fire and so forth. Different trees make different demands on, and different contributions to, the fertility and moisture resources of the soil. They have different properties, many of them still imperfectly understood. It is only reasonable therefore that they should be studied cooperatively, by botanists, plant pathologists, plant chemists, hydrologists, pedologists and ecologists. This is what is now being done at a number of forestry research centers, such as INEAC (Institut National pour l'Etude Agronomique du Congo Belge) and EAAFRO (East African Agriculture and Forestry Research Organization).

---

[26] The local processing of wood is dealt with in Chapter 10 on "Industrial Progress."

Government Control

If there is one resource that belongs to the people it is the forest, for every man has need of it and uses it when he can for its shelter, soil, fruits, game and stored-up waters, if not always for its wood. Unfortunately the line dividing use from abuse is vague and difficult to patrol. Sometimes it cannot even be recognized until it has been crossed and the damage done. Further, what is use at one time is abuse at another; and, worse, what is use under one management may easily become abuse under another. But once abused, a forest quickly becomes a tyrant. Upon occasion governments, too, can become tyrants, but at least they are in a better position than individuals or corporations to organize the needful forest-controlling strategy and to muster the men and money necessary to give effect to it. So far, those African governments which have assumed the initiative in such matters have given ample evidence that they are not tyrannically disposed.

Multiple Use

Forests are finite, and in many areas they are being destroyed faster than they are being replaced. On the other hand there appears to be no end to the uses to which they can be put, or to the users of them. It is logical therefore that the forests should be made to work harder — or, better, that their users should learn how to get more out of them while maintaining them in good order. Most Africans still need instruction in this art, for whether they are pastoralists or bush-fallowers, they tend to think of forest as a single exploitable resource rather than a combination of resources which, if wisely employed, are self-renewing and permanent.

The lumberman's attitude is not very different. He has his eyes on the trees to the neglect, generally, of the ground, and he is seldom interested in more than one type of tree for more than one type of use. In most African forests this makes for phenomenally high wastage of wood and low operating efficiency. In the Atlantic Ocean basin rain forests, Aubréville reports, "the average volume of wood per hectare . . . may be estimated at 300 cubic meters, of which about 100 might be used commercially. Current yields, however, are hardly more than 10 to 15 cubic meters per hectare, and 30 cubic meters under the most favorable circumstances." [27] To get out those 30 cubic meters of hardwoods, lumbermen may have to destroy or damage most of the 270 cubic meters of other woods surrounding them. Yet all of that wood has value: as forage, as mulch and anchorage for the soil, as a reservoir of moisture, as a screen against scorching wind and sun, and, sooner or later, as firewood. It also has chemical value — so much that Egon Glesinger was persuaded to argue a few years ago that tropical forest industries might some day out-

[27] *Loc. cit.*, p. 368.

strip their middle- and high-latitude competitors "by converting a richer and more abundant crop of raw materials into a larger range of products than even the most venturesome wood chemist has yet dared to contemplate." [28] It is true that not everybody shares Glesinger's optimism, but having in mind the rapid shrinking of the extra-tropical forests of the world, the development of processes that now make it possible to break down the chemical constitution of hardwoods as easily as that of softwoods, and the enormous hydroelectric potential of tropical Africa, it can scarcely be doubted that its forests will one day provide the basis of local integrated industries similar to those now operating in North America and Europe. Indeed, the beginnings of such industries can already be reported.

[28] *The Coming Age of Wood,* Simon & Schuster, New York, 1949, p. 59.

CHAPTER 7

The Waters of the Land

THE WATER REGIONS

IMPROVEMENT OF THE WATER SUPPLY

WATER POWER

O F all resources none is more essential than water. Yet even in a "well-known" country like the United Kingdom, nobody knows exactly how much water is available for the sum of human, animal and vegetable needs, let alone exactly how it fluctuates from year to year and from place to place, or how adequate the supply is likely to be for the growing demands made upon it. In tropical Africa the number of unknowns is larger still.

The rainfall, which, apart from underground seepages from the sea and some small ancient accumulations in the core of the earth, is the father of all waters, is quite unknown for many areas, and very imperfectly known for many others. It cannot be known accurately until there are many more — thousands rather than hundreds more — recording stations, and all of them have at least a twenty-five-to-thirty-year run of observations on their books.

With the exception of the Nile, the regimen of the great rivers — the "watermains" of the land — is still pretty much of an unknown also. We can make a lot of general statements about these rivers. We know, for instance, when they are normally in flood and how high the rise, what are their periods of low water and even, for some points on some rivers, how much water passes a given point on a given day. But only for the Nile do we yet have hydraulic data covering a long enough span of years in enough detail to enable an engineer to calculate how much water can be diverted for the purpose of, say, irrigation without at any time impairing the river's other functions.

How much water is retained in the rocks and subsoil of the earth is likewise unknown. Large parts of the region remain *terra incognita* so far as their water-catching and water-storing capacity is concerned; the same is true of the level of the water table — the level at which permanent water may be found. Practically nothing is known about the rate at which water is being lost by such processes as desiccation, induced by man and nature alike, and erosion, not the least of whose effects is to increase the run-off and evaporation factors and decrease the percolation factor in the hydrologic equation.[1] Similarly, there is a dearth of precise data concerning areal and seasonal variations in the size of these factors. It is still necessary to take refuge in such generalizations as "run-off is probably between 2 and 12 per cent of rainfall; percolation between 2 and 40 per cent, while evapotranspiration may be anything between 40 and 96 per cent."[2] Nor are we likely to be able to discard such loose generalizations until vastly more agricultural and forestry research stations are engaged in collecting data. Meantime, by using these figures, it is possible for two men to arrive at radically different conclusions about the water resources of a given region.

THE WATER REGIONS

In the absence of precise, even approximate, water resource figures, it would be pointless to attempt a detailed division of tropical Africa into water regions. The most we can hope to do is to indicate the general distribution of (1) those areas which, on the face of it, have all the water they can use; (2) those areas which have less than they can use part of the time; and (3) those areas which have less than they can use all of the time. In the first category we can place the Guinea-Equatorial and east African rain forests, the perennial swamplands and lake regions; in the second category we can place the better-watered parklands, or savannas, and the seasonal swamps; and in the third category, the deserts, semideserts, and the poorly watered savannas and scrublands. No categories, of course, are proof against exceptions.

THE PERENNIALLY WELL-WATERED REGIONS

Rain Forests

The rain forests are the one place where the annual rainfall is characteristically in excess of plant water needs.[3] This does not necessarily mean that a rain forest is a place that always has more water than it can use. It could conceivably be a water deficit area if the run-off factor were large and the percolation factor small; but in a mature rain forest this would be

[1] The hydrologic equation states the fact that precipitation = run-off + evapotranspiration + percolation + water held in the soil.
[2] L. Dudley Stamp, *Africa: A Study in Tropical Development*, John Wiley & Sons, New York, 1953, p. 89.
[3] See Figure 4, p. 52.

a most unlikely situation, since the very nature of such a forest makes for a continuous downward movement of water into the subsoil, and from the subsoil to the streams and rivers which drain the region.

The ability of a mature rain forest to have and to hold water in excess of its needs is attested by every traveler who has walked through one, whether in the Liberian back country, the Ondo Province of Nigeria, the Mayumbé massif of the lower Congo valley, or the Ruwenzoris. In the rainy season, or seasons, it can "rain" within the forest even when it is not raining outside, for each story of vegetation acts as a catchment surface and "filtration plant" from which beads of moisture are passed slowly earthward. Even in the dry months (if there are any, which is not always the case) the forest air is heavily laden with evaporated and transpired moisture, the water table remains high — indeed, it may scarcely change — and the streams continue to be amply supplied by the dripping sponge of earth that enfolds them.

Where man has made clearings and failed, in doing so, to secure the soil against erosion and excessive solar radiation, the equalizing effect of the forest on run-off is impaired. There the ground dries out rapidly between rains, the run-off factor increases, and the percolation factor decreases with consequent lowering of the water table in the dry spells and flooding in the wet spells. The equalizing, or reservoir, function of a rain forest is also impaired, of course, in hilly and mountainous country, for no forest cover on earth can long hold out against the force of gravity. And the gravity pull of a six-inch rain falling on even a 3 per cent slope — to say nothing of a 30 per cent slope — is considerable, for a six-inch fall weighs over 388,000 tons a square mile, or roughly 600 tons an acre. In some rain forest areas, for instance around the base of Cameroons Mountain, such weights have to be accommodated at frequent intervals. Under these circumstances the balance between run-off and percolation can be quickly upset, and once upset is not easily, cheaply or quickly restored. What is more, the effects of the upset are not confined to the areas upset. Loss of water balance (which implies a loss of water resources) in the hills will almost certainly mean loss of water balance in the valleys. And loss of water balance in the valleys means loss of further forest land through periodic flooding and resulting change in the ecological conditions needed for the maintenance of the forest.

It is understandable that African governments faced with such a sorry chain of causation have their eyes turned to the hills whence come both their help and their undoing. Today there is hardly a watershed in the rain forest country, and in a good many less lavishly forested areas, that is not under strict supervision.

It follows from all this that, length for length, width for width, and gradient for gradient, the most useful rivers in tropical Africa are, with the single exception of the Nile,[4] the rivers of the rain forests. This is true whether they are judged from the standpoint of power,[5] irrigation, navigability, sanitation and public health, or the support of fish and wild-life.

Because of the size of the annual rainfall — it is of the order of 60 to 80 inches — there is naturally little call for irrigation within the rain forest zone. However, outside this zone there are few areas that could not use supplementary irrigation waters to advantage in their agriculture. Of those that have already learned to do so, most rely on rivers that are fed, in part or wholly, from a rain forest "reservoir." To name only five of the more important: the middle Niger, which draws heavily on the waters of the Fouta Djallon Mountains; the Logone (Chad), which taps the Cameroon Highlands; the Tana, which drains the forest slopes of Mount Kenya; the Bahr-el-Jebel (Mountain Nile), which drains the Lake Albert–Lake No region; and the Ruzizi, which comes out of Lake Kivu whose waters are continually being replenished from the surrounding forested reservoirs.

Although it would be wrong to say that the only tropical African rivers used for year-round navigation are those in the rain forest, it would not be wrong to say that without the rain forest there could be no year-round navigation. For it is only in the rain forest that the annual rainfall is well enough distributed to make for an equalized river flow, and ample enough in the months of minimum fall to keep the flow at a level acceptable to modern craft. Where these conditions extend beyond the confines of the rain forest, it is solely by courtesy of the forest and its sustaining surface and subsurface waters. The rivers most used as waterways are the Niger, the Congo and its numerous sectionally navigable tributaries, and the White Nile, all of them beneficiaries of rain forest waters.[6]

What of the sanitary value of the rain forest rivers? Quite clearly, in a still largely sewerless part of the world, a full river serves human necessity better than a half-empty one. And because a full river is always on the move, it is less hospitable than a half-empty one to mosquitoes, snails, flukes and other carriers of disease. True, full rivers can overflow their banks and create areas of stagnant water; but of all African rivers, those of the rain forest, with their "built-in" regulating system, are the least subject to extensive flooding.

Then, again, a full river serves animal needs better than a half-empty one, and a river with a well-regulated flow better than one given to alternate flooding and shrinking. A full rain forest river not only provides land animals with an abundance of water, it provides the water at a level that

[4] An exceptional river in almost every respect, the Nile derives no small part of its waters from lakes and swamps fed by streams issuing from heavily forested country.

[5] The use, actual and potential, of rivers for power is dealt with in a later section of this chapter.

[6] See pp. 441ff. for an account of these waterways. See also Figure 16.

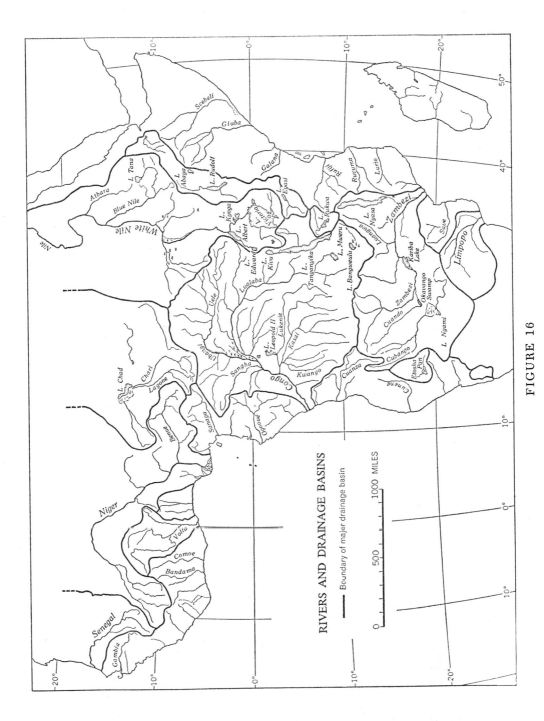

RIVERS AND DRAINAGE BASINS

——— Boundary of major drainage basin

0   500   1000 MILES

FIGURE 16

229

enables the animal to do its drinking under cover of bush or tree, and in cool shade. It provides fish and aquatic animals with more than enough food, for the production of organic and inorganic waste proceeds faster in a rain forest than anywhere else on earth.

Perennial Swamps

For every square mile of tropical Africa that catches the eye because of its relief, there are a dozen so flat that the eye cannot tell their lay without a map. Some of the land is so flat that water stops running on reaching it. Most of the land occupied by perennial swamps, however, has enough of a gradient to keep water moving, if only very slowly.

These swamps come in a great range of sizes, elevations and climatic contexts, but most of them have at least four qualities in common. First, they serve as run-off regulating systems. In the rainy seasons they take in water faster than they pass it on. This is partly because they use some of the intake to make good the losses, notably through evapotranspiration, incurred in the dry season, and partly because of the frictional drag exerted on the flow of the water by the dense and often thickly matted vegetation growing in them. By way of compensation, in the dry season (or, failing a dry season, in the drier months of the wet season) they release more water than they receive, in the manner of the rain forest. As always there are exceptions. One of these is the Okavango swamp of Bechuanaland, which has no run-off. Although many streams feed the swamp, none leaves it; what "surplus" water it has from time to time is consumed by the sands of the deserts that hem it in on three sides.

Second, because swamps typically have a high ratio of surface area to volume, the ratios of evapotranspiration to run-off and of evapotranspiration to percolation are also high. In some areas they are high enough greatly to impair a swamp's water resource value. According to Frank Debenham's report prepared for this study, it is claimed that the northern channels of the Bahr-el-Jebel swamp in the southern part of the Republic of Sudan manage to give back to the mainstream only about half the water this swamp receives at its southern end, and that the hundred-mile-long main channel of the Okavango swamp loses, by evapotranspiration alone, 90 per cent of its water intake.

Third, the perennial swamps, like all swamps, fluctuate in size from season to season, or from year to year, their regulating power notwithstanding. For obvious reasons these fluctuations tend to be least in the well-watered equatorial zone and greatest at or near the arid tropical margins. Their economic importance is twofold: they govern the siting of settlements dependent upon the swamps as a source of food, both fish and game; and they govern the distance to which cattle need to be taken for water in the dry season.

Fourth, and arising out of these periodic fluctuations, most perennial swamps have three clearly marked zones. Their outer margins are under water for only a short part of the year, following on heavy local rains or the seasonal flooding of their feeder streams. As the water subsides a sward of tussock-type grasses appears. These provide seasonal range for many pastoral groups and many species of game. The Bangweulu Flats, belonging to the Northern Rhodesian swamplands of the same name, constitute one of the most extensive areas of this kind in tropical Africa; they are seldom flooded for more than a week or so at a time, and seldom more than once a year.

Next comes a zone which is usually water-covered, or at least water-logged, for a much longer period. In the vast Sudanese swamplands of the Bahr-el-Jebel and Bahr-el-Ghazal, this is known as *toich* land, beloved of the cattle-keeping Dinka, Shilluk and Nuer for its succulent grasses, and by game for its tall, protective bamboo-like thickets.

The innermost of the three zones is occupied by the true swamp. Here there is water all the year and, on that account, an abundance of aquatic vegetation, including "floating" grasses. Starting from any firm anchorage they can find, these grasses spread outward into open water where they break loose from their moorings, or are torn loose by passing craft and floodwaters, to become floating islands, or *sudd* [7] as the phenomenon is called in the southern Sudan.

The water regime of these perennial swamps is more complicated than the rainfall regime might lead one to suppose, for the islands of floating vegetation frequently grow large enough to block channels and cause flooding, which, in turn, produces new channels, new blockages and new flooding. It follows that no survey made of a perennial swamp remains up to date for very long. It also follows that some parts of a swamp are likely to get more floodwaters over a period of years than others, only to be starved of them in a subsequent period.

The human consequences of such changes can be considerable, as the Unga people living on the Lunga Plain, a sandy island in the Bangweulu swamps, have reason to know. The island, always much reduced in size during the flood season, became gradually more and more inundated until in the late 1940s most of its inhabitants had to be removed to the "mainland," where they found themselves among unfriendly people and away from the fish supply on which they had largely depended. The cause of the flooding was simple enough. One of the main feeder streams had altered its course, and was now directing its flow onto the Lunga Plain. The remedy for such flooding is not so simple. For one thing, in an area which is either under water or more or less resting on water, surveyors have a hard time establishing gradients as a preliminary to remedial

[7] Literally meaning "barrier" (from *saadat*, an embankment), this Arabic word was originally used to describe the blockage of navigable channels by floating vegetation; by extension the area within which the blockage occurs has come to be called by the same name.

measures. For another, because the gradients are slight and subject to change through blockage by floating vegetation and sedimentation, an engineer can seldom be sure that any new channels and spillways he may construct will be anything more than temporary palliatives. And for a third, the local materials he has to work with, mostly sands and clays, sometimes prove better suited to the raising of new crops of floating grass than to the canalizing of floodwaters.

In this particular instance, the engineers were able to construct a channel with a sufficient gradient to encourage the floodwaters using it to erode and so deepen and stabilize its central portion, and with a sufficient capacity to relieve the Lunga Plain of the worst of its seasonal flooding. The new channel is, of course, subject to the same seasonal and yearly fluctuations as the old one. It is also subject to the same "sudding." Further, it is almost certain to become blocked unless properly maintained or, what amounts to the same thing, regularly navigated, for nothing inhibits the growth of large current-blocking islands of swamp vegetation as satisfactorily as constant disturbance of the water surface.[8]

Of tropical Africa's many hundred perennial swamps, the largest are the following:

1. West Africa: the Niger "delta" above Timbuktu, and the Lake Chad margins.

2. East Africa: the Bahr-el-Jebel and Bahr-el-Ghazal valleys, Lake Kyoga (in Uganda, and only partly swamp) and Malagarasi swamp (in Tanganyika).

3. Central Africa: Lakes Bangweulu, Mweru, Mweru Wantipa and Okavango; the Kafue Flats, and the middle Congo and upper Lualaba valleys.

The aggregate mean area occupied by these swamps exceeds 100,000 square miles.

Great Lakes

As a water resource, actual and potential, the great lakes of tropical Africa rank well below the perennial swamps. The lakes occupy much less of the country (approximately 75,000 square miles), and several of them are too saline, or brackish, to be of much use either for domestic or for agricultural purposes. In this category are Rukwa, Manyara, Eyasi, Balangida, and Natron (in Tanganyika) and Magadi (Kenya). Besides, few of the great lakes, even the fresh-water ones, have a big outflow, and

[8] In his paper on the water resources of tropical Africa Frank Debenham remarks that among the reasons advanced for the late-nineteenth-century blockage of one of the western distributaries of Lake Ngami, at the southern end of the Okavango swamp, is the slaughter of its hippopotamus herd. The local inhabitants of the region used the muskets the white man gave them to such effect that after a few years not enough hippopotamuses were left to keep the muddy waters of the channel stirred up, and so clear of floating vegetation.

outflow rather than size — whether measured in three dimensions or two — is what largely determines the utility of a fresh lake as a water resource. Some of the great lakes have a very small outflow. The mean discharge from Lake Nyasa, the third largest lake in Africa, is only about 170 cubic meters a second. The mean outflow of Lake Tanganyika, the second largest lake in Africa, is rather less; the Lukuga River which carries the outflow is in fact so insignificant that it was not discovered until several years after the lake, and even then (1874) the sluggish stream was so obstructed by papyrus and reeds that its discoverer, Commander V. L. Cameron, managed to pass along it for a distance of about five miles only.

It is not difficult to see why African lake discharges tend to be small when we consider the typically small size of their catchment areas — smaller in the case of the Rift Valley lakes than that of the great perennial swamps — and the fact that most are situated in thirsty land. The catchment areas of lakes like Rudolf (in Kenya), Tanganyika and Nyasa get a comparatively small supply of moisture and quickly lose most of it to the atmosphere. In this respect, too, the lakes are typically worse off than the swamps; in other words, the ratio between discharge and intake tends to be higher in swamp catchment areas than in lake catchment areas.

In the case of more than one lake a third factor makes for temporarily small discharges. Exactly what this factor is, was for long obscure. At first it was supposed that the discharges varied because of variations in the rainfall and rate of evaporation occurring over the catchment basins. However, this supposition is no longer widely supported, because it has become clear in the case of Lake Nyasa, the most notable example of the phenomenon, that the local variations in rainfall and evaporation could not be correlated, either for amplitude or for incidence, with variations in discharge from that lake, which have ranged from nothing at all to 14,000 cubic feet a second and have followed no known climatic cycles. It is now believed that the Nyasa variations are due to periodic blockage similar to that occurring in swamps. As aquatic vegetation accumulates and traps silt, a 50-mile-long "sill" forms in the shallow bed of the upper Shire River, the lake's outlet. As the level of the sill rises, so does the level of the lake and the pressure of the lake water on it. In time the sill can no longer support the pressure and breaks, as sometimes happens with man-made earth dams, with consequent increase in the rate of discharge and lowering of the lake to the level of the river bed or the residual portion, if any, of the sill. With the return of low water, the blocking process starts again. The consequence of these fluctuations of lake discharge are serious for both the Nyasa lake-shore dwellers and the few inhabitants of the Shire valley. What can be, and is being, done to control the discharge is discussed in a later section of this chapter.[9]

[9] See pp. 250-51, 262.

Considered from the water resource standpoint, or from almost any other, the most important lakes are those of the Victoria Nile and Mountain Nile, that is, Lakes Victoria, Edward, George and Albert, and that hybrid water body — half lake, half swamp — known as Lake Kyoga. These are the lakes that, along with the riparian swamps, regulate and virtually control the supply of water reaching the region above Khartoum, and do most of the regulating and controlling of the low-season discharge below Khartoum. Without these natural reservoirs, the Jebel Aulia Dam on the White Nile and the system of dams on the lower Nile between Aswan and the Mediterranean would be quite inadequate to supply the water needs of Egypt, and the White Nile in its middle and upper Sudanese course would be subject to seasonal flooding on a disastrous scale. As Egypt and the Sudan have both known for a long time, the political power that holds the headwaters of the White Nile holds a resource as necessary to their existence as air or earth. Their lands are still "the gift of the Nile"; and Uganda, in whose keeping are nearly all the White Nile's headwaters, has the power to do nearly all of the giving and withholding. Every year these headwaters give roughly 22 billion cubic meters of water as their contribution to the well-being of the Nile valley. Much of it is lost en route through the Sudanese swamps, but even as far downstream as Aswan the White Nile's contribution to the lower Nile's discharge is, on the average, never less than about 37 million cubic feet a day; at its maximum, it is well over 100 million cubic feet a day.[10]

The biggest giver by far is Lake Victoria, its average annual discharge into the Victoria Nile being about 21 billion cubic meters, or only about 5 per cent less than the discharge of Lake Albert into the same river (but called Albert Nile) much farther downstream. The size of the discharge, though enormous by African lake standards, is not so surprising when we realize, first, that Lake Victoria has a superficial area of nearly 27,000 square miles, or more than three times the size of Massachusetts, making it the largest lake in Africa and the second largest fresh-water lake in the world; second, that it lies in one of the rainier parts of central Africa (at some shore stations and on the Sese Islands the average annual rainfall exceeds 80 inches); and, third, that the lake is fed by a number of streams, notably the Kagera, that add considerably to the water volume available for river discharge, irrigation and other productive uses.

The balance sheet in Table 12 summarizes the best guesses so far made concerning the water income and expenditure of the major lakes. It is the work of H. E. Hurst, for many years Scientific Consultant to the Egyptian Ministry of Public Works. The magnitude of Lake Victoria's contribution

---

[10] Although only some 16 per cent of the average annual discharge of the Nile at Aswan comes from the great lakes region of east Africa, around the time of minimum discharge (mid-May) only some 16 per cent of the Nile's discharge at Aswan does *not* come from this region.

Table 12

ESTIMATED ANNUAL
INFLOW AND OUTFLOW OF MAJOR LAKES

(*Billion Cubic Meters*)

LAKE	TOTAL INFLOW AND OUTFLOW	INFLOW HOW DERIVED	AMOUNT	OUTFLOW HOW DISBURSED	AMOUNT
Victoria	114.0	Rainfall on lake	98.0	Evaporation	93.0
		Tributaries	16.0	Outlet: Victoria Nile	21.0
Albert	29.6	Rainfall on lake	4.6	Evaporation	7.6
		Tributaries	25.0	Outlet: (Albert	
		Victoria Nile [a]	19.7	Nile)	22.0
		Semliki River	3.6		
		Other	1.7		
George and Edward	5.6	Rainfall on lake	3.4	Evaporation	3.6
		Tributaries	2.2	Outlet: Semliki River	2.0
Kyoga	32.1	Rainfall on lake and swamp	8.0	Evapotranspiration	12.4
		Tributaries	24.1	Outlet: Victoria Nile	19.7
		Victoria Nile [a]	20.6		
		Other	3.5		

Source: H. E. Hurst, *The Nile: A General Account of the River and the Utilization of Its Waters,* Constable & Company Limited, London, 1952, pp. 247ff.

[a] Mainly from Lake Victoria.

to the Nile's water economy is clearly seen when its outflow is compared with the inflow and outflow figures for the other contributory lakes.

From the water resource standpoint the most important fact brought out in the table is the enormous size of the evaporation entries. With the sole exception of Lake Victoria, the entries under evaporation are greater than those under rainfall.[11] With the exception of Lake Victoria, therefore, the east African lakes make pretty indifferent reservoirs — so indifferent, indeed, that to dam up the outlets of any of them except Lake Victoria would be to increase the amount of water lost by surface evaporation without increasing commensurately the amount of rain falling on the

[11] If the mean annual evaporation off the surface of Lake Victoria is as high as some investigators are beginning to think it is, there may even be some question about that lake. See H. O. Walker, "Evaporation from Lake Victoria," *Weather,* December 1956, p. 382.

enlarged lake surfaces. It remains true, nevertheless, that control of these lakes is necessary if the fullest possible use is to be made of Nile waters in the Republic of Sudan and in Egypt.

THE SEASONALLY WELL-WATERED REGIONS

Savanna (including dry forest)

It is difficult to characterize simply that vast area, occupying well over half of tropical Africa, which suffers from alternating surpluses and shortages of water; for although such surpluses and shortages stem from a single cause, they assume very different dimensions in different places — so different that the casual observer can easily be deceived into thinking that in some places there are no shortages, and in others no surpluses. However, in characterizing the larger part of it as savanna we probably come as near to the truth as we are likely to get in a single identifying word, for however we construe savanna botanically, all of it consists of grasses, bushes and trees adapted to conditions of alternating dryness and raininess. The fact that there are wide areal variations in the plant associations found in savanna country is of little importance for our purpose. What is important is that in all savanna country there are times when the rainfall is not enough to maintain the water balance of the soil at the optimum, and times when, even if there is not too much, there is at least enough to so maintain it.

We are dealing, then, with country in which, apart from the presence of exotic waters (waters, that is, that have their origin in "outside" lakes, swamps and rain forests), more water is to be had on a seasonal than on a perennial basis. Just how much is to be had in any given locality, and what ratio the seasonal supply bears to the perennial, will depend on a number of factors. Foremost among these is the rainfall.

While, as we saw in Chapter 2, plant associations do not always march in step with isohyets,[12] it can be said that in general the annual rainfall over the savanna country ranges between about 25 and 60 inches, with the mean between 30 and 35 inches. Rainfalls of more than 60 inches tend to be associated with rain forest, that is, with perennial water supplies; rainfalls of less than about 25 inches with thornbush and scrub, that is, land where the optimum water balance is seldom if ever obtained and where, as a result, even ground water is scarce. Generally, also, the greater the savanna rainfall, the longer is its seasonal spread, the shorter the period of surface water shortage, and the higher the permanent water table; and conversely. In parts of southern Nigeria there are "park" savannas (whether natural or induced by the burning of rain forest it is not always easy to decide) where the rainfall is more than 60 inches, the

12 An isohyet is a line drawn through points having the same mean amount of precipitation for any specified period.

wet season seven to eight months long, and there is never any serious shortage of ground water, either for domestic or for agricultural use. In parts of northern Nigeria, on the other hand, there are short-grass savannas where almost all of the year's rainfall of about 30 inches comes in four to five months and where, for most of the rest of the year, water can be had only by digging for it and life hangs on the flow of a well or a bore-hole.

Many factors can easily give the lie to a man's expectations of water yield based on considerations of rainfall. The porosity of the soil is almost certainly the most important of these. And the range of porosity of savanna soils is wide. In the short-grass savannas of northern Nigeria, for instance, the soils are characteristically light, sandy and absorbent. Here, in consequence, the run-off is relatively small, percolation is large, and most of the concentrated 30-inch rainfall can be put to productive use. Moisture not taken up by plants during their wet-season period of growth passes on to the subsoil, where it forms a reservoir to be drawn upon during the long months of drought. The fact that parts of northern Nigeria support among the densest populations in tropical Africa, including a number of its largest cities (e.g., Kano, Zaria, Katsina and Maiduguri), is evidence of the satisfactory water-holding qualities of their savanna soils.

The lower Sobat valley in the Republic of Sudan, although it receives about the same rainfall as the short-grass savannas of northern Nigeria over roughly the same period of time, has no such concentrations of population except in the vicinity of the river itself. The main reason for this difference would appear to lie in the fact that the soils of the Sobat plains consist of fine clays, so impervious to water that a well sunk only a few yards from a perennial stream may receive little water by seepage from it. As soon as the rains begin, the cracks which formed during the dry season — ranging in size up to six inches across and four feet deep — fill up with a compound of sticky, swelling clay and ash left over from the dry-season bush fires, a compound that is almost as resistant as putty to the seductions of rain water and just about as well suited to vehicular traffic. Consequently most of the later rains are either returned to the atmosphere or sent down to the Sobat as run-off.

Colloidal clays of this kind are not confined to the Sudan. In Debenham's words, "Many of the dambo-clays and vlei-clays [i.e., swamp clays] of southern Africa come into this category and go through the same process of swelling in the wet season to complete impermeability and cracking in the dry season." Almost the only good thing to be said for them is that they do make excellent sealing material for ponds and open tanks for the storage of rainy-season waters.

Another factor that can influence the supply of savanna water is the structure. Areas of basin drainage, of which there are several in the savanna zone, tend to promote the accumulation of salt in the waters issuing from them in springs, wells, bore-holes, etc. Areas underlain by deeply fissured or porous rocks, such as the Wajir and Garba Tula districts of Kenya, frequently lose most of the rain falling on them to subterranean levels that are beyond the reach of the homemade well and bore-hole.

Still another factor is the incidence of fire. Bush fires are destructive at the best of times. Savanna fires not only destroy the season's crop of leaves from deciduous trees and bushes, and the standing growth of cured grasses, they also destroy part of the humus layer of the topsoil, thus accelerating the rate of evaporation.

Finally, the human uses, or abuses, to which the land is put have an important bearing on the capacity of the soil to hold water. Soil that is continually being disturbed by hoeing, plowing and the pounding of hooves is continually losing moisture from its top layer to the air by evaporation, and from its intermediate and lower layers to its top layer by capillary action. Once loosened and dried out, such soil is easy prey to erosion by wind and rain. In large areas of east Africa the annual loss of soil through erosion is equaled in the hierarchy of evils only by the annual loss of water through the accelerated run-off that comes in its wake. There are hillsides in the Somalilands and Kenya, for instance, which shed water almost as quickly and completely as a pitched roof.

While savanna water is "where you find it," like gold it is more easily found when you know where to look for it. In the wet season, it usually takes very little finding, except in badly eroded country of the kind just mentioned. Then rivers are high to overflowing, the level of wells and bore-holes rises, ponds and natural depressions fill up with muddy run-off waters, and springs increase their yield. In the dry season, most rivers other than those that draw upon the waters of the perennially wet regions retreat into their sandy, silt-laden beds, ground water levels fall, ponds and depressions dry out, and the yield of springs declines, sometimes catastrophically. As every savanna dweller knows, at such times it is not always possible to find water where you expect to find it; but, as he also knows, where there is greenness in grass and new growth in trees and bushes, there is moisture. Accordingly, to seek out the areas of verdure is as likely a way as most of finding water. The presence of trees and bushes in an area otherwise devoid of them, of tall trees and bushes in an area of dwarfed vegetation, and of a thick sward in an area of sparse and discrete grasses, all bespeak the presence of underground water either in abnormal amount or at less than normal depth. Some would wish to carry the connection between plant association and water supply much further, claiming that the depth of the dry-season water table can frequently be correlated with the dominants found in a given plant association. The trouble with this, however, is that a man might die of thirst while establishing a correlation, for many savanna trees go down a very long way for their water.

Seasonal Swamps

Many of the seasonal swamps occur inside the savanna (including dry forest) zone, but enough occur outside it to warrant their separate mention.

In origin seasonal swamps are much the same as perennial swamps. They arise wherever the lay of the land, the soil, the vegetation and the climate conspire to make rainy-season waters congregate in a locality faster than they can disperse, or be dispersed. The main respects in which they differ from the perennial swamps are in regard to duration, size and role of vegetation. Depending on their physical location, they may last from a few weeks, as in the semi-desert foothills of the Ethiopian Highlands, to almost the full year, as in some of the more humid parts of Tanganyika and the Rhodesias. In a year of subnormal rainfall, those in the semi-desert areas may be swamps only in name. In a year of more than normal rainfall, those in the humid zones may turn "perennial." As for size, they are mostly small; and those that are large have neither the area nor the volume of the large perennial swamps. If they had, the chances are that they would be able to survive the rigors of the dry season and so change their category. Being seasonal they offer very little scope for the development of true "aquatics" and *sudd*. Their place is taken by reeds, sedges and damp-loving bushes which, because they must survive a dry season, are firmly and deeply rooted. As a result, the seasonal swamps produce little in the way of shifting channels and the drowning and drying that accompanies the shifting. And because reeds, sedges, etc., do not produce channel blockages as readily as *sudd*, seasonal swamps do not grow upstream by ponding back the incoming waters as fast as perennial swamps. On the other hand, they do not seem to have much difficulty in growing downstream. Indeed, one of the strangest characteristics of seasonal swamps (and also of some perennial swamps) is their ability to grow down a slope, a phenomenon that is no doubt due partly to their shallowness and the consequently greater frictional drag of the soil, and partly to their large population of rooted plants, which likewise slows down the surface movement. In some places, such as Kigezi in Uganda, swamps have been found on slopes with a gradient high enough to produce a four-knot current in a free channel.

But, fluctuating and ephemeral as they are, seasonal swamps are far from being a negligible source of water. While they last, they supply the irrigation and household needs of their shoreline inhabitants, and drink for the game and — provided they are not in tsetse fly country — for the domestic animals that seek them out. In the dry season they may frequently be exploited for their subsurface supplies through shallow wells and water holes; many seasonal swamps can be made to yield a year-round water supply in this way.

The exact number of such swamps is unknown, partly because no attempt has ever been made to count them and partly because their number is not constant. As the result of changes in the water balance of a catchment area, induced by such things as deforestation, soil erosion, cultivation and river control, new ones are always being formed and old ones drying out. Some, in these days, are being drained for permanent use as pasture or crop land. But their total number is certainly more than 10,000, and could conceivably be more than 100,000 if account were taken of every patch of land known to be under water from time to time.

Their distribution comes as near to being pan-tropical African as that of any discontinuous physical phenomenon. At the same time it is very far from being uniform. For obvious reasons the very wet and very dry areas have the smallest number of such swamps, and the areas of high, seasonally concentrated rainfall have the largest. This is to say that most of them are found in the south of the Belgian Congo, Angola, Mozambique, east Africa, Nyasaland and the Rhodesias. In the north of Northern Rhodesia aerial surveys show that up to one quarter of the land surface is shared between dry *dambos,* or seasonal swamps, and wet *dambos,* or perennial swamps. Even if — as is not improbable — the wet *dambos* have the lion's share, this still leaves the northern half of the territory with something like 25,000 to 30,000 square miles of seasonal swamps.

THE PERENNIALLY ILL-WATERED REGIONS

Perennially ill-watered regions constitute the largest of the three major water regions. Precisely how much perennially ill-watered land there is is a matter of dispute, for want of adequate rainfall and evaporation data or an objective definition of the term. However, very approximately it can be said that the area in which there is, on the yearly average, insufficient water to meet the demand is of the order of 3.25 million square miles, or about two fifths of the land surface of tropical Africa. In about one third — perhaps more — of this area, the rainfall is so small as to be inconsequential; this is the domain of the true desert. The rest may be designated as semi-desert.

Semi-desert

Throughout the region of semi-desert the annual rainfall is generally less than 15 inches and in many localities less than five; it is unreliable in occurrence — annual fluctuations of almost 100 per cent from the mean are not unknown; and it is torrential in nature — a year's rainfall can come in a shower. Very little of the rain stays where it falls; the little that does soon evaporates into the arid air or sinks out of sight.

All that is out of sight is not out of circulation, however. In fact, as Debenham reminds us, a semi-desert often makes more efficient use of its meager water income than many better-endowed areas.

No coarse-grained rock can withstand for long a direct sun heat of up to 200°F by day and a drop to near freezing point by night. The individual crystals, each with a slightly different rate of expansion, work themselves loose and flake off as sand or chips of rock . . . Into this rock waste such rain as falls sinks rapidly to the best place for water in such a climate — underground. The proportion of the rain which sinks into the ground is higher in a sandy desert than anywhere else . . . probably well over 50 per cent in a heavy storm.

Once underground, the rain is protected from heavy evaporative loss by the overlying mantle, which, because it is full of air pockets, makes a good insulator. Finding it again, however, can often be a trouble. Some of it, of course, is never found again; it is simply swallowed up by the earth. The best place to look for the rest is in low ground, since all water running freely obeys the law of gravity. The troughs between fixed sand dunes, the outer margins of the "fans" that form at the foot of mountains, and the beds of seasonal streams — these are the kinds of places where ground water congregates and comes to the surface.

In sinking through the top of a new dune, rainstorm waters pick up some of the finer wind-blown particles and carry them toward its base. If this process goes on long enough, it brings about a stratification of the dune into an upper, extremely porous sand zone and a lower, water-shedding zone of fine clays mingled with coarser sands. Thereafter, percolating storm waters on reaching this zone are constrained to move sideways to the outer margins of the dune, rather than earthward. This constraint is well known to the dune dwellers and frequently exploited by them in such crop-raising and pastoral activities as they are able to follow. Typical of this regime is the country beloved of the Baggara tribes in southwest Kordofan and southeast Darfur (Republic of Sudan), where the annual rainfall is about 10 inches, and around the borders of the Kalahari, where animals take more advantage of it than humans.

In the aggregate, foothill fans probably provide a more abundant source of water than sand dunes. They have a heavier rainfall, since even in deserts mountains "attract" clouds and clouds precipitate moisture, and they also receive run-off from their parent rocks. Like the dunes they hide most of what they receive. In some cases, it is true, they hide it too well; but in others, a majority, they conduct it to points on their outer margins where it can be turned to good account. The way of water through a foothill fan is such that the amount of water penetrating to the attenuated extremities of the fan increases gradually over a period of time, thanks to the "sealing" of the ground by the suspended sands and silts. With each outward extension of the "sealed" zone goes an increase in the ratio of horizontally to vertically moving run-off waters and so in the amount of water penetrating to the extremities of the fan. Paradoxically, therefore, the farther the source of the water, the nearer the supply.

These fans are widely distributed. They are found at the base of almost all the mesa-like hills and mountains that pierce the desert and semi-desert skyline. They are especially common in the Sahara and bordering parts of the Republic of Sudan. They are also found in the Somalilands, Ethiopia and the northern part of Kenya. They are uncommon in the much less well articulated landscapes of the Kalahari and Namib deserts of Southwest Africa and Bechuanaland. Although much exploited, as, for example, by the Nuba people of the mountains of the same name in Kordofan and the Arabic-speaking tribes of northern Sudan, they are probably the one underexploited source of ground water in arid Africa. It is not every society that has acquired the knack of tapping this underground supply at its most rewarding points, or of using what it taps with efficiency.

The most widespread source of water in this half-dead, half-living world is, again paradoxically, the "dry" stream. It is found wherever rain falls; it may sometimes be found even where no rain is known to fall, if the floodwaters it carries are strong enough to push it out beyond the receiving zone. It goes by different names in different parts, the most usual being wadi or *oued, khor,* or, more simply, sand river. The dry stream provides, so to speak, the guttering of the semi-desert world. Like most gutters, it is more often empty than full, and when full, given to spillage. For if there is one desert water rule that is more often honored in the observance than in the breach it is this: all storm waters sooner or later exceed the capacity of their beds to contain them, to the undoing of their dependent peoples. But unlike the man-made gutter, the wadi does not pass on all it receives. Often it holds back as much as, if not more than, it passes on. The part held back replenishes the depleted water table. Unfortunately, not all of this water is as useful as one could wish. Much of it does not stay around long enough to raise a crop or support a settlement, and most of the spillage waters, for example those feeding the Saharan *sebkhas* (small ponds), are brackish. Where it is durable and fresh, it is the very water of life — of man and beast, as well as plant.

Of possibly similar origin and serving a similar function, if generally less "serviceable," are the pans which cover so much of the Kalahari. They are shallow depressions that gather up the occasional storm waters falling in their catchments. They have, to quote Debenham, "more rounded outlines than one would expect if they were filled-in ancient channels or wadis, yet they tend to run in chains or series in many places. Usually one side of the depression is higher than the other, denoting, no doubt, that the drifting sand of a more arid epoch was held up by vegetation or moisture on the windward side." Their flat-as-a-pancake surfaces consist for the most part of the finest of fine silts, or

loess (windborne) soils, that hold water more efficiently than the surrounding sands. However, because of their low depth-to-volume ratio
they seldom manage to hold it for more than a few weeks. They are
also inferior to the wadi in another respect: once their surface water has
disappeared, practically none can be had by digging for it. The subsoil is damp, but rarely saturated. About the only way water can
be squeezed from it is by following the primitive, and now almost
obsolete, practice of the Bushman woman. She searches for the dampest
spot she can find in the pan and hollows it out with her hand to arm's
depth, inserts into the hole a hollow grass stem which she surrounds with
fine grass or roots, then fills in the hole with earth. After waiting an hour
or so, she starts sucking at the exposed end of the stem. At the end of
ten to twenty minutes of very visible effort she will, with luck, begin
drawing water; this she will transfer to an ostrich egg or a container of
similar size against the day of need. A clever trick, to be sure — but
not half as easy as turning a tap or lifting a pump handle, which some
Bushmen are now more than pleased to do.

Desert

The exact size of the water resources of the tropical African deserts
is unknown, and perhaps unknowable. Since these lands have no regular
rainfall, they have no regular "domestic" waters other than those derived
from dew and fog, and therefore next to no waters amenable to direct
measurement. Their waters are of "foreign" — exotic — origin. They
mostly travel by underground courses, that can only be surmised, from
distant mountains and plateaus the run-off from which is not known, to
oases, wells and bore-holes whose yields are still, with few exceptions,
unmeasured. Those that travel overground can, of course, be measured,
but almost the only surface "supply line" of any consequence to a desert
is the Nile, and the yield of this river in its desert section (northern
Sudan) is capricious. About all that is known with assurance is that few
deserts are bone dry; that many deserts have more ground water than is
being, or has ever been, put to productive use; and that the use of such
water almost always poses problems.

Perhaps the nearest tropical Africa comes to complete aridity is in the
Namib Desert. This is the desert that skirts the coast of Southwest Africa
from the Orange River to the Cunene River in southern Angola. Almost
the only moisture it can lay claim to, other than subsurface waters, of
which little as yet is known, is the fog which forms over the cold adjacent waters of the Benguela current and is carried inshore periodically
by westerly winds. Once in a while the fog is thick enough to amount to
drizzle and to bring into being a short-lived crop of herbaceous plants
that provide food and moisture for migratory game.

In the Sahara there are large elevated areas that likewise have no regular expectation of rain, but get nightly falls of dew during the cooler months of the year. As a source of water supply for man such falls have an almost negligible value, but for many desert animals (including several species of gazelle and lizard) and plants they are life-giving.

Foolish as it would be to imply that nothing is wrong with any of the deserts that a good system of artesian wells and bore-holes cannot put right, it is arguable that a great deal more, and better, use could be made of their ground water supplies. This is thought to be especially true of the Ahaggar and Tibesti Mountains. The windward slopes of these mountains, for all their remoteness from the sea, have a high enough rainfall to support tree growth, a very rapid run-off because of the large expanse of bare rock offered by them, and no surface drainage to speak of. Opinion is divided on what happens to this water. Possibly, as some have suggested, part of it penetrates as far afield as the oases of the northern and southern Sahara. If it does, so much the better for the oases dwellers. But certainly not all of it can get that far, and, in any case, there must be less wasteful ways of using scarce water than to let it disperse through 800 miles of deeply fissured, leaky underground channels. To draw off some of this water closer to the mountains would seem to be the beginning of water wisdom, and of prosperity, for the people living there. They might have to dig a long way to reach it, however; for, to give the converse of our earlier paradox, the nearer the source, the farther — down — the supply.

Depth is only one of the problems the water seeker in the desert has to contend with. Salinity can be a very serious problem. Even in the valley of a river like the Nile 20 per cent of all wells dug are said to be too saline for drinking purposes. And the farther one goes from a fresh-water source, the greater the incidence of undrinkable springs, wells and bore-holes, and the higher their salinity. Then, in areas where ground water is pumped to the surface, it frequently happens that the longer the pumping goes on, the saltier the water becomes. In some maritime areas none of the ground water is drinkable. Nor is it merely a question of the water having too much salt. Much of the ground water of the Sahara contains other chemicals, such as iron and manganese oxides, that fur the walls of wells and bore-holes. If left undisturbed, this furring process will bring about a complete stoppage of the water supply, within ten years in many instances.

Temperature is another problem. Water that is brought up from considerable depths, as artesian waters are, may be too hot for the convenience of the plants and animals needing it. The temperature of water derived from many of the deeper Nile valley wells is over 100°F.

Lastly, there is the problem of knowing where to look for the ground water. In the desert even the most accomplished dowsers have trouble in divining water a thousand feet or more below a clueless surface.

IMPROVEMENT OF THE WATER SUPPLY

By now it must be apparent that most of tropical Africa has water problems. Alternating seasonal surpluses and deficits ill serve the needs of
man and beast, and perennial surpluses can be almost as impeding as
perennial deficits. Deficits spell dryness, dearth and economic instability;
surpluses spell waterlogging, flooding and lost economic opportunity.

To solve these problems is easier said than done. In the first place, it
is often difficult to persuade the African cultivator or pastoralist that
the only way to stop flooding in the valleys is to stop overworking, and
eroding, the hills. Second, the scale on which nature operates over much
of this part of the world is too large for water problems to be amenable
to attack on the parochial level; yet frequently the financial resources
required to tackle such problems on a scale commensurate with
the need are lacking. Third, because water is used for many purposes,
conflicts of interest understandably arise when a water development
scheme is proposed. A dam built to supply the turbines of a hydroelectric power plant can easily be construed by farmers as a water-stealing
device, just as the canalization of a marsh for the purpose of decreasing
surface loss of water can easily be seen by fisherfolk as a threat to their
livelihood. Fourth, the manipulation of an existing water source can
easily produce as many physical problems as it solves. Although dams
do not "steal" water, they often steal fertility by trapping the silt on
which floodland farmers rely for the renewal of their exhausted soils;
likewise, the canalizing of a marsh may cause it to disappear entirely.

Yet much can be done to make better use of water already available
in an area, if not always to increase the amount available.

A number of simple water-conserving devices are now in common use.
One of the most satisfactory of these is the "subsand" dam. Where the
sand bed of a river is underlain at no great depth by an impervious formation, the construction of a cement barrier across it is a sure way of holding
back some of the water that would otherwise escape downstream. The
water held back can be drawn off as needed through a stop-cock or a
length of tubing inserted in the face of the barrier. The fact that this
water lies below the surface of the sand (for in time the bed of the
sand rises to the top of the barrier) means that the loss of water by
evaporation is much smaller than it would be in the case of an "open"
dam of the same water capacity. In the postwar period many hundreds
of such barriers have been thrown across the beds of rivers in British
East Africa and central Africa. They cost little to build, for labor is
cheap — often freely given for this sort of community enterprise — and
the stream bed is full of rock rubble and sand needed for the making of
the concrete. Cement is the only major item of expense, and in a simple
structure of this kind a few bags of cement go a long way. Upkeep costs
are negligible, except when the sand becomes infiltrated by fine silts that

decrease its water-carrying capacity — as happens periodically in areas which are subject to topsoil erosion.

The principle of the subsand dam can be applied equally well to springs. In the rainy season almost every steep hillside in tropical Africa has a spring line, that is, a level where ground water comes to the surface because it has come up against a layer of rock that stops its further downward percolation. Often all that a man needs to do to increase the seasonal life of such a spring — perhaps even to make it perennial — is to dig a broad V-shaped trench in front of it, fill the trench with clay from the nearest anthill, and insert a short length of pipe through the apex of the V into the parent rock beyond. The waters of the spring will then remain "on tap" behind the trench instead of seeping downhill uselessly, and can be drawn off as required.

Scarcely less effective as a water conserver is the check-weir. Its primary purpose, as its name suggests, is to stagger the floodwater flow of the stream across which it is thrown. It is built of boulders, tree trunks, brushwood, sods, and anything else that comes handy. To serve its purpose efficiently it should be placed where the run-off tends to be greatest, that is, near the headwaters. The more check-weirs there are on a stream, the more effective the staggering is likely to prove. So far, however, they have not been nearly as popular with the African as the subsand dam, perhaps because it is difficult to persuade him that the raising of the water table which results from the checking of the run-off has the same effect on the dry-season yield of a river as the damming of the river itself. It is equally difficult to convince some Europeans that a seasonal stream can have its high-water period extended and its dry period reduced, or even eliminated, by the building of such rough-and-ready devices at close intervals along it.

The check-weir technique can also be used to advantage in areas formerly covered by marsh. To stop the deep soil erosion that is likely to follow in the train of a disappearing *dambo*, engineers are coming to look with increasing favor on the use of "no-fines" cement dams. Being made solely of cement and gravel, such dams allow water to pass through while checking its velocity enough to make it drop its silt load. In this way the eroded gulley above the dam gradually fills up and a new *dambo* is formed.

Another device of great use in flattish country is the open tank, so placed as to receive the run-off of as much as possible of the land surrounding it. In the old days, tank digging was inclined to be laborious, for it was impracticable to go down any depth when all the excavating had to be done by hand and hoe. It was also inefficient, since a shallow tank soon dries out in a climate where the dry season lasts six to eight months and the loss of surface water by evaporation during that period may be as much as ten inches a month. Now that mechanical excavators can be put onto the job, tank digging has become much easier. The past few years have seen an increase in the number of large, deep tanks, especially in the semi-arid Somalilands, where they are used to irrigate grain crops and keep cattle alive in the dry season, and in northern Kenya and the central part of the Republic of Sudan, where they are used to water stock. The Sudanese believe that with the help of such tanks they will eventually be able to strengthen the present feeble economy of an area covering 300,000 square miles. In the whole of tropical Africa there are probably not less than 2 million square miles of land that would stand to gain from a tank-digging program. Most of this is found in the "horseshoe" of plateau country that hems in the rain forest on three sides.

Among the many other simple devices in common use are the following, all of them as much soil- as water-conserving in function: contour plowing and ridging of hillsides; planting of soil-fixing grasses and crops wherever run-off is high; afforestation and reforestation of watershed areas; and the basin-listing of level land (to increase percolation).

These, then, are ways of conserving water. What of the ways of increasing the amount available to deficit areas? Almost every territory already has a program of well digging, bore-hole drilling and water pumping, and in quite a few territories the scale of the program is impressive. Between 1951 and 1955 the government of northern Nigeria built 4,900 concrete-lined wells and 167 bore-holes. Eventually it expects to have one water point (not necessarily a ground water point) for every 500 persons. In the Eastern Region of Nigeria more than 12,000 water points were provided between 1946 and 1956. The government of the then Gold Coast made available to rural communities more than 2,000 wells and 65 bore-holes between 1950 and 1955. In Nyasaland more than 500 successful bore-holes were sunk in rural areas between 1950 and 1956. In Tanganyika, at the end of 1956, gravity pipelines and hydraulic pumps were yielding more than 12 million gallons a day, and bore-holes about as much again.

Although not many Africans yet know how to maintain properly even the simplest kinds of hydraulic equipment, there is no lack of appreciation of its advantages. The water that comes out of a pump is usually perennial. The labor involved in getting it from a pump is much less than that involved in getting it from a spring or a stream, for, so far as possible, wells and bore-holes are placed where they are most needed, that is, near villages and grazing grounds. And many Africans have already come to see that a pumped water supply enables them to lead healthier and more substantial lives.

The Makonde water development scheme in the Southern Province of Tanganyika epitomizes the problems of a community living in a water deficit area and the benefits that accrue when the water pump is brought to its aid. The Wa'Makonde settlers of the Makonde plateau, driven there by hostile neighbors, had as their sole supply of water during the four-month-long dry season springs issuing near the base of the plateau's thousand-foot southern escarpment. At first they settled near the edge, but as their numbers grew and they spread farther and farther back, some had to walk 24 miles a day eight months a year to get water. In 1952 the government began piping water from a small pumping station at the spring line to Newala two and a half miles away on the edge of the plateau. In 1954 the pipeline was carried six miles farther over the plateau. Encouraged by the readiness of the Wa'Makonde to pay a nominal charge for the water so obtained, the government set up a water development corporation in 1955. The Makonde Water Corporation, as it is called, is now engaged in piping water all over the plateau, so that nobody living there will be more than an hour's walk (still enough, to be sure) from a metered, automatic water dispenser. The people with water are able to spend more time cultivating their land, and the additional crops they are getting more than cover the cost of the water. They are no longer under a strong compulsion to crowd, and exhaust, the plateau margins adjacent to the springs. They have time for leisure and for the development of community interests that arise when men build their homes around a focal point — and on the Makonde plateau nothing is more "focal" than a water point.

But, as we have already hinted, the problem of improving the water supply does not everywhere lend itself to the installment approach, or to rule-of-thumb techniques.

The problem of increasing the delivery of water from the upper White Nile system to the droughty down-river areas is an example. At the present time approximately half of all the water reaching the Sudd region is evaporated. To increase the discharge rate of the great Nile lakes without at the same time decreasing the evaporation rate in the Sudd would clearly be of very little advantage to the irrigation farmers of the Nile valley. No less clearly, the problem of decreasing this rate over an area that is more fluid than solid and covers some nine to ten thousand square miles is hardly likely to be solved by small patchwork operations, let alone by Africans equipped with hoes and canoes. It can be solved only by treating the White Nile as a single hydrological unit and by exposing it to the kind of engineering undertaken in the Tennessee valley.

So far the engineers have not been given the approval of the riverside governments, or the money, they need to put their ideas to work, but nobody doubts that they will be given both, or that the scale of their planning, and the nature of it, matches the scale and nature of the phenomena they are seeking to control. In a word, what they propose to do is to build a canal from Jonglei (7°N) to a point downstream between the mouths of the right-bank tributaries of the Bahr-el-Zeraf and the Sobat. This canal would be able to carry about half the amount now going into the Sudd and deliver nearly all of it to the White Nile, for the evaporation loss from a 16-foot-deep, 390-foot-wide and 175-mile-long canal would, it is estimated, be no more than a tenth of what it now is from the surface of the Sudd and the channels of the Bahr-el-Jebel between the same two points. There would be a further saving as well, since with so much water diverted into the Jonglei Cut (as the planners call it), there would be much less flooding of the Bahr-el-Jebel and the Sudd, and so a much smaller evaporating surface for the sun and the air to work upon.

To reap the maximum profit of such a scheme, it would be necessary to stabilize the now seasonally irregular flow of water, both through the cut and through the existing channels. The best way to do this, it has long been agreed, is by increasing the storage capacity of the Bahr-el-Jebel's headwater lakes. And this can now be done. Thanks to the building of the Owen Falls Dam across the Victoria Nile at Jinja, the maximum level of Lake Victoria is theoretically capable of being raised by more than four feet. If and when it is raised by this amount, the lake will constitute the largest reservoir in the world, with an area of considerably more than 27,000 square miles, and have a usable capacity of about 100 billion tons or 80 million acre-feet.[13] From such a vast "storage tank," it would be possible, in the long run, to bring Lakes Kyoga and Albert to the level where any increase in the discharge from Lake Victoria would lead to a like increase in the discharge from these lakes, and so in the volume of water delivered to the Bahr-el-Jebel and the Jonglei Cut. We say "in the long run" with good reason, for the topping-up process might well take the better part of a hundred years to complete. Once it was complete, though, the region's biggest water problem, that of decreasing the surplus of the wet season and the deficit of the dry season, would have been solved. H. E. Hurst, one of the chief minds behind both Century Storage (as the lake regulation scheme is called) and the canalization of the Sudd, has summarized the expected changes in the following words:

> The effect . . . will be to produce more uniform conditions on the Bahr-el-Jebel and in the swamps, but they will be different from those now existing. The average regulation will send down approximately two-thirds of the [annual] supply during the months January to June, and the other third in the remainder of the year . . . The general result will be to make the annual supply very much more uniform, but to invert the seasons by making the discharge of the low season high and that of the high season low. The rainfall on the swamps and neighbouring country will not be altered. This change of the régime of the river will have far-reaching effects on the country and the life of its inhabitants, as far even as Kosti [13°N].[14]

[13] See H. E. Hurst, *The Nile: A General Account of the River and the Utilization of Its Waters,* Constable & Company Limited, London, 1952, p. 153. An acre-foot is the amount of water that will cover an acre to a depth of one foot.

[14] *Ibid.,* p. 307.

Water supply problems of comparable magnitude are posed by Lake Nyasa. To begin with, it is a large lake, with a superficial area of over 11,000 square miles, and a catchment area of nearly 50,000 square miles. Its waters, like those of Lake Victoria, are of interest to more than one territory. Tanganyika, Mozambique and Nyasaland share its shores, and Mozambique and Nyasaland share its outlet, the Shire River. But what gives magnitude to its water problems is not so much its size and international significance, as its erratic habits, the causes of which have already been described. Between 1912 and 1950 the level of the lake fluctuated more than 20 feet; in few years was the seasonal fluctuation less than three to four feet. Such departures from the mean are inconvenient not only for the people who live beside the lake, but also for shipping services. Some of the jetties built at a time when the lake was low are now completely submerged, and some of those built at a time when the lake was higher than it is now are unusable because of the shallowness of the water.

Partly because of these fluctuations and partly because of the changes in the height of the "sill," the lake is subject to large and unpredictable fluctuations in the rate of discharge, as noted earlier. The economic significance of these fluctuations has so far not been very great, the population of the lower Shire valley being small, backward and only loosely attached to the river. But it is their future significance that concerns the planners. Certainly no scheme for the development of the Shire valley, whether for irrigation, navigation, power or manufacturing, could succeed unless it were assured of a constantly large water supply.

The satisfactory regulation of these lake and river waters is not likely to be easy. No matter how satisfactory their plans may appear to the layman, engineers know that all it would take to wreck them is an unbudgeted fluctuation or two, and they have little enough information for sound budgeting. Just as troublesome is the difficulty of reconciling the multiple interests that would need to be served. Granted that everybody could be made to agree on where to place the dam or dams without which there can be no regulating at all; it would be another matter to get general agreement on the height at which the impounded lake waters should be stabilized. The level best suited to the needs of navigation is not necessarily the level most likely to maintain a rate of discharge sufficient to keep the sill from clogging up periodically; and the level best suited for this purpose is not necessarily the level capable of delivering enough water to supply a hydroelectric plant below the dam and irrigation channels still farther downstream. Then there is the matter of cost. The scheme recently proposed by Sir William Halcrow & Partners, and well received by most interests, is estimated to cost approximately £78 million. This is a large sum in any country; in a small country of less than 3 million people, and a poor one at that, it sounds like a very big, and burdensome, sum.[15]

WATER POWER

RESOURCES

The water power resources of Africa, though as yet not accurately measured, are known to exceed by a handsome margin those of any other continent. According to the estimates of H. K. Barrows,[16] they amount to about 274 million horsepower, or about 41 per cent of the world total. If we credit northern and southern (i.e., extra-tropical) Africa with 15 million horsepower, as Debenham believes it is reasonable to do, this leaves tropical Africa with about 259 million horsepower, or slightly over 37 per cent of the world total. This compares with estimated potentials of 151 million horsepower for Asia, 77 million for North America, 75 million for South America, 74 million for Europe, and 21 million for Australia and Oceania.

At first glance the figure for tropical Africa is scarcely credible, since such large parts of the region are waterless either periodically or permanently. However, since most of the parts that do have permanent water have it in abundance, since their area is considerable, and since most of them are located well above sea level, together they constitute a vast "head" of water. In these parts the two indispensable terms in the water power equation — water and slope — are well represented. The parts best served are those contained by the 60-inch isohyet and the 1,000-foot contour line, as Figure 17 shows. Within these limits the most favored localities are, first, those which have a well-distributed rainfall; second, those with large watersheds, preferably watersheds which straddle the heat equator and so receive floodwater at different seasons; and third, those whose mainstreams have conspicuous constrictions and breaks of slope, as these provide the likeliest power sites.

It follows that the area with by far the largest water power potential is the Congo basin. Its catchment area of approximately 1.6 million square miles is the largest in the whole of Africa. Further, over most of this area the rainfall is very well distributed, as African rains go; only in the southern and northern extremities is the rainy season less than six months long, and over almost half of the area it is more than eight months long. Then, because it lies astride the heat equator, the dry season of the northern tributaries is the wet season of the southern, with the result

---

[15] In 1956 a temporary low-level earth dam wall was constructed across the Shire River at Liwonde. Damming the river at this point has facilitated site investigations for a permanent barrage (at Matope), and the carrying out of surveys and pilot irrigation schemes in the lower Shire.

[16] *Water Power Engineering*, McGraw-Hill Book Company, New York, 1943, pp. 4ff.

that the mainstream is constantly being "topped up" with the floodwaters of one tributary or another. Again, because the rainfall is well distributed and heavy, most of the catchment area is covered by either forest or marsh, or both, that serve further to stabilize the water yield by lessening the run-off, and to safeguard the bed of the river against one of the engineer's worst enemies, excessive siltation. And, for full measure, the course of the Congo is broken at several points by falls and rapids, the biggest break of all occurring where the volume of the river is at its greatest and its flow most uniform, namely, between Stanley Pool (just below Léopoldville) and Matadi. Here, in a distance of 220 miles the Congo descends more than 800 feet in a series of 32 falls and cataracts, and develops an electricity potential of 114 million horsepower — about half as much again as the water power potential of the North American continent. More than a thousand miles upstream the so-called Stanley Falls — a series of seven rapids spread over a distance of nearly 60 miles — have a mean flow of approximately 470,000 cubic feet per second, or more than twice the flow over Niagara.

The water power potential of the entire Congo basin has been put at 168 million horsepower, one fourth of the estimated world potential. This clearly places the Congo in a class by itself. At the same time it leaves the rest of tropical Africa with a potential not far short of 100 million horsepower, which, by any yardstick, is a lot of power. Much of this is available in the river basins of the Nile and the Zambezi.

The energy equivalent of the Nile's falling waters has never been satisfactorily measured. The reason for this is threefold: ignorance of the cyclical variations in the flow of some sections of the river; ignorance of the degree of attrition which the potential would suffer from proposed irrigation schemes or by evaporation from the surface of storage reservoirs; and ignorance of where and how the energy could be tapped to the greatest advantage. But the order of magnitude of the potential is suggested by the following recent estimates of power available in the nearly 1,000-mile section of the valley between Khartoum and the Egyptian border: [17]

	(Thousand Kw.)	
	Primary Power (available at all seasons of the year)	Secondary Power (available at certain seasons only)
Fourth Cataract	500	450
Semna	500	380
Fifth Cataract	200	190
Sabaloka (Sixth Cataract)	100	80
	1,300	1,100

[17] Supplied by John H. G. Lebon, University of Khartoum.

For the valley as a whole, the corresponding figures could hardly be less than five times as great as these, and they could conceivably be much greater still.

To judge from such partial calculations as have been made of the power potential of the Zambezi basin, it is of the same order of magnitude as the Nile. The cascades and falls of its left-bank tributary, the Shire River, are believed to be capable of developing more than 2 billion kilowatt-hours annually; the Kafue River, its other large left-bank tributary, is believed to have an even bigger potential — 2.6 billion kilowatt-hours approximately; while the mainstream itself has a rate of flow through the Kariba Gorge roughly equivalent to that needed to produce 6.5 billion kilowatt-hours of electric energy annually. Besides these, there are hundreds of smaller power sites, not to mention the Victoria Falls, which, along with the rapids below, have a low-water potential of about 750,000 horsepower.

This still leaves a large power potential unaccounted for. It is contained in the hundreds of smaller, tumultuous but permanent rivers that take their rise in high ground and hack their way to the coast through breaches in the rim of the bordering plateaus. As is to be expected in view of its generally heavier rainfall, the Atlantic seaboard has a larger number of such rivers than the Indian Ocean seaboard. To name only a few: the Konkouré of the Republic of Guinea; the Volta of Ghana; the Sanaga of the French Cameroons; the Kouilou of the Republic of the Congo; and, in Angola, the Dande, Cuanza, Catumbela and Cunene rivers. On the Indian Ocean side of the continent, almost the only rivers of any consequence are the Revue, Incomati and Movene rivers of Mozambique. The rivers in the other territories have plenty of falls and rapids, but little water. The power potential of the Rufiji, Ruvu, Pangani and Malagarasi, four of the largest rivers in Tanganyika, has been put at a very modest 40,000 kilowatts, on minimum flow. The potential of the Tana in Kenya has been put at something over 100,000 kilowatts. That of the Juba in Somalia and the Awash in Ethiopia could scarcely be more.

PRESENT INSTALLED CAPACITY

For reasons that may or may not be related to the much advertised absence of the wheel, the idea of turning falling water to account in everyday life, was slow in occurring to the indigenous peoples of tropical Africa. Even today they are not greatly drawn to the idea, for it is still possible to travel through most tropical African territories without coming upon a single waterwheel. And those who have tried to sell a bush community the advantages of, say, a water-powered flour mill have frequently met with incomprehending dismay or outright opposition. Why spend money which is scarce to save labor which is abundant?

Why take away from a woman a task which becomes her as much as child-bearing, and is as necessary if she is to be kept out of mischief? A man's argument, no doubt; but the woman has hers, too. Why be beguiled into giving up a companionable backyard task like pounding out the evening meal of maize or manioc? Would not then the husband, or the white man, find another less congenial chore with which to occupy her newly acquired spare time?

Up to now water power has been white man's power, but, as the figures in Table 13 show, very little of it has been harnessed and used. As of

Table 13

INSTALLED CAPACITY OF PUBLIC
AND PRIVATE HYDROELECTRIC PLANTS, 1949-1957

(*Thousand Kilowatts*)

TERRITORY	1949	1953	1954	1955	1957 [a]
Angola	2.23	3.55	4.67	11.69	16.00
Belgian Congo	n.a.	275.00	284.90	326.00	616.70
French Cameroons	Nil	16.00	16.26	22.70	65.40
Ethiopia	2.68 [b]	5.88	5.88	7.76	7.76
Eritrea	0.72	0.72	0.72	0.72	0.72
French Equatorial Africa	Nil	13.80	15.00	18.60	18.60
French West Africa	0.40	14.80	14.80	10.60	7.60
Kenya	6.70 [b]	15.60	17.30	25.40	25.90
Malagasy Republic (Madagascar)	9.00	13.30	13.30	14.90	19.00
Nigeria	n.a.	15.50	19.50	19.50	19.80
Northern Rhodesia	35.00	34.00	37.00	37.00	40.00
Nyasaland	n.a.	0.15	0.30	0.30	0.60
São Tomé, Príncipe	0.20	0.16	0.19	0.20	n.a.
Southern Rhodesia	2.00	2.00	2.00	1.00	1.00
Tanganyika	13.10	19.20	19.20	19.20	19.10
Uganda	Nil	Nil	30.00	60.00	90.00

Source: Data from United Nations, *Statistical Yearbook, 1958*, New York, 1958, pp. 258-59.

[a] Provisional or estimated.   [b] 1950.   n.a.: not available

about 1957 the installed capacity of all the hydroelectric plants in tropical Africa was approximately 950,000 kilowatts, or less than 1/250 of the estimated potential and less than two fifths of the total installed electric energy (more than 1.4 million kilowatts of which is raised thermally). Of the 29 territories reporting to the United Nations, only three, the Belgian Congo, the French Cameroons and Uganda, had more than 50,000 kilowatts of installed capacity; nine were producing no hydroelectric power at all.

Anomalous as this situation appears to be, the explanation of it is not hard to find. In the first place, with the exception of the scattered mines and towns, the demand for bulk power of any kind has been weak until the past few years. Second, it has proved possible to satisfy most of the demand through the medium of thermal plants, which are inexpensive to build and can be run on inexpensive local supplies of wood or coal, or, at the coasts, on sea-borne oil. Third, many of the technically most promising water power sites are either too remote from the power markets to have been capable of profitable development or too large to have been capable of development on a scale matching the modest demand.

As a result, interest in hydroelectricity has been confined to those mining centers and towns which are near falls and rapids tailored to their needs and far from other feasible sources of power. Two such places are the Katanga Province of the Belgian Congo and the Broken Hill region of Northern Rhodesia.

The Katanga copper industry, the largest consumer of hydroelectric power in tropical Africa, is located more than 700 miles from a coal field and farther still from a seaport. However, in the Cornet and Koni Falls on the Lufira River, and in the rapids of the Zilo Gorge on the Lualaba, and the Lukuka Falls 20 miles farther downstream, the industry has a most handy and manageable water power resource. The Cornet Falls are only 40 miles from Jadotville and the Zilo Gorge is only 16 miles north of Kolwezi, where much of the power is needed. All four sites lend themselves well to exploitation: they are small enough to be harnessed at unastronomical cost, yet large enough to produce significant amounts of power, and of such volume, width and slope as to keep the cost-to-yield ratio low.

The Broken Hill (zinc-lead-vanadium) mine of Northern Rhodesia likewise has no local coal, and it long ago outgrew the capacity of the local forests to keep it going with wood fuel. Very early its operators realized that their only hope of staying in business was to harness the ample water power resources of the surrounding region. Thanks to the plants erected at Mulungushi in 1924 (the first in the whole of tropical Africa) and at Lunsemfwa twenty years later, they have been able to retain their hold on a strongly competitive metal market, and, at the same time, sell enough power to meet the needs of the government township of Broken Hill.

Other towns which by the late 1950s had come to rely largely or wholly on hydroelectric power were Douala, the commercial capital of the French Cameroons, which is supplied by the Edea plant on the nearby Sanaga River; Jinja, the second largest town and fast-growing industrial center of Uganda, which has a power station, the recently opened Owen Falls Hydro-Electric Scheme, at its doors; Luanda, the capital of Angola, which is already outstripping the 19-million-kilowatt-hour output of the Mabubas plant on the lower Dande River; Stanleyville, which uses power from the nearby Tshopo plant; Léopoldville, which now gets power from the nearby Zongo plant; Zomba, the small administrative capital of Nyasaland, whose needs are met by a diesel-hydro plant with less than 1,000 kilowatts of installed capacity.

But the day of small things is passing, if not in Zomba, at least in many localities. Almost every territory is now committed to development programs that call, along with everything else, for greatly increased amounts of power. Power is needed in the towns for the lighting of homes and businesses, and for the running of public utilities and factories. It is needed in the country for the running of new mines, lumbering concessions, plantations, farms and village workshops. And although few people are simple enough to believe that the "magic" of electricity can transmute African disease, poverty and backwardness into health, wealth and progress, none supposes that any such changes can be brought about without it.

Where is all this power to come from? No doubt some of it will come from wood, which is still widely used in steam engines. In the Belgian Congo, for instance, about 6 million cubic meters of fuel wood are being consumed annually at the present time on the railroads and waterways, and in industrial plants. No doubt, too, some will come from oil, domestic and foreign. More will obviously come from coal, for the proven resources of Southern Rhodesia, Nigeria, Tanganyika and Mozambique are large and capable of economical exploitation and shipment. Some, perhaps, will come from atomic reactors yet to be constructed — which would be reasonable enough considering the reputed size of the region's contribution to the world supply of fissionable materials. Nevertheless, judging from the blueprints and the building programs either under way or recently completed, it is almost certain that, for many years to come, much of it will be derived from falling water.

HYDROELECTRIC PROJECTS

The list of hydroelectric projects is already long and is continually being added to. As Figure 17 and the following partial list show, such projects are no country's monopoly. Furthermore, no one interest has a monopoly of the power produced by them.

Ethiopia

About 50 miles from Addis Ababa on the Awash River is an excellent dam site which the Ethiopians, with the help of Italian reparations money and technology, are now developing. When complete, the Coka Dam Scheme, as it is called, will have an installed capacity of 61,500 horsepower, and an annual electricity potential of approximately 100 million kilowatt-hours. This power will be used to meet the rapidly growing needs of Addis Ababa and Diredawa.

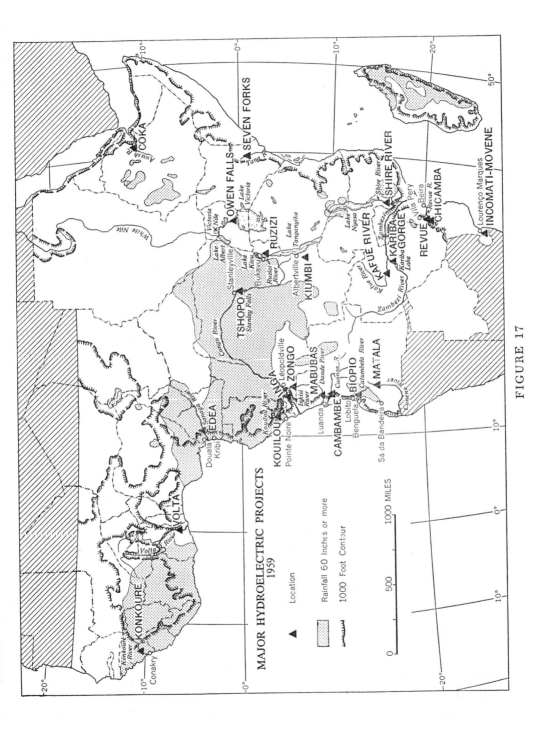

MAJOR HYDROELECTRIC PROJECTS
1959

▲ Location

░ Rainfall 60 Inches or more

〰 1000 Foot Contour

0   500   1000 MILES

FIGURE 17

257

Areas of French Influence

Here two projects are especially notable:

1. *The Edea project.* The output of this French Cameroons plant, located on the lower Sanaga River near Douala, is being increased from 100 million to one billion kilowatt-hours annually. This increase is considered necessary to satisfy the needs of the rapidly expanding industries of the Douala-Edea-Kribi triangle, and the no less rapidly expanding population of African laborers, artisans, tradesmen and their families attracted to the region by them.

2. *The Kouilou project.* This Republic of the Congo project calls for the building of a plant at the Sounda gorge on the Kouilou River. The plant would produce approximately 800,000 kilowatts of power. In addition to serving the expanding commercial and industrial needs of the port of Pointe Noire (including the 200,000-ton-capacity aluminum plant which the French Péchiney group is planning to build) it would also serve the agricultural and industrial needs of the up-and-coming Niari valley, which forms part of the Kouilou River system.

The Republic of Guinea

The lower valley of the Konkouré River, which enters the Atlantic conveniently near the growing port of Conakry, is to be dammed at Souapiti. Enough power — approximately 3 billion kilowatt-hours — will be generated here initially to make possible an annual aluminum production of 100,000 tons; later the installed capacity will be increased to meet the needs of a 250,000-ton production.

Belgian Areas

The Ten Year Plan (1950-1959) for the development of the Belgian Congo and Ruanda-Urundi provided for the construction of stations to serve the power and lighting needs — European and African, domestic, industrial and public service — of four of the largest urban centers: Léopoldville, Stanleyville, Bukavu and Albertville.

1. The largest of the four, the Zongo station, situated some 90 miles southeast of Léopoldville on the Inkisi River, began to deliver power in 1955. In addition to relieving Léopoldville of its former partial dependence on foreign power (from the Djoué plant near Brazzaville), the Zongo plant enables the city to supply more electricity more cheaply to its population of over 300,000 and its several hundred European industrial and commercial establishments. When complete the plant will have an installed capacity of 31,500 kilowatts.

2. The Tshopo station, situated just below the Stanley Falls, also came into operation in 1955. It delivers most of its power (present installed

capacity: 13,300 kilowatts) to the rapidly growing industrial and commercial city of Stanleyville.

3. The Ruzizi plant, on the river of the same name, began to deliver its first units of power to Bukavu in 1957. Its initial installed capacity is 17,750 kilowatts.

4. Work on the Kiumbi plant, serving Albertville, is behind schedule. As before in the African tropics, the "irresistible" powers of the planner have been confronted by the "immovable" facts of the environment. Plans to use the Kitimba Falls as the site of the Ruzizi plant had to be abandoned when the ground was found to be too porous. The geology of the Kiumbi area has proved almost as disconcerting.

Far outstripping these in size and economic significance is the Inga project. At the Inga rapids, between Léopoldville and Matadi, the hydroelectric potential is estimated to be more than 25 million kilowatts, about twenty times the potential of the Hoover Dam. The present blueprints call for the construction of a dam and power plant capable of generating 3 million kilowatts at "a few centimes per kilowatt," [18] which would make it the cheapest electricity in the world. It is the expectation of the planners that "Inga will bring into being a vast industrial setup which may become the Central African equivalent of the Ruhr." [19] It is also contended that "through rational irrigation and canalization," Inga will speed up the agricultural development of the Congo; and that it "will produce enough electricity for the electrification of the neighboring territories." [20]

Portuguese Areas

At least six projects — four in Angola, two in Mozambique — are either under way or now complete in Portuguese Africa.

1. The 19-million-kilowatt-hour output of the Mabubas plant near Luanda has recently been stepped up to 56 million kilowatt-hours.

2. The newly completed dam at Biopio on the Catumbela is now putting 38 million kilowatt-hours of energy annually at the disposal of the Lobito Bay–Benguela district.

3. The Matala project on the Cunene is still in course of construction. When complete it will have an annual output of approximately 69 million kilowatt-hours, and will be able to supply the southern cities of Sá da Bandeira and Moçâmedes (Mossamedes) with a large part of their needs. Among other things, it is expected to contribute to the development of a long-overdue meat-processing industry and the newly introduced karakul pelt industry.

[18] A. Buisseret, Belgian Minister of Overseas Territories; see *The Belgian Congo Today* (Brussels), Vol. VI, No. 3, 1957, p. 14. There are 100 centimes to the Belgian franc; about 50 francs to the dollar.
[19] *Loc. cit.* A similar claim is being made for the Kariba project.
[20] *Ibid.*

4. The latest and largest power project to be undertaken in Angola is located in the Cuanza valley which drains the region to the southeast of Luanda. The dam, being built by the French Péchiney group at Cambambe, is expected to impound enough water to produce nearly 4 billion kilowatt-hours annually. The first phase of this development (delivering 700 million kilowatt-hours for use in an aluminum plant) is expected to be complete by 1962.

5. In Mozambique, the first — two-turbine — phase of the Revue project was completed in 1956. Most of the approximately 45 million-kilowatt-hour production goes to the nearby Vila Pery (which has a textile mill), to Dondo (which has a cement and fibro-cement plant) and to the port of Beira. Eventually, the Revue plant will have five turbines with a combined potential of about 135 million kilowatt-hours, most of which will be absorbed by Beira. In 1957 work was begun on a new dam at Chicamba. When complete, this will impound approximately 1.6 million cubic meters of water — enough for all the foreseeable needs of the Revue valley–Beira area.

6. The Incomati-Movene project, still in its early stages, is only partly concerned with the generation of power. A reservoir being built in the Movene valley in the extreme south of Mozambique will be able, with the aid of additional supplies tunneled in from the Incomati River, to provide irrigation water for 120,000 acres of seasonally dry land lower down the valley. At the same time it will provide a 140-foot head of water capable of generating annually in the turbines at its base about 72 million kilowatt-hours of energy. Most of this power will be transmitted by overhead lines to Lourenço Marques and neighboring districts.

Areas of British Influence

For the most spectacular hydroelectric projects we must go to those territories which own varying degrees of allegiance to the British Crown. Several such territories have long been interested in developing the water potential within their borders, but it is only since World War II that they have commanded the political significance, economic stability and financial resources — to say nothing of the spokesmen — with which to do something about it. Even now it is by no means sure that all of these territories command enough of these assets to get beyond the talking stage in every case. For the fact is that the viability of undertakings of the size of the Owen Falls, Volta, Kafue, Shire and Kariba projects hangs on more than demonstrable proof that power can be produced for so much, and that it will be bought by so many in such amounts that the capital costs will be amortized over a given number of years. It hangs no less on good will, integrity, efficiency and faith in the future — things that are undemonstrable to the point of being imponderable.

So far, only two of the largest projects have gone much beyond the blueprint stage. These are the Owen Falls project in Uganda and the Kariba Gorge project in the Federation of Rhodesia and Nyasaland.

1. *The Owen Falls project.* The construction of the Owen Falls Dam across the Victoria Nile near its outlet from Lake Victoria was begun in the late 1940s for the primary purpose of providing power for the rapidly expanding but coalless economy of Uganda.[21] The first phase of the project was completed in 1954 with the putting into service of two of the planned ten turbines (turbo-alternators). By 1957 four more had been put into service. The remaining four turbines are expected to be in operation by 1960. The station will then have a generating capacity of approximately 150,000 kilowatts. With estimates of the country's power needs in the 1960s greatly exceeding this figure, the Uganda Electricity Board, which administers the scheme, has already decided to build a second plant at Bujagali, a short distance downstream from Owen Falls. This plant will have an annual output of about 830 million kilowatt-hours.

2. *The Kariba Gorge project.* As we have seen, the Zambezi is one of Africa's greatest water power resources. And of all the power sites along its course, and those of its tributaries, none is more inviting than the Kariba Gorge. By damming the gorge to a height of approximately 400 feet, as the federal government of Rhodesia and Nyasaland began to do in 1955, the hydrologists believe that it will be possible to obtain a continuous discharge, even in very dry years, of not less than 37,000 cubic feet per second, or enough to generate 1,000 megawatts at a load factor of 74 per cent. To raise this vast amount of power, it will be necessary to construct two powerhouses, one on each bank of the river below the dam, with a total installation of sixteen 77-megawatt units. The cost of constructing the dam and installing eight of the sixteen units has been put at roughly £80 million; the cost of the complete scheme at £113 million. (On the basis of this latter estimate power could be delivered to the receiving stations at slightly less than one cent a unit.) The first Kariba power, about 140 megawatts, is due to become available in 1960. By 1962 the first powerhouse should be operating with all eight units. Probably another two years will elapse before all sixteen units are operating. Most of the initial output will be used on the Copperbelt, which has been hard put to it in recent years to keep its smelters going on local wood, Wankie coal, and electricity borrowed from the Katanga. Much of the remainder will be used in the larger industrial centers of Southern Rhodesia, which also have become more accustomed to dearth than to plenty in the postwar years.

3. *The Kafue River project.* Unlike the Zambezi at Kariba, which forms the border between Northern and Southern Rhodesia, the Kafue lies entirely in Northern Rhodesia. Between the section known as the Kafue

---

[21] The secondary purpose the dam is likely to serve as a regulator of the lake's run-off waters is discussed on p. 249.

Flats and its confluence with the Zambezi, the Kafue has an average gradient of 3 per cent and a total descent of 1,950 feet. The mean flow is thought to be enough to generate 400 megawatts at a load factor of 74 per cent. To realize this potential, it would probably be necessary to build two power stations, the upper having a gross head of 1,532 feet and the lower a gross head of 395 feet.[22] The cost of the two-station scheme has been put at approximately £55 million, which would make it possible to deliver power to the receiving stations at approximately half a cent a unit. Estimates of the time required to bring both stations into service have varied from four to seven years. Until March 1, 1955 it was generally supposed that this power project had first priority with the federal government, but on that date the government announced its decision to shelve it, for the time being at least, in favor of the Kariba project.

4. *The Shire River project.* This, too, is still only a blueprint project, and a somewhat faded blueprint at that. Not that the need for it can be, or is, questioned by anyone. It is needed for many reasons, some of which have already been dealt with. It is simply that no country with a low per capita income can expect to finance all at once all the "development" it would like to have. To implement the power part alone of this project would, it has been estimated, take not less than £40 million; for the harnessing of the 1,300-foot head of water between the outlet of Lake Nyasa and the Shire marshes would call for no less than five separate power stations, in addition to a low-head dam. However, when completed these stations would be able to develop some 2.1 billion kilowatt-hours of power at very low cost — not more than one cent a kilowatt-hour. But even cheap power does not always find a purchaser, especially when the purchaser is poor. At present there is little demand for extra power in Nyasaland. And it is probable that, by the time there is, Kariba will be able to supply it, at no capital cost to the Federation or the purchasers.

5. *The Seven Forks (Kenya) project.* To relieve Kenya of the necessity of having to rely heavily on imported power, and to make adequate provision for the expected continuing rise in domestic demand, the East African Power and Lighting Co., Ltd., is planning to develop a site on the Tana River. At Seven Forks, about 70 miles from Nairobi, some 100,000 kilowatts of energy can be developed and distributed to the main consuming centers, at a cost considerably less (so it is believed) than that now being paid for Owen Falls power. However, it is not planned to begin work on the dam before the early 1960s.

6. *The Volta project.* Ghana's hopes of developing hydroelectric power on a large scale are pinned on the Volta River. If the necessary capital

---

[22] However, some believe it would be more economical, though it would doubtless take longer, to build a single underground station so placed as to be able to use the full head.

can be raised, the Ghana government will undertake the construction of three dams, the largest being near Ajena, 70 miles above the mouth of the Volta. Here a sufficient head of water would be formed to warrant the installation of a power plant with a generating capacity of approximately 617,000 kilowatts. On the basis of present reckoning only 50,000 kilowatts of this would be available for public services; the rest would be used to turn locally available bauxite into aluminum at the rate of approximately 210,000 tons a year. This scheme is so self-evidently in the industrial interest of the country and the sterling area as a whole (in which very little aluminum is now produced), that it is to be hoped the money for it will soon be forthcoming. But £309 million — the figure quoted in the report of the Preparatory Commission [23] — is a lot more money than the Ghana government can raise within its borders or any foreign investor, corporate or government, has so far been willing to invest in a country with so little experience of "bigness" and its attendant temptations.[24]

[23] See *The Volta River Project: Report of the Preparatory Commission*, 3 vols., H.M.S.O., London, 1956.

[24] Since this chapter was written, the Ghana government has announced the signing of a contract with Kaiser Engineers and Contractors Incorporated for carrying out "preliminary work on the Volta project." On the basis of its own surveys, the Kaiser company believes that the project can be put into effect for approximately £100 million, and that it will deliver more power more cheaply than the earlier surveys indicated. The government has also announced that a European consortium has offered to build all three dams for the sums proposed by the Kaiser company and to obtain the extra financing needed to complete the project.

CHAPTER 8

Food from the Water

TYPES OF FISHING

GROWTH OF COMMERCIAL FISHERIES

FISH FARMING

TRENDS AND PROSPECTS

Aｌｔｈｏｕｇｈ a complete count has never been taken, it would appear that tropical Africa is almost as rich in species of fish as it is in species of trees. Where counts have been taken, the figures are imposing. As long ago as 1867 David Livingstone reported the vernacular names of no less than 39 species caught by the fishermen of a single lake, Mweru, located on the Belgian Congo–Northern Rhodesia border.[1] Some other central African lakes are now known to be better endowed. Lake Nyasa, for instance, has at least 200 species of fish. The riverine and coastal waters do not lag far behind. A recent five-week survey of Belgian Congo waters yielded 26 different "table" species alone. A 1952 report of the Food and Agriculture Organization listed 150 varieties taken off the coast of Somalia; and more than 170 varieties are said to be landed in the ports of Kenya.

But, as with most species of trees, most species of fish have up to now commanded little commercial interest. Where a demand for fish has existed, it has been on a small scale, and for a small number of varieties. Over wide areas there has been no demand. This is partly because fish do not "travel" well in the tropics. Unless treated, they lose condition in a matter of minutes. The usual African treatment, while it prolongs their marketable life, does little to enhance their quality, taste or appearance. There can, in fact, be few less inviting sights, and smells, than those of the open stands of blackened, fly-ridden and rotting fish found in most village markets of west and central Africa. Another reason for the lack of demand is that many sections are poorly served with lakes, ponds and

[1] *The Last Journals of David Livingstone in Central Africa* . . ., Harper & Brothers, New York, 1875, p. 199.

rivers or are remote from the sea, or both. And some of the inland waters are subject to seasonal and secular fluctuations that would jeopardize any economy dependent on their aquatic life. Moreover, fish are widely regarded as a food of last resort. Those groups of cattle-keeping Turkana (northern Kenya) that eat fish — not all do — do so only in bad seasons when they cannot live off their animals; yet their ranging grounds go down to the shores of Lake Rudolf, which abounds in fine fish. The Galla of Ethiopia, many of whom combine cultivating with stock raising, will eat fish only if they are too poor to afford meat and bread.

Many pastoralists will not eat fish at all. Some of the Somali regard fish as plebeian food. Their fish-eating coastal neighbors are known to them as Rer Manyo, a derogatory term signifying merely "common occupation." "Speak not to me with the mouth that eateth fish" is a Somali taunt. The Nandi (Kenya) and some of the Ndebele (Southern Rhodesia) groups consider fish to bear too close a resemblance to snakes and lizards. Many cultivators, including some of the Ibo-speaking peoples of southern Nigeria, shun fish, believing they embody the souls of their ancestors. Even where the eating of fish is not forbidden unconditionally, it may be proscribed in a wide range of circumstances. Among the Lele of Kasai (Belgian Congo), for example, fish must not be eaten by pregnant women, nor used in the making of certain medicines. It is held important not to offend the spirits which inhabit the same environment, and sometimes the same body, as the fish.

Even so, we must be careful not to underestimate the importance of fish in tropical African diets. It has long been a staple food for such peoples as the Ovimbundu of Angola, the Bakuba of the Belgian Congo, the Lozi, Kazembe and Ila of Northern Rhodesia, the Yao and Tonga of Nyasaland, the Shilluk of the Republic of Sudan, and almost all coast and lake shore dwellers. It has provided many other groups with a seasonal source of food, and has been an irregular item of food in the diet of many more. All told, it is probably no exaggeration to say that fish have formed a significant part of the traditional diet of at least one third of the peoples of tropical Africa.

With alternative sources of animal protein scarce and expensive in most of the wooded zones, and with the population almost everywhere increasing faster than the supply of the alternatives, more and more people are becoming interested in fishing, either as a source of food or trade, or both. Some people, including the Kikuyu, for whom fish were traditionally taboo, are turning to fish for other reasons. They argue that if the Europeans eat fish, fish must be good; that if they buy and sell fish, it must be because there's money in it; and that if they bother to stock the mountain streams with trout, it must be because there's fun to be had in catching them.

TYPES OF FISHING

Whatever may have been the limitations of the primitive African fisherman, lack of ingenuity was not one of them. Unlike his cousin the cultivator, he developed a remarkable variety of techniques for the furtherance
of his ends. The Lokele (of the Stanleyville region of the Belgian Congo)
and the Lozi (Northern Rhodesia) developed at least twenty different ways of catching fish. The Luena (Angola–Northern Rhodesia
border country) did even better: they developed twenty different kinds
of fish trap alone. Most of the techniques used by African fishermen may
have been cruder than those employed by the modern sports fishermen,
but they were every bit as cunning and, in many instances, more effective.

SEA FISHING

The coasts of tropical Africa are among the least inviting in the world.
Most of them are beset by offshore bars or coral reefs, and by strong
currents and persistent ocean swell that make small-boat operations
hazardous. Most of them are subject to strong surf caused either by
onshore prevailing winds or by daytime sea breezes. Except for some
favored stretches they lack natural shelter and good harbors. On the other
hand, most of their waters are rich in fish.

While some sea fishing is done from the shore, more is done from
canoes or other kinds of craft. It is done mostly by the men, and most
men who live on the coast are fishermen part of the time. Some of them
are full-time fishermen. Fishing practice, rather naturally, varies from
group to group and often, within a group, from place to place. However,
common challenges have produced many common responses, including
an almost uniformly high degree of manipulative skill and adaptation to
local conditions. Both of these features are well exemplified in the practices of the fishermen of Ghana. The way of a Fanti or Ga fisherman
with a cast net has often been portrayed. And it deserves to be, for it has
poetry in it as well as power and skill. Sometimes he will use the net in
the surf, where he stands waist-deep waiting for the propitious moment,
when he flings the bell-shaped, weighted net with the flowing rhythmic
movement of a discus-thrower or a lassoer. He then withdraws the
top of the bell gently, letting the weights at the rim close together over
the sandy bottom, until at last he can gather up the whole net and the
fish within it. At other times, he will use the net from the bow of a canoe,
a stance requiring agility as well as grace.

The skill of these fishermen in adapting themselves to differing environmental circumstances has been characterized by F. J. Pedler in his
recent study of the economic geography of west Africa. He contrasts the
methods used on the shallow, surf-pounded coast to the west of the

Ankobra River with those used on the rocky coast to the east, where the broken coastline tames the surf:

The western boats must be launched and beached in very heavy surf, and they must be hauled a long way up the beach beyond the reach of the tide. They are 25 or 30 feet long, with 3 feet of beam and a depth of 4½ feet from the gunwale to the bottom. The thwarts are stout planks. The boats are tarred black, are not usually decorated, and do not carry sail. The paddles are long and spear-shaped. The eastern boats, which must be handier to navigate among the rocks, are shorter, and have thwarts of bamboo. The wood is not tarred, and gay designs and slogans are painted on it. A lateen sail is rigged, and the paddles have three prongs. Two or three hooks on lines are [trolled] when the canoe is at sea. The western men make very long drift-nets with the object of catching everything that swims within 18 or 20 feet of the surface of the sea. The fish are caught by getting their gills entangled in the mesh, and in order to secure a varied catch the nets are made in sections of different-sized meshes . . .[2]

The same regard for the niceties of habit and habitat may be observed wherever Africans have turned to the sea for a livelihood. Where fish can be had in shallow lagoon and estuarine waters, traps, often made of bamboo, are commonly used. Sometimes, as along parts of the Guinea coast, these extend for great distances, simulating underwater fences. Where very big fish, such as shark, are sought, it is customary for nets as large as 600 by 6 feet to be used; these nets may have half-hitches in place of knots, thus allowing the mesh to widen or contract according to the strain. In the rather less exposed waters off the northeastern seaboard, flat polygonal basketwork traps are commonly employed, in addition to fence traps, throw nets and lines.

The full list of fish taken, one way or another, off these African coasts is long, confusing (because the nomenclature is mostly the work of amateurs and varies from place to place), and of little significance to any but ichthyologists. Many of the species have only local, vernacular names. Some do not have even that; they are just fish that happen to get caught.[3]

Varieties that rate high with commercial fishermen off the west African coast are barracuda, bogue, drum, halfbeak, "sardine" (*Sardinella* spp., notably *S. aurita* and *S. cameronensis*), mackerel (*Caranx* spp.), meagre, mojarra, mullet, prawn, red snapper, sailfish, sea bream, shark, tarpon, threadfin, tuna and weakfish.

Off the coast of Angola, anchovy, bream, crayfish, dolphin, eel, mackerel, mullet, muraeno, porpoise, "sardine," shad, shark, shrimp, skate, sole, swordfish, torpedo fish, tuna, turbot and whiting are all caught in marketable quantities.

Off the east African and Malagasy coasts, anchovy, barracuda, bass,

[2] F. J. Pedler, *Economic Geography of West Africa*, Longmans, Green & Co., Ltd., London, 1955, pp. 48-49.

[3] Once in a while some very remarkable fish happen to get caught; for example, the coelacanth, a "fossil" fish that had supposedly been extinct for millions of years, has been taken several times off the Comores Islands and Madagascar since 1952.

billfish, catfish, grouper, dogfish, dolphin, horse mackerel, kingfish, marlin, milkfish, mullet, octopus, sailfish, "sardine," sea bream, sea perch, shark, snapper, spinefoot, threadfin, tuna, and shellfish of many kinds are among the commoner catches.

Several species of whale are also found off different sectors of these coasts, notably in and near the cold waters of the Benguela current which flows northward along the Angola coast.

RIVER FISHING

There is scarcely a river in tropical Africa that is not fished at some time or other, but in very few rivers is fishing more than a small-scale enterprise serving more than local needs. Many of the rivers are too small and too subject to variations in flow to be good fishing rivers. Many flow through unhealthy and poorly inhabited country. Many carry a discouragingly high percentage of fish, such as the mud-skipper, the climbing perch, the lung fish, the globe fish and the electric fish, notable more for their peculiar appearance and habits than for their culinary uses. Many have crocodiles, whose capacity for breaking nets and robbing traps — and catching the fisherman — does nothing to commend fishing as a career, or fish as a staple.[4]

In spite of all this, most of the large rivers are well worth fishing. The Congo has several species of fresh-water herring (*Pellonula* spp.), elephant-snout fish or mormyrid, flying fish (e.g., *Pantodon buchholzi*), catfish, barbel (*Barbus caudovittatus* and *holotaenia*), perch (especially *Lates niloticus*), spiny eel and tiger fish (or water leopard). Some tiger fish scale 100 pounds. The perch may run well over 200 pounds. Most of these types of fish are also found in the upper Nile, the Niger, the Volta and the other big rivers of west, equatorial and central Africa. Where fresh-water crabs are found, as they are in many streams, they, too, are much used for food. In recent years many of the smaller, higher streams of equatorial and central Africa, notably in Kenya, Tanganyika and the Federation of Rhodesia and Nyasaland, have been stocked with trout and other sporting fish.

Fresh-water fishing techniques show much the same refinement as those developed by salt-water fishermen. In general they are well adapted to the nature and size of the fish, the configuration and flow of the river, and the availability of materials.

The Luapula peoples who live alongside the river of that name in Northern Rhodesia use spears when fishing the clear, shallow marginal

[4] Though the crocodile population has been greatly reduced in the past decade or two (thanks in the main to the demand for crocodile skins on the European and American markets), it is still large enough in many rivers and lakes to keep fishermen at bay. At times the banks below the Murchison Falls on the Victoria Nile are covered with crocodiles, actually lying on top of one another for lack of room.

pools, and conical wickerwork baskets set in rocky falls or in the openings of a weir when fishing the faster-flowing mainstream. The Lozi of the same territory change their fishing methods with the seasonal changes in the flow of the Zambezi. When the river is rising (December through February) they employ "non-return" traps set in reed fences; when the river falls (April through July) they use fish-dams and fences at the base of which fish tend to congregate and become easy prey for net, line and trap. When the waters are low (September through November) they use trawl and gill nets for the bigger pools, and, for the smaller "pans," fish spears and sticks. This is the season of the communal battue, when whole villages turn out for the systematic slaughter of the fish that have been caught, so to speak, with their fins down. Variations of the net-and-basket-trap techniques are numerous and are found almost everywhere.

Also in very general use in the drier areas is a "dope" technique. For this the fisherman uses a poison or stupefacient strong enough, when thrown into the water, to immobilize the fish and bring it to the surface. It is obviously calculated to give its best results in small rivers, or in the low-water pools found in many of the bigger rivers. A wasteful and dangerous technique, it has already been banned, officially, in some territories. Among others to use this device are the WaGosha of Somalia, who prepare an extract of the euphorbia tree for the purpose; the Ovimbundu of the Cunene River region of Angola; and the Azande of the Equatoria Province of the Republic of Sudan.

Less generally employed practices, found in many widely separated areas nevertheless, are night fishing with torch and spear, as among the Dinka and Nuer of the upper White Nile; and hook-and-line fishing, as among the Kyedye of central Nigeria and the Ndebele of Southern Rhodesia, who apparently learned the art from Europeans.

Unlike sea fishing, river fishing is done almost as much by women as it is by men. In some groups it is done exclusively by the women, at certain times of the year if not always. This seems to be the case among the Tikar of the Bamenda region of the British Cameroons, the Lotuko of the southernmost part of the Republic of Sudan, and the Lele of the Kasai Province of the Belgian Congo. It is more customary for the women to do certain kinds of fishing only, and for the men to do the rest. Among the Ovimbundu the men usually do the line fishing, the women the basket-trap and poison fishing. Among the Luena the men fish in the streams with traps, nets and weirs, the women in the shallows with long, hand-operated sweeping baskets.

The division of labor between the sexes is not everywhere as clear cut as it used to be. Among the Luchazi, near neighbors of the Luena, the women can often be found assisting the men in the weir and trap fishing, and in some Ovimbundu districts both men and women fish with nets and weirs. Other changes are coming about, too. Most Lokele fishermen now make nets with nylon cord; some even have outboard motors fitted to their canoes.

LAKE FISHING

The great inland lakes of tropical Africa rank among the largest in the world. The only fresh-water lake larger than Lake Victoria is Lake Superior. The next ten tropical African lakes aggregate about 40,000 square miles — even more when Lake Chad is in good shape, for at its maximum it is nearer 10,000 than 5,000 square miles in area; thus they are on a par with Lakes Huron and Michigan. With the exception of Lake Kivu in the Belgian Congo and some smaller ones, these lakes are extremely well served with fish, both in regard to species and total numbers. And most of the species are pleasant to the palate. Further, most of the lakes can be easily fished and are surrounded by country that is well populated — in some cases densely so — by people accustomed to eating fish and generally unaccustomed to obtaining their animal protein in any other form. Notwithstanding, most of the great lakes were fished in a rather desultory fashion until recently, the average catch being but a small fraction of the potential yield and seldom traveling far from its point of origin. This state of affairs still applies to most of the lakes, though it is changing.

The majority of the fish taken from the lakes of east central Africa belong to the same families as those found in the rivers, so that catches contain everything from lung fish, elephant-snout fish and catfish to spiny eels. The most sought-after fish, and possibly the most abundant, belong to the Cichlidae and Clupeidae families. The Cichlidae are related to the perches. Of the many representatives of this family the most important are those belonging to the genera *Tilapia* and *Haplochromis*, both of which yield species of very great food value, well regarded by Africans, Asians and Europeans alike. Lakes George, Nakivali and Kachira in the Western Province of Uganda, which must be accounted among the world's most productive lakes, are particularly rich in *Tilapia*, as are Lakes Nyasa and Bangweulu. At their prime the various species of *Tilapia* can stand comparison, in taste and texture, with the best lake fish of North America, but it is not every eater who gets them at their prime. They run up to 20 inches in length and three pounds in weight. Lake Victoria is also rich in *Tilapia*, but seemingly richer still in *Haplochromis*. These are much smaller, being more like a sardine; but they are highly esteemed for all that. The Clupeidae are best represented in Lake Tanganyika, the inshore waters of which abound in species akin to salt-water herring and sardine. The deeper waters of the lake, though still scarcely tapped, are known to be well endowed with edible fish, including not less than 34 genera of Cichlidae.

The gear employed by most lake fishermen is little different from that employed by most river fishermen. The fishing craft are mainly hand-propelled plank canoes and dugouts, sometimes carrying an auxiliary sail. For shallow-water fishing, as around the margins of the great lakes and in the swamps of Lake Chad and Lake Bangweulu and the Sudd of the upper White Nile valley, shore seine nets, basket traps, small throw nets and even spears are common stock-in-trade. For deeper water there are gill nets, trawl nets, long-lines and hook-and-line fishing. Most of the gear is still homemade and handmade.

On the larger lakes the old order is beginning to pass. Thus, because of the difficulty of obtaining paddlers and the high wages commanded by them, many Uganda and Tanganyika fishermen are now fitting their canoes with outboard motors; some already have modern, fully powered fishing vessels. More and more lake fishermen are buying machine-made nets of nylon and other types of synthetic fiber to take the place of the traditional flax or bark-cloth nets and those which have been hand-braided from sewing-cotton or cord stripped from old motor tires.

GROWTH OF COMMERCIAL FISHERIES

The buying and selling, or bartering, of fish in tropical Africa has only during the past generation become a commerce in the usual sense of the word. Even today it is not a big or widespread commerce. It occupies a significant monetary role in the economy of scarcely more than half a dozen territories. In all but a very few areas, however, it is becoming more important.

One reason for this growing interest is that almost every government now realizes it has a serious malnutrition problem on its hands and is intent on doing something about it. Over large parts of the region fish appears to constitute the one food capable of turning a poor diet into a decent one, for it supplies not only much needed animal protein but also calcium, fat and vitamins. Another reason is that almost every awakened African is set on having a better diet. Though fish is seldom his preferred meat, he is coming to see its virtues and demanding more of it. Now that millions of Africans have spending money, many of them for the first time, they are using increasing amounts of it for the purchase of more and better food. Ships, trucks, trains and planes are now available in sufficient numbers to enable fish producers to move their supplies expeditiously to where they are needed. Then, too, in a world where crops soon tire the soil and animal dung is scarce (and often put to non-manurial uses), fish manure is beginning to look like the answer to many agronomic problems. And fish meal could certainly do something to improve the meat and milk yield of most African cattle.

Up to now it is the waters of the west coast and the great east and central African lakes that have given rise to most of the commercial fisheries. Of the two, the fisheries of the west coast are the more important. The coastal fisheries have several advantages over those of the great lakes, such as their earlier start, the economies accruing from water transportation, the large aggregate purchasing power of the west African countries, and the fact that there has been very little resistance among the peoples of west Africa to the "eat more fish" campaign. Indeed, in some territories, Sierra Leone and Ghana for instance, the demand far exceeds the available supply.

WEST COAST FISHERIES

The west African fisheries have grown out of the seemingly haphazard hand-to-mouth operations of individual fishermen, and their organization still is rather rudimentary and inefficient. There are few large fishing companies or combines, and fewer fishermen's unions (none of any size), and generally there is no tie-up between producers, middlemen and processors, no guaranteed prices or wages, and no social security legislation.

Some of the more important west coast fisheries are described in the following paragraphs.

Ghana

The best, and worst, features of the west coast fisheries are probably seen most clearly in Ghana, where commercial fishing has been established many years and is a major economic activity. Though it is difficult, if not impossible, to obtain precise figures of the Ghana salt-water fish harvest, it is officially put at about 20,000 tons. Considerable as this figure is — it represents a per capita consumption of nearly 10 pounds a year — it is not enough. Even after adding in the presumed large, but incalculable, amount of fresh-water fish, the country still finds it necessary to import more than 10,000 tons of fish from neighboring territories and Europe. The bulk of the domestic harvest is gathered in one or other of three ways: by drift and ring net (mainly *Sardinella aurita* and *S. cameronensis*); by shore seine net (mainly *Caranx* spp., or horse mackerel, drum, threadfin and barracuda), and by line (mainly tuna, shark, sailfish, red snapper and bream).

Involved in the catching of this large tonnage of sea fish are some 8,000 canoes and some 60,000 fishermen. Most of the canoes and nets are owned by individual Africans who hire crews by the season and pay by results, usually at the rate of one third of the season's takings. Out of their two-thirds share the owners must pay all capital and maintenance costs, which are quite heavy. The cord and netting for a seine net nowadays run to between £400 and £500; a seven-to-eight-man canoe, the normal type, costs upward of £60.[5] With luck the canoe may last eight to ten years; the net, with careful repairing, may last longer. Even so, repairs and depreciation will come to between £50 and £100 a year, which means that at prices prevailing in the early 1950s — about sixpence a pound on the beach — the owner of a single canoe and net could expect to have an income of as much as £200. Though this is not the biggest kind of money to be made in Ghana, it is good money, so that it is understandable if many of the hired hands resent having to live on about one tenth of it.

It is possible that the growth of interest in cooperative ownership of canoes and nets stems partly from this resentment. No doubt another reason why the fishing community now collectively owns canoes and nets in a number of Ghanaian villages is that the margin of profit has been narrowing in recent seasons. Fishermen, wooed away to more rewarding occupations, have had to be replaced by more expensive and sometimes less efficient help. Consequently it is becoming increasingly difficult for the individual owner to find the capital necessary for "motorizing" his business with European-style fishing vessels, without which he is unlikely to increase his profits.[6] Unless, of course, he can do something meanwhile about the highly unsatisfactory arrangements for marketing and distributing fish.

At present fish landed at Accra, Sekondi and elsewhere passes, on the average, through the hands of four traders before it reaches the customer. Even smoked fish sold at the coast will probably be handled by three traders. Fish that travels any distance upcountry may be handled by as many as six. As each trader reckons to make up to 50 per cent profit from his transaction, the total markup is seldom short of 200 per cent and may be as much as 600 or 700 per cent. Attempts to bring these figures down by getting traders to deal in bigger quantities are seldom successful. More fish merely means more traders, a matter the "little man" may deplore but can do nothing much about. Likewise there is nothing much he can do about the tight control of prices habitually exercised by the wholesale buyers. As things now are, even if changes were made in the standard fishing methods so that the haul per fisherman was greater, "there is no indication that the costs of retailing would fall. Given the present high demand for fish, to make any appreciable difference in the retail price, new methods of marketing would have to be devised."[7] All of this provides good grist for the cooperative mill.

[5] See Pedler, *op. cit.*, p. 50.

[6] Not that motor vessels are necessarily the answer. Before now, dugout canoes have been found to ride out strong winds and negotiate heavy surf better than power boats.

[7] Rowena Lawson, "Some Economic Problems of Development in the Gold Coast Fishing Industry" in *Report of Annual Conference — Economics Section* of the West African Institute of Social and Economic Research, held at Achimota, April 1953, mimeographed, pp. 131-32.

At most other places along the Guinea coast, commercial fishing is less organized and, to a Westerner's eye, still less efficient. In many areas the catch is simply traded — fresh, dried or smoked — in the nearby markets for agricultural produce. With the exception of the Republic of Senegal, the business is generally conducted on a smaller scale than in Ghana.

Nigeria

Nigeria, which has the largest population of any tropical African country and the largest potential market for fish, has up to now had one of the smallest sea fisheries. Unlike the Ga and Fanti of Ghana, the Fanti of Liberia, and the Sherbro of Sierra Leone, the Yoruba, Ijaw and other coast dwellers of Nigeria have shown no particular fondness for open-sea fishing. They do most of their fishing in the sheltered lagoons and ample waters of the Niger delta. However, recently efforts have been made by the Fisheries Section of the Department of Commerce and Industries and the Western Region Production Development Board to encourage sea fishing by helping fishermen to obtain more suitable craft and equipment.

A striking effort has been made by one Nigerian group to develop cooperative fishing. It began in the late 1940s as an attempt by a small group of Yoruba-speaking fishermen, "influenced by Bible reading and under the guidance of three outstanding local men," to break away from the old tribal system of living and "strive for a fuller life and better conditions." [8] The site chosen for the attempt was an unpromising stretch of foreshore about a hundred miles east of Lagos. Today the Apostle Community, as it is called, of Aiyetoro ("The World Is at Peace") is a progressive, well-run, thriving town of some 3,000 people. Yet it is still deeply committed to cooperation — or, as the leaders of the community prefer to think of it, apostolic Christianity. All profits derived from fishing are placed in a community chest and used for the benefit of the group as a whole. "No money is credited to individuals. Instead they get free rent and excellent housing, clothes in great variety, free food in abundance and, recently, even free electric light." [9] They have discovered that when people are willing to put community above compound, and industry before idleness, the cooperative principle can be made to work.

European-Run Fisheries

The interest of Europeans in the fish resources of the "African" Atlantic goes back a long way. As early as the fifteenth century the Portuguese, and perhaps the French, had learned something of their size and promise.

[8] *The Times British Colonies Review,* Third Quarter 1957, p. 19.
[9] *Ibid.*

Since 1500, there has hardly been a year when the fishing grounds off the Guinea and equatorial coasts have not been visited by "outsiders" from Western Europe and the Canary Islands. Some of the grounds are still fished from European ports, but as this kind of fishing contributes next to nothing to the trade of the neighboring African countries, it can be omitted from consideration here.

The fishing done by European boats based on west and equatorial African ports, in contrast, already makes a useful contribution to the revenues of several territories and is making a bigger one with the passing of almost every year. The most important centers of this type of fishery are St. Etienne, St. Louis and Dakar in Senegal, Libreville in the Gabon Republic, Pointe Noire in the Republic of the Congo, and Moçâmedes, Porto Alexandre, Baía dos Tigres, Benguela, Baía Farta and Luanda in Angola. In addition to supplying fresh and dried fish to the local markets, most of the companies send fish and fish products abroad. By methods often more picturesque than practical, Angola currently produces more than 100,000 tons of dried fish and fish products a year. Most of it is exported, mainly to neighboring territories, but some of it goes farther afield, to the Union of South Africa and to east Africa. The output is increasing, as the market grows and more interest is being taken in the commercial possibilities of tuna and other large fish. The same is true of the Gabon Republic and the Republic of the Congo, where several firms have recently been established to exploit the seemingly very considerable fish oil and whale oil potential of the deeper Atlantic waters. Companies have also been established (at Pointe Noire and Libreville) to catch and process shark and other large fish for which African fishermen have no particular use.

The economic importance of the Angolan fisheries may be judged by the fact that in the past few years the value of fish and fish products has been second only to coffee on the country's export list. In 1957 fish meal alone contributed 382.3 million escudos (approximately $13.5 million) to the revenues of the country, or slightly more than 10 per cent of the the total.

As is to be expected, the European-run fisheries are more highly organized than the African. This is especially true of the Angolan fisheries, most of which are manned and owned by Europeans. The dozens of fishing and fish-processing companies in each of the main ports are grouped together in syndicates belonging to a national federation. The main purpose of these syndicates is to regulate the sale and fix the price of all fish entering the ports, and to decide a premium and discount scale appropriate to the amounts and types of fish available. The syndicates also have the sole control of the sale of dried and smoked fish, whether destined for the domestic or the foreign market. In the neighboring republics of the French Community the arrangements concerning this kind of thing are left rather more elastic.

EAST AND CENTRAL LAKE FISHERIES

Commercial fishing on the great lakes of east and central Africa is a comparatively new undertaking. There was very little of it before the last war or even as lately as 1950 on some lakes, for instance, Lake George. An exact measure of its growth is difficult — almost impossible — to obtain, since very few Africans keep accounts and most of the lake fishing is in African hands. But the upward trend is unmistakable. Thus, whereas the annual Lake Tanganyika catch of dagaa (the local name for the small "whitebait" belonging to the Clupeidae family) was estimated officially to be "around 1,500 tons" in 1951, by the late 1950s it was estimated to be about 4,000 tons. Again, whereas the annual value of Uganda's fisheries was put at nearly £300,000 in 1951, by the late 1950s it was over £1.2 million, which, after the cost-of-living factor has been taken into account, still represents a real value increase of more than 200 per cent. And in Nyasaland, whereas in the late 1930s the weight of the Lake Nyasa catch taken by commercial, that is, non-African, firms was only 200 tons or so, in the late 1950s it was more than 3,000 tons. The fisheries of most of the other large lakes of east and central Africa and also some of the small ones appear to have shared this trend.

Because of the uncertainties of African-derived statistics, it is a little risky to rank the lake fishery territories in order of importance. However, there can hardly be any doubt that the four most important territories are Uganda, Tanganyika, Kenya and Nyasaland, and that Uganda is the most important of the four.

Uganda

All of Uganda's many lakes are rich in fish, but the bulk of the estimated 35,000-ton catch comes from four: Lakes Victoria, Edward, George and Albert. The catch is varied, with ngege (*Tilapia* spp.) making up most of it. The 3,500 or so fishing craft employed commercially on the lakes consist mainly of hand-propelled plank canoes and dugouts. Here and there, as on Lake George, motor vessels and canoes powered with outboard engines are proving their worth and so are coveted by more and more of the estimated 20,000 Africans who find full- or part-time work catching and distributing fish. The few Europeans in the industry are concerned with research, development, marketing and control work, the distribution of nets, and the trade in crocodile skins (which for the purpose of convenience rates as fishery). A number of Asians also find employment in the industry. Most of the fishermen are small operators owning a single canoe or maybe two, a minimum of gear and very little capital. Until 1954, when the African Loans Fund was set up, they lacked credit facilities. But the good prices of recent years have enabled many of them to invest in better types of gear.

Most of the catch goes onto the domestic market, but an increasing amount finds its way into other east African territories and the Belgian Congo. In the late 1950s about one tenth of the total catch was exported, either in dried or frozen form.

Much of the credit for the development and expansion of Uganda's commercial fisheries during the postwar years goes to The Uganda Fish Marketing Corporation. TUFMAC, to call it by its initials, was incorporated as a public company in October 1948, with a very modest initial capital of £50,000 (later increased to £107,187), of which a part is owned by individual Africans or African local governments and the rest — the major part — by the Uganda Development Corporation Limited, a government-controlled body. The aim of TUFMAC has been to "provide a steady long-term market at an assured price" and, to this end, to develop fisheries wherever, with the exception of Lake Victoria (which is under another agency), they are deemed to be an economic proposition. So far its chief project has been the development of the Lake George (Western Province) fisheries. Under the legislation covering these fisheries, TUFMAC purchases all its supplies of fish from individual, licensed African fishermen operating on the lake. It collects the catches daily from the fishing villages, paying an agreed price for every pound of fish caught. It supplies fishing gear and food at prices below those prevailing on the retail market. It assists the fishermen financially with the purchase of canoes and gear; and in general it seeks "to provide a useful service as well as a useful livelihood to the local community." [10]

The processing is done at Kasenyi on the shores of the lake. Here equipment is available for blast-freezing and cold storage, and for salting and smoke curing. Equipment for the manufacture of fish meal from waste products — hitherto consumed by pelicans, cranes and other convenient lake-shore scavengers — came into operation in 1955. From Kasenyi fresh fish now go by truck to all the larger towns of the protectorate and quick-frozen fillets by air to towns throughout east Africa. Most of the dried-fish output goes over to Ruanda-Urundi and the Belgian Congo. To handle the preparation of the daily catch TUFMAC employs some 400 Africans, Asians and Europeans, for all of whom housing and other services are provided. In recent years TUFMAC has been paying the Lake George fishermen over £50,000 annually for their catch.

Some of the credit for the present satisfactory state of Uganda's lake fisheries must also go to the protectorate government's Game and Fisheries Department, which supervises the development and control of all fisheries with the exception of those of Lake Victoria. The primary aim of this department is "to provide all local fish requirements from the

---

[10] A. G. Jones, Chairman of TUFMAC, in *Natural Resources, Food and Population in Inter-Tropical Africa*, edited by L. Dudley Stamp, Geographical Publications Ltd., London, 1956, p. 100.

country's own resources." This aim it pursues by a variety of means: by
introducing and popularizing improved methods of catching and processing, by opening up new fisheries and restocking old ones with quick-grow-
ing species, by sponsoring courses of instruction in better boat building
and demonstrating the advantages of power-boat fishing, by keeping the
crocodile population under control, and, not least, by running experimental and demonstration fish farms. For Lake Victoria the Lake Victoria
Fisheries Service, an East Africa High Commission agency which serves
the needs of Kenya, Tanganyika and Uganda, performs somewhat similar
functions.

Tanganyika

Unlike Uganda, Tanganyika has few lakes of any size, but what it has
are highly productive. In the middle and late 1950s, Lake Tanganyika,
Lake Rukwa and the territorial waters of Lake Victoria alone yielded an
estimated 50,000 tons of fish annually, or almost 50 per cent more than
the estimated catch from Uganda's lakes. Most of the catch consisted of
dagaa and species of *Tilapia,* and was marketed within the territory.
There was a small export of sun-dried dagaa and smoked *Tilapia* across
Lake Tanganyika to the Belgian Congo and Ruanda-Urundi. The total
value of the catch from all lakes was put at over £2 million, or considerably more than that of the Uganda catch.

Most of the fish are taken inshore, and by methods and gear identical
with those used by Uganda fishermen. Easily maneuvered and "sea-
worthy" as the dugout canoe can be, it was not designed for use on lakes
as large and squally as Lakes Tanganyika and Victoria. Consequently,
the deep-water fish resources of these lakes are as yet almost untouched.
They are not likely to remain so much longer, however. Such experimental fishing as has been done in them has given results that leave no
room for doubt about their money-making possibilities. Trawl nets used
in conjunction with echo-sounders have enabled motor fishing vessels to
obtain catches of up to 400 pounds in thirty minutes. There is already
talk of the possibility of a 30,000-ton "crop" being taken from each of the
two lakes annually without risk of overfishing them.

Kenya

By comparison with those of Tanganyika and Uganda, the lake fisheries
of Kenya are small. The Kenya waters of Lake Victoria yield about 3,000
tons of fish a year, Lake Rudolf between 300 and 400 tons, some smaller
lakes another 400 tons or so, making a total of less than 5,000 tons, or
about one tenth of the Tanganyika production. Efforts are being made
to increase this figure, which represents an annual per capita consumption
of less than two pounds; but progress is slow. There is still con-

siderable resistance to the idea of eating fish among many groups, especially the cattle keepers, for whom, traditionally, the only good food is food derived from animals. Then, too, the lakes of Kenya, excluding Victoria, cover only a little over 5,000 square miles, and are not extremely rich in fish species. However, there is always the Indian Ocean, with its 170-odd varieties of commercial fish, most of them flourishing within a net's cast of the coast.

Nyasaland

The main sources of fish in Nyasaland are Lake Nyasa and Lake Chilwa. Officially it is estimated that the annual catch from these two lakes and the lower Shire River has been averaging around 5,500 to 6,500 tons in recent years, but in the absence of reliable statistics of African landings, even official figures are no more than first approximations. The landings made by commercial, mostly Greek, firms are known; in 1956 they amounted to nearly 3,000 short tons, mostly species of *Tilapia* and nearly all taken from the southeast arm of Lake Nyasa. The commercial firms generally work with imported tackle and power craft of the motor cruiser type. They favor the use of shore seine nets and open-water ring nets. Gill netting and hook-and-line fishing are also employed, but on a smaller scale. The mainstay of the African fisheries is still the dugout canoe, the shore seine net and, in the northern part of Lake Nyasa, the open-water net suspended between two canoes. The shallow waters of Lake Chilwa are fished by Africans using staked-out gill nets.

Some of the commercial catch is sold fresh at the point of landing. Some is shipped fresh by truck to the large centers of population in the Southern Province. But most is sun-dried and then either hot-smoked or dry-salted for sale as rations to the tea estates and other large employers of African labor. Nowadays only a small quantity is exported, mainly salt fish, to the Copperbelt of Northern Rhodesia.

The greater part of the African catch is sold on the beach or bartered for other foodstuffs, or is distributed among crew members. What fish is caught in excess of local requirements and the personal needs of the fishermen is generally bought, sun-dried or salted, by African hawkers who work the inland areas and the towns on foot or by bicycle. There are thousands of such small middlemen; but, broadly speaking, fishing for the Nyasaland African is not a major commercial undertaking. It is rather "a subsistence activity with a commercial side to it, which becomes more prominent towards the south end of the Lake [Nyasa]." [11] In the past few years, though, some African fishermen have begun to take notice of the profits made by their European colleagues, and to tear a leaf out of their ledgers.

[11] *Nyasaland, 1953,* Colonial Reports, H.M.S.O., London, 1954, p. 76.

EAST COAST FISHERIES

With very few exceptions, the fisheries of the east coast are still of little consequence. Long stretches of this warm-water coast are fringed by coral reefs which are death to net fishing, whether by seine, trawl or stake. Where the waters are fished, it is usually in a desultory fashion by indigenous fishermen whose interest is primarily in feeding themselves. The few commercial fisheries are small by Atlantic coast standards and, so far as can be surmised from existing knowledge, small in relation to the resources of the areas fished. Those of the Republic of Sudan, Somalia, British and French Somaliland, the Malagasy Republic and Tanganyika are especially small. The Tanganyika government, in fact, seems scarcely aware of the existence of any such fishery within its jurisdiction; for in its 1954 report to the United Nations the government declared that it is still "too early to state whether there is any likelihood of establishing a commercial fishery on these [Tanganyika coast] waters." [12] The marine fisheries making the most substantial contribution to the domestic economy are those of Kenya, Zanzibar and Pemba, and Mozambique.

Kenya

The estimated production of the marine fisheries of Kenya in the late 1950s was about 5,000 tons, or roughly the same as that of its inland fisheries. Almost all of this tonnage was taken inshore, between the inner and outer line of reefs which flank the coast, by small craft (mostly canoes) using a wide assortment of tackle, mostly indigenous in design and materials. The use of goggles in underwater spear fishing is about the only concession most fishermen have been able, or willing, to make so far to foreign ways. The catch per fisherman is low; generally the daily amount marketed is not more than 10 to 12 pounds. Only a few handle as much as a hundredweight a day. Most of the catch is disposed of at the point of landing, either directly to consumers or to African and Asian middlemen who peddle it in Mombasa or upcountry markets. However, some now goes to the freezing and cold-storage plants which have been installed at Malindi, Shimoni and Mombasa, and some is shipped by rail, in ice, to Nairobi.

Zanzibar and Pemba

The marine fisheries, the only ones, of Zanzibar and Pemba annually yield about 2,000 tons of fish, with a market value in recent years of between £100,000 and £150,000. It is obvious therefore that most of the 5,000 fishermen on the two islands cannot possibly make more than a bare

[12] *Report by H. M. Government . . . to the General Assembly of the United Nations on Tanganyika . . . for the Year 1954*, H.M.S.O., London, 1955, p. 45.

living out of the business, or afford to use up-to-date gear. A part-interest in an outrigger canoe, or a dugout, and a net are the average extent of their capital stock, and a few shillings a week their average earnings. Those who work with the larger fishing dhow do somewhat better. The types of fish caught are much the same as those of the Kenya coast fishermen. Among the more important are spinefoot (or chafi), mullet, milk fish, crayfish, shark and octopus. As transportation is no great problem — the islands are small and the local demand for fish usually exceeds the supply — most of the catch is sold fresh.

Mozambique

Mozambique's commercial fisheries rank in size between those of Kenya and the islands of Zanzibar and Pemba. The annual catch is around 3,000 metric tons, and is made mainly by Africans working inshore from canoes, rowboats and sailboats. Most Mozambique Africans have an entirely justified fear of the open waters of the Mozambique Channel, which is frequented by typhoons and other dangerous winds and is well populated with sharks. European interest in the territory's fisheries has grown of recent years, especially since a cold-storage plant was established in Lourenço Marques in 1951. Already a considerable number of motor vessels are in service, mostly in the colder and more productive waters at the southern end of the Mozambique Channel. The range of fish taken is wide and includes swordfish, grouper, squid, bream and various species of shellfish. But the waters fished do not appear to be productive enough, or the fishermen energetic enough, or the fish esteemed enough, to meet the domestic demand; there is still a large importation of sardines from Portugal and crayfish from the Union of South Africa.

FISH FARMING

Fish farming, which bears the same relation to fishing as stock raising does to hunting, has been practiced with great success in the Far East for centuries. In tropical Africa it is still an innovation. But of all the innovations aimed at increasing the basic food supplies of that vast territory, none better deserves to be publicized or supported.

For consider some of its merits in the context of that environment. Fish, being cold-blooded, grow at a rate related to the temperature of the water in which they live. Tropical waters, being warm the year around, make for faster growth and maturation than mid-latitude waters with their sharp seasonal fluctuations of temperature, provided, as is generally the case, there is a parallel rate of growth of fish food. So favorable to fish growth are such waters that they can be made to sustain annual yields of one ton or more of fish to the acre; under particularly favorable circumstances they can be made to yield more than two tons an acre. There are few other ways of producing so great a weight of high-protein food in so small an area, and none that is practicable in tropical Africa.

Furthermore, there are few more simple ways of growing food. The principles of fish farming can readily be grasped by any intelligent — not necessarily literate — man, and the practice of them is not irksome. Fish ponds may be of almost any size and shape, though for efficient use of sunlight they should not be more than a few feet deep. Once made, they can last for years with reasonable care and immunity to flood and drought. Indeed, they are theoretically capable of lasting forever.

There are other advantages to fish farming. It is free from the hazards and frustrations of natural fishing with its dependence on the weather, the unpredictable movements of shoaling fish, and plain luck. Since the fish are captive, they can be taken at will, and in the required amounts. Then, fish farming can generally be practiced where there is a demand for fish, thereby all but eliminating transportation and middleman costs, which, as we have seen, are the bugbear of much African commerce in fish. Again, it takes up very little room. An acre pond should be able to provide a community of 50 persons with a half a pound of fish a week, even if it yields only half a ton a year. One million acres yielding one ton a year could provide 43 million people with one pound of fish a week, and 4 million acres — less than 6,300 square miles — could theoretically keep the whole population of tropical Africa in animal protein. Further, fish farming is not fussy about the room it takes up. Fish thrive as well in a pond constructed on sterile sands as in one constructed in valley alluvium, even better if the sun can get at it more readily. Then, again, unlike most African "crops," fish do better the longer they stay in the same place. The more a pond is nourished with fertilizer and the remains of its unconsumed plant and fish life, the greater its reserve of fertility grows. In time the fertility may grow to the point where it can sustain two "crops" — fish and rice, a form of "intertillage" the Chinese have been practicing with marked success for many generations. And, not the least of its advantages, fish farming is generally well adapted to those hot and humid areas which are the breeding ground of the tsetse fly, where alternative sources of animal protein are not easily or steadily available.

Naturally, the need for fish farming is not everywhere the same. Much less, though maybe still something, can be said for fish farms along the margins of the great lakes of east Africa and the Gulf of Guinea than on the "fly"-infested bush of the Rhodesias, or on the grass savannas of northern Nigeria, and the southern part of the Republic of Sudan. Likewise, the feasibility of fish farming is not everywhere the same. It is difficult to keep fish ponds topped up in regions where the evaporation greatly exceeds the rainfall, as it does over the drier savanna country.

It is difficult to maintain fish ponds in areas underlain by porus rock and in areas subject to flash floods that submerge low-lying ponds and even sweep them away. In some needy areas the people have a long-standing prejudice against the eating of fish. However, in plenty of areas the need for fish farming is matched by its feasibility, and in not a few both are matched by the skills, the manpower and the money necessary to make it a business proposition.

Though some fish-farming work is being carried on in most of the territories, few, if any, of them can be said to have put it on a commercial footing so far. Those that have come nearest to doing so are Southern Rhodesia, the Belgian Congo (including Ruanda-Urundi), Nigeria and Uganda. In all of these fish farming is being actively promoted by government agencies.

In 1954 in Uganda, for instance, the African local governments of Kigezi and Ankole, heavily populated areas faced with food problems, voted money for the establishment of demonstration fish farms on the lines of the central government's farm at Kajansi near Entebbe. These farms did their job. Within five years more than 4,000 small ponds — some as small as one eighth of an acre — had sprung up. Today their owners are catching and eating their own *Tilapia zillii*, a fast-growing fish which has the additional merit of battening on the weeds that would otherwise quickly choke the pond waters.

In the Belgian Congo fish farming has been part of the "battle for better food" engaged in by the implementers of the Ten Year Plan. "There is now a total of more than 100,000 [individually owned] ponds covering a total surface of 10,000 acres, which in 1956 yielded 2,000 tons of fish." [13] Even so, this is regarded merely as a start. "There is plenty of room for more ponds and it is expected that, with the natives learning all the tricks of the modern multiplication of fish, production will rise from 1,000 to 6,000 and even 8,000 pounds per hectare." [14]

In Southern Rhodesia interest in fish farming is being quickened as much by the irrigation as by the food possibilities of the ponds and dams. By 1956 over 40,000 acres of dam water were available for both purposes. The lowest yields obtained from experimental ponds have been about 400 pounds an acre a year. Where properly managed, some ponds have yielded two tons an acre, [15] so that an annual "crop" off the existing pond acreage of the order of 80,000 tons is already within the bounds of possibility. And there is no reason to suppose that the pond acreage will remain

[13] *The Belgian Congo Today* (Centre d'Information et de Documentation du Congo Belge et du Ruanda-Urundi, Brussels), Vol. VI, No. 3, 1957, p. 34.
[14] *Loc. cit.*
[15] *Report of the Secretary to the Federal Ministry of Agriculture, for the year ended 30th September, 1956,* Salisbury, 1957, p. 43.

stationary. It could be increased to 400,000 acres in the next ten years without too much difficulty.

The fish family in which the greatest interest is being shown by the fish-farming experts is the Cichlidae, begetters of the various species of *Tilapia*. These fish have many of the qualities needed for pond culture, since they are hardy and, to a large degree, plant and plankton feeders. They are also easy to breed. If they have one disqualification, it is that they often find it hard to grow, under conditions of maximum yield, beyond the weight of half a pound. The morale of few African fishermen is long sustained by fry of this size. Perhaps the solution in such cases lies in periodically introducing pike or other cannibals, into well-stocked fish ponds! [16]

TRENDS AND PROSPECTS

Up to now, fisheries have had a rather undistinguished career in tropical Africa. In few areas have they played the part of principals; in most they have been cast as extras; in some they have had no role at all. But this is changing, and it does not take any great power of prophecy to tell that today's extra is destined to become tomorrow's principal in more and more places. For the fact is that there is no cheaper, more reliable or more conservative way of making good the average African's protein deficiency than by providing him regularly with fish. Further, in an environment where food preservation is one of the housewife's greatest problems, not many foods keep longer (we can hardly say better) than smoked or dry-salted fish. Alternative ways of supplying this deficiency, whether over the shop counter or from the slaughter yard, usually cost the consumer more. Over very large areas, of course, alternative ways of providing animal protein in adequate amounts simply do not exist. In some areas even vegetable proteins are at a premium.

Increasing effort is being devoted to the business of making Africans more fish-minded, and fish more widely available. The mounting size of the catch taken from the waters of many territories is testimony to the effectiveness of the effort being put into the first of these aims. So is the growing attention being paid by many African fishermen to the preparation of their catch for market, and by African women to its cooking. So also is the growing outlay by Africans on more and better fishing gear. In some recent years the value of the fishing gear imported into Uganda has been roughly 20 per cent of the value of the protectorate's catch.

[16] The problems of fish farming in tropical Africa are dealt with at some length in a recent publication (No. 25) of the Scientific Council for Africa South of the Sahara: *The 2nd Symposium on African Hydrobiology and Inland Fisheries, Brazzaville, 1956,* Commission for Technical Cooperation in Africa South of the Sahara, London, 1957.

The second aim is being promoted in a number of ways: by scientific investigations into the spawning and feeding habits and the migrations of fish, both of the seas and lakes; by the systematic search for new fisheries and fishing methods, including the design of better boats and tackle and the development of loan associations to enable fishermen to buy such boats and tackle; and by the development of superior transportation, distribution and marketing facilities. Although this aim is not being promoted as vigorously or as thoroughly in some territories as in others, all but a very few territories are doing something to make fish more widely available. Thus, fishery surveys either have been or are being carried out off the coast of almost every west and east African territory. And several of the "great lakes" territories have been working on their own fish potential, and how to realize it.

Nyasaland completed in 1956 a two-year survey of Lake Nyasa, for the purpose of discovering which of the 200 varieties of fish inhabiting it are of economic value and what are the best ways of getting them into the net. (This is not as simple as it sounds since many of them live in the open waters of the lake, which have never been fished by the African; their preferences in the matter of nets are accordingly still unknown.)

Uganda has recently opened up a number of new fishery stations on its smaller lakes. Among these are Rwensama on Lake Edward and Rwengara on Lake Albert. It has also started a controlled fishing experiment on Lake Nyamisigeri, near the Kazinga Channel, to determine the maximum sustained yield of the area, and in the hope of being able to apply the findings to the neighboring larger and already much fished Lakes George and Edward. In Uganda, too, there are now places where qualified African carpenters can take courses in the art of building better types of fishing vessels.

Zanzibar has been experimenting successfully with powered fishing boats. These can reach more distant and richer fishing banks and still market their haul while it is in good condition. They can handle far more fish traps than an outrigger or ordinary dugout canoe, and, unlike the fishing dhow, they are not at the mercy of variable or contrary winds. To overcome the problem of financing such boats, the Zanzibar government has made their purchase possible with the help of loans repayable from earnings over a five-year period.

In Ruanda-Urundi, under their Ten Year Plan, the Belgians have been promoting fish-pond culture and lake stocking by means of demonstration farms and teaching programs, as the result of which the production of fish has been raised almost tenfold.

In Ghana and other west African territories attention is being given to the training of Africans to run seagoing motor vessels (some of which are equipped with echo-sounding equipment) and to run cooperatives, which, it is believed, will provide a much needed incentive to fishermen to catch more fish.

In Sierra Leone research and educational work aimed at making de-hydrated fish more attractive to local palates has been going on for several years with some success.

Another, and related, trend is the increasing interest being taken in the local processing of fish and the by-products of such processing. As the catch increases, so does the volume of fish offal and non-table varieties of fish for which the average fisherman has no use. So also does the volume of fish for which no fresh market can be found. True, much of this surplus can be cured for subsequent consumption, but since neither of the customary methods of curing fish — smoking and dry-salting — extends their keeping period by more than a few weeks, waste is almost bound to occur here too. In many European, Asiatic and North American countries fish falling into these categories have long been canned, or else processed along with the offal of the marketed fish for oils, fertilizer, cattle meal and other valuable commodities.

Up to two decades ago the demand for such commodities in most tropi-cal African countries was small and met by imports, if not very cheaply, at any rate more cheaply than it could have been by local concerns. But with the large demands of the present time, and the patently larger needs, the case for the establishment of local fish-processing plants grows stronger. Imports of fish and fish products into Ghana alone amounted to over £2 million in 1958. The imports of fish and fish products into Nigeria are higher still, running to roughly £8 million in 1958. Those into the Belgian Congo and Ruanda-Urundi were valued at almost half a billion francs, or some $10 million, in 1958. While part of the import con-sists of varieties of fish not found in tropical African waters and suffi-ciently well regarded to be able to hold their own against any local com-petitor, most of it consists of fish products that could be duplicated domestically, or at least within the borders of tropical Africa.

To reach the growing market for canned fish, several factories are now in operation. Ghana has an experimental plant that produces a canned fish of the herring type (*Sardinella*) for which the demand is keen. The west African members of the French Community have a number of small canning plants, notably at St. Louis and St. Etienne. The domestic need they were set up to meet in wartime continues to grow. Angola has canneries at Moçâmedes and Benguela serving both the export and the domestic markets on an increasingly large scale. Other plants, planned or in building, are considered to have good prospects.

The prospects for establishments processing fish and fish offal for meal, oil and fertilizer are generally thought to be better still, assuming — and it is still quite an assumption — that the demand for these things can be made effective by an advancing standard of living. Fish oil, especially liver oil, being rich in Vitamin A, could make a great contribution to the health of children and adults suffering from malnutrition. A fish meal ration could do wonders for the looks of most African cattle, and fish fertilizer could do equally much for most African landscapes. Already there are flourishing plants for the manufacture of fish oil and fish meal in west Africa and Angola, from which territory more than 94,000 tons of fish meal were exported in 1957. And, as noted earlier, Uganda already has, at Kasenyi, a fish meal plant using the offal formerly consumed by the resident pelicans and cranes. Similar plants are projected for several other territories, to the certain advantage, it would seem, of their lands and peoples, if not of their pelicans and cranes.

CHAPTER 9

The Mineral Realm

THE PAST HUNDRED YEARS

THE PROBLEMS OF PROSPECTOR
AND DEVELOPER

MINERALIZED REGIONS

MINERAL RESOURCES AND
PRODUCTION

TRENDS AND PROSPECTS

Until recently, the African was not much interested in the mineral wealth of his lands. For the most part he was quite unaware of it. There were, it is true, some notable exemplars of the art of smelting and moulding iron, copper, tin and gold, but these were in the habit of practicing their art in seclusion and keeping the sources of their supply hidden from all but the initiated few. Also, their sources were small, and the techniques of working them so laborious that, even had they wanted to, they would have found it next to impossible to make their products widely known.

The outsider's interest in the mineral wealth of tropical Africa goes back a long way, though it is only in the past generation that his interest in it has come to be matched by an appreciation of its magnitude. In the opinion of many, the interest in gold — the first to be quickened and the last to be quenched in any explorer's or prospector's breast — is at least as old as the Pharaohs. Near some ancient gold workings in western Ethiopia hieroglyphs have been found of a kind said to have been current in early dynastic times, and the gold taken from these workings is held to be indistinguishable from the gold taken from Egyptian tombs of the same period. Further, there are those who contend that the Old Testament references to "the whole land of Havilah where there is gold" and "the gold of Ophir" have a central African, perhaps a southern African, context. Even if the interest in African gold cannot positively be said to date back to antiquity (and the evidence is capable of more than one interpretation), it surely goes back to the Middle Ages. It is written large on the earliest extant maps of Africa, dating from the fourteenth and fifteenth centuries, in their references to "River of Gold" and "Gulf of Gold" and their pictures of men grubbing in river sands. It is found in the writings of Arabic travelers to sub-Saharan Africa as early as the twelfth century. And it supplied the main motive for many of Christendom's navigators — French, Portuguese, Flemings, Danes and others — in west African waters from the fifteenth century onward. While few of those who went to the African tropics, by land or by water, during this era made as much from gold as they did from slaves, they made enough to keep alive the belief that there was more gold in the hills of Africa than the Africans, or anybody else, had taken out of them. It simply needed finding, and digging.

THE PAST HUNDRED YEARS

The finding and digging began in earnest in the second half of the nineteenth century. To start with, the search, whether for gold or for baser minerals, was haphazard; prospectors played their hunches, and lost more often than they won. Among the lucky ones were those who listened to the African and learned where he got his metal supplies. But as more became known about the geological constitution of the region, prospecting became more methodical and increasingly successful.

The massive Kambove copper deposit on the Katanga was discovered in 1892. In 1900 the Comité Spécial du Katanga entrusted to Robert Williams, a British engineer, and to Tanganyika Concessions, Ltd. (incorporated in the previous year) the exclusive rights over the whole highly mineralized area of southern Katanga. By 1906, the year in which the Union Minière du Haut-Katanga was launched, the importance of the Katanga had been well established. Well to the north of it a large tin deposit was discovered at Manono in 1912. Major discoveries were also made south of the Belgian Congo border. In 1895 Sir Edmund Davis and Cecil Rhodes formed the forerunner of the Rhodesia Copper Company, in whose holdings the site of what was to become the Broken Hill (zinc-lead-vanadium) mine was discovered in 1902. In that year William Collier, a prospector, discovered the Roan Antelope [1] and Bwana Mkubwa [2] copper outcrops. In the Republic of the Congo (then the

---

[1] So named because Collier found it as the result of shooting a roan antelope bull; the rock on which the antelope was standing when killed was stained green with copper.

[2] In Chinyanga, one of the African languages widely spoken in Northern Rhodesia, the name means "The Big Master."

Middle Congo Province of French Equatorial Africa) the Mindouli copper mines came into production in 1910, following the organization of the Compagnie Minière du Congo Français.

Meanwhile important deposits of other minerals were being discovered — coal in Southern Rhodesia; coal, mica and graphite in the Malagasy Republic; potash in Ethiopia; diamonds in Angola; diamonds, manganese and bauxite in Ghana. By the outbreak of World War I minerals were beginning to figure in the export trade of several territories.

While World War I acted as a tonic to some mineral interests, it acted as a depressant to others. From 10,700 metric tons in 1914, the copper production of the Union Minière du Haut-Katanga rose to 27,500 tons in 1917. The military needs of the allies also led to the development of the Ethiopian potash deposits, one of the very few sources of potash available to them; to a greatly increased graphite production in the Malagasy Republic and the start of its mica production; and to the expansion, in the later stages of the conflict, of the German East Africa mica production. But most of the other mining enterprises, in both German and allied Africa, languished, and little new prospecting was undertaken.

The period between the two world wars was one of fluctuating fortunes for the miner and prospector. Faced with the necessity of rebuilding homes, services and industries destroyed during the war, the colonial powers were unable to give a high priority to their African territories. The ex-German territories fared perhaps worst of all, for none of the trustee powers was anxious to put scarce money into enterprises the future of which was clouded with legal uncertainty. For some years following the return of Great Britain to the gold standard in 1925, even well-established gold-mining enterprises found difficulty in attracting new money, and, in some instances, in making money; so that gold prospecting became more of a memory than a means of livelihood. Then, early in the 1930s, came the world depression — an ill wind indeed to the tin, copper and other base-metal enterprises, barely yet out of their swaddling clothes, though one that blew some good to the gold-mining industry.

Nevertheless, the status of minerals and mining was advanced more than it was retarded during these decades. In the Belgian Congo, the Union Minière du Haut-Katanga, with more courage than conviction of success, embarked upon its vast Jadotville project, completing the copper concentration plant in 1921 and the hydro-power installation at Cornet Falls on the Lufira in 1920. In 1925, at Kipushi, near Elisabethville, the Prince Léopold mine began producing copper, along with considerable amounts of silver and zinc. In 1934 the Géomines Company (Compagnie Géologique et Minière des Ingénieurs et Industriels Belges) installed a tin smelter, using power from a hydro-plant on the Luvua River, at Manono. In Northern Rhodesia, through the combined efforts of the British and American interests which later became known as the

Rhodesian Selection Trust Group, and the Anglo American Corporation of South Africa, a new copper domain was established. By 1932, the output of the Copperbelt, as the area came to be called, was already greater than that of the Katanga mines. In the present Republic of the Congo, mining for lead and zinc began in 1933, and mining for diamonds about the same time, the depression notwithstanding. In Nigeria the first columbite-tantalite mine went into production in 1933. In Sierra Leone, important discoveries of diamonds, gold, platinum, iron ore and chromite were made in the 1920s, and from 1926 onward minerals began to figure conspicuously in the country's export trade. In Uganda mining for tin ore began in 1927. Before the outbreak of World War II Angola, Ghana, the Republic of Guinea and Tanganyika were exporting diamonds, and Ghana manganese as well.

World War II was for most mining concerns a time of unprecedented growth, and growing pains. There was scarcely a mineral in production, other than gold, that was not classified as "strategic," and gold continued to have its uses. Several minerals which up to 1939 had been little more than curiosities in African museums became the subject of intense interest. Among these were Angolan mica, Malagasy quartz, Ugandan tungsten, Ghanaian bauxite and, most interesting of all, Belgian Congo uranium-radium. At the same time the demand for tin, tantalite, columbite, copper, cobalt, zinc, manganese, iron and industrial diamonds rose higher than it had ever been. It says much for the industry that these demands were largely met. In addition to wrestling with labor shortages — many tropical African territories furnished contingents of Europeans and Africans for active service — the industry was short of rolling stock and shipping and, in many instances, machinery and maintenance facilities. This was especially true of the colonies administered by countries that were either enemy-occupied or repeatedly bombed. In the circumstances, the installation in the Belgian Congo, at Lubumbashi, Elisabethville, by the Union Minière du Haut-Katanga of a converter for the production of blister copper, thereby relieving the company of the necessity of exporting the semi-concentrated ore (or matte), was an achievement of the first order. No less notable were the establishment, in 1941, of a copper concentrator at Kolwezi to the northwest of Elisabethville and the development of an electrolytic copper-leaching process; the conversion of a Congo steel foundry into a tin smelter to provide additional facilities for the processing of tin ore to the metal state; and the creation of an iron and steel industry in Southern Rhodesia.

The years since World War II have been a time of great, though not uninterrupted, expansion for most established mining concerns (other than gold, which is still prevented from running loose in the world market), and one of lively activity by government and private geologists and the promoters of new mining concerns. Cobalt and copper production have set new records. Activity in manganese, iron, industrial diamonds, chrome and zinc has increased greatly. And there has been an almost undignified scramble for such "jet-age" minerals as lithium salts, pyrochlore (containing niobium), monazite, columbite and tantalite. There has also been a greatly stepped-up search for petroleum wherever the rock structure gives so much as a hint of a promise.

THE PROBLEMS OF PROSPECTOR AND DEVELOPER

Tropical Africa is no place for the sourdough equipped with a hammer and a hunch. Since much of it is covered with thick bush or dense forest, the going is slow and painful, and it is possible to wander for days looking for clues to what lies beneath. Where the vegetation presents no problem, the weathered rock frequently does, for in the wet tropics weathering is capable of transmuting primary rock into secondary compounds that cunningly conceal their parentage. To be a successful prospector in such country calls for much patience, or, what amounts to the same thing, ample resources.

As many modern-day developers have discovered, the African wilderness continues to exact quite a price from those who would probe its riches and exploit them. And while the currency in which the price is paid has altered since the days of the early pioneers, the price does not get any less. On the contrary, it gets higher, so much so that the keeping of running costs within manageable limits is now, for many mining companies, the primary problem.

Modern mining being what it is, a highly complicated strategy for the winning of the earth's ores in the speediest, cheapest and least drudging fashion, it has to lean heavily on the high-priced skills of geologists, cartographers, chemists, engineers, laboratory technicians, artisans and administrators — plus those of the airman, since aerial photography and surveying are playing an increasingly important role in geological prospecting. As few of these skills have been acquired by Africans, they have to be imported from a distance, mostly from the Union of South Africa and Europe. This, of course, costs more than passage money alone. Salaries and perquisites have to be attractive enough to compensate for the isolation and discomforts of life at a tropical mining site. The costs of unskilled labor may be lower per worker than they are on a European or an American mine, but they are not greatly different per unit of work after a reckoning has been made of the generally lower efficiency of African labor and the substantial fringe benefits it receives in the way of free or subsidized food, housing, medical care and so on.

Labor costs are only part of the problem. Most of the mines are a long way from the sea or other navigable water. Many are, or were to start with, a long way from railways, roads, towns, power stations and similar services. Some, like those in the Katanga-Copperbelt region, were even a long way from places that could meet their food requirements satisfactorily. Mining supplies and ores are costly to ship under the best of conditions; when the supplies have to be brought by sea from Europe or North America and by road or rail from a coast that may be more than a thousand miles away, and when ores have to be shipped back over the same route, freight rates can quickly price a product out of the market.

Most mines have also to reckon with heavy depreciation charges. Wet-season damage to installations and equipment from flood and rust can be costly, and the roads in the wet season can quickly degenerate into quagmires. Dry-season damage from dust can be almost as costly. African dust can penetrate the tightest machinery and the most closely sealed oil caps; there are no more effective saboteurs of machinery than the quartzite sands that veil so much of the face of Africa. Both wet- and dry-season troubles are aggravated by the inability of most indigenous workers to deal with machines that have ceased to go.

Capital over the years has been almost as much of a problem as costs. The developers of a new concern have to find money not only for mining and processing plants and the technical, scientific and other skilled services indispensable to their efficient use, but also for roads and perhaps railways, for power installations, for the provision of housing, for the financing of social welfare facilities, and for all the other benefits which nowadays are held to be necessary components of a major mining enterprise. It is one thing for a geologist to prove that, over a given number of years, an African mine will produce wealth enough to reward the investor's faith in such an enterprise; it is another to find the investor — government, corporation or individual — willing to underwrite it. In some places mining capital has been scarce simply because governments have done little to attract it. Thus, it could be argued that until recently neither Liberia nor Ethiopia was in any shape to play host to foreign investors. Until a few years ago, some territories, including those of Portuguese Africa, showed no more than a lukewarm interest in their mineral potential. Some have traditionally preferred to spend their money on other types of economic development. In the "settler" areas of Kenya, and more recently in other parts of that country, the government's primary interest has been to build up stable agricultural communities. With few exceptions, tropical African governments are acting more and more on the premise that the chief end of publicly raised capital is to better the lot of the man on the land.

Finally, numerous technical problems have had to be overcome. There has been a need to develop methods of systematically sampling mineralized areas and ore bodies possessed of special characteristics, in order to ascertain the feasibility of working them at a profit. In some cases new methods of mining, or modifications of standard methods, have had to be developed to suit local conditions or labor. The discovery of new metallurgical processes has been the key to the successful operation of more than one mine, the most notable instance of which has been the use of "flow sheets" for the recovery of cobalt from certain types of ore. Thomas G. Murdock, whose working paper has furnished the bulk of the information contained in this chapter, says:

The existence of ably staffed research departments on all the larger mines is proof enough of the importance attached to the solution of problems in the field of ore beneficiation, reduction and refining of the recovered metal. And the development of an integrated operation has often called for investigations into the recovery of waste products, the manufacture of sulfuric acid and of explosives, and the location of sources of water, refractories, fuels and fluxes.

MINERALIZED REGIONS

The best defined of the many mineralized regions of tropical Africa are the following:

1. *The Katanga–Northern Rhodesian copper region.* This is one of the world's largest copper bodies, perhaps the largest. From end to end it is over 250 miles long, and in places more than 50 miles wide. Although it is being developed as two almost completely separate economic entities, it is one in physical features, geology and mineralization. It consists of a partially worn-down peneplain, composed of ancient shales, limestones, conglomerates and other sedimentary formations. The northwesterly-southeasterly trend line of these formations is interrupted here and there by geological faults. Some of the copper ores are associated with cobalt, and some with zinc. Other minerals found in this region are uranium, cadmium, silver, gold, platinum, palladium and germanium. The ores are for the most part oxidized and appear as impregnations, concretions and deposits in the sedimentary formations. In zones unaltered by surface waters, sulfide ores predominate; these take the form of small veins, impregnations or spots. The mineralized zones frequently differ in appearance from the nonmineralized zones, from which they are separated by faults.

2. *The kimberlite region of east central Africa.* In size this constitutes, in Murdock's opinion, "a metallogenic province without parallel anywhere in the world." Including "skips," it may be said to run practically the whole way from the Tropic of Cancer to the Tropic of Capricorn. Its major components are located in Tanganyika, Angola, and the Katanga and eastern Kasai regions of the Belgian Congo. Unlike the Katanga–Northern Rhodesian copper region, it has no unity of surface relief, geological formation or mineralization. What unity it has derives from its turbulent structural history. The volcanic cataclysms to which it has been periodically subjected left a rich legacy of "pipes" and other bodies of kimberlite that accommodate most of Africa's diamonds. So far the principal mining developments have been associated with the "alluvials," that

is, with those diamonds which have been weaned away from their host by the forces of denudation and running water. As there is good reason to believe that there are still far more diamonds in the kimberlite than ever came out of it, the prospects of this mineral region would seem to be almost as durable as its major product.

3. *The Great Dyke of Southern Rhodesia*. This pencil-shaped formation is anything from three to six miles wide and runs in a north-northeast line for more than 320 miles. For part of its course it is as conspicuous physically as it is geologically; in its northern section it forms the Umvukwe Range, rising fifteen hundred feet above the otherwise almost featureless veld. Geologically, the Great Dyke represents the exposed hardened remains of an ancient outflow, along a structural cleavage line, of viscous materials derived from the magmatic womb of the earth. The "remains" consist of such things as dolerites, norites, peridotites and schists, which, between them, house one of the most varied assortments of minerals to be found anywhere on the continent. Its precious minerals include emerald, platinum, gold and silver. Its base metals include chromium, nickel and iron ore, and its nonmetallic minerals, asbestos and limestone.

Of several smaller mineralized regions the best defined and most notable are:

a. The Southern Rhodesian coal fields lying to the south of the Zambezi in sedimentary formations dating back to Palaeozoic times, and forming part of what geologists call the Karoo system.

b. The manganese occurrences of Ghana, the Belgian Congo, the Gabon Republic and Angola, most of which are secondary; that is, they are the product of the mechanical and chemical processes that take place when rock with a slight manganese content is exposed to air and water.

c. The west coast — Sierra Leone, Liberia and the Republic of Guinea — iron fields, where mechanical and chemical processes are likewise responsible for much of the mineralization that has gone on in the deeply decomposed basement complex.

d. The tin fields (and their associated minerals) of Nigeria, the Belgian Congo, Tanganyika and Uganda, in all of which the intrusion of acid granites into ancient schists and quartzites is apparent.

e. The gold fields of Ghana, Southern Rhodesia, the Belgian Congo, Ethiopia and Tanganyika, which can likewise boast of a venerable geological ancestry, even though the alluvial deposits in them are in the habit of keeping younger company.

MINERAL RESOURCES AND PRODUCTION

In times such as these any mineral resource survey is bound to be out of date long before it is published. For scarcely a week passes without the announcement of some major new find, or some impressive addition to the proven resources of a known deposit; and, of course, many finds and additions are not announced. What follows, therefore, is in the nature of a progress report giving the state of generally available knowledge of tropical African minerals and mining around 1957-1958.

METALS

FERROUS METALS

Ferrous metals are widely distributed in tropical Africa. In addition to iron ore, which is being mined on an increasing, though by world standards still exceedingly small, scale, the following ferrous metals are found and worked in significant quantities: manganese, chrome, cobalt, columbium, nickel, tungsten and vanadium. So far there have been no reports of important bodies of molybdenum.

Iron Ore

The vast bulk of the current production of iron ore comes from the three west African territories of Sierra Leone, Liberia and the Republic of Guinea. As Figure 18 and Table 14 show, increased output in these territories and in Southern Rhodesia, the only other sizable producer, has

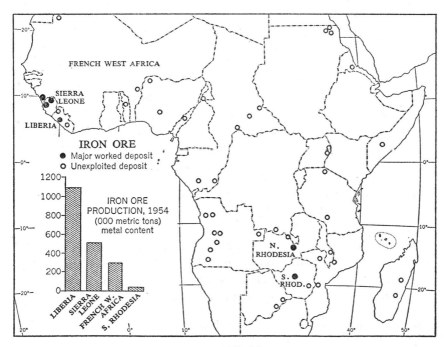

FIGURE 18

Table 14

PRODUCTION OF IRON ORE, 1938-1957

(Iron Content; Thousand Metric Tons)

TERRITORY	1938	AVERAGE 1945-1949	AVERAGE 1950-1954	1955	1957 [a]
Total	525	549	1,365	2,318	2,798
Per cent of world total [b]	0.7	0.7	1.0	1.3	1.4
Republic of Guinea (French Guinea)	—	—	99	325	544
Liberia	—	—	540	1,163	1,337
Southern Rhodesia	—	8	32	46	74
Sierra Leone	525	541	694	784	843

Source: United Nations, *Statistical Yearbook, 1958,* New York, 1958.

[a] Preliminary figures.   [b] Including U.S.S.R.

doubled tropical Africa's share of the world total during the past ten years or so.

Sierra Leone. The major deposits are located near the Tonkolili River, and near Lunsar in the Marampa chiefdom of the Port Loko district.

The Tonkolili deposits, which lie about 80 miles northeast of Marampa, consist mostly of high-grade (more than 60 per cent iron content) hematite. As the deposits have not been fully prospected, "it is not possible to estimate the quantity of ore available but it is expected considerably to exceed 100 million [long] tons." [3] So far there has been no exploitation of these deposits.

The more accessible Marampa deposits consist mostly of hematite, containing up to 65 per cent iron, with attractively low silica, phosphorous and sulfur contents. "It is understood that the reserves of soft ore at Lunsar are in the region of 20 million [long] tons, but this is probably a very conservative estimate." [4] Most of the output goes to the United Kingdom, West Germany, the United States and the Netherlands. The Lunsar workings are linked with the seaport of Pepel by rail.

Liberia. The Bomi Hills deposits were prospected during World War II. Their development began in the late 1940s and the first shipment of ore (to the Republic Steel Corporation, via Baltimore) took place in 1951. The ore consists of roughly two-thirds magnetite and one-third hematite, and averages over 68 per cent iron. At the present production rate of under 1.5 million metric tons a year, the estimated reserves of 35 million tons, suitable for open-hearth processing, should be good

[3] J. D. Pollett, *The Geology and Mineral Resources of Sierra Leone,* H.M.S.O., London, 1952, p. 18.

[4] *Ibid.,* p. 17.

for at least a generation. A railroad has been built between the mine and the Free Port of Monrovia.

The Mano River deposits, located along the Sierra Leone border, are larger than those of the Bomi Hills, though their metal content is somewhat lower (averaging about 53 per cent). The National Iron Ore Company Ltd., in which the Liberian government is the largest shareholder, has recently been formed to develop them. It expects to begin shipments in 1961, and to work up to an annual production of about 4 million tons of ore by 1965.

The Mount Nimba deposits, located about 170 miles from the coast (at Buchanan), are being developed by the Liberian American-Swedish Minerals Company and the Bethlehem Steel Corporation. When complete (about 1963), the facilities for production and shipment are expected to make possible an annual export of up to 10 million tons of high-grade ore.

Republic of Guinea. The ore deposits are among the largest in tropical Africa. The only deposit worked on any scale at present is at Conakry. Its mineral content ranges from 50 to 70 per cent. The French first became interested in the possibility of exploiting these extremely accessible ores before World War I, but it was not until 1949 that the Compagnie Minière de Conakry began operations, and not until 1953 that the first shipments were made. The annual production, which in 1957 was still only slightly over 500,000 metric tons, could, so it is stated, be easily increased to a million tons, and probably to 3 million, without additional capital investment. Each of the three ore-bearing layers is capable of being worked by open-pit methods. There are other deposits west of Satadougou and Beyla.

Southern Rhodesia. The commercial mining of iron ore here began in 1946.[5] From a mere 128 short tons in that year the production rose to over 74,000 in 1957. At present the only ore body being worked is that at Redcliff near Que Que. The ore is mostly high-grade hematite and limonite, yielding up to 65 per cent iron. The proven reserves are said to be not less than 50 million tons.

Elsewhere in Southern Rhodesia there are numerous deposits of fair to high-grade ore, for which there has been no commercial call up to now. One of the more promising of these, from the standpoint of grade, access to power supply, transportation facilities and market, is located in the Sabi valley near the Makushwe and Malilongwe coal fields. Exploratory work on these deposits was recently undertaken by South African companies as part of the government's economic survey of that area. Early estimates put the high-grade reserves at 14 million tons, the total reserves at 53 million.

[5] The Rhodesian Iron and Steel Commission — now the Rhodesian Iron and Steel Company (Pvt.), Ltd. — was established in 1942, but during its early years it was concerned only with production from scrap metal.

Northern Rhodesia also has large deposits, but so far they have been worked on an extremely small scale. Most of the output has come from the Mwomboshi mine and has been used in the Broken Hill lead and zinc plant, as a reagent.

Many other territories are known to have workable ore bodies, but in almost none of them is the iron being worked except by African blacksmiths for the making of simple tools, utensils and implements. A catalogue, by territories, of the major known deposits follows.

Angola. Iron ore has been discovered at many points, notably near Zenza do Itombe, Vouga, Saia, Nova Lisboa, Dongo, Chitado and in the Alto Zambeze district. Although these ores have good properties and medium to high mineral content, most of them are too far from transportation facilities to be of economic interest at the present time.

Bechuanaland. At least three large ore bodies have been found: at Mogobane (a high-quality hematite); in the Tati district; and in the south of the protectorate (siliceous banded ironstones).

Belgian Congo. The total reserves appear to be extremely large, but have not yet been systematically investigated. The chief deposits, in the form of common oxides, hematite, magnetite and limonite, are located in the Uele, Kibali-Ituri and southern Katanga regions.

Republic of Dahomey. There are large deposits at Banjeli, northwest of Bassare.

Ethiopia. Although there are numerous verified occurrences, Murdock reports that "the indicated reserve is small and the occurrence is of such a nature geologically that the prospects for their economic exploitation are not very good."

French Cameroons. "Rather abundant" magnetic iron ore bodies have been identified east of Dschang.

(French) Togo. Important deposits have been located at Kompa and Kandi.

Gabon Republic. The most promising deposits are located in the extreme northeast of the state at Boka-Boka near Mekambo. Here several hematite bodies have been proved, the largest having an estimated 6 billion metric tons of recoverable ore averaging 40-45 per cent metal and rising in places to over 65 per cent.[6] An international syndicate, of which the Bethlehem Steel Corporation is a leading member, is planning to develop some of these deposits in the future. The first step in the undertaking is the construction (now under way) of a 400-mile railway from Boka-Boka to Kango, near Libreville, whence the ore will be shipped overseas.

Malagasy Republic. Small quantities of magnetite ore of excellent grade

[6] According to information supplied in 1958 by Dr. P. Moussa, Director of Economic Affairs in the General Secretariat of the French Community.

are found in many places on the plateau, for example, in the region of Ambositra and Fianarantsoa and to the east of Tananarive.

Mozambique. At Tete there is a large magnetite ore body with a high titanium content that would require electric furnace treatment. At Milange there is a high-grade magnetite (up to 70 per cent iron), and at Lucite, near Melsetter on the Southern Rhodesian border, a hematite deposit of very good quality.

Nigeria. In the vicinity of Lokoja, at the confluence of the Niger and the Benue rivers, lies an extremely large ore body running to "perhaps as much as 1,000 million tons." The phosphorous content is high and the iron content only around 50 per cent; but the ore body is favorably disposed for open-cut mining and for gravity transport to the Niger.

Nyasaland. A high-grade hematite ore body (up to 69 per cent mineral content) extends from the southwest side of Mlanje Mountain to the Portuguese border.

Somalia. "Ferruginous minerals occur in great quantity," but so thinly in any given area as to offer very poor prospects at the present time.

Republic of Sudan. Five high-quality ore bodies have been disclosed by government geologists. Unfortunately, all five lie at least a hundred miles northwest of Port Sudan and between 15 and 45 miles from the sea, in most inhospitable country. Other deposits have been found in the province of Bahr-el-Ghazal and near Umm Keddada in eastern Darfur.

Tanganyika. Many ore bodies have been confirmed, but most of them are magnetites with a troublesome percentage of titanium. Those located in the Njombe district to the north and northeast of Lake Nyasa and near the eastern shore of Lake Tanganyika are considered to have the largest potential.

Uganda. Large bodies of high-grade magnetite have been confirmed between Mt. Elgon and Tororo. According to Murdock, "Now that the development of hydroelectric power from the source of the Nile is a reality, the possibility of exploiting these deposits is being investigated thoroughly."

Cobalt

Economically important deposits of cobalt have so far been found in only three territories (Figure 19). In all three the deposits occur in association with copper ore bodies. In two, the Belgian Congo and Northern Rhodesia, their exploitation has been undertaken for a number of years; in the third, Uganda, production began only in 1958. From an annual average of nearly 7,700 metric tons of recoverable cobalt in 1950-1954, the tropical African output rose to more than 9,400 metric tons in 1957, when it represented about three fifths of the world total.

Belgian Congo. Of the three producers, the Belgian Congo is by far the largest. It is, in fact, the largest cobalt producer in the world, ac-

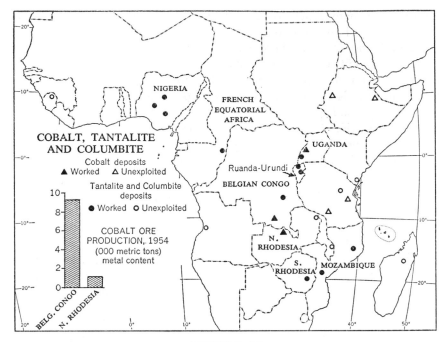

FIGURE 19

counting in 1956 for nearly 9,100 metric tons and in 1957 for over 8,100 tons. The chief cobalt-copper ore bodies are located in the Kolwezi region of the Katanga field. The ores occur in impregnated veins, or mineralized sands, in the form of oxide or sulfide compounds; their structure and cobalt content tend to be very irregular. After concentration at Kolwezi, the poorer ores are treated in a leaching and electrolysis plant, and the richer ores in an electrothermal plant, both at Jadotville. About half of the output of these plants consists of highly refined cobalt granules; the rest consists of an alloy (cobalt-copper-iron) which is sent to the Olen plant in Belgium and to the United States for final separation. In 1952 the Katanga cobalt reserves were put at approximately 225,000 metric tons.

Northern Rhodesia. Very much smaller though it is, the Northern Rhodesian cobalt output is the world's fourth largest. Until 1956 nearly all of the output came from the Nkana mine, belonging to the Rhokana [Anglo American] Corporation, and until 1952 it was all marketed in the form of a high-grade cobalt-copper-iron alloy. Since then a steadily increasing proportion of the Nkana output has been in the form of high-quality electrolytic cobalt. The results obtained with the electrolytic method are considered so satisfactory that it is likely to supersede the older one in the not very distant future. The annual output of the Nkana mine is currently (1958) about 1,500 short tons of cobalt.

The recently opened Chibuluma mine, affiliated to the Rhodesian Selection Trust, had an output of over 650 short tons of cobalt in 1958, its second full year of operation. The Chibuluma reserves are put at 6.6 million short tons averaging 0.5 per cent cobalt. Those of the still undeveloped Baluba mine are put at 70 million short tons averaging approximately 0.2 per cent cobalt.

Uganda. Deposits are located at Kilembe in the eastern foothills of the Ruwenzori Mountains. Although estimates of workable reserves are not yet complete, about 13.5 million long tons have already been proved in the five copper-cobalt ore bodies under development. As soon as cobalt recovery can be shown to be a paying proposition, it is planned to install a processing plant capable of giving an annual production of 900,000 pounds (450 short tons) of cobalt. The ore will be crushed and concentrated at the mine portal and the resulting concentrates "piped" to Kasese, the railhead. Here they will be roasted and leached and shipped by rail as a cobalt oxide to Mombasa. Power for the project will be supplied by the Mobuku Hydro-Electric Scheme located about 25 miles from Kilembe.

Cobalt is also found in Ethiopia, east of Nejo in Wollega, and in the Chercher region, but the known occurrences in these localities are not large enough or sufficiently continuous to encourage hopes of exploitation. Deposits have been reported in Tanganyika, near Njombe and in the Uluguru Mountains.

Chrome Ore

Although chrome ore is reported as existing in workable quantity in many territories, only in two is it mined on any scale. These are Southern Rhodesia, an easy leader, and Sierra Leone (Figure 20). Together these two territories have contributed in recent years between 15 and 20 per cent to the world output of chrome ore. Preliminary figures of their 1958 output credited them with more than 275,000 metric tons (chromic oxide content).

Southern Rhodesia. Based on its estimated chromic oxide content, the output of chrome ore from Southern Rhodesia is the third largest in the free world, being exceeded only by that of the Philippines and Turkey. Between the early 1900s, when chrome mining began, and 1950, Southern Rhodesia's production totaled almost 6 billion short tons, or one sixth of the total chrome ore output during that period. Since 1950 it has been between one sixth and one quarter of the free-world output of chromic oxide. Most of the deposits being worked are of metallurgical grade, containing 48 per cent or more chromic oxide and having a chrome-to-iron ratio of nearly 3 to 1, in some cases more. There are also large deposits of refractory and chemical grade ores. The chief deposit, one of the world's largest, is at Selukwe just to the west of the Great Dyke in the Southern

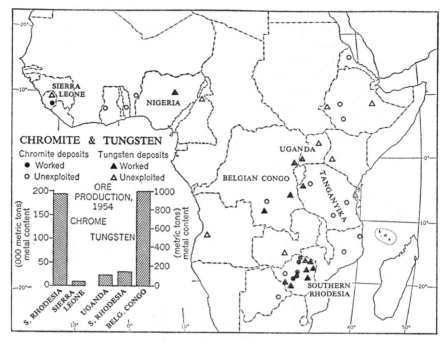

FIGURE 20

Rhodesian Midlands. It occurs in various types of ore body, the chief of which lends itself to large-scale, low-cost mining methods. A second and genetically very different deposit is found in the Great Dyke, which contains numerous bands or layers of chromite. Thin though they are, these layers in the aggregate represent a very large reserve of metallurgical and chemical ores. The total probable reserves of chrome ores of all grades have been put at 2 billion short tons.

By far the larger part of the output is sent 500 miles by rail to Beira for export, mainly to the United States and the United Kingdom. Transport, loading and unloading charges are accordingly heavy, amounting on the average to between 25 and 35 per cent of the cost to the consumer. Given adequate railway- and port-handling facilities (and they have greatly improved in recent years), there is said to be no reason why an annual output of 600,000 tons of ore should not be possible from the existing mines.

The amount of local processing done is still comparatively small, but it is increasing. Already there are several crushing and concentrating plants at Selukwe, Spotts and other points along the Great Dyke, and a small ferro-chrome plant at Gwelo.

Sierra Leone. Chromite was first found here in 1929 by government geologists. Of the several important occurrences that have been brought to light since then, the most important are those now being mined in the Kambui Hills north of Hangha on the Freetown-Pendembu railway. The ore has a lower chromic oxide content (43-44 per cent) than Southern Rhodesia's, but the ratio of chrome to iron is satisfactory. Further, much of the ore is suitable for beneficiation; much of it can be improved to 50 per cent and still maintain the favorable chrome-to-iron ratio. At the beginning it was mined by open-cast methods, but these have ceased to be economical.

Production, which began in 1937, has always been on a small scale. In the first twelve years or so it averaged little more than 10,000 long tons a year. In the middle and late 1950s it fluctuated between 6,000 and 10,000 tons (chromic oxide content). The mines are run by Sierra Leone Chrome Mines Ltd., a company that holds "a special exclusive prospecting license over 1,893.42 square miles of country that includes most of the known deposits." [7] Most of the ore is shipped to the United States for use in the ferro-chrome, refractory and chemical trades.

No data on reserves have been published, but they are unquestionably large.

The existence of extensive chromite deposits has also been confirmed in other parts of west Africa and in Mozambique.

West Africa. Chromite has been known to exist in Togo since 1907 and in Dahomey since 1936. The most promising occurrences in Togo are in the region at Atakpamé, which places them near the railway that runs upcountry from Lomé. Their chromic oxide content averages around 40 per cent. In Dahomey several deposits have been identified in the Tanguiéta region and it is considered likely that there are others thereabouts; all of them are believed to be of good quality, but as they are about 180 miles from railhead, at Parakou (the present terminus of the Benin-Niger railway), and as Parakou is 275 miles from the port of Cotonou, their immediate economic prospects can hardly be rated very high.

Mozambique. The two most promising known occurrences in Mozambique are those near Alto Ligonha and near Porto Amélia. In each case the chromite could be easily concentrated by gravity separation in jigs, but the Alto Ligonha deposit is not as high in grade as the Porto Amélia one, while the latter is much farther away from the places where it could do the most good.

Other territories from which there have been confirmed reports of chromite deposits are Bechuanaland, the Belgian Congo, Ethiopia (including Eritrea), Ghana, Kenya, the Malagasy Republic and Tanganyika.

Manganese Ore

More than 95 per cent of the total output of manganese ore in tropical Africa comes from two territories, Ghana and the Belgian Congo (Figure 21). Of the two, Ghana has always been the more important producer,

[7] Pollett, *op. cit.*, pp. 22-23.

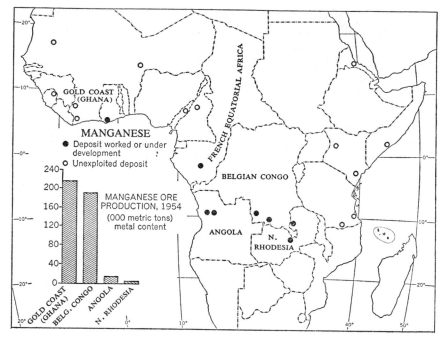

FIGURE 21

though, as Table 15 shows, the Belgian Congo has greatly shortened its lead in recent years. The Angolan and Northern Rhodesian outputs have also increased since World War II, but they are still tiny.

Ghana (then the Gold Coast) began mining manganese during World War I, and quickly became one of the world's major producers. For a

Table 15

PRODUCTION OF MANGANESE ORE, 1938-1957

(*Mn Content; Thousand Metric Tons*)

TERRITORY	1938	AVERAGE 1945-1949	AVERAGE 1950-1954	1955	1957 [a]
Total	176	367	466	513	517
Per cent of world total [b]	12.1	33.4	20	19.7	17.8
Angola	—	2	25	13	10
Belgian Congo	4	3	82	231	183
Ghana (Gold Coast)	172	361	357	260	309
Northern Rhodesia	1	[c]	2	8	14

Source: United Nations, *Statistical Yearbook, 1958,* New York, 1958.

[a] Preliminary figures.

[b] Excluding U.S.S.R. If U.S.S.R. is included, the 1955 percentage of world total is approximately 11.

[c] Less than 500 metric tons.

while, during World War II, it was the largest supplier of manganese ore for metallurgical uses to the United States, Canada and Great Britain. For a while, too, it supplied the whole of the "battery" ore used in Great Britain and the bulk of that used in the United States. With the postwar rise of other producing areas, in Africa and elsewhere, its percentage contribution to the world's supply has been steadily slipping, from approximately 15 per cent in 1946-1950 to less than 11 per cent in 1957.

Apart from a few thousand tons, all the exported ore comes from the Nsuta mine near Tarkwa, about 40 miles by rail from the port of Takoradi. The bulk of the ore shipped is of metallurgical grade, assaying (after "sintering" in a local plant) at least 50 per cent manganese. The quite appreciable remainder is of chemical or battery grade. The reserves at Nsuta are estimated at over 10 million long tons of proven ore, with an average mineral content of 52 per cent.

The rest of the Ghanaian output comes from much smaller deposits located near Axim to the south of Tarkwa.

Belgian Congo. Production in the Belgian Congo was very small before World War II, and came from the Kasekelesa mine situated near Lufupa on the Lobito Railway. Although much more extensive deposits had been discovered in the upper Lulua valley around 1929, nothing much was done about them, except to prospect them, until 1950 when mining operations were begun. Transportation difficulties kept down production in the first years of operation, but these have been overcome with the improvement of facilities on the Lobito Railway. The ore is of metallurgical grade, assaying up to 52 per cent manganese, and is mined in open cuts with the aid of power shovels. Possible reserves are of the order of 10 million metric tons of ore.

Angola. The first manganese discovery dates back to 1916. Production began soon after (at the Quichinje mine near Dondo), but was very small down to 1948. Since the opening of the Quitota mines, it has shown a marked increase. These mines are situated near Quizenga on the Luanda-Malanje railway line. The deposits average about 50 per cent manganese, are worked by open-cut methods along a series of benches, and are shipped, untreated, to the railway by truck. There are other producers in the same district. Soon there may be several more, for promising deposits have been located in a belt extending roughly southeastward from Golungo Alto for a distance of about 60 miles to Pungo Andongo, athwart the Luanda-Malanje Railway.

Northern Rhodesia. Manganese, associated with iron, has been noted in a number of localities. The most important occurrences appear to be in the Fort Rosebery area. In 1956 the Bahati mines produced nearly 40,000 long tons of manganese ore.

Three other territories are known to be well endowed with accessible manganese ore. These are Ethiopia, the Gabon Republic and Somalia.

Ethiopia. Although known for many years, the Ghedem Mountain deposits, located near Massawa in Eritrea, were not investigated closely until about 1940. From the reports it appears that there are at least ten deposits which might be worked, perhaps for their iron as well as their manganese content. However, the reserves are small by any but Ethiopian standards.

Gabon Republic. Of the several known occurrences, Murdock reports that "the only ones which appear to be of any importance are those in the Franceville region. These are perhaps the most important manganese deposits in all of tropical Africa, and, perhaps, in the world." While exploration is still in progress, indicated reserves already run to "150 million [metric] tons of ore, containing from 40 to 50 per cent manganese." [8] A company in which the United States Steel Corporation has a 49 per cent interest, Compagnie Minière de l'Ogooué (Comilog), was formed in 1953 to exploit them. Initially (around 1961) the output is expected to be of the order of 500,000 metric tons a year, rising later to a million tons. To get the ore from the mine to the Congo-Océan Railway, it has been necessary to build a 175-mile line from a point near Dolisie to M'Binda, and 50 miles of *téléféric,* or overhead cable transportation, from M'Binda to Moanda where the mine is.

Somalia. Recent exploration by the Minerals Research and Development Corporation has confirmed the existence of a coastal deposit which has been estimated at 5 million short tons. A further reserve of another 5 million tons is believed to exist in the same area.

There are also some deposits of manganese in the following countries: Bechuanaland, the French Cameroons, the Sudanese Republic (formerly French Sudan), the Republic of the Ivory Coast, the Republic of the Upper Volta, Kenya, the Malagasy Republic, Mozambique, Nyasaland, Sierra Leone, Southern Rhodesia, the Republic of Sudan and Tanganyika. But the deposits are generally small and of low grade. Those of Bechuanaland (near Ramoutsa) were worked for a time in the late 1950s.

Columbite and Tantalite

Columbium and tantalum are two rare metals for which demand has grown dramatically in recent years. Columbium (now more usually called niobium) is an essential ingredient of many high-temperature alloys, and tantalum of many types of electronic equipment. Almost all of the United States supply of both metals is imported, and the world supply has seldom been adequate since before World War II. Up to 1953 most columbium and tantalum had come from the pentoxide minerals columbite

[8] *France Actuelle* (Paris), April 1957.

and tantalite, but in that year a process was developed whereby columbium could be extracted from pyrochlore. Tropical Africa is easily the world's largest source region of columbite and tantalite, though it no longer enjoys the near-monopoly it had during the 1946-1950 period. Nevertheless, with the recent discovery of several substantial deposits of pyrochlore, it stands a good chance of keeping its lead over the other producing areas. At present the two important producers are the Belgian Congo and Nigeria (Figure 19).

Belgian Congo. Here both columbite and tantalite are obtained as by-products of tin mining. The largest producer of both are the Géomines plants at Manono and Kitotolo, where about 5 per cent of the heavy minerals recovered are pentoxides of columbium and tantalum. The largest occurrence of columbite as a principal mineral is near Lake Sake in Ruanda-Urundi. Until a premium price plan was announced under the minerals-purchasing program of the United States government in mid-1952, there was little interest in raising production. Since then, production has increased considerably, not least on tin properties which might otherwise have been in financial difficulties.

Nigeria in recent years has produced more than four fifths of the world's supply of columbite. From almost nothing in 1933, the annual output of concentrates rose to more than 2,000 long tons in 1944. In 1955 it stood at more than 3,000 tons. Since then it has dropped to less than 2,000 tons. As in the Belgian Congo, the greater part of the output comes from ores that are mined, or that used to be mined, primarily for their tin content. The chief producing regions are the Plateau Province, where the columbite occurs in association with both cassiterite (tin ore) and wolframite in a lode deposit, and Egbe in the Kabba Province, where it occurs along with tantalite.

Pyrochlore deposits have been recorded from at least six areas in Nigeria, one of which — the Lirvei-n-Kano Hills occurrence — appears to be of major importance. "Although the vertical extent of this deposit has still to be investigated," Murdock notes, "it is clear that reserves of pyrochlore-bearing granite probably amount to hundreds of millions of tons, so that it is possible to count on the production of pyrochlore on the scale of several thousand tons annually should the need arise."

Of secondary importance as producers of columbite and tantalite are the following:

Uganda. The very small columbite-tantalite production of Uganda comes from the Ankole and Kigezi areas. A large apatite-pyrochlore deposit, at present unworked, is located at Sukulu, near Tororo. The reserves "are estimated to be of the order of 200 million tons." [9] It is believed that the pyrochlore could be recovered as a by-product of a chemi-

[9] *Uganda, 1956*, H.M.S.O., London, 1957, p. 73.

cals and fertilizer plant which Sukulu Mines Limited has had under study for some time.

Mozambique. Both tantalite and columbite occurrences have been noted in several parts of this Portuguese province. An extensive area of pegmatite (one of the host rocks) has been located in the northern part of the Quelimane district, approximately 160 miles from the port of Lumbo. The ore is low grade; only occasionally does its columbite content reach 50 per cent. Further, it commonly occurs in large chunks, which are difficult to handle. In 1952 a promising alluvial deposit of columbite was discovered at Vila Machado, on the Beira-Umtali road. So far most of the territory's small production has come from workings within the large concession area held by Empresa Mineira do Alto Ligonha and from the Inchope tin field.

Southern Rhodesia. For several years a small amount of tantalite has been produced in the Bikita district east of Fort Victoria. Most of it occurs in association with cassiterite, beryl and lithium minerals.

Malagasy Republic. The principal reported occurrences of tantalite are near Lake Alaotra, Mampangabe and Ambatofotsikey. Some high-grade columbite is found in the same general area. The production is extremely small.

Republic of the Congo. Since 1945 there has been a very small "by-product" output of columbite and tantalite in the Mayoko gold-mining region. Occurrences have also been reported and confirmed on the Mayumbé plateau.

Territories with confirmed occurrences, but with little or no commercial production to date, include Angola, the French Cameroons, Kenya, Northern Rhodesia, Nyasaland, Sierra Leone, British Somaliland, the Republic of Sudan and Tanganyika.

Tungsten

Tungsten has been reported in at least twelve territories and is mined in five (Figure 20), but nowhere does it hold a high commercial rank. In 1938 the total tropical African output was about one per cent of the estimated world total. However, as Table 16 indicates, the percentage has risen since World War II. Given the maintenance of the present world demand, and the continued denial of Chinese tungsten to many of its onetime purchasers, both the relative and absolute rating of the region as a tungsten producer is likely to go on improving.

Belgian Congo. The colony is easily the largest and the fastest growing of the five producers. Its tungsten output was more than six times larger in 1957 than in 1950 and accounted for more than four fifths of the total tropical African output. Most of the ore comes from the Ruhengeri area of Ruanda-Urundi, but it is mined in several places and found in several more, generally in association with cassiterite. Because the type

Table 16

PRODUCTION OF TUNGSTEN ORE, 1938-1957

(*WO₃ Content; Metric Tons*)

TERRITORY	1938	AVERAGE 1945-1949	AVERAGE 1950-1954	1955	1957 [a]
Total	232	379	880	1,176	1,643
Per cent of world total	1.0	3.5 [b]	4.4 [b]	4.4 [b]	4.8 [b]
Belgian Congo	4	239	599	942	1,423
Nigeria	29	3	8	—	—
Southern Rhodesia	198	57	145	123	90
Tanganyika	—	5	19	14	11 [c]
Uganda	1	75	109	97	119

Source: United Nations, *Statistical Yearbook, 1958,* New York, 1958.

[a] Preliminary figures. [b] Excluding China. [c] 1956.

of rock — intrusive granite — in which it occurs is common in the Congo, the chances of its being found in still other localities are considered good.

Southern Rhodesia. Here scheelite and wolframite, two of the commonest hosts of tungsten, also have a wide occurrence. Hartley, Mazoe, Bulawayo, Wankie, Umtali, Marandellas and Melsetter all have useful deposits in their vicinities of either the one or the other. A part of the present small and declining output of tungsten comes from gold mines, as a by-product of the gravity concentration of scheelite, which most frequently occurs in association with gold.

Uganda. Deposits of wolframite, located in the southern part of Kigezi, are believed to be the northern continuation of the Ruanda-Urundi deposits. Although they were discovered in 1931, not much use has been made of them. The ore body is extensive and of excellent quality, however. Given more efficient mining and beneficiation methods, it ought not to be difficult greatly to increase the present output.

Nigeria's production of tungsten has recently been small to the point of being negligible, and it shows no signs of growing. Most of the accessible and easily worked deposits in the tin fields of the Jos Plateau, where the output has come from, have apparently been exhausted.

Tanganyika. The one producing mine is located in the Karagwe tin-mining area (Bukoba district). Tungsten minerals, notably scheelite and wolframite, have been reported and confirmed in several other areas, but their development is unlikely while prices remain at their present level.

Territories with proven but as yet unworked occurrences include Angola, Ethiopia, the French Cameroons, Kenya, Mozambique, Northern Rhodesia and Sierra Leone.

Vanadium

Minute quantities of vanadium are found all over the earth's crust, but deposits in which the concentration is high enough to justify mining and recovery are few. The only territory in tropical Africa where its occurrence favors production at the present time is Northern Rhodesia, and there only in one locality.

The existence of vanadium in the Broken Hill mine was established as far back as 1902; however, it was not exploited until 1922 and it was not until 1931 that a plant designed especially for the production of fused vanadium oxide began operations. In 1945 the Broken Hill ore body still had an estimated 15,000 long tons of recoverable vanadium oxide in it. Exploration since that date is believed to have raised this figure considerably. Even so, the immediate prospects for the ore are not considered to be very bright. According to the producing company, the Rhodesia Broken Hill Development Company, it is becoming increasingly difficult to maintain a continuous supply of vanadium-bearing material of a high enough grade to warrant using the existing leaching plant. There has been no significant production of vanadium ore in the colony since about 1952. The company's hope of staging a vanadium "come-back" depends mainly on the success of new processes for the recovery of low-grade tailings.

Besides Northern Rhodesia, the following territories have reported the existence of vanadium-bearing ores: Angola, the Belgian Congo, the Republic of the Congo, Ethiopia and Mozambique.

Molybdenum

So far molybdenum has been reported from at least eight territories, but it has not been produced in any of them. Nor is there any indication that any of the occurrences might lead to a commercial development. As Murdock reports, "The fact that a little molybdenum goes a long way and that the world's production is concentrated in the United States [more than 90 per cent in 1957] has meant that there has been little incentive for a wider search for molybdenum minerals or exploration of the known African occurrences, most of which are clearly of little or no economic importance."

The territories, and localities, in which these occurrences have been confirmed are as follows: the Belgian Congo (near the confluence of the Lufira and the Lualaba rivers, in the Kilo-Moto gold region, and at Kalima in the Maniema district), Ethiopia (in Wollega, northeast of Nejo, in the valley of the Didessa, and not far from Harar along the Harar-Jijiga highway), the French Cameroons (in the Mungo region south of N'Kongsamba, and in the Mayo Darlé tin deposit), Kenya (near Maralal and in North Nyanza), Sierra Leone (on the Mapoko River in the Tane district), British Somaliland (in the northwestern part of the protectorate), Tanganyika (on the Lupa gold field, near Lake Rukwa, and off the Mwanza-Musoma road near Nyasirori) and Uganda (in the Toro district, along the line of the recently opened Kampala-Kasese railway line).

Nickel

Nickel-bearing ore bodies of economic importance are scarce in tropical Africa, as they are in most other parts of the world. In only one territory, Southern Rhodesia, have the known deposits been of sufficient merit to justify development. The first to be developed were those located on the Noel claims in the West Gwanda region. Down to the end of 1939 when the ore became unprofitable to work, a total of some 3,260 short tons of nickel concentrate had been produced. The mine has since been re-opened, but it remains a very small producer, too small to be listed in the United Nations *Statistical Yearbook*. Recently nickel has been found, in association with platinum, in the Great Dyke, at Ingondoma, 50 miles west of Gatooma. The ore body is said by the Rio Tinto Corporation, which has done most of the exploratory work, to resemble that of Sudbury, Ontario, and to be one of the largest in the world.

Other territories in which sizable nickel ore bodies have been found are Bechuanaland, the Belgian Congo, Ethiopia, the Malagasy Republic, Northern Rhodesia, Nyasaland and Tanganyika.

BASE METALS

It is for its minerals in the base-metal group that tropical Africa is best known. In addition to copper, the dominant member of the group, the following metals are produced in amounts ranging from insignificantly small to globally important: antimony, arsenic, beryllium, bismuth, cadmium, germanium, lead, mercury, selenium, tin and zinc.

Copper

In tropical Africa's mineral economy copper has long been king, and judging from all the indications it is likely to remain so for some time. Of the several producing areas, by far the most important are the Copperbelt of Northern Rhodesia and the adjacent Belgian Congo province of Katanga (Figure 22). On the basis of smelter production, in the first nine months of 1958 these areas ranked second and fifth as world producers of copper.[10] The commercial significance of copper to these territories is seen in the fact that, in recent years, it has supplied, by value, as much as four fifths of the total exports of Northern Rhodesia and one third of those of the Belgian Congo.

[10] The United States ranked first, Chile third and Canada fourth; figures for the U.S.S.R. are not available.

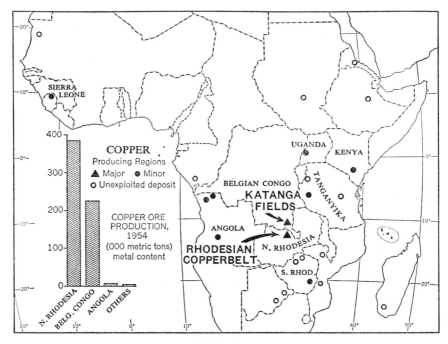

FIGURE 22

Although no other tropical African territories come within hailing distance of these two producers, several others have a useful and growing copper output. In the 1950s the total tropical African production amounted to between one fourth and one fifth of the world supply, exclusive of the U.S.S.R., as Table 17 shows.

Northern Rhodesia. Practically the whole of this territory's vast copper output comes from six mines: Mufulira, Roan Antelope, Rhokana,

Table 17

PRODUCTION OF COPPER ORE, 1938-1957

(Thousand Metric Tons)

TERRITORY	1938	AVERAGE 1945-1949	AVERAGE 1950-1954	1955	1957 [a]
Total	378	363	537	586	670
Per cent of world total [b]	20.0	18.2	24.7	21.5	21.9
Angola	—	[c]	2	3	5
Northern Rhodesia	255	212	333	348	423
Belgian Congo	124	151	202	235	242

Source: United Nations, *Statistical Yearbook, 1958,* New York, 1958.

[a] Preliminary figures.   [b] Excluding U.S.S.R.   [c] Less than 500 metric tons.

Nchanga, Chibuluma and Bancroft. When all six are running at full capacity (the last two came into production only in 1956 and 1957 respectively), the Copperbelt will have an output potential of roughly 500,000 short tons. In years to come it may have an even higher potential, since there are several other properties, such as Baluba and Chambishi, that hold promise of profitable operation, given high prices and demand.

Down to 1956 the power needs of the mines were met, not always adequately, by the Wankie coal field 500 miles to the south of the Copperbelt, by local wood supplies and imported coal and oil. Since the end of that year, however, the mines have been able to draw some hydroelectric power from the Belgian Congo's Le Marinel station on the Lualaba River. By the early 1960s they expect to begin drawing heavily on the Kariba station now under construction on the Zambezi.

Among them the various copper companies operate six large flotation concentrating plants, three reverberatory smelting plants and one leaching plant for the treatment of oxide concentrates. Following recent extensions and modernization, the capacity of the largest smelter, at Nkana, is now approximately 20,000 short tons of copper a month, which enables it to smelt the concentrates from all three mines (Nchanga, Bancroft,[11] and Rhokana) in the Rhodesian Anglo American group. Recently, too, the capacity of the leaching plant has been raised from 25,000 to 40,000 short tons a year. In addition, the Copperbelt has three electrolytic copper refineries, at Nkana, Mufulira and Ndola. The refinery at Nkana, jointly owned by Rhokana and Nchanga, now has a nominal capacity of about 130,000 long tons a year; the Mufulira unit has a capacity of about 100,000 long tons. The Ndola refinery has an initial capacity of 55,000 long tons. When, with the help of an extension which is under construction, its capacity has been doubled, it will be able to handle all of the Roan Antelope production.

Reserves are now considered to be in excess of 700 million short tons of ore averaging 3.7 per cent copper and so capable of yielding more than 25 million short tons of metal. If the current explorations yield only a tithe of their sponsors' hopes, the reserves may well prove to be much higher than this figure.

Belgian Congo. The Katanga copper mines are all operated by a single corporation, the Union Minière du Haut-Katanga. On the whole the grade of the ores, both sulfides and the oxides into which the surface deposits have weathered, is slightly higher than it is on the Copperbelt, and higher than that of the average American and Chilean ores. Further, much of the ore is capable of being worked by open-pit methods. The sulfides are obtained at the Prince Léopold mine at Kipushi, the only underground

[11] Mining operations were stopped on March 31, 1958, under an agreement by the members of the Rhodesian Anglo American group to reduce the combined outputs of their three mines by 10 per cent. Operations were re-started in 1959.

mine, and from the bottom of some of the open pits. The oxides are obtained from several large open pits in the Kolwezi region, notably from the Musonoi, Ruwe, Kolwezi and Kamoto mines. The sulfides are treated by smelting in water-jacket furnaces at Lubumbashi (Elisabethville), and the oxides by leaching and electrolysis at Shituru (Jadotville).

The large amount of power needed to run all these concerns comes from four hydroelectric plants, the Francqui and Bia, both on the Lufira, and the Delcommune and Le Marinel, both on the Lualaba. Their combined capacity is rated at between 2 billion kilowatt-hours (minimum flow) and 2.8 billion kilowatt-hours (maximum flow).

Including amounts used in the making of zinc concentrates and copper-cobalt alloy, the Katanga output is now (1958) roughly 250,000 metric tons a year, divided almost equally between electrolytic and blister copper. This gives Katanga about 8 per cent of the total world output and makes it the Belgian Congo's largest money-maker.

Although Katanga is the only area in the Congo where copper is presently produced, it may not always remain so. For several years the Bamoco Syndicate, in which the Union Minière has a substantial interest, has been examining copper occurrences in the Madimba area of Bas-Congo, with promising results, so it is said.

Angola. Copper occurrences are widely reported in this Portuguese province, but the majority of them do not appear to be exploitable. Many are of a purely secondary nature and have neither the grade nor the persistence needed for successful operation. Those of primary origin are on the whole poorly mineralized and of small size. The best of the known prospects are near Cuma west of Nova Lisboa, at Bembe about 150 miles northeast of Luanda, and near Quibocolo about 75 miles northeast of Bembe. Most of the province's small production comes from the last-named region, where an oxidized ore body, principally malachite, is being mined by the Empresa do Cobre de Angola.

Kenya. The small copper output of recent years has come from the Macalder-Nyanza mines in South Nyanza. The present output is about 200 long tons a month.

Tanganyika. Here, too, the small output of copper comes from a single mine, the Mpanda in the Western Province, where copper occurs in association with lead, silver and gold. The ore body has been put at some 5 million tons, assaying on the average 0.61 per cent copper, 6.48 per cent lead, 118.7 grams of silver per ton and 2.1 grams of gold per ton. Copper-bearing ores are also found in the Mpwapwa district.

Southern Rhodesia. Not since 1925, when the only important copper mine, the Falcon, was closed down, has copper been a large item on the mining list. However, in recent years much exploratory work has been carried out in the Lomagundi fields, notably in the Copper King, Copper Queen and Silverside mines. Even some of the old dumps at the Falcon and elsewhere have been assayed and found to possess enough copper to warrant its recovery. And since 1955, there has been a small production of copper concentrates at Umkondo in the Sabi valley. As the company responsible for this development, the Messina (Transvaal) Development Company, Ltd., already has a smelter at its Messina mine a few miles inside the Union of South Africa, the concentrates are taken there for refining. In the north of the country, near Sinoia, Rhodesia Copper Ventures Ltd., a subsidiary of the Messina firm, is developing another sizable ore body. The Messina firm is also developing a mine — the Alaska, about 70 miles northwest of Salisbury — that is expected to yield about 2,600 long tons of copper concentrates annually.

Uganda. The principal occurrence of copper is at Kilembe in a narrow valley on the southeast flanks of the Ruwenzoris. Although the presence of copper here has been known since 1906, it was not until 1952 that the Legislative Council of Uganda and the East African Central Legislative Assembly approved the construction of the railway westward from Kampala to Kasese, without which the Kilembe ore could have found no economic outlet. The mine came into production in 1956. The projected rate of ore extraction will give the mine an annual output of some 10,000-11,000 long tons of blister copper. In 1957, the first full year of operation, production was 7,467 long tons; in 1958 it was 10,831 tons. After crushing and concentration at the mine portal, the ore is piped to Kasese, the railhead eight miles down the valley. There it is roasted before being sent to Jinja for smelting. The probable reserves of workable ore (averaging 1.91 per cent copper) are of the order of 13.5 million tons.

Of the presently non-producing territories, the following have copper deposits of more than conversational interest:

Bechuanaland. The most important of the fifteen or so reported occurrences are those in the old Bushman mine in the Bamangwato Reserve (abandoned since 1918), and at the Rainbow mine and Selkirk in the Tati district.

Republic of the Congo. For a while there was a small output from the Mindouli mines in the Niari valley, but the ore body is now worked out. However, a number of copper occurrences have been confirmed in the surrounding country. Although the reserves so far disclosed are small, French interests believe that they warrant development.

Ethiopia. The Italians investigated a deposit in the Chercher area west of Harar that may some day be worth developing. The deposit at Adi Rassi, south of Asmara, appears to be the most important of the several known in Eritrea. Before the Abyssinian War put a stop to its plans, an American mining company had established the existence here of some 400,000 tons of 3 per cent copper ore and 2 million tons of 1.75 per cent ore.

Islamic Republic of Mauritania. Intensive investigations carried on since 1952 in the region of the Akjoujt oasis have disclosed the existence of an ore body said to be "the largest ever found in the French Community." Indicated reserves are in excess of 35 million tons, averaging 2 per cent copper. Several problems have so far stood in the way of developing this deposit, not the least being that of increasing the scanty water supply.

Mozambique. Between 1913 and 1921 some copper was produced near Vila Manica. There is believed to be still plenty of profitable ore below the levels worked at that time. There are also substantial ore bodies in the Tete region.

Republic of Sudan. From ancient times the outcrops of oxidized copper ore in the Hofrat en Nahas area of the Bahr-el-Ghazal Province attracted the attention of local metal workers. Although these outcrops are now known to be underlain by sulfide ores they have not yet been worked commercially.

Tin

Of all the base metals, tin is perhaps the most widely distributed in tropical Africa. It is commercially produced in nine territories, and occurs in some of the others (Figure 23). In the postwar period, the region has supplied 13 to 14 per cent of the world total. As Table 18 shows, only two territories are large producers. Between them the Belgian Congo and

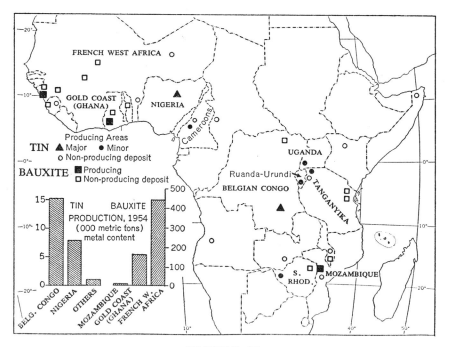

FIGURE 23

Table 18

PRODUCTION OF TIN CONCENTRATES, 1938-1957

(*Sn Content; Metric Tons*)

TERRITORY	1938	AVERAGE 1945-1949	AVERAGE 1950-1954	1955	1957 [a]
Total [b]	19,522	24,509	23,035	23,670	24,331
Per cent of world total [c]	11.6	20.0	13.8	13.2	13.8
Belgian Congo	9,824	14,289	14,489	15,270	14,510
Nigeria	9,121	9,926	8,383	8,289	9,766
Tanganyika	215	114	58	42	15
Uganda	362	180	105	69	40

Source: United Nations, *Statistical Yearbook, 1958,* New York, 1958.

[a] Preliminary figures.

[b] Excluding a number of small producers.   [c] Excluding U.S.S.R.

Nigeria continue to account for over 95 per cent of the output, as they have done for a long time.

Belgian Congo. The tin region of the Belgian Congo, Africa's largest producer, lies mostly to the southeast and east of the Lualaba River and includes parts of the Orientale and Kivu provinces, Ruanda-Urundi and the northern part of Katanga Province. For many years the bulk of the production came from placers, but the attention of the mining companies has been turning more and more to lode tin, the reserves of which are very large. Mining methods vary. Pick-and-shovel operations are still common in some localities, but, generally speaking, electrically powered tools are superseding hand tools. The old-style sluice is still used for recovering tin on some of the smaller mines, but gravity concentrating plants, with jigs and tables, are in use on the larger properties. While there are still a considerable number of small operators, the bulk of the output is now in the hands of a few companies, the most important of which are the Symétain Company (the largest producer), which operates in the Manlema district (Kivu), and Géomines, which has a smelter at Manono (Katanga).

In the past decade the output has averaged between 14,000 and 15,000 metric tons a year. This is about twice as much as in the years immediately preceding World War II, though about 10 per cent less than at the peak of the wartime boom.

Nigeria, now in second place, was in earlier days a considerably larger producer than the Belgian Congo. From 1910, when tin mining began, down to 1958, the production of concentrates totaled nearly 500,000 metric tons, valued at over £130 million or about nine tenths of the value of all minerals produced in the colony during that time.

Apart from a few hundred tons from the Lirvei-n-Kano Hills and in the Nasarawa Division of Benue Province, almost all the tin ore comes from the Jos Plateau area. The early workings were alluvial, the ore being obtained by the panning of stream beds, and the largest mines on the Plateau are still based on alluvial rather than lode deposits. However, many of the known alluvial deposits appear to be approaching the end of their working days, and it is doubtful whether the output can be maintained at the present rate for another ten years unless major new discoveries are made or advances in technology make it profitable to exploit deposits of considerably lower grade. Accordingly the attention of the large companies is being turned more and more to lode mining. It appears likely that in the future these companies will be engaged mainly in underground operations, "with private operators continuing to work surface deposits of small extent, or in rocky valleys, where mechanical aids would be uneconomic or impracticable." [12]

Hand labor still accounts for about half the tonnage of tin-bearing ground treated, but African-operated electric gravel pumps, draglines, bulldozers and tractors are slowly taking business away from the pick-and-shovel brigade.

The seven other producers are all very small and show no signs of getting much bigger. The biggest of them is Uganda.

Uganda's postwar output has been fluctuating — downward more than upward — between about 40 and 200 long tons of metal. The ore comes from placer and lode deposits, in the Ankole and Kigezi districts, and the greater part of it is handled by a single company, Kagera Mines Ltd.

French Cameroons. The output of approximately 80 long tons comes from a single deposit, at Mayo Darlé, situated to the south of Banyo. There are, however, many "interesting indications" of tin in other areas, which is not surprising in view of the broad similarity, in structure and rock types, between large parts of the territory and the tin-yielding Jos Plateau.

Tanganyika. Here the production comes largely from the Karagwe region of Bukoba district in the Lake Province. Most of the ore comes from residual or alluvial deposits, but increasing attention is being given to the exploitation of vein tin. There are less extensive deposits near Ngara on the Ruanda-Urundi border, the output from which has so far been negligible.

Southern Rhodesia. Most of the output comes from the Gwaai tin fields in the Wankie district. These fields are extensive — about 40 miles from end to end — and consist of a narrow but persistent belt of metamorphic rocks that have been intruded by small veins of cassiterite. At first only the alluvial deposits were worked; now the veins are being exploited. There are also some mines in the Fort Victoria and Salisbury areas that

---

[12] K. M. Buchanan and J. C. Pugh, *Land and People in Nigeria,* University of London Press, London, 1955, p. 183.

continue to yield a little metal. Most of the territory's production finds its way to a small smelter in Bulawayo.

Republic of the Niger. When this state produces tin, as it does not do every year, it comes from the mountainous Air country lying to the north-east of Agades.

Mozambique has a large area of cassiterite-bearing rock at Inchope on the Beira-Umtali road, but only a minute output. Lack of water has so far been the chief obstacle to its development, but new methods of separation might circumvent this obstacle.

Northern Rhodesia has four small mines in the Choma area where some tin is being produced by primitive methods.

Other territories in which tin is found, but not mined commercially at present, are Angola, the Central African Republic (Ubangi-Shari), the Republic of the Congo, the Dahomey Republic, Kenya, Nyasaland, Sierra Leone and Somalia.

Lead

Although occurrences of lead have been reported from almost every territory in tropical Africa, the Broken Hill mine in Northern Rhodesia continues to be, as it has long been, the only large lead producer. (See Figure 24 and Table 19.)

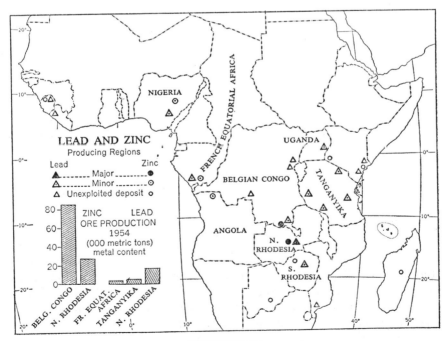

FIGURE 24

Table 19

PRODUCTION OF LEAD ORE, 1938-1957
(*Pb Content; Thousand Metric Tons*)

TERRITORY	1938	AVERAGE 1945-1949	AVERAGE 1950-1954	1955	1957 [a]
Total	8	14	19	24	22
Per cent of world total [b]	0.5	1.1	1.4	1.2	1.1
Belgian Congo	5	1	[c]	[c]	—
French Equatorial Africa	3	2	3	3	2
Northern Rhodesia	[c]	11	14	16	15
Tanganyika	—	—	2	4	5
Nigeria	—	—	[c]	[c]	1

Source: United Nations, *Statistical Yearbook, 1958*, New York, 1958.

[a] Preliminary figures.   [b] Excluding U.S.S.R.   [c] Less than 500 metric tons.

Northern Rhodesia. Notwithstanding its age — now about fifty years — the Broken Hill mine continues to yield well, although seldom straining the 18,000-ton capacity of its smelter. The reserves, of both oxides and sulfides, are believed to be nowhere near exhaustion. And after they are exhausted, "mining" activity could very well continue for some years, thanks to the mountainous tailings, in which the percentage of lead is anywhere from 7 to 14 and the percentage of zinc even higher.

Tanganyika. The most important occurrences yet disclosed are at Mpanda, 200 miles southwest of Tabora. Here a lead-silver-copper-gold ore body has been developed by Uruwira Minerals Ltd. To facilitate the opening of this rather remote region, the Tanganyika government agreed in 1945 to finance the construction of a branch line to the mine from Kaliua on the Central Line. This line was opened in 1950. As the region round about is highly mineralized, there are good chances that the line will prove to have been a sound investment. However, the lead reserves at Mpanda are already showing signs of exhaustion.

Republic of the Congo. When the quite small reserves of the M'Fouati mine in the Niari valley have been exhausted, the nearby Hapilo deposit, now being developed, is expected to replace it as the country's major source of supply.

Nigeria. The existence here of lead, and zinc, has been known for many years, but it is only quite recently that the occurrences have been closely studied. Now that they have been, it is being said that they will probably prove eventually to be far more extensive and valuable than the Nigerian tin resources. The main deposits lie in a 350-mile stretch of country that straddles the provinces of Benue, Ogoja and Adamawa.

Southern Rhodesia. Here lead, like silver, copper and antimony, is a gold-mining by-product. Most of the small and intermittent output comes from a single mine, the Penhalonga.

Belgian Congo. So far lead has come mainly from the Kengere mine (southwest Katanga) and from the flue dusts trapped by the Lubumbashi smelter where the complex copper sulfide ores from the Prince Léopold mine are treated. Production has been small for many years, and in some recent years nil. There are also lead deposits, as yet unworked, in the Kasai and Bas-Congo regions, in Ituri, and on the west shore of Lake Kivu.

Uganda has some small deposits near the edge of the Rift Valley. The most promising of these is considered to be the Kitaka deposit on the Ankole-Toro border. "This interesting deposit has not been systematically explored or developed but continues to produce easily-won mineral from rich pockets of ore." [13] In 1954 it produced 67 tons of galena (lead sulfide); in 1956, 121 tons.

A few territories must be counted as possible producers in the not too distant future. One of these is Kenya, where lead occurs at several places in the Coast Province. In Liberia along the Sierra Leone border there are indications of extensive lead deposits. Mozambique, too, may become a producer, for lead is found in Vila Manica in a number of gold reefs. In Sierra Leone lead occurs in the Sula Mountains in promising amounts and situations.

Zinc

Although zinc occurs in many territories and is mined in several, only in two is it of major importance (Figure 24). Of the two, the Belgian Congo is now responsible for about three quarters of the total tropical African production. Northern Rhodesia produces all but a fraction of the remainder, as Table 20 shows.

[13] *Uganda, 1955,* H.M.S.O., London, 1956, p. 57.

Table 20

PRODUCTION OF ZINC, 1938-1957
(*Zn Content; Thousand Metric Tons*)

TERRITORY	1938	AVERAGE 1945-1949	AVERAGE 1950-1954	1955	1957 [a]
Total	20	61	125	130	134
Per cent of world total [b]	1.8	3.5	5.4	5.0	4.8
Belgian Congo	6	41	101	102	104
French Equatorial Africa	1	c	—	—	—
Northern Rhodesia	13	20	24	28	30

Source: United Nations, *Statistical Yearbook, 1958,* New York, 1958.

[a] Preliminary figures.   [b] Excluding U.S.S.R.   [c] Less than 500 metric tons.

Belgian Congo. The entire output comes from the Prince Léopold (Kipushi) mine of the Union Minière du Haut-Katanga. Although this is primarily a copper mine, the sulfide ores are associated with zinc, which is recovered by differential flotation, yielding concentrates of about 52 per cent zinc. Some of the concentrates are roasted, at Jadotville, and yield sulfuric acid necessary for the hydro-metallurgical treatment of the oxidized copper-cobalt ores. Both roasted and raw concentrates have in the past been exported to Belgium for further treatment. Since the middle of 1953, however, the Société Métallurgique du Katanga (Métalkat) has been producing zinc ingots at its newly installed leaching and electrolysis plant at Kolwezi. This plant has an annual capacity of about 36,000 metric tons of metal.

Northern Rhodesia's zinc likewise comes from a single source, the Broken Hill lead-zinc property. The ore body, containing both sulfide and oxide ores, has an average zinc content of about 22 per cent.[14] Although between 91 and 95 per cent of the sulfide zinc (and between 85 and 88 per cent of the sulfide lead) is recovered in the flotation mill, the tailings average between 15 and 20 per cent zinc (and between 7 and 14 per cent lead). At the present time these are being stockpiled for recovery either when the mine is exhausted or when the market justifies the undertaking. After concentration, the zinc is reduced to a very high-grade metal in a nearby electrolytic plant. The annual capacity of this plant is approximately 30,000 short tons of slab zinc. The total zinc output of the Broken Hill mine through 1957 was well over 500,000 long tons.

The other producing territories are:

Angola. Here zinc is a by-product of the small copper-mining operations of the Empresa do Cobre de Angola located to the east of S. Salvador do Congo.

Republic of the Congo. Zinc is produced along with lead by the Compagnie Minière du Congo Français at M'Fouati in the Niari valley. With the approaching exhaustion of this ore body, interest is expected to shift to the Hapilo mine to the west of M'Fouati, where there is a large sulfide body.

Nigeria. As indicated under lead, very little use is at present being made of the country's extensive lead-zinc deposits. Most of the small output continues to come from the Zurak mine, located near the Jos Plateau–Adamawa provincial boundary. Since World War II considerable interest has been shown by commercial concerns in the lead-zinc deposits near Abakaliki in the Eastern Region. To date, however, the necessary capital has not been forthcoming.

Territories with zinc deposits that hold possibilities for the future in-

[14] The oxidized ore which forms a thick shell above and around the sulfide body contains between 1 and 2.5 per cent vanadium, which adds considerably to its value.

clude Bechuanaland, Kenya, the Malagasy Republic, Sierra Leone and Southern Rhodesia.

Beryllium

Deposits of the oxide mineral beryl, from which beryllium is most commonly obtained, are found in many parts of tropical Africa, but because of their generally low mineral content, few of them have so far proved commercially attractive. Those that have usually occur in association with other commercial minerals, such as feldspar, mica, quartz, cassiterite, and columbite and tantalite.

Southern Rhodesia. In recent years Southern Rhodesia has become an important supplier of beryl. By the end of 1953 the output exceeded 1,700 short tons, around one fifth of the world total. Since then, however, it has declined (to 577 tons in 1957). Most of the output comes from Bikita, which is 45 miles by road from Fort Victoria. The remainder is supplied by a large number of small operations in the Mtoko, Miami and Salisbury-Enterprise areas. With new occurrences being reported almost every year, the immediate prospects of the industry are considered good. No estimates of reserves are as yet available, largely because of the capricious mineralization that characterizes beryllium-bearing rocks.

Malagasy Republic. The output comes mainly from the Tananarive region, near Fitampito, Ankazobe and Antsirabe, and to the west of Fianarantsoa. The increased production of the past few years has been made possible through the opening of new roads and the installation of light mechanical mining equipment.

Mozambique. Beryl is found in many places. The present output is derived principally from numerous small workings dispersed over the 2,000-square-mile concession of the Empresa Mineira do Alto Ligonha, inland from Lumbo. Deposits of beryl have also been observed in the Mocuba and Ribaue areas.

The small Uganda production comes from Kigezi. Although it has risen sharply in recent years, it is not expected to go on rising for long. On the contrary, it is reported that as opportunity for "open-pitting" decreases, production will decline.

The new, and still quite small, Belgian Congo production comes from the Katumba area of northern Ruanda-Urundi, which is being developed by the Société des Mines d'Etain du Ruanda-Urundi, and from Kivu. The mineral has been reported in other localities.

In the past few years Northern Rhodesia and British Somaliland have also been small beryl producers.

Other territories known to have beryl deposits are Ethiopia (including Eritrea), Kenya, Somalia and Tanganyika.

Antimony

Up to now tropical Africa has given no indication of being well endowed with deposits of this metal. Occurrences have been reported from only five territories, and production — 114 metric tons in 1958, or well under one per cent of the world total — from only one, Southern Rhodesia. Most of this is a by-product of gold mining in the Midlands (Hartley-Gwelo) area.

Other known deposits are in Sierra Leone, Tanganyika, Uganda and the French Cameroons.

Arsenic

Here again tropical African production is very small, and Southern Rhodesia accounts for all of it. Currently it averages less than 400 metric tons annually, or about three quarters of one per cent of the world production. Like antimony, arsenic is found mainly in association with gold. The most propitious occurrences are in the Champion and Hydra group of gold properties near Gwanda, and in the Umtali area. In recent years the only producer of arsenic has been the Que Que roasting plant, where crude arsenic is obtained from flue gases during the roasting of arsenical gold concentrates. The output has been disposed of locally for the preparation of cattle dips and wood preservatives.

Arsenopyrite, the mineral from which the metal comes, is also found in Angola, the Belgian Congo, Ethiopia, the French Cameroons, Kenya, Sierra Leone and Tanganyika.

Bismuth

Bismuth is an uncommon metal and its distribution in tropical Africa appears to be extremely limited. Occurrences of it have been reported from five territories, namely, the Belgian Congo, Mozambique, Southern Rhodesia, Tanganyika and Uganda, but only those of Uganda are considered to be very extensive. None of the territories has so far made more than a token contribution to the world supply of bismuth. The total production of tropical Africa during recent times has seldom exceeded 8 metric tons of bismuth ore in any one year and at its maximum represented less than one per cent of the world total. Of the two leading producers, Mozambique is now more important than Uganda.

The two main producing areas in Mozambique are Ribaue and Alto Ligonha. In the Belgian Congo bismuth is found, in its native state and as a sulfide or carbonate, in Ruanda-Urundi and Maniema. It is recovered as a by-product of tin mining by the Compagnie Minière des Grands Lacs Africains and the Société des Mines d'Etain du Ruanda-Urundi.

The most interesting deposits in Uganda are those, discovered quite recently, in Kigezi at the Rwanza mine. With the improvement of transport facilities in this mountainous and heavily forested country, the mine was due to come into commercial production in 1959. Other deposits, some of which are being worked, are located in the Muramba and Kayonza areas.

Bismuth-bearing ores were often reported by the early gold miners in Southern Rhodesia, but none have been worked since 1948. In Tanganyika occurrences of bismuth have been reported in the Uluguru Mountains, and the Lupa and Musoma gold fields.

Cadmium

At the present time cadmium is obtained in only two territories, the Belgian Congo and Northern Rhodesia. In both it is a by-product of the smelting and refining of zinc-bearing ores.

In the past the Belgian Congo output, averaging between 5,000 and 7,000 kilograms in recent years, has come from the Prince Léopold mine at Kipushi near Elisabethville. But since 1953 cadmium has also been produced in the newly installed electrolytic zinc plant at Kolwezi. The even smaller Northern Rhodesian output (less than 20 short tons in 1958) comes from the Broken Hill mine.

Cadmium-bearing ore is also found in the Bangwaketse Reserve of Bechuanaland, but its metal content is said to be discouragingly small.

Germanium

The chief tropical African source of this metal which in recent years has become very important in the electronics industry is the Belgian Congo. In 1954, the first year in which it was produced, 1,095 kilograms of germanium oxide were recovered from the flue dusts of the Lubumbashi copper smelter at Elisabethville. In 1958 more than twenty times this amount was recovered. These dusts, which are constantly being trapped in the smelter flue, are now sent to Kolwezi for beneficiation and thence to Belgium for the recovery of electronically pure germanium oxide.

The only other territory where germanium is known to exist is Northern Rhodesia. Its presence in the Sable Antelope mine at Mumbwa was announced in 1954, and since then its potentialities have been under study.

Mercury

The mineral literature of tropical Africa has very little to say about mercury. For a while a small amount of the metal was produced at the Pilgrim mine, 40 miles north-northeast of Bulawayo, Southern Rhodesia, but there has been no record of any production since 1940. The only other territories where it has been found are Kenya, Tanganyika, Ethiopia (including Eritrea) and Somalia.

Selenium

The most important commercial source of selenium is the anode mud or slime produced in the course of refining blister copper electrolytically. To date the only tropical African production has come from the electrolytic refinery at Nkana on the Northern Rhodesian Copperbelt. In recent years the production has averaged between 40,000 and 50,000 pounds, or approximately 3 per cent of the world total. (The selenium content of Belgian Congo copper is recovered at Olen in Belgium and reported as Belgian output.)

LIGHT METALS

Under this heading come aluminum, lithium, magnesium, titanium and zirconium, all of them of significance to the manufacturers of metallic materials with a high strength-to-weight ratio. The fast-growing interest in such materials, especially by the aviation and ballistic missile industries, is reflected in the intensive prospecting and exploration programs that have been carried out in recent years, in the plans being made for the local reduction of tropical African ores — now exported in their raw state — and in the production figures given in the tables that follow.

Aluminum Ore (Bauxite)

This was the first of the light metals to attract outside attention, and it is still the most important, from the standpoint of both tonnage and revenue. Even so, its true importance is to be measured not so much by current output as by future reserves, which are enormous. Those of Ghana and the Republic of Guinea alone have been assessed at about 400 million long tons, or approximately one fifth of the known world reserves and not less than one quarter of the known reserves of the free world. At the present time, tropical Africa's contribution to the world supply of bauxite is about 3 per cent. It is made by three territories, Ghana, the Republic of Guinea and Mozambique. (See Table 21 and Figure 23).

Republic of Guinea. Bauxite deposits are very widespread, being found almost wherever there are soils of lateritic origin. The only places where they are exploited at present are in the Iles de Los and Boké regions. Although not as extensive as most, the Los deposits have the advantage of being near the port of Conakry, whence the ore is shipped abroad, mostly to Canada, for processing. Like Ghana, the Republic of Guinea is planning to have its own aluminum industry. To this end hydroelectric stations are now being built at Souapiti and Amaria on the Konkouré River. By 1961 they are expected to be delivering enough power to

Table 21

PRODUCTION OF BAUXITE, 1938-1957

(*Thousand Metric Tons*)

TERRITORY	1938	AVERAGE 1945-1949	AVERAGE 1950-1954	1955	1957 [a]
Total	[b]	19	331	614	559
Per cent of world total [c]	—	1.6	1.9	4.0	3.2
Republic of Guinea (French Guinea)	—	2	181	493	366
Ghana (Gold Coast) [d]	—	13	121	118	188
Mozambique	[b]	2	29	3	5

Source: United Nations, *Statistical Yearbook, 1958,* New York, 1958.

[a] Preliminary figures.   [b] Less than 500 metric tons.
[c] Excluding U.S.S.R. and China.   [d] Exports.

make possible an annual production of 480,000 metric tons of alumina. It is hoped later to increase the capacity of the plant to 1.2 million metric tons a year.[15] Agreement for the building at Fria, by an international consortium (in which the Olin Mathieson Chemical Corporation and the Péchiney group hold the major interests), of a factory capable of producing this amount of aluminum was reached in 1957.

Ghana. With an estimated 230 million long tons of high-grade ore (averaging about 53 per cent Al_2O_3), Ghana has an almost unrivaled bauxite reserve. The largest deposits are at Yenahin, 40 miles west of Kumasi. Smaller but still very significant ores are at Awaso 55 miles northwest of Dunkwa, and at Mount Ejuanema above Nkawkaw. "There are some 200 million tons at Yenahin on the flat tops of high hills over a distance of some 20 miles, the bauxite being 20-50 feet thick. The Awaso deposits, with 30 million tons, are up to 70 feet thick: those at Mount Ejuanema are about 20 feet thick and contain about 4 million tons."[16] Until the Volta River project[17] materializes, only the Awaso deposit is being exploited, and the bauxite is shipped through Takoradi. The Awaso output in recent years has been running about 150,000 tons.

When the Volta River project does materialize, the output of bauxite could be greatly increased, for in addition to the continuing needs of overseas processing plants, there would be the needs of the smelter at Kpong.

[15] In the French Cameroons, which has no bauxite to speak of, aluminum is shortly to be manufactured from ore imported either from the Republic of Guinea or from France. The smelter will use some of the excess power generated at the Edea hydroelectric station.

[16] R. J. Harrison Church, *West Africa,* Longmans, Green & Co., Ltd., London, 1957, p. 408.

[17] See pp. 262-63.

Using electricity to be made available by the power station on the lower Volta River, this smelter would have an annual capacity, to begin with, of 80,000 long tons of aluminum ingots, or more than three times the present output of aluminum in the sterling area. Its ultimate capacity would be about 210,000 long tons.

Mozambique. Bauxite has been worked on a small scale for some years for the manufacture of refractory bricks and aluminum sulfate. The source of the supply is a large, high-grade, low-silica deposit well located with regard to road and rail transport in the Penhalonga–Vila Manica region. With some hydroelectric power already available at the Revue Falls, near Vila Pery, and much more capable of being developed there, it is possible that Mozambique will begin producing its own aluminum, on a modest scale, before long. Preliminary cost estimates suggest that locally produced metal should be able to hold its own with imported metal.

The only other territories in which bauxite has been found in amounts sufficient to give it commercial interest are the Belgian Congo, Nyasaland, Sierra Leone, Southern Rhodesia and Tanganyika.

Lithium

Lithium is the lightest of the metals known as yet. In addition to its obvious military uses, it is being increasingly used, along with its compound salts, in the making of ceramics and enamels, lubricants and cosmetics, in air-conditioning plants, and even in the food industry. The four most important land [18] sources of lithium are spodumene, lepidolite, petalite and amblygonite. So far significant occurrences of these minerals in quantity have been reported from only six territories and the commercial working of them from four, namely, Southern Rhodesia, Mozambique, the Belgian Congo and Uganda. But with exploration barely begun in many promising areas — and wherever there is pegmatite (a rock partial to "dykes" and other igneous intrusions) there is promise — additional occurrences are certain to be disclosed in the coming years. All but a small fraction of the present output comes from Southern Rhodesia and Mozambique, and their output has fluctuated widely.

Southern Rhodesia. The largest known concentration of the four lithium minerals is in the pegmatites of the Bikita tin field, about 45 miles east of Fort Victoria. Lepidolite is found in the Bikita Quarry, once worked for its tin. Amblygonite occurs in small, irregular and scattered patches, as does spodumene. Most of the petalite comes from a single mass situated to the north of the Bikita Quarry. Bikita Minerals (Pvt.) Ltd., the organization most responsible for this mining development, has had a checkered career. After a modest start in the early 1950s, when the annual produc-

[18] Lithium can also be obtained from the compound dilithium-sodium phosphate, which is present in brine.

tion averaged only a few thousand tons, the company stepped up production to 82,000 short tons in 1955. Since then the demand (mainly American) for lithium has fallen off so sharply that the company decided in April 1959 to put the mine on a care-and-maintenance basis early in 1960.

Lithium minerals are also found in some tin-bearing areas of Mashonaland, and in the Filabusi district of Matabeleland.

The probable reserves of readily available lithium minerals are not yet known with precision. One estimate puts them at 1.5 million short tons. Another puts those of the Bikita area alone at well over 3 million short tons.

Mozambique. The only lithium mineral produced is lepidolite. This is worked by open-cut methods at Nahipa and other pegmatitic areas on the large concession of the Empresa Mineira do Alto Ligonha. In spite of difficulties in keeping the grade of ore up to a commercially satisfactory level (3 per cent LiO_2), the demand for it has encouraged the company to enlarge the scale of its operations.

Belgian Congo. Lithium minerals are known to occur in large quantities in several parts of the colony. The principal representative of the group is spodumene and its principal known occurrence the tin-bearing granitic pegmatite at Manono-Kitotolo. The company — Géomines — responsible for the development of this deposit has spoken of it as "perhaps the most important known reserve of spodumene in the world." Having successfully tackled on a pilot scale in Belgium the problem of producing lithium carbonate from this ore body, the company was in 1957 planning to construct a commercial plant on the spot. Since in this instance spodumene will be a by-product of tin washing, the company will not be required to bear the heavy costs of ore extraction, transportation and crushing. The availability locally of electric power is expected to further cheapen the cost of production.

In the past few years there has been a small but growing output of amblygonite in the Katumba area of Ruanda-Urundi.

Uganda's likewise small output of amblygonite comes from the Mubende area, where the mineral occurs in boulder form that makes for easy and economical recovery.

The two territories where lithium minerals have been reported but not as yet mined are Kenya (sporadically in the pegmatites of the basement complex) and Tanganyika (northeast of Dodoma).

Magnesium

All of the more important magnesium-bearing minerals are widespread in tropical Africa. However, the mining of them is reported in only four territories, namely, Southern Rhodesia, Tanganyika, Kenya and Ethiopia, and there only on a small scale. At present the only territory with a significant output is Southern Rhodesia, which has been producing anywhere from 2,500 to 15,000 metric tons in recent years.

Southern Rhodesia. Magnesite occurs at several points along the Great Dyke. Of special interest is the ore body lying to the southeast of Gatooma in the Umsweswe valley. So far this has been worked mainly for export to the Union of South Africa, where it is used in the manufacture of refractory bricks.

Tanganyika. The output, amounting in the last few years to no more than 300 metric tons annually, comes from a high-grade magnesite deposit in the Longido region of the Northern Province. Other magnesite deposits are located in the Dodoma, Kondoa and Pare districts and in the Lupa gold field area. Another potential source of magnesium is the mother-liquor at present rejected in the process of crystallizing salt at the Uvinza (Kigoma district) brine springs. It has been estimated that at present the equivalent of about 100 long tons of magnesium chloride goes to waste annually.

Kenya. Magnesite is found and intermittently exploited in the Mtito Andei area of Machakos. Other deposits have been identified in the Northern Province.

Ethiopia. Magnesium chloride occurs as a constituent of certain potassium minerals which have been worked on a small scale in the Salt Plain of the Danakil depression.

Titanium

Up to now tropical Africa has been a very unimportant supplier of ilmenite and rutile, the main sources of titanium. There are good reasons for this, the chief being that the high cost of transporting bulky and low-value ores has put a premium on the resources of those parts of the world that are handy to the great centers of manufacturing. Unfortunately, large though they are, most of the known tropical African sources are very unhandy. But with the yearly development of new uses for this tough, lightweight metal, notably to reduce metal fatigue in high-speed aircraft, there is little reason to suppose that the producing areas will long remain at their present levels of output, or at their present number.

Of the many known occurrences of titanium minerals, the most impressive are those in the French Cameroons, the Republic of Senegal and Gambia.

French Cameroons. Rutile occurs, in both alluvial and hard-rock situations, within an area of about 20,000 square miles encompassed by the Edea-Yabassi-Bafia–Nanga Eboko–Doumé-Sangmelima-Edea polygon. The ore is high grade, reaching 98 per cent TiO_2 in some places, or superior to most of the world's known deposits. The alluvial deposits have been put at 50,000 metric tons. No firm figure is as yet available for the less easily recovered hard-rock deposits; however, they are believed to be abundant. The output of rutile has been very uneven. For a while during World War II it exceeded 3,000 metric tons a year; in the postwar decade it tailed off to almost insignificant figures. At the present time the few small producers are hampered by their seeming inability to compete with Australian rutile on the European market.

Republic of Senegal. Titanium sands containing both ilmenite and zirconium are found along the coast near Rufisque, extending to the mouth of the Saloum River and, south of Gambia, near the mouth of the Casamance River. During World War II these areas produced between them up to 13,000 metric tons of ore a year. Their output is now down to less than 25 per cent of this figure.

Gambia. Large deposits of ilmenite, clearly related to those of Senegal and Casamance, have recently been found near Cape St. Mary, to the south of Bathurst. To develop them, Gambia Minerals Ltd., a subsidiary of Imperial Chemical Industries Ltd., has built a 15-mile railway (the only one in Gambia) to link the mining site with the extraction plant. This plant, in turn, has been linked by road to the government road system and so to Bathurst, the territory's port. The first shipments of ilmenite were made in 1956. Unfortunately for the small and struggling economy of the colony, these deposits are not expected to last more than ten years or so at the present, quite modest, rate of extraction; and they are proving so costly to extract that the company can pay only a small revenue to the government.

Among the many other territories from which reports of titanium minerals have been forthcoming are the following:

The French Community. Ilmenite is found in the southern part of the Republic of Dahomey southwest of Abomey, and in the Republic of the Upper Volta southwest of Diapaga. Of these two deposits, the latter is almost certainly the larger and the richer, but it is also the more remote from means of transport. Rutile deposits, with an average TiO_2 content of 95 per cent, have been discovered in northern Dahomey at Djougou, Kouandé and Birni. Some of these are thought to be capable of profitable development.

Mozambique. Ilmenite and rutile deposits have been found in the Tete region. The grade of both is high, the former averaging 98 per cent and the latter 90 per cent TiO_2.

Nyasaland. Ilmenite is reported as being "ubiquitous" in stream sands and as being present, along with rutile, in the Port Herald area. The total possible reserves of ilmenite and magnetite (with which it is frequently associated) have been put at roughly a million tons. Most of the ore is so scattered and its grade so indifferent, however, that its recovery is not considered feasible at the present time.

Sierra Leone. Titanium minerals, mainly ilmenite, occur in the hills behind Freetown and Waterloo, and near York. They are also found in the gravels of the Little Scarcies River.

Uganda. Titaniferous magnetite is an important constituent of a number of so-called iron ores in the Bugisu district. As a result of recent tests, these ores are regarded as being of possible future economic interest.

Zirconium

Zircon and baddeleyite, from which zirconium is obtained, occur widely in African beach sands and river gravels, often in association with alluvial gold, ilmenite, tin and diamonds. So far the output of them has been very small and almost entirely limited to the Republic of Senegal. Here zircon occurs in association with the ilmenite sands. The two minerals are obtained from the same workings, thus keeping costs low and giving the territory a little advantage over some of its possible competitors. The supply greatly exceeds the foreseeable need.

Other territories possessing deposits that may some day attract commercial attention are the Belgian Congo, Kenya, the Malagasy Republic, Mozambique, Nyasaland, Tanganyika and Uganda.

PRECIOUS METALS

It was precious metals that brought the early prospectors, and many of the early explorers, to tropical Africa. Although the focus of interest of most modern explorers and prospectors has shifted, there is still plenty of gold, silver and platinum in the hills of Africa, and it is still making some men and nations rich.

Gold

Gold is one of the most widely distributed metals of tropical Africa. It is known to occur in every territory in the region, and is being produced in many of them (Figure 25). However, three territories account for more than 90 per cent of the current production. There is no mistaking the identity of the chief producers in Table 22. Ghana, still living up to its former name, is an easy first; in most years its output is about one-third larger than that of Southern Rhodesia and about twice as large as that of the Belgian Congo, the territories ranking second and third on the list. The table also suggests that some of the smaller producers, and even some of the larger ones, are having a struggle to keep going in the face of rising production costs and a steady gold price.

Ghana. The chief lode mines are at Obuasi (the largest producer over the years), Prestea, Bibiani and Konongo. The chief "banket" (gold-bearing conglomerate) mines are at or near Tarkwa. In addition there are large alluvial workings on the Ankobra River. Barring any serious aggravation

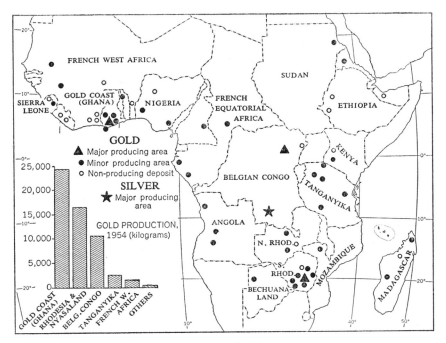

FIGURE 25

of the present cost-price squeeze, "the future of the . . . industry seems to be assured," Murdock reports. "The ore bodies are large and above average grade; the mines are relatively shallow, the geological environment favors persistence in depth, and there is every prospect that other important deposits will be discovered."

Southern Rhodesia. Gold is widely distributed. Most of the occurrences are small, however. In the past decade or so some of the smallest, non-mechanized mines have been forced out of business, but the output as a whole has been well maintained because of increased activity by the larger, mechanized and more efficiently run concerns. At nearly £7 million in 1958, gold ranked, among Southern Rhodesia's minerals, second only to asbestos (over £8.5 million) as a revenue earner, and made a handsome contribution to the sterling area's gold reserves.

The chief gold-producing districts in Southern Rhodesia at present are Gwelo, Hartley, Bulawayo, Salisbury, Gwanda, Umtali and Fort Victoria. Most of the mines are on the healthy high veld, and near the main railway line. Lode gold makes up the greater part of the output and its relative importance is likely to increase with the years. Although the grade of lode ore is generally lower than that of reef gold or quartz vein gold, the ore bodies are larger and cheaper to work. Several such low-grade deposits have been opened up by the bigger operators in the past few years.

Table 22

PRODUCTION OF GOLD BY
PRINCIPAL PRODUCERS, 1938-1957
(*Kilograms*)

TERRITORY	1938	AVERAGE 1945-1949	AVERAGE 1950-1954	1955	1957 [a]
Total	76,102	53,483	54,722	53,593 [b]	56,687 [b]
Per cent of world total [c]	7.7	7.8	6.9	6.4 [d]	6.2 [d]
Bechuanaland	580	188	26	17	6
Belgian Congo	14,723	10,035	11,178	11,506	11,640
French Cameroons	483	369	105	16	339
Eritrea	156	84	33	5	100 [e]
Ethiopia	500	1,440	506	n.a.	n.a.
French Equatorial Africa	1,207	2,070	1,610	1,448	957
French West Africa	3,994	149	63	18	10
Ghana (Gold Coast)	20,993	18,863	22,379	21,373	24,584
Kenya	2,146	833	430	296	227
Liberia	59	452	147	21	16 [e]
Malagasy Republic (Madagascar)	421	97	53	31	26
Mozambique	281	163	38	39	39 [e]
Nigeria	772	128	39	21	12
Northern Rhodesia	34	64	67	69	124
Southern Rhodesia	25,346	16,660	15,745	16,320	16,703
Sierra Leone	947	47	68	15	12 [e]
Republic of Sudan (Anglo-Egyptian Sudan)	276	104	64	47	199
Tanganyika	2,546	1,688	2,160	2,337	1,682
Uganda	638	49	11	14	11

Source: United Nations, *Statistical Yearbook, 1958,* New York, 1958.

[a] Preliminary figures.　[b] Partial total.
[c] Excluding U.S.S.R., mainland China, Romania and some small producers.
[d] First approximation.　[e] 1956.　n.a.: not available

Belgian Congo. The principal gold mines of the colony are located in the provinces of Orientale and Kivu. Only small quantities come from Kasai and Ruanda-Urundi. The total output is divided almost equally between the yield from hard-rock and alluvial and other surface workings. About 80 per cent of it comes from two concerns, the Société des Mines d'Or de Kilo-Moto and the Compagnie Minière des Grands Lacs Africains. Here, as in many other parts of tropical Africa, the trend is toward mechanization. Without it, the future of most mines could only be described as bleak. As it is, some of the poorer deposits cannot much longer be worked at a profit.

Since their numerical rating is not as constant as that of the "Big Three," the rest of the producing territories will be dealt with in alphabetical order.

Angola. Almost all of the recorded output comes from alluvial deposits. The chief of these are at Maiombe in the Cabinda enclave. There are also many smaller deposits. Indeed, most Angolan rivers have some gold in their beds, though not often in quantities that warrant commercial recovery. The quantities that can be profitably recovered with the help of machinery are, however, considered large enough to keep the industry going at its present low level for a very long time.

Bechuanaland. Gold is the most important of the few minerals known to exist in recoverable quantities. The present output comes from the Tati district in the northeast of the protectorate.

Ethiopia. Gold has been produced commercially in Eritrea at least since before the end of the nineteenth century. The major operations have been located in the semi-arid valleys of the Anseba and Gash and the Asmara region. Since World War II the output has been very small. In Ethiopia proper the beginnings of gold mining go back so far that they are lost to recorded history. Some of the deposits were certainly being worked in early Old Testament times. For all that, there is still a great deal of alluvial and vein gold left in the country, notably in the provinces of Wollega, Illubabor and Gojjam and near the town of Adola in the province of Sidamo-Borama.

French Cameroons. Of the many known alluvial deposits the principal ones are located in the region stretching to the north and south of Bétaré Oya, from Meiganga to Batouri. Until the 1957 gold strike in the Mboscorro area, the output was small. Since then it has increased spectacularly (125,000 grams were offered for sale to the French authorities in a single six-week period), but the scale of the individual operations remains small, and the mode extremely primitive.

The French Community. The principal of many producing areas in what used to be French Equatorial Africa are the Mayumbé Mountains of the Republic of the Congo, Yakola in the Central African Republic, and Ndjolé and Mimongo in the Gabon Republic. In the past the main interest has been in placer gold. Now it seems to be shifting to vein deposits. One of the most important of those worked is in the Haut-Sanga district of the Central African Republic. Very large amounts of gold are still to be had in the river beds, but dredging and washing machinery is expensive and the current margin of profit in the industry rather too small to tempt most private investors.

Though there have been many gold-mining operations in the Malagasy Republic, few have enjoyed more than a passing prosperity. Today reef mining has practically ceased, and almost the entire production comes from river deposits worked, either in pans or primitive sluices, by indigenous miners who sell their pickings to the European owners of gold-mining concessions. The main fields are located in the region of the Tsaratanana Mountains, Miandrivazo and Marovato.

In the west African states of the French Community most of the gold likewise comes from alluvial or placer deposits which are generously scattered throughout the territory. The chief producing regions are the Bambouk district of the Sudanese Republic (formerly French Sudan) and near Natitingou in the Republic of Dahomey.

Republic of Guinea. Most of the small output comes from Siguiri.

Kenya. The most important mine is the Macalder in the Kavirondo region adjacent to the eastern shore of Lake Victoria. In the surrounding country there are estimated to be some 8,000 square miles of auriferous rock.

Liberia. Alluvial gold is taken, mostly by very primitive sluice box and pan methods, from many stream beds. Hard-rock gold has been reported from at least three different areas, but development is retarded by many things, not least perhaps by government legislation. For some years the government has required that all gold mined in the country be sold at a rather low fixed price to the Bank of Monrovia. When the monopoly first went into effect the visible exports of gold "fell off one half . . . indicating, in all probability, that the rest of it left the country by smuggling." [19]

Mozambique. The once important gold fields near Vila Manica now have only one sizable operation, the Braganza mine. Most of the operations have been marginal and short-lived. In recent years the chief producers have been the Empresa Mineira do Alto Ligonha and the Companhia de Mozambique, but even they are no longer doing a very big business in gold. Again, here is a territory where almost all the rivers have some alluvial gold in them and rich lodes are reported from many places, but one where it is hard to find enough high-grade gold in any one place to justify the heavy capitalization necessary to put the industry in a strongly competitive position.

Nigeria. The chief gold-bearing areas are in the Oyo and Calabar provinces, where they are associated with basement complex schists. The small output is derived largely from scattered alluvial deposits. Where lodes and veins are worked, it is mostly by open-cast methods. According to Murdock, "the general geological setting does not appear to be favorable for the existence of important lode deposits comparable, for example, with those in Ghana."

Northern Rhodesia. Of recent years a significant part of the territory's small gold output has come from the "waste" copper slimes of the Copperbelt smelters. Some gold has also come from Chumbwe near Lusaka, and from the vicinity of Mumbwa. Gold is also present in the Broken Hill area, north of Serenje, and between Kasama and Abercorn, but it is un-

[19] R. Earle Anderson, *Liberia: America's African Friend,* University of North Carolina Press, Chapel Hill, 1952, p. 262.

likely to be mined in these localities while the depression of the gold industry lasts.

Nyasaland. In the past, small amounts of alluvial gold have been worked in the Ncheu district, and there are indications of alluvial gold in other areas. On the whole, however, Nyasaland is not gold country — one of the very few tropical African territories of which this can be said.

Sierra Leone. While alluvial gold in paying amounts has been worked for centuries in neighboring parts of west Africa it was not until 1926 that its existence on a large scale was established in Sierra Leone. The principal workings to date have been to the northeast and southeast of Magburaka and in the Sefadu and Lake Sonfon districts. As yet very little prospecting for lode deposits has been carried on, but there is no reason to suppose that such deposits will not be found. All alluvial gold has its origin in hard — parent — rock; being, by reason of its weight, a reluctant traveler — and a one-way traveler at that — its location is often an important clue to the whereabouts of the parent. One such parent body, at Baomahun at the southern end of the Kangari Hills, has been estimated to have a probable reserve of over 56,000 long tons of ore, averaging 5.3 pennyweight of gold per ton. Sometimes, of course, there is no longer any "parent" — it has been weathered away.

Republic of Sudan. It is probable that less gold is now mined in this section of the Nile valley than was mined there in early Egyptian times. For the gold fields are too far from water and transportation facilities to attract the modern mining corporation. The three mines that have yielded most of the small Sudanese output of modern times are at Umm Nabardi in the northeast of Kassala Province, and the Gebeit and Oyo mines in the Red Sea hills. In 1958 the only places where gold was mined were Duweishat and Bir Kateib, in the extreme north of the country.

Tanganyika. In terms of capital invested and labor employed gold mining takes pride of place in the country's mining industry. For a while, around 1938, gold was second only to sisal in the list of exports. Since World War II the industry has suffered, as in most other territories, from having to sell its product at a price bearing little relation to production costs, and gold currently occupies a low place in the list of investment opportunities. The principal hard-rock gold-producing areas are the Geita mine, located in the district of the same name at the southern end of Lake Victoria, the Musoma field, the Singida district of the Central Province, and the Lupa field in the Chunya district of the Southern Highlands Province. The Lupa field is also the most important source of alluvial gold in the country. Alluvial gold occurs, and is worked spasmodically, in several other localities, including Dodoma, Morogoro and Lindi.

Uganda. In the past a good deal of alluvial gold was obtained in the Toro district. However, most of this has now been worked out, and the "parent" from which it came has not been discovered. The small present-day output comes mainly from the Busia area on the Kenya border. This is regarded by many as the area of greatest potential, for in mineralization and geological setting it has much in common with the neighboring Kenya and Tanganyika gold fields.

Silver

The total silver production of tropical Africa has fluctuated from around 140,000 to 150,000 metric tons in recent years, and the ratio it bears to the world's total has varied from about 2 to 3 per cent. A part of it is recovered as a by-product of gold mining, and a much larger part as a by-product of base-metal refining; nowhere is silver mined for its sake alone.

Of the producing countries listed in Table 23, the Belgian Congo is a

Table 23

PRODUCTION OF SILVER, 1938-1957

(*Metric Tons*)

TERRITORY	1938	AVERAGE 1945-1949	AVERAGE 1950-1954	1955	1957 [a]
Total	106	145	153	143	116
Per cent of world total [b]	1.3	3.1	2.7	2.4	1.9
Belgian Congo	97	134	139	127	95
British West Africa [c]	1	1	1	1	1 [d]
Northern Rhodesia	3	6	10	12	18
Southern Rhodesia	5	3	3	2	2

Source: United Nations, *Statistical Yearbook, 1958*, New York, 1958.

[a] Preliminary figures.
[b] Excluding U.S.S.R., Czechoslovakia, Romania and a few small producers.
[c] Nigeria, Ghana, Sierra Leone.　[d] 1956.

very easy first. Most of the output comes from Katanga, where it is recovered either from the blister copper or from the slimes of the Jadotville-Shituru electrolytic refining plant. In both cases, the refining of the metal is done in Belgium. A small amount is also recovered in the processing of gold ores taken from the Kivu and Orientale provinces.

The other producers, in alphabetical order, are Bechuanaland (silver is found alloyed with gold in the Tati and Monarch districts), Ghana (also in association with gold), Kenya (in association with gold in Nyanza and with base-metal ores, such as galena, in Coast Province), Mozambique (associated with gold, near Vila Manica and Tete), Nigeria (alloyed with lead, in the Abakaliki Division of Ogoja Province and Zurak in Adamawa Province), Northern Rhodesia (derived from two sources, the Broken Hill lead-zinc property and the Nkana copper slimes, the output from the latter being by far the larger), Southern Rhodesia (virtually all of the output is a by-product of gold mining), Tanganyika (the gold mines are again the main benefactor, but the recently developed Mpanda lead-copper mine has been producing sizable amounts of by-product silver) and Uganda (from the Busia area, near the Kenya border).

In addition, there are occurrences of silver, but at present no production, in Angola, the Republic of the Congo, Ethiopia, Nyasaland, Sierra Leone, British Somaliland and Somalia.

Platinum Group

Besides platinum, this group of metals contains palladium, iridium, osmium, rhodium and ruthenium. Notwithstanding their wide distribution in tropical Africa, the production of these minerals has so far been small and confined to the Belgian Congo, Ethiopia and Sierra Leone. Most of the output has consisted of platinum.

Ethiopia has been for many years the chief tropical African producer of platinum. The source of its supply is the Yubdo area of the Wollega Province, where the ore occurs in both the weathered and native — hard-rock — state. Estimates of the reserves of platiniferous rocks and gravels in this area range all the way from 12 to 60 million cubic yards, the latter being regarded as the most reasonable. Even if the recoverable platinum content is assumed to be as low as one gram per cubic yard, this gives a metal reserve of possibly 60,000 kilograms. At the current rate of exploitation such a reserve would last several hundred years.

Belgian Congo. Palladium and platinum used to be found in association with gold at the Ruwe mine, near Kolwezi in Katanga, but this deposit now seems to have been worked out. They are also found in the gold mines of the Orientale and Kivu provinces. Currently the output is almost negligible; what there is is derived from the refining, in Belgium, of copper products.

Sierra Leone. The chief deposits are found in the stream and beach gravels of the lofty Freetown peninsula and its low-lying perimeter. So far only the stream gravels have been worked.

Of the presently non-producing territories, the one that offers the greatest promise is Southern Rhodesia. This territory has long been known to possess large platinum deposits, but hitherto the refractory nature of the ore has presented serious extraction problems. However, those most interested in promoting these deposits now claim that the problems are not unsolvable. If the claims can stand up to the buffetings of the open market place, the 70-square-mile area in the Belingwe district is likely to see a great deal of activity. The recoverable deposits here have been tentatively put at some 80 million short tons and are believed to contain, besides platinum, exploitable amounts of nickel and copper.

Other territories in which platinum-bearing ore bodies have been found

are Nyasaland (near Blantyre and Ncheu, and in Angoni) and Tanganyika (in the Njombe and Mpanda areas).

INDUSTRIAL MINERALS

Under this heading are grouped together the large and growing number
of nonmetallic minerals (exclusive of fuels) that enter into the manufacture of such things as abrasives, bearings, refractories, chemicals, in-
sulation and construction materials, and cutting tools. While the full range
of tropical Africa's offerings in this category has still to be revealed, it is
clearly substantial, comparing well with those of other and better-explored
territories.

Diamonds [20]

The importance of tropical Africa to the world's diamond users can be
gauged from the following statistic: in 1957 the region accounted for
over 80 per cent of the world's output of gem and industrial diamonds.
The comparative standing of the several producers of industrial diamonds
and gem stones is given in Table 24 and Figure 26.

Belgian Congo. Over the years the colony has been the largest producer
of both types of diamonds. The Kasai field was the first to be developed,

[20] For convenience, both gem stones and industrial diamonds are dealt with here.

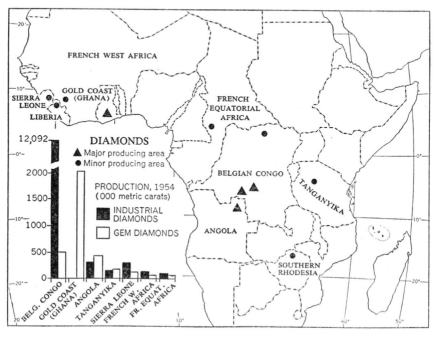

FIGURE 26

Table 24

PRODUCTION OF DIAMONDS, 1938-1957

(Thousand Metric Carats)

G & I: Gems and industrial diamonds.   I: Industrial diamonds only.

TERRITORY	1938		1949		AVERAGE 1950-1954		1955		1957 [a]	
	G & I	I	G & I	I	G & I	I	G & I	I	G & I	I
Total	9,925	1,691 [b]	12,285	10,042 [b]	16,216	12,552 [b]	17,262	15,279 [b]	21,105	18,438
Per cent of world total	85	18 [c]	86	85 [c]	88	81 [c]	80	82 [c]	81	81
Angola	651	280	770	330	725	352	743	304	864	350
Belgian Congo	7,206	n.a.	9,649	9,100	12,108	11,646	13,041	12,413	15,647	15,016
French Equatorial Africa	16	13	123	98	169	98	137	90	109	70 [d]
French West Africa	62	50	95	76	215	154	318	210	300	150
Ghana (Gold Coast) [d]	1,297	898 [e]	963	n.a.	2,320	n.a.	2,276	2,114	2,931	2,650 [e]
Sierra Leone	690	450	494	330	497	222	420	n.a.	863	n.a.
Tanganyika	4	4	191	108	182	80	325	148 [d]	391	202 [d]

Source: United Nations, *Statistical Yearbook, 1958*, New York, 1958.

[a] Preliminary figures.   [b] Partial total.   [c] First approximation.   [d] Exports.   [e] Partly estimated.   n.a.: not available

and it continues to be one of the most important. From the numerous small workings in the gravels of the lower Kasai River and its tributaries there come annually about 600,000 carats, equally divided between gems and industrials. But the bulk of the present-day industrial output comes from the Bakwanga gravel deposits, east-southeast of Luluabourg. A third, and much smaller, producing area is the Uele basin in the extreme north; here the diamonds are recovered from gold mine "waste."

Ghana. The main fields lie in the Birim valley and to the south of Tarkwa. They consist of old stream bed gravels buried beneath a 2-to-10-foot mantle of younger deposits. In the larger properties the stripping of the overburden and the separation of the diamonds from the washed concentrates are done mechanically. More primitive methods are in use on the smaller African-leased properties. The production of both gem stones and industrial diamonds has increased significantly in the past decade. In 1957 it was more than three times as large as in 1948.

Angola. The fields here are in the Dundo area of the northeast adjacent to the Congo's Kasai fields. They represent the rich legacy of a long-lost river system that once spewed its diamantiferous gravels across the countryside. The recovery methods employed by Companhia de Diamantes de Angola, which has a diamond monopoly, are generally simpler and call for more hand labor than those employed by the Belgians; but this does not greatly affect the company's competitive power, for in Angola labor is cheap and can be had for the commanding.

The other main producers are together responsible for about 30 per cent, by value, of the total diamond output.

Central African Republic. The chief mines — all alluvial — are at Bria and in the Carnot-Berbérati-Nola region.

Republic of Guinea. The principal known occurrences are located midway between Kissidougou and Beyla. Approximately two thirds of the output consists of industrial stones. When the present modernization programs are completed, the output of both industrials and gems is expected to rise sharply.

Liberia. Except for a short-lived attempt by the Liberian government to produce diamonds in the 1930s, commercial interest in diamonds was negligible until about 1952. At the present time Liberia has several licensed diamond exporters and a small, but rising, production of both gem and industrial stones. During 1953, the first year for which figures are available, 3,243 carats were exported. In 1956 more than one million carats of industrial diamonds were exported. Most of the diamonds come from upcountry, near the Sierra Leone border.

Sierra Leone. The richest of the known deposits lie within the Bafi-Sewa River drainage system. Within this area the most productive mining centers to date are those in the Sierra Leone Selection Trust's concessions in Kono and Tongo. Although a good deal of detective work has been carried out, the pipe or pipes that fathered the alluvial diamonds have not been found. Most of the diamonds recovered are small, between 2 and 3 carats, and of gem quality. Considerable as the recorded production is, the actual production is much greater. The difference represents the "take" of the illicit diamond diggers and buyers whose highly ingenious but unsavory strategems annually cost the country a not-so-small fortune.[21]

Southern Rhodesia. Notwithstanding the existence of diamantiferous kimberlite pipes and gravels, Southern Rhodesia has never greatly excited the diamond seeker. The total recorded output down to 1952, covering a period of about half a century, was less than 16,000 carats. Since then the production has been negligible.

Tanganyika. Although diamonds were reported near Mabuki in the Kwimba country, to the south of Lake Victoria, before the first world war, and were produced off and on between the two wars, it was not until the Williamson era that diamonds became big business in the territory. The now famous Mwadui kimberlite pipe near the village of Luhombo, 20 miles northeast of Shinyanga, was discovered by the late Dr. J. T. Williamson in 1940. Thereafter, notwithstanding wartime difficulties, the output of diamonds expanded rapidly, if a little unsteadily. So far, all of the production has come from the superimposed gravels. It remains to be seen whether the Mwadui pipe — or any other known kimberlite pipe in the area — has any diamonds left in it and, if so, whether they are present in payable amounts.

Diamonds are reported to occur in several other territories. In the French Cameroons they have been found in almost all of the gold-mining properties, though not in sufficient concentrations, it appears, to warrant the cost of installing washing and separating machinery. In Mozambique diamonds were discovered in 1953 in the Lebombo Mountains near the Swaziland border. There have been vague and, in some instances, conflicting reports of diamonds in the Republic of Sudan, Ethiopia and Bechuanaland.

Asbestos

Tropical Africa produced an estimated 120,000 metric tons of asbestos in 1957, compared with 95,600 metric tons in 1955 and an annual average of 74,000 in the preceding five years. The region at present accounts for about 9 per cent of the free-world total.

Southern Rhodesia has for many years been a large producer of asbestos,

[21] The smuggling of diamonds out of Sierra Leone has grown to be such a business that in 1956 "over £ 6,000,000 is estimated to have been lost to revenue . . ., more than half the total value of all exports from the country during the year." (*The Times British Colonies Review*, Second Quarter 1957, p. 19.)

with a very long lead over the other producing territories. The lead is lengthening, thanks largely to strong world demand for high-quality (low-iron-content) asbestos, remunerative prices, and the ease with which the mineral can be mined. In 1955 asbestos ousted gold from its long-held position as the most valuable mineral in the Southern Rhodesian economy — a distinction it continues to enjoy.

Most of the recent increases in output have occurred on the larger properties producing long fibers of spinning grade. The largest of these properties are located at Shabani and at Mashaba, some 30 miles northeast of Shabani.

The smaller operators, who for the most part produce only short grades of fiber, have not been doing so well for themselves in the postwar period. They have found it difficult to meet the more and more exacting requirements of the market with the small and obsolete mills most of them have. They are also finding it difficult to pay the high wages and provide the fine facilities and accommodations which the new, heavily capitalized mines can afford — a situation not confined to the small asbestos operator, needless to say. Some of them have already been forced to close down. Others are doing their best to stay in business by pooling their resources, natural and technical.

The total annual capacity of the territory's asbestos plants, large and small, was more than 130,000 short tons in 1957. Reserves are generally accepted to be well in excess of the figure of 7 million short tons arrived at in 1928, for drillings have disclosed the existence of ore bodies unsuspected at that time. The Shabani area alone is still reckoned to have more than a million short tons of spinning-grade fiber.

Apart from the small amount which is used locally in the asbestos cement industry, the output is shipped overseas, mostly to the United Kingdom, the United States, India, France and Germany.

The remainder of the tropical African output, a very small percentage of the total, comes from Bechuanaland (near Kanye), Kenya (near Voi), the Malagasy Republic (the Betioky, Antsirabe, Maevatanana and Tamatave areas) and Mozambique (near Vila Manica).

Among the territories reporting, but not yet producing, asbestos are the Belgian Congo, Ethiopia, Nyasaland, Sierra Leone, Tanganyika and Uganda.

Graphite

Some graphite is found in most countries of the world. There are known deposits of it in eleven tropical African territories and some production in four of them.

Of the four the Malagasy Republic is an easy first; it is, in fact, one of the world's major sources of high-quality graphite needed for crucible work. Of the many deposits, those in the east central part of the island — the Tamatave-Vatomandry-Moramanga triangle — are the principal sources of supply. Production methods are still mainly of the pick-and-shovel type; and because most of the producing companies are small, averaging not more than 15 tons a month, modernization schemes make only slow progress.

Elsewhere production is very small and intermittent. In Kenya the most promising of the several widely separated deposits are those near Tsavo about 100 miles northwest of Mombasa, and at Thika. In Mozambique the most valuable, it would seem, of the several known deposits is at Itotone, some miles inland from the port of Lumbo. It is of high quality, and lends itself to simple flotation treatment. Tanganyika has major deposits in the Morogoro, Mpwapwa, Handeni, Lindi and Mahenge districts. The Morogoro deposits have been put at a million short tons of ore, from which possibly 50,000 short tons of graphite could be recovered by flotation.

The presently non-producing territories are the Belgian Congo, the Central African Republic, Ethiopia, the Republic of Guinea, Northern Rhodesia, Nyasaland and Southern Rhodesia.

Barite

The geological literature of tropical Africa contains very few references to barite. The only territories in which it has so far been reported are Bechuanaland, the Belgian Congo (where it frequently occurs in association with copper), Kenya (in the Coast Province), Nyasaland, Northern Rhodesia (to the south of the Kafue River east of the railway), Southern Rhodesia (in the neighborhood of Que Que) and Tanganyika (near the mouth of the Malagarasi River and in the Lupa gold field). The sole producer is Southern Rhodesia, which in recent years has had an output of between 100 and 300 short tons, amounting to less than one tenth of one per cent of the world output.

Bitumens

Occurrences of native bitumens and related materials are reported in several areas, particularly along the western seaboard. So far they have been worked only in Angola, the Belgian Congo and the Republic of the Ivory Coast. The output is small and is used almost entirely for local road surfacing.

In Angola, deposits of bituminous materials are found in the sedimentary (Cretaceous) formations that flank the coast from Maiombe in the Cabinda enclave to a point beyond Moçâmedes in the south. In the aggregate these deposits are capable of supporting a large multipurpose processing plant. In recent years the average annual output of bitumens has been around 20,000 metric tons.

The most promising Belgian Congo occurrences are in Bas-Congo, near the Cabinda enclave, and on the shores of Lake Albert. After extensive laboratory testing, the Bas-Congo deposits are now being developed commercially.

In the Republic of the Ivory Coast there are several occurrences of bitumen-bearing sands in the Eboinda region, near Assinie. The beds containing them range from three to ten feet in thickness and from 6 to 35 per cent in bitumen content. There has been some exploitation of them since 1952.

Bitumen is also present in parts of the Republic of the Congo (Pointe Noire, the principal port, takes its name from the asphaltic limestones found in its vicinity), the Malagasy Republic and Tanganyika.

Clays

There are clays of most kinds in tropical Africa. Even such special-purpose clays as kaolin, or china clay, are quite widely distributed. As for the common clays used in making brick, they can be had in almost any termite mound, and these can be had almost everywhere; indeed, the only thing commoner than termite mounds in many parts of Africa are the termites that built them. So far, most of the clay extraction has been done by Africans for their own immediate ends, which are not primarily commercial. Production figures are accordingly hard to come by; where they exist, they are incomplete and therefore misleading. Production of china clay is better recorded, but very few territories have yet begun to exploit their resources, and those that have are not yet significant producers.

The following territorial summary deals mainly with special-purpose clays that are found in significant quantity.

Belgian Congo. Kaolin is widely intermingled with the tin deposits of Katanga, Maniema and Ruanda-Urundi. It is also abundant in the provinces of Léopoldville, Equateur and Kasai.

Republic of the Congo. Lateritic clays, of varied chemical constitution and quality, are especially abundant in the Niari and Djouah river systems.

Ethiopia. Kaolin occurs in commercially useful amounts at various points and is exploited on a small scale, for a ceramic plant in Asmara. Laterized clays are found in many districts and are used locally in the making of pottery.

Kenya. Ceramic clays occur at many places in the Central and Coast provinces.

Nyasaland. Small deposits of kaolin occur in Ncheu and Kota Kota, and much larger deposits of red marl, suitable for tiles and piping as well as bricks, occur near Chiromo. Refractory clays, from which fire brick of good quality has been made, are present on the Zomba Plateau, while clays well suited to the requirements of the Portland cement industry are present in the Chiromo area and in the north of the country.

Sierra Leone. Large deposits, put at several million tons, of whitish multipurpose clays exist in the Lungi area. Their proximity to Freetown and the coast is likely to enhance the chances of their being worked in the near future.

Southern Rhodesia. Fire clays have been produced here for some years, primarily for use as refractory bricks by the Wankie Colliery Company. In the mid-1950s the annual production of fire clay exceeded 70,000 short tons, making Southern Rhodesia the largest, by far, of tropical African producers.

Tanganyika. Kaolin occurrences have been reported at several points, notably at Pugu (on the Central Line), where for a while a pilot plant for the manufacture of a good-quality refined clay was in operation.

Corundum [22]

Despite the competition of manufactured abrasives derived from other mineral sources, corundum and garnet continue to be in demand as natural abrasives. Both minerals are widely distributed in tropical Africa, as the following partial list of reported occurrences shows:

Angola. Garnet has been found in several places (notably near Quicabo, northeast of Luanda), though not as yet in payable quantities.

Belgian Congo. Both corundum (Maniema district of Kivu and southern Katanga) and garnet (Boma, Katanga and Ituri) are fairly abundant.

Republic of the Congo. Corundum is present and has been produced, intermittently, on a small scale in the Mayoko region.

Ethiopia. Garnets have been reported near Harar and the Somalia border.

Kenya. Corundum has been reported near Mtito Andei and the Tanganyika border.

Malagasy Republic. Alluvial deposits of corundum have been exploited off and on for some years in the region of Tamatave, Ambositra, Moramanga and Vatomandry. In the Ambositra and Ampanihy regions garnets exist on a scale that makes their exploitation feasible.

Mozambique. Corundum, in workable amounts, has been found at Zobue on the Nyasaland border, Vila Pery and in the Tete area.

Northern Rhodesia. Corundum-bearing schists are present in two areas in the southeastern corner of the territory, and several garnet bodies have been found near Lubombo on the railway line between Kafue and Mazabuka.

Nyasaland. Garnets have been found in the Port Herald area, and rich

---

[22] For convenience garnet is coupled with corundum, since both minerals are primarily used for the same purpose, the manufacture of abrasives.

patches of weathered corundum have been found and worked from time to time near Mwanza in the southwest.

Sierra Leone. Corundum fragments and crystals occur in many stream beds.

Southern Rhodesia. There is at Concession, near Salisbury, a massive (perhaps 250,000 short ton) corundum reef which as of 1956 was being worked at the rate of about 500 short tons a month. There are also a number of garnet occurrences.

Tanganyika. Workable deposits of corundum are reported in the Dodoma district and elsewhere, and garnet occurrences in the Uluguru Mountains, near Newala to the southwest of Mtwara, and along the Tanga railway line.

Diatomite

As its name indicates, the essential constituents of diatomite (or diatomaceous earth) are the fossil remains of diatoms, microscopic marine and fresh-water vegetable organisms. In its purest form it is chalk-like in appearance, light in weight, porous and friable, and can be used for heat- and sound-proofing, fillers, filtration media and abrasives. The list of its uses is continually growing. Not the least important of those to which it is being put locally is that of tick-repelling whitewash, a boon that only habitués of mud huts can fully appreciate. Up to now diatomite has been reported in five tropical African territories, but only in Kenya has it been produced on a commercially significant scale, notably at Gilgil and Magadi.

The other territories in which deposits are known to occur are Bechuanaland, the Belgian Congo, Tanganyika and Uganda.

Feldspar

Feldspar, chiefly used as a ceramic flux, is a common constituent of the earth's crust. Payable deposits are, however, comparatively uncommon. Few have been found in tropical Africa; fewer still have been worked, perfunctorily at that.

The main occurrences are in the Belgian Congo (in Bas-Congo, and in the tin-bearing areas of Ruanda-Urundi and the Orientale and Kivu provinces), Ethiopia (in Eritrea, and in the pegmatite dikes around Harar and to the southeast of Diredawa), Kenya (in the Central Province), Mozambique (near Gondola) and Tanganyika (in the Lupa gold field and near Dodoma).

Fluorspar

Like feldspar, fluorspar is used mainly in specialized industries, such as the manufacture of fluorine, lenses and fluxes, that are not extensively developed in tropical Africa and that can be supplied more cheaply from less remote sources. Consequently very little use has yet been made of the several known deposits of fluorspar.

These deposits occur in Bechuanaland (in the Kanye area), the Belgian Congo (in Katanga and Ituri), Kenya (in the Kisumu district), Nyasaland (on Chilwa Island), Sierra Leone (at Songo near Freetown), Southern Rhodesia (in the Wankie district, where the deposit has been worked on a small scale since 1938 for use in the Bulawayo iron and steel plant) and Tanganyika (where fluorspar occurs widely as an accessory mineral in the younger granites).

Gypsum

Gypsum falls into much the same category of demand as fluorspar; it "travels" badly and can be used profitably only near its place of origin. So far tropical African countries have not had much occasion to develop gypsum-using industries. When they come to do so, however, they will not need to look far for their raw material. Already a number of likely deposits have been reported upon.

One of these is a deposit in southern Angola, near Benguela, which has been worked from time to time for use in the manufacture of plaster of Paris and cement. Another is in Bechuanaland, in the Palla Road area. The Belgian Congo has deposits of gypsum in Katanga, where it is used locally for plaster of Paris and cement. In Ethiopia a small amount is produced in the Danakil Salt Plain for use in the Diredawa cement plant and for other purposes. Kenya has gypsum near El Wak and Garissa in the Northern Province; Nyasaland, in the Chiromo area. In British Somaliland some of the world's greatest reserves of calcium sulfate minerals are found, at not great distance (20 miles or so) from the port of Berbera. In Southern Rhodesia the shales of the Wankie coal-mining area are a source of gypsum. In Tanganyika deposits occur at various points, but most promisingly at Mkomazi, about 100 miles by rail from Tanga. This deposit is believed to contain more than 100,000 long tons of high-quality gypsum. At the present time it is worked on a very small scale (about 5,000 tons a year).

Kyanite (and related minerals)

Aluminum silicate minerals, of which kyanite is perhaps the commonest, are used in the manufacture of special kinds of refractories. So far the world demand for such minerals has been largely met by non-African sources. The only tropical African territories producing them commercially are Bechuanaland, Kenya, Nyasaland and Tanganyika. The amounts produced are small and subject to wide annual fluctuations. For a time in the early 1950s Kenya had an annual output ranging up to 12,000 long tons of kyanite and related minerals. In recent years the output has fallen off badly. However, a government report speaks of the likelihood of Kenya's regaining before long "its position as one of the principal sources in the world of this important mineral." [23]

Several kyanite ore bodies have been found in Kenya. One of the largest is located near Taveta, in the Coast Province, and so within easy reach of rail and the port of Mombasa. Deposits, as yet unworked, of sillimanite, a related mineral, have been found in the Machakos and Maralal areas, and in the Northern Province.

In Bechuanaland in the past few years, a kyanite deposit has been developed about eight miles from Francistown. The deposit is large and of high grade, but the output is very small (around 2,000 metric tons annually).

Kyanite is widely distributed among the "basement" gneisses of the Kirk Range in the Ncheu district of Nyasaland. The ore bodies are extensive and can be worked cheaply by open-cut methods. Several mining leases have been negotiated in the past few years; for a time (between 1952 and 1954) there was a small export of kyanite.

Aluminum silicate minerals have also been reported in quantity in the following, as yet non-producing, territories: Angola (in a number of "basement" areas, for example at the Cambaça mica mine south of Quicabo), the Belgian Congo (also in a number of places, but most promisingly along the Katanga–Northern Rhodesia border), Northern Rhodesia (in the Lusaka-Zambezi area) and Tanganyika (in the Pare district among others).

Mica

Mica occurs in various forms, each of them having its uses. Sheet mica has long been used for stove and furnace windows and is being used increasingly in the electrical and electronic industries. Scrap and flake mica are ground for use as an insulating material, a lubricant and an absorbent. Although tropical Africa contributes relatively little — between 1 and 2 per cent — to the world supply, it does provide some of the best-quality mica known.

At one time or other mica has been produced in eleven of the territories, and it is found in several others. A brief recital of the more important known deposits follows:

Angola. The occurrences of mica in payable form appear to be confined to an area of crystalline rocks situated along the middle course of the Dande River near Quicabo, northeast of Luanda. Expansion of the modest operations of the mines in this area is impeded by the inadequacies of the existing transportation facilities and labor supply, and the lack of a large local market for the unexportable scrap.

[23] *Commerce and Industry in Kenya, 1958,* Government Printer, Nairobi, 1958, p. 39.

Belgian Congo. Scrap mica is found in parts of Ruanda-Urundi, and sheet mica, in readily recoverable form, in many of the country's tin ore bodies.

Ethiopia. Deposits of mica have been reported in several provinces, notably in Wollega (Nejo region) and Harar (Jijiga), and in Eritrea.

French Cameroons. "Books" of white mica 4 to 6 inches thick have been found north and northwest of Yaoundé, and southwest of Bafia.

Kenya. A very little sheet mica is produced, intermittently, in the Central Province and the West Suk district.

Malagasy Republic. Mica deposits are generously scattered over the island and many of them have been or are being worked. The bulk of the output — easily the largest in tropical Africa — is derived from prismatic deposits, weighing up to several scores of tons apiece, in the Benato and Fort Dauphin areas. As a result of the mine-modernizing campaign that has been under way for some years past, the general quality of the product has been greatly improved.

Mozambique. Excellent "ruby" mica is found at Entre Rios and Alto Ligonha. For a while there was some ruby mica production at Gondola on the Beira-Umtali road. There are also mica deposits at Netia, to the northwest of Lumbo.

Northern Rhodesia. Mica is found in many places and mined, on a very small scale, in several. The more important of these are in the Lundazi, Petauke, Fort Jameson, Lusaka and Choma districts.

Nyasaland. From time to time prospectors have been interested in, and have worked, a number of mica occurrences, notably in the Kirk Mountains; but with the "creaming off" of the more accessible and attractive exposures, production has ceased.

Southern Rhodesia. Over the years there has been a considerable mica output in this territory. However, since shortly after World War II, the output of both sheet, or block, mica and the much less sought-after waste and crude mica has declined. In 1953 the value of the mica output was only about one third of what it was in 1946. At present prices it barely pays to work the waste and crude grades, which alone are abundant. The chief deposits are located at Miami (northwest of Sinoia) and to the northeast of Salisbury near the Mozambique border.

Tanganyika. Good commercial quality mica has been marketed from many "basement" localities. The principal producing areas are in the Bagamoyo, Korogwe, Mbeya, Morogoro, Mpanda, Mpwapwa and Rungwe districts. The eastern producers are the largest; their proximity to the seaports from which most of the product is shipped abroad gives them a considerable advantage over their more westerly competitors.

Pyrite

Pyrite, or iron sulfide, is widely distributed throughout tropical Africa, but known occurrences of economic importance are very few. Only one, the Iron Duke mine in the Mazoe district of Southern Rhodesia, has been exploited on any scale. In the past few years its output (used in the manufacture of sulfuric acid at Broken Hill in Northern Rhodesia) has fluctuated between 20,000 and 40,000 short tons.

Useful deposits occur in Angola (at the Bembe copper mine), the Belgian Congo (at the Kipushi copper mine near Elisabethville, and in the Luena coal field), Kenya (in the Kakamega gold fields and on a copper-gold property in South Nyanza), Northern Rhodesia (in the Luangwa River system, and in the King Edward mine southwest of Lusaka), Sierra Leone (in the Tonkolili district), Tanganyika (in all the gold fields) and Uganda (in the Kampala area).

Salt

Salt was without doubt the first mineral to be exploited commercially in tropical Africa. Primitive man managed to get along remarkably well without most minerals that we now deem indispensable, but not without salt. And because salt is not to be had everywhere, trade in salt early developed between the "haves" and the "have-nots." Some of the oldest African travelers' tales to come down to us tell of the silent barter that was carried out in the sub-Saharan savannas by negroes willing to trade their alluvial gold for Arab salt. It is safe to say that this salt trade was not confined to the sub-Saharan savannas, and that Arabs were not the only salt traders. On the contrary, it is likely that wherever there were salt seas, or brackish lakes and springs, and drying winds, there were the makings of an indigenous salt trade; as there still are.

Table 25 lists, for several recent years, the recorded salt output of the

Table 25

PRODUCTION OF SALT, 1938-1957

(Thousand Metric Tons)

TERRITORY	1938	1949	AVERAGE 1950-1954	1955	1957 [a]
Total (partial)	279	283	407	404	349
Angola	n.a.	41	50	58	52
Eritrea	167	79	177	184	167
Ethiopia	n.a.	n.a.	14	15	15
French Somaliland	52	68	64	20	2
Kenya [b]	3	19	19	26	23
Mozambique	6	10	11	14	n.a.
Republic of Sudan (Anglo-Egyptian Sudan)	38	44	50	52	54 [c]
Tanganyika	10	15	17	26	26
Uganda	3	7	6	9	10

Source: United Nations, *Statistical Yearbook, 1958,* New York, 1958.

[a] Preliminary figures.   [b] Sales.   [c] 1956.   n.a.: not available

major producing territories. Some part of the output of most salt-producing territories is used for chemical purposes, but by far the larger part of the total output continues to serve man's timeless need.

None of the producing territories in tropical Africa occupies a significant place among the world's suppliers of salt. Even the three largest — Angola, Eritrea and the Republic of Sudan — produce among them less than one per cent of the total world output. The chief producing areas in these territories are: in Angola, Lobito, Capolo, Moçâmedes, Porto Alexandre, Ambriz, Ambrizete and Cacuaco; in Eritrea, Massawa and Assab; in the Republic of Sudan, the Red Sea lagoons. In all of these the salt is produced by the evaporation of sea water pans. In some other areas, including the Katanga region of the Belgian Congo, the Danakil Salt Plain of Ethiopia, the Lake Chad region of the Republic of Chad and the Katwe region of Uganda, commercial quantities of salt are recovered from terrestrial sources such as saline lakes and springs and salt beds.

Soda Ash

The only territory where the production of soda ash is important at the present time is Kenya. In the postwar period the output, from deposits located at Lake Magadi in the Rift Valley southwest of Nairobi, has been between about 75,000 and 125,000 long tons. These deposits, worked since 1919, continue to be Kenya's most valuable mineral resource. There are geologically similar, but unexploited, deposits in Tanganyika in the vicinity of Lakes Natron, Manyara, Balangida and Eyasi.

Sulfur

Native sulfur has been reported in several localities. In some it occurs in association with gypsum (as in the Cabo Ledo and Dombe Grande areas of Angola); in others, with volcanic rock (as in Kivu in the Belgian Congo, the Awash valley in Ethiopia, and the Kilimanjaro region of Tanganyika). So far none of these deposits has been worked commercially.

Talc, Soapstone and Pyrophyllite

These minerals also occur in several parts of tropical Africa, notably in the Belgian Congo, Kenya, Northern and Southern Rhodesia, Nyasaland and Tanganyika. They have been reported in Bechuanaland and Ethiopia as well. Off and on talc has been produced in Kenya, Southern Rhodesia and Tanganyika, but the output has been small and in recent years the only deposits to be worked continuously have been those of South Kavirondo in Kenya.

Vermiculite

While greatly resembling mica in appearance and properties, the various minerals belonging to the vermiculite group are quite differently derived and so for the most part differently located. The chief established tropical African occurrences of these minerals are as follows: Ethiopia (near Harar), Kenya (in the Central Province at various points, and West Suk), Mozambique (Tete), Southern Rhodesia (near Salisbury), Tanganyika (in the Korogwe district) and Uganda (near Busumbu). There has been a small, spasmodic output of the mineral in Kenya, Southern Rhodesia and Tanganyika. Occurrences, of no great importance at the present time, have been reported from Angola, Bechuanaland, Nyasaland, Sierra Leone and Somalia.

Other Nonmetallic Minerals

The list of nonmetallic industrial minerals found, and worked, in tropical Africa includes, in addition to those already mentioned, a wide variety of gem stones, quartz crystals and building material. The distribution of each of these is wide — wider no doubt than our present knowledge of their occurrences. Because few territories keep adequate records, any territorial comparisons one might make would be misleading, if not odious. The most we can say is that the Belgian Congo, the Malagasy Republic, Nyasaland, Southern Rhodesia and Tanganyika appear to be especially well endowed with gem stones (the recently developed emerald mine at Belingwe in Southern Rhodesia is said to be the world's largest); that Angola, the Belgian Congo, the Malagasy Republic, Mozambique and Tanganyika are the territories in which the most promising quartz crystal deposits have yet been found; and that the supply of building materials (including limestone for cement) promises to be no major problem in any of the territories, such as the Rhodesias, the Belgian Congo and British East Africa, where the demand for them is mounting sharply.

FERTILIZER MINERALS

Up till now little use has been made of mineral fertilizers by the farmers of tropical Africa. Most farmers have acted on the assumption that the soil is an expendable resource, to be worked till exhausted or destroyed and then abandoned. This has been almost as true of European as of African farmers. Such attempts as have been made to lengthen the productive life of a piece of land — and, as we saw earlier, there have been some notable ones — have leaned heavily on fertilizers of non-mineral origin, such as wood ash, compost and animal manure. About the only farmers to use mineral fertilizers on any scale have been those engaged in growing tobacco and other "hungry" but rewarding cash crops capable of absorbing the high cost of shipping bulky materials over long distances.

With the growing emphasis on higher farm productivity and continuous land use, and the dearth over large areas of fertilizers of animal and vegetable origin, there is a growing call for handy African supplies of mineral fertilizer, especially phosphates and potash. Fortunately, such supplies exist. Some of them are already being worked on a modest but increasing scale. Others will almost certainly be worked in the near future. Together they represent an enormous reservoir of fertility that must be freely tapped if the land of tropical Africa is to go on yielding its fruit in due season, and in amounts commensurate with the need.

Phosphate

Phosphate comes in many natural guises — in limestones, sandstones, shales, igneous rocks and guano; in nodules, veins, sediments and residual weathered compounds. Most phosphate rock belongs to the apatite group of minerals and has, as its main chemical ingredient, calcium phosphate. The territories at present producing phosphates are listed in Table 26. Together they produce less than one tenth of one per cent of the world total.

Table 26

PRODUCTION OF PHOSPHATE ROCK, 1938-1957

(*Thousand Metric Tons*)

TERRITORY	1938	AVERAGE 1945-1949	AVERAGE 1950-1954	1955	1957 [a]
Total [b]	—	—	20	14	7
British Somaliland [c]	—	—	0.4	0.2	0.2 [d]
French West Africa	—	—	14	8	1.0
Malagasy Republic (Madagascar)	6	—	1	3	3 [d]
Tanganyika	0.1	—	0.2	0.1	—
Uganda	0.1	—	4 [e]	3	3

Source: United Nations, *Statistical Yearbook, 1958,* New York, 1958.

[a] Preliminary figures.
[b] The percentage of the world total is less than 0.1 in each column.
[c] Phosphatic guano.   [d] 1956.   [e] 1951-1954 average.

Phosphate deposits of one kind or another have a wide distribution in tropical Africa. In Angola the chief of the known occurrences are in the Cabinda and Moçâmedes areas. Preliminary analyses indicate that the calcium phosphate content averages between 60 and 80 per cent. In the Belgian Congo phosphate rock is found in the Mayumbé region of Bas-Congo and at Katumba in northern Ruanda-Urundi; bat guano, in the caves of the Ituri and Bas-Congo districts. The Republic of the Congo has deposits near Holle on the Congo-Océan Railway. The Malagasy Republic has a number of small widely scattered deposits. In the Republic of Senegal there are large deposits at Taiba on the outskirts of Thiés and in the Senegal valley near Podor and Matam. A start was made on the development of the Taiba deposits in 1957. The Republic of the Niger has deposits in the Niger valley about 60 miles north of Bourem. Phosphates are also found in Nigeria, about midway along the railway line between Lagos and Abeokuta; in Nyasaland, in Ncheu district and near Fort Johnston; and in Southern Rhodesia, in the Dorowa area of the upper Sabi valley. In Togo there is a sufficiently large, high-quality deposit near Lomé to warrant plans for a million-metric-ton annual output. In Uganda, apatite deposits near Tororo are believed to contain several hundred million tons of phosphate rock and to be among the largest in the world. Occurrences in Tanganyika are reported near Nagaga in the Masasi district, near Babati (Galappo) and Kisaki (to the south of Morogoro), and in the Mbeya district. British Somaliland has extensive coastal deposits of phosphatic guano.

Potash

Potassium-bearing materials [24] are widely distributed in tropical Africa, but not many of the known deposits are considered to be of great interest. The only one to be worked commercially is the carnallite and sylvite deposit located at Mt. Dalol in the Danakil Salt Plain of Ethiopia, but the output has never been large and has declined considerably in recent years. The almost insufferable daytime heat of the plain, the dearth of local supplies and the high cost of putting the product on the foreign market (it has to go first by road, then by dhow, then by ocean steamer) constitute a powerful trinity of obstacles to its increase.

Of the other deposits the most promising are those found in the Kivu Province of the Belgian Congo, along the coast of the Gabon Republic, and in the Lake Rukwa–Ivuna Salt Pans area of Tanganyika.

Other Fertilizer Minerals

So far such interest as the farmers of tropical Africa have shown in chemical compounds has been largely confined to phosphates and potash. But as the needs of tropical soils and plants become better understood they can be expected to show increasing interest in others as well. Among those which are almost certainly destined to become more important, as fertilizers or as "conditioners," or both, are manganese sulfate and mag-

---

[24] In ordinary agricultural and industrial parlance the various compounds of potassium are referred to as potash, a term going back to the time when the potassium carbonate needed by glassmakers and others was obtained by leaching plant ashes with water and then evaporating the solution in iron pots.

nesium sulfate, limestone, gypsum and vermiculite. From what is already known of the mineralization, it should not be impossible for the region to meet its foreseeable needs of any of these commodities. Whether it will in fact meet them will depend on economic rather than geological factors.

RADIOACTIVE MINERALS

For reasons that need no underlining, the minerals in this group are more often talked about than seen, and, more often still, not talked about. Specific details about their occurrence are difficult to obtain; statistics, either of production or estimated reserves, are virtually unobtainable. In the circumstances, it is possible only to summarize such meager information as has been released for general consumption.

Angola. The only authenticated reference to the occurrence of radioactive minerals in this territory concerns torbernite, a copper-uranium phosphate found near Cuma on the Benguela Railway.

Belgian Congo. The presence of uranium-bearing ore was first established (near Elisabethville) in 1913. The famous mine at Shinkolobwe, near Jadotville, was discovered two years later (April 10, 1915) and for many years was reputed to be the principal source of uranium for the free world. There are several other uranium deposits within the copper-yielding zone, from which radium is extracted.

Ethiopia. There have been some reports, at present unverified, of the occurrence of radium near Diredawa.

Malagasy Republic. The island of Madagascar appears to be uncommonly well endowed with radioactive minerals. Uranium deposits are found in several localities, most notably perhaps in the Antsirabe region. The radioactive sands at Behara near Fort Dauphin are now producing undisclosed quantities of fissionable material on behalf of the French Atomic Energy Commission. The already prospected thorium sands found along the east coast from Manakara to Vatomandry are considered large enough to make the Republic one of the leading thorium producers in the world.

Mozambique. Samples of radioactive rock have been gleaned from several areas. The most extensive deposits seem to be located to the north of Tete; here a gravity concentrator mill has been erected to treat 100 tons of davidite a day. According to Murdock the radioactive constituent in the ore is proving "comparatively difficult to treat in later chemical processes," so that the economic success of the mill is far from assured. Various radioactive rocks are under investigation in the Alto Ligonha district. In August 1958 a heavily capitalized company (Companhia do Uranio de Moçâmbique) was formed to expedite the prospecting of radioactive minerals.

Nigeria. Present-day interest is centered on the radioactive granites of the Jos Plateau and the Lirvei-n-Kano Hills. In one area, exceeding 200 acres in extent, the granites are known to have a high concentration of both niobium and uranium. If the extraction problems can be overcome, there will be work here, it is said, for a plant capable of handling 3,000 long tons of ore daily. Such a plant could produce, by Murdock's report, "about 100 tons of uranium and 2,000 tons of niobium annually."

Northern Rhodesia. In 1952 "a significant discovery of uranium" [25] was made in the Mindola ore body of the Nkana mine. Somewhat tardily, in February 1957, "this occurrence was brought into production as feed for the Federation's first uranium plant, operated by the Rhokana Corporation." [26] Surveys are being undertaken in the belief that similar occurrences will be found in other parts of the Copperbelt.

Nyasaland. The radioactive sands discovered near Monkey Bay have come in for a lot of attention since 1955. They are considered to constitute a "useful source of thorium for British atomic power stations in future years." [27] Several other promising deposits of radioactive minerals have also been found recently, notably along the east shore of Lake Nyasa between Fort Johnston and Fort Maguire, and in the Mwanza area of the Southern Province.

Southern Rhodesia. Low-grade radioactive thorite has been reported in the pegmatitic rocks of the Beitbridge region at the Transvaal border, and a tantalum oxide–columbite deposit, containing uranium and thorium, has been found about 10 miles from Salisbury in the Enterprise district. Uranium-bearing ores have also been reported (and many claims registered) in the Zimunya Reserve, about 20 miles south of Umtali. In 1958 the United Kingdom Atomic Energy Authority began mapping the whole of the colony for radioactive minerals.

Tanganyika. Although no very newsworthy "prospects" have yet been disclosed, pitchblende is known to occur in the Uluguru Mountains and in some of the mica mines. Allanite, containing, among other things, small amounts of thorium, has been reported in a number of granitic areas of the territory. But presumably the United Kingdom Atomic Energy Authority finds the prospects, such as they are, not unpleasing, for it has opened an office in Dodoma.

RARE EARTHS

Under this heading are grouped together the mineral compounds from which are derived panthanum, cerium and the other chemical elements whose atomic numbers lie between 57 and 71. The rare earths most widely found in tropical Africa up to now are monazite, a native phosphate of the cerium group of metals (atomic numbers from 57 to 62), bastnaesite

[25] *The Times British Colonies Review,* Fourth Quarter 1957, p. 8.
[26] *Loc. cit.*
[27] *Nyasaland, 1956,* H.M.S.O., London, 1957.

and pyrochlore. So far the production of rare earths has been reported from only a few territories, notably the Belgian Congo and the Malagasy Republic.

Among the reported occurrences of these minerals, the following would seem to be the most significant: Belgian Congo (in the Maniema and Ubangi areas — monazite), Central African Republic (in the Ouaka district — monazite), French Cameroons (in the Batouri region — monazite), Kenya (in the coastal sands about 40 miles southwest of Mombasa — monazite associated with a large columbite deposit), Malagasy Republic (in the Fort Dauphin region — monazite and bastnaesite), Nigeria (in some of the tin- and columbite-bearing areas — monazite), Nyasaland (in some of the old volcanic vents, known as "ring structures," which pock the surface of the Central and Southern provinces — monazite and pyrochlore), Ruanda-Urundi (about 18 miles southeast of Usumbura — bastnaesite), Somalia (in the sands of the lower Juba River — monazite) and Tanganyika (in the Mkata region near Morogoro — monazite; and in the Panda Hill region of the Southern Highlands Province — pyrochlore).

MINERAL FUELS

On the basis of present knowledge, tropical Africa has as small an endowment of coal and petroleum as any area of its size in the world. It is possible that surveys now in progress will disclose hitherto unsuspected deposits, but not even the most optimistic petroleum geologists expect to uncover a new East Texas field or a new Kuwait; and the chances that any new major coal fields will be brought to light are likewise not rated very highly.

The fact is that most of the region is not mineral fuel country. Both coal and petroleum need for their formation a long-lasting sedimentary environment, and immunity from structural disturbance and metamorphizing heat and pressure. Such conditions were rarely met with in tropical Africa until recent geological times and then only in a few quite small areas, not all of which, even so, became active coal or oil producers. The areas that did, however, are far from negligible, and though they may never rank among the world's great fuel sources, or producers, they are assured of an important place in the economy of the regions round about them.

Coal

Of the two mineral fuels, coal appears to be the more abundant. There are important fields in six territories, and lesser ones in at least four others. The total indicated coal reserves of these territories are of the order of 100 billion long tons, if account is taken of the sub-bituminous fields, which are far more extensive than the bituminous fields.

Table 27

PRODUCTION OF COAL, 1938-1957

(*Thousand Metric Tons*)

TERRITORY	1938	AVERAGE 1945-1949	AVERAGE 1950-1954	1955	1957 [a]
Total	1,510	2,380	3,464	4,728	5,384
Per cent of world total [b]	0.1	0.2	0.3	0.3	0.3
Belgian Congo	42	105	265	480	433
Mozambique	96	13	110	172	270
Nigeria	328	581	619	761	828
Southern Rhodesia	1,044	1,681	2,470	3,315	3,853

Source: United Nations, *Statistical Yearbook, 1958,* New York, 1958.

[a] Preliminary figures.   [b] Including U.S.S.R.

As Table 27 shows, the present output of tropical African coal is very small by world standards, and virtually limited to four territories. The token output of the Malagasy Republic is excluded.

Southern Rhodesia is easily the largest of the main producers. Its Wankie field, located on the railway line connecting Bulawayo with Victoria Falls and the Copperbelt, is one of the largest in Africa. The proven reserves of good-quality coking coal in this field are known to exceed 800 million tons, and it is likely that they exceed one billion. Wankie also has large reserves of poorer coal suitable for raising steam, generating electricity and manufacturing by-products. With the coal output still (in 1958) below 4 million metric tons, the Wankie colliery can expect to be in business a long time.

There are a number of other fields in the colony. The two largest of these, located in the valley of the lower Sabi River, are estimated to have some 4.5 billion tons of non-coking semi-anthracite, and 250 million tons of bituminous (coking) coal. Although these fields are a good many miles from a railway and much farther from a market where they could compete on equal terms with coal either from Wankie or the Union of South Africa, interest in them is growing.

Nigeria, the second largest producer, gets its coal from the sub-bituminous deposits found in the Cretaceous rocks of the Enugu-Udi scarp region, 120 miles north of Port Harcourt. Until a few years ago the reserves in this field were thought to be no more than 16.5 million tons; now they are thought to be "capable of meeting national requirements for a very long time." [28] At present most of the output is used in steam engines, the biggest consumer being the Nigerian Railway. In the coming years it is hoped that part of the output will be used for the manufacture of

[28] Buchanan and Pugh, *op. cit.,* p. 182.

gas, tars, oil and other distillation products. There are also extensive, but as yet unexploited, lignite fields in the Tertiary rocks of the eastern part of Benin Province.

Belgian Congo. Third on the producing list, the Congo has two known coal fields, the Lukuga and the Luena, both in eastern Katanga and both of sub-bituminous grade. While their proven reserves are modest (around 50 million tons), the probable reserves are said to be of the order of "several hundred million tons." Most of the small output comes from the Luena field and is used on the copper mines and the railways. If experimental distillation work now being done on the Lukuga field lives up to its promise, one of the most important future uses for its coal will be as raw material for the local manufacture of synthetic liquid fuels.

The Belgian Congo also has a number of lignite fields, for example in the Thysville area, but none of these is being worked at present.

Mozambique. The output comes from the Moatize bituminous field near Tete, which has a reserve estimated to be in the neighborhood of 700 million tons. Most of the present small tonnage is used to supply the Tete-Beira railway and ships bunkering at Beira, for which purpose it is far from ideal on account of its friability. Laboratory tests indicate that it could be used to better advantage in the manufacture of gas and oil. Coal-bearing formations have also been identified at Vila Cabral to the east of Lake Nyasa, and in the south of the country in the neighborhood of the new Limpopo Railway line.

Malagasy Republic. The output, still largely for experimental purposes, comes from the Sakoa field, near Tuléar. Although the field is large, possibly amounting to several hundred million tons, its prospects cannot be considered very bright. It is situated in the semi-arid southwest of the island, where food and water supplies are scarce, local demand is negligible and export a problem. The coal is bituminous but non-coking. A number of other fields belonging to the same Permian series of rocks have been identified, but not explored.

Territories with proven reserves but either no recorded or no significant output of coal include:

Bechuanaland. Bituminous coal seams, said to lie less than 300 feet below the surface, to extend for "hundreds of miles," and to be among the richest in Africa, have been located in the Bamangwato Reserve.

Northern Rhodesia. Large deposits of "promising" bituminous coal have been found in parts of the Zambezi valley.

Nyasaland. Coal-bearing areas (mostly sub-bituminous) have been identified near Chiromo and Chikwawa in the south, and in Livingstonia in the north.

Tanganyika. Large deposits of non-coking, but otherwise acceptable, coals occur in the Njombe and Songea districts (the Ngaka-Kitewaka fields), and smaller deposits in the Rungwe district (the Kiwira-Songwe fields) and the Ufipa district. The total proven reserves of these fields are reported to be in excess of 400 million tons, and the indicated reserves about the same size; however, nothing much can be done about their exploitation until they are linked by a railroad to the more developed parts of the territory.

In addition, the following territories have large, but still poorly explored, deposits of lignites: Angola, Ethiopia, French Cameroons, Kenya and Sierra Leone.

Petroleum

At present (1959) petroleum is being produced commercially in only three countries in all of tropical Africa: Angola, the Gabon Republic and Nigeria. But if the amount of geological and geophysical exploration being carried out has any indicative value, these producers should soon be joined by others. In the past few years exploration programs have been launched in almost a score of territories. So far most of the sponsoring companies have said very little about their findings (perhaps because there has been very little to say), but some have thought well enough of them to extend the scale of search. And more than one company has found enough oil to warrant heavy capital investment in mining and processing plants.

The major developments of the past few years are summarized below.

Angola. After three years of drilling in the Luanda area, petroleum was struck at Benfica in April 1955. In September 1956 the first tanker load left Luanda for processing in Portugal. While the operators have made no official statement concerning the likely extent of the field, they set up an exploitation company, capitalized at over $31 million (U. S.), and have recently completed the construction of a local refinery with an annual capacity of approximately 100,000 metric tons. Other successful drillings have been made in the regions of Cacuaco and Quicama (near Cabo de S. Braz). By August 1958 the Angolan wells were yielding about 320 metric tons of crude oil daily.

Belgian Congo. The presence of petroleum has been recognized in the sediments of the Rift Valley (Lake Albert region), along the Lualaba valley from Ponthierville to Stanleyville, and in the central Congo basin. Of the three areas, the third is believed to hold the most promise. Since 1955 large parts of it have been systematically surveyed by seismic, gravimetric and magnetic methods.

Republic of the Congo. The existence of an oil reservoir has been established in the Pointe Noire area, which has a geological structure similar to that of the well-endowed Port Gentil field in the Gabon Republic (see below).

Ethiopia. In 1945 the Sinclair Petroleum Company was granted exclusive oil-prospecting rights in the Empire. As of 1958 no strikes had been reported. Among the areas being explored are the coastal belt, including that of Eritrea and the offshore Dahlak Islands, and the Ogaden region.

French Cameroons. The existence of petroleum-impregnated sedimentaries in the Douala area has been recognized for many years. Some of the local inhabitants were using these sedimentaries as a source of lighting fuel long before the European introduced them to the kerosene lamp. Although there was intermittent investigation of the area in the early part of the century, it is only since World War II that a proper test-drilling program has been carried out. Several drills have struck gas (in large enough amounts, apparently, to satisfy the foreseeable domestic and industrial needs of the region for at least a generation), but down to 1958 none had struck oil in promising amounts.

Gabon Republic. At several points along the Gabon coast and the course of the Ogooué River gas and oil have been found in quantities that stirred the prospector's imagination and secured his sponsor's continuing interest. Much of the attention has centered on the Port Gentil area, where the existence of a major reservoir has been confirmed. The Port Gentil field is believed to be capable of an output of as much as 5 million metric tons annually. In 1958 it yielded 450,000 metric tons of crude oil.

Gambia. An investigation, by D'Arcy Exploration Company, of the Gambia River basin was begun in 1956.

Ghana. The Gulf Oil Corporation of the Gold Coast began drilling in the extreme west of the country in June 1956.

Kenya. The Geological Survey has been following up studies made in the Wajir-Mandera district in the 1930s. Several promising structures have been identified.

Malagasy Republic. Desultory exploration in the 1930s proved the presence of several oil-bearing strata not too far from the surface in the Ankavandra-Morafenobe area, and westward of it. Since 1946 an extensive geophysical survey of the sedimentary areas has been carried out and a drilling program drawn up. Hopes are high that oil will be found in paying quantities.

Mozambique. In the opinion of the Gulf Oil Company (which in 1948 signed a contract with the Portuguese government giving it the right to prospect), the Sul do Save and lower Zambezi districts are the most likely parts of southern Africa in which to find oil. This opinion is founded largely on the fact that almost the whole of the region is floored by marine sedimentary rocks that abound in ammonite fossils — the kind that elsewhere has often spelled oil.

Nigeria. Over the past few years the Shell-British Petroleum Development Company of Nigeria Limited has sunk several wells in the coastal sedimentaries and carried out an extensive seismic exploration of the navigable waterways of the Niger delta. After a long run of disappointments, in the course of which the company spent approximately £30 million, strikes were made in August and September 1956 at Oloibiri in the Niger delta east of Port Harcourt. The first commercial shipments of crude oil from this field were made early in 1958, and in 1959, with the coming into production of new wells, output was expected to reach 600,000 tons. In 1959 Mobil Exploration Nigeria, Inc. (an affiliate of the Mobil International Oil Company), obtained an exploration license from the Nigerian government covering an area of some 4,000 square miles.

Republic of Senegal. Some indications of oil have been found in the western part of the state, and conditions in the central part are considered to warrant further exploration.

Somalia. Oil indications have been found, from time to time, in several localities. Following some years of geological and geophysical work, in 1956 the Sinclair Somal Corporation started well drilling near the coastal town of Obbia. Since then it has drilled several other wells, all of them dry; nothing dismayed, the corporation has announced its determination to stay in Somalia for at least two or three more years. The Italian firm Mineraria Somala and the Standard Vacuum Oil Company are also carrying out large-scale explorations.

Republic of Sudan. The British Petroleum Company has been doing some prospecting work, mainly in the coastal plain of the Red Sea, since the end of 1954. Data on its findings are meager and, on the whole, discouraging.

Tanganyika. In the mid-1950s explorations were conducted by the D'Arcy-Shell Exploration Company on the offshore island of Mafia. Although the test well was sunk to a depth of more than 11,000 feet, no oil was found. The company's focus of interest has since shifted to the Kilwa district and to the island of Zanzibar (see below).

Uganda. For many years oil seepages have been reported at various points around the Lake Albert shores. However, wells sunk in the 1930s failed to produce anything but more seepages. After the end of World War II, the government financed further exploration of this region — likewise to no avail. So far no oil companies have elected to carry on where the government left off.

Zanzibar. In 1956 the D'Arcy-Shell Exploration Company began drilling for oil at a point about 10 miles north of the city of Zanzibar on the island of the same name. With the disappointing experience of Mafia behind them, the engineers were disposed not to overrate their chances of finding oil in a geologically similar situation. So far their disposition has been fully justified by the findings — or, rather, the lack of them.

TRENDS AND PROSPECTS

If there is one conclusion that may be drawn from the foregoing survey, it is that the wartime and postwar surge of interest in tropical Africa's mineral resources shows no signs of slackening off. Indeed, the African bush was never fuller of exploration parties, all hopeful and all laden with ore samples. And not without good reasons. Highly mineralized region that it is, the chances are that somebody will come upon another Kilembe, if not another Katanga; another Mboscorro, or even another Mwadui; another Bomi Hills, or perhaps another Shinkolobwe, in its still unexplored areas. In the second place, mining companies in these days are well aware that minerals are not renewable resources. For them, exploration must go hand in hand with exploitation. Then, too, many of the world's industrial nations are in growing need of such essential minerals as copper, iron ore, uranium and tin — all of which tropical Africa has, they would like to believe, in unwanted abundance. Nor should the desire of the territorial governments to raise the standard of African living be underrated in this connection; nor yet the determination of the newly independent nations to see that the mineral wealth of their lands is used increasingly for the good of their peoples.

Up to now, most mining enterprises have been conducted by foreigners in the pay of foreigners who were interested primarily in making money for other foreigners — their investors. True, a part of the foreign money put into such enterprises has gone to work for Africans in the form of wages, allowances, amenities and taxes. And in some cases foreign money has been put into processing plants and secondary industries designed to turn out goods for African use. But the sums plowed back are much smaller than those which have been taken out of the region in the form of ores, concentrates and refined metals. While most African leaders do not need to be told that the development of the mineral wealth of tropical Africa would have been impossible on any other basis (for, like Americans and Europeans, they appreciate the necessity of holding out to the investor the prospect of rewards commensurate with the risks), they do not believe that their people are getting enough for their mineral heritage. And, almost to a man, they are determined to do something about it.

Nevertheless, for many years to come most of the mines will almost certainly continue to be operated at the managerial and technical levels by non-Africans. For there are not enough African geologists, mining engineers, chemists and executives to fill these positions, and not enough training facilities. And because domestic capital, private and public, is still scarce, the bulk of the capital for new mining developments and for the modernization and expansion of existing mines will almost certainly continue to come from foreign money markets — which means that there will continue to be a heavy export of mining profits. Then, again, there can be little doubt that most of the new money will continue to be put into enterprises reckoned by the investors to be the surest money-makers; some of these, of course, may well be quite different from those considered by a territory's residents to be the best for their economy.

At the same time, it cannot be doubted that the mining industry will become more and more "domesticated." Already many mining administrations are deeply committed to African training programs and other equally important aspects of African advancement. This is particularly true of those in the Katanga-Copperbelt region. Mining and finance corporations are seeking increasingly to find capital for the development of local secondary industries based on locally processed minerals. By doing so, they are building up the local money market and helping not only to decrease the dependence of the would-be manufacturer on outside aid and control, but also to reduce the region's dependence on outside demand for its minerals — a dependence that has more than once brought distress and bewilderment to African mine workers: Elisabethville, capital of Katanga, was but one of several ghost towns in the African jungle in the early thirties. Meanwhile the voice of the African is becoming increasingly influential in mining counsels. As mine labor becomes better organized, the pattern of African advancement in the Katanga-Copperbelt region is being repeated in other places. More and more corporations are finding themselves discussing wages and fringe benefits with their workers, and even profits, shareholding and the "Africanization" of the directorate.

What, then, are the immediate prospects of the region's mineral development? There is, almost certainly, more of every metal and nonmetallic mineral still underground than has ever come out. Mineralogically, tropical Africa promises to be as rich as any of the other great regions of the world, not excluding North America and the U.S.S.R. Fuels are almost the only major group of minerals in which the region is poorly off, but with abundant water power and fissionable material, this poverty is more a challenge to invention than a serious limitation. Among the minerals that are likely to make, or keep, the grade of the globally significant are asbestos, bauxite, chrome, cobalt, columbite, copper, diamonds, ferroalloys (including manganese and tungsten), gold, graphite, iron ore, lead, lithium minerals, rare earths and radioactive (fissionable) metals, tin and zinc. These and many other minerals will continue to be sought after by almost every nation that has smelters, stockpiles, defense plants, factories and reactors.

The uneven distribution of the mineral wealth among the territories is, however, bound to be a continuing cause of concern to those charged with planning. In those territories where minerals dominate the economy and provide much of the budget, politicians and company directors have reason to be anxious lest the market for these minerals should collapse, or the supply of them should fail. In those territories where minerals promise shortly to dominate the economy and to finance a greatly enlarged budget, the authorities face the problem of exploiting their good fortune without destroying what is worth preserving in the present order. And the "have-nots" — those territories which so far have found little exploitable mineral wealth — are fearful that the "haves" will outpace them in the march toward economic stability.

This preoccupation with economic stability is now widespread. While there is no agreement on how such stability is to be attained, there is a growing feeling that it will require, in Murdock's words, "a certain de-emphasis on mineral activity in those areas where mining is at present of prime importance," and a countervailing emphasis on it in those areas where agriculture is at present of prime importance. There is also a feeling, amounting to a conviction in some quarters, that it is possible to pay too big a price for the tapping of a country's mineral potential. The development of such wealth behind the walls of a high tariff, or other protective device, is felt to be especially undesirable since, to quote Murdock again, "no area is economically self-sufficient in all respects, and such devices would almost inevitably lead to counter ones" — if they did not collapse under their own incubus.

As more and more territories come of age politically, the task of fashioning economies that are at once strong and supple, self-generating and interdependent, becomes increasingly pressing. And it is a task that calls for gifts of mind as well as of "matter." It is indeed fortunate that so many of these territories have the latter. The former may well prove the harder to come by. But happy indeed is the nation that has both, for its standard of living will surely rise even as its economy will surely be stabilized.

CHAPTER 10

Industrial Progress

THE COMING OF THE FACTORY

PRIMARY PROCESSING

SECONDARY INDUSTRY

NATION BUILDING

SURVIVAL OF INDIGENOUS CRAFTS

PROBLEMS OF THE MANUFACTURER

To make a thing by hand (we have almost forgotten that this is the root meaning of "to manufacture") was, for long, the only way to get anything in tropical Africa. And because there were few specialists and next to no surpluses, almost every African was of necessity a manufacturer. His very survival hung upon his ability to make an axe and a hoe and to wield them, to hollow out a canoe and paddle it, to handle clay and fire it, and to fashion skins, bark or fibers into clothes.

The manipulative skills thus acquired — possessed, to be sure, by all primitive, preindustrial peoples — are helping the African today to span the centuries between his simple unmechanical world and the world of the assembly line, the hydraulic press and the acetylene torch. Already many thousands have shown that dexterity, fastidious regard for detail, a sense of timing, and a feeling for tools are not so much matters of environment as of habitude and knack; and that proficiency in the traditional arts and crafts can be turned to account in the sawmill, the foundry and the copper mine. Some Africans, indeed, already have their own sawmills and foundries, and some have long mined their own copper.

But ability to work in an industrial plant is one thing. Ability to operate the plant in competition with long-established firms in other parts of the world is another thing. For most such firms are handy to supplies of power and raw materials, and, because of the size of their markets, are in a position to exploit to the full the advantages of mass-production techniques. They can also draw upon large reservoirs of skilled labor, long legacies of managerial competence, and, in most cases, ample money markets for the funding of their development programs.

Even if the plant can compete "on paper" with overseas producers, it may not in practice be able to make a living doing so. Most Africans still have little need to buy and little to sell, and their purchasing power is feeble. Fifty dollars (or its equivalent) is more money than most of them are accustomed to see at one time; a hundred dollars will buy most — in some cases all — of the things they highly prize. The number of industries that can thrive in such a rarefied atmosphere is limited. It is true that some Africans think in much bigger denominations, but generally there are not enough of them in one place to excite the imagination of market researchers. It is equally true that some Asians and Europeans in Africa earn big money and spend it, but, with few exceptions, their distribution is too diffuse and their attachment to the home country too strong to encourage overseas manufacturers to put capital into the building of local factories.

Nor is this all. Many Africans are still of two minds about the merit of some of the white man's inventions. They have yet to be convinced — to take a case in point — that it is better to have a kerosene lamp, the working of which they do not understand and the oil for which is costly and has to be toted by hand or head over many laborious miles, than to sit around a charcoal brazier and a burning taper. Or that it is healthier to walk encumbered with the white man's clothes through the wet bush, with no prospect of drying them, than to go naked and so be at once more comfortable and less likely to catch a cold. Others are not yet sure that it is possible to have the white man's goods without losing the black man's consolations. In the words of Esther Warner's Johnny:

[The "wants"] eat a man up from the inside. Just like bug-a-bugs (termites) eat up a stick of wood! . . . I have got everything I need and more besides . . . I get rice because I take care of you. You sew fine clothes for me because you would feel shame if I did not look fine past all other stewards. I get sweet soap from you because . . . you do not want me to smell like a crocodile . . . I get enough money besides to wear a gold coat on my tooth and to buy stockfish and to make play. What more can a man want? [1]

The Firestone Plantations in Liberia have hundreds like Johnny even after a generation of coaxing.

In the circumstances, it is not surprising that the industrial development of tropical Africa should so far have been slow and patchy, or that there should still be a widespread disposition among industrialists to believe that it is uneconomic for these low-income countries to manufacture their own bicycles, banjos, umbrellas, ball-point pens and other

[1] Esther Warner, *Seven Days to Lomaland*, Houghton Mifflin Company, Boston, 1954, p. 39.

sought-after consumer goods that can be imported advantageously. Rather it is surprising that industry in the region should have made the progress it has, and made it with so little fanfare and such seeming ease and profit.

THE COMING OF THE FACTORY

The factory is a comparative newcomer to tropical Africa. For hundreds of years the economic life of the region was centered on the garden plot, the cattle kraal, the artisan's workshop and the village market. With the arrival of the European enterpriser, the center shifted to the mine, the plantation, the forest and the farm. Their products were needed to fill the widening maw of Europe's factories, and the expanding grasp of the people who manned them. As other parts of the world outgrew their colonial straitjacket and began to consume more and more of their own wealth, the European demand for Africa's resources soared. By World War II, tropical Africa was supplying a sizable part of Western Europe's requirements of such industrial commodities as sisal, palm oil, hardwood timber, copper, tin, diamonds, gold and manganese, and large amounts of such foodstuffs as cocoa, cane sugar, peanuts, coffee and tea. As yet very little processing of any of these commodities was done locally.[2] The main economic function of an African colony was still considered to be that of supplier of primary produce, the proceeds of which could be used to pay for the colony's requirements of manufactured goods and services.

It is probably true to say that this still represents the viewpoint of the majority of investors in tropical Africa. But it is no longer shared by the African elite or, for that matter, by many of the African governments. In the first place, World War II made it impossible for importers to satisfy the demand for manufactured goods. Shipping space was scarce and priority was given to war matériel — a two-way traffic, for there were armies, navies and air forces in tropical Africa as in Europe. And the convoy casualty rate, in the early years of the war, merely served to emphasize the undesirability of so great dependence on the outside world.

To escape from this dependence, many European companies put up industrial plants on tropical African soil; indeed, some companies had

[2] While "manufacturing" is sometimes taken to embrace all the activities involved in transforming a raw material into a commodity for direct consumption, or further processing, the initial processing — sorting, cleaning, refining, etc. — is usually considered to be a part of the production of that raw material. For present purposes, the manufacturing process is considered to begin when the product has reached a state in which it can be moved to another establishment for further treatment. The divide between the two types of process may be held to occur where the commodity passes from an economic unit specializing in primary production to one that specializes in transforming raw materials.

already done so before the war. Among these plants, there were several for the processing of perishable and bulky commodities such as foodstuffs, lumber and cotton, and several for the repair and maintenance of machinery and transport equipment.

In the second place, and following on their wartime experiences, the governments of tropical Africa have come to see that countries with broadly based economies are assets in peace as in war, since they are less likely to need underwriting than countries dependent for their revenues on a couple of crops; and that their peoples are much less likely, on that account, to "waste long nights in pensive discontent." In the past decade or so most of these governments have been willing to back their convictions with substantial amounts of risk capital.

In the third place, almost all of Africa's "new men" — the Nkrumahs, the Azikiwes and the Mboyas — are in favor of industrialization. Trained in Europe and North America, they know that it is the most highly industrialized countries that are the giants in the world; and they are tired of being counted among the pygmies. With few exceptions, the things they want for their peoples, such as shoes and suits, hospital and school equipment, electric generators and plumbing, come out of factories. The fact that most of these things can be made more cheaply, and better, elsewhere is immaterial. Being nationalists, these leaders regard continued dependence on imports as continued economic exploitation and servitude, or, in short, as colonialism, the ghost of which they are determined to lay. Further, they know that without the application of machine power and inanimate energy to the production of goods it will be impossible to close the gap in productivity per man between their countries and the countries they seek to emulate.

In the fourth place, there is the fast-growing body of world opinion, of which the United Nations and its specialized agencies form an important part, that sees in industrialization not only an answer to the poverty, malnutrition and unrest prevalent in underdeveloped countries, but also an antidote for international ill will which battens on such conditions. For industrialization does not merely mean factories, which may or may not be economic, but roads, railways, ports, airports, dams that provide irrigation water and navigation as well as power, conservation projects (since factories cannot endure without an uninterrupted flow of raw materials), and health and education programs (since without them no factories are likely to have, and hold, an efficient labor supply).

Considerable differences of opinion still exist, of course, between one tropical African government and another, to say nothing of differences between governments and governed, concerning the degree of industrial development feasible in a given territory and the tempo at which such development should proceed. But few would be likely to dissent from the view expressed by Paul Béchard, onetime High Commissioner of the Republic, at the opening of the *Grand Conseil* of French West

Africa in 1950, that "the simultaneous development of agricultural production and the creation of processing industries . . . provide the foundation for social progress and raise the standards of living of the . . .
people which is the [French government's] supreme objective." Whether
the two together are sufficient to secure the superstructure as well as the
foundations of social progress is another, more contentious, matter.

Most of the establishments to be found in tropical Africa at the present
time are concerned with either primary processing or secondary industry.

PRIMARY PROCESSING

Before almost any commodity is marketable, it needs processing. This
is true whether the commodity is a tree trunk which may only need lopping, a pineapple which may only need stripping of its leaves and crating,
or a diamond which merely needs washing, grading, appraising and
securing against loss. The country that has no processing plants is therefore in a pretty poor way of business, or, what amounts to very much
the same thing, not interested in business. The opposite also applies.
While there are still large areas of tropical Africa that have no processing
plants, they are small in comparison with those that do, and they are
getting smaller year by year. Simultaneously, the range of processing
done in such plants is getting larger.

Broadly speaking, the commodities processed fall into four classes:
foodstuffs, industrial crops, timber and minerals.[3]

FOODSTUFFS

Most of the traditional foodstuffs (including beverages) of the African
are still processed at home. This is true particularly of the rural areas,
though even in many of the towns it remains the custom for the womenfolk to do their own hand processing of manioc, rice, maize, millet and
palm oil, and for the men to make their own beer and wine from millet,
sugar cane and palm. Of recent years, however, with the coming of the
plantation, the mine and the town, and the attendant separation from
their families of the menfolk, who are not in the habit of using grindstones
and pestles and mortars, or, in many cases, of raising their own food
supplies, there has been a notable shift of food processing from the farm-
stead to the factory. Today, all the larger cities and some of the smaller
ones have grain mills, bakeries, dairies, slaughterhouses and meat dressing, packing and canning plants, and vegetable oil refineries. Generally
they are small plants and work for the domestic market, indigenous and
nonindigenous. The larger ones work primarily for the export market.
Outstanding among these are the oil-processing plants of Unilever Limited
and the Compagnie Générale des Oléagineux Tropicaux.

---

[3] The mining industry has been dealt with in Chapter 9.

Palm Oil

Early in the twentieth century, the demand in Europe and North America for vegetable oils, for industrial and edible uses, brought Lever Brothers Limited, as the firm was then called, to tropical Africa, where large areas are covered with stands of oil-bearing palms, notably the Guinea oil palm (*Elaeis guineensis*). It quickly became apparent that, to exploit this great resource profitably, it would be necessary to do most of the oil extracting on the spot. The oil [4] contained in the fleshy mesocarp of the palm fruit is perishable. Delay in extracting it increases its content of free fatty acids, thereby impairing its quality and increasing the cost of refining it. Consequently it was important to place the crushing mills as close as possible to the center of the main palm-producing districts. In these mills the fruit is sterilized, stripped, washed and cooked, and its kernels extracted and separated from the residual fiber, which, in some instances, is used as fuel to run the mill machinery.

Not all the local oil processing is done in large modern mills. In Nigeria and other parts of west Africa much of it is still done in small mills using manual methods less than satisfactory to either the seller or the buyer. Often the oil is extracted too late to be of top quality, and the proportion obtained is an unrewarding 50 to 55 per cent as against 90 to 95 by modern milling methods. However, some increase in the efficiency of peasant methods (up to 65 per cent) has been apparent during recent years, largely as a result of the introduction of hand presses. To obtain greater efficiency still (up to 85 per cent), several governments have set up small power mills in different parts of their territories. Those in British West African territories are known as Pioneer mills. Though designed and built by the United Africa Company Limited (a member of the Unilever group), these mills are being run by government departments, with the expectation that they will be handed over later to African bodies. Those in the areas of French influence are government-financed, but run on a commercial basis and leased to private firms. On the whole the French have made rather less progress in this field than the British, who, in turn, have lagged behind the Belgians.

Until World War II, next to no processing of the separated palm nut was done before export. All that was usually done was to crack the nuts, an operation performed by women by hand, and to ship the kernels to European and American factories for crushing and conversion into soaps and fats. Two mills had been established for the purpose in Nigeria (at Lagos and Opobo) by Lever Brothers Limited before 1914, but they were closed down in 1915. Small quantities of palm kernels were subsequently crushed in Nigeria and the Belgian Congo to supply oil to the soap factories established by the same corporation in these

[4] Known as *palm oil*, as distinct from the *palm kernel oil* obtained from crushing the seed of the fruit.

countries. Since 1939 there has been a marked increase in the number, and output, of kernel-crushing mills in the Belgian Congo. Between 1939 and 1944 the number of such plants rose from one to seven, and the output from 420 to 7,500 metric tons. In 1948 the export alone of palm kernel oil totaled more than 17,500 metric tons as against 100 in 1939; in 1958 it was nearly 58,000 metric tons. More than 95,000 metric tons of oilseed cattle cake were exported in 1958 as against less than 3,000 in 1939.

Other Vegetable Oils

Manufacturing industries based on other locally produced oils, such as cottonseed oil and peanut oil, have also made considerable headway in the Belgian Congo in the past two or three decades.

While, as yet, there has not been a comparable development of palm kernel processing in west Africa, peanut processing has made remarkable strides, most notably in the territories formerly known as French West Africa. Even before World War II Senegal was exporting more than 5,500 metric tons of peanut oil a year, in addition to prodigious amounts (more than half a million metric tons in 1938) of whole peanuts, shelled and unshelled. During the war the capacity of the oil mills in French West Africa, and particularly those in Senegal, was increased. By 1946 the region was exporting approximately 36,000 metric tons of peanut oil, the largest quantity exported from any country in that year. By 1957 the figure had risen to almost 100,000 metric tons. In that year about one third of the total peanut exports, measured in oil equivalents, were shipped in the form of oil, against less than 3 per cent in 1938. Today the processing of the peanut crop in the Republic of Senegal and its onetime French neighbors is as mechanized as it is in France. The refining of the processed oil is, however, still done in France, and practically the entire output of this region goes there. In addition to oil, the larger mills manufacture soap, mainly for domestic consumption, and cattle cake, some of which is exported.

In Nigeria, the chief peanut producer in British West Africa, the large-scale processing of peanuts for their oil has made much less progress to date. This is partly because there has generally been enough peasant-produced oil to satisfy the domestic market, partly because of the grave deficiencies of transportation, and partly because, as R. J. Harrison Church reports in his paper prepared for this study, "the few small mills have had their peanut purchases restricted by the Northern Regional Government anxious to retain its pre-eminent place in the world peanut markets, upon which so large a part of the country's revenue depends."

Other Foodstuffs

Also in quite recent years a marked increase has occurred in the processing of milk (for cheese and butter), fruits (for their juices), meat (for canning and refrigeration), cereals (for flour) and other foodstuffs that formerly were almost unknown to the African and that the European could only obtain expensively, and irregularly, through importers. This is especially true of the Federation of Rhodesia and Nyasaland, Kenya and the west African members of the French Community.

INDUSTRIAL CROPS [5]

Until the white man came, almost the only reasons an African had for growing crops were those of the ancient Psalmist — to "bring forth food out of the earth, and wine that maketh glad the heart." Most of the other things he might require of the living earth from time to time — grass for thatch, lianas for twine, bamboo for poles, bark for cloth, poisons for spears and arrows, herbs for medicine — could be obtained without cultivation, as could, in fact, some of his basic foodstuffs.

Cotton

The one "industrial" crop that appears to have been widely grown by Africans in pre-European times was cotton. Cotton (*Gossypium* spp.) was known in the "horn" of Africa in antiquity,[6] and the art of weaving cotton has been known among most of the grassland and savanna dwellers for a long time. Leo Africanus, writing early in the sixteenth century, found the merchants of Jenné, a town on the Niger above Timbuktu, doing an active trans-Saharan trade in cotton. Three centuries later, Henry Barth discovered that the cotton cloths woven and dyed by the Hausa craftsmen of Kano, Katsina and Zaria were in demand as far north as Tripoli and as far west as "the shores of the Atlantic." With few exceptions (one of the more notable of which is provided by the Yoruba of southern Nigeria) neither cotton cultivation nor cotton weaving was carried on in the rain forest country.

"Cottage"-type cotton manufacturing is still carried on in many localities. In some, as, for instance, the Laki Islands of Lake Zwai in Ethiopia, it is the men who do the weaving; in others, as, for instance, in the eastern part of the Yoruba country of Nigeria, it is the women. Here a horizontal loom only capable of making long, narrow strips of cloth, no more than five to six inches wide, is employed. There a vertical loom, capable of weaving cloth four to five feet wide, does duty. Elsewhere, as in the region of west Africa lying to the south of the Sahara, a treadle loom is fa-

[5] Excluding vegetable oils.

[6] "It is even possible that a *Gossypium* was first taken under the care of man in Africa . . .": Carl O. Sauer, *Agricultural Origins and Dispersals,* American Geographical Society, New York, 1952, p. 78.

vored. In the hands of the gifted, such looms, for all their simplicity, can turn out fine fabrics, but in these days it takes more than skill to produce fabrics that can compete, in color, pattern and price,[7] with factory-made cottons.

Most of the credit for encouraging cotton manufacturing in tropical Africa goes to the Belgian Congo government, which as far back as 1921 issued a decree protecting the interests of cotton producers and insuring the industrial exploitation of the commodity. Eight years later the Usines Textiles de Léopoldville began production. Today Utexleo (as the corporation is called) employs between 4,000 and 5,000 Africans, working three eight-hour shifts, in its spinning, weaving, dyeing and printing establishments. Its 46,000 spindles make it one of the largest cotton factories in the whole of Africa. In 1957 it produced 5,700 metric tons of cloth in a great range (between 600 and 700) of designs, many of them created by African artists. Together this mill and two smaller textile plants, in Elisabethville and Albertville, meet about half of the domestic demand for cottons.

Though progress in the domestic manufacture of textiles has been more spectacular in the Belgian Congo than in any of the other territories, the trend is general. Since 1938-1939 the consumption of ginned cotton, including imports, in tropical Africa has more than trebled. Up to now the most important developments have been in the following territories:

Angola. A small mill, operating 10,000 spindles and employing over 600 workers (550 of them Africans), was opened in Luanda in 1946. Its production of cotton cloth increased from 140,000 meters in that year to over 2 million meters in the late 1950s; its production of cotton blankets, from approximately 3,000 to over 300,000.

Ethiopia. Four mills, with a total of 175,000 spindles, were in operation by the late 1950s. These mills have a rapidly growing output of yarns and fabrics; between 1950 and 1957, production rose from approximately 200 metric tons to over 4,500.

The French Community. For many years there have been mills in Dakar (Republic of Senegal) and Bouaké (Republic of the Ivory Coast). Under the postwar development plans of the French Union the output of these mills was stepped up greatly and the range of goods (mostly yarns, threads and blankets) manufactured in them widened. More recently a textile plant, designed to supply most of the unbleached and dyed fabrics needed by the people of the Central African Republic, has been established at Bouali, near Bangui. In addition, several plants, two in the Central African Republic, have been built for the processing of cottonseed for oil.

---

[7] "A piece of cloth 20 inches by 80 inches in blue and white stripe . . . requires two or three full days' work . . . and then is only likely to fetch eighteenpence." See Daryll Forde and Richenda Scott, *The Native Economies of Nigeria,* Faber & Faber, London, 1946, p. 79.

Mozambique. The territory's first cotton mill, about 125 miles west of Beira, at Vila Pery, went into operation in 1953. When all of its more than 400 looms and nearly 15,000 spindles are working at capacity, the mill is able to produce annually about 2,500 tons of yarn and cloth, including bleached, dyed and stamped materials. The power for the plant comes from the generators of the Revue River hydroelectric scheme.

Nigeria. A number of small and rather primitive mills have for several years been producing a coarse but popular cloth known as "Kano." Under the government's present development program provision is made for a considerable expansion of this output, and for the manufacture of a wider range of cotton goods. Since 1957 a fully automatic spinning and weaving mill has been in operation at Kaduna. On a three-shift system, this mill is capable of turning out about 12 million yards of cloth a year. An extension now (1959) in hand is expected to increase the mill's output by about one half. At the same time, the federal government, through its Department of Commerce and Industries, is seeking to give the "cottage" industry a new lease on life by encouraging narrow-loom weavers to turn over to the broad loom, and by teaching them, at textile centers dispersed throughout the country, the latest techniques of hand spinning and weaving. Upon completion of their training, spinners and weavers can purchase reliable equipment with the help, if need be, of loans. For some years shortage of yarn constituted a serious obstacle to increased production, but the introduction of improved methods of spinning has done much to remove it.

Southern Rhodesia. The most important textile unit is the Cotton Industries Board (a nationalized — federal — concern until 1959) at Gatooma. This board, besides doing research work in cotton culture, operates a ginnery capable of handling some 40 million pounds of cotton a season, and two spinning mills with a total of 42,500 spindles. The chief products of the factory are cotton wool and a variety of cotton yarns (over 5,000 tons in 1957). The bulk of the yarn is sold to local factories weaving cotton blankets and piece goods. The surplus is exported, mainly to the Union of South Africa.

Republic of Sudan. In the Zande district of Equatoria Province, in the extreme south of the country, the Equatoria Projects Board has been engaged, for some years now, in "an experiment for the social emergence" of the indigenous Azande people. The establishment in 1951 of a cotton spinning and weaving plant at Nzara was regarded as an indispensable part of this experiment, since the cloth it produces in excess of local needs provides the Azande people with their most salable "export" — to central and northern Sudan — and consequently their chief source of purchasing power. At full capacity the plant can turn out between 2 and 3 million yards of unbleached — loom state — cloth a year, but such an output does not begin to satisfy the country's demand for cheap-grade cloth. Nor has it often been attained since 1955, when this part of southern

Sudan became disaffected. A much larger plant is being built in the Khartoum area; it is expected to come into operation during 1960.

Uganda. As part of the country's postwar development program made possible by the Owen Falls hydroelectric power station, a large textile plant has recently gone into operation at Jinja. Owned by the Nyanza Textile Industries Limited (a partnership between the Calico Printers Association of Manchester and the Uganda Development Corporation Limited), the plant specializes in khaki drill and shirtings. In September 1958 the weaving department was producing cloth at the rate of more than 10 million yards a year, and new machinery was being ordered to cope with the demand.

There is also a small cotton textile mill in Somalia, at Mogadishu.

Sisal

Of the numerous other vegetable fibers grown in tropical Africa — the list includes flax, jute, Congo jute (*Urena lobata*), Deccan hemp or kenaf (*Hibiscus cannabinus*), ramie, piassava and sisal — the only one that is processed, or cultivated, locally on a large scale is sisal.

The processing of sisal consists in extracting the fiber from the leaf of the plant (*Agave sisalana*), with the aid of a decorticator. After washing, drying, brushing and baling, the fiber is ready for manufacture. As all these operations have to be carried out before the cut leaves harden, they have to be done where the plant is grown. The fact that between 96 and 97 per cent of the leaf is of no use in the manufacture of sisal products provides a further reason for placing the processing establishment as close as possible to the source of raw material.

While by far the greater part of the processed fiber is exported, in some territories a small amount is retained for conversion into binder twine, sacking and other bulky products. The first factory built for this purpose, in the early 1930s, near Tanga in Tanganyika, did not outlive the depression. Just before World War II a second attempt was made to manufacture sisal goods in east Africa, this time at Ruiru, near Nairobi, in Kenya. During the war it did good business in camouflage nets, hessian, cordage and sacking (including sandbags). It is still in business. Its bags are now so satisfactory in quality that they are replacing jute bags as containers for an increasing range of local products.

More recently, both Mozambique and Angola have begun to turn a little of their sisal fiber into rope and sacking. But in none of the territories where the crop is grown are the prospects for the establishment of openly competitive fabricating plants very good. To be economic, such a plant must be large, much larger than is warranted by the sisal production of most of the countries in question or by the size of the local markets for their products. Without the help of tariffs, sisal factories in these countries would stand little chance against the large, conveniently located plants of Europe and North America. Where the sisal-producing territories are likely to do themselves more good is in converting some of the present unused residue of the fiber-extracting process. This residue contains a number of useful substances, including wax, glucose, pectates and various acids. From an industrial point of view probably the most important of these substances is sodium pectate, a gelatinous mass used by the food, cosmetics and pharmaceutical industries, and known to have considerable possibilities in the textile industry. Up to now, the commercial recovery of these "waste" products has been undertaken in Europe and North America only. However, since their raw material, even when dried, is bulky, and the finished products, by comparison, light, compact and valuable, there would appear to be some advantages in setting up local extracting plants — all the more so since, with very little doctoring, part of the dehydrated waste could be made into a cattle feed for which almost every animal in Africa would be the better.

Since the decortication of the sisal leaf has to be done on the spot, most of the plants doing this work are located in British East Africa (Tanganyika had well over 200 in 1958) and Portuguese Africa (mainly Angola and Mozambique). The rest, accounting for not more than about 5 per cent of the total output, are in west Africa, the Malagasy Republic and the Belgian Congo.

Other Industrial Crops

As for the other industrial crops processed, partly or wholly, in tropical Africa, some have never been very important. Some were formerly more important than they now are. On the other hand, some are gaining ground, and may soon rank with cotton and sisal.

Cinchona Bark [8]

Until the advent of synthetic compounds, quinine, derived from the bark of the cinchona tree, was the main specific for malaria. The chief African producer of it has always been the Belgian Congo. Until World War II the bark was shipped for treatment abroad. Then, in 1943, an extraction plant, formerly in commission in England, was imported by the Congo government and erected near Bukavu. This plant is capable of producing 12 tons of quinine a year, an amount well in excess of the Congo's present consumption. The rest of the bark crop — about 90 per cent of it — is exported in its raw state. Production in the other territories, mainly Tanganyika, is small. Although many residents of the malarial tropics continue to swear by quinine, the demand for it has slackened

---

[8] As this is taken from the cinchona tree at regular intervals, it is here regarded as a crop; similarly with gum arabic and rubber.

noticeably since the introduction of paludrin, atebrin and similar compounds.

Essential Oils

Of the many herbaceous plants, shrubs and trees that yield volatile oils as against fixed oils like castor oil, a number are raised and processed commercially in tropical Africa. The more important include clove oil (from Zanzibar, Pemba and the Malagasy Republic), cedarwood oil [9] (almost exclusively from Kenya), geranium oil (Belgian Congo, the Malagasy Republic, Tanganyika and Kenya), lemon grass oil (Belgian Congo, the Malagasy Republic and Tanganyika) and citrus oils (Tanganyika, Southern Rhodesia and west Africa). Most of the expressing and distilling of these oils is done perforce at or near their place of origin, in small, simply equipped factories.

Fixed Oils [10]

The list of crops yielding fixed oils that are cultivated and processed in Africa is long and getting longer. To the stock varieties, such as coconut, oil palm, peanut, cottonseed, benniseed (or sesame), have been added in quite recent times tung, sunflower, castor seed, linseed and soybean. As the oil content of most of these seeds is small in relation to the total bulk of their pods, obvious gains are to be derived from the preliminary processing of them locally, and this is generally done. In some cases, too, the later stages of the processing are also carried out locally; this is true not only of palm oil but also, increasingly, of tung oil [11] and peanut oil. With the growing clamor for industrialization, it can scarcely be doubted that more and more of such processing will be done in the country of origin. The action of the (British) Colonial Development Corporation in underwriting the cost of a tung-processing mill in the Vipya plateau region of Nyasaland and of the Tanganyika government in stimulating the manufacture of soaps, paints and varnishes from locally processed coconut oil is indicative of the trend.

Rubber and Other Gums and Resins

As most gums and resins, including the highly sought-after gum arabic and copal of tropical Africa, are resistant to heat, moisture and insects,

[9] Unlike the others, this is not a "crop," but a by-product of the sawmill. Strictly speaking, it belongs to the later section dealing with timber, but for convenience it is inserted here.

[10] It is difficult to draw the line between oils for industrial uses and those for nonindustrial uses. Just as part of the output of palm oil, peanut oil, etc., goes into chemical and other manufacturing establishments to produce a wide range of nonedible substances, so a part of the production of the oils specified under this heading is destined for pharmaceutical and other "edible" uses.

[11] A special-purpose oil, seldom used alone, but of great value industrially when blended with other oils, notably linseed oil.

and at the same time contain in highly concentrated form the ingredients that make them commercially valuable, they travel well. Local processing, beyond cleaning and grading, is therefore seldom necessary. In many instances it is not even feasible, since, with the major exception of rubber, these substances do not form a large part by weight of the manufactured articles — varnishes, paints, pharmaceuticals, candies, adhesives, mucilages, etc. — into the making of which they go. And, further, as most of these manufactures call for a skilled labor force, cheap power, large ready-to-hand markets and high standards of living, all of which are still uncommon in tropical Africa, there is little likelihood that more than a small fraction of the African output of these raw materials can be processed locally, at least for some time to come.

The position with rubber is different. The latex of *Hevea brasiliensis,* the main source of vegetable rubber, is liquid in form and subject to change of state with churning and, from the manufacturer's point of view, deterioration. Its rubber content is low, running between 30 and 40 per cent by weight. The rest is waste. Shipment of it overseas in its raw state would be highly uneconomic. Consequently, some preliminary processing of the latex is always done on or near the plantation. This processing may be one of the following kinds: concentration in solid form either as "ribbed smoked sheet" or as crepe; concentration in liquid form as preserved latex, which is increasing in demand for the manufacture of foam rubber; or concentration in powdered form. The initial step in the concentration process is the same, namely, the coagulation of the latex by acetic, formic or other acids.

The processing of sheet rubber, still the commonest raw kind, requires no great skill or elaborate machinery; it can be done equally well by the small indigenous grower and the large foreign-owned corporation. The manufacture of crepe rubber calls for heavy power-driven machinery, which in turn calls for capital outlays and large centralized processing plants such as those operated by the Firestone Plantations in Liberia and, cooperatively, by the peasant producers of Nigeria, the French Cameroons and elsewhere.

The making of preserved latex is done with the aid of either centrifuges or driers, which increase the dry-rubber content to about 62 per cent in the case of the centrifuged and "creamed" latex and to about 75 per cent in the case of the evaporated concentrate.

With the popularization among Africans of crepe rubber shoes and other rubber goods in recent years, a small but growing proportion of the output of crepe and preserved latex is being retained for further processing rather than shipped abroad.

Most of the preshipment processing of rubber is done at Harbel in Liberia, where nearly half of the entire African "crop" is handled; in the Yangambi, Mayumbé and Coquilhatville districts of the Belgian Congo;

the Warri and Benin provinces of Nigeria; the Dizangué district (near Edea) of the French Cameroons; and the Cabinda enclave of Angola.

Pyrethrum and Other Insecticides

The extraction of poisons from plants is a skill almost as old as man, but it is only recently, with the demand for insecticides, that it has become a commercially important one. Of all the vegetable sources of such poisons, the feverfew flower, or pyrethrum (*P. cinerariaefolium* and *P. roseum*), is without question the most valuable; for while it destroys lice, bedbugs, fleas, mosquitoes, flies, ants, caterpillars and aphides, it does not harm warm-blooded animals. It has been especially valuable in controlling infection on African coffee plantations. Its role in the economic and social life of the humid tropics is therefore substantial, and continues to expand, notwithstanding severe competition from chemical insecticides. In Tanganyika almost the only processing done on the spot is the drying (either in the open air or in specially constructed sheds) and pressing of the flower into bales. However, in Kenya and the Belgian Congo (including Ruanda-Urundi), the largest African producers, a large part of the crop is factory-processed for the active constituent, pyrethrin.

Other vegetable insecticides are grown and processed on a small scale in some territories. Establishments for the conversion of nicotine (*Nicotiana rustica*) into an impure nicotine sulfate exist in the Federation of Rhodesia and Nyasaland and in Uganda, but the production, never large, has fallen off owing to the increasing popularity of chemical insecticides with the same general toxic range. Production and extraction of derris (*D. elliptica* and *D. malaccensis*) has lagged in recent years for the same reasons.

Wattle Bark

With the decline in importance of quebracho and chestnut as major sources of vegetable tannin, increasing attention is being paid to wattle, which grows as well and as rapidly in many parts of highland Africa as in its native Australian habitat. Although wattle bark is exported "raw" from more than one territory, its low ratio of tannin to total bulk constitutes a powerful argument in favor of on-the-spot processing. And this is being done more and more. Already wattle bark extract is one of Kenya's major products, ranking as high as fourth on the colony's export list in 1957. Since 1956 it has occupied a place also on the list of Rhodesian manufactures. At Melsetter and Inyanga, both in the Eastern Highlands of Southern Rhodesia, the Rhodesian Wattle Company, Ltd., now has factories capable of producing 33,500 tons of extract in the ten-month working season. By the end of 1958 the company had exported approximately 11,000 tons of extract. A wattle extract factory was opened in Tanganyika (near Njombe) in 1958.

TIMBER

As we saw in Chapter 6, it is no easy matter to exploit tropical woods. The man who tries to do so soon finds himself up against many obstacles, including the characteristically great complexity of species in the rain forest, the limited utility of the primary species by comparison with those of middle and high latitudes, the difficulty of moving timber over tropical terrain often poorly supplied with roads and well supplied with swamps and unbridged rivers, and, not least, scarcity of labor.

Nevertheless, most African territories can point to a rising curve of lumber production and a steady expansion of lumber-processing operations. These processing operations are of many kinds. In one territory alone — the Federation of Rhodesia and Nyasaland — they cover the manufacture of such things as brooms and baskets, ceiling and plaster boards, cardboard boxes and cartons, fencing, plywood and veneers, parquet flooring, pulp and paperboard, chipboard, paper bags, wrappers and toilet rolls. In these respects, as in many others, the Federation holds an impressive lead over most of the other territories, for which lumber processing mainly means sawmilling and the manufacture of veneers and plywoods.

Lumber

Prior to 1939 most of the timber felled was shipped as logs, round or squared. The mills which existed at that time generally worked for the large mining corporations and railroads, producing pit props, railroad ties and construction lumber. Here and there, as in Nigeria and the then Gold Coast, a small amount of sawn lumber was produced for the local market and for export. On the whole, wartime circumstances favored the sawmilling industry. Not only had a large military demand to be met, especially in British and French tropical Africa, but local substitutes had to be found for the softwoods formerly imported. After the war, high shipping charges made it desirable to export lumber rather than logs, and booming economies and development programs created a strong domestic demand for many types of prepared woods. New sawmills were erected in several territories, notably in the Gabon and Middle Congo provinces of the then French Equatorial Africa, the Gold Coast, Nigeria and the Belgian Congo. Since the war, also, the sawmills have tended to diversify their product. In many cases, it is now no longer confined to lumber, railroad ties and the like but includes such things as roof shingles, tool handles and the frames for prefabricated houses. A measure of the rapid postwar expansion of sawmilling is contained in the fact that already by 1949 the aggregate lumber exports of French Equatorial Africa, French West Africa and the French Cameroons, the principal prewar exporting group, were by weight more than double the 1938 volume of about 357,000 metric tons.[12] By 1958 the export of lumber from French Equatorial Africa alone had reached nearly 800,000 metric tons.

But expansion has not everywhere meant modernization. In many areas sawmilling equipment is out of date, the quality of the work indifferent, and the basis of operations inefficient by modern standards. Few mills as yet produce really first-class lumber. Very little wood used locally is seasoned, and even wood intended for export is often only air-dried; not much of it is impregnated with creosote or other preservatives, or even planed and dressed before shipment.

Veneers and Plywood

The postwar development of veneer and plywood manufacturing has been no less striking than the expansion of sawmilling. In some ways, it has been more remarkable, because the domestic market for such products is still uneconomically small, the manufacture of veneers and plywood makes heavier demands on the skill of both management and labor, and the products have to compete on the export market with those of longer-established and better-located European and North American firms. But there are at least two advantages to the local processing of wood for such purposes. The lumberman is able to be more selective, picking only those logs that he highly esteems for the purpose; and he can do the peeling of them before they have a chance to get discolored or otherwise damaged by weather and handling.

Before the war, so far as can be ascertained, no peeling (veneer) or plywood plants existed in tropical Africa. Since the war, such plants have been set up in a number of territories. One of the most successful is located at Lemba in the Mayumbé region of the Belgian Congo. Among the many commercial species of hardwood to be found in this region is *Terminalia superba*. As pointed out in Chapter 6, veneers made from this wood, known in the trade as Korina, are in great demand by manufacturers of modern furniture, especially in the United States.

Impressive as are the postwar increases in the output and variety of processed woods, tropical Africa still occupies a very humble place on the list of the world's wood processors — notwithstanding the fact that it contains probably at least 10 per cent of the world's accessible timber of merchantable quality. In 1957 it supplied not more than 3 per cent of the

---

[12] United Nations, "Review of Economic Conditions in Africa" (Supplement to *World Economic Report, 1949-50*), New York, 1951, p. 38.

world's lumber, or about half the amount supplied by "woodless" Japan. Its contribution to the world's supply of other types of processed wood was considerably smaller.

SECONDARY INDUSTRY

The line between primary processing and secondary industry is clear enough in theory; in practice, too, it is generally not very difficult to decide where, along the processor's way, the adding of a new function or characteristic transfers a commodity from one lane to the other. But the point of making such distinctions when describing the manufacturing activities of still very young countries can well be questioned, if only because both types of enterprise are frequently carried on under the same roof and many workers divide their time between the two. Here we are more concerned with the fact of a spreading industrial umbrella than with the debate as to where its primary shaft ends and its secondary ribs begin.

Characteristics

The list of industries supported by processed raw materials is, of course, longer in some territories than in others. In the Federation of Rhodesia and Nyasaland, for instance, it contained in 1958 more than 250 items; in Kenya, more than 125; in Somalia, not more than 25. But whether long or short, the list is highly illuminating. It tells as much about cultural sophistication as it does about economic development, as much about human resourcefulness as about physical resources.

Some of the industries can be explained quite simply as the invention of necessity. People who build towns in the African tropics soon find themselves needing the services of the tinker and the tailor, the butcher and the baker, and still, in some places, those of the candlestick maker. Some others can just as easily be construed as an expression of the settler's determination to live as well, and as comfortably, in the African tropics as his compeers live in France, Belgium, Portugal or Great Britain. The ice, gas and electricity plants, the brick and cement factories, the cabinet shops and the printing presses are witness to this determination. Some are financed by old-established European corporations eager to increase their business domain and able to put large sums into the doing of it. More than one soap, brewing, canning, boot-and-shoe and metallurgical enterprise falls into this category. Some are the outcome of nothing more substantial than a man's hunch that there was room for the thing he could make with his own hands on his own place, be it costume jewelry, confectionery or a carved elephant. Some owe their existence to considerations of a more political and prestigious kind. To a people emerging from the colonial cocoon, few vistas are more attractive than those glimpsed between belching chimney stacks and from the end of a moving assembly line.

Almost the only generalizations that can be made about these industries are:

1. Their number and economic significance are growing. There were many times more secondary industries in the Federation of Rhodesia and Nyasaland, Kenya, the Belgian Congo and Ghana in 1958 than in 1938. In Kenya alone the number increased more than tenfold, and the contribution of such industries to the national income of the territory was by 1958 almost double what it had been as recently as 1947. Over the same period the gross annual output of manufacturing industry in and around Salisbury, Southern Rhodesia, rose from £8.3 million to £36.5 million.

2. Their spatial distribution is very uneven. Large areas, including Ethiopia, Bechuanaland and the hinterland of Portuguese Africa, have almost none. Others, such as the periurban areas of Nairobi, Léopoldville, Salisbury and Bulawayo, are almost as well served as cities of comparable size in the American Middle West. As of June 1958, Salisbury, for instance, had over 400 factories within its civic jurisdiction.

3. The markets they supply are usually domestic, and often local. Comparatively few of them as yet straddle a political frontier.

4. The fuel and power requirements of most secondary industries are quite small; so also are their labor requirements.

5. Although most of these industries were started by Europeans or Asians for Europeans and Asians, they are coming increasingly to serve African needs, to be manned by Africans and, here and there, to be owned by Africans. For several years now the printing presses of Ghana and Nigeria have done most of their newspaper and textbook business with Africans, and have employed Africans as compositors, proofreaders and editors. Some of the wealthiest men are African newspaper owners. The growing role of the African in secondary industry is scarcely less apparent in the "settler" countries. The Rhodesian Plough and Machinery Company's plant in Bulawayo, Southern Rhodesia, works almost exclusively for the African hand hoe and mouldboard plow market, and for every European in the plant there are more than a score of Africans. The same is true of a hundred other Rhodesian factories. And in almost every large town in every territory there can now be found self-employed African woodworkers making furniture of excellent quality for both the African and non-African markets.

Favorable and Unfavorable Factors

As to the types of secondary industry being developed, most fall into two categories: those concerned with the manufacture of essential consumer goods, and those concerned with the maintenance of essential services.

What is deemed essential depends very much upon a people's material standards. The European has long regarded suits of clothes, footwear, cigarettes, confectionery and bottled beers as essential, and is prepared to go to great lengths, even in wartime, to keep the supply of them flowing. To the African, until recently, these commodities mattered little, for he had other ways of adorning, refreshing and amusing himself. So long as the demand for such things was weak and diffuse, it was cheaper to import them than to manufacture them. But, as we have seen, material standards are changing all over Africa. Today there is scarcely an African who is immune to the appeal of shoes, suits, cigarettes and other European-style "essentials," or who lacks the means of obtaining some of them. With the consequent increase in demand for such things has come the desire to undertake their manufacture locally. To the businessman local manufacture spells (albeit erroneously upon occasion) lower costs and increased consumption; to the administrator it spells new sources of taxation and revenue (partly offset, it is true, by the reduction in import duties); to the consumer, better living.

Whether or not factories are set up depends on many circumstances besides desire and demand. Among others, it depends on the labor supply, the industry's fuel and power requirements, its access to an adequate water supply and other public utilities, the size of the market, the availability of raw materials other than fuel, and what we might call the confidence factor, that is, the willingness of investors to put money into a given industry in a given territory.

Other things being equal, favorable circumstances for local manufacture may be said to exist when:

1. The raw materials are available on the spot; for this gives the local product a protection against imports equal at least to the cost of transporting the raw material. The manufacture of such commodities as cement and beer often turns on this circumstance.

2. The industry produces a commodity more bulky and fragile than the materials of which it is made; for this affords a similar protection, irrespective of whether the raw materials themselves have to be imported. Furniture, hollow ware, such as crockery, kitchen pots, etc., and most kinds of assembly work fall in this category.

3. No markedly unfavorable circumstances are present.

Unfavorable circumstances may be said to exist when:

1. The raw material for the product has to be imported and loses weight in the process of manufacture; for then the transport factor is on the side of production in the country which has the raw material. Many foundry products come under this head.

2. The fuel requirements are large and have to be transported great distances (in most industries the cost of fuel is less than 2 per cent or so

of the value of the finished article, but in certain industries it is much —
up to ten times — higher). Some chemical commodities, newsprint and
steel (which is a primary industry and not now under consideration) fall
in this group.

3. The local market is very small, as, with very few exceptions, it is in
the case of things like typewriters, railroad engines and automobiles.

4. Very special skills are required, as in the case of watches and other
precision instruments.

5. The ratio of capital to labor is abnormally high, as with almost all
types of chemical and metallurgical work.

6. The tariff structure favors the local importer rather than the local
manufacturer. (Thus, one of the reasons why the Federation of Rhodesia
and Nyasaland has only bicycle assembly and not bicycle manufacture
plants is that the import duty on bicycles from the United Kingdom is
so low that it pays the British manufacturers *not* to set up local manufacturing plants.)

Marginal circumstances may be said to exist when:

1. The industry has to import a raw material which neither loses nor
gains much bulk in the processing, as in the case of the manufacture of
cigarettes and cotton goods.

2. The requirements of capital, skill and fuel are quite modest, as they
are in the footwear and confectionery industries.

3. The local demand is considerable but periodic rather than constant,
as in the case of hoes, axes and other simple foundry products.

While it does not follow that "favorable" industries are invariably set
up before industries in the "marginal" category, or that "unfavorable"
industries always are unable to attract capital, the trend is increasingly
toward rational development. No African government hoping to create a
climate congenial to investors can afford to have sickly industries on its
hands. True, what is a sickly industry in one territory may be a healthy
industry in a second. At the same time most of the economic differences
between territory and territory are little more than skin deep. These may
bewitch the passer-by, but they must never be allowed to blind the
planner or the investor to the basic, systemic, similarities of form, function and need.

Taking the region as a whole, the most commonly produced consumer
goods are beverages (fruit drinks, beer, tea, coffee); cotton clothing;
earthenware; food products (canned vegetables and fruits, edible oils and
fats, sugar and molasses); salt; soap and candles; and furniture.

Consumer goods that are as yet less widely produced (though not
on that account to be considered marginal) are bread, biscuits and cakes;
books and newspapers; chemicals; confectionery (excluding chocolate [13]);

---

[13] In none of the lower-lying parts of the African tropics has the storage of either
raw cocoa or processed chocolate been found practicable. For this the constant heat
and high humidity must be held largely responsible.

crockery and glassware; footwear; hardware (buckets, chains, nails, nuts and bolts, etc.); jewelry; leather goods; paints and varnishes; tobacco and cigarettes.

In the consumer services field, the commonest industries are those concerned with the care and repair of automobiles, bicycles, clothes (including dry cleaning), radios, etc., and the supply of water, gas and electricity.

NATION BUILDING

In most territories, the list of highly favorable industries is still short. The list of localities where such industries stand to succeed is also short. Some territories, like Ghana and the Republic of Sudan, have considerable purchasing power by African standards, but little in the way of industrial raw materials or fuels. Territories like Tanganyika and Angola have plenty of raw materials and fuel (coal in the former, oil in the latter), but only a low purchasing power. Others, like the Somalilands, would appear to have little of either. Very few are as fortunate as the Belgian Congo and Nigeria, with their diversified physical resources, including fuels, and their large exports of industrial crops and strategic minerals. Even so, because of the vastness of these territories, their still very inadequate transportation services and their patchy economic development, the number of places in them where secondary industries of even the most favorable kind can be set up with good prospects of success is small. For Nigeria, they number perhaps a score at the most; for the Belgian Congo, ten or a dozen.

In most territories, too, the list of not so highly favorable industries is still short. By the time the ordinary consumer has satisfied his need for a shirt and trousers, a little extra food, some candles and salt, a stick or two of furniture, and a bicycle, he has usually run out of ready cash. If he has some left, it is by no means certain that he will spend it on other kinds of goods. Many passably well-off Africans like nothing better than to buy more of the things they already have.

But both lists are growing, if slowly. As the standard of living rises and consumers are educated in the uses of a well-equipped kitchen, toolshed and workshop, and their field of choice — still small in most places — is enlarged, it is certain that many now marginal industries will move over into the favorable class.

What will happen to the now unfavorable industries, secondary or primary, is less clear. Their future may well be shaped more by considerations of politics, prestige and military strategy than by those of profit and loss. Even now it would seem that such considerations are not unimportant in the minds of some of tropical Africa's nation builders.

Take, for instance, the case of the small Rhodesian iron and steel industry — the only one of its kind in tropical Africa. As everyone knows, the logistic requirements of the iron and steel industry are such that very few places in the world can meet them satisfactorily. The production of pig iron — the first step in the manufacturing process — requires iron ore, coking coal and fluxing stone. The smelting of the iron to make steel — the second step — calls for metal scrap, limestone and sometimes burnt lime, fluorspar, ferroalloys and spiegel, a mixture of iron, carbon and manganese. Both steps call for prodigious amounts of water. Since most of these materials are bulky and of low value by weight, they are unable to stand heavy freight charges. At Redcliff, the site of the Rhodesian plant, iron and limestone are available locally, but coal has to be railed in from Wankie, approximately 350 miles away. Most of the metal scrap comes from still farther afield — from the Copperbelt; and the other ingredients also have to be brought in from a distance. Since no large perennial rivers are handy, the water supply is not all that it might be. Further, there is no large market for the products of the plant and no large local supply of labor, skilled or unskilled.

It is hardly surprising therefore that the Rhodesian industry — a nationalized concern down to 1957 — had to rely for many years rather heavily on government largesse and protective tariffs to keep going, and that its annual output of crude steel as of 1958 was still well under 100,000 metric tons and its output of pig iron and ferroalloys smaller still. Granted, production of both is rising, but even at 200,000 metric tons each, the steel and pig iron outputs would be very far below the amounts which would enable the plant to "equal the low domestic costs of any of the large scale production units" [14] in other parts of the world. Certainly it is difficult to see how the industry, unaided, can hope to cut much of a figure on the export market. The remoteness of the Federation from the sea and from large manufacturing centers that provides it with a measure of protection against imports of iron and steel is its own guarantee that the industry will have to operate on a short tether. The commissioners reporting to the Southern Rhodesian government in 1954 on the present state and future prospects of the industry were unanimous on this point.[15]

But this is not to say that anybody in the Federation is disposed to dismantle the plant. On the contrary, its new owners, the Rhodesian Iron and Steel Company (Pvt.), Ltd., announced plans, in December 1957, for increasing the output of steel to 150,000 (long) tons by 1960 and later to 250,000 tons. More recently still, plans for the building of two new rolling mills have been announced. With these plans the people of the Federation are clearly in sympathy, for no country on the eve of political independence — as many of its European leaders believe themselves to be — is going to throw away the garment which, in this steel-clad world, is reckoned to carry the best guarantee of security and respectability.

[14] *Report of the Commissioners Appointed to Inquire into the Iron and Steel Industry of Southern Rhodesia,* Salisbury, Southern Rhodesia, 1954, p. 3.
[15] *Ibid.,* p. 4.

Much the same considerations, we may assume, have influenced the thinking of nation builders in Ghana and elsewhere in tropical Africa. The Volta River project is a case in point. At the start its promoters were convinced that it could be made to produce power and aluminum competitively with existing world producers, and some of them still avow their belief in its ability to do so. But it is not without significance that almost every time a group of experts examines the economics of the project it comes up with higher costs and lower returns. In its 1956 report the Preparatory Commission suggested that the costs of putting the scheme into full working order could well be £309 million instead of, as announced in 1952, £144 million, with a comparable increase in the cost of delivered power. Such a prospect, needless to say, did not sit well with the aluminum companies interested in the scheme. After studying the 1956 report, Aluminium Limited, the chief of these companies, was constrained to say that the report had "affected the attractiveness of the Scheme so that on the 1952 framework the prospective return on capital in the proposed aluminium company is now substantially lower than estimated at that time." True, it went on to say that it believed the project could still be "developed satisfactorily," but only if arrangements could be made "for the financing and the division of responsibilities and risks which would be satisfactory under present conditions." All of which, when stripped of its diplomatic verbiage, sounds uncommonly like the "retort courteous" of a banker to a loan applicant of doubtful credit.

But economic feasibility is no longer the only, if indeed the primary, issue. The government and people of Ghana have come to believe in the project as in an article of political faith. The key to national greatness is industry; the key to industry is power; and power, whether for aluminum, agriculture or utilities, can only be obtained in quantity from the Volta River. More than this, a dam near Ajena and an aluminum smelter at Tema have become symbols of an economic revolution, which will lift all men to a higher and better way of life.

As we saw earlier, the scheme — or, rather, a modified version of it — will come to pass. So, too, in the course of time will others of similar political and national consequence to other tropical African territories.

SURVIVAL OF INDIGENOUS CRAFTS

Few of the traditional artisan skills possessed by the African are as widely found, or as elegantly practiced, today as they were a generation ago. In some districts woodworking is almost a lost art. In others it is rare to find a good potter. For every woman who carries a pitcher fired in her own compound, two carry gasoline containers made in Europe or America. The tourist in search of authentic metal ware will often find that what purports to be a nice specimen of Hausa inlay work carries a

British or a Belgian trademark. The fact is that a man may have reservations about the merits of kerosene lamps and business suits without being averse to buying European mass-produced hoes and cooking pots to save himself the trouble of fashioning his own — especially when he can earn the money for such things in a nearby plantation or town with less effort than would be required to make them. This must be reckoned as gain, even though it involves a loss of skill.

But it is open to question whether the loss of artisan skill, which almost every student of African man deplores, would have been as great had the travelers, traders, missionaries and administrators of the late nineteenth and early twentieth century had higher artistic standards. As Harrison Church says in his working paper:

> The initial decline in craft goods coincided with the Victorian age in Europe, during which massive quantities of shoddy bric-a-brac were exported to Africa . . . That age all too often produced Europeans who scorned local art forms and wished to replace them with nineteenth-century "Gothic," Birmingham brass and Manchester calico.

To many Europeans of this epoch African craft goods, like African art works, were objects of disdain. To others they were just funny — the work of inept children. And to the more prudish Europeans (of whom tropical Africa has had its share), some of the craft goods carried more than a suggestion of evil, for were they not wrought in the dark places of the earth, "full of the habitations of cruelty"? Were not their makers kin to the shameless artists — sometimes, indeed, the selfsame artists — whose imaginations bodied forth shapes and symbols unfit to be seen in any Victorian drawing room?

The strictures notwithstanding, much good craftsmanship — along with an unconscionable amount that isn't good — has survived, especially in west Africa. The craftsmen of Kano still do notable work with leather, cloth, silver and gold; those of Bida with glass and silver; of Benin City with brass and wood; of Awka with wood; of Ikot Ekpene with rafia; of Akweti with embroidered cloth — to take examples only from Nigeria. As notable in other west African territories are the makers of camel and goat hair blankets (Sudanese Republic and Republic of the Niger), of brass and rafia goods (Abomey in the Republic of Dahomey), of cottons interwoven with gold thread (Keta in Ghana), of straw-embroidered, leather-covered bottles and boxes (Sierra Leone and the Republic of Guinea), and of leather and inlaid wood (Sudanese Republic). Farther east, in the Republic of Sudan, the city of Omdurman is still famed for its workers, mostly Egyptian and Syrian immigrants, in silver, leather and ivory. In Darfur the art of rug weaving is still practiced on a small scale. But once south of the northern savannas, such skills are either entirely lacking or very rare. Over large parts of east and central Africa almost the only medium of craft work is rafia.

Where attempts have been made to foster indigenous craftsmanship, they have seldom been conspicuously successful. True, the French have succeeded, through an artisans' school established for the purpose, in improving the filigree work done in the Sudanese Republic. Likewise the British have helped many Nigerian and Ghanaian weavers to find larger markets for their narrow-loom cloth. And in every territory the tourist market for handmade "Africana" of all sorts is growing. But a craftsman who would gladly make a wooden stool for the chief of his tribe or a length of gold-threaded cloth for a friend's favorite wife will not readily work five days a week from nine to five making stools and weaving cloth for people who mean nothing to him, who have no interest in why he works the way he does, who want to use the products of his skill for purposes they were never intended for, and who, likely as not, will do him down at the first opportunity.

Even if this were not the case, it would be difficult to feel cheerful about the future of traditional African craftsmanship so long as Africans with money prefer to spend it on non-African merchandise.

PROBLEMS OF THE MANUFACTURER

The manufacturer, big or small, who operates a factory in tropical Africa has to wrestle with many problems. Some of them, of course, are not peculiar to Africa or to the tropics. There is nothing parochial about wage disputes, strikes and depressions; they have a habit of cropping up in Nagasaki, New York and Nairobi. The siting of a new factory can be just as much of a headache for the New Englander as for the Nigerian. Bottlenecks can play havoc with textile production schedules as readily in Lancashire as in Léopoldville. The manufacturer in Kenya, Nigeria or the Belgian Congo is likely to find, however, that his labor, location and production problems are not resolved as easily, and do not stay resolved as long, as those of his North American, European and Oriental colleagues. And he may also find that he has to reckon with other problems about which the mid-latitude manufacturer knows very little. It is these that are of interest here. Broadly they are of four kinds: environmental, cultural, "colonial" and capital.

The Environmental Problem

The environment is a factor in every manufacturing equation, but in the tropics it assumes larger dimensions than elsewhere. The almost constant heat that hustles a plant through its cycle of growth slows a man at his work.[16] The moisture that feeds forests and sustains rivers also rusts

[16] Reliable statistical evidence of the "slow-down" is hard to come by. An investigation conducted some years ago in Australia showed that wharf workers in the tropical

machinery, rots raw materials and bedevils the life of the warehouseman. The combination of the two encourages the processes of fermentation, mold formation and structural deterioration in almost every harvested and processed crop. It all but precludes, as we have seen, the possibility of manufacturing chocolate in the cocoa belt of west Africa.

It is true that large parts of the African tropics have too little, rather than too much, moisture; most of these, however, are disqualified on that account from raising the kind of crop that is in great industrial demand. It is equally true that large parts of the African tropics are high enough above sea level not to require air conditioning; but most of these are situated well inland, away from cheap water transportation, and often remote from fuel, labor and basic raw materials. The factories that are being built in such areas — they are many — can hardly do more than serve a local market.

The environment of the region spells more than heat and moisture. It also spells difficult terrain — palisaded coasts that obstruct the railroad engineer, gradientless plateaus that flood and parch by turns, insidious jungle that can swallow up a fresh-cut path in a season, unsheltered harbors and unaccommodating rivers — a terrain that is easy to abuse, and hard to subdue. It spells disease that impairs the quality of an animal's hide and a man's labor; that can undermine almost overnight the economic security of a people (as the "swollen shoot" cocoa disease and "sudden death" clove disease succeeded in doing); and that can consign a fourth of a continent to a milkless and largely meatless existence. For the land it spells disease as well — the cancer of the earth's skin which we call erosion. In addition it frequently spells shortage of mineral fuels where they are most needed, and the use of inefficient or costly alternatives.

The Cultural Problem

While nobody questions the manufacturing ability, actual or potential, of the ordinary African, a great many people question his willingness to work steadily for any manufacturer other than himself. Some would doubtless go further and question his willingness to work steadily for himself. The African has never been cumbered with an abundance of things. Though he is quick to see merit in many of the newfangled things around him, he is often inclined, it seems, to see more merit in other people's using those things than in using them himself. This disinclination to become entangled in a web of other men's spinning does nothing to simplify the manufacturer's task. On the contrary, it complicates his

port of Townsville accomplished about 11 per cent more work in the cool season than in the hot, and that they did from 5 to 10 per cent less work than their fellows of the same ethnic stock in Brisbane, 9° farther south. Similar differentials might be expected to exist in African ports.

task in at least two ways. It keeps the effective demand for manufactured goods small, and the labor turnover high; in consequence it keeps operating costs high. Small demand tends to mean small factories that find difficulty in competing with the large factories abroad in technical efficiency and per unit production costs. Where there are large factories, they are prone to run into problems of supply of raw material, transportation and labor, as well as problems of demand. High labor turnover means higher costs of recruitment, training and supervision; at the same time, it makes for lower demand since many workers stay only long enough to buy the one or two things on which they have set their fancy.

To entangle the African in the manufacturer's web is often more easily said than done. To give him higher wages may merely increase the manufacturer's costs without proportionately increasing the African's productivity, since there are still many laborers whose response to higher wages is not more work, but less. To offer him cheaper goods frequently leads to the same end. To remove the factories from the towns, where most of them are, to the countryside, where most of the laborers come from, might alleviate, even if it did not solve, the problem of high labor turnover, for the African knows no greater deprivation than to be parted from his kin. A few places, indeed, already have rural industries (an example is the Bata shoe factory at Limuru in the Kenya Highlands) that draw the bulk of their labor supply and raw materials from the surrounding countryside, and have no difficulty in paying their way. But all the time there are so few places where it is relatively easy to assemble raw materials (because of roads, rivers and railways), to fabricate goods (because of power resources and skilled labor) and to sell them (because of banking and credit facilities and effective demand), it is difficult to see how the average producer's primary aims — to lower costs and increase sales — are likely to be furthered by a "rustication" of manufacturing industries. On the contrary, as Charlotte Leubuscher has reminded us, they are likely to be frustrated more than furthered by such a policy. "While hardly ever can the location of an industry be traced to a single factor, there is a growing tendency towards moving industries nearer to the market of the manufactured goods." This, she says, is explained "by the increasing specialisation in manufacture and differentiation in consumption and by the growing proportional importance of distribution costs resulting from it, as well as by the better assessment of the market which proximity allows." [17]

However, this does not mean that the African will forever remain on the periphery of the buyer's market, a man of few wants and in no particular hurry to satisfy them. Hundreds of thousands of Africans have already settled for the white man's juju, his sewing machines, suits,

[17] *The Processing of Colonial Raw Materials: A Study in Location,* H.M.S.O., London, 1951, p. 180.

bicycles, radios, watches, medicines and contraceptives, and have decided that while these things may not always work any better than their own brands of magic, and take more understanding and paying for, they have their uses. Given time and tutelage, all the peoples of Africa will assuredly come to see their uses. The African's motivations, after all, are those of the rest of mankind: fear of ill-health, danger, loneliness, ostracism; love of home and family; and desire for leisure, prestige and power. The enterprisers and advertisers can be relied on to see to it that his motivations are duly exploited. Their own incentives for doing so are obvious: unless he has wants, he will not work in their factories, mines and plantations; unless he has money, he cannot buy their wares.

The "Colonial" Problem

In large parts of tropical Africa the helm is still a long way from the bridge. Much of the economic navigating is therefore done by remote control. Even such independent territories as Liberia and Ethiopia are not wholly free to chart their own courses; without American and, to a lesser extent, European help, their economies would not long remain on an even keel. In some territories the overseas direction continues to be substantial, we might almost say total. In Portuguese Africa, for instance, most matters relating to the development of the local economy are still referred to Lisbon, and most policy decisions are made by Portuguese officials. The private businessman is welcome, but he is subject to direction, even correction. In many other territories, the metropolitan hold on the economy is less firm. In places like Kenya and the Federation of Rhodesia and Nyasaland, it is barely perceptible. Their tax concessions to industry, their trading restrictions and tariffs are of their own devising — more or less.

But if the traditional concept of the colonial bond, as a *quid pro quo* arrangement whereby the mother country gives protection in return for "room and board," is changing — and it is — some by-products of it continue to be important. One of these is the continuing desire of metropolitan manufacturers to have access to cheap raw materials of which the colonies have been big providers and which have enabled them to stay in the export business, often against all comers. In his paper on Angola written for this study, Cecil Scott points out the kind of anomaly — or, as some would have it, injustice — to which this leads:

> Farmers have been prevented from obtaining the full benefit of the rise in world prices by government decree obliging them to sell a percentage of their crops to Portugal at lower rates. This percentage varies according to the crop and from year to year. There is no reciprocal benefit, by way of lower prices for goods imported from Portugal. Thus, in the ten-year period between 1939 and 1949 the cost of cotton textiles increased by 224 per cent, whereas that of raw cotton went up by only 61 per cent. In spite of this, cotton planters were obliged to send 100 per cent of their exports to the mother country.

Another by-product of the tradition was a rather leisurely and uphol-stered approach to the business of living. To get almost anybody, other than missionaries, to make a career in the African tropics in the early days of the colonial epoch it was deemed necessary to offer not only good salaries, but long and frequent furloughs, first-class passage, free medical attention and early pensions. No doubt it was necessary to offer "fringe benefits" of this type in a world sans antibiotics, sans airplanes, sans ice-boxes, sans everything save courage and dedication. But habits once formed are hard to break. Most business and government establishments, consequently, still go in strongly for such benefits — along with, in many cases, free education, free accommodation and free fun. If these things continue to be necessary to attract and keep the right people in the manu-facturing industry, then it is obvious that sooner or later the cost of pro-viding them will have to be passed on to the consumer. They cannot for-ever be paid for by the African's cheap labor. African rates of pay are already rising, in some cases quite sharply,[18] and with them the living standards of many Africans in industrial employment. In time, they will demand many more of the "European" amenities for themselves and their children.[19] To the usual factors in the cost equation, therefore, the in-tending manufacturer must frequently add — to use the naval phrase — a hard-lying allowance.

The Capital Problem

It would be foolish, certainly, in the light of the foregoing analysis, to belittle the problem of persuading investors that the African tropics are healthy for manufacturing industry. So long as the prudent company can look for a painless 10, perhaps even a 15 per cent return on money put into mineral or manufacturing developments in the Americas, he is unlikely to be interested in putting it in places which run up large bills for man-agement, plant maintenance, labor recruitment, training and housing, services and taxes, where corporations live in a symbiotic relationship with governments which some day may terminate that relationship in their favor. So long as the metropolitan countries have to underwrite expensive defense schemes at home and develop export markets outside the sterling area, they, too, are unlikely to devote scarce money to the purpose of increasing the output of manufactured commodities that al-ready move slowly. And, with some notable exceptions, the African is as yet in no position to undertake his own industrial financing. Although many Africans earn extremely good money, some of which they are in the habit of putting into savings banks to accrue interest, the extended family system makes saving difficult for most of them. As Harrison Church

---

[18] See pp. 598ff.
[19] Be it said to their credit, many of the mining and plantation companies have anticipated the demand.

reminds us, "In a polygamous family there are many relatives, and the tradition of family aid is strong . . . The calls on the pocket of the wage earner are especially numerous if, during his apprenticeship, he was helped by family loans."

Serious though these problems are, they need occasion no distress. What has been done already can no doubt be done again, and on a bigger, more effective scale. Indeed, as we have seen, industrial expansion is taking place with startling rapidity in more than one territory in more than one category of goods. Doubtless it will go on doing so as more Africans become more interested in "things," and either more willing to work for them or better able to buy them, or both. But it will be a long time before the average African ceases to be a producer of agricultural goods; and talk of an African industrial revolution on the European or North American scale is an extravagance while the agricultural productivity of the average African remains low and almost stationary. So long as it does, the market for manufactures must remain small, and its rate of expansion slow; in such circumstances the employment of a large number of people in manufacturing is possible only with the help of large subsidies. Similarly, because low-income farmers can provide capital only by dint of depressing their already low standard of living, the financing of manufacturing industry must remain dependent on foreign capital and, in large amounts, it can be attracted only on unfavorable terms. A low and almost stationary output means also that there is little chance of decreasing the size of the agricultural labor corps, and without this all plans for a rapid industrialization must collapse, since labor is already far from plentiful in many places.

It cannot be very far wrong, therefore, to conclude that the key to the industrial future of tropical Africa lies not so much in the mines, the rivers or the plantations — or even in the rising purchasing power of the doctors, teachers, truck drivers and other select groups — as in the fields and on the grazing lands, and in what the millions of Africans who tend them make of them. What they do make of them will depend as much, probably, on what they feel is socially acceptable as on what is economically possible. As Malthus observed long ago:

. . . the powers of production, to whatever extent they may exist, are not alone sufficient to secure the creation of a proportionate degree of wealth. Something else seems to be necessary in order to call these powers fully into action . . . Unless the estimation in which an object is held, or the value which an individual, or the society places on it when obtained, adequately compensates the sacrifice which has been made to obtain it, such wealth will not be produced in future.[20]

[20] Thomas R. Malthus, *Principles of Political Economy*, William Pickering, London, second edition, 1836, p. 361 (London School of Economics reprint, 1936).

CHAPTER 11

The Changing Route Map

FACTORS IN THE DEVELOPMENT
OF TRANSPORTATION SERVICES

RAILROADS

THE INLAND WATERWAYS

PORTS AND OCEAN SHIPPING

ROADS

AIRWAYS

THE TREND

THE business of getting about, and moving things about, has never been an easy one in tropical Africa. In many places and for most people it has long been extremely hard. Neither the waters nor the land were made for easy movement. Enemies, both men and beasts, and disease; ignorance and fear; language barriers — all these stood in the way. Yet many Africans were doing a quite remarkable amount of moving about and carrying before the European arrived.

Most of the moving about was done on foot, and most of the carrying on the head or back, since the use of animals for lading and hauling was ruled out in many areas by the tsetse fly. Exactly how many people and how much merchandise were involved in this traffic we have no means of knowing, but the figures were certainly not small. For a time, in the closing years of the eighteenth century, the ships engaged in the west African slave trade had cargo space for approximately 100,000 slaves; and as late as the 1850s, 15,000 slaves a year were sold in the Zanzibar market alone. Around 1860 not less than 500,000 caravan porters were passing annually through the single Arab trading center of Tabora in Tanganyika. If only one in three of them carried loads, at the standard rate of 50 to 60 pounds a man, they would have been hauling between 4,000 and 5,000 tons of freight a year. Before the end of the nineteenth century people were traveling the length and breadth of tropical Africa along paths beaten out of the bush by human feet, slave and free.

Today, amid all the talk of a transport revolution in Africa, it is easy to forget that the major thoroughfares are still these paths. Indeed, it is probable that more people use the paths of Africa today, and use them more often and for greater distances, than at any previous time. It is probable also that these paths carry more freight than they ever did before the roads and railways came. There is hardly an "African" commodity that does not begin or end its journey on a path. Here it is cocoa or coffee; there, cotton or manioc; elsewhere, cashew or kola nuts; and almost everywhere, cooking pots and cupboards, fruit and firewood, salt and sewing machines. It is the women who do most of the carrying, and many of them seemingly make light of loads that a six-foot American male would have difficulty in lifting off the ground. Some of them habitually carry burdens of up to a hundredweight, for hours on end.

Nor are these paths in any danger of being swallowed up by the bush. They may be formless and unplanned, but they are friendly and serviceable, linking family with hamlet, hamlet with village, and village with town. They may be narrow and ungraded, but as a rule they are cool and shady, easy on the foot traveler, and by no means hard on the cyclist. They cost next to nothing to make or maintain; they can go almost anywhere, and they take almost anything the African is able to buy. They are, in fact, very well adapted to most of his present needs.

To say this is not to belittle the place of the highway, railway, airline or waterway in the transportation net of tropical Africa, or to suggest that the African has no need of such things. On the contrary, their place is yearly becoming more important and the need of them more clamant. Yet it is well to underline the continuing strength and utility of some traditional African ways of doing things, which the modern planner is liable to forget in his preoccupation with the task of pushing "civilizing" concrete, steel, brick and stone into every likely nook and cranny.

FACTORS IN THE DEVELOPMENT OF TRANSPORTATION SERVICES

The company or government that seeks to develop any kind of transportation service in tropical Africa quickly finds itself faced with considerations of more than usual variety and perplexity.

Physical

To start with, the developing agency must face the fact that few of the physical circumstances of the country are in its favor, any more than they were in favor of the traveling African of precolonial days. Rivers that suffer from a markedly seasonal flow, to say nothing of shoals, shifting channels, cataracts and falls, hold no greater attraction for the operator of steamboats than of dugout canoes. Coasts devoid of shelter and exposed to heavy surf may not be greatly feared by the cargo ship owner, but neither are they greatly loved. Offshore lightering and the building of breakwaters are expensive and reduce, sometimes eliminate, profits.

As for the rain forest, its prodigal rains and vegetation can be more of a disability to the man who builds a road than to the man who "builds" a path. A storm can wash a road away in a night; a fallen tree can block it for hours, perhaps days, on end. Sooner or later most motorists in the rain forest have the disagreeable experience of narrowly missing death from the falling of an overaged giant across their path. (Some have had the even more disagreeable experience of not missing it.) In the savannas the road user must reckon on alternating seasons of mud and dust, unless he is lucky enough to be motoring on an all-weather surface. In the deserts he must be prepared for heavy wear and tear on all mechanical equipment, for the necessity of carrying emergency supplies of all kinds with a consequent reduction of pay load, and for the occasional flash flood.

The railway builder and operator must make still more generous provision for exigencies of this kind, as the cost of railway accidents, whether in money or prestige, comes very high; a poorly constructed culvert, a flood-weakened bridge or an unreported landslide can wreck more than a train.

Most curbing of all perhaps are the physical circumstances faced by the company which seeks to run an airline. The storms that can wreck a train with their floods can overturn a plane with their turbulence. Airlines know better than to schedule any but long-distance, high-altitude flights at night, when the storms cannot easily be seen and are often at their worst. Because of the torrential rains of the forest belt the only satisfactory ground facilities, such as concrete or tarmac runways, are those that are costly to build and maintain. Because of the high temperatures and high humidity characteristic of the same belt, plane equipment must be sealed against heat and moisture and often air-conditioned. For flights over the deserts and in the dry season it must also be sealed against the dust which sometimes rises 15,000 feet into the air. And because of the thin air of the high plateaus of east and central Africa, where much of the airline business is located, the pay load with which a plane may take off is substantially lower than that it would be permitted to have at sea level. In some areas the pay load is also reduced by the necessity for carrying emergency stores of food and water in case of a forced landing.

Economic

The economic factors that must be taken into account by the transportation planner are no less important. Predominant among them are factors relating to costs. These are a compound of many ingredients, of which perhaps the most sizable are materials, labor and servicing, wear and wastage, the quality of service offered and the availability of return loads.

By now it may be taken as axiomatic that the building of a road, railway, port or airfield in tropical Africa costs as much as, if not more than, it does in most other parts of the world; and that it costs more than its sponsors said it would. Almost everything needed for it has to be brought in from a distance — all the mechanical equipment, much of the raw material (the steel and concrete, for example), the food supply and housing facilities, and also the capital, for not many governments or companies are able to finance such projects locally. All of this is expensive.

European (expatriate) labor is expensive because it has to be wooed away from work that can be done in more congenial surroundings, and the only way to do this is by offering special inducements. African (local) labor is expensive because its output is generally low, its quality frequently indifferent and its need of supervision well above the average; furthermore, it frequently has to be recruited at some distance from the place where it is needed.

Expenses for depreciation are high. The life expectation of a bus in Nyasaland is only about half of what it is in the United Kingdom — eight years as against fifteen or so; and during that time it is likely to be out of service more often than a British bus. While Africans have taken well to driving trains, trucks and steamboats, they have in most cases yet to show the same interest in looking after them. It is still uncommon to find a good repair man, let alone a man who is capable of keeping things from going wrong.

There are other kinds of wastage that come high in price, such as roads, ports, airfields and railways built in the wrong places, or at the wrong time. Among the more recent instances of this kind of thing was the building in the years following World War II of the "peanut" port of Mtwara and its feeder railway to Nachingwea in southern Tanganyika. It is likely to be several years before either does half the business its planners expected of it. Some years earlier, it was found necessary to realign the railway between Sekondi and Kumasi in Ghana at a cost almost equal to the original construction cost.

A no less important factor in the cost equation is the quality of the service provided, itself a compound of several factors, notably timing, flexibility and hazard. The quality factor is especially important for freight shippers. Since the physical transportation of freight forms only part of the service of distribution, the use of the "cheapest" means of transportation does not necessarily result in the most satisfactory kind of distribution, which — to employ the words of the trade — is the kind that puts "the right goods in the right place at the right time." And the right time is when the goods are wanted. Commercially this coincides with the time when the reward for efficient distribution is at its highest. To gather this peak reward the merchant must be able not only to forecast the occurrence and size of the peak demand, but also to have the goods on hand when the demand comes. The timing of transport operations is therefore a matter of great concern both to the merchant and to the community. It follows that the cost of transportation can rarely be considered separately from the accuracy of its timing.

But timing is still more of an art than a science, and one that takes long to acquire. It is, furthermore, an art in which even the experts can give an amateurish performance — and one in which before now the amateurs have outclassed the experts. In tropical Africa there are still no experts in such matters, for the country is commercially very young, but some of the amateurs are doing pretty well. For instance, in 1951, an enterprising Nigerian company decided that it would pay to "air lift" groceries, such as tea and sugar, and other items of wide appeal to a city (Fort Lamy, near Lake Chad) which was temporarily cut off by high floodwaters. During the course of a three-month period the company flew in a thousand tons of such goods, to its very evident advantage and that of the city.

This, of course, may rightly be taken to be a testimony as much to the importance of flexibility as of timing. Increasingly, in tropical Africa as elsewhere in the world, shippers of freight are becoming impressed by the importance of flexibility. The greater the flexibility, the greater the proportion of operating time the goods spend in traveling and the smaller the proportion spent in waiting to be loaded and unloaded. But the most flexible types of vehicles, such as trucks and airplanes, are generally the most expensive. While expense may not greatly matter in the shipment of articles of high value and small bulk, such as precious metals, engine parts, ladies' wear and phonograph records, it matters enormously in the shipment of things like cement and peanuts and, under normal circumstances, of things like tea and sugar as well. Not the least of the transporter's everyday problems is to determine the point at which the advantages of speed and convenience are canceled out by the disadvantages of cost and hazard. Each medium of transport — rail, road, air and water — has its own critical point.

An excellent illustration of the importance attached nowadays to the flexibility factor is provided by the practice of the United Africa Company in using motor vehicles rather than trains on its west African oil palm plantations. Its reasons for doing so have been stated as follows:

It is largely a matter of time: speed in loading and unloading, acceleration, deceleration — in short, the greatest possible movement during operating time. One of the chief aims of the plantation manager is to sterilize the palm fruit as soon as possible after picking. At one extreme, each fruit bunch as it is cut down could, if necessary, be rushed to the sterilizing plant without any delay whatsoever. At the other extreme, the whole of a day's fruit harvest could be loaded on to a single railway or road train serving all parts of the plantation. The first method would be absurdly expensive in transport costs; the second might be the cheapest form of transport, but it would result in inferior production since the first bunches picked would not be sterilized at the mill until the end of the day. A mean must be struck between these two impossible alternatives. The fruit must be brought to the right place (the mill) at the right time (before deterioration sets in), at the right cost.

The size and power of the transport vehicle are material factors. Current experience suggests that the method best suited to combine the right timing with the right cost in oil palm plantations is road transport, using 5-ton tipping lorries (without trailers) developing in the neighbourhood of 80 brake horse power.[1]

The third "quality" factor, hazard, is frequently the most critical. Delays can be inconvenient, even costly, but they are most unlikely to be as inconvenient or as costly as damage. In tropical Africa things in transit damage rather easily, from cement that gets wet and peanuts that go moldy to bricks that arrive broken and meat that spoils. The most flexible and "timely" services, unfortunately, are not always those with the highest safety ratings. On the contrary. Trucks, generally speaking, offer the most flexible and timely services, but they have an appallingly bad safety rating in many parts of the region — which may help to explain why their operators often display large notices invoking the help of Providence. Resolving the comparative importance of such hazards in the various media of transportation open to him, and in relation to the other two "quality" factors, keeps many a shipper working overtime.

Perhaps the most important single factor in the cost equation is the availability of return loads. It is an important factor whether the "vehicle" is a woman's head, a canoe, a bicycle, a truck, a steamer, a train or an airplane. It is also one of the most intractable. If a return load does not exist, there is nothing much anybody can do about it; to wait around until one turns up can be more costly than to make the return trip without one. If a return load does exist, it may not be suited to the type of vehicle. To take an obvious case: flatcars and trailers used for bringing hardwood lumber down to the coasts of west and equatorial Africa are clearly not suited to the carrying of gasoline or chinaware upcountry. Even if a return load of the right kind is available, there is only a slim chance that it will be available when needed and take up the right amount of space. In many parts of tropical Africa, freight movements tend to be extremely lopsided. The produce that leaves a given area is generally much greater in bulk, though not necessarily in value, than the merchandise that enters it. In the twenty-year period 1933-1952 the excess of exports over imports in the foreign trade of Nigeria was more than 19 million tons, or only about 25 per cent less than the total import tonnage.

Often the inequality of internal commodity movements is even more

----

[1] *Statistical and Economic Review* (United Africa Company Limited, London), September 1954, pp. 22-23.

marked than that suggested by the gross foreign trade tonnage. This is
the case, for instance, in those territories where a large proportion of the
people and most of the wealth are concentrated at or near the coast, such
as Ghana and Nigeria. The coastal localities naturally tend to be bigger
consumers of imports than the less densely peopled and less prosperous
upcountry localities. Their contribution to the export market, on the
other hand, is seldom proportionately bigger, because many of their inhabitants are "nonproductive" workers in government and commerce, a
circumstance that serves to increase the gap between inbound and outbound tonnages and so to aggravate the shipper's problem of finding
return pay loads.

In the absence of return freight loads it is sometimes possible for shippers to use their empty space for the carriage of passengers. And, provided the price is right, there are always plenty of people willing to
travel, seats or no seats. While some of them — the migrants — are just
one-way travelers, most of them are on a two-way trip. From this it might
be supposed that, in "riding rough," they were merely filling up one
vehicle to empty another, and doubtless this is sometimes the case. Frequently, however, the passengers travel back as "supplementary freight"
in a vehicle already loaded to capacity. This may not be good for the
vehicle, but it saves the operator, or somebody else, the trouble and expense of running additional carriers that are empty half the time; and
since it is easy on the pocket, the passengers seldom complain.

The still very low average per capita income of the employed African
worker is a factor all transport planners must reckon with. In some
territories it is not much more than $50 a year; in few is it more than $150.
This does not leave much of a margin even for cut-price travel on a truck,
and most Africans accordingly still do most of their traveling on foot.
But with real incomes rising all over tropical Africa the outlook for the
transport operator is anything but dismal. Nobody has to "sell" the
African on travel, or on the advantages of shipping his produce and
merchandise by modern means. A visit to the massive bus terminals of
Accra, Dakar, Lagos and a dozen other west African towns provides convincing evidence of the growing use being made of motor transport, even
by the "small man." Nor is he reluctant to spend money, when he has it,
traveling in style, for this begets prestige and puts him on an equality, in
the eyes of the beholder, with the Europeans in his land. In the Gezira
region of the Republic of Sudan, when the money is good, cotton growers
think nothing of going by taxi to Khartoum, a hundred miles away, for a
day's shopping or visiting. On the Congo-Océan Railway in the Republic
of the Congo, it is not uncommon to see almost as many Africans riding
first class as third class. The first-class seats in the buses of Nyasaland are
also well patronized by Africans when the money is good. Some of the air
services in west Africa are now used as much by Africans as they are by

Europeans. Nevertheless, the density of traffic and the returns remain low by modern operating standards.

In many sections the operators' troubles are frequently compounded by the marked cyclical nature of traffic. The cycles are of two kinds. First, there is the "cash" cycle. Because most Africans still live from hand to mouth they tend to do most of their local traveling around pay-day. As paydays in the larger enterprises occur only once or twice a month, many of the bus and train companies are called upon to carry vastly more traffic at such times than at others. Second, there is the "crop" cycle. Notwithstanding the absence of well-marked thermal seasons, there is, in most parts of tropical Africa, a recognized time to sow and a recognized time to reap. This is particularly true of those areas with a seasonal rainfall regime and where, in the absence of irrigation, crops must be raised in the rainy months. Though not all of the crops will ripen at the same moment, the spread is seldom very great. Few crops are any the better for being stockpiled in the farmyard; and some, such as cotton and tobacco, quickly become the worse for it. So it comes about that almost all of the heavy demand by farmers for freight space on truck and train occurs during the dry season, and that the shorter the dry season, the more concentrated the demand, since with the onset of the next rains, the farmer needs to give his attention to other matters. In some territories passenger services feel the incidence of this crop cycle almost as much as freight services. The Nyasaland (Bus) Transportation Company, for instance, takes in as much as three quarters of its yearly revenue during the six months June through November, the main cropping season. Its revenue in September, the peak of the season, is often more than twice what it is just before the season starts.

Social and Political

Some other factors also have to be borne in mind by planners and operators of transportation services. Among these are group habits and attitudes, ethical standards, government policy and nationalism.

Group habits and attitudes obviously need to be studied by anyone planning to run a passenger bus service in a multiracial community, for it cannot always be assumed that, because the people need such a service and have the money to use it, they will do so in sufficient numbers to warrant its capitalization. This may be a fair assumption for such cities as Lourenço Marques and Luanda, where Europeans work and mix fairly readily with the Africans and where the standard of living of the European is not very much higher than in Portugal. It would not be a fair assumption, however, for such cities as Nairobi and Salisbury. There almost every European seems to think that a car is as essential for getting about as a suit of clothes, and consequently is seldom seen without one. Even the newly arrived immigrants, not many of whom had cars of their own or could have managed without buses in the old country, quickly fall into this way of thinking. Nor should the planner exclude from his reckoning the possibility that the Africans in a multiracial community may, from time to time, decide that they, too, can manage without buses. Very effective bus boycotts have on occasion been organized in some of the larger cities.

On the delicate question of ethical standards it need only be said that there is a widespread feeling they need lifting -- a feeling not confined to those who do business in tropical Africa, of course. While the experience of individual companies differs considerably, it is impossible to travel far without discovering that many transportation companies are concerned about the toll which thefts of money and stores take of their net incomes. Such companies still refuse on that account to allow Africans to serve either as storekeepers or as ticket agents and inspectors.

The part played by governments in developing transportation services has varied both in time and place. In territories like Liberia there was no government policy until quite recently and, perhaps as a consequence, no modern means of transportation. Even today what means of transportation exist in Liberia are largely the gift of private corporations. Mostly, however, the initiative in such matters has come from governments. It is government money, legislation and survey work that has made possible most of the railways and highways and almost all of the airfields in tropical Africa; without it there would have been next to none.

But although indispensable to the development of such facilities, governments seldom strike their critics as being indispensable to the running of them; or if indispensable, at least not unexceptionable. If the tariffs are not exorbitant (and they are often considered to be), the chances are that the rolling stock is inadequate, or the service is too slow, too infrequent and too irregular, or the spoilage of goods is excessive. Here and there, the governments' role has been unpopular for an additional reason. Faced with high capital and operating costs and needing every passenger and pound of freight their railways could carry, some governments have put almost penal restrictions on anybody who sought to provide an alternative transportation service by road or river or other means. At one time vehicles operating in Nigeria on roads parallel to the railway had to pay double the ordinary rate of road tax. In Ghana "there were even instances of the removal of road bridges over rivers, which — whether that was the intention or not — effectively discouraged the use of the roads for the transport of goods." [2] Elsewhere, where government-controlled railways have discovered that they could not "lick" their competitors, they have sometimes bought them out, thereby restoring the monopolistic *status quo*.

With the rise of African nationalism in recent years a new factor has

[2] See *ibid.*, p. 16.

been added. The world over, investors are interested as much in matters of security and "recovery" as they are in matters of yield. Remembering what has happened elsewhere in the world when nations have slipped their colonial moorings, some investors are more than a little cool toward the idea of putting new money into long-term African transportation projects. Confidence in the future of such projects is not generated by talk of expropriation and "Africa for the Africans," or by disclosures of lack of efficiency and integrity in the handling of public moneys.

It is clear, then, that the development of modern transportation services in tropical Africa poses plenty of problems — enough, some might feel, to discourage the most courageous of men from tackling the job. But the truth is that the region already abounds in monuments to the ability of men to solve even the toughest of problems when they have to, and that not the least of these monuments are its railroads, highways, ports and airways.

RAILROADS

The long-delayed European penetration of the interior of Africa took place at a time when the railroad was still regarded as the logical and almost the only means of bringing law and order to a raw country, of opening it up to the missionary, the administrator, the prospector and the settler, and of making its resources available to the outside world. For in 1885, the year that marks the real beginning of railroading in tropical Africa,[3] there were few paved roads in the world, no "Tin Lizzies," trucks or trailers, and no airplanes. Had the penetration been delayed yet another thirty years or so, the great age of rail would have been nearing its end, and the story would have been rather different. By the end of World War I, the auto was already beginning to challenge the supremacy of the "iron horse on civilizing rails" in the minds of men. By the 1930s, the challenge was beginning to be apparent on the ground as well. More roads were being built than railways, and only those railways were being built that were regarded as having exceptional commercial promise.

As the map (Figure 27) shows, the major railroads of tropical Africa may be grouped conveniently under the following regional headings: (1) west Africa, (2) Congo basin and margins, (3) central Africa, (4) the Malagasy Republic, (5) east Africa and (6) northeast Africa (including the upper Nile valley).

[3] An abortive attempt to build a railroad along the Nile valley south of Wadi Halfa had been made ten years earlier.

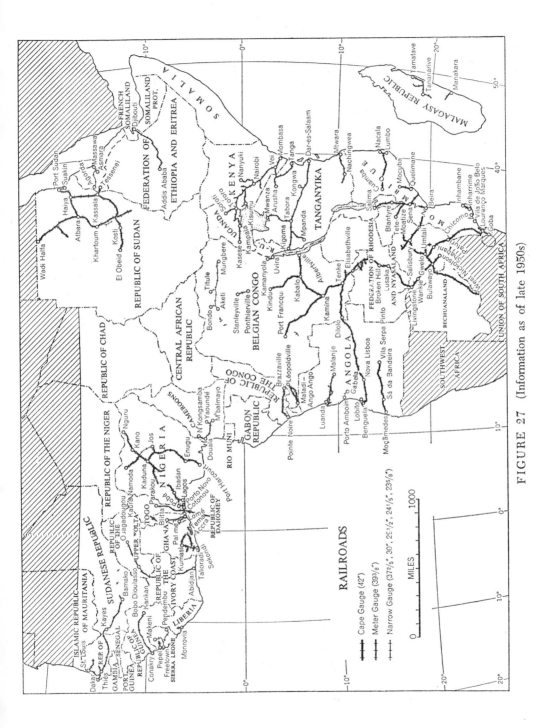

FIGURE 27 (Information as of late 1950s)

WEST AFRICA

The French Community and the Republic of Guinea

The meter-gauge line connecting Dakar with the Senegal River port of St. Louis was the first railroad to go into service in tropical Africa. Its main intended function was military, for there were at that time (1885) still many unpacified tribes in the immediate hinterland of the coast.

To extend their sphere of effective control, the French began about the same time to build a line from Médine, at the head of barge navigation on the Senegal River to Koulikoro, beyond Bamako on the Niger. It was not completed until 1906.

In the following year, work was begun on a line that would obviate the necessity of using the Senegal River — highly seasonal in its flow — as a link in the Dakar-Niger transportation chain. By linking Kayes on the Médine-Koulikoro line with Thiés on the Dakar–St. Louis line, it made the navigable central Niger valley a part of the economic watershed of Dakar. Since it was opened in 1923 a number of small spurs have been added near the western end of the line, for the purpose of tapping the important agricultural areas located in the vicinity of Dakar.

No other part of this west African region has seen as much railroad building. All that the map of the other French and formerly French territories shows today is a number of rail tentacles that insinuate themselves inland at several points along the coast without ever seeming to find their mark.

Going from west to east, these meter-gauge tentacles are as follows:

Conakry-Kankan. From the engineering standpoint this is the most remarkable of all west African lines, for it crosses the dissected, wet and forested Fouta Djallon mountain system.

Abidjan-Ouagadougou. Although begun in 1903, this line did not reach Bobo Dioulasso until 1934 and Ouagadougou until 1955. From time to time there has been talk of extending it northwestward beyond Bobo Dioulasso toward Ségou in the upper Niger valley.

Lomé-Anécho, Lomé-Palime, Lomé-Blitta. The first two tentacles of this three-tentacle system were built by the German Togoland administration in the early years of the present century for the purpose of opening up the rich hinterland of Lomé, the territory's capital and major port. The third, and longest, tentacle was built for strategic reasons. Without it the Germans could not hope to hold the interior of their colony in the event of war, for they were flanked by the British on the west and the French on the east. In their day the line went only as far as Atakpamé; after it came under French control it was extended to Blitta.

Cotonou-Parakou. Begun in 1900, the line reached its present terminus only in 1934. If it is someday continued to Malanville (a distance of over 250 miles by road), the name by which the line has long been known — the Benin-Niger — will at last be founded on fact.

Porto Novo–Pobé. This little line was begun in 1907 and finished in 1913. Later, in 1930, a tie line was added between Porto Novo, the capital of Dahomey, and Cotonou, its major port.

Since World War II the most important of these railway lines have been extensively refurbished; tracks and roadbeds have been improved, better rolling stock has been brought into service, wood- and coal-burning locomotives have been replaced by diesel and diesel electric engines and railway cars. Most of the funds for this modernization program were provided by FIDES (Fonds d'Investissement pour le Développement Economique et Social) and the Caisse Centrale de la France d'Outre-Mer.

The French Cameroons

When, following World War I, the former German colony of Kamerun was divided into two mandated areas, one administered by France and the other by Great Britain, France got the part with the railways. These consisted of two meter-gauge lines: the Northern Railway, built between 1906 and 1911; and the Central Railway, built between 1910 and 1914. The Northern Railway, which runs from Bonaberi, across the Cameroons River from Douala, to N'Kongsamba, roughly a hundred miles to the north, through the difficult but fertile foothill country of the Cameroon Highlands, was built to serve the needs of the German planters (mainly coffee) and was the only privately owned railway in the German colonial empire. The Central Railway had its origin in the desire of the German authorities to link Douala with the Lake Chad area, but when the German occupation ended it had only reached Eseka. The French realigned the last few miles and carried it forward to its present terminus, Yaoundé, the capital of the country, in 1927; they also added a short branch line from Otellé to M'Balmayo on the navigable Nyong River.

Commonwealth West Africa

The railway systems of this region broadly follow the habit of the French lines, which is to say, they are "dead-end" lines. At their smallest the systems consist of single tentacles; at their largest, of several ramifying tentacles. In almost every case the base of the tentacle is a coastal port, and its extremity an inland town of commercial or mining importance. None of the systems is linked with those in neighboring territories; none so much as crosses a frontier. Each exists to serve fairly specific territorial needs and the main axis of each runs more or less at right angles to its piece of coastline.

Sierra Leone has two railway systems — one, the larger, government owned, the other owned by a private iron-mining company, the Sierra Leone Development Company Limited.

The government railway, which runs from Freetown to Pendembu with a branch from Bauya to Makeni, was built a bit at a time between 1895 and 1915. To make construction as cheap as possible and to prevent the possibility of its being linked up with a line in the adjacent French territory, a narrow, 30-inch gauge was chosen.

Over the years it has played an important economic and administrative role, but not even its best friends are convinced that it has much of a future, as it stands. Its capacity is, by modern railroaders' standards, small to the point of being uneconomic. Part of its rolling stock is antiquated. All its schedules are slow; the express passenger train that runs between Freetown and Pendembu averages 18 miles an hour — when on time. Some of the railway's numerous critics are of the opinion that Mr. Emett, whose railway caricatures enlivened the pages of *Punch* for many years, got his ideas from Sierra Leone; others incline to the converse of this opinion. And every year sees it facing stronger competition from autos and trucks and, along the southern waterways, from launches.

The iron company's line, which was opened in 1933, has a 42-inch (Cape) gauge. It runs between the mine at Lunsar in the Marampa iron field and the loading port of Pepel on the Sierra Leone River, about 14 miles upstream from Freetown. There is talk of extending the line inland if and when the company decides to develop its concession in the northern part of the Tonkolili district.

In proportion to its size, *Ghana* is less well supplied with railways than either Sierra Leone or Nigeria. Its only railways are in the southern third of the country, and as of 1958 had less than 600 route miles of track. The starting point of the system was the port of Sekondi, from which a line was built, first to Tarkwa — a gold-mining region — in 1901, and then, in 1903, to Kumasi, the capital of the newly created Ashanti Protectorate. Later some small branch lines were added to aid the opening up of nearby mineralized areas, and part of the main Kumasi line was realigned to favor the new and much more satisfactorily situated port of Takoradi, three miles to the west of Sekondi. A second line, linking the capital city and surf port of Accra with Kumasi and so, circuitously, with Takoradi, was built by very easy stages between 1908 and 1923. A third line, the Central Province line, was opened in 1928; this runs northeast from a point on the main Takoradi-Kumasi railway north of Tarkwa to Kade. Its extension between 1954 and 1956 to Kotoku on the Accra-Kumasi line cut the rail distance between Takoradi and Accra by almost half. During the same period the new seaport of Tema was linked by rail to Accra and the section between Tarkwa and Takoradi was double-tracked to ease the congestion of freight traffic (mostly minerals, cocoa and hardwood timbers) moving southward along the main and branch lines to Takoradi.

A railroad to serve the Northern Region has been talked about, off and on, for forty years. But the chances of its ever materializing are now considered to be negligible, for today practically every Ghanaian commodity can be transported competitively by road.

Nigeria, one of the largest territories in tropical Africa, and the most populous, is served by nearly 2,000 route miles of rail, most of it on Cape gauge. Although by European and American standards this represents a very low mileage-to-area ratio, the system does cover most of the economically important regions of the country, which is more than can be said for those of its neighbors. Only the mountainous southeastern and semi-arid northeastern areas of the country, and the United Nations Trust Territory of the British Cameroons (which is administered as an integral part of Nigeria), are not served by it.

The start of the system was a line, built between 1898 and 1901, linking Lagos with Ibadan. Between 1904 and 1912 the line was carried northward to Kano, via Ilorin and Zaria. Later in the second decade the newly opened tin mines at Jos were linked by a light, 30-inch-gauge railway to Zaria, and the first section of a second north-south railway was opened to traffic. This gave the Enugu coal field direct access to the deep-water harbor of Port Harcourt, at the eastern end of the Niger delta. In 1927, the Port Harcourt–Enugu line was extended to Kaduna on the Lagos-Kano line, and a Cape-gauge line was put through to Jos. Since then only two major additions have been made to the system: a branch line from Zaria to Kaura Namoda, and an extension of the main line from Kano, formerly the terminus, to Nguru. Both of these lines, which were completed by 1930, serve important cash crop farming areas.

Like the other west African railways, those of Nigeria have often been called upon in the past fifteen to twenty years to perform tasks in excess of their prewar strength. Among the more conspicuous evidences of their postwar "underfitness" were the peanut pyramids of Kano. For a while it seemed possible that these pyramids would become as permanent a feature of the skyline as those of Gîza. In its 1954 report on the country, the International Bank for Reconstruction and Development indicated some of the steps that would need to be taken before the railways are equal to their tasks. These included the use of more powerful diesel and diesel electric locomotives, more rolling stock and heavier track, though not, for the time being at least, a double track.

That a country of the size and importance of Nigeria needs additional route mileage is evident. The most urgent need is for a 400-mile line linking Maiduguri, in the extreme northeast of the country, with the Port Harcourt–Kano line at Kuru, near Jos, thereby opening to development the large and still barely tapped agricultural resources of Bauchi and Bornu provinces. The building of this line, authorized in 1956 and financed partly by the International Bank, began in 1958.

Liberia

Until the late 1940s the Republic of Liberia had no railways, and it probably would not have had one then but for the improvements to the port of Monrovia carried out by American contractors under an agreement with the United States Navy in the period 1943-1948. As a result of these improvements, it became possible to consider exploiting, for foreign shipment, the vast iron ore deposits of the nearby Bomi Hills region. Thanks to the Liberia Mining Company Limited this possibility was not long in being realized, for by 1951 the 45-mile railway between the mine and Monrovia was complete and the first ore shipments were being made. In most years since then the line has carried a million or more tons of ore.

THE CONGO BASIN AND MARGINS

It did not take the nineteenth-century explorers long to decide that the Congo basin and its perimeter would never amount to much without railways. These alone, they argued, could tie together the navigable waters of the area into an economically rewarding transportation network. So it came about that almost all of the early lines were in the nature of portages, for the carrying of goods and passengers either around rapids and falls or from one river or lake to another.

The most important of these "portage" lines are the following:

Ango Ango–Léopoldville. The Matadi-Léopoldville section of this Cape-gauge railway [4] was opened to traffic in 1898, its function being to circumvent the 220-mile stretch of rapids between Stanley Pool, the downstream end of the navigable middle Congo, and the head of ocean-going navigation. During World War I, it was extended four miles below Matadi to the river port of Ango Ango, in order to serve vessels that would be endangered by passing through the narrows near Matadi. After the Ten Year Plan for the Belgian Congo came into operation in 1950, some sections of the line were double-tracked and steam power was replaced by diesel electric locomotives. The whole line will be electrified as soon as the necessary hydro-power installations are complete. It is owned by Otraco (Office d'Exploitation des Transports Coloniaux), a government-controlled corporation.

Stanleyville-Ponthierville. As its name implies — Compagnie des Chemins de Fer du Congo Supérieur aux Grands Lacs Africains (CFL) — this portage line was built around the series of rapids and falls culminating in the Stanley Falls to facilitate traffic moving between the lakes of the Rift country of east Africa and the Congo basin. This is still its primary function, for it generates little local traffic. Above Ponthierville the

---

[4] Originally a two-foot six-inch gauge.

Lualaba — as the main stream of the Congo is called in its upper section — is navigable by river steamers as far as Kindu.

Kindu-Kongolo. This, the second link in the CFL chain of railways, was built in order to bypass the rapids-strewn section of the Lualaba between these two points.

Kabalo-Albertville. With the laying (in 1915) of the portage line, also along the Lualaba, from Kabalo to Kalemie (later Albertville), the CFL could claim to have lived up to its name; for this made possible, for passengers and freight alike, scheduled travel between the Atlantic and the great lake of Tanganyika.

Kongolo-Kabalo. The last links in the CFL chain were completed in 1939 with the opening of the railway bridge across the Lualaba at Kongolo and the line from Kongolo to Kabalo. Since then the CFL has operated in two sections: Stanleyville to Ponthierville, and Kindu to Albertville.[5]

Aketi-Bondo. This narrow-gauge, 60-centimeter line, the Vicicongo (short for Société des Chemins de Fer Vicinaux du Congo), runs from the head of navigation (Aketi) on the Itimbiri tributary of the Congo north to Bondo, a small river port on the navigable Uele tributary of the Ubangi River. It is in the center of an agricultural area that has grown steadily in importance since it was opened in 1928. Today branch lines serve the outlying Mungbere coffee and cotton area and the Titule cotton area.

Uvira-Kamanyola. The aim of the builders of this Cape-gauge line was to link Lakes Tanganyika and Kivu, but the link has never been forged; nor is it likely to be, now that there is a hard-topped motor road between Uvira and Bukavu, the line's intended terminus on Lake Kivu.

Important as these tie lines were in helping to give the infant Congo a circulation system, they were not enough to give it the cohesion and strength it needed for the giant-sized task of making its resources available cheaply to a world that needed them in ever larger volume. Nor were they enough to enable the Belgian government to realize its self-appointed task of turning the Belgian Congo "from wilderness to civilization." Consequently, very early in the present century some of the Congo's more farsighted boosters began to urge the building of through lines that would obviate the need for expensive, time-consuming break of bulk. Among these was Robert (later Sir Robert) Williams. His primary ambition was to make a success of a British company — Tanganyika Concessions, Ltd. — which had acquired an interest in the Katanga copper mines. The construction of the two most important railways serving the Congo basin, the BCK (Compagnie du Chemin de Fer du Bas-

---

[5] CFL steamers operate on the lake between Albertville and Kigoma, the western terminus of the Central Line of Tanganyika. They also operate upstream from Kabalo to Bukama, where the main line of the Compagnie du Chemin de Fer du Bas-Congo au Katanga (BCK) crosses the Lualaba.

Congo au Katanga) and the Benguela Railway, was in no small degree due to his initiative.

BCK, which today operates more than 1,500 miles of Cape-gauge railway, was founded in 1906, a time when the "Cape-to-Cairo Railway," brain child of Cecil Rhodes and Robert Williams, was being pushed northward from Lusaka and Broken Hill. In 1909 it reached Sakania on the Katanga border. From here BCK carried it forward to Elisabethville (1910), and later (in 1918) to Bukama, with marked effect on the shipments of copper ore to South African and Mozambique ports. Realizing that it could not hope to match these shipments on existing routes through Belgian Congo territory (that is, down the Lualaba to Kabalo, thence to Albertville, Kigoma and Dar-es-Salaam by way of the Central Line of Tanganyika), BCK decided to push its Bukama line northwestward to Port Francqui on the navigable Kasai. This it did during the years 1923-1928. In this way it acquired an all-Congo route that needed only two transshipments — rail to boat at Port Francqui and boat to rail at Léopoldville — in place of the four needed on the Dar-es-Salaam route. Three years later (1931), BCK completed a line from Tenke, between Elisabethville and Bukama, to Dilolo on the Angolan border, where it linked up with the Benguela Railway. Any disadvantages this western route might have because of its international character were more than compensated for by the fact that it did away with the necessity for break of bulk.

The Benguela Railway had its origins in a company founded by Williams at the beginning of the century. However, it was not until 1914 that agreement was reached with the Belgian government on where it should cross the Angolan–Belgian Congo border, and not until 1927 that it reached Dilolo. Through passenger and freight services between Lobito, its coastal terminus, and Elisabethville have been in operation since 1931. The domestic portion of the Benguela line is over 800 miles long and has its headquarters at Nova Lisboa high up on the healthy Angolan plateau. With the exception of the treeless "thirsty country" of the coastal escarpment, where imported coal had to be used, wood has been the railway's main fuel. But since 1955 a number of oil-burning locomotives have been in service, and it is probably only a matter of time before the entire line comes to rely on oil fuel. While the Belgian Congo makes heavy demands on the railway (over the years it has come to handle most of the heavy freight traffic in and out of Katanga), the Rhodesias continue to ship most of their exports southward, as in the early days of the century.

The advantages of through rail transport continue to be sought wherever they are considered feasible. Among its many other provisions, the Belgian Congo's Ten Year Plan of 1950-1959 provided for (1) the construction of a Cape-gauge [6] line (completed in 1957) linking Bukama

---

[6] The Cape gauge was chosen in order to make it uniform with the gauge of the routes serving the Katanga from the south and west.

directly with Albertville, thereby eliminating the existing break of bulk at Kabalo and the long and slow river haul between these two towns; and (2) the change-over of the whole of the CFL system to the Cape gauge, in the interests of both present efficiency and possible future construction. (The change-over on the Kindu-Albertville line was made in 1955 in a mere ten days.)

With the exception of the short lake crossing from Albertville to Kigoma there is now, therefore, an all-rail connection between Katanga and the Indian Ocean. Whether there will ever be a second all-rail connection between Katanga and the Atlantic Ocean is uncertain. The construction of the "missing link" between Port Francqui and Léopoldville has long been under study, but it would be no easy or inexpensive task. Most of the projected route lies over wet ground subject to seasonal flooding from the Kasai River, many of whose tributaries would need to be bridged at considerable cost. Further, such a line would have to compete with the long-established, efficiently run and comparatively cheap water route between the two towns.

The only other railways in the Congo basin and its margins are the Congo-Océan (CFCO) of the Republic of the Congo, and the Luanda-Malanje, Moçâmedes–Vila Serpa Pinto and Porto Amboim–Gabela lines of Angola.

The Cape-gauge Congo-Océan Railway serves several functions. Like the Léopoldville–Ango Ango line, it links the Congo (at Brazzaville, the present capital of the Republic of the Congo) with the Atlantic (at Pointe Noire), and so carries a good deal of traffic, both passenger and freight. Like the BCK, it hauls minerals that originate along the line. But one of its most important functions is to open up the Niari valley, through part of which it runs; and this it is doing very successfully.[7] The roadbed is one of the smoothest in Africa; the scenery in places is quite spectacular, and on some of the level stretches the streamlined diesel electric trains are able to travel at more than 60 miles an hour.

The construction of a second railroad in the territories formerly known as French Equatorial Africa is expected (1959) to start very shortly. It will link Bangui on the navigable Ubangi River with the important cattle-raising region near Bongor in the Republic of Chad. It is expected to follow the M'Poko and Logone valleys as far as possible.

The three domestic Angolan lines were designed primarily for the purpose of moving goods to and from Atlantic coast ports. The most important of the three is the meter-gauge Luanda-Malanje line. The government, which owns it, is now (1959) extending the line eastward to Lui. Eventually it hopes to continue the line to Portugalia on the Belgian Congo border. The flanking country is high and generally healthy, of increasing agricultural interest, and well mineralized. Also in the

[7] See p. 187.

planning stage is a line that would link Luanda with Uige and later with Nóqui, near Matadi.

Next in importance, but potentially of greater importance, is the now Cape-gauge railway that runs upcountry from the port of Moçâmedes. It is also state-owned. The Huila Plateau which it serves is, according to Cecil Scott in a paper prepared for this study, "one of the few places in Africa where European peasant farmers have been able and willing to use their own labor on the land instead of being dependent on Africans. They have formed a happy and prosperous community here for many generations." The soils are of more durable fertility than most tropical African soils, and the climate, by reason of the elevation (averaging about 4,000 feet), more temperate than tropical. The region is also well endowed with minerals. The government hopes before long to continue this line from Vila Serpa Pinto (to which it has only recently come) to the border of Northern Rhodesia.

The smallest of the three lines runs inland from Porto Amboim. It has a narrow, 60-centimeter gauge, is privately owned, and exists largely to serve the coffee-growing center of Gabela. There is talk of its being extended eastward to Cela, the headquarters of a large government settlement scheme.

CENTRAL AFRICA

The story of railways in central Africa is bound up with the name of the British South Africa Company. Founded in 1889 by Cecil Rhodes, the primary purpose of this company was to bring the lands north of the Limpopo River, with their presumed vast resources, within economic reach of the miner, farmer, forester and merchant. Everybody was agreed that the best way to do this was to push railways into the territory. Even before the century was out, the Cape Railway had been carried northward to Bulawayo, and a line opened between Salisbury and Beira, the most accessible ocean port for the territory controlled by the British South Africa Company. By World War I, the major part of the present central African network had already been built.

The Rhodesias and Bechuanaland

Today, a single system, the Rhodesia Railways, serves these three territories.[8] Bulawayo, the largest railway junction in the entire region, is its headquarters. It is here that the line from the south forks, one fork going north to the Belgian Congo where it joins up with the BCK, the other going northeast to Mozambique. The northern fork serves the

---

[8] Although the section of the "Cape-to-Cairo" line south of Mahalapye, Bechuanaland, is (1959) operated by the South African Railways and Harbours Administration, it is owned (as far as the Union of South Africa border) by the Rhodesia Railways.

Wankie colliery, Victoria Falls–Livingstone, Lusaka (the capital of Northern Rhodesia), Broken Hill and the Copperbelt. The northeastern fork serves the larger towns of the Southern Rhodesian Midlands (Gwelo, Que Que, Gatooma and Salisbury) and, with the help of spur lines, some smaller urban settlements. It ends at the border town of Umtali, where the Mozambique line from Beira comes in. In the absence, as yet, of any tie line between the two forks, traffic between Beira (or Lourenço Marques) and the Copperbelt has to be routed through Bulawayo, thereby enhancing the latter's nodal importance.

All told, the Rhodesia Railways operate about 2,750 route miles of Cape-gauge track. Up to and during World War II, they had no great difficulty in keeping pace with the needs of the territories they served. But they were in no shape to meet the phenomenal (and largely unexpected) postwar expansion of mining, commerce and industry, for they found themselves with a legacy of deferred maintenance on their hands, and a shortage of serviceable equipment, capital and personnel. And when they began to cast around for new equipment, capital and personnel, they had to make their bids in a strongly competitive, and therefore expensive, market. The story of the first ten postwar years was one of trials, if not of errors — and in the opinion of many there were some errors, too. Passenger trains habitually ran behind schedule and not infrequently broke down along the way. Freight trains had neither the tonnage capacity nor the engine power to shift all the traffic offered, with the result that marshalling yards and storage sheds became cluttered with goods that everybody wanted but nobody could have.

Earnest efforts were made to grapple with the problem. In 1946 the system was nationalized. The operational efficiency of almost every major department was increased. Long-range projections were made of tonnages and passenger demands, and purchasing plans laid accordingly. Large sums of scarce money — more than £30 million in all — were found for capital equipment. And the working and living conditions of the company's army of employees (between 8,000 and 9,000 Europeans and 20,000 Africans) were greatly improved.

Thanks to these and similar measures, the Rhodesia Railways were able to report annual increases in every type of traffic. Even so, the performances were not up to the territories' needs, and it became necessary to take more radical measures.

One of the Railways' worst problems in the early postwar years was jamming of traffic on the Beira route. Sometimes this was due to lack of wharfage space and handling gear; sometimes it was due to difficulties on the Mozambique section of the railway, and sometimes to the failure to clear traffic to and from Umtali, the border station. To relieve the pressure on both the port and the Railways, a traffic phasing plan was put into operation in 1949. While it has not always been successful (let alone popular with those importers whose goods, consigned to Beira, were diverted to Durban, or even to Capetown, to keep a jam from forming), it has enabled the port to work more smoothly and the trains to be used to better advantage.

But the fact remained that the Federation of Rhodesia and Nyasaland still had only one handy port through which to channel its import and export trade. Moreover, it was a port that was already cramped and incapable of physical expansion equal to the expected needs of both Mozambique and the Federation. Accordingly, it was decided to build a line, known as the southeast connection, from Bannockburn on the Shabani spur line near Bulawayo to link at Pafuri on the Mozambique border with a line being built from Guijá near Lourenço Marques by the Portuguese authorities. This line, begun in 1952, was opened to traffic on August 1, 1955. For imports in particular, Lourenço Marques provides the Federation with a convenient alternative to Beira and the Union ports.

Among other suggestions for additional railway outlets that have come up repeatedly for discussion are the building of (1) a line about a hundred miles long between West Nicholson, the present terminus of a railway spur running southeast of Bulawayo, and Beitbridge, where a South African Railways branch line giving access to Lourenço Marques terminates; (2) a much longer line westward across Bechuanaland to link the Copperbelt line either with Walvis Bay via the existing railway system of Southwest Africa or with the Moçâmedes–Vila Serpa Pinto line of Angola; (3) a still longer line from Kapiri Mposhi, some 40 miles north of Broken Hill, northeastward across Northern Rhodesia to join one of the existing lines in Tanganyika; and (4) a line from Sinoia northwest of Salisbury to Kafue, south of Lusaka. This line, generally referred to as the Sinoia-Kafue cutoff, would provide a direct connection between the Copperbelt and Beira, reducing the rail mileage between the two by more than 500 miles.

The fact that, notwithstanding all the progress of the postwar years, the performance of the Rhodesia Railways is still open to criticism has given rise to two other possibilities. These are the use of motor trucks to "pick up the slack" if no more; and electrification. That trucks could do it nobody doubts. That the roads and bridges could stand it is very doubtful indeed. And it is equally doubtful if the economy could stand it, for the rates quoted in recent years by road transport operators are anything up to ten times those in force on the railway. As for electrification, it would eliminate the consumption of about a million tons of coal a year. It would greatly ease the watering problem, which is acute along many of the drier sections of the country. On the other hand, the cost would be exceedingly burdensome to a country already carrying a heavy debt load. To electrify the main line completely would, it has been estimated, necessitate an expenditure of probably not less than

£100,000 per route mile. The electrification of the proposed Sinoia-Kafue cutoff alone would cost about £35 million.[9]

For the time being, most people in the Rhodesias seem willing to believe that the nationalized, modernized and expanded Rhodesia Railways system will be able to cope with its responsibilities given, on the one hand, a continued steady flow of investment capital [10] and, on the other, no more delays in deliveries of locomotives and rolling stock, no further difficulties in recruiting staff, and no unexpected increases in the freight demands made upon it.

Nyasaland

The Nyasaland railway system extends from Salima near the southwestern end of Lake Nyasa to Beira and is about 600 route miles long. It is owned by three companies: the Trans-Zambesia Railway, which operates inside Mozambique territory; the Central Africa Railway, which operates across the Mozambique-Nyasaland border; and the Nyasaland Railways, which operates inside Nyasaland. All three lines are on the Cape gauge, and all three are privately owned and administered by one general manager at Limbe in southern Nyasaland. There are no railways at all in the Central and Northern provinces of Nyasaland. Traffic on the system is very small in relation to that carried by the Rhodesia Railways, but it has grown sharply during the postwar years. Freight volume on the Trans-Zambesia Railway, for instance, rose from 176,000 tons in 1945 to almost 850,000 tons in 1957. Comparable increases were reported over the same period by the other two lines. To carry this additional traffic, new locomotives and rolling stock have been brought into service.

Mozambique

Unlike the Rhodesias, Mozambique has nothing that can be dignified by the name of network. Its several separate railway systems are all in the nature of tentacles. The smaller of these tentacles appear to clutch very little; the larger ones reach out from the ports of Beira and Lourenço Marques across their domestic borders to lay their grip on the landlocked territories of Nyasaland, Southern Rhodesia and the Transvaal.

Beira, as we have already seen, is the Federation of Rhodesia and Nyasaland's main port. Most of the business handled by it has to do with

[9] Estimates of Sir Roy Welensky in a speech before the Kafue Valley Regional Development Association in Lusaka, Northern Rhodesia, on April 15, 1955.

[10] In recent years much of this capital has come from United States government agencies. In 1951 a loan of £5 million was made by the Economic Cooperation Administration. In 1954 the Foreign Operations Administration made a loan of the sterling equivalent of $10 million. The International Bank for Reconstruction and Development helped the financing of the southeast connection (Bannockburn to Pafuri) with a $17 million loan.

goods moving to and from the Federation, by way of either the privately owned Trans-Zambesia Railway or the government-owned Beira Railway Company. Lourenço Marques, as we have also seen, is likewise the terminus of two international lines. Of the two, the line to Ressano Garcia, on the Transvaal border, where it joins up with the South African Railways system, is still the more important; it carries a large part of the Transvaal's export of coal, chrome ore and citrus. However, the amount of domestic traffic carried by these four "international" lines is not negligible, and it is growing yearly with the development of the flanking areas. Thus, the fertile Limpopo valley through which the newly completed line from Lourenço Marques to the Southern Rhodesian border passes is now the center (at Guijá) of a large colonization project. And since the completion of the spur lines to the Moatize coal basin at Tete and the Sena sugar estates, the Trans-Zambesia Railway has been doing an increasing shipping business in these commodities.

What is true of the international lines is also true of most of the domestic lines. Going from south to north, these are as follows:

Lourenço Marques–Goba, near the Swaziland border.

Lourenço Marques–Vila Luiza. This line is being extended to Manhiça.

Both of these lines are Cape gauge and government-owned. Much of their revenue is derived from the banana and tourist traffic they carry.

Vila de João Belo–Chicomo. This is a 75-centimeter line serving an expanding timber- and crop-producing community lying near the coast to the northeast of Lourenço Marques.

Inhambane-Inharrime. This Cape-gauge line serves a nearby coastal district with a somewhat similar economy and need.

Santa Ana [11]–Tete. This Cape-gauge line was built (1947-1950) to make possible the development of the important Moatize coal field.

Caia [12]–Marromeu. This 36-inch-gauge privately owned line works largely for the Sena sugar estates.

Quelimane-Mocuba. This Cape-gauge line serves the sisal plantations of the coastal plain.

Nacala and Lumbo-Cuamba. This unfinished Cape-gauge line is potentially one of the most important. Its main eastern terminus, Nacala, has one of the best deep-water harbors in Africa. The territory it taps is attractive both climatically and agriculturally. Already the line handles a substantial freight traffic in cotton, rice, peanuts and cashew nuts, mostly African-grown. When it reaches Catur and Vila Cabral (this section is now, in 1959, under construction), it will open up a large "settler" region hitherto in an economic backwater. There are plans to continue the line to the eastern shore of Lake Nyasa and so to give landlocked Nyasaland a second outlet to the coast.

[11] Near Chindio on the Trans-Zambesia Railway.
[12] On the Trans-Zambesia Railway near the south bank of the Zambezi River.

THE MALAGASY REPUBLIC

The first line — the Tananarive–Côte Est Railway — was constructed between 1901 and 1913 from Brickaville, near Andevorante, to Tananarive, the capital, and from Brickaville to the main port of Tamatave. In 1923 a branch line linked Moramanga, about midway between the coast and the capital, with the fertile and densely populated Lake Alaotra area. In 1923 also a branch line was run southward from Tananarive to the resort town of Antsirabe. This meter-gauge system of roughly 440 route miles was dieselized, and modernized generally, in the early years after World War II. It has a lively downgrade traffic in rice, manioc, peanuts, hides and skins, canned foods, mimosa bark, coffee and cloves. Its upgrade freight consists largely of cement, iron and steel goods, machinery, foodstuffs and beverages.

The only other line, also meter gauge, links Fianarantsoa, the largest town in the southern part of the plateau, with the open-roadstead port of Manakara, a distance of roughly a hundred miles. Unlike its neighbor to the north, this line has not fulfilled its builders' expectations. Its chief outbound sources of revenue are graphite, rice, peanuts and coffee. Inbound traffic is similar in kind to that on the Tananarive–Côte Est line.

For all their smallness, these two lines serve four of the eight largest cities and the two most populous districts of the Republic. In recent years they have handled between 40 and 50 per cent of the goods entering the country and about 20 per cent of the exports.

EAST AFRICA

The East African Railways and Harbours administration supplies the main transport facilties for the three territories of Kenya, Tanganyika and Uganda. The railway system, which is meter gauge throughout, comprises (1) the Kenya-Uganda Line running from Mombasa to Kasese, with branch lines to Kisumu, Kitale, Magadi, Nanyuki, Solai, Soroti and Thomson's Falls; (2) the Tanga Line running from Tanga to Moshi and onward to Arusha, and joined at Kahe Junction to the Voi branch of the Kenya-Uganda Line; (3) the Central Line that runs from Dar-es-Salaam to Kigoma with a connection from Tabora to Mwanza and a branch line to Mpanda; (4) the Southern Province Line running from Mtwara to Nachingwea and Masasi. All told, the system totals roughly 4,000 route miles. The Railways and Harbours administration has its headquarters in Nairobi, and regional offices in Tanganyika and Uganda.

The Kenya-Uganda Line

Construction of a railway almost 600 miles long between Mombasa and Kisumu on the shores of Lake Victoria was begun in the 1890s with the twofold purpose of facilitating the running of the newly acquired

British territories (including the stamping out in them of the still active Arab trade in slaves), and of making money. The line was built over a period of six years at a cost of £8 million and many hundred lives. For nearly two decades its operations were anything but businesslike. By the early 1920s, however, confidence in its future and that of the territories it served had grown to the point where its backers were ready to start building a line from Nakuru to Kampala, that would obviate the lake-crossing from Kisumu and provide a through rail link between Uganda and the coast. This extension was completed by 1931. The main line was carried westward another 200 miles or so in 1956, bringing its total length to over 1,080 miles. Kasese, the new terminus, is the shipping point for copper from the Kilembe mines in the foothills of the Ruwenzori Mountains.

The branch lines cater to the needs of certain agricultural and mining communities that have sprung up to the north and south of the main line. The chief of these are the Konza-Magadi line, important for its carbonate of soda traffic; the Nairobi-Nanyuki line, serving Kenya's Northern Province cattle trade and a large section of her Kikuyu and European Highlands, and the Tororo-Soroti line, running through the cotton country of eastern Uganda.

It is a large system by tropical African standards, and it plays a large role in the life of the region it serves. While nobody would question the past necessity of having such a dominating figure in the cast, many have come to question the wisdom of allowing the Railways and Harbours administration to go on "running the show." Among the criticisms commonly leveled against it are, first, that it has operated so long without competition it has become "the worst type of vested interest"; second, that it has used monopoly powers to block road haulage of passengers and freight; third, that the services it offers are both indifferent and inadequate; and, fourth, that its employees work on the assumption that the customer is generally wrong. The railway, on its side, can claim that each year sees it carrying more goods and passengers with greater safety and speed than it did forty years ago; [13] that its long-range modernization plans have been carried out to the point where, in certain respects, there is capacity to spare; that, to improve the service still further, it is planning to introduce electric and diesel electric locomotives on the busier sections of the main line; [14] that it is in business as a common carrier and as such must be given a degree of protection from road competition, especially since its rates are based on a differential tariff which allows the administration to carry some of the major export commodities hundreds of miles to the ports at below cost so that they may be able to compete in price on the world's markets;

[13] It is now possible to travel the 330 miles between Mombasa and Nairobi in about twelve hours. The railway is still having trouble with the elements, and an occasional derailment by hippopotamuses on the lesser used lines.

[14] The first deliveries of diesel electric locomotives are promised in 1960.

and, lastly, that its relations with the public have seldom if ever been happier than at the present time.

The Tanga Line

The Tanga-Moshi part of this line was built by the Germans before World War I for the purpose of giving access to the fertile and healthy Kilimanjaro-Meru region. The link with the Mombasa line, from Kahe Junction to Voi, was built by British forces in furtherance of their 1915-1916 German East African campaign. Today it carries most of the coffee and other agricultural exports of the Moshi-Arusha district, since Mombasa is better equipped to handle these than Tanga.

The Central Line of Tanganyika

Built between 1905 and 1914 by the Germans, this line runs from Dar-es-Salaam on the coast to Kigoma on the eastern shore of Lake Tanganyika. One of the Germans' reasons for building it was the hope that they could siphon off some of the Katanga mineral traffic. To this end they gave the Belgians generous facilities at both the ocean and lake terminals. However, as we have seen, the "Indian Ocean" route out of Katanga was subject to even more time-consuming and money-losing breaks of bulk than the "Atlantic Ocean" route through the Congo. The Central Line therefore was never greatly favored by the Union Minière, and after the opening of the Benguela Railway in 1931, was seldom used for copper shipments. It continues to be used by eastern Congo importers of heavy manufactured goods, such as autos and trucks, and by exporters of bulky agricultural and forestry products.

Like the Kenya-Uganda Line, the Central Line runs through long stretches of unremunerative country. Unlike the Kenya-Uganda Line, though, it has few feeder lines. The longest of them, and the most valuable, is the one from Tabora to Mwanza on Lake Victoria. In 1948 a short spur, from Shinyanga to Mwadui, was added to this line in order to meet the equipment and supply needs of the Williamson diamond mine at Mwadui. Also of recent origin — it was completed in 1949 — is the branch line that goes southwest from Kaliua to Mpanda, where Uruwira Minerals Ltd. has developed a lead-copper-silver-gold mine. Another company is showing interest in a nearby area, so that the economic outlook for this line is considered to be getting steadily better.

The Southern Province Line of Tanganyika

This short line was originally designed to meet the needs of the (British) Overseas Food Corporation, one of whose major projects was the development of the Nachingwea region for the mechanized production of peanuts. The first section of it, from Mkwaya at the head of Lindi

Creek to Ruo and Nachingwea, was opened in 1949. A second section was opened in 1954 when the new port of Mtwara, to the south of Lindi, was linked with Ruo.[15] A third section, from Chilingula to Masasi, was opened in 1958. Although the OFC project failed, the Tanganyika Agricultural Corporation, which took over its plant and plowed-up lands, is convinced that there is nothing wrong with the idea of mechanized general farming in this region, and that the project can be made a profitable one, given the necessary time and transportation facilities. Now that TAC has the transportation, it hopes the time will not be long before it can be used to good advantage. Others, who do not altogether share the courageous opinion of TAC, are hoping that it will not be long before the much discussed scheme for an extension to the rich coal areas at Ngaka in the Songea district is acted upon.

NORTHEAST AFRICA

The three railway systems of northeast Africa are entirely separate from those of east Africa, west Africa and the Congo basin, and, for that matter, Egypt. The largest of the three, and the only one that can be called, with any truth, a network is the Sudan Railways. The other two are not much more that tentacles — dead-end lines — stretching from their coastal bases on the Red Sea and the Gulf of Aden inland and up the Ethiopian-Eritrean Highlands.

The Sudan Railways is a government-owned Cape-gauge system of more than 2,000 route miles. Its main functions are to provide bypasses along the cataract-ridden section of the Nile between Khartoum and the Egyptian border, to give Khartoum, the commercial and administrative capital, direct access to Port Sudan on the Red Sea, and to link together the other large towns in the savannas of the middle third of the country.

The first line of the present system was built in 1897-1899.[16] It ran from Wadi Halfa, near the Egyptian border, southward, chord-fashion, across the base of the great westward-bending arc of the Nile, to Abu Hamed, and thence, paralleling the Nile on its eastern bank, to Khartoum. Over the years this line has come to be regarded, by those who know their railways, as one of the best in the world for service and cuisine, and, notwithstanding the great daytime heat, for comfort also. In 1905-1906 a branch line was built between Atbara, situated about midway between the Fifth and Sixth cataracts, and Suakin on the Red Sea; it was later extended northward to the much more commodious harbor of Port Sudan

[15] As Mtwara will be able to take all the traffic that is likely to be offered, the Mkwaya-Ruo section of the railway has been abandoned.

[16] The railway construction before this time was negligible. In 1875 the British began building a line upstream from Wadi Halfa, but they succeeded in laying only 30 miles of track. Later they added another 90 miles, only to abandon it all in 1905.

(opened in 1909). Subsequently lines were built from Khartoum southward through the Gezira cotton country to Wad Medani and Sennar on the Blue Nile; from Sennar westward across the White Nile at Kosti to El Obeid in Kordofan (opened in 1912); from Sennar northeastward to Kassala, near the Eritrean border, and on to Haiya (opened in 1926) to join the Atbara–Port Sudan railway, and from Sennar to Singa some miles upstream. There are also a number of shorter spur lines. Lines now under construction, or planned, will extend the system to Ed Da'ein and Nyala in Darfur, to Aweil and Wau in the province of Bahr-el-Ghazal and from Singa to Er Roseires near the Ethiopian border.

The Franco-Ethiopian Railway may be a poor second to the Sudan Railways in length and traffic, but it is second to none in the whole of Africa for scenery and engineering skill. Starting from the French Somaliland port of Djibouti in the Gulf of Aden, it winds its meter-wide way through wadis and ravines, and over escarpments and plateaus, until at an elevation of over 8,000 feet it reaches Addis Ababa, its Ethiopian terminus. Although French-owned, only 70 of the nearly 500 miles of track lie in French Somaliland. Almost thirty years in the building (1897-1926), it is at once an indispensable and inadequate lifeline; indispensable because it is one of the very few surface links which the mountain-girt Ethiopian Empire has had with the outside world, and inadequate because it is incapable of carrying a large enough volume of traffic at a low enough tariff to serve the necessities of a poor country. The trains are small, slow and infrequent; and the cost of shipping goods, such as hides and coffee, by them from Addis Ababa to Djibouti is anything up to three times the cost of shipping them from Djibouti to Europe and America.

The Eritrean Railway is a narrow-gauge (95 centimeter) Italian-built line. It runs inland from the Red Sea port of Massawa to Asmara (the capital of Eritrea), Keren and Agordat. There are plans to continue it westward one day to Tessenei, where it would link up with the Sudan Railways. From Massawa to Asmara the railway runs parallel to a macadam road and a *teleferica* (cableway) built by the Italians. Like the Franco-Ethiopian Railway, it is more remarkable for its scenery and engineering (it also has to climb 8,000 feet to get onto the plateau) than for its effectiveness. In addition to poor service and high operating costs, it has, from time to time, to cope with armed attack. As recently as 1951, "all trains on the railway had to be escorted . . . and in one administrative division, authority appeared to be divided between the British Army and a local Robin Hood."[17] Since Eritrea became federated with Ethiopia in 1952, the mantle of the British Army has fallen on the shoulders of people better versed, from long familiarity, in the business of banditry.

[17] Sir Duncan Cumming, "The U.N. Disposal of Eritrea," *United Empire*, March-April 1953, p. 67.

A summary of the ranking, by passenger and freight traffic, of the various territories will be found in Table 28.

Although the total route mileage of tropical African railroads has grown by many hundreds of miles since the end of World War II, it is (1959) still less than 25,000 miles. Taking the land area of the region as approximately 8.5 million square miles, this gives a rail density of one mile for every 340 or so square miles. By any criterion this is a low figure,[18] one

[18] Corresponding figures for the nontropical areas of Africa are one mile for every 60 square miles; for continental United States, one mile for every 18, and for France, one mile for every 8.

Table 28

RAILROAD TRAFFIC,
BY REGION AND TERRITORY, 1948 AND 1957

REGION AND TERRITORY	1948		1957 [a]	
	MILLION PASSENGER-KILOMETERS	MILLION NET TON-KILOMETERS	MILLION PASSENGER-KILOMETERS	MILLION NET TON-KILOMETERS
West Africa				
French West Africa	313	345 [b]	449	593 [b]
French Cameroons	68.6	54.0	87.2	109.8 [b]
Sierra Leone	51.0 [c]	27.2 [c]	73.3 [d]	30.7 [d]
Ghana (Gold Coast)	269	207	247	300
Nigeria [e]	525	1,076 [b]	738	2,015 [b]
(French) Togo	50.8	10.9	69.8	7.5
Congo basin and margins				
Belgian Congo	143	1,994	353	2,717
French Equatorial Africa	26.2	73.7	50.9	141.4
Angola	78.1	479	94.4 [f]	1,141 [f]
Central Africa				
Northern & Southern Rhodesia [g]	n.a.	2,868 [b, h]	n.a.	6,575 [b]
Nyasaland	n.a.	n.a.	n.a.	105 [b]
Mozambique	74.1 [i]	263 [i]	175.3 [d, j]	1,672 [d, j]
Malagasy Republic (Madagascar)	81.6	81.6 [b]	153	131.1 [b]
East Africa				
Kenya, Uganda & Tanganyika [k]	n.a.	1,470 [b, h]	n.a.	2,746 [b, h]
Northeast Africa				
Republic of Sudan (Anglo-Egyptian Sudan)	n.a.	607	n.a.	1,514
Ethiopia [l]	52.1	118	45.6	139
Eritrea	19.8	14.1 [b]	12.7	14.5 [b]

Source: United Nations, *Statistical Yearbook, 1958*, New York, 1958.

[a] Provisional.   [b] Including service traffic.   [c] 1951   [d] 1956.
[e] Twelve months beginning April 1 of year stated.   [f] 1955.
[g] Excluding Vryburg-Bulawayo line.   [h] Excluding livestock.
[i] State railways only.   [j] Including Beira-Umtali line.
[k] Including road and lake services.   [l] Including traffic from Djibouti to Ethiopian border.
n.a.: not available.

that spells physical isolation, economic anemia, strategic vulnerability —
in a word, underdevelopment. And, if anything, the facts are worse than
the figures suggest. Much of the mileage is poorly engineered, equipped
and operated. Some of it has outlived its usefulness; some never was
very useful. Very little of it was laid down with an eye to the coordina-
tion of adjacent territories' needs, let alone transcontinental needs. While
it provides access to many important places, it provides interconnection
between very few of them. Among some early colonizers, interterritorial
connection was regarded rather in the nature of a contagion to be avoided
than as a consummation to be sought, and more than one government
chose a gauge different from its neighbors' to insure that there would be
no contagion. In his paper prepared for this study Hibberd V. B. Kline,
Jr., writes: ". . . this fear of the creation of international lines was a persistent factor in route development until post-World War II times, when
cooperation in the transport field reached the point where international
conferences were held on the subject."

Even now, apart from crossings of domestic borders, such as those between Northern and Southern Rhodesia, there are not yet ten international rail links in the whole of tropical Africa. The only transcontinental
route — not that anybody makes a practice of crossing the continent by
it — is the one running from Benguela in Angola through Katanga to
Livingstone, Bulawayo and Beira (or Lourenço Marques). There is still
no "Cape-to-Cairo Railway," and no prospect of one.

But if the political fragmentation of the region during the latter part
of the nineteenth century and the rivalries to which it gave rise can be
blamed for the idiosyncrasies of the railways, they can scarcely be blamed
for their inadequacies. These are the progeny of a more mixed parentage
— between Dame Nature and the transport planner. Nature is notori-
ously disregardful of human expectations, and her tropical African
standards of adequacy differ greatly from those current in Europe and
North America. As for the transport planner, his ignorance of his partner
has all too frequently been equaled only by his inability to give her what
she needed to make a railway thrive. For while some of his troubles are
born of the environment — physical, economic and social — as many or
more derive from a "general reluctance . . . to put larger capital investments into nonproductive, though basic and vital, activities than are
needed for minimum performance," as Kline puts it. And where money
is short, equipment suffers; for example, lightweight rails and light locomotives tend to be ordered in place of heavy-duty ones. Revenue-earning capacity is thereby reduced; for lightweight rails and locomotives
are incapable of taking heavy axle loads and long trains.

It is not without significance that at the present time such matters as the
realignment of right-of-way, the improvement of roadbed quality and of
traffic control devices, the provision of additional passing loops, and the re-

placement of obsolescent locomotives, cars and rails are high up on the agenda of almost all companies. And there can be no doubt that the companies which have been able to find the money for modernizing programs have already begun to reap the benefit of them in lowered operating costs, better schedules, and kinder words from their customers.

At the same time it would be wrong, and grossly unfair, to leave the impression that the story of tropical Africa's railways up to now has been largely one of idiosyncrasy and inadequacy. Some of them have performed prodigiously. For instance, during the years of World War II the mean daily movement of freight cars on the Kenya-Uganda Line would have borne comparison with that of many American lines in that period. Since the war it has surpassed the American average. The Rhodesia Railways, despite "aging" problems, have not failed to turn in, year after year, steadily increasing figures of shipments of coal, copper and other minerals. Many other railways, of which no prodigies were asked or expected, have gone about their daily business doing what was scheduled, which was usually a great deal more than their critics gave them credit for. And all of them, from the least to the largest, have played a part in the great and continuing "revolution of rising expectations," the African's no less than the Asian's and the European's. They have been, in truth, "civilizing rails."

THE INLAND WATERWAYS

Like the railways, the inland waterways are a thing "of shreds and patches," and of rather more shreds than patches. As the accompanying map (Figure 28) indicates, most of the shreds are on or near the coast, the patches in the interior. As it also shows, in practically no instance are the coastal shreds joined to the interior patches; the falls and rapids which interrupt the smooth descent of almost every tropical African stream from the interior highlands to the coastal lowlands keep the two apart most effectively.

THE COASTAL WATERWAYS [19]

As befits its more ample rainfall, the Atlantic side of the continent has far more useful rivers than the Indian Ocean side. Between the Senegal in the republic of the same name and the Cunene in southern Angola there are at least 36 rivers that are navigable in their lower courses by launches and, in many cases, bigger craft, at least for part of the year. Between the Juba in Somalia (there are no navigable streams to the north of it) and the Incomati in southern Mozambique, there are not more than seven or eight.

[19] Including intracoastal waterways formed by lagoons, deltas, etc.

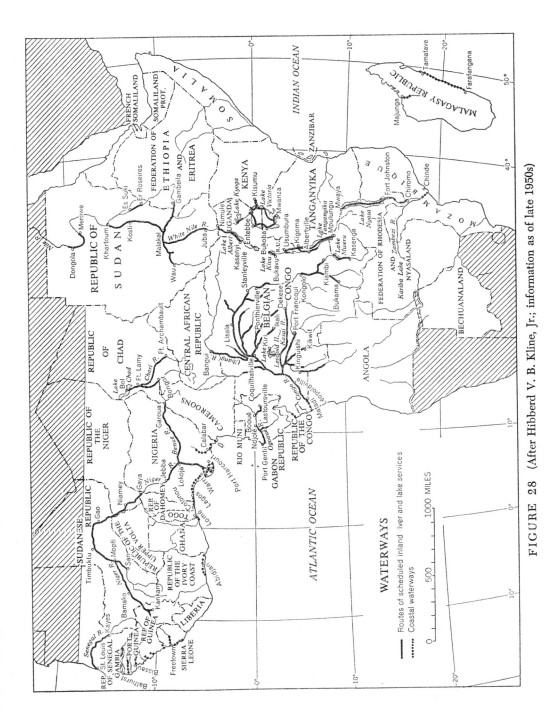

FIGURE 28 (After Hibberd V. B. Kline, Jr.; information as of late 1950s)

435

Atlantic Coast Waterways

Along the section of the coast between the Senegal and the Congo most of the rivers are short and their courses ungraded — still in process of having their irregularities of slope removed. Because of the marked seasonality of the rainfall and consequent fluctuations of water volume, few — even of the "graded" rivers — are of sustained usefulness. In their seaward margins few of them are immune to the hazards of heavy surf and shifting sand bars and channels.

Going from north to south, the chief waterways are those associated with the following rivers:

The Senegal. In at least one respect the Senegal is unique among tropical African rivers, for it is the only one that affords uninterrupted passage from the coast deep into the interior. From St. Louis, the port at its mouth, it is navigable upstream for a distance of approximately 500 miles. However, the steamer season usually lasts only from July through October, the floodwater months. For the rest of the year small launches can normally ascend as far as Kayes, but larger vessels can get no farther than Podor. It was this serious seasonal curtailment of navigation that impelled the French to build the Dakar-Kayes railway link that now takes much of the upper Niger basin freight traffic. St. Louis is the nearest to Europe of all ports in western tropical Africa; but its offshore bar and associated difficulties of approach rob it of the advantage which, in this respect, it has over Dakar.

The Saloum. South of Cape Verde and Dakar the Saloum River, though also somewhat obstructed by shifting bars, is navigable upstream as far as Kaolack. Kaolack's rail connection with the Dakar-Niger railway and its proximity to major peanut-producing areas account for most of its present-day importance.

The Gambia. Viewed casually from the coast, the multimouthed Saloum and the Gambia are all of a piece; and, indeed, they are so closely connected that small craft navigate freely, through their distributaries, from one system to the other. Yet there is no mistaking the Gambia's mainstream; at its mouth it is wide and deep and has a charted 27-foot channel. Above Bathurst, located on the southwest side of the entrance, the Gambia is navigable at high water for vessels of 15-foot draft as far as Kuntaur. Vessels drawing not more than five and a half feet may reach Basse. With no road system to speak of, the people of Gambia are extraordinarily dependent on this arterial waterway. No fewer than 56 "wharf towns" line its banks and enjoy direct, if slow, connections with Bathurst. Several of the larger can claim direct connection with European ports by virtue of the large shipments of peanuts they are able to offer ocean-going vessels.

The Casamance. Where it enters the sea, the Casamance is six miles wide, but most of its mouth is choked with sand bars. Through one of the larger gaps, ships drawing 15 feet may pass and proceed to the peanut port of Ziguinchor. River vessels drawing up to five feet are able to reach Sedhiou.

The Cacheu and the Geba. These are the principal rivers of Portuguese Guinea. The former provides a 12-foot channel for a distance of approximately a hundred miles and the latter a five-foot channel for a distance of 70 miles.

The Nunez, the Pongo and the Mellacorée. These are the three most serviceable rivers in the Republic of Guinea. The Nunez, the northernmost, is navigable as far as Victoria, for vessels drawing 19½ feet; and as far as Boké for vessels drawing seven feet. The Pongo, to the southeast, can take vessels of 16-foot draft to Boffa at high tide. At other times sand bars tend to restrict shipping movements. The Mellacorée, the southernmost of the three, is navigable for about the same distance, to the small port of Benty, for ships of about the same draft.

The Sierra Leone. The large estuary of the Sierra Leone River provides one of the most commodious deep-water harbors in Africa. Upriver from Freetown, its ocean port, there is an assured year-round 20-foot channel to Pepel, the port from which the country's iron ore is exported. Above Pepel, the river is available only to shallow-draft launches.

Although none of Sierra Leone's rivers give access "in depth," the Great and Little Scarcies, the Sherbro and the Moa, helped by a system of coastal backwaters, lagoons and deltas, give considerable access "in width." Altogether more than 500 miles of motor launch routes are operated, more or less on schedules, on the inland waterways of lowland Sierra Leone.

South and east of the Sherbro River as far as the equator, the coastline is affected by the eastward sweep of the Guinea current. Off the Ivory Coast and at other places this current occasionally exceeds three knots during the "monsoon" months (May through July generally). Most of this "Guinea" coast is also troubled by strong surf. The consequent choking up of river mouths with sand bars, spits and shoals constitutes a serious barrier to navigation. The few rivers that are accessible to seagoing vessels usually have been made so by artificial means.

None of Liberia's rivers is navigable except by small African craft and launches; and but for the Assinie and Vridi Canals which have been cut across the coastal sand bars, none of the Ivory Coast rivers would be much use either. As it is, most of the navigable mileage is in the lagoons rather than the rivers.

Ghana is scarcely better served. There is a little steam launch traffic on the Tano, the Ankobra and the lower Volta rivers, but no seagoing traffic on any of them. Except at Takoradi and Tema, both artificial deepwater harbors, all ships must stay outside the line of surf, and be loaded and unloaded by lighters.

Conditions along the Togo and Dahomey coasts are no better. Between the open ocean and the rivers lies a sand bar backed by shallow lagoon waters. Apart from the lagoons, only two of the rivers, the Mono in Togo and the Ouémé in Dahomey, rank as waterways; they can carry small launches inland for distances of 60 and a hundred miles respectively. Only Porto Novo, Dahomey's capital, lying on the inner shore of a large lagoon and connected by navigable channels westward to Cotonou and eastward to Lagos, is deep enough to accommodate ocean-going vessels.

Once into Nigeria the picture quickly changes. Almost all of its many streams are navigable by modern power craft. The intracoastal waterway of the Niger delta, which links Lagos in the west with Opobo in the east, has a minimum depth of four and a half feet. The main distributaries of the Niger have much more and can be navigated by medium-draft vessels. The Escravos River has a "least depth at low water springs [tides] with a smooth bar" of 15 feet; so, too, has the Forcados River. The corresponding figures for the other major outlets are: Nun, 9 feet; Bonny, 19 feet; and Opobo, 6 feet. The island port of Lagos and its mainland twin, Apapa, are available for vessels with a draft of 27 feet. The smaller channels and creeks are, together, scarcely less important, for they provide the only natural routeways between the close-spaced delta settlements; and "in some areas traveling canoe 'shops' provide the only contact with the merchandise of other regions." [20]

The mainstream of the Niger is considered navigable as far upstream as the railway bridge at Jebba. At high water — July through October as a rule, though, especially in west Africa, river "rules" are flexible — vessels drawing seven feet may make the entire trip without difficulty. In September and October vessels of 12-foot draft may reach Lokoja, at the confluence with the Benue. In these months the Benue itself is usually navigable by shallow-draft vessels (drawing not more than five feet) as far as Garoua in the French Cameroons. At low water there is less than four feet of water above Lokoja, and not always much more below. Most of the freight business on the Niger and the Benue is done in tugs and barges.

To the east of the Niger River system of waterways lies the entirely separate Cross River system. As far as Calabar it can accommodate vessels drawing up to 19 feet. From July through October vessels drawing 10 feet are able to reach Ikom, 200 miles above Calabar. In September, the peak of the high-water season, vessels drawing not more than seven and a half feet may go another 85 miles to Mamfe in the British Cameroons. At low water vessels drawing more than six feet can seldom ply more than 150 miles upstream.

Going east from the Cross River the lowlands of the Niger-Benue basin give place to the Cameroon Highlands, whose streams are too torrential

[20] K. M. Buchanan and J. C. Pugh, *Land and People in Nigeria*, University of London Press, London, 1955, p. 221.

to rank as waterways. The lower Bimbia River comes nearest to doing so, for its banana, rubber and cocoa port of Tiko can be reached by medium-sized cold-storage vessels.

To the east of the British-French Cameroons border lies the large estuary of the Cameroons River.[21] Of the several rivers that feed the estuary, the Mungo, the Vouri and the Dilamba are navigable for distances up to 50 miles. In periods of high water launches can pass southward from this estuary through the Kwakwa Creek to the Sanaga River, the lower reaches of which are navigable by small craft. South of the Sanaga are the Nyong, the Muni and the Gabon rivers; of these the first offers some 35 miles of navigable waterway, the second about 20 miles, and the third (including tributaries) more than a hundred miles. From the Ramboé tributary of the Gabon it is possible to pass, by canoe or small launch, into the system of the Ogooué River.

The Ogooué. The lower Ogooué is a sluggish braided stream greatly given to flooding its low-lying borders during the rainy season. Its 50-mile-wide delta is a maze of creeks, shifting channels and lagoons. Only two of its channels are much used by power craft. Both of these lie to the south of Cape Lopez and Port Gentil. The bigger of the two can take 50-to-100-ton barges as far upstream as Lambaréné except at times of very low water.

Between the Ogooué and the Congo lie many hundreds of miles of creeks and lagoons navigable by canoe and other small craft, but only one river of any size. This is the Kouilou, which in its upstream section is called the Niari; it is navigable, by launches, for some 50 miles.

The Congo. Seen from the ocean, the Congo [22] has a most welcoming look about it. It is wide and deep — over 100 fathoms in the offing — completely free from guile. It is one of the few rivers in the whole of Africa that manages not only to get all its own mud and sand dumped well out to sea, but also to prevent the mud and sand of other rivers being dumped in its approaches. The welcome is short-lived. Above Boma, 50 miles upriver, the unhurried waters of the estuary give place to strong currents and whirlpools, and the outstretched arms of its bordering shores become a vise. By the time seagoing vessels reach the Devil's Cauldron, below Matadi, another 30 miles upriver, the navigation of the Congo has lost all its charm. Above Matadi the river becomes entirely unnavigable, and remains so as far as Stanley Pool, at Léopoldville.

South of the Congo, the Atlantic coast fares badly for waterways. The Angola uplands crowd the coastal plain, thereby restricting the areas in which rivers stand a good chance of being navigable. And toward the south of Angola, aridity gets the upper hand, so that such streams as the

[21] "River" is a misnomer; it is a 230-square-mile estuary of other rivers.
[22] The interior — plateau — section of the river is dealt with later.

Cunene cannot be navigated for more than a few weeks at a time. The only river in the entire country that has enough water to take a decent-sized barge is the Cuanza, south of Luanda. In a good season it is navigable upstream for about 125 miles; but since such seasons are rare, its role in the economic life of the area is small.

Indian Ocean Coast Waterways

The same can be said for all of the waterways that link the Indian Ocean coast of tropical Africa with its hinterland.

Along the whole of the Mozambique section only four rivers — the Incomati, the Limpopo, the Macuse and the Zambezi — are capable of handling barge traffic. Up to now only the Zambezi has had to handle such traffic on any scale. During the high-water season, usually December through August, the lower Zambezi [23] is navigable for barges of four-foot draft as far as the coal mines at Tete. Since the completion of the all-rail route to Tete, however, it has lost almost all its coal barge traffic. The Shire, the Zambezi's navigable left-bank tributary, can also take shallow-draft vessels, and in the old days a sternwheeler service was available over part of its course; but its importance also has declined since the coming of the Trans-Zambesia Railway. The only sections of the Shire much used today are those between Fort Johnston and Mpimbe, where the Nyasaland Railways cross the river, and between Chikwawa and Chiromo, a flourishing cotton area.

The Ruvuma, on the Mozambique-Tanganyika border, and the Rufiji in central Tanganyika can take small craft only, and then only in their lowest reaches in a good season. The elusiveness of good seasons probably explains why the authors of a 1949 United Nations report decided that "Tanganyika has no navigable rivers, except for a section of the Lukuledi [which enters the sea at Lindi]." [24] The Lukuledi itself is not sufficiently navigable to rank as such in the official government handbook of the territory.

In Kenya, the only navigable river is the Tana. In a good season it can be ascended some 400 miles, but in a poor one for not more than 150 miles. Because of the seasonal and annual fluctuations of flow, the scheduling of regular services on the river is next to impossible. As for the Juba (Giuba), the northernmost of the Indian Ocean coast waterways, small craft may ascend it for 400 miles between the months of May and

[23] The only section of the upper Zambezi where water transport has been developed on any scale is that between Livingstone and Mongu in Northern Rhodesia. Here a government organization, known as the Zambesi River Transport, operates a combined truck and barge system. Some power barges have recently been purchased with the object of speeding up the rather poor service. Most of the downstream freight is hardwood timber for the Livingstone sawmills.

[24] United Nations, Department of Economic Affairs, *Transport and Communications Review*, April-June 1949, p. 41.

December. Only the first dozen miles or so are usable throughout the year, and then only by vessels drawing not more than three or four feet of water.

Malagasy Coast Waterways

The mountainous nature of the wet eastern side of the island of Madagascar and the seasonal flow of the rivers on the drier western side have prevented river transport from becoming important. The only river port worthy of the name is Marovoay, which is the regular head of (small barge) navigation on the west coast river Betsiboka above the ocean port of Majunga.

Of more consequence is the line of lagoons extending from Foulpointe to Farafangana along the middle section of the east coast. The work of breaching the transverse barriers (*pangalanes*) between these lagoons was begun in 1897 and is still in progress. When complete, the canal will have a length of approximately 400 miles and will be able to accommodate barges of 300 metric tons burden. Over most of its length at present, Hubert Deschamps reports in his working paper, "the traffic is hindered by the water plants which sometimes completely block the canal and the rocky sills . . . [and] is made up of 20-ton barges which run between Mahanoro and Tamatave; it reaches about 50,000 metric tons annually."

THE WATERWAYS OF THE INTERIOR

These may be divided into five systems: the basins of the middle and upper Congo, the Niger and the Nile, the Great Lakes and the Chad basin.

The Middle and Upper Congo Basin

On any score, this is the biggest and most useful of all the waterways of tropical Africa. In the Belgian Congo section alone there are reckoned to be more than 8,000 miles of navigable waterways, of which approximately 800 miles consist of lake routes, 1,650 miles of large-barge routes and 5,600 miles of small-barge routes.[25] Léopoldville is the downstream terminus of the Belgian Congo part of the system, Brazzaville of the part belonging to the Republic of the Congo and the Central African Republic. Both ports have boat building and maintenance yards. From them regular services fan out to every navigable creek and channel of the Congo system. Three of the most important, and longest, are those from Léopoldville to Stanleyville, at the head of navigation on the middle Congo (nearly 1,100 miles upstream), to Aketi on the Itimbiri (about 1,000 miles upstream), and to Bangui on the Ubangi (about 750 miles

[25] "Large-barge" routes can handle vessels drawing between six and seven feet and "small-barge" routes vessels drawing between three and five feet.

upstream). On some of the smaller streams only freight services are run; on most of the larger ones, both passenger and freight services are available. In many cases, the schedules are complementary to those of the railways that tie together the navigable sections of the system. Until recently all schedules were slow; boats traveled by day only, there being no markers to enable them to travel by night, and in any case the nights were needed for refueling. But with the introduction of faster, oil-burning vessels and of markers and buoys coated with imported luminous paint, schedules on many of the bigger streams are being greatly speeded up. The Léopoldville-Stanleyville run that used to take eleven days upstream and seven days downstream can now be done in seven and five.

All told, well over 1,000 power vessels operate on Congo basin waters. Most of the freight and passenger vessels run between 1,000 and 1,300 metric tons burden, and have cabin and dining room accommodation. Sternwheelers are particularly well adapted to the shallow waters and the necessity of going alongside jettyless banks to take on fuel and cargo.

The bulk of the passenger and mail business and much of the freight business done on the waterways of the middle Congo and its tributaries are in the hands of Otraco. The quite remarkable coverage of the regular services run by this government-controlled organization is shown in the following excerpt from a recent issue of the "Traveler's Guide to the Belgian Congo and Ruanda-Urundi":

Otraco's Scheduled River Services

(a) *Léo-Stan.* Congo River Mail Service. Regular weekly services. Steamers leave Léo at dawn on Wednesday and arrive at Stan the following Wednesday. On the return trip steamers leave Stan on Thursday and arrive at Léo the following Tuesday.

(b) *Léo-Coquilhatville.* Congo River Mail Service. Regular fortnightly service. Steamers leave Léo at dawn on Saturday and arrive at Coquil. the following Friday. On the return trip steamers leave Coquil. on Saturday and arrive at Léo the following Wednesday.

(c) *Léo-Pt. Francqui.* Kasai River Mail Service. Regular fortnightly service. Steamers leave Léo at dawn on Thursday and arrive at Pt. Francqui on the following Wednesday. On the return trip steamers leave Pt. Francqui on Thursday and arrive at Léo the following Monday.

In addition to these principal services, Otraco operates regular services on the navigable tributaries of the Congo and Kasai rivers.

On the Lualaba (i.e., upper Congo) the scheduled services are run by the Compagnie des Chemins de Fer du Congo Supérieur aux Grands Lacs Africains (CFL).

Most of the vessels operating from river ports in the Republic of the Congo and the Central African Republic belong to the Compagnie Générale de Transports en Afrique and the Compagnie Française du Haut et Bas-Congo.

Although still slow by comparison with road and rail travel, and not as greatly used for passenger traffic as they used to be, the Congo basin waterways have no difficulty in attracting freight traffic. Over most of the flood-ridden, marshy sections, they provide the only satisfactory medium for the transportation of goods in bulk. Since they cost little to "build," need little in the way of repairs [26] and are much easier on the equipment than either roads or railways, they are likely to go on doing so.

The Middle and Upper Niger Basin

Although there is no physical interruption between the waterway of the lower Niger and that of the middle and upper Niger, not much traffic has moved between them since the French abandoned the right of free navigation on the Nigerian section of the river in 1904.

The middle and upper reaches of the Niger River system are divisible into two main sections, those above and below Bamako. Above Bamako, where the railway from Dakar reaches the river, small-steamer services can be operated during periods of high water — normally July through November — as far as Kouroussa on the mainstream and as far as Kankan on the Milo, a right-bank tributary. Below Bamako steamer services can normally operate from July through December between Koulikoro (the terminus of the Dakar railway), Kabara (the river port for Timbuktu) and Gao, and sometimes to Ansongo. Between Ansongo and Niamey river traffic is impeded by rapids, except at very high water. Below Niamey the river is readily navigable as far as Gaya near the Nigerian border. The only navigable tributary in the whole of this Koulikoro-Gaya section is the Bani, which comes into the Niger at Mopti. During high water small vessels can get up the Bani as far as San.

Formerly, these two navigable sections of the Niger were operated independently, being separated by the rapids between Bamako and Koulikoro, a break of about 60 miles. However, since its inauguration in 1929 the Sotuba Canal has carried steamers around these rapids. Thanks to this and the Costes Canal that circumvents the Sansanding irrigation dam about 150 miles below Koulikoro, it is now theoretically possible for small steamers to travel a distance of approximately 2,350 miles on the Niger, from Kouroussa to the Gulf of Guinea. But to do it might take a very long time. Because of the slowing action of the great swamps and lakes above Kabara on the flow of the mainstream, the floodwaters that leave Kouroussa in, say, August are unlikely to reach the Nigerian border before the following June, and the lower Niger, below the Benue-Niger confluence, until September — thirteen months after they began. Without these floodwaters it is doubtful if any powered craft could make the journey.

---

[26] For a while the water hyacinth (*Eichhornia crassipes*), an exotic, gave shipping a good deal of trouble. However, thanks to systematic spraying (with 2-4-D), the pest is now under control on the most frequented waterways.

The Middle and Upper Nile Basin

With five of the six great cataracts strewn along its course, the northern Sudanese section of the Nile is of very limited use to shipping. Steamer services operate between Wadi Halfa, the border town, and El Shallal near Aswan in upper Egypt, that is, between the First and Second cataracts, but none between the Second and Third. Above the Third Cataract there is a high-water steamer service between Kerma and Karima; during the low-water season the service runs from Dongola to Karima to connect with the Karima–Abu Hamed rail services. Between Karima, just below the Fourth Cataract, and Khartoum, well above the Sixth Cataract, the Nile is little used except by small craft.

From Khartoum the Blue Nile is navigable to the Sennar Dam, a distance of roughly 200 miles. Above the dam it is navigable during the high-water season — usually from late June to early December — as far as Er Roseires near the Ethiopian border. But nowadays there are no scheduled steamer services on the Blue Nile.

The White Nile is continuously navigable, and at all times of the year, for more than a thousand miles above Khartoum. A fortnightly steamer schedule is maintained between Juba in Equatoria Province and Kosti, which has railway connections with Khartoum. Upstream from Juba the White Nile is rendered unnavigable by rapids and falls as far as Nimule on the Uganda border. From here the Albert Nile, as this section of the river is called, is navigable 200 miles upstream to Lake Albert.

The Sobat, which joins the White Nile a few miles above the important river port of Malakal, is navigable in the flood season as far as the Ethiopian trading post of Gambeila, one of the still few recognized points of entry into Ethiopia from the Sudan. In a normal navigation season three round trips are made — in May, June and September — between Gambeila and the Nile ports.

The Bahr-el-Ghazal is navigable the year around to Meshra'er-Req, and a regular service is maintained from Kosti. From July to October the head of navigation is farther upstream, at Wau.

All the steamers on the Sudanese section of the Nile and its tributaries are owned and operated by the Sudan Railways.

The Great Lakes System

Of the dozen or so water bodies that make up the great lakes of east and central Africa, six only do a regular scheduled freight- and passenger-carrying business; these are Lakes Albert, Kivu, Nyasa, Kyoga, Tanganyika and Victoria. The rest are waterways only in the sense that those who live around their shores use them to get about, to catch and market fish and, in the case of Lakes Edward and George, for showing off their aquatic wildlife.

Lake Albert. From Butiaba, the southern terminus of the East African Railways and Harbours administration steamer service in that area, ships ply regularly down the Albert Nile to Nimule and around the 2,000-square-mile surface of the lake. There is also a de luxe motor launch service, mainly for the benefit of tourists, to and from the Murchison Falls. Passengers and goods coastward-bound are transported by road over the 75-mile stretch between Butiaba and Masindi Port on Lake Kyoga. There are no Belgian Congo services on the lake.

Lake Kyoga provides the link, by sternwheel steamers, with railhead at Namasagali, besides serving the cotton-producing areas of Kachung and other smaller ports.

Lake Victoria. With an area of roughly 27,000 square miles, Victoria is by far the largest of the great African lakes. It also does by far the largest shipping business. Having an unnavigable outlet and only one navigable tributary, the Kagera, and this too shallow and short to be of great consequence, Lake Victoria derives most of its importance as a waterway from the services it is able to provide a number of major producing and consuming areas in east Africa that have either no alternative or no competitive surface links. Fronting onto the lake are Entebbe, the administrative capital of Uganda; Port Bell, Kampala's port and linked to it by railway; Jinja, a rapidly growing industrial center; Kisumu, the home port of the lake steamer service, the terminus of an important branch of the Kenya-Uganda Line and the nearest rail point to Mombasa; Mwanza, the lake terminus of the Mwanza branch of the Central Line in Tanganyika; and the small trading ports of Bukoba on the west shore and Musoma on the east shore.

All these ports are linked by regular power boat services — 2,780 route miles of them in all. There are currently six passenger vessels in service on the lake, besides many tugs and lighters that carry nothing but freight. Only two vessels have a burden of as much as 1,200 tons. A fast passenger vessel — it will circle the lake twice a week — has been ordered, and should be commissioned in 1960. Power boat services are run by the East African Railways and Harbours administration. Since World War II there has been a more than 100 per cent increase in the freight traffic carried on this lake, and a larger increase in passenger traffic. A number of dhows also operate on the lake, but their importance, both relative and absolute, has greatly declined since the 1930s.

Lake Kivu. This is the highest of the great lakes of east and central Africa (4,830 feet above sea level), one of the smallest, and one of the least used. The only scheduled steamer service is the one, run by Otraco, between the ports of Bukavu at the southern end of the lake and Goma and Kisenyi at the northern end. Since the lake is surrounded by some of the most beautiful and salubrious country in the whole of Africa, there is hope that its role as a waterway will not always remain so modest.

Lake Tanganyika. For such a large body of water — it is about 450 miles long and between 30 and 45 miles wide — Lake Tanganyika does a very small shipping business. CFL operates a weekly connection between the two railheads, Albertville on the Belgian Congo side and Kigoma on the Tanganyika side, as part of its service to Usumbura and Uvira. CFL steamers also call regularly at several other points. The East African Railways and Harbours administration operates scheduled steamer service between Kigoma and the Northern Rhodesian lake port of Mpulungu, from which there is a road connection with Abercorn and the Copperbelt. In addition both organizations run some small freight steamers and lighters. These and a few African- and Asian-owned dhows that do a small nonscheduled business make up the total freight fleet of the lake.

Lake Nyasa. This, the southernmost of the great African lakes, is a slightly scaled-down version of Lake Tanganyika, being about 360 miles long and anything from 15 to 50 miles wide. Its western and southern shores belong to Nyasaland, the southern half of its eastern shore to Mozambique and the northern half to Tanganyika. Unlike the other great lakes, Lake Nyasa is subject to very considerable changes of level.[27] Since these changes were first measured around the turn of the present century, the level of the lake has fluctuated 24 feet, with serious commercial consequences. A drop of as little as six feet leaves some port installations high and dry; a rise of the same order just as surely drowns them.[28]

At the present time the principal lake steamer services are those between Fort Johnston, at the outlet of the lake on the Shire River, and Chipoka where the Nyasaland Railways system touches the west shore of the lake; and between Fort Johnston and Mwaya at the northern end of the lake in Tanganyika. Both services are operated by the Nyasaland Railways. A number of African-owned dhows also ply the lake, picking up cargo where they can find it. Most of the other lake craft — canoes, sailboats and motorboats — are engaged in the fish trade.

In the first postwar decade the tonnage of goods carried on the lake increased by roughly two thirds. Given improvement of the primitive harbor facilities, stabilization of the lake level, and more cargo capacity, the second decade should see a much more spectacular increase.

Lake Bangweulu. The last of the great lake waterways, and the least developed commercially, is Lake Bangweulu. Though much used by African fishing craft, its swampy and rather unhealthy margins, fluctuating level, easily choked channels, and its location in an economic backwater of Northern Rhodesia, do not commend themselves to the opera-

[27] See pp. 233, 250.
[28] Not the least of the reasons why the backers of the Shire valley development project (see p. 262) are in a hurry to get going is their desire to plug the "sink" before the level gets any lower.

tors of modern craft. During the two world wars, however, some use was made of its more navigable channels in shipping heavy supplies between Northern Rhodesia and Tanganyika.

The Chad Basin

Of all the navigable waterway systems here considered, the Chad basin is the most isolated. Until the coming of the airplane it was in fact one of the most isolated parts of inhabited Africa. Even today it has no rail or all-weather road links with the outside world. And since it is an area of inland drainage its waters drain away from rather than toward neighboring river systems. The only way a Chad canoe can get down to the sea is for it to be portaged from the headwaters of the Logone River (which, with the Chari, provides Lake Chad with most of its water) to those of the nearby Benue.

The navigability of the basin is not as great as the maps would suggest. There is a vast difference between the size of the lake at high water and at low water, and it is usually the high-water Chad that is shown on the maps.[29] Even at high water, much of the lake is too shallow to be navigable by any but the smallest local craft. And where the water is permanent and deep, it is often so cluttered with reeds and swamp grasses as to be almost impassable by power boats. The most useful reaches of the waterway are those to the north of the Chari delta and in the "Mesopotamian" area above Fort Lamy, where the Logone and the Chari share a common flood plain. The maximum route mileage available to small steamers (the largest using the basin have a freight capacity of about 10 tons) is roughly 1,250 miles. Longboats and canoes can cover about the same distance at low water and between three and four times as much during high water. The steamers can usually get up the Chari as far as Fort Archambault between August and December; in a good season small craft can get up as far as Batangafo on the Bahr Sara tributary. The Logone is less used, but is considered navigable by launches as far up as Bongor between July and November, and by smaller vessels as far as Gore. Very little use is made of the lake itself, except by local fishermen.

PORTS AND OCEAN SHIPPING

It is customary to refer to the coasts of tropical Africa as, at best, uninviting and, at worst, positively forbidding; and to assume that their tardy penetration stemmed directly from this circumstance. Though doubtless

[29] Since 1953 the lake has been rising rapidly. In 1956, for the first time in more than seventy years, it was sending water into the Bahr-el-Ghazal (*not* the Bahr-el-Ghazal of the Republic of Sudan) that in the old days regularly carried the lake's overflow waters into the Bodele depression lying to the northeast.

some parts of both the Atlantic and Indian Ocean coasts take a lot of penetrating, both coasts have plenty of hospitable anchorages, as the Arabs, the Portuguese and their competitors were not slow to find out. These anchorages may not always be very conveniently located with regard to the hinterlands they serve, and few of them are either deep enough or commodious enough to rank high among the world's great natural harbors; but for the most part they are no worse than those found around the coasts of Australia, Arabia or India. Together they are more than able to handle the region's coastwise and foreign trade. Very few of the territories with ocean frontage lack the rudiments of at least one "natural" port. As Figure 29 shows, no such territory is portless, or compelled to divert its trade through a neighbor's shipping channels.

The French Community and the Republic of Guinea

While the long insistence of the French on the economic and administrative dominance of Dakar may have been unfortunate in some respects, it has been responsible for the development of its natural harbor into a first-class port. At the present time ships drawing nearly 33 feet may enter it at any tide. The almost three miles of harbor quays have a minimum of about 21 feet of water alongside. Some of the quays have 30 feet. Almost all of them are equipped with feeder lines from the Dakar-Niger railway, traveling cranes and oil-bunkering facilities. All told there is sheltered anchorage behind Cape Manuel of Cape Verde Peninsula and the island of Gorée for about 60 ocean-going vessels. In recent years the port has been handling over half of the import and export trade of the west African territories of the French Community. Most of its business falls into the category of general merchandise; peanuts and peanut oil form a large part of the exports, petroleum and coal a large part of the imports.

Next in rank comes Abidjan. Though opened only in the summer of 1950, it is already a major port by west African standards. As of 1958 it had nearly a mile of deep-water berthing and all the usual conveniences. Like Dakar, it is linked by rail with its hinterland. In time it is expected that Abidjan will come to do as much business as Dakar, since potentially the Republic of the Ivory Coast is one of the richest in west Africa. Most of the outbound traffic consists of agricultural produce, such as coffee and cocoa, and hardwood timbers; most of the inbound traffic consists of fuels and manufactured goods.

Other sizable ocean ports, each with rail access to the interior, are Conakry in the Republic of Guinea and Cotonou in the Republic of Dahomey. Conakry, on Tumbo Island (which is tied to the mainland by a rail-and-road bridge), is an improved natural harbor. It has about 1,500 feet of pier with a minimum-depth clearance of 21 feet, modern loading and unloading facilities, and a cold-storage depot. Most of its export trade is in bananas, coffee, palm kernels, bauxite and iron ore; most of its im-

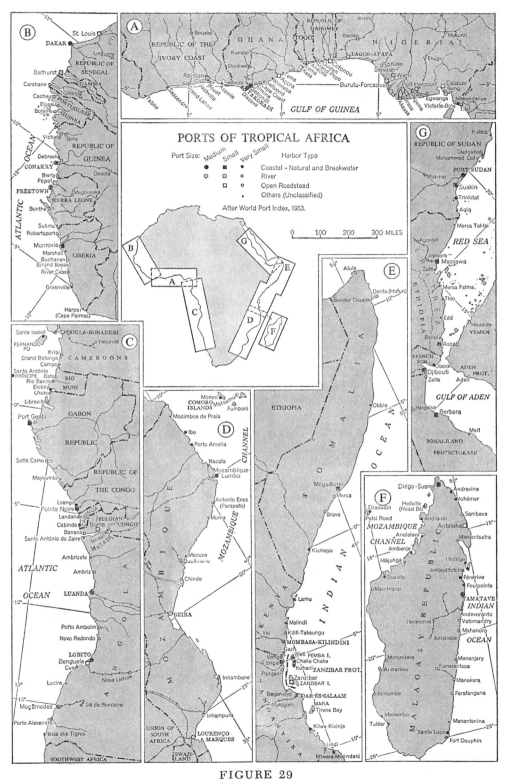

PORTS OF TROPICAL AFRICA

Port Size: Medium Small Very Small   Harbor Type
● ▣ •   Coastal – Natural and Breakwater
◐ ▢ ◦   River
▢ ◦   Open Roadstead
•   Others (Unclassified)

After World Port Index, 1953.

0   100   200   300 MILES

FIGURE 29
449

ports consist of manufactured goods and petroleum products. The ore dock has 37 feet of water alongside and can accommodate two freighters. The port of Cotonou is less well equipped and does a much smaller business, the exports consisting largely of coffee and palm products, and the imports being much the same as in the other west African territories.

Commonwealth West Africa

Each of the constituent territories can claim to have at least one modern port. Gambia and Sierra Leone have obtained theirs by using broad river estuaries; Ghana by building two long, overlapping breakwaters in an open roadstead; Nigeria by developing a lagoon.

Gambia's port of Bathurst is located on the estuary of the Gambia River. Although the site has been used as an anchorage for over three hundred years, it was not until 1952 that seagoing ships were able to load and unload at a deep-water wharf. This wharf provides a 24-foot clearance at low tide. The bulk of the port's small export business is in peanuts, the colony's only important cash crop; its imports consist largely of textiles, petroleum and foodstuffs.

Freetown, in Sierra Leone, is located on the south bank of the broad and deep estuary of the Sierra Leone River. The capacity of the harbor is enormous, there being almost no limit to the draft of vessels using it, or the number. However, until 1954 there was no quay long enough and deep enough to allow even two freighters to tie up alongside. The port does a growing export business in palm products (oil and kernels), coffee, cocoa, chrome ore, peanuts and piassava. Its imports consist mostly of manufactured goods and fuels. The only other ports in Sierra Leone are Pepel, built to handle the country's iron ore export trade; Bonthe on Sherbro Island, chiefly important for its export of palm kernels and palm oil; and the open roadstead of Sulima, which has a small export trade in piassava.

All port facilities in Ghana are at present administered by a government agency, the Railway and Harbours administration, but under the terms of the Second Development Plan (1959-1964) the administration of the two entities will be separated. Takoradi, opened in 1928, handles most of the country's export trade in cocoa, manganese, bauxite, and hardwood logs and sawn lumber. It can accommodate the largest vessels plying along the west African coast. Since 1951, a number of additional deep-water and shallow-water berths have been built, along with new marshalling yards and facilities for cargo handling and storage. Construction of a second artificial harbor, at Tema in the Eastern Region, began in 1954. Its first berth was opened to seagoing ships in 1958. The port is expected to become fully operative in 1961.

All the other Ghana ports — at least 27 coastal towns have served as "ports" at one time or another — are open roadsteads that have to contend with the ever-present surf and swell. Only one, Accra, has even a small breakwater. Notwithstanding, most of the cargo has to be carried directly from ship to beach and from beach to ship. The range of cargoes handled in this way is equaled only by the ingenuity of the men who handle them. Nobody knows how many crates were lost in the sands before the surfboat crewmen mastered the technique of balancing them athwart the bulwarks of their temperamental craft. But many cars and many other valuable cargoes are still brought to shore in this way — not that anybody regards it as a satisfactory method, especially for commodities, like cartonned foodstuffs, cocoa and cement, that do not improve by being seasoned with salt water. Despite the hazards, Accra has handled as much as 375,000 tons of freight in the course of a year. In time Accra is likely to be superseded as a port by Tema, as shelterless Sekondi was by Takoradi.

Lagos, the federal capital and chief port of Nigeria, is located on an island in a sheltered lagoon at the one point in the miles of coast between Dahomey and the Niger delta where there is a gap in the fringing sand banks. By dint of constant dredging, a deep channel is maintained through the gap from the open ocean to the port installations. These installations are in two parts. On the east side of the lagoon are the islands of Lagos and Iddo, connected with each other by road bridge and with the mainland by causeway. The Ijora wharf on Iddo is used principally for the unloading of coal brought by sea from Port Harcourt. The customs wharf at Lagos can accommodate three freighters. To the west of the lagoon is the mainland town of Apapa, which handles the bulk of the traffic, is served by the railway, and has a small floating dock and oil storage facilities.

The overwhelming importance of Lagos to the commercial life of the country is seen in the share of trade it handles. It does two thirds of the total volume of the country's seaborne trade, and it handles larger quantities of cocoa, hides and skins, palm products and peanuts than any other Nigerian port.

The only other port of major consequence to the country is Port Harcourt on the Bonny River at the eastern side of the Niger delta. Originally intended to serve as the outlet for the Enugu coal field, it has come to serve a much wider hinterland with the extension of the railway northward to the Jos Plateau and Kaduna. In addition to coal, it exports considerable quantities of metal ores, palm produce and peanuts.

Nigeria has nine other seaports, all of them small. Two of the nine, Warri (about 25 miles up the Warri River) and Burutu (on an island near the mouth of the Forcados River), are really private ports, the first belonging to the John Holt Line, Ltd., and the second to the United Africa Company Limited. They serve as collecting and transshipment centers for some of the tin, cotton, peanuts, palm products and hides produced in the upstream areas of the Niger-Benue system. The remaining seven, which serve more local functions, are Sapele on the Benin River, principally important for timber and rubber; Koko, a palm port, also on the Benin River; Degema, a palm port on the Bonny River; Forcados, below Burutu on the river of the same name, also a palm port; Calabar, a palm port on the Cross River; and the British Cameroons "plantation" ports of Tiko and Victoria, which are mainly concerned with the export of bananas, rubber and cocoa.

Other West African Territories

The only other west African ports of any rank are Bissau in Portuguese Guinea and Monrovia in Liberia.

Bissau stands on an island in the estuary of the Geba River. It has a single deep-water wharf at which it handles most of the colony's small foreign trade in peanuts and palm products.

The American-built Free Port of Monrovia has a 2,000-foot deep-water wharf, capable of accommodating up to nine cargo vessels at a time. Since its opening in 1948 it has come to take most of the business formerly done by the little surfboat ports of Robertsport, Marshall, Buchanan, River Cess, Greenville and Cape Palmas. Its principal outbound cargoes are iron ore and rubber (latex); its principal inbound ones, manufactured goods and fuels.[30] The Liberian American-Swedish Minerals Company is developing Buchanan to serve its iron-mining operations.

The French Cameroons

The French Cameroons has two seaports, Douala and Kribi, and a river port, Garoua, on the Bénoué. Of the three, Douala is by far the largest. Formerly vessels had to anchor 25 miles off the town, but a dredged channel now enables seagoing ships to tie up alongside a deep-water quay. In common with most other Atlantic coast ports, Douala's traffic has increased considerably in the postwar period. In 1948 the port was handling only about 250,000 metric tons of traffic; in 1958 its exports alone amounted to well over 300,000 metric tons. Most of the export trade consists of agricultural produce, such as cocoa, coffee, bananas, palm products, rubber, cotton and peanuts. The import trade is made up largely of manufactured goods, in both the capital and the consumer categories, and fuels.

Kribi and Garoua, small as they are in comparison with Douala, play a far from negligible role in the commercial life of the territory. Kribi is primarily concerned with the export of timber and cocoa from its

---

[30] Although a large number of ships are registered at Monrovia (in 1958 their gross tonnage passed the 7-million-ton mark), few of them ever use their home port — the only Liberian thing about many of them being the flag.

expanding hinterland. Garoua is the chief outlet for the produce of northern French Cameroons. The facilities of both ports have been enlarged and modernized in the past few years.

The Gabon Republic and the Republic of the Congo

This region also has three main ports, Libreville, Port Gentil and Pointe Noire. The last of these far outstrips the others in traffic, handling on the average about half of the total seaborne traffic of the region. The port of Pointe Noire was built between 1934 and 1939 to serve the Congo-Océan Railway, which in turn was built to serve the rich Niari valley and to make the then French Equatorial Africa independent of the Belgian Congo route to the Atlantic. Behind its mile-long sea wall it provides more than 160 acres of sheltered water, berthing space alongside the quay for a dozen or so seagoing ships, and cargo-working facilities as up to date as any to be found in tropical Africa and capable of handling over a million tons of traffic annually. In recent years the trade volume handled has been of the order of a third of a million metric tons. Pointe Noire's chief exports are hardwoods, palm kernels and palm oil, cotton and minerals; high on the list of imports are cement, fuels, foodstuffs and beverages.

Libreville and Port Gentil are much less adequately equipped. Notwithstanding, they both do a sizable timber export business. When the present port development program of the administration is complete Port Gentil will have a modern deep-water port comparable to Pointe Noire's, and Libreville a large protective sea mole. The same program provides for the building of quays at the open roadstead of Mayoumba, and at Ovendo on the Gabon estuary.

Spanish Guinea (Fernando Po, Annobón and Rio Muni), the Portuguese enclave of Cabinda, and São Tomé and Príncipe are all without modern ports. The best they can offer in the way of shipping accommodation are open roadsteads and landing beaches (e.g., at Bata and Benito in Rio Muni) and partially sheltered bays (e.g., at Santa Isabel on Fernando Po).

The Congo Estuary

The estuary of the Congo River is partly in Belgian Congo and partly in Angolan territory. Of its six ports, Matadi, Boma, Ango Ango, Banana, Nóqui and S. António do Zaire, the first is easily the best equipped and the largest.

The port of Matadi, first developed by a private railway company, has been administered since 1936 by Otraco. It is far from ideally situated. The stream runs very strongly offshore — between 10 and 11 knots at the flood — and its level fluctuates as much as 23 feet. Ships approaching its quays must negotiate the dangerous narrows and whirlpools of the Devil's Cauldron. The port has very little room for landward development, moreover, partly because of its rocky, hilly site and partly because of the proximity of the Angolan border. Until the late 1950s its needs exceeded its resources. Now that the building program of the Ten Year Plan for the Belgian Congo is complete, Matadi's needs and resources are at last in reasonable balance. Its three deep-water quays (alongside depths of 25 to 31 feet) have a total berthing length of more than a mile and its freight storage sheds cover several acres.

Four miles downstream from Matadi is the out-port of Ango Ango, built (from 1926 onward) to handle the Congo's petroleum needs, and to avoid taking such highly inflammable cargo through the Matadi narrows.

Still farther downstream, on the north bank, lies the port of Boma, which until 1923 was the capital of the Belgian Congo. Today it derives most of its relatively small importance from the fact that it is the terminus of the railway to Tshela, serving the right-bank section of the Bas-Congo district. Both port and railway are operated by Otraco.

The last of the Belgian Congo seaports, Banana, is situated on the north bank, right at the entrance to the estuary. In the old days a bustling slave port, it is now a sleepy little place that comes alive only when its quarantine and pilotage services are needed. It has very few bananas.

The two Portuguese ports on the Congo estuary are Nóqui and S. António do Zaire. Nóqui lies on the south bank downstream from both Matadi and Ango Ango. Hitherto of little importance and with few facilities, it is now being enlarged and modernized in preparation for the business in minerals and agricultural and forestry products that will be channeled to it when its hinterland has better means of transportation. S. António do Zaire, an open roadstead, occupies a position on the south bank corresponding to that of Banana on the north bank. It does a small local business in fish and palm products.

The Angola Coast

Lobito, the country's chief port, outranks its competitors because it is the terminus of the Benguela Railway, a system that serves the Katanga Province of the Belgian Congo as well as the productive highlands of central Angola. Although the port of Benguela was nearby, it was passed over by the planners of the railway in favor of Lobito's safer anchorage behind the long sand spit which parallels the shore. This sand spit — the "gift of the sea" as the Portuguese call it — forms a natural breakwater some three miles long and up to 400 yards in width. The harbor it all but encloses is approximately two square miles in area, and ranges in depth from 18 to 100 feet. The L-shaped quay which has been built at its southwestern end is capable of berthing five or six ocean-going vessels of 35-foot draft.

Since its opening in 1928, the port has seldom been hard-pressed. Not until 1954 did its volume of trade reach the port's estimated capacity of approximately a million metric tons, and even this figure is far below the estimated 3.5-million-ton capacity which the port will have when the present long-range development program is complete.[31] How soon the port will need such a capacity will depend largely on the transport and tariff policies of the Belgian Congo and, possibly, of the Federation of Rhodesia and Nyasaland. Lobito is very advantageously placed as an outlet for Katanga and the Copperbelt, but it is improbable that its advantages could be fully exploited save at some loss of traffic to both Matadi and Beira. Most of its traffic at present is made up of goods in transit either to or from Katanga and the Copperbelt. The domestic outbound traffic consists largely of agricultural produce (maize, beans, manioc, rice, sisal, etc.), fish and salt; the inbound traffic largely of fuels, wines and liquors, cement and general manufactured merchandise.

Luanda, the second port and the capital of Angola, is concerned exclusively with domestic trade. Because of the larger European population living in its hinterland and in the city itself than in Lobito and in the Angolan part of its hinterland, the value of Luanda's domestic trade is larger than that of Lobito. Its exports are made up largely of coffee, palm oil, oilseeds and other agricultural produce; its imports are very similar to those of Lobito. Like Lobito it enjoys the advantages of a sheltered, deep and commodious anchorage; it has berthing facilities for up to six ocean-going vessels, and good railway connections with the interior.

Moçâmedes is at present a rather poor third to Lobito and Luanda. Salt, fish, and fish meal and oil are its leading exports; its imports are much the same as those of Lobito and Luanda, but the amounts imported are quite small. However, its business is expected to expand when the Moçâmedes Railway, which at present taps only one or two productive areas, is carried eastward toward the Northern Rhodesian border. In expectation of bigger things to come, a breakwater and a quay, complete with modern handling and storage facilities, were built in the mid-1950s, coming into service in 1957.

Besides these three international ports, there are many that carry a small coastwise trade. The chief of these are, in order of occurrence from north to south, Ambrizete, Ambriz, Porto Amboim, Novo Redondo, Benguela (now almost a ghost port), Cuío, Lucira, Porto Alexandre and Baía dos Tigres.

[31] W. A. Hance and I. S. van Dongen, "The Port of Lobito and the Benguela Railway," *Geographical Review*, October 1956, p. 462.

The Indian Ocean and Red Sea coasts of tropical Africa differ physically from the Atlantic Ocean coasts in two important respects. First, because they are considerably warmer than the Atlantic coasts (which are washed by the cool Canary and Benguela currents), they have provided the coral polyp with a congenial environment in which to breed. Coral reefs, accordingly, border long stretches of the coast, providing shelter for small craft at the same time as they deny it to large craft. Second, because these coasts are on the whole drier than the west coast, few of their river mouths are either deep enough or wide enough to have the makings of satisfactory harbors. By way of partial compensation, they do have a number of large, well-placed, deep-water bays that have lent themselves to port development.

The Malagasy Republic

The finest bay on the island, and one of the finest natural harbors in tropical Africa, is Diego-Suarez in the extreme north. However, because of its remoteness from the economic hub, its mercantile functions are few and small. Down to 1959 most of its importance had been derived from the presence of the French naval and naval-air base.

The chief port is Tamatave. It was selected in 1897, says Kline, as "the site most amenable to improvement in the neighborhood of the most productive part of the country — the Merina area with its great city and capital of Tananarive." Since 1927, when they were badly damaged by a tropical cyclone, the port installations have been extensively rebuilt, enlarged and modernized. They now include two long moles and steel piers with more than 1,500 feet of deep-water dockage. The port does a large coastwise collecting and distributing business in addition to handling more than half of the island's overseas trade.

Other ports engaged in overseas trade are Majunga at the mouth of the Betsiboka River (on the northwest coast) and Tuléar near the mouth of the Onilahy River (on the southwest coast).

There are some 15 other ports along the coasts, all of them engaged almost exclusively in local shipping.

Mozambique

One of the finest bays on the whole of the east coast provides the setting of Mozambique's major port, Lourenço Marques. Three well-marked, dredged channels link its 12 square miles of completely sheltered anchorage with the open ocean, 25 miles downstream. Along its 7,300-foot quay 21 vessels of 30-foot draft can berth at one time. The facilities provided for both day and night working of cargo are much above the tropical African norm. They are very well run and seldom strained.

Long a major outlet for the agricultural and mineral products of the Transvaal and the not inconsiderable traffic generated in the Limpopo and Incomati valleys, Lourenço Marques has been serving recently as an outlet for the agricultural and mineral products of the Rhodesias. The chief domestic exports are cotton and cottonseed, sugar, cashew nuts and timber; the chief domestic imports, textiles, machinery (including motor vehicles), wines and fuels. In 1957-1958 the volume of goods moving through Lourenço Marques was of the order of 5 to 5.5 million short tons annually. These figures are considerably higher than those of the early 1950s and reflect in large measure the increased use which the Federation of Rhodesia and Nyasaland has been making of the southeast connection. As we saw earlier, this has given the Bulawayo region of Southern Rhodesia a direct rail link with Lourenço Marques.

Beira is the second largest port in the province. Since the beginning of the century it has been the major port for the two Rhodesias and Nyasaland, a minor port for the Belgian Congo, as well as the port for its own quite large hinterland. Unlike most of the others in east Africa, it is a river port, being situated on the Pungwe River about 15 miles from the open sea. Its newly lengthened quay has an alongside depth of 33 feet and accommodates several ocean-going vessels. One of the berths is served by a conveyor belt three quarters of a mile long with an ore-carrying capacity of 400 tons an hour. Liquid fuel can also be loaded and unloaded at this berth by means of pipelines connected with shore installations.

Like those of Lourenço Marques, the facilities for the handling and storage of general merchandise are modern and well run; but unlike those of Lourenço Marques, they have proved less than adequate in the postwar years to meet the demands made upon them, even though they have been and continue to be worked on an almost round-the-clock basis. Some of the inadequacies have been removed, it is true, as a result of the introduction of traffic phasing [32] and the expansion of both port and rail capacity, but others remain. Wharf accommodation is still small by ordinary standards. The harbor is difficult to enter and leave, especially at neap tides, when the minimum depth on the bar is only about 16 feet; and it shows an unfortunate tendency to shoal. Then, too, the Beira Railway is still hampered by its inability to take more than a 15-ton axle load. In the middle and late 1950s the port was handling about 3 million short tons, which was virtually its capacity. Most of the outbound Rhodesian and Nyasaland traffic consists of minerals, tobacco, tea and other agricultural crops, and the inbound traffic, of manufactured goods and fuels. The domestic trade is broadly similar to that of Lourenço Marques.

The oldest port in the province, Mozambique, founded in the early sixteenth century, is no longer as important as it used to be. It is still used by a number of shipping lines, but apart from its historical interest

[32] See pp. 423-24.

and its deep anchorage — it can accommodate ships drawing 28 feet — it has little to commend it. It is situated on an offshore coral island (of the same name) that generates little traffic, and whose chief function is that of an entrepôt. All goods moving to and from the mainland have to be transshipped at the port of Lumbo, which is small, poorly equipped and incapable of the expansion required to meet the fast-growing needs of this northern "frontier" region.

The port destined to serve most of these needs is Nacala, situated roughly 50 miles north of Lumbo. For

Nacala has beyond doubt the finest harbor in eastern Africa and one of the best in the world. Its entrance is approached through the wide and deep bay of Fernão Veloso, and is completely sheltered, half a mile wide and 200 feet deep. Within is an enclosed water area eight miles long and from two to four miles wide, nowhere less than 36 feet deep, and with deep water close to the shore along the eastern side of the harbor.[33]

The Portuguese have already begun to turn these assets to account by making Nacala the terminus of the railway that formerly ended at Lumbo and by constructing a two-berth deep-water wharf. Another wharf and a large drydock are planned.

Still farther north lies another fine natural harbor, Porto Amélia. This is expected to become the fourth port of the province. Work has already started on the construction of a two-berth deep-water wharf.

In the absence of north-south land lines, Mozambique, like Angola, makes much use of coastwise shipping. Serving its ends are a large number of small craft and small ports. Between Lourenço Marques and Beira are Vila de João Belo, on the Limpopo River, and Inhambane, the terminus of the railway to Inharrime. Between Beira and the island of Mozambique are Chinde near the mouth of the Zambezi River (before the completion of the railway to Beira in 1922 this port handled the bulk of Nyasaland's overseas export and import trade), Quelimane at the terminus of the railway line to Mocuba, and Macuse, Moma and António Enes. North of Porto Amélia are the tiny ports of Ibo and Mocímboa da Praia.

British East Africa

The major seaports along this section of the east coast are Kilindini in Kenya, and Dar-es-Salaam, Tanga and Mtwara in Tanganyika.

Kilindini — the port for Mombasa — is the most important of the three. After Nacala it has the largest expanse of sheltered deep water (its name means "the place of deep waters"), and after Lourenço Marques the largest business, of any Indian Ocean port falling within the limits of this study. Its spacious haven is capable of accommodating vessels of up to

---

[33] H. C. Brookfield, "New Railroad and Port Developments in East and Central Africa," *Economic Geography*, Volume 31 (1955), p. 64.

45,000 tons burden and 760 feet in length. Although well equipped by prewar standards, it was gravely embarrassed by the postwar boom. For several years it was customary to see more vessels idling their time away in the stream than tied up alongside. Frequently vessels had to wait for days, even weeks, before they could be berthed; and when their turns came, the turn-around time was distressingly long. The port is now a model of streamlined efficiency. Extensions to the deep-water berths and lighterage wharves have been made and additional cargo-handling equipment brought into service at a cost of $20 million in the last few years. By 1958 there were more than 4,700 feet of general cargo quays capable of berthing eight ocean-going vessels drawing up to 32 feet. There were also jetties for handling bulk and cased oil, and ample storage sheds. All of these facilities were served by modern equipment. Three additional deep-water berths were under construction.[34]

Including transshipments, nearly 2 million tons of general cargo and more than a million tons of oil were handled by the port in 1958. The principal domestic exports were coffee, cotton, soda carbonate, sisal, oilseed and cake, wattle and tea. More than 50 categories of goods were represented in the imports, the chief being fuels, textiles, iron and steel manufactures, machinery and motor vehicles.

Dar-es-Salaam is also blessed with a sheltered deep-water anchorage. Its harbor is, in fact, as near to being landlocked as any in the world. But it is not as commodious as Kilindini and not as well equipped. Until the middle 1950s it was subject to all the delays and other disadvantages of a lighterage port. Now it has three deep-water quays, one of which is owned by the Belgians, under the terms of a free-port agreement with the Tanganyika government. The volume of Belgian Congo traffic moving through the port and over the Central Line to Lake Tanganyika has grown substantially in recent years. Dar, as everyone calls it, also handles a fair amount of dhow traffic, both coastwise and foreign (mainly with Arabian ports).

Tanganyika's second port, Tanga, is little more than a roadstead serving a limited, though very important, function. It is through Tanga that a large part of the sisal crop of the territory is exported. The port is linked by railway with the rich agricultural region around Mounts Kilimanjaro and Meru, where much of the territory's coffee crop is grown; however, a good deal of the trade of these areas is handled through Mombasa over the Kahe Junction–Voi branch line.

Mtwara is the newest and, as yet, the smallest of the four major ports of British East Africa. But if its promoters' hopes for it come true, it may

[34] All existing harbor facilities are on the "Island." Mombasa remained an island until 1940 when the linking bridge was filled in to become a causeway so as to prevent any infiltration of Japanese submarines into the waters adjacent to the mainland. A further link with the mainland, providing rail connection with the new marshalling yard at Changamwe, has recently been completed.

well become one of the largest. Its construction was undertaken in 1948, in conjunction with that of the Southern Province Line, for the main purpose of providing the Tanganyika Groundnut Scheme with transportation facilities commensurate with the expected crops. When it became apparent that the scheme as originally planned was not going to succeed, interest in the port flagged. It was opened officially only in 1954. Its facilities include a deep-water general cargo quay and up-to-date mechanical handling gear and storage sheds. The waters of the almost completely enclosed harbor are deep enough to allow large ships to come and go at any tidal stage. So far neither the facilities nor the waters have suffered from congestion. The Tanganyika Agricultural Corporation, the successor to the Overseas Food Corporation which administered the original Groundnut Scheme, is one of its main users, but the firm's exportable crop surpluses are still small, as also are its needs of capital equipment and supplies.

The port could probably be kept quite busy if the Southern Province Line were carried westward from its present terminus, to Songea and round the head of Lake Nyasa by way of Njombe and Mbeya; for these highland areas are cool and well watered, capable of great agricultural development, and the Songea area is endowed with mineral wealth, including coal. If such a rail line were carried still farther southwestward, as has been proposed, to Northern Rhodesia, to link up with the Rhodesia Railways, Mtwara might even become congested.

The rest of the British East African seaports are all of minor rank. Most of their business is coastwise or between the offshore islands and the mainland. Much of it is done in dhows and smaller craft. Going from south to north, these ports are Mikindani, Lindi and Mkwaya (all of which are being superseded by Mtwara), Kilwa Kivinje, Bagamoyo,[35] Pangani, Mombasa Old Harbour (which does a brisk dhow traffic with places as far away as the Malagasy Republic, the Persian Gulf and India), Kilifi, Malindi and Lamu, not forgetting the ports of the islands of Pemba and Zanzibar (which has a quay for vessels of less than 18-foot draft).

The Somalilands

Somalia. In all of tropical Africa there is probably no more inhospitable coast than that of Somalia. Most of it is desert or semi-desert. Fresh water and food are both hard to find. Except at one point, sheltered anchorage is unobtainable, and if there was ever a coast that needed shelter it is Somalia's during the summer monsoon when the prevailing wind is onshore and an ugly swell is often running. The significance of this seasonal condition for shipping deprived of shelter is seen in the 1949 ruling of the Somaliland administration that between June 1 and

[35] For long this was *the* slave port of east Africa. Its name, meaning "lay down your life (or heart)," was then all too appropriate.

September 15 all ports between the Kenya border and Cape Guardafui were to remain closed except Mogadishu and Kismayu, which were open "subject to weather," and that between June 1 and August 31 all the ports on the Gulf of Aden were to remain closed.

The main port is Mogadishu, the capital of the territory and the outlet for its one large cultivated area, in the Uebi Scebeli. Its traffic (exports, mainly bananas; imports, fuels and manufactured goods) is handled by lighters. Kismayu, near the mouth of the Juba River, is the only port offering sheltered anchorage, but so far it has done little about exploiting its uniqueness. Other small ports, or rather open roadsteads, used mainly by sailing dhows, are Brava, Merca and Obbia on the Indian Ocean, and Alula and Bender Cassim on the Gulf of Aden.

British Somaliland. The only port of any consequence is Berbera, which is occasionally visited by small ocean-going vessels and has regular connections by dhow with Aden. Dhows also work out from the two open roadsteads of Mait, in the east, and Zeila, in the west of the protectorate.

French Somaliland. The one good port in the whole of the Somalilands is Djibouti. Situated on the south side of the Gulf of Tadjoura, it is commodious and, except during the "monsoon" months of June, July and August when high seas frequently run, may be entered, and left, in any wind or water. The harbor proper is an artificial one, formed by jetties. Loading and unloading facilities are on the primitive side, for the port has no deep-water quay and all vessels must anchor offshore. For many years Djibouti was the "natural" outlet for the highlands of Ethiopia and handled most of its export and import trade. To encourage the Ethiopians to continue using it after their federation with Eritrea, the French eliminated all customs duties on goods passing through Djibouti. While the Ethiopians continue to use the port, and the railway that feeds it, they are giving greatly increased attention to their newly acquired Eritrean ports. The chief domestic shipments from Djibouti are salt and hides; the chief "transit" shipments, coffee, hides and skins, and grain; the chief imports (domestic and transit), textiles and other manufactured goods, and fuels.

When the French occupied this section of the coast in the nineteenth century, Obock, lying at the northern entrance of the Gulf, was its main port, but its fortunes declined rapidly after Djibouti became the terminus of the Franco-Ethiopian Railway.

The Red Sea Coast

The African coast of the Red Sea may not be troubled by wind and swell, but it offers little attraction to the sea trader. It is hot, hotter at times than any other part of the African coast; it is dry, having no permanent streams and few wells; and it has next to no cultivated areas, so that the victualing of ships is a problem. Further, it is fringed by coral reefs that are more ornamental than useful. Even so, neither the Eritrean nor the Sudanese section of the coast is as badly off for ports as the Somaliland sections.

In Eritrea, Massawa, designed by the Italians to serve as a civil and naval port, is able to accommodate large vessels without difficulty. So far its physical facilities more than meet the needs of its hinterland, which, thanks to the Italian-built railway, includes the capital of Asmara and the surrounding plateau. No doubt, in time the Ethiopians will succeed in extending this hinterland to take in the northernmost perimeter of their highlands, but Massawa could never become a serious contender for the business of the central (Addis Ababa) highlands. The land distances involved are too great, and the terrain altogether too rugged.

The port that is much more likely to compete with Djibouti is Assab, located in southeastern Eritrea near the French Somaliland border. The development of Assab from an open roadstead to a real deep-water port with jetties was undertaken in the late 1930s by the Italians as part of their colonization program. Although it is still far from being a first-class port, it is already connected by a truck road to Addis Ababa, and its further improvement is high on the list of the country's development plans.

The other mainland ports, all of them very small and used only by local craft, are (going from south to north) Beilul, Edd, Thio, Marsa Fatma, Zula and Marsa Taklai. There are also a number of small ports on the offshore islands.

The premier port of the Republic of Sudan is Port Sudan. It owes its status to three things: the existence of a large natural harbor; easy passage through the offshore coral reef belt; and an assured water supply in the bed of a wadi (Khor Arba'at) about 20 miles to the north. It lies at the northern terminus of the railway line from Khartoum. Its main deep-water quay has a minimum clearance of 28 feet; up to 33 feet of water is available on the bunkering quay. Its handling and storage facilities are modern, spacious and well run. Through the port goes nearly 90 per cent of the Sudan's external trade, including most of the ginned cotton and cottonseed.

Of much greater antiquity is the now largely ruined and deserted port of Suakin, lying 40 miles to the southeast. For centuries this was the pilgrim port for Mecca, and one of the main Red Sea slave ports. It still does a little "trade" in pilgrims; but, judging from the rate at which its buildings are being dismantled and carted away, the port will shortly lose what little remains of its ancient airs and architecture, as well as its trade.

Other, smaller dhow ports along the Sudanese section of the Red Sea coast are Aqiq and Trinkitat south of Suakin, and Mohammed Qol and Dungunab north of Port Sudan.

ROADS

It is more difficult to talk usefully about the roads than about the railways and waterways of tropical Africa.

To begin with, there is the matter of definition. What is a road to one man is a track to another, and what is a motorable road in the dry season may well be an impassable track in the wet season.

Then there is the matter of documentation. Unlike most railways and waterways, which require a lot of survey work, financing, organizing and publicizing, and so get into everybody's files, most roads are built without fanfare, and often without very much of anything except local initiative and labor. All travelers in Africa come upon roads that don't exist on the maps or in the official files. (On the other hand, it is only fair to say that most travelers sooner or later have the worse experience of hunting in vain for roads that are on the maps, and, presumably, in the official files.) The fact is that roads are nowadays being built in so many places and so rapidly that mileage statistics are obsolete before they are printed — and probably wrong to start with. And what is true of mileage statistics is truer still of traffic statistics. Whereas all railway and shipping companies keep records of their carriers, the passengers and goods hauled by them, their gross and net revenues, and so on, only the larger motor transport companies do so; and a notable proportion of the road transportation business is in the hands of small operators. Even if all the companies kept satisfactory records, it would still be impossible to obtain the total volume of traffic, passenger or freight, over a given stretch of road, since there would be no means of ascertaining the volume of traffic created by owner-drivers. In some parts of tropical Africa this is quite heavy, for the only way many Africans can manage to maintain a car is by plying it for hire among their friends.

The matter of description also presents problems. Tropical Africa already has more than a third of a million miles of "motorable road." No territory, it is true, has nearly as much as it would like; but all territories have some. In one or two instances the road mileage claimed by a territory is even more than the railway mileage for the region as a whole. It is clear therefore that it would be impractical, in a study of this size, to describe in detail the courses and characteristics of the roads. All it is practical to do is to indicate what the threads in the seemingly pattern-less weave of land routes are made of, how strong or how weak they are, where they run, and what functions they perform.

Most tropical African roads fall into the "dirt" category. The material used in the making of them is, so far as possible, the local soil. Where it is available, coarse-textured soil of the type usually spoken of as laterite is favored. It has the double advantage of being porous, so that it dries quickly after rain, and of being handled easily. Its main disadvantages are its tendency to corrugate with heavy use, to "pothole" badly during heavy rains, and to turn to dust in the dry season. Maintenance costs are consequently high. And because most of these roads are maintained by unskilled and inadequately supervised crews, their quality, even when new, is inclined to be poor. Machine maintenance of such roads is still regarded by many highway engineers as uneconomic; but where the efficiency of road crews is low, as it frequently is, and labor is scarce, the gains of mechanization almost certainly outweigh the losses.

In places where the local earth is unsuitable, as, for example, in regions of unconsolidated sands and silts, or where the traffic is heavy or is carried in heavy trucks, either gravel or hard-topped roads become necessary. Both types need more engineering, more materials and, of course, more money. Their cost depends, among other things, on the amount of bridging, embanking and draining to be done, on the nature of the bedrock, on the articulation of the terrain, and on the proximity of the necessary supplies and labor crews. Because these are such variable factors, average construction cost figures are frequently meaningless. In British East Africa, the average cost of building a mile of first-class road is said to be between £8,000 and £10,000,[36] but in any given hundred miles of first-class road, the unit cost could well range between £200 and £20,000. In 1955 in the then French Equatorial Africa, one mile of road with a high tonnage capacity was said to cost anything up to $184,000.[37] In west Africa, where the physical conditions are generally more favorable, the average is much lower, about £2,000 a mile,[38] but even here the range in unit cost is large, say between £50 and £5,000. Actual construction costs have a habit of running higher than estimated costs everywhere, sometimes very much higher.

Once built, both gravel and hard-topped roads tend to be less expensive to maintain than dirt roads. Maintenance is never cheap, however, partly because most materials have to be brought in from a distance, partly because of the heavy wear and tear on highway machinery, and partly because of the rapid deterioration of the road margins which follows from the fact that most of the gravel and tarred roads are one lane wide, so that the soft shoulders must be used for passing and parking.[39]

So far no territory has managed to build more than a small mileage of first-class hard-topped or gravel roads. Nowhere is the ratio of such roads to the total higher than about 1:13; in some territories it is less than 1:200. But everywhere there is a clamant need for them. They are needed not only to make good the more serious gaps in the other surface

[36] A. G. Thomson, "Cheap Roads for Africa," New Commonwealth, February 15, 1954, p. 178.
[37] "The Franco-African Transportation System . . .," African Affairs (Ambassade de France), April 1955, p. 3.
[38] Thomson, loc. cit.
[39] In Ghana, a fairly representative country, annual maintenance costs were estimated in 1954 to be over £200 per mile for tarred roads and £167 per mile for gravel roads.

— railway and waterway — systems, and to foster economic and social development of all kinds, but also to reduce the appallingly high cost of maintaining vehicles on the dirt roads. The situation in a fairly typical part of west Africa has been described as follows:

Trucks must enter a repair shop, or receive emergency repairs on the road, after a run of 300 to 400 miles. Standard passenger automobiles must be garaged, for minor adjustments at least, after a day's run. Springs, shock absorbers, axles, steering parts, etc., must be replaced frequently.[40]

The most that can be expected from a heavy-duty truck, on the dirt roads of any territory, is about two years' profitable service. If it gets regular care from skilled mechanics, it may last three years; if it gets the more customary hit-or-miss treatment, it may have to be written off after one year.

Beyond any question it is the fast depreciation of motor vehicles of all types that continues to constitute the main deterrent to their wider use. Even so, the number of registered vehicles (passenger and commercial) has risen sharply in recent years. In Nigeria, for instance, it rose from less than 1,500 in 1938 to approximately 40,000 in 1957; between 1950 and 1957 alone it rose by more than 25,000. In Southern Rhodesia the number rose from 19,500 in 1937 to over 85,000 in 1957. As Table 29 shows, the total number of registered vehicles in tropical Africa increased by more than 200 per cent between 1948 and 1957.

Because of the high costs involved in building better roads and the seeming improbability that either governments or corporations will be able to build enough to match the demand, a good deal of thought is being given to the possibility of making wider use of "roadless" vehicles. The jeep and the Land-Rover and others of their kind have demonstrated their roughshod riding abilities. What these can do for the trackless bush, why should not the "weasel" and the "snocat" do for the sand, and the "swamp buggy" for the flood plains? There are many who believe they can, with modifications. R. G. Letourneau, Inc., a pioneer in the field of unconventional vehicles, has already developed a 35-ton roadless freight carrier, each wheel of which is independently driven by an electric motor. Such vehicles might one day help to solve the problem of freight transportation in such dry areas as Bechuanaland and southern Angola, the Somalilands and the southern flanks of the Sahara. They can, it is claimed, ride through deep mud. Buoyed up by their huge low-pressure tires, they might manage even to traverse streams.

Meanwhile, the roads of tropical Africa are in no danger of being outmoded, primitive though most of them are.

For convenience, and with some reason, the major strands in the road net may be divided into warp and woof strands. The former run roughly

---

[40] U. S. Department of Commerce, *Transportation and Electrical Energy in French West Africa*, World Trade Series, No. 543, February 1954, p. 14.

Table 29

MOTOR VEHICLES IN USE, BY TERRITORY, 1948 AND 1957

(*Thousands*)

TERRITORY	1948			1957 [a]		
	TOTAL	PASSEN-GER CARS	COMMER-CIAL CARS	TOTAL	PASSEN-GER CARS	COMMER-CIAL CARS
Total (partial)	206.4			638.4		
Angola [b, c]	6.5	3.9	2.6	30.4	21.4	9.0
Belgian Congo	17.1	6.8	10.3 [d]	57.3	33.8 [e]	23.5 [e]
British Somaliland	0.4	0.1 [f]	0.3 [f]	0.7	0.3	0.4
Eritrea	3.3	1.1	2.2 ⎫	22.9	16.7 [h, e]	6.2 [h, e]
Ethiopia	4.7	3.2 [g]	1.5 [g] ⎭			
French Cameroons	4.9	0.8 [g]	4.1 [g]	23.4	6.8	16.6
French Equatorial Africa [b]	3.2	n.a.	n.a.	23.2	8.4	14.8
French Somaliland	0.4	0.2 [g]	0.2 [g]	1.5	1.0 [i]	0.5 [i]
(French) Togo [b]	0.3	0.1 [f]	0.2 [f]	2.6	0.9 [i]	1.7 [i]
French West Africa [b]	20.8	6.6	14.2	80.8	34.3	46.5
Gambia	0.6	0.3	0.3	1.2	0.5	0.7
Ghana (Gold Coast) [b]	n.a.	n.a.	n.a.	28.3	13.4 [i]	14.9 [i]
Kenya [b, j]	21.5	12.2	9.3	60.5	49.6	10.9
Malagasy Republic (Madagascar) [b]	13.6	7.2	6.4	31.1	15.5 [k]	15.6 [k]
Mozambique [c]	10.9	7.8	3.1	24.1	19.0 [i]	5.1 [i]
Nigeria [l]	14.2	6.9 [f]	7.3 [f]	40.1	20.2	19.9
Northern Rhodesia [b, m]	9.5	5.3	4.2	40.2	27.2	13.0
Nyasaland [b]	2.4	1.4	1.0	8.1	4.4	3.7
Portuguese Guinea [b, c]	0.4	0.2 [n]	0.2 [n]	n.a.	n.a.	n.a.
Ruanda-Urundi	n.a.	n.a.	n.a.	4.5	2.6 [e]	1.9 [e]
São Tomé & Príncipe [b, c]	0.4	0.2 [f]	0.2 [f]	0.6	0.4 [o]	0.2 [o]
Sierra Leone	1.1	0.9 [f]	0.2 [f]	4.8	3.0 [i]	1.8 [i]
Somalia (Italian Somaliland) [k, p]	3.4	0.7 [f]	2.7 [f]	4.7	1.8	2.9
Southern Rhodesia [b, m]	39.0	26.0	13.0	85.2	64.4 [e]	20.8 [e]
Republic of Sudan (Anglo-Egyptian Sudan)	7.0	3.0	4.0	20.1	10.0	10.1
Tanganyika [j, k]	13.9	8.6 [n]	5.3 [n]	25.2	18.0	7.2
Uganda [j, k]	6.2	3.7	2.5 [q]	25.9	20.7	5.2 [q]
Zanzibar & Pemba [j]	0.7	0.4	0.3	2.0	1.4	0.6

Source: United Nations, *Statistical Yearbook, 1958,* New York, 1958.

[a] Provisional.
[b] Including police cars.
[c] Figures refer to "light" and "heavy" vehicles.
[d] Excluding buses.
[e] Excluding vehicles exempt from taxation.
[f] 1950.
[g] 1949.
[h] Including Eritrea.
[i] 1956.
[j] Light commercial vehicles are included with passenger cars.
[k] Excluding government vehicles.
[l] Including British Cameroons.
[m] Including military vehicles.
[n] 1951.
[o] 1955.
[p] Including vehicles no longer in use.
[q] Excluding tractor and semi-trailer combinations.   n.a.: not available.

north-south, that is, longitudinally, and the latter roughly east-west, or latitudinally, across the region. The pattern they make may be seen in the accompanying map (Figure 30).

MAJOR LONGITUDINAL ROUTES

Trans-Saharan

Five motorable roads span the Sahara, linking tropical Africa with North Africa. The westernmost of the five leaves Agadir on the coast of southern Morocco, strikes overland for Tindouf in the extreme west of Algeria, crosses the Islamic Republic of Mauritania near the border of Spanish West Africa and comes out to the coast again at St. Louis at the mouth of the Senegal River. From here it goes on to Dakar. This is commonly known as the Mauritanian Road, or Route Number 1. It can be used the year around.

The second route, known as the Tanezrouft Road, runs almost due south from Colomb Béchar in western Algeria through the waterless Tanezrouft to Bourem on the great bend of the middle Niger, and thence downstream to Niamey. During the cool season, buses are operated regularly over the whole of its 1,750-mile length.

Still farther east, and roughly parallel, lies the Hoggar Road. Leaving the Saharan Atlas Mountains at Laghouat in Algeria, it passes through In Salah, Tamanrasset and Agadès to end at Zinder. This 1,700-mile route likewise has a cool-season bus service.

The fourth route, actually known to the French as Number 5, runs from Gabès on the coast of Tunisia to Remada and thence across the Libyan border to Ghadames. From here it goes south, keeping to the Algerian side of the border, to Fort Gardel, and thence to Fort Lamy on the upper Chari River. Up to now this has been the least used, because the most difficult, of the French Saharan routes.

The fifth route lies wholly in Egyptian and Sudanese territory, and follows the line of the Nile valley from Port Said (or Alexandria) through Cairo upstream as far as Idfu, where it strikes across the desert, following a more direct route than the river, to Wadi Halfa. Here it forks, one branch following the Nile, the other following the railway, to Khartoum.

Trans-equatorial

Beyond the Sahara the range of longitudinal routes open to the motorist is more restricted. He can either take "the high road" through British East Africa or "the low road" through the Congo basin.

If he crosses the Sahara by the Hoggar Road he can get onto the low road by striking south from Zinder to Kano and thence to Fort Lamy. If he crosses by Number 5, he can avoid the still rather indifferent section between Kano and Fort Lamy — though he may well regard any road as

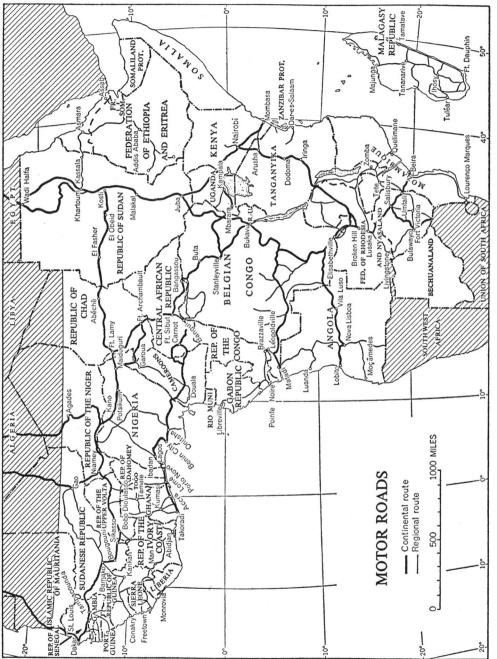

MOTOR ROADS

—— Continental route
—— Regional route

0   500   1000 MILES

FIGURE 30 (After Hibberd V. B. Kline, Jr.; information as of late 1950s)

an improvement on Number 5! From Fort Lamy the road goes southeast to Fort Archambault and Fort Sibut, thence to Bangassou on the border between the Central African Republic and the Belgian Congo. At this point it is possible, with the help of small hand-operated ferries, to go by car around the eastern perimeter of the Congo system to Buta, Stanleyville, Walikale and Bukavu.[41] From Bukavu the road goes southwest to Kasongo and Kamina. From Kamina it keeps fairly close to the line of the BCK railway as far as Sakania on the Northern Rhodesian border. Throughout its course across the Belgian Congo, this route can be used by motor traffic at all seasons. A few miles inside Northern Rhodesia, at Kapiri Mposhi, it joins the Great North Road, Africa's leading aspirant to the title of transcontinental highway.

Although it is not everywhere known as the Great North Road, this road is the one generally followed by motorists seeking to "do" the continent from Cape to Cairo. Its Saharan section runs from Cairo to Khartoum, as already described. Above Khartoum it keeps to the east bank of the White Nile as far as Malakal; thence it goes across country to Juba. Largely because of the existence nearby of good, complementary river and rail services, neither the Egyptian nor the Sudanese government has so far felt inclined to spend much money on its section of the road. In some places it is difficult for the motorist to tell whether he is on or off the road; and in most places it would be foolish for him to expect to find gas stations and other services.

From Juba the main route to the south (there is an alternative route across the Belgian Congo border to Faradje and Beni) goes via Nimule on the Uganda border, Gulu, Soroti, Tororo (Uganda), Eldoret (Kenya), Nairobi, Arusha (Tanganyika), Dodoma, Iringa to Tunduma on the Northern Rhodesian border, and thence to Kapiri Mposhi. The quality of the British East African section varies greatly from place to place, and from season to season. It tends to be better in Uganda and Kenya than in Tanganyika, where, for the most part, it runs through thinly populated territory. Even so, it may be traversed throughout its entire length at all seasons by motorists equipped with a sturdy vehicle, a generous repair kit, emergency gasoline and food supplies, and ample patience.

From Kapiri Mposhi the Great North Road follows the line of the Rhodesia Railways through Broken Hill and Lusaka to Kafue; here it strikes southeastward to Salisbury, crossing the Zambezi at Chirundu by means of the long Otto Beit suspension bridge. From Salisbury it goes to Bulawayo, Gwanda and West Nicholson, and thence into the valley of the Limpopo River, which it crosses at Beitbridge. Here it joins the road system of the Union of South Africa. At its best the Rho-

---

[41] Until 1954 when the Stanleyville-Bukavu road was completed, it was necessary to travel via Beni on the edge of the Albert National Park. From Beni (a coming crossroads town) there are roads to Juba in the Sudan, to Fort Portal and Kampala in Uganda, and to Bukavu.

desian section of the road is as good as any two-lane highway in America, but not all of it is yet at its best. Most of the Southern Rhodesian section has been modernized during the postwar period and can be taken at speed except after periods of heavy rain, when some of the low-level bridges are "out." The Northern Rhodesian section was for many years something of an endurance test for motorists and motors, but it is steadily being improved.

As there are road links between the two most westerly trans-Saharan routes and the two trans-equatorial routes, it is theoretically possible to cross the continent longitudinally by not less than five routes. The main way stations and very approximate mileages of these routes are listed in Table 30.

Table 30

MAJOR LONGITUDINAL ROADS

ROUTE	MILES	ROUTE	MILES
Tangier-Capetown	10,450	Algiers-Capetown	8,100
Tangier-Tindouf	900	Algiers-Laghouat	275
Tindouf-Dakar	1,500	Laghouat-Hoggar Road-Kano	1,875
Dakar-Bamako-Niamey	1,500	Kano-Beitbridge	4,675
Niamey-Kano	600	Beitbridge-Capetown	1,275
Kano-Fort Lamy-Bangassou-Buta-Stanleyville-Bukavu-Elisabethville-Kapiri Mposhi	3,750	Gabès-Capetown	7,300
Kapiri Mposhi–Beitbridge	925	Gabès-Chad (Fort Lamy)	1,800
Beitbridge-Capetown	1,275	Fort Lamy–Beitbridge	4,225
		Beitbridge-Capetown	1,275
Oran-Capetown	8,700	Port Said (Alexandria)–Capetown	6,900
Oran–Colomb Béchar	400	Port Said (Alexandria)–Wadi Halfa	900
Colomb Béchar-Tanezrouft-Niamey	1,750	Wadi Halfa–Juba	1,500
Niamey-Beitbridge	5,275	Juba *-Nairobi-Kapiri Mposhi-Beitbridge	3,225
Beitbridge-Capetown	1,275	Beitbridge-Capetown	1,275

* By taking the Beni-Bukavu-Kapiri Mposhi "alternate," this section is shortened by approximately 225 miles.

MAJOR LATITUDINAL ROUTES

The major "woof" strands in the road net run from Dakar across the savannas south of the Sahara to Kosti on the White Nile above Khartoum, from Takoradi in Ghana to Mombasa on the Indian Ocean, from Matadi on the lower Congo to Mombasa, and from Lobito in Angola to Beira in Mozambique. (See Table 31.)

Table 31

MAJOR LATITUDINAL ROADS

ROUTE	MILES	ROUTE	MILES
Dakar-Kosti	4,080	Matadi-Mombasa	2,650
Dakar-Bamako	775	Matadi-Thysville	150
Bamako-Niamey	730	Thysville-Luluabourg	725
Niamey-Kano	600	Luluabourg-Bukavu	625
Kano–Fort Lamy	550	Bukavu-Mbarara	350
Fort Lamy–Geneina	600	Mbarara-Mombasa	800
Geneina–El Fasher	225		
El Fasher–El Obeid	400	Lobito-Beira	2,450
El Obeid–Kosti	200	Lobito-Dilolo	1,150
		Dilolo-Elisabethville	225
Takoradi-Mombasa	4,750	Elisabethville-Salisbury	700
Takoradi-Lagos	500	Salisbury-Umtali	175
Lagos-Mamfe	550	Umtali-Beira	200
Mamfe-Yaoundé	600		
Yaoundé-Bangui	750		
Bangui-Beni	1,325		
Beni-Mbarara	225		
Mbarara-Mombasa	800		

Dakar-Kosti. Over most of its course, this road has a dirt surface of varying degrees of "passability." It is at its best where it is hard-topped, as, for instance, between Dakar and Kaolack. It is at its worst from Fort Lamy to Kosti, where the route followed is very roughly the one beaten out over the centuries by Moslems making the pilgrimage to and from Mecca. During World War II this section acquired a new importance as a safe back-door route for the haulage of aviation gasoline to allied bases in the Middle East. However, the first stage, Fort Lamy to Abéché, is frequently impassable in the wet season because of the prevalence of deep sand and "black cotton" soils which become slithery with use. From Abéché to Geneina vehicles have to contend with sharp grades in addition to deep sands. Between Geneina and El Fasher lie the mountains of Darfur and, in places, more deep sand. This section of the road is difficult enough in the dry season, when high-gear driving is possible for only about 20 per cent of the distance; in the rains it is considered impassable. From El Fasher to En Nahud, the road winds badly, often through "bottomless" sand. Along with many other African roads, it has the local reputation of providing "the worst ride in the world." From En Nahud onward the going is easier, yet it is often possible to make better time off the road than on it because of the potholes and corrugations developed during the rains.

No traffic regularly moves from end to end of this approximately 4,000-mile route. But there is a substantial volume of interurban traffic, both passenger and freight, on the Dakar–Fort Lamy stages, and a lively lorry traffic from El Obeid westward to El Fasher, Geneina and Fort Lamy. This has long been caravan country. Many of the towns along its way were "ports" for trans-Saharan trade before there were any ports on the Guinea coast to the south of them. Some go on doing a caravan business, but more derive the bulk of their present-day importance from the agriculture and industry carried on around them. As the various government development schemes being undertaken in this sub-Saharan region increase in momentum, so will the commercial role of the Dakar-Kosti road, if only because there is no feasible alternative to it.

The distances of the main stages of this road as given in Table 31 are approximate. Just how approximate they are may be gauged from the fact that no two sources agree. Thus, whereas Kline's figure for the distance between Dakar and Fort Lamy comes to 2,655 miles, Pedler's is 2,400 miles; and whereas Kline makes the distance between Niamey and Fort Lamy 1,150 miles, Pedler makes it 800.[42]

Takoradi-Mombasa. This latitudinal strand in the road net is still in process of being spun; Takoradi simply happens to be its present western end. It can only be a matter of time, however, before it is carried through the Republic of the Ivory Coast, Liberia, Sierra Leone and the Republic of Guinea to Dakar, for the coastal towns of this region sorely need to be linked by land, as well as by sea. Like its more northerly counterpart, this route serves no transcontinental functions, and is most unlikely ever to do so; there are much faster and safer ways of getting people, and much cheaper ways of getting goods, from one coast to the other. Its main function is still to carry goods and passengers from one part of a given territory to another, and this it is performing with increasing despatch and economy.

From Takoradi, an all-weather road, much of it tarred, runs eastward along the coast to Accra, Lomé, Grand Popo, Porto Novo and Lagos. At Lagos the road turns inland — the watery expanses of the Niger delta are wide enough to dampen the enthusiasm of any road engineer — to Benin City and Onitsha on the east bank of the Niger. From Onitsha the all-weather road continues to Enugu and thence to Mamfe in the British Cameroons. Most of the Nigerian section is now hard-topped. The section from Mamfe to Douala and Yaoundé, across the Cameroon Highlands, is much poorer and presents major problems in the rainy season, that is, during most of the year. From Yaoundé [43] the route goes eastward to Bangui. This section is generally passable, even in the rains. At Bangui it joins up with the trans-equatorial route that comes in from Fort Archambault

[42] See F. J. Pedler, *Economic Geography of West Africa*, Longmans, Green & Co., Ltd., London, 1955, pp. 115ff.

[43] Yaoundé and Douala are actually well to the south of the "direct" Takoradi-Mombasa route, but because of their size, importance and sheer attractiveness, they are the most obvious towns hereabouts for way stations.

and, for a time, stays north of the Ubangi River to connect with Beni in the Kivu Province of the Belgian Congo, and across the Uganda border at Kasindi, and thence to Mbarara, Kampala, Nairobi and Mombasa. Although all-weather properties are claimed for most of the central and east African sections of this route, they are not discernible in some sections.

Matadi-Mombasa. Like its southern neighbor, this route runs across the waistline of tropical Africa. From end to end it is not much more than 2,600 miles long. For more than half of this distance it follows the route of the Takoradi-Mombasa road, and, like that road, serves functions that are primarily interurban and intraterritorial. From Matadi on the lower Congo it runs inland over the escarpment of the Crystal Mountains to Thysville, Kitwit and Luluabourg, where it is joined by the road from the Katanga region. From Luluabourg it continues northeastward to Bukavu, thence north to Rutshuru following the line of the western Rift Valley. From Rutshuru it goes to Kabale and Mbarara, where it joins up with the Takoradi-Mombasa route. Although most of the Belgian Congo section has still to be hard-topped, the going is generally good; few stretches of it present serious problems to the motorist, even in wet weather.

Lobito-Beira. This route traverses an even narrower part of the "waist," and a more accommodating one. Notwithstanding the fact that much of it still has a rather unkempt, dirt surface, the journey of some 2,400–2,500 miles from coast to coast can usually be made in five to six days. Among its environmental advantages is the fact that it lies well to the south of the zone of long and heavy rains and therefore south of the great forests and swamps. For most of the way it keeps to well-drained uplands that offer easy grades and abundant road metal of a lateritic type, and present few serious bridging or ferrying problems. For several hundred miles it runs along or near the Congo-Zambezi watershed, one of the most inconspicuous watersheds in the world. It crosses the Rift Valley, moreover, in one of its least noticeable places.

In its Angolan and Katanga sections, the road keeps fairly close to the Benguela Railway, passing through the railway towns of Vila General Machado and Vila Luso in Angola and Dilolo, Kolwezi, Tenke and Elisabethville in the Belgian Congo. At Kapiri Mposhi in Northern Rhodesia it joins up with the Great North Road, following it southeastward to Salisbury. Here it turns east onto the newly rebuilt Umtali road (one of the finest in Africa), which keeps close to the Salisbury-Beira railway. The final, short Mozambique section of the road, down to the Indian Ocean port of Beira, has recently been improved, and now runs its Rhodesian neighbor a close second for comfort and engineering excellence.

THE TERRITORIAL ROADS

Although the volume of traffic in passengers and goods moving between territories over these roads is increasing year by year and is already quite considerable in some sections, their most important functions continue to be regional and intraterritorial and are likely to remain so for many years to come. For what the ordinary African needs most is ready transport for his goods and person to and from his local market, or from one market to the next. Most of the journeys he undertakes, either as a buyer or as a seller, are less than 25 miles — probably nearer 10 miles — in length. For such the feeder road is more serviceable than the throughway. When he undertakes journeys for noncommercial reasons, as when he goes visiting, he is unlikely to go very far either, since in tropical Africa a man's friends are mostly those of his own household and tribe. For the African who goes to more distant places — mines, factories and service camps — interterritorial roads and through bus services certainly have their uses; but so do airways and chartered planes, and in recent years they have been used increasingly by the recruiters of mine labor.

It is not surprising to find therefore that the interest of the road builder continues to be focused primarily on roads that facilitate movement between neighboring communities, that open up new areas to agricultural and mining settlement, and that tie together already existing strands — railways, waterways or highways — in a given region's transportation net.

The following summary of the present road situation in the various areas, and of plans to improve it, will serve to illustrate these points.

WEST AFRICA

The French Community and the Republic of Guinea

Of the approximately 50,000 miles of road, at present only about one fourth are regarded as passable the year around. Less than 1,000 miles have a rock or gravel base, and less still have a hard, tarred surface. But with the continued investment of large sums of money in the area's *infrastructure*, the mileage of all-weather roads is yearly rising. Generally the best roads are the *routes federales* which link the larger towns, those that reach out into the periurban "support" areas of the larger towns and ports, such as Abidjan, Bamako and Dakar, and those that serve as feeders to the railway lines.

Commonwealth West Africa

Each of the four territories — Gambia, Sierra Leone, Ghana and Nigeria — is still inadequately supplied with all-weather roads.

Gambia has a few miles of improved road in the vicinity of Bathurst, but elsewhere its roads are for dry-season use only.

Sierra Leone has some mileage of tarred road near Freetown. Its other roads are nearly all of dirt construction, and subject to interruption in the long wet season because of potholing, washouts and the flooding of ferry crossings. Most of the mileage consists of feeder lines to the Freetown-Pendembu railway; the eastern and northern sections of the protectorate have almost no roads worthy of the name.

Ghana gave little thought to its roads in times past, except those, e.g., in the Takoradi-Kumasi-Accra triangle, that would serve to build up the revenues of the railways. Even today there are few reliable wet-weather roads north of Kumasi. Southward, Kumasi is now linked by all-weather roads with Takoradi and Accra, which are themselves linked by "fast" roads. In the entire territory, there were in 1958, out of a total of approximately 8,500 miles of trunk and other motorable roads, about 1,650 miles of tarred roads and 2,500 miles of gravel roads.

Nigeria's main road arteries tend to be complementary to both the railways and the waterways, and accordingly more often run at right angles to, than parallel with, them. Here again the south has fared much better than the north, some parts of which are still 50 miles or more from a motorable road. Of the three regions, Eastern, Western and Northern, the Western is the best provided for. It has a little over half of the country's mileage of hard-topped road. Although the Eastern Region has only about four miles or so of road to every 1,000 square miles of territory — an extremely low density even for tropical Africa — its system of main roads is, in the opinion of the International Bank for Reconstruction and Development, "practically complete." [44] Certainly it does not appear to have much difficulty in meeting the demands that are being made upon it. In the three regions as a whole there were approximately 37,000 miles of motor road in 1958, of which rather more than 4,000 were hard-topped.

Liberia

It is scarcely an exaggeration to say that until World War II Liberia was a country without a mile of decent road. Its only motorable road was the one linking Monrovia, the capital, with the Firestone Plantations, but not even the missionaries who used it called it decent. With the coming of the military air base and, later, the civil airport at Robertsfield, and the opening up of the Bomi Hills iron mine, a number of short service roads were built. A road has also been put through from Monrovia to Ganta and N'Zérékoré (just inside the Republic of Guinea). This road is already carrying considerable freight, most of it either coming from or going to the agriculturally important N'Zérékoré district, for which Monrovia is the obvious port of lading. [45]

[44] *The Economic Development of Nigeria: Report of a Mission Organized by the International Bank for Reconstruction and Development,* Johns Hopkins Press, 1955, p. 501.

[45] Formerly the only link this region had with the coast was that provided by the roundabout road and railway system of Sierra Leone and its port of Freetown.

As time goes by, and the people of the Liberian back country get the habit of producing salable crop surpluses, this road will undoubtedly come to be as important for Liberia's economy as for Guinea's.

That it takes more than one trunk road and a few branch roads, totaling in 1958 not more than 2,000 miles, to redeem the life of a country from economic lethargy, the Liberian government fully realizes. In the past few years it has pledged a substantial proportion of its budget for road construction; it has also taken a loan of $12 million for the same purpose from the United States Export-Import Bank. In 1956 it announced the start of a 150-mile road that will make the northern section of the country, with its timber and mineral resources, accessible to Monrovia.

Portuguese Guinea

The Portuguese have long appreciated the administrative importance of roads. Roads simplify the problems of control, especially in a country where the terrain is, more often than not, on the side of the governed. They also simplify the problem of what to do with the recalcitrant and the criminal. And in default of cash, they can be made to provide every man with a means of settling his government's tax claims against him. The road net of Portuguese Guinea may not be the best in tropical Africa, but it is one of the densest. It is especially dense in the coastal sections, where the majority of the people live. Most of the roads are narrow and made of earth, but regular maintenance makes movement over many of them possible the year around.

The Cameroons (French and British)

In both of these trust territories the road builder faces problems of more than usual severity, particularly in the southern areas with their rugged, mountainous terrain and their long and heavy rains. In many localities the road builder's problems are compounded by shortage of labor and lack of suitable road material. Not surprisingly, good roads are scarce. In 1958 the British Cameroons had roughly 2,000 miles of motorable roads. Away from these, travel was almost exclusively on foot, with consequent slowing down of the administrative machinery. In one section, the Mamfe Division, the majority of the people still lived several days' walk from a road. In the same year the French Cameroons had about 7,000 miles of motorable road, mostly in the drier central and northern districts; but since the territory is nearly five times the size of its British neighbor, its mean road density was even lower.

But the position in both territories is improving. In recent years the French have given Fort Lamy an all-weather link with Bonaberi (near Douala), and Douala an all-weather link with Bertoua. They have been able to tar the road between Bonaberi and Loum, and between Douala and Edea, the site of the recently opened hydroelectric plant on the Sanaga River; to build a new and shorter road between N'Gaoundéré and Garoua; and to erect a road-and-rail bridge across the Vouri River at Bonaberi. The British have been able to link more effectively such towns as Victoria, Kumba, Mamfe and Enugu (in eastern Nigeria); Mamfe and Calabar; Mamfe and Bamenda. They have also been able to improve the British Cameroons section of the Maiduguri–Fort Lamy road.

Even so, at the present rate of new construction, it will still be many years before either territory can claim to have an all-weather net capable either of serving its administrative needs efficiently or of providing its peoples with economic opportunities equal to their needs and the country's resources.

THE CONGO BASIN AND MARGINS

The French Community

As in the French Cameroons, the road net is denser in the central and northern districts than in the south. Wherever possible, the swampy and heavily forested Gabon Republic and Republic of the Congo have relied on their ready-made routeways — the Congo, Ubangi, Sangha, Ogooué and other rivers. The Central African Republic and the Republic of Chad, being much drier, have few navigable rivers and present fewer road-building difficulties. Besides the main interterritorial roads linking Fort Lamy and Fort Archambault with Bangui and the Belgian Congo, and Yaoundé with Bangui, the only other roads at present in regular use by motor vehicles are those between Pointe Noire, Dolisie and Brazzaville, serving the Niari valley, whose transportation needs are increasing yearly, and between Libreville, Ndjolé, Lambaréné, Dolisie and Pointe Noire. Improved all-weather roads are under construction between the manganese mines at Franceville and the Niari valley, and between Berbérati, Ouesso, Gamboma and Brazzaville.

The Belgian Congo (including Ruanda-Urundi)

With so much of the territory heavily forested, seasonally or perennially swampy, subject to floods and erosion, and generously supplied with navigable water, the Belgian Congo government has tended, naturally enough, to build roads only where there are no lakes or rivers to serve its purpose. Most of the early roads, like the railways, were in fact bond servants to the waterways. Notwithstanding the almost explosive growth of the country's economy and the need for more rapid and more flexible surface transportation services, the road has not yet escaped from its bondage. Many believe it may never do so. Be that as it may, the government's ten-year plan to construct an 8,750-mile network of all-weather roads that would be largely independent of both waterways and railways had to be superseded, mainly because of unrealistic cost estimates, by a modest effort to improve existing roads and to build new ones which would serve to enhance the usefulness of the water-rail net. The main roads built or improved under the revised plan, other than the interterritorial ones already referred to, are those between Boma and Tshela in Bas-Congo and between Bukavu and Uvira.

In addition to government-built roads, there are a number of company-built ones that serve mining and industrial needs. Notable examples are those of Kilo-Moto, which operates approximately 1,600 miles of truck roads; Symétain, with a 130-mile system; Forminière, which operates a truck route in the vicinity of Tshikapa on the upper Kasai; Géomines, which now uses trucks instead of trains between Manono and Muyumba on the Lualaba; and Sogefor, the company operating the hydroelectric power plant at the Cornet Falls near Jadotville.

The rapidly growing use made of Belgian Congo roads is reflected in the following statistics: between 1950 and 1957 the number of motor vehicles more than doubled (to over 57,000); between 1946 and 1952 the number of bicycles increased sevenfold; and between 1947 and 1953 gasoline consumption rose by some 1,300 per cent.

Angola

Like Portuguese Guinea, and for much the same reasons, Angola has long believed in the utility of the road. In pre-World War II days, its road system was one of the most comprehensive and satisfactory in tropical Africa. If its best roads no longer compare favorably with the best in other territories, its worst roads continue to be better than the worst found elsewhere. Both best and worst are continually being renovated. Vehicular traffic is still subject to serious interruption on most roads in the rainy season, but in the dry season almost any part of the province can be reached by truck. With the exception of the one important interterritorial road running east from Lobito, the better roads tend to run longitudinally, linking the various railway tentacles. The chief of these roads goes from Nóqui near Matadi (with which it is linked) to Luanda, Porto Amboim, Lobito, Benguela, Sá da Bandeira and Moçâmedes. Another much used highway connects Portugalia and the diamond-mining area in the extreme northeast of the country with Vila Luso on the Benguela Railway. So far only the roads in the vicinity of Luanda and Lobito have been tarred.

CENTRAL AFRICA

The Federation of Rhodesia and Nyasaland

Exclusive of roads in municipal areas, there are well over 50,000 miles of road in the three territories. Of these, over half are in Southern Rhodesia, 30 per cent in Northern Rhodesia and the rest in Nyasaland. Only a small proportion of the main roads are hard-topped and capable of accommodating two lanes of traffic comfortably. A considerable mileage of the all-weather highways continues to consist of narrow parallel strips of tarmac, or bitumen, separated by dirt or turf, as it has done since the early 1930s.

In the postwar period the volume of road traffic has grown impressively. Since 1949 motor vehicle registrations in Southern Rhodesia have been increasing by 6,000 to 12,000 a year, and at present there is one such vehicle to less than every two Europeans. In the first postwar decade the route mileage of the Road Motor Services division of the Rhodesia Railways increased from 1,794 to 3,573; the number of miles run annually, from 758,585 to 2,673,469; the freight hauled annually, from 91,393 to 270,848 tons; the number of passengers carried annually, from 123,557 to 218,132. Already by 1949 the wear and tear on Southern Rhodesia's roads had become so great that "the country was faced with the possibility of the complete collapse of the main road system."[46] Since then the most traveled trunk roads, including the interterritorial road from Beitbridge to Salisbury and Umtali, have been converted into modern two-lane highways, and many of the more important local roads, especially in the agricultural and industrial Midlands area, have been much improved. Today it is probably true to say that the country has one of the best road nets in tropical Africa. Not that it has much cause for complacency. Traffic loads continue to increase faster than the long-range projections on which the road improvement programs were based. In some sections of the country they are increasing too fast for the good of the pavement; here the turf is frequently in better shape than the tarmac strips which separate it.

In Northern Rhodesia, at the end of World War II, the road situation was extremely bad. Most of the roads were of poor-quality dirt construction, and poorly maintained. In the whole colony there were not more than 50 miles of hard-topped roads outside of the towns. While the demand for heavy-freight transport since then has steadily grown, it has not grown as fast as in Southern Rhodesia. It has been found possible therefore to concentrate on modernizing the trunk routes without risking the collapse of the less important roads. Besides the interterritorial Great North Road referred to earlier, there is now a satisfactory road between Kafue and the Livingstone–Victoria Falls area where it links up with a road from Bulawayo via Wankie, and another between Barotseland in the west of the country and Livingstone, Lusaka and the Copperbelt. An improved road runs from the Copperbelt to the hitherto rather isolated Fort Rosebery area west of Lake Bangweulu, via the pedicle of Katanga.

[46] Sir Roy Welensky, "Railway, Road and Air Plans for Central Africa," *New Commonwealth*, January 24, 1955, p. 57.

For long the roads of Nyasaland, with a single exception, could be classified only by degrees of badness. The exception was the Zomba-Blantyre-Mlanje road, which had an all-weather surface even in pre-World War I days, and was then said to be the longest stretch of macadam road in Africa. There was always the Lake. It was much easier, more pleasant and usually not any slower to get about by lake than by road, and the upkeep charges of lake transportation were not such as to embarrass an impecunious government. But even a country blessed with a lake the size of Nyasa needs passable roads if it is to go forward economically and socially.

It is now getting them. Since the end of World War II the road linking Zomba, the administrative capital, with the twin towns of Blantyre and Limbe — the commercial capital — and the tea-growing regions of Cholo and Mlanje has been rebuilt. The northern extension of this road, to Mzimba and Tunduma (where Nyasaland, Northern Rhodesia and Tanganyika meet), is being improved to take truck traffic the year around. Other roads being remade or improved are those from Salima, the northern terminus of the Nyasaland Railways system, to Lilongwe, a growing farm community in the Central Province; and from Fort Jameson (just inside Northern Rhodesia) northward to Mzimba and southeastward to Lilongwe, Dedza and Zomba.

In many parts of the Federation the need for new bridges is second only to the need for new and reconstructed roads. Scarcely a rainy season passes without one or more of the highways being cut by floods that rise above the parapets (where they exist) of the characteristic, low-level bridges. In the mid-1950s it was not unusual for the Salisbury-Bulawayo road to be impassable at two or more bridging points simultaneously. Where the roads have no bridges at all and the streams have to be crossed by "drifts" or fords, they can, upon occasion, be lethal as well as impassable, for it doesn't take much of a rise in water level to submerge the ordinary British passenger car. But to eliminate all "drifts" and to replace all low-level bridges by high-level ones on all the roads of the Federation would cost millions of pounds which at present are needed for other things.

Mozambique

Assiduous road men though they are, the Portuguese have still a long way to go before they can claim to have covered their east African province with a good road net. Out of a total of not more than 25,000 miles, only about 2,500 rank as "first-class," that is, all-weather roads; and of this mileage only about 10 per cent is tarred. The rest of the roads, including the rest of the first-class ones, are made of earth. The second- and third-class roads are often little better than seemingly haphazard dirt tracks that become unusable after rain. The amount of new road building, as distinct from road maintenance, that is going on is small.

Apart from the interterritorial roads, the two most important of which are those going from Lourenço Marques to Ressano Garcia (for Johannesburg) and from Beira by way of Dondo to Vila Manica (for Umtali), the main roads are those between Beira and the Tete coal field region, between Quelimane and Milange, between Nacala, Lumbo and Mandimba, and between Lourenço Marques and Beira. Whole sections of the province, notably the northern interior, are still virtually roadless, a state of affairs the Portuguese have felt under no great compulsion to alter. The few people who live there seem more interested in getting out than in going back. Moreover, it is a region that has so far yielded few minerals or other sure sources of wealth.

The Malagasy Republic

Madagascar is nightmare country for road travelers, many of whom continue to echo the sentiments A. Martineau expressed in 1894 when he wrote, "There is nothing like the paths of Madagascar to discourage a traveler from having anything to do with the country." Within its borders the island has virtually every type of problem to be found in tropical Africa in the way of climate (including tropical cyclones), terrain, vegetation and drainage. It also has some of the worst gradients. Notwithstanding, many miles of good road have been built in the past fifty years or so. Today there are approximately 20,000 miles of improved road, of which over 10,000 miles are said to be passable at all seasons. However, says Kline, "as in many other African territories, these figures greatly exceed the route mileage in common use."

The best roads are those linking the capital, Tananarive, with (1) Majunga, the west coast port, (2) Ihosy and points south and southwest, and (3) Tamatave, the country's major port, on the east coast. There are still large roadless areas in the far north and west central portions of the island.

EAST AFRICA

Kenya, Tanganyika and Uganda

Because roads seek out people and the people of British East Africa are most unevenly distributed, the road net varies widely in density and quality from place to place. In so far as the net can be said to have any pattern to it, it is the pattern of gossamer — patches of intricate tracery held together loosely by single threads. Some of the threads, as, for instance, the interterritorial roads already spoken of, are stouter than others; but all of them are liable to break under stress of storm and flood, and, as in other parts of tropical Africa, many of them periodically break through sheer attrition of their modest strength. This is not to say that the roads of British East Africa are worse than those of west or central Africa, but only that they are set in an environment that makes greater demands on them and is, at the same time, insufficiently rewarding to allow of large expenditures on their upkeep. There are exceptions of course. Among them are (1) Buganda, many parts of which furnish an excellent-quality *murram* (a type of laterite) for the making of dirt roads that require comparatively little upkeep and are at the same time good revenue producers; (2) the European Highlands of Kenya; (3) the north-eastern shores of Lake Victoria; and (4) the foothill country of Mounts Kenya, Kilimanjaro, Meru and Elgon, which while it makes substantial demands on the road builder generates large amounts of taxable traffic. But just because these are regions of high increment, they must contribute to the upkeep of the regions of stringency around them, with the result, among others, that their roads are often not as good as those in comparably endowed parts of west and central Africa.

"Despite improved [road building] methods and mechanization since the war, it would seem that, at the rate permitted by present finance, many years will elapse before [British] East Africa has a system of modern roads adequate to its needs." [47] Although these words were written in 1952, their validity stands. Money — or the scarcity of it — is still the crux of the region's road transportation problem. Some of the more obvious consequences of this fact can be seen in the following figures. In 1958 the mileage of roads of all classifications in Kenya was put at approximately 24,500. Less than 500 miles were tarred; the bulk of the rest, over 15,000 miles, was unsurfaced. In the same year Tanganyika, more than two thirds as big again, had roughly 26,000 miles of road, of which less than 4,000 miles ranked as "main road" and not more than 500 miles were hard-topped. In Uganda there were some 11,000 miles of road; roughly 3,000 miles were accounted to be all-weather road, but less than 500 miles were hard-topped.

In all three British East African territories [48] most of such moneys as have been made available in recent years for road work have been put into realigning and improving the surfaces of existing roads, rather than into the building of new ones. And they have been used to good effect, as anybody can see. The Nairobi-Nakuru-Molo (Kenya) and Kampala-Tororo (Uganda) sections of the interterritorial road from Mombasa to the Belgian Congo, and the Moshi-Arusha road in northeastern Tanganyika, are now among the best in Africa.

[47] G. T. Dow-Smith, *British East Africa: Economic and Commercial Conditions in British East Africa, April 1952*, Overseas Economic Surveys, H.M.S.O., London, 1953, p. 116.

[48] Although Zanzibar and Pemba are also part of British East Africa, they are omitted from this discussion because neither of them has more than a few dozen miles of road.

NORTHEAST AFRICA

The Republic of Sudan

The Sudanese road net is one of the most open-meshed in Africa. Indeed, it is an exaggeration to speak of it as a "net," since it consists of the two interterritorial roads previously described, some feeder lines to these roads and to the Sudan Railways, and very little else except caravan trails. Over most of the southern — savanna and *sudd* — half of the land, and over nearly all of the desert and scrub northern half, there are no formal roads. Trucks and cars using such motorable tracks as they can find will do well to have on board repair kits, food and water supplies — and navigating instruments. Figures of road mileage are hard to come by, but it is improbable that the entire country has more than 10,000 miles of improved road, or more than three or four hundred miles of hard-topped routes. Apart from the longitudinal Wadi Halfa–Khartoum-Juba-Nimule road and the latitudinal Geneina-Kosti road, neither of which can rank as motorable the year around, the only trunk roads over which motor services operate with any degree of regularity are those of Equatoria Province (where a nine-month rainy season has made all-weather roads a necessity), and between Khartoum and Kassala, where connection is made with the Ethiopian system. There is still no satisfactory road between Khartoum and the Red Sea, or between any Nile valley town and the Red Sea.

Ethiopia and Eritrea

Before the Italian occupation of 1935-1941 Ethiopia and Eritrea were all but roadless, and not without some reason. There may be more inaccessible countries in the world, but none that hold less attraction for the road builder. Even the Italians were nonplussed by some of the canyons they ran into, for they were too wide to bridge and too steep to climb. But at least they did manage to build about 3,000 miles of high way in the two territories, much of it capable of taking heavy truck traffic.

Unfortunately, from 1941 to 1951 very little maintenance work was done, with the result that Ethiopia became almost a roadless country again. In 1951, however, the Ethiopian government negotiated a four-year contract (later extended to six years) with the United States Bureau of Public Roads to rebuild the system, the money for the task coming mainly from the International Bank for Reconstruction and Development. Since 1951 most of the existing roads have been gone over. Pavements have been widened and resurfaced with crushed rock, and bridges reconstructed. Now it is possible to motor in comparative comfort from Addis Ababa to the Eritrean port of Assab, to Asmara and the larger port of Massawa (via Dessye on the Assab road), to Jimma and Gambeila near the Sudan border, and to the Kenya border at Lake Rudolf via the line of the Rift Valley.

In addition to the Italian-made net, there are, according to Kline, "perhaps 2,000 miles of roads and tracks under local jurisdiction that may be 'jeepable' or usable by trucks." Large parts of the two territories have never seen a jeep or a truck, however, and are most unlikely to see one unless they get it by parachute. Even on some of the highways a car still has curiosity value. Although it has grown sharply in this past decade, the total number of registered motor vehicles in Ethiopia and Eritrea was only about 20,000 in 1958.

The Somalilands

None of the three Somali territories has much to offer in the way of motor roads. Few of the roads that carry motor traffic were intended for the job, as motorists discover sooner or later. Of those that were, the road running inland from the port of Mogadishu in Somalia to the Ethiopian border via Villagio Duca degli Abruzzi is easily the best. This and the much shorter road going from Mogadishu to the farming center of Afgoi in the valley of the Uebi Scebeli are the only two hard-topped roads in Somalia, but neither is kept in a very good state of repair.

British Somaliland claims to have about 2,000 miles of road that can be used by wheeled traffic; however, next to none of this is all-weather road. Only in the dry season — here lasting the greater part of the year, to be sure — can the principal towns of the colony, Berbera, Zeilah, Burao, Erigavo, Las Anod, Hargeisa and Borama, be reached easily.

French Somaliland has about a thousand miles of road, almost all of it inferior and most of it useless in wet weather.

AIRWAYS

Of all the modern means of transportation the airplane is at once the most, and the least, flexible. It can fly almost anywhere, but it can land almost nowhere. Unlike the train, the river boat and the auto, the plane is under no compulsion to follow a narrowly defined route. There are air lanes, it is true, but no pilot is compelled to follow these at the risk of jeopardizing his plane in fog, hail or electrical storm. Every pilot is, however, under the strongest possible compulsion to keep to the scheduled stops; unscheduled stops spell emergency, or disaster. Consequently, a discussion of airways as a means of transportation, in Africa or otherwise, is basically a discussion of airfields, their ground facilities, their areal distribution and their traffic.

Civil aviation got its start in tropical Africa shortly after World War I. During the next two decades it made such steady progress that by the outbreak of World War II it was possible to fly to almost every major town within the tropics, and also to a great many minor ones. Although the war put a stop to most commercial flying, it did not stop the development of flying. On the contrary. Hundreds of allied aircraft were engaged in ferrying, reconnaissance and training work. Many new airfields were built. New and badly needed meteorological knowledge was accumulated. And, by no means least, government departments, mining corporations, mission societies, and ordinary individuals who had previously looked upon flying as a luxury, began to be impressed by its conveniences and economies. Today more than a score of the world's major airlines operate between tropical Africa and Europe, Asia and North America. There are many more airlines that operate scheduled internal services, to say nothing of small taxi and charter companies. There are international airports at all the main cities, and many quite small cities are equipped to handle long-distance flights. All told there are well over 500 airfields that have either scheduled or charter services or both. The main continental air routes are shown in Figure 31 and the main regional air routes in Figure 32.

With the exception of one or two of the smaller and poorer territories, such as Gambia and Portuguese Guinea, each territory is also served by an internal air service. These services are mostly supplied either directly by the appropriate metropolitan carrier, or through a local subsidiary set up for the purpose. Two of the largest "domestic" networks are those of Sabena and East African Airways. Sabena operates over some 16,000 route miles and has more than 40 scheduled stopping places. In 1958 its short-haul planes carried more than 120,000 passengers and flew more than 4.5 million miles. Since July 1957 another Belgian line, Sobelair, has also been operating domestic services.

East African Airways operates over the British East African territories of Kenya, Uganda, Tanganyika and Zanzibar and, to a more limited extent, in Nyasaland, Mozambique, Northern and Southern Rhodesia, the Union of South Africa and the United Kingdom. It has the use of more than 30 airfields, and in a recent year (1957) carried well over 100,000 passengers in addition to mail and cargo.

Central African Airways provides much the same range of services within the Federation of Rhodesia and Nyasaland and bordering territories.

In Mozambique and Angola, the Divisão de Exploração dos Transportes Aéros (known as DETA in the former province and DTA in the latter) maintains across-the-border services from its Mozambique fields to Salisbury, Durban and Johannesburg, and from its Angolan fields to Pointe Noire and Léopoldville, along with its purely internal services.

In Commonwealth West Africa, the West African Airways Corporation serves every important town in Gambia, Sierra Leone, Ghana and Nigeria (including the British Cameroons). In Nigeria alone it operates out of

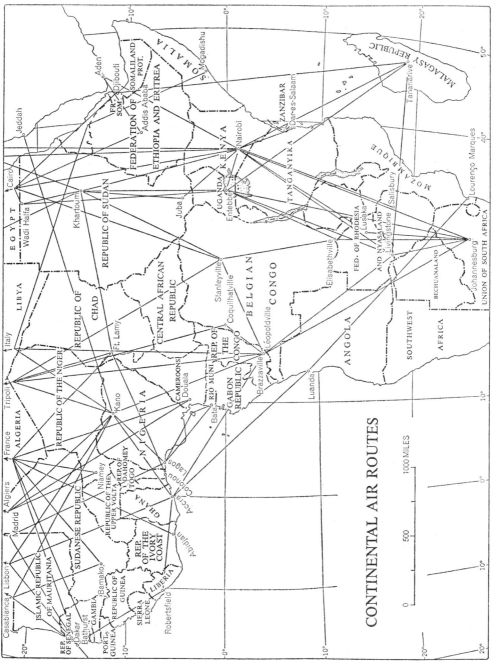

FIGURE 31 (After Hibberd V. B. Kline, Jr; information as of late 1950s)

CONTINENTAL AIR ROUTES

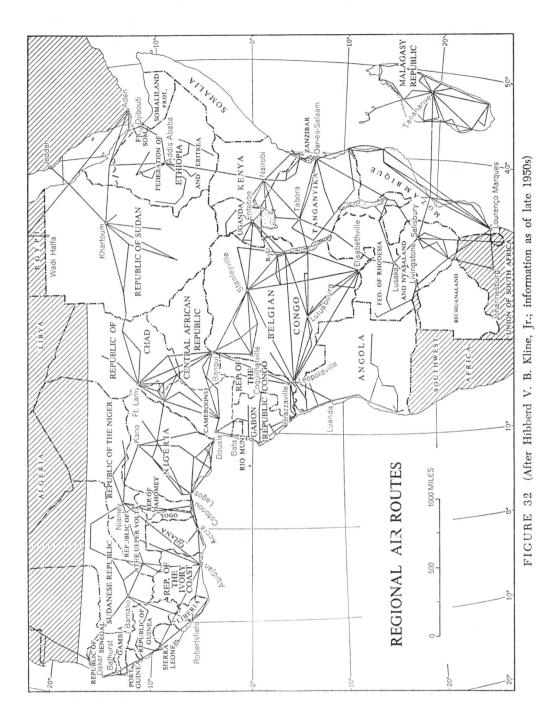

REGIONAL AIR ROUTES

FIGURE 32 (After Hibberd V. B. Kline, Jr; information as of late 1950s)

487

at least 28 airports. It also operates transcontinental services to Jidda (near Mecca) in Saudi Arabia for the benefit of the large west African Moslem population.

The territories belonging to the French Community and those that formed part of its predecessor, the French Union, though much larger in size, are well covered by the regional services of Air France, TAI (Compagnie des Transports Aériens Intercontinentaux) and UAT (Union Aéromaritime de Transport). The Gabon Republic also has a number of internal services operated by a local company, Transports Aériens du Gabon. All told, more than a hundred places are linked by these services. In the Malagasy Republic, Air Madagascar provides internal service to places not covered by Air France.

In the northeastern section of tropical Africa, most of the local services are run by the following companies:

1. Ethiopian Air Lines, an affiliate of Trans World Airlines, which in 1957 flew nearly 3 million miles and nearly 40 million passenger-miles, and which, notwithstanding the unsurpassed difficulty of the Ethiopian terrain, has not had a serious accident in its history.

2. Sudan Airways, which has internal flights linking its farflung cities — Port Sudan is all of 800 miles from El Fasher, and Wadi Halfa more than 1,200 miles from Juba — and a number of international flights, for example, to Cairo, Jidda and Gambeila.

3. Aden Airways, which operates between a number of Red Sea ports and the "horn" region.

4. Misrair (Egyptian), which is also active in the Red Sea region.

5. Alitalia, which links together the main towns of Somalia and its near neighbors.

It is hard for a North American to appreciate the present significance of air transport to tropical Africa, unless he happened to live there before there was any. If there were no airlines in the United States, we should still be able to live rather well. But if there were no airlines in tropical Africa, most of the Europeans living there would quickly find a difference. Mail and newspapers that now take less than twelve hours to go from Brazzaville to Fort Lamy and from Nairobi to Salisbury would take as long as twelve days. Government furloughs that now enable officers living in the deepest bush to spend not less than eleven weeks out of an allotted twelve at home might give them less than a month there.[49] Delegates to interterritorial conferences who can now reach any centrally located town almost overnight would be spending weeks — perhaps months — in travel that no government or private agency could possibly

[49] In 1930 a district officer stationed in the Darfur region of the then Anglo-Egyptian Sudan reckoned on having to spend 63 days out of his 84 days' furlough in traveling. In 1955 his successor needed to spend not more than four days out of the 84 traveling.

look upon with favor. And, not least, the feeling of well-being that has come to remotely situated people who know they are only a few hours from "the outside" — from relatives, friends, medical care and supplies of all kinds — would quickly evaporate.

Probably nowhere in the world is the civilizing function of the airplane so apparent as it is in tropical Africa. Certainly there is no more air-minded group of people than the Europeans who work or live there, and who are, in the main, people of a high enough earning power to be able to afford air travel. In the Belgian Congo three in every four Europeans travel by air, if not habitually, at least occasionally, and the ratio is of much the same order in the Federation of Rhodesia and Nyasaland. The ratio in the United States is one in eight or so.

It is not only the European who has come to appreciate the uses of the airplane. In some parts of tropical Africa Europeans commonly find themselves outnumbered on internal or interterritorial flights by non-Europeans. This is particularly true of west Africa. Here so much of the passenger business is generated by the African that the airlines have long since learned to pay court to him — and *her*, for the woman trader plays a very powerful role in west Africa. Much of their advertising is directed at the African, and many of their flights are specially priced for his benefit. Even on international flights, non-Europeans — Asians, Arabs and Africans alike — are yearly providing a larger proportion of airline revenues. Non-European traffic is especially heavy between British East Africa and India, between west Africa and Saudi Arabia (Jidda for Mecca), and between the various African and European seats of government, higher education, commerce and industry.

And because ground transportation services are, in general, still far from adequate, most airlines do a significant amount of freight and mail carrying.[50] The range of goods carried as air freight is already quite wide, and getting wider. It includes (1) foodstuffs, such as fish (e.g., from Lake George in Uganda to Kampala and Nairobi), meat (e.g., from Chad to Brazzaville), coffee and vanilla (from the Andapa district of the Malagasy Republic to Tananarive), dairy produce and eggs (e.g., from the Kivu district to Katanga); (2) agricultural raw materials (mostly in sample lots) such as cotton, wool, mohair, oilseeds and tobacco; (3) minerals, notably gold (from Kenya and Tanganyika) and diamonds (from Tanganyika); (4) manufactures, such as machine tools and replacements, fashion and sports goods, and even farm equipment (e.g., small carts are now being flown, crated, from Southern Rhodesia, where they are made, to British East Africa); and (5) such miscellaneous goods as phonograph records, medicines, periodicals, pedigree bulls and day-old chicks.

A measure of the increasing use being made in tropical Africa of the

[50] Those that do not could if they had the carriers. Some of the smaller companies do not have enough planes to be able to undertake new services, and do not as yet make enough profit to be able to buy more.

airplane as a freight carrier is given in the following operating figures of the Central African Airways Corporation:

Revenue Traffic in Thousand Ton-Miles

Year	Freight Other Than Mail	Mail
1949	346	165
1953	577	322
1954	706	297
1955	735	333
1956	733	372
1957	861	400

THE TREND

It is many years since Lord Lugard affirmed that "the material development of Africa may be summed up in one word — transport." It was, of course, a vulnerable generalization, but it did serve to remind the slow-footed colonial rulers of the time that, no matter how well endowed a land may be with soils, forests, waters and minerals, these things might as well not be there unless people can get at them. The point is still well taken. Indeed, the "get-at-ableness" of things and people was never more important than it is today. In a thousand businesses, from the overnight trucking of fluid milk to the "packaging" of tours for hurried holiday makers, it is the first condition of survival. This is as true of tropical Africa as it is of North America or Western Europe.

Whereas fifty years ago the emphasis in African transportation developments was on the opening up of the continent to the outside world, today it has shifted to the opening up of the continent to itself. As we have seen, important surface links are still being forged between inland mine, plantation or factory and river or seaport, as are air links between almost every large city in Africa and the cities of Europe, Asia and North America; and many more are planned. But what the working and awakened inhabitant of the region is more interested in is transportation that helps to increase his "share in the equity" — that gives him a wider field of economic opportunity, makes him a more effective supplier of goods and services, and, most of all, puts him within reach of the local market. For, as Lord Hailey recognized in 1938, "the local market is the most potent agency for stimulating agricultural production, and for encouraging the specialization which is essential for the creation of local crafts or industries." [51] It is also an important primer of capital, he went on to say, for "the larger finance of a country must have its basis in the innumerable petty transactions of small centers of this nature."

[51] *An African Survey*, Oxford University Press, London, 1938, p. 1610.

What is most urgently needed, it follows, is more and better roads. True, the African worker will gladly use the railways when they serve his purpose, and the airlines when he has the price of a ticket. But trains and planes are long-distance haulers, while most of his concerns — such as the shipping of surplus crops to the nearest point of sale, the buying of a shirt, the search for a job and the visiting of kin — are local. For these the road serves him best. It is companionable; it draws all men unto it. It is convenient; a man can stop when and where he likes, even if he is traveling in a "mammy lorry." It is flexible; it is not in bondage to gradients, nor is it fastidious about foundations and fill. Also, it is generally economical. As we have seen, building and maintenance costs of all-weather highways can sometimes be high, but those of the much more extensive secondary and less-than-secondary roads that feed them are low. In some territories many such roads are made and kept in repair by either voluntary or pressed labor using only hand tools.

The mileage of local road networks can therefore be expected to go on increasing almost everywhere in tropical Africa, and especially in those regions which derive a large part of their revenues from peasant-grown crops, notably in Ghana, Nigeria and west Africa generally, the Malagasy Republic, Uganda and Tanganyika. (In the Congo basin, the waterways are likely to go on taking a good share of the traffic in locally grown produce, especially among the riverside tribes, for whom water is as much a part of the environment as land, and a lot easier to travel by.) The local road networks can also be expected to grow in serviceability. As the volume of local trading increases, more spending money will become available. Much of this will certainly be used to buy bicycles, cars and trucks. The resulting increase in road traffic density will automatically lead to a rising demand for better-engineered, all-weather pavements, and better maintenance of them. And we can be sure that the taxing authorities will spirit away some of this additional spending money to satisfy the demand.

Then, again, as more and more peoples reach political adolescence, the focus of their attention, we may take it, will shift from their parents to their neighbors' children. Among other things, this will assuredly lead to the building of new interterritorial highways and the improvement of the few that already exist. Such highways will serve functions that were of little consequence to colonial powers. In many cases they will link people of the same ethnic background, for the existing political boundaries of tropical Africa are notorious dividers of kindred, tribe and tongue. In many cases they will link economies that are complementary and invite integration by transport.[52] In some cases, too, they will link "ideologies" and doubtless further the common political designs of their makers.

[52] The "integration" argument is one of those being used by the sponsors of the African International Highway — a first-class motor road that would link the Cape with Kenya (perhaps Cairo as well). Among other things it would enable the Fed-

What of the still large gaps in tropical Africa's transportation net? The "netless" areas of the southern half of the Republic of Sudan, the Somalilands, inner Angola, Bechuanaland and elsewhere? The "breaks" in the net arising from the early preoccupation of governments with being linked by rail to the sea rather than to their landward neighbors? Here, likewise, the road builder would seem to have an important role to play, initially at any rate. In their report on the feasibility of linking the Rhodesian and British East African railway systems, Sir Alexander Gibbs & Partners came to the conclusion that "the correct approach to the problem [might well be] to allow road transport to carry the burden hitherto borne by the low cost [railway] line and to postpone rail construction until traffic has begun to build up to such a point" [53] that it is capable of absorbing the cost of constructing a high-quality railway.

There are those who would go further and contend that, with railways almost everywhere finding the going tough, the railway-building era is as good as over, even in so new a land as tropical Africa. This is not to say that the lines now on the drawing boards will never be built, for some of them are needed to enable existing lines to operate more rationally and profitably. (The proposed west coast "extension" of the Rhodesia Railways through southern Angola or Southwest Africa provides a case in point.) But to look for a railway renaissance that would bring forth the long-dreamed-of Cape-to-Cairo railway or a Dakar-to-Djibouti railway would be unwarranted; new births are not induced by old hopes.

If not more railways, more airways then? Here the prospects are good, for several reasons. First, and more negative than positive, much of tropical Africa is ill-suited to surface forms of transportation; it is riven with canyon-like valleys, spattered with lakes and marshes, pocked by ancient eruptions, given by turns to flood and drought, and, furthermore, its key centers of population and production are hundreds of miles apart. Second, the airplane has already proved its worth in tropical Africa as a medium- and long-distance hauler of passengers, freight and mail; it has even shown, in some territories, that it can earn its keep. Third, the rate of annual increase in the volume of air traffic is almost everywhere greater than the rate of annual increase in the volume of railway and waterway traffic; here and there it is greater than the increase in the volume of road traffic. Fourth, while most of the traffic is still generated in the European and Asian sectors of the economy, the African sector is

---

eration of Rhodesia and Nyasaland and British East Africa to reduce, by more than half, the time now taken to ship goods between them, and so be in a much stronger position to serve one another's trade needs. Already the governments of the territories through which this highway would pass are talking of standardizing "regulations affecting licensing, customs and immigration, [with a view to] increasing the flow of trade." (*Africa Weekly*, August 21, 1957.)

[53] *A Development Survey for the Central African Railway Link*, Sir Alexander Gibbs & Partners (London) and Overseas Consultants, Inc. (New York), October 1952.

growing steadily in importance. It is not without significance that several of the great industrial corporations now offer African laborers, recruited from a distance, free air transport. Fifth, tropical Africa is rapidly acquiring a strategic status of the first order. To the Western powers it offers elbow room, the possibility of defense in depth, and ready access to the trouble spots of the Middle East and Europe (Mombasa, for instance, is nearer to Moscow than Seattle is to Vladivostok). It also offers vital war supplies of almost every kind. Whether its people wish it or not, such a region must be adequately served by military airfields. Where there are military airfields, there are employees and their families to be flown, freight to be shipped, and aircraft to be serviced — all of which makes business for the civil airways. And last, in every continent, "going by air" has all but ceased to be the monopoly of the moneyed and the hurried. It is fast becoming the mode for the administrator, the engineer, the educator, the businessman and the tourist; likewise for mail, perishables, business samples, urgently needed replacements and parts, and an ever-widening range of goods which are high in value and low in bulk. It is a trend that tropical Africa shows no signs of reversing.

CHAPTER 12

Merchandise, Marts and Marketing

EXTERNAL TRADE

INTERNAL TRADE

THE ADVANCEMENT OF THE AFRICAN
IN TRADE

O<small>VER</small> most of tropical Africa the rudiments of business were lacking until fifty to seventy-five years ago. Either there were no goods or services that people wanted at prices they were willing to pay, or there were no means of bringing the two together. Banking and currency were unknown. The yield of the land being mostly meager and always uncertain, prudence demanded that, when there were food surpluses, they should be conserved so far as possible to cushion future shortages. Little else was available for sale or exchange. The making of bark cloth, earthenware pots and metal spearheads was time-consuming and tiring, and the rejection rate was inclined to be high.

Since there was little specialization of economic activity, most of the goods to be had were of the same kind. Accordingly, they were not readily disposable. The man with a storehut full of yams obviously had little use for his neighbor's surplus yams; and although the woman with a collection of household pots could always use another, she would almost certainly prefer that it be one made in the home, for the ability of a household to keep itself in pots was as much a point of honor as its ability to keep itself in food.

It followed that few people were able to acquire much in the way of purchasing power. True, a full storehut of yams spelled greater wealth than a half-empty one, but it was not very negotiable wealth. All a man could do with it was eat it or trade it for somebody else's not very negotiable bananas or maize. Nor was it very durable wealth. Neither yams nor bananas nor any other crops keep for more than a few months in the humid tropics when stored in African fashion. Cattle were more durable and more negotiable, but in an environment subject to a dozen endemic and epidemic scourges few men were willing to exploit the purchasing power of their prestigious herds for any but very compelling reasons.

Transport difficulties were a major obstacle to trade. The only ways in which goods could be brought to people who wanted them were extravagant of effort and subject to wastage.

Consequently the volume of business remained very small for centuries. What there was, was confined to "goods" that provided their own transportation, such as slaves and cattle, or that had a high ratio of value to weight and were imperishable, such as gold and ivory. Bulky goods, such as hardwood timbers and base metals, and perishables, such as cotton and grain, attracted little custom.

Over much of tropical Africa the rudiments of a lively business are still lacking. In some areas they are lacking because the people have next to nothing to dispose of, and therefore next to no purchasing power. In others are they lacking because there are next to no serviceable means of transportation for handling surpluses, and therefore next to no market.

Important changes have taken place in the past generation, nevertheless. There is scarcely a road, railway or navigable waterway that is not carrying at least twice the volume of freight it was carrying before World War II, a territory that does business with less than twenty-five of the great trading nations, a main street in any town that does not display at least a dozen world-famous agency signs, or a village that does no business at all with the outside world. Indeed, hardly a family in the whole of tropical Africa does not possess some foreign article — if only a discarded gasoline can, a "pop" bottle, a piece of cast-off clothing, or a faded Sunday newspaper.

Because the story of tropical Africa's commercial penetration, whether by slave trader, ivory hunter, seeker of cash crops, cabinet woods and metals, or by road and rail builder, is essentially the story of foreign initiative, and because without it there could have been no significant increase in internal trade, it is appropriate to begin by dealing with external trade.

EXTERNAL TRADE

At the present time — the figures are for 1957 — tropical Africa is responsible for about 3 per cent, by value, of the free world's export trade [1] and about 3.3 per cent of the world's import trade. By way of com-

---

[1] Gold (bullion, unrefined gold, ores, etc.) is excluded from the reckoning since its movement affects monetary rather than material resources. Data in this chapter were prepared before the United Nations issued the *Economic Survey of Africa Since 1950* and the 1958 edition of the *Yearbook of International Trade Statistics*. Figures in those sources differ only slightly in most instances from those here used; in some instances they are on a different basis. The later figures are incorporated in the appendix, Volume II, pp. 445ff.

parison, the United Kingdom's share of the world's export trade is — also in 1957 — more than 9 per cent, and of the import trade, more than 10 per cent. The corresponding figures for the United States are about 21 and 12. Small though the region's percentages are, they are bigger than they were in prewar years, as Table 32 shows.

Table 32

PER CENT, BY VALUE, OF FREE WORLD'S
MERCHANDISE TRADE, 1937-1957

YEAR	EXPORTS	IMPORTS
1937	2.6	2.0
1938	2.1	1.8
1948	3.2	2.9
1950	3.3	2.9
1951	3.4	3.0
1952	3.6	3.6
1953	3.6	3.4
1954	3.8	3.6
1955	3.5	3.5
1956	3.4	3.3
1957 [a]	3.0	3.3

Source: Based on United Nations, *Yearbook of International Trade Statistics, 1957,* Volume I, New York, 1958.

[a] Preliminary figures.

More important is the increase, over the same period, in the value of trade. Tables 33 and 34 give a measure of this increase. These statistics make impressive reading. True, the evil genie of inflation has had a hand in the making of them, but efficient felon though he is, he is merely an accessory after the fact. Even if we credit him with having halved the purchasing power of tropical African currencies in this period, there is scarcely a territory that has not more than doubled the real value of its imports and exports, and most territories have done much better than this. Especially noteworthy are the relative increases registered in both the import and the export fields by such territories as the French Cameroons, Angola, Liberia and the territories known until 1958 as French Equatorial Africa, and the absolute increases registered in such places as the Belgian Congo, Nigeria, Ghana, the territories now constituting the Federation of Rhodesia and Nyasaland and those formerly constituting French West Africa.

COMPOSITION OF EXPORTS

The export trade of most of the territories has been built up on a narrow base. In some of them the base has been provided by a single commodity — copper in Northern Rhodesia, peanuts in Gambia, cotton in the Sudan, rubber in Liberia, and so on. In a number of others it has

Table 33 (With Opposite Page)

EXTERNAL MERCHANDISE TRADE:
EXPORTS, BY TERRITORY, 1937-1957

(*Millions of Dollars; f.o.b.*)

G: General trade.   S: Special trade.

TERRITORY	1937	1938	1948	1950
Total	589.1 [a]	414.8 [a]	1,698.2	1,829.1
S French Cameroons	10.7	7.3	36.0	46.8
S French Equatorial Africa	9.8	6.6	50.3	39.6
S French Somaliland	5.4	2.5	8.7	6.5
S French West Africa	50.8	37.4	155.0	177.3
S Malagasy Republic (Madagascar) [b]	23.9	23.6	50.0	71.0
S (French) Togo	3.1	1.9	9.7	8.7
S Belgian Congo [c]	74.3	52.1	245.4	260.7
S Angola	15.5	14.9	59.5	75.4
S Mozambique	13.0	7.9	39.7	37.0
S Portuguese Guinea	1.7	1.4	5.2	4.4
S São Tomé and Príncipe	2.1	1.5	8.8	7.3
G Federation of Rhodesia and Nyasaland [d]	86.5	74.6	209.6	242.0
G British Somaliland	1.4	1.0	1.8	1.8
G Gambia	3.5	1.6	9.0	6.4
G Ghana (Gold Coast) [e]	60.6	32.2	203.0	192.3
G British East Africa [f]	68.3	55.0	168.2	200.7
G Nigeria [g]	95.0	46.5	251.8	252.6
G Sierra Leone	13.4	11.3	21.7	21.9
G Zanzibar	4.3	4.1	8.4	13.8
S Republic of Sudan (Anglo-Egyptian Sudan)	43.8	29.5	98.7	95.1
S Eritrea	n.a.	n.a.	7.5	8.2
G Ethiopia [h]	n.a.	n.a.	31.3	28.5
S Somalia (Italian Somaliland)	n.a.	n.a.	3.1	3.5
S Liberia	2.0	1.9	15.8	27.6

Source: United Nations, *Yearbook of International Trade Statistics,* 1956 and 1957 editions, Volume I, New York, 1957, 1958.

G *General trade* includes in imports all merchandise unloaded in the country, whether for home consumption or re-export. It likewise includes re-exports in export figures. Usually it does not record direct-transit trade in either imports or exports.

S *Special trade* includes in imports merchandise unloaded for home consumption, plus goods custom-cleared from warehouses. It records as exports only national (or domestic) produce exported, plus foreign products re-exported after transformation or supplementary treatment. It also includes re-export of foreign products which have been cleared by customs and reported as imported.

Table 33 (Continued)

1951	1952	1953	1954	1956	1957 *
2,523.4	2,602.2	2,624.6	2,865.0 ᵃ	3,138.6 ᵃ	2,818.4 ᵇ
65.0	63.1	74.8	87.1	75.1	81.3
61.1	56.8	55.1	71.5	79.3	82.4
11.8	9.7	13.2	12.4	12.3	n.a.
221.2	229.7	267.3	332.9	343.3	328.3
77.1	93.6	84.8	91.6	93.1	86.2
15.4	11.9	15.6	24.4	13.3	11.8
387.1	391.1	398.3	397.0	534.7	472.3
110.9	95.7	122.9	102.9	114.4	115.7
43.6	46.4	56.4	55.0	52.9	65.1
5.0	6.5	6.3	n.a.	n.a.	n.a.
7.5	6.8	8.6	8.6	6.0	n.a.
274.5	357.3	394.9	411.1	508.9	437.2
2.5	2.9	3.0	3.5	3.7	3.8
9.4	11.1	8.0	8.5	7.1	12.0
233.6	216.0	225.4	294.2	222.5	229.1
319.3	346.6	255.2	281.6	335.6	331.5
336.2	362.7	347.8	418.7	376.9	355.6
28.1	29.9	33.4	31.8	36.9	51.5
17.0	13.0	22.1	16.6	16.3	16.4
180.3	122.8	127.5	116.0	191.8	138.2
14.0 ⎱ 47.0 ⎰	42.9 ˡ	68.2 ˡ	64.5 ˡ	60.9 ˡ	n.a.
4.2	6.5	4.8	8.7	9.1	n.a.
52.1	37.2	31.0	26.4	44.5	n.a.

The distinction is important only for countries with extensive intermediate trade (e.g., industrial countries which import goods and distribute them among other countries), which does not as yet apply on a large scale to any tropical African country.

ᵃ Partial total (because of gaps in data).
ᵇ Beginning 1952, excluding the Comoro Islands.
ᶜ Including Ruanda-Urundi.
ᵈ Figures exclude trade between component territories.
ᵉ Including British Togoland.
ᶠ Excluding Zanzibar.   ˡ Federation of Ethiopia and Eritrea.
ᵍ Including British Cameroons.   * Preliminary figures.
ʰ Year ending about December 12.   n.a.: not available

Table 34 (With Opposite Page)

EXTERNAL MERCHANDISE TRADE:
IMPORTS, BY TERRITORY, 1937-1957

(*Millions of Dollars; c.i.f.*)

G: General trade.   S: Special trade.

	TERRITORY	1937	1938	1948	1950
	Total	493.8[a]	408.5[a]	1,669.1	1,713.9
S	French Cameroons	10.4	6.2	42.4	60.4
S	French Equatorial Africa	9.7	8.4	52.7	76.5
S	French Somaliland	7.2	4.3	16.6	12.7
S	French West Africa	62.2	46.9	177.5	241.0
S	Malagasy Republic (Madagascar)[b]	18.9	17.4	77.7	86.1
S	(French) Togo	3.2	2.1	7.4	9.3
S	Belgian Congo[c]	41.4	36.8	191.1	187.9
S	Angola	9.7	10.2	48.5	57.9
S	Mozambique	19.3	21.5	71.5	57.5
S	Portuguese Guinea	1.6	1.3	7.4	4.5
S	São Tomé and Príncipe	0.9	0.8	4.4	3.8
G	Federation of Rhodesia and Nyasaland[d]	62.5	71.9	240.2	231.3
G	British Somaliland	2.6	2.7	4.2	3.2
G	Gambia	3.7	2.0	9.3	8.2
G	Ghana (Gold Coast)[e]	62.1	38.4	126.5	134.8
G	British East Africa[f]	57.5	49.7	236.2	199.5
G	Nigeria[g]	72.3	42.1	169.1	173.2
G	Sierra Leone	9.0	7.0	20.1	18.9
G	Zanzibar	6.1	4.9	10.9	10.4
S	Republic of Sudan (Anglo-Egyptian Sudan)	31.5	31.6	91.6	77.6
S	Eritrea	n.a.	n.a.	11.6	11.5
G	Ethiopia[h]	n.a.	n.a.	38.9	29.5
S	Somalia (Italian Somaliland)	n.a.	n.a.	4.5	7.6
S	Liberia	2.0	2.3	8.8	10.6

Source: United Nations, *Yearbook of International Trade Statistics,* 1956 and 1957 editions, Volume I, New York, 1957, 1958.

G *General trade* includes in imports all merchandise unloaded in the country, whether for home consumption or re-export. It likewise includes re-exports in export figures. Usually it does not record direct-transit trade in either imports or exports.

S *Special trade* includes in imports merchandise unloaded for home consumption, plus goods custom-cleared from warehouses. It records as exports only national (or domestic) produce exported, plus foreign products re-exported after transformation or supplementary treatment. It also includes re-export of foreign products which have been cleared by customs and reported as imported.

Table 34 (Continued)

1951	1952	1953	1954	1956	1957 [*]
2,463.7	2,823.6	2,608.6	2,789.2 [a]	3,209.0	3,365.6
94.3	106.6	80.4	92.9	95.2	98.4
104.2	115.0	84.6	95.3	117.3	140.9
15.1	20.1	24.7	10.4	9.0	n.a.
350.5	349.5	315.7	380.3	381.3	417.3
131.4	133.6	129.3	137.4	132.0	141.5
13.3	13.3	11.9	15.5	15.4	15.6
309.1	400.6	363.4	370.8	415.7	436.1
75.7	91.4	84.7	95.8	110.0	124.0
71.6	75.9	80.0	85.6	95.2	104.2
5.6	7.6	5.6	n.a.	n.a.	n.a.
5.2	4.7	4.1	4.4	4.6	n.a.
318.4	347.4	328.3	350.8	445.9	496.9
4.6	5.8	5.3	6.6	7.8	11.3
11.2	10.4	6.2	7.3	10.4	13.3
178.6	186.5	206.6	198.9	249.0	270.4
291.3	338.9	296.2	328.9	374.7	392.4
236.8	317.2	303.2	319.4	427.8	425.6
23.0	28.8	31.1	36.1	64.7	79.1
14.3	14.0	16.4	15.1	17.0	18.1
120.5	177.1	145.6	139.1	129.7	180.5
16.4 ⎱ 42.1 ⎰	46.4 [i]	55.6 [i]	64.4 [i]	63.2 [i]	n.a.
13.4	14.7	11.0	11.5	16.1	n.a.
17.1	18.1	18.7	22.7	26.8	n.a.

The distinction is important only for countries with extensive intermediate trade (e.g., industrial countries which import goods and distribute them among other countries), which does not as yet apply on a large scale to any tropical African country.

[a] Partial total (because of gaps in data).

[b] Beginning 1952, excluding the Comoro Islands.

[c] Including Ruanda-Urundi.

[d] Imports f.o.b. Figures exclude trade between component territories.

[e] Including British Togoland.

[f] Excluding Zanzibar.

[g] Including British Cameroons.

[h] Year ending about December 12.

[i] Federation of Ethiopia and Eritrea.

[*] Preliminary figures.

n.a.: not available

been built up on various combinations of two commodities. Examples are cocoa and palm products in Nigeria, tobacco and tea in Nyasaland, cotton and copra in Mozambique. In few territories has the export trade been built up on more than two commodities. As recently as 1948 the combined value of the two largest export items exceeded 50 per cent of the total exports in all but eight out of 24 territories.

And the base is still narrow. For, while almost every territory is yearly increasing the range of its offerings on the export market, almost every territory still relies heavily on the earning power of one or two commodities. A comparison of the 1948 and 1957 figures in Table 35 shows that as many territories (12) became more dependent on their two leading export commodities as became less dependent on them. It also shows that as many territories derived at least half of their export revenues from a single commodity in 1957 as in 1948. In the circumstances it is not surprising that the status of most second- and third-string commodities continues to be rather lowly. In both 1948 and 1957 second-string commodities contributed one fifth or more of the total export revenues of less than half the territories. The number of territories in which third-string commodities contributed one tenth or more of the total export revenues was less in 1957 than in 1948.

What emerges no less clearly from this table is the continuing dependence of tropical African countries on primary products for their revenues.

Primary Products [2]

Organic

Of the two main kinds of primary products, organic and inorganic (or mineral), the former occupies by far the more important place in the export trade of tropical Africa. In 1948 an organic commodity headed the export list of 22 out of 24 territories. In 20 out of the 24 an organic commodity occupied second place. In only one territory (Northern Rhodesia) did organic commodities account for less than one third of the export revenues. In all the rest they accounted for at least half of them.

Of the 20-odd different organic commodities (mostly crops) listed in the 1948 columns of Table 35, cotton (including seed) holds pride of place. Cotton was the chief money earner in four territories (Kenya-Uganda, the Republic of Sudan, French Equatorial Africa and Mozambique),

[2] Included under the heading "primary products" are such processed commodities as tobacco, sisal fiber, sawn wood and copper. As in Chapter 10, the manufacturing process is regarded as beginning when a product has reached a state in which it can be moved to another establishment for further treatment, that is, when it passes from an economic unit specializing in primary production to one that specializes in transforming raw materials.

the second largest money earner in two, and the third largest in two. Cocoa was the chief money earner in four territories (Togo, Nigeria, Ghana and the French Cameroons) and the third largest in one. Coffee was the chief money earner in two territories (Ethiopia and Angola), the second largest in four and the third largest in one. Tobacco headed the list in two territories (Nyasaland and Southern Rhodesia), peanuts in two (French West Africa and Gambia), palm kernels and oil in one (Sierra Leone), bananas in one (Somalia), cloves and clove oil in one (Zanzibar), skins and hides in one (British Somaliland), sisal in one (Tanganyika), and rubber in one (Liberia — the only territory where a wood product occupied first place).

The 1957 columns are as notable for their likenesses to the 1948 columns as for their differences from them. Organic commodities continue to hog the export market, heading the list in 21 (out of 24) territories, occupying second place in 19, and third place in 18 territories. The ten leading exports of 1948 are the ten leading exports of 1957. Almost all of the organic commodities listed in the 1948 columns are listed in the 1957 columns. Again, in one territory only (Northern Rhodesia) do organic commodities account for less than one third of the export revenues, and in all but one or two they account for more than half of them.

There are good reasons for the "sameness" of these lists. Commodities such as cotton, coffee, tobacco and cocoa are already high-priority purchases with most people in the world. Their per capita consumption is therefore not as liable to violent fluctuations as the per capita consumption of raw materials (such as sawn timber and copper) for capital goods. Neither high prices nor depressions stop people from consuming beverages, smoking and wearing clothes. There is the fact, too, that since World War II the demand for most tropical African staples has generally been ahead of the world supply — a fact on which almost all the governments have bolstered themselves, but on which none may pillow their heads. Then, with regard to such crops as rubber, cocoa, coffee and sisal, it must be remembered that the growing period is long and costly; once they have come to maturity their growers cannot afford not to keep them on the export list. And with regard to some others, such as gum, peanuts and cotton, there is the question of finding alternative exports; in many parts of tropical Africa they simply do not exist.

There is nothing immutable about the export status of a given animal or vegetable product, of course. Seasonal fluctuations of yield can be an unstabilizing factor of large dimensions. Market favor and fashion can play havoc with projections of demand, and the varying incidence of profit to the grower can play similar havoc in some areas with projections of supply.

The differences between the 1948 and 1957 columns provide illustrations. Easily the most important of these is the change in the status of coffee. Between 1948 and 1957 it became the ranking export in two more

Table 35

PRINCIPAL EXPORTS AS PER CENT OF
VALUE OF TOTAL EXPORTS, SELECTED TERRITORIES,
1948 AND 1957

TERRITORY	1948 COMMODITY	PER CENT	1957 COMMODITY	PER CENT
Angola	Coffee	31	Coffee	44
	Beans	12	Diamonds	12
	Diamonds	11	Fish and meal	14
Bechuanaland	Cattle	72	Meat	49 [a]
	Hides, skins	10	Sorghum	9 [a]
	Butter	6	Beans, pulses	6 [a]
Belgian Congo (inc. Ruanda-Urundi)	Copper	29	Copper	32
	Cotton	14	Coffee	13
	Palm oil	12	Cobalt	6
British Somaliland	Skins, hides	62	Sheep, goats	55 [a]
	Sheep, goats	28	Skins, hides	40 [a]
	Gums	3	Gums	? [a]
Ethiopia and Eritrea	Coffee	20	Coffee	67
	Hides, skins	18	Oilseeds	8
	Oilseeds	6	Hides, skins	9
French Cameroons	Cocoa	46	Cocoa	38
	Bananas	19	Coffee	19
	Palm oil, kernels	12	Bananas	9
French Equatorial Africa	Cotton	48	Wood, veneers	43
	Wood, veneers	20	Cotton	29
	Gold	8	Coffee	4
(French) Togo	Cocoa	23 [b]	Cocoa	35+
	Coffee	15 [b]	Coffee	30+
	Palm oil, kernels	12 [b]	Palm oil, kernels	9+
French West Africa	Peanuts, oil	44	Peanuts, oil	39
	Coffee	14	Coffee	26
	Cocoa	8	Cocoa	10
Gambia	Peanuts	96	Peanuts	95
	Palm kernels	2	Palm kernels	3
Ghana (Gold Coast)	Cocoa	75	Cocoa	56
	Gold	10	Gold	11
	Manganese	5	Timber	11
Kenya-Uganda	Cotton	29	Coffee	38+
	Coffee	20	Cotton	27+
	Sisal	10	Tea	5+
Liberia	Rubber	81 [c]	Rubber	68 [a]
	Palm oil, kernels	13 [c]	Iron ore	18 [a]
	Gold	2 [c]	Palm oil, kernels	2 [a]

Table 35 (Continued)

TERRITORY	1948 COMMODITY	PER CENT	1957 COMMODITY	PER CENT
Malagasy Republic (Madagascar)	Meat (and preparations)	20	Coffee	42
	Coffee	16	Vanilla	6
	Hides, skins	11	Tobacco	6
Mozambique	Cotton	23	Cotton	25
	Copra	22	Sugar	17
	Sisal	12	Cashew nuts	12
Nigeria (inc. British Cameroons)	Cocoa	29	Palm oil, kernels	26
	Palm kernels	19	Cocoa	21
	Peanuts	16	Peanuts, oil	20
Northern Rhodesia	Copper	85	Copper	92 [d]
	Zinc	5	Zinc	2 [d]
	Lead	4	Tobacco	2 [d]
Nyasaland	Tobacco	54	Tobacco	39 [d]
	Tea	32	Tea	21 [d]
	Cotton	9	Maize, flour	12 [d]
Sierra Leone	Palm kernels	41	Iron ore	35 [g]
	Diamonds	22	Palm kernels	21 [g]
	Iron ore	21	Diamonds	10 [g]
Somalia (Italian Somaliland)	Bananas	41 [e]	Bananas	60
	Hides, skins	19 [e]	Hides, skins	8
	Cotton	12 [e]	Charcoal	5
Southern Rhodesia	Tobacco	45	Tobacco	33 [d]
	Gold	18	Asbestos	12 [d]
	Asbestos	11	Gold	12 [d]
Republic of Sudan (Anglo-Egyptian Sudan)	Cotton	68	Cotton, cottonseed	58
	Cottonseed	10	Gum arabic	10
	Gum arabic	7	Peanuts	10
Tanganyika	Sisal	64	Sisal	27 [a]
	Cotton	8	Coffee	19 [a]
	Coffee	6	Diamonds	11 [a]
Zanzibar	Cloves, oil	42 [b]	Cloves, oil	83
	Coconut oil	29 [b]	Coconut oil	9
	Copra	21 [b]	Copra	3
Federation of Rhodesia and Nyasaland	Copper	58 [f]	Copper	54
	Tobacco	17 [f]	Tobacco	18
	Asbestos	4 [f]	Asbestos	5

Sources: United Nations, *Yearbook of International Trade Statistics, 1957; The Statesman's Year-Book, 1957,* Macmillan & Co., Ltd., London, 1957; and various H.M.S.O. publications.

[a] First half of 1958.   [b] 1949.   [c] September 1949–August 1950.
[d] 1953 (last year before Northern Rhodesia, Nyasaland and Southern Rhodesia federated).   [e] 1953.   [f] 1954 (first year of Federation).   [g] 1956.

territories (Kenya-Uganda and Madagascar), and its average percentage contribution to the export revenues of the ten territories in which it was one of the three major exports was 31 (as against 17 in the seven territories in which it was one of the three major exports in 1948). Alone among the "big five" (cotton, cocoa, coffee, tobacco and peanuts), it either maintained or improved its percentage in every one of the territories in which it was a major export. Among major exports that improved either their rank or their percentage standing, or both, during the ten-year period were vanilla (in Madagascar), sugar (in Mozambique), fish and fish meal (in Angola), wood and wood products (in Ghana, Somalia and French Equatorial Africa), cloves and clove oil (in Zanzibar) and cashew nuts (in Mozambique).

But relative gains must be balanced by relative losses. These were spread over a wide field that included sisal, cotton, palm kernels and oil, and hides and skins. Thus, sisal disappeared from the list of the three leading exports in Mozambique and Kenya-Uganda, and lost ground in Tanganyika. Cotton disappeared from the leading export list in Nyasaland, Somalia and the Belgian Congo and dropped rank in French Equatorial Africa, Kenya-Uganda and Tanganyika. Palm kernels and oil disappeared from the Belgian Congo and French Cameroons list and dropped rank in Liberia and Sierra Leone. Hides and skins disappeared from the Bechuanaland and Madagascar lists, and dropped rank in British Somaliland and Ethiopia.

However, it is not only the major export crops that are subject to the ebb and flow of fortune, though it is true that because of their characteristically disproportionate size, these are the ones where the ebb and flow matters most. The difficulty, of course, is to predict the direction of fluctuation, and the extent of it, in a given period. So far this difficulty does not seem to have been overcome. Just as in a tropical African drought all forecasts of rain are likely to fail, so in a tropical African boom all forecasts of export demand tend to have a rather low reliability index. For that matter, forecasts of export demand in tropical African depressions have not been infallible. Anyone venturing opinions on export trends therefore runs the risk of being contradicted by the event. Nevertheless, that risk must be taken.

It is fairly certain that few if any of the ranking exports will be able to go on bettering, or even maintaining, their high percentage standing on the present lists. No matter how great the demand for a given commodity, no country can afford to have its export business dominated by one product. Such domination means wealth and power for the few only: not all parts of Ghana can grow cocoa, or of the Republic of Sudan cotton, even if everybody in these territories wanted to grow them, which is far from being the case. For the many it means stringency, and for their rulers hypertension. A one-string fiddle is a difficult instrument at the best of times; and when the string goes, the music stops. A violin, on the other hand, is good for a tune even with its E-string broken. It will undoubtedly take a long time to diversify the economy of farm and forest to the point where every territory has even four good strings to work with, but the time must surely come, and every government is set upon doing something to speed its coming. Liberia, after having for years derived virtually all of its export revenues from rubber, is building up bit by bit an export trade in cocoa, coffee, piassava, palm kernels and wood (to say nothing of diamonds). Northern Rhodesia, which has been another "one-string" performer — and an exceedingly nervous one on that account — is slowly adding to its resources such exportable commodities as tobacco, cotton, rice, peanuts, maize and meat.

Some commodities will undoubtedly suffer a more severe loss of status than others, as measured by their percentage rating on the exports list. Indeed, this is already taking place. Using the recent short-term shifts as trend setters (a risky tactic, to be sure), it would look as though the following commodities are headed for the sharpest relative losses: cotton (because of increases in its cultivation in other parts of the world, and the growing competition of synthetic fibers); palm kernels and oil (because of easier-to-produce substitutes like peanuts and soybeans); rubber (because Liberia — the only country where it is raised on any scale — is engaged in an economic base-broadening enterprise); sisal (because of overproduction or, to put it differently, cheaper alternatives); and such foodstuffs as cereals and sugar. The reason for the last is that almost the first thing an African does with extra money is to buy food with it; and the foods he is especially partial to are those made from maize and wheat (which have accounted for most of the export trade in cereals), and those made from sugar.

Commodities that seem likely to fight the toughest rear-guard action are coffee and cocoa (because the places where they grow in tropical Africa are as well adapted to them as any in the world and the diseases that afflict them are now mostly under control); cloves (because there are so few other things — besides coconuts — that Zanzibar and Pemba, the main producers, are suited for); meat (because the demand within tropical Africa is steadily growing and can best be met by interterritorial shipments from the "haves" to the "have-nots"); wood and wood products such as plywood and veneers (because, for many commercial woods and most by-products, the region is the largest and best repository in the world); and, by no means least, the peanut (because of its unparalleled versatility, ease of cultivation, suitability to large parts of tropical Africa, and ability to stand rough handling).

Few of the major export commodities in the organic category are likely to decline in absolute importance. There are no parts of the world where such commodities as cotton, coffee, cocoa, peanuts, cashew nuts, cloves and hardwood timber can be raised more cheaply or easily — a fact that also applies to many of the minor export commodities, such as pyrethrum, wattle bark extract and benniseed. Moreover, the per capita world consumption of almost all of these exports is increasing and is likely to go on doing so, short of a major world calamity. Then, too, few tropical African governments could get along without the contribution these commodities make to their exchequers, and the rest of the free world has every reason to see that these governments do continue to get along.

Inorganic

Only eight of the commodities or groups of commodities listed in the 1948 columns of Table 35 are minerals. In only two territories (Northern Rhodesia and the Belgian Congo) does a mineral — copper in each case — head the export list; in only four (Northern Rhodesia, Sierra Leone, Ghana and Southern Rhodesia) does a mineral occupy second place on the list; and in only seven (Northern Rhodesia, Liberia, Sierra Leone, Ghana, Angola, French Equatorial Africa and Southern Rhodesia) does a mineral occupy third place.

Of the commodities or groups of commodities listed in the 1957 columns, only seven are minerals. In only three territories, namely, the Federation of Rhodesia and Nyasaland (thanks to the Northern Rhodesian copper production), the Belgian Congo (copper) and Sierra Leone (iron ore), does a mineral occupy the ranking position. In five territories a mineral occupies second rank; and in four, third rank.

The importance of tropical Africa's mineral trade must not be underestimated on this account. As Table 36 shows, in 1948 minerals provided at least half of the export revenues of two territories, at least one quarter of the revenues of four territories, and not less than 10 per cent of the export revenues of nine territories. In 1957 the corresponding figures were three, four and seven (or eight, if we continue to regard the two Rhodesias separately). Bearing in mind the sharp increases over this period in total export revenues, this means that the monetary contribution of minerals to the export trade has become very substantial. In both the Federation of Rhodesia and Nyasaland and the Belgian Congo, it exceeded $250 million in 1957; in the region as a whole it was not far short of $1 billion.

Where there have been recent declines in the export status of minerals, as a rule they have been small. The territories most affected by them are the large gold producers: Ghana, Southern Rhodesia and the Belgian Congo. With the official dollar price of gold remaining stationary, since before World War II, at $35 per fine ounce, and with almost all other commodity costs spiraling upward, gold miners have had little incentive to maintain their prewar rate of expansion and have failed to do so. Whereas Southern Rhodesia's gold exports amounted to 49 per cent of the total exports in 1938, they amounted to only 12 per cent in 1953 (the last year before federation); the corresponding percentages for the Belgian

Table 36

MINERAL EXPORTS AS PER CENT OF
VALUE OF TOTAL EXPORTS, SELECTED TERRITORIES,
1948 AND 1957

TERRITORY	1948	1957
Angola	11	13
Bechuanaland	2	6 [b]
Belgian Congo (including Ruanda-Urundi)	50	58
British Somaliland	a	a
Ethiopia and Eritrea	a	a
French Cameroons	1	a, b
French Equatorial Africa	13	6
French West Africa	a	2
Gambia	Nil	a, b
Ghana (Gold Coast)	18	30
Kenya-Uganda	5	4 [c]
Liberia	2	24 [b]
Malagasy Republic (Madagascar)	4	3
Mozambique	11	a
Nigeria	8	7
Northern Rhodesia	94	d
Sierra Leone	43	66
Somalia (Italian Somaliland)	a	a
Southern Rhodesia	39	d
Republic of Sudan (Anglo-Egyptian Sudan)	Nil	a
Tanganyika	10	15 [c]
Federation of Rhodesia and Nyasaland		63

Sources: United Nations, *Yearbook of International Trade Statistics, 1957; The Statesman's Year-Book, 1957,* Macmillan & Co., Ltd., London, 1957; and various H.M.S.O. publications.

[a] Less than 0.5 per cent.   [b] 1956.   [c] First half of 1958.
[d] Became part of Federation of Rhodesia and Nyasaland in January 1954.

Congo were 22 and 3, and for Ghana 43 and 10. The 1957 figures for the Belgian Congo and Ghana were 3 and 11 respectively. Even so, the total value of the gold exports from these three producing territories was greater in 1957 than it was in 1938. The most striking recent development in the mineral export trade has been the greatly increased importance of cobalt, iron ore, asbestos, chrome ore, diamonds and copper.

Secondary (Manufactured) Products

The development of manufacturing industries has already been discussed in another chapter. While most of these industries are concerned only with satisfying domestic demand, many have begun to do a useful export business.

The country offering the most striking example of this is the Federation of Rhodesia and Nyasaland; the industries most closely concerned, textile and clothing; and the biggest external customer, the Union of South Africa. In 1957, the Federation exported, under the general heading of "fibers, yarns, textiles and apparel," manufactured goods of domestic origin to the value of over £3 million (over £4.7 million in 1955). More than five sixths of this business was done with the Union of South Africa. The range of goods exported is indicated by the following items, all of which figured prominently on the Union's purchase list: outer garments, shirts, singlets and undervests, pullovers, jerseys and other apparel, cotton piece goods, furnishing drapery, haberdashery, twine, textiles for surgical purposes, textile bags, and cotton yarns for further manufacture. Exports in these categories were not confined to the Union; Bechuanaland, Southwest Africa, Angola, Kenya, Mozambique and the Belgian Congo were also important customers. Small consignments of outer garments, shirts and the like went to the United Kingdom and Yugoslavia. And two pounds sterling's worth of "other apparel" — an entry that leaves room for the imagination — got as far as Japan.

Nor were the secondary exports confined to textiles. Of the almost 100 classes of goods listed in the Federation's "Annual Statement of External Trade, 1957" as being exported to the Union of South Africa in that year, more than 60 can be classed, without semantic strain, as manufactures; of these only 17 belong to the textile category. The range of the non-textile exports is wide, including cigarettes, cutlery, enamelware, steel windows and doors, radios and phonographs, paints, pharmaceutical preparations, footwear, jewelry, suitcases and optical instruments. For a country barely fifty years out of the bush, it is an impressive list, one that says as much for the caliber of the men who have peopled it as for the geographical advantages it has conferred upon them.

So far the only other territories that have done much to exploit their advantages, acquired and inherited, human and physical, to the same end are Kenya and the Belgian Congo, and in neither is manufacturing industry as well established as it is in the Federation. Kenya's manufactured exports consist of such things as beer, cigarettes, cement, confectionery, insecticides, sisal bags and sacks, clothing, footwear, aluminum hollow ware, meat preparations, sugar, steel doors and windows, nails and hurricane lanterns. Most of its export business is done — in roughly even amounts — with its neighbors, Tanganyika and Uganda. The Belgian Congo's export trade in manufactured goods includes soap, cotton fabrics, casks, bottles, jute sacks, small craft, shoes, blankets, quinine, derris and cement; and most of it is likewise done with its neighbors.

A few other territories do an export business in a much more limited range of manufactures. The Republic of the Ivory Coast exports to its west coast neighbors such things as soap, cordage and canned fruit. Angola exports fertilizer (from fish) to the Union of South Africa and a certain amount of dried and canned fish to the Belgian Congo. Uganda exports cigarettes and some cotton piece goods to Kenya, Tanganyika and Ruanda-Urundi. Mozambique exports small amounts of soap and beer (mainly to Angola), cigarettes (mainly to Portuguese Guinea), cement (to Swaziland and Portugal), glycerine (to the Union of South Africa) and pottery.

Each year sees an increase in the amount of export business being done in such categories of goods.

COMPOSITION OF IMPORTS

The import lists of the several territories have, understandably, always been longer than their export lists. The needs of new, underdeveloped lands cover almost every category of goods, and are virtually without number. However, because of the poverty of the African, the scarcity of public and private capital, and, with some notable exceptions, a lack of awareness of the potential of the region, the list was for many years pared of everything but the necessities of a low-level economy. It consisted of goods of the type still referred to in some parts of southern Africa as "kaffir truck" — shoddy blankets, cotton piece goods, hollow ware, footwear and trinkets, and such other consumer goods and capital goods as were needed by the small European and Asian communities and the rather grudging territorial governments.

Today, things are different. The African is interested in an ever-widening range of goods and is learning how to find the money that buys them. The European and Asian communities are larger than they used to be, on the whole well to do, and disposed to live as well as any European and Asian communities in the world. Governments and corporations alike are spending very large sums on development work that requires almost every type of equipment a fertile technology can devise. These facts do much to explain why a country like Ghana had over 100 items and groups of items on its 1957 import list, and the Federation of Rhodesia and Nyasaland well over 300.

At the same time the composition of imports into tropical Africa continues to reflect its generally underdeveloped status. This is brought out in Table 37. From this analysis we see that food, textiles and capital goods make up approximately three quarters of the region's imports; that, of these three import groups, the food group is the smallest and the most stable, the capital goods group the largest [3] and getting larger — mostly at the expense of the textile group.

---

[3] The role of imported capital goods is undoubtedly greater than the figures suggest, since they leave out of account motor vehicles and parts, without which few capital development projects get very far these days.

Table 37

COMPOSITION OF IMPORTS, 1951-1956

	1951	1952	1953	1954	1955	1956
	AMOUNT (MILLIONS)					
Total imports	$1,644.5	$1,914.6	$1,683.8	$2,121.4	$2,113.1	$2,319.6
Capital goods ᵃ	670.0	870.2	718.4	904.9	941.3	1,160.4
Textiles	400.8	384.1	289.9	379.1	328.9	327.8
Foods and beverages (including tobacco)	179.4	190.7	207.5	240.2	250.4	263.7
Other imports	394.3	469.6	468.1	597.2	592.3	567.7
	PERCENTAGE DISTRIBUTION					
Total imports	100	100	100	100	100	100
Capital goods ᵃ	41	45	43	43	45	50
Textiles	24	20	17	18	15	14
Foods and beverages (including tobacco)	11	10	12	11	12	11
Other imports	24	25	28	28	28	25
	OTHER IMPORTS: AMOUNT (MILLIONS)					
Total	$394.3	$469.6	$468.1	$597.2	$592.3	$567.7
Basic (raw) materials	22.1	22.9	19.5	31.0	28.1	27.2
Mineral fuels	27.5	60.1	61.3	57.0	54.7	41.6
Chemicals	78.5	88.0	77.4	114.7	122.8	121.7
Other manufactures	227.1	249.0	243.3	323.4	311.6	308.6
Miscellaneous	39.0	49.6	66.6	71.1	75.1	68.6
	OTHER IMPORTS: PERCENTAGE DISTRIBUTION					
Total	100	100	100	100	100	100
Basic (raw) materials	6	5	4	5	5	5
Mineral fuels	7	13	13	10	9	7
Chemicals	20	19	17	19	21	21
Other manufactures	58	53	52	54	53	54
Miscellaneous	10	11	14	12	13	12

Sources: United Nations, "Economic Developments in Africa, 1954-1955" (Supplement to *World Economic Survey, 1955*), New York, 1956; and *ibid.*, 1955-1956 (1956 Supplement), and 1956-1957 (1957 Supplement).

ᵃ Includes metals and metal manufactures, machinery and transport equipment.

Food Imports

It is difficult to generalize about the composition of the imports in the foodstuffs category. The demand for imported foodstuffs (including beverages) varies from country to country, in range no less than in amount. In some territories the demand, as measured by the value of food imports in relation to the value of total imports, is consistently large, and the range of foodstuffs imported consistently wide. In some others the demand, as measured by the same criterion, is much smaller, while the range of foodstuffs imported remains very wide. In still others both the size and the range of the demand are small. Further, the demand within a country varies from year to year. In a good year it is likely to soar, for much the same reason as the demand in the United States for imported caviar and whiskey increases in a good year. The newly franchised of every land find satisfaction in "display" buying, and there is no quicker way, in most of Africa as elsewhere, of winning friends and influencing people than by keeping an impressive table. In a bad year, of course, the demand for imported foodstuffs drops. Of all the necessities of life, food is the one most quickly "improvised" from local resources.

Perhaps the nearest one can come to a helpful generalization is to say that the range of food imports varies with the size and standard of living of a territory's European and Asian populations. Thus, Kenya, the Federation of Rhodesia and Nyasaland, the Belgian Congo and other territories with sizable and well-to-do European populations import an extremely wide range of foodstuffs. In the best Belgian Congo restaurants it is possible to choose different dishes each day for a week or more without eating anything that was "home-grown" except the salads and the strawberries, which may have come from Kivu. The fish will probably have been flown in from the North Sea, the meat from Kenya or the Republic of Chad, the peas and asparagus from Belgium, the cheese from Holland and the wines from France or Italy. The flowers decorating the table may also have been imported — from the greenhouses of Brussels. On the other hand, countries like Gambia, Sierra Leone, British Somaliland and Bechuanaland have very small and not conspicuously wealthy nonindigenous populations. With the exception of certain items, their desire for imported foodstuffs and beverages is not matched by their ability to consume them in quantities that warrant their importation.

As for the degree of dependence of a country on imported foods and beverages, this appears to be a function of its people's scale of values and opportunities. The dependence tends to be heavier in a country like Liberia than it is in, say, Ghana, and heavier in Ghana than it is in, say, the Federation of Rhodesia and Nyasaland. For many years Liberia derived the bulk of its revenues from the export of a single, inedible commodity: rubber. Though the base of her economy has been broadened in the postwar period, neither peasant nor plantation food crops have been responsible for very much of the broadening. The average Liberian laborer still finds it more congenial to earn money tapping rubber or shovelling iron ore and to buy imported sugar, flour, meat and even vegetables with his earnings than to raise these commodities himself. And until about 1955 the cocoa grower of Ghana saw no good reason for living the life of a drudge, cultivating yams, sugar cane and corn, when the "golden" cocoa pod provided him with an almost effortless economic superiority, including the means of buying a wide range of imported canned and cartonned goods. The Federation of Rhodesia and Nyasaland, on the other hand, has long laid the emphasis in its economy on the cultivation of food crops, with the result that in recent years foodstuffs and beverages have constituted only about 8 per cent, by value, of the total imports. (See Figure 33.)

Though every government in the region is encouraging its people to grow more food, not many governments can yet point to a measurable percentage decline in the import of foods and beverages. On the contrary, in several territories the percentage has grown over the past ten to twenty years. This may be due in part to the difficulty of growing foodstuffs in large areas of tropical Africa — and certainly it can be formidable in countries like Liberia. It may also be due in part to the difficulty of finding farm labor in areas which are suited to large-scale food raising. But to some extent it would seem to be due to the desire of Africans with money, even those with the equivalent of only a few dollars in their pockets, to eat and drink the things a European eats and drinks. A man is what he eats and drinks — so the thinking still goes in many a mind. Accordingly, if the European is a smarter man than the African — if he can make stronger "magic," can earn more money and have more leisure in which to enjoy it — it must be because of what he eats and drinks. But what he eats is mostly not what the African grows and eats, and what he drinks still less so. This may help to explain the rising African demand for canned goods, packaged cereals, refrigerated meat, butter and condensed milk — to say nothing of beers and, where they are legal, other beverages such as wines and spirits. Most of these items are imports.

Textile Imports

The import of textiles also differs widely from country to country and from year to year, so that here, too, almost any generalization is subject to recall on short notice. What is clear — beyond the fact of the sharp postwar decline in the percentage contribution made by textiles to the total imports (see Table 37) — is, first, that the bulk of the textile import continues to consist of cotton piece goods; second, that most of the imported lines are of the "bargain basement" kind — cheap calicoes, ginghams, hessians, denims and so on; third, that the ratio between good-quality and poor-quality imports is growing; and, fourth, that it will continue to grow.

The first is natural enough, for one of the prime necessities of modern life is clothing. In most parts of tropical Africa this necessity is well served by lightweight blouses, dresses, trousers and shirts made of cotton; and because village labor is cheap, Africans find it more convenient as a rule to buy the material of their choice for making up than to buy the finished

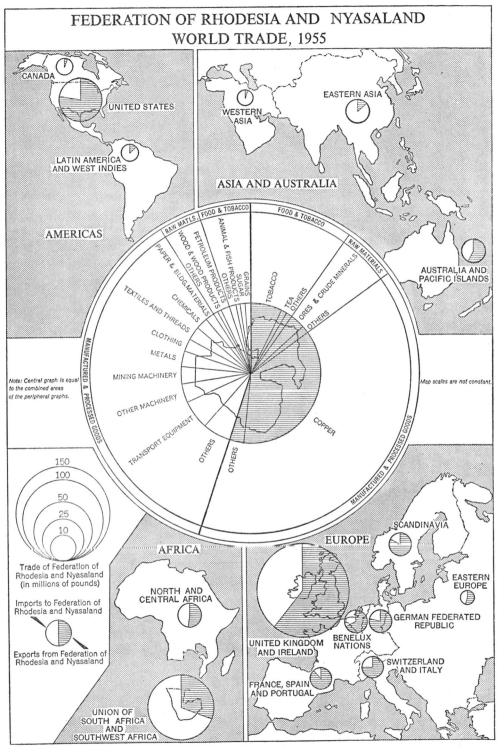

FEDERATION OF RHODESIA AND NYASALAND
WORLD TRADE, 1955

FIGURE 33

article. The second is natural also, because the average African's spending power is still very limited. And the third and fourth are understandable when we bear in mind the postwar growth of factories in the Belgian Congo, Angola, Mozambique, the Federation of Rhodesia and Nyasaland and elsewhere for the making of mostly cheap-grade cottons, and the many indications which the wealthier African gives of being a lavish spender on clothes. Most cities already have a brisk African trade in high-priced lines, including satin, silk, nylon and other synthetic fabrics, as well as fine cottons.

To get an idea of the range of textile goods imported, one need only glance down the columns of the annual statement of external trade of the Federation of Rhodesia and Nyasaland. The following list contains only those articles belonging to the category of "fibers, yarns, textiles and apparel" which were imported in amounts exceeding £250,000 during the year 1957. It reads: hats and caps; outergarments; hosiery; shirts; singlets, undervests and other underclothing; other clothing; jute and hessian bags; blankets and rugs; cotton piece goods; cotton thread; carpets and floor rugs; napery and other furnishing drapery; haberdashery, millinery and minor articles of attire; silk and rayon piece goods; woolen piece goods; textiles for surgical purposes; cotton waste yarns and other yarns for further manufacture. If the Federation is not representative of tropical Africa, its lead at least is being followed wherever governments are concerned with raising their people's sights and giving them the means of reaching what they see. It may still be a long time before Bechuanaland offers much of a market for imported silk piece goods, or Liberia for imported bed linen and towels, but who, fifty years ago, would have thought otherwise about the Rhodesias?

Capital Goods Imports

As the preceding table shows, not only are capital goods an easy first on the import list, but their lead, both absolute and relative, over foodstuffs and textiles is getting longer. There is no reason to suppose that it will stop getting longer in the next few years, for all the governing authorities agree on the need for capital development. Whether it takes the form of dams, wells, drainage projects, terracing of hillsides, or what the French call *infrastructure* — roads, railways, etc. — capital development calls for gear that is not to be had locally. In time, no doubt, it will be found convenient and economic to manufacture many kinds of capital gear within the borders of the country needing them. Southern Rhodesia is already manufacturing some such items, including part of the steel that has gone into the Kariba plant. But no government is likely to feel that its interest in the foreseeable future would best be served by following a "Made in Tropical Africa" line of thinking to the point of autarky. For one thing, no government is likely to command the capital necessary to build the plants for such goods; and for another, there are so many better places in the world for making them.

Important as capital goods are in any modern scheme of development, they are not as basic to a country's existence as foodstuffs and textiles. Accordingly, territorial differences in the percentage contribution of capital goods to total imports are much wider than they are in the case of foodstuffs and textiles. Their contribution to the total tends to be large where much or most of the export business is derived from minerals, as in the case of the Belgian Congo and the two Rhodesias. It tends to be smaller in territories that get their revenues mainly from non-mineral sources of wealth, as, for example, Mozambique, the French Cameroons and the Republic of Sudan. It tends to be smallest in those that are still searching for the bootstraps with which to lift themselves economically, such as Ruanda-Urundi and Somalia. In saying this we are not forgetting that large amounts of capital goods have from time to time been imported into countries like Ruanda-Urundi and Somalia by governments and corporations, in the belief that every pump needs priming, and the more unpromising the pump's location the greater the need of priming fluid. Nor are we forgetting that in some territories the notion of pumping back, in the form of capital improvements, profits made on the mines, plantations and forests is still little more than a notion.

With capital goods as varied as the capital needs they serve, and no two capital needs exactly alike, no useful purpose would be served by attempting an enumeration of them. Suffice it to say that about 90 per cent fall into the following categories: agricultural implements and machinery (tractors, plows, harrows, harvesters, etc.); electrical gear (transformers, turbines, power cable, pylons); locomotives, rolling stock and parts; metals (mainly iron, steel, copper) and metal goods (mining equipment, piping, galvanized sheets); motor vehicles (passenger, commercial), parts and accessories; and transport building and maintenance equipment. Because these categories would be most unlikely to occupy the same relative standing in more than two or three territories in the whole region — and then perhaps only for a year or two at a stretch, such has been the fitful demand for capital goods in most of the territories up to now — it would be pointless to give them anything but an alphabetical rating.

However, if there is one category of capital goods that stands at or near the top in more countries than any other, it is motor vehicles and their parts and accessories. This is true of "roadless" countries like Liberia and Ethiopia no less than of countries like the Federation of Rhodesia and Nyasaland, Angola and the Belgian Congo. And if there is one category that is improving its position everywhere faster than the others, it is agricultural implements and machinery. Whereas the demand for mining, electrical and other nonagricultural types of machinery stands in pretty close relation to the needs of a few comparatively expensive development schemes which, once complete, will require little in the way of capital replacements, the demand for agricultural machinery is less dependent on the availability of large sums of corporation capital than it is on the individually small but cumulatively large investments of enlightened farmers and cooperative societies. The demand for such machinery is, therefore, more broadly based. With so much of tropical Africa still to be reclaimed from its wasteful self, and so few of the waste places amenable to hoe-in-the-hand techniques, agricultural machinery promises to go on being a steadily expanding entry on the capital imports list.

Other Imports

Imports other than those in the foodstuffs, textiles and capital goods categories are, as Table 37 shows, far from negligible. In most territories, the majority of the items consist of such things as leather and rubber goods, glassware, hollow ware and ceramics, wood and paper products, and prefabricated houses. The balance is made up of chemicals, mineral fuels, basic raw materials (such as mineral ores and concentrates, lumber, cotton and cement), and miscellaneous goods.

The recent changes shown in the table seem to be conspicuously free from trends, other than that of impressive growth. If the percentage decline of the "other manufactures" category is significant, it may reflect the diversification of local manufacturing industry in the postwar period. The fact that the percentage of "other imports" consisting of "basic (raw) materials" has not risen need not be taken as contradictory, since domestic raw materials are employed in most of the domestic plants now engaged in manufacturing.

DIRECTION OF TRADE

It is only in recent years that ample and fairly uniform trade data have become available for most tropical African countries, but it is still difficult to obtain from some of them the data necessary for a direction-of-trade analysis. Tables 38 and 39 give such an analysis for the main trading entities for a recent five-year period.

From these tables it is clear that tropical Africa does the bulk of its commodity business with countries in the Organization for European Economic Cooperation, that is, with Western Europe. For the five-year period in question, two thirds of its imports came from OEEC countries and nearly three fifths of its exports went to them. And the ratios were well maintained throughout the quinquennium. It is no less clear that trade, import and export alike, still tends to "follow the flag," that is, to move between mother country and colony (or protectorate, or overseas province, or trusteeship). While this quasi-domestic type of international trade reached its highest percentage level in the trade moving between

Table 38

ORIGIN OF IMPORTS, 1950-1954
(*Per Cent*)

TERRITORY AND YEAR	OEEC COUNTRIES [a]	METRO-POLITAN COUNTRY	DOLLAR AREA	STERLING AREA [b]	OTHER AFRICAN COUNTRIES
Total [c]					
1950	65.8		10.1	34.8	11.6
1951	66.9		8.0	30.7	11.1
1952	65.9		9.6	33.0	11.0
1953	66.5		8.6	34.4	12.3
1954	66.8		7.9	31.2	12.3
Belgian Congo					
1950	58.9	39.2	25.9	10.2	8.9
1951	62.3	40.1	23.1	9.8	7.6
1952	61.5	39.2	25.6	9.1	7.0
1953	63.1	40.0	23.9	7.5	7.1
1954	62.8	36.9	20.1	7.8	8.2
Sterling area countries					
1950	61.0	51.9	5.9	61.0	15.1
1951	60.6	45.3	4.7	54.6	15.4
1952	61.4	47.6	6.0	56.3	14.8
1953	62.3	49.5	5.3	58.8	15.8
1954	60.2	44.4	4.8	54.1	16.4
French franc countries					
1950	75.6	70.1	9.6	3.1	7.6
1951	77.9	71.9	5.8	3.3	6.5
1952	77.0	66.4	6.9	5.4	7.0
1953	77.8	67.3	5.6	4.8	8.2
1954	79.1	67.7	4.7	3.9	7.6
Portuguese Africa					
1950	70.2	39.9	15.8	20.2	6.8
1951	71.4	40.9	14.5	17.0	7.0
1952	72.5	39.5	13.5	18.9	7.0
1953	72.1	39.4	15.3	17.9	6.2
1954	71.8	38.0	18.3	16.1	5.4

Source: United Nations, "Economic Developments in Africa, 1954-1955" (Supplement to *World Economic Survey, 1955*), New York, 1956.

[a] Countries in the Organization for European Economic Cooperation, the chief of which are: France, United Kingdom, Belgium and Luxembourg, Portugal, West Germany, Italy, Netherlands.

[b] Mainly United Kingdom, India and Hong Kong. Sterling countries in Africa are included under "other African countries."

[c] Excludes imports of Liberia, Ethiopia and a few small territories.

Table 39

DESTINATION OF EXPORTS, 1950-1954

(*Per Cent*)

TERRITORY AND YEAR	OEEC COUNTRIES [a]	METRO-POLITAN COUNTRY	DOLLAR AREA	STERLING AREA [b]	OTHER AFRICAN COUNTRIES
Total [c]					
1950	56.2		13.5	38.0	7.8
1951	59.1		12.4	37.6	8.5
1952	58.4		11.9	39.3	7.9
1953	56.6		14.5	37.2	7.7
1954	57.1		12.7	35.8	7.7
Belgian Congo					
1950	78.7	58.5	13.0	13.0	5.5
1951	81.3	56.1	12.2	12.0	6.1
1952	80.1	57.2	12.9	10.4	4.6
1953	78.6	56.7	16.5	8.6	3.8
1954	75.6	53.4	16.3	9.3	6.1
Sterling area countries					
1950	65.4	53.5	17.7	59.5	8.3
1951	67.6	53.1	15.8	58.9	8.4
1952	68.6	54.2	13.7	61.8	7.5
1953	68.3	55.4	16.2	61.0	7.1
1954	71.3	52.4	12.6	57.9	7.2
French franc countries					
1950	80.8	70.1	2.7	3.4	7.8
1951	79.2	69.4	2.6	3.5	10.6
1952	81.0	68.1	3.2	2.1	11.5
1953	79.4	65.8	4.3	2.2	12.3
1954	78.5	65.0	8.4	2.4	9.8
Portuguese Africa					
1950	72.8	31.9	11.4	11.5	10.4
1951	75.4	22.2	10.7	13.6	9.8
1952	63.4	32.3	21.1	15.5	9.5
1953	63.3	25.2	26.1	17.5	7.5
1954	66.0	25.7	20.6	16.2	8.6

Source: United Nations, "Economic Developments in Africa, 1954-1955" (Supplement to *World Economic Survey, 1955*), New York, 1956.

[a] Countries in the Organization for European Economic Cooperation, the chief of which are: France, United Kingdom, Belgium and Luxembourg, Portugal, West Germany, Italy, Netherlands.

[b] Mainly United Kingdom, India and Hong Kong. Sterling countries in Africa are included under "other African countries."

[c] Excludes exports of Liberia, Ethiopia and a few small territories.

France and the territories then under her control, it reached its greatest volume in British territories. (The high sterling area percentages are, in large part, a reflection of this.) In the 1950-1954 quinquennium, the mean annual value of exports from the British territories of the Gold Coast, Nigeria, the Federation of Rhodesia and Nyasaland, Sierra Leone, the Anglo-Egyptian Sudan, Tanganyika and Uganda came to the equivalent of approximately $1.4 billion, or about 58 per cent of the exports from all the areas covered by the tables; and of this export business roughly 54 per cent was carried on with the United Kingdom. The corresponding import figures were $1.1 billion, 49 per cent and 47 per cent.

By contrast, the amount of trade done in this period with the dollar area was very small — less than one seventh of the total export trade and less than one tenth of the total import trade. In both cases most of the business was done with the United States. Likewise, very little of it was done within the African continent, the percentages being less than 12 for imports and less than 8 for exports. It is only fair to point out, however, that these figures do not take full account of movements of goods across African frontiers by migrant workers and others of less honorable calling.[4] These movements may have been individually small but they were unquestionably large in the aggregate. As for general trends, it is always tempting to read significance into percentage shifts, however slight. Some of the shifts during this period are really not so slight or insignificant when we remember the inertia of international trade movements, and the strength of the ties — strategic, fiscal, political and sentimental — that bind one territory to another and sometimes keep them bound even in the face of economic logic.

If these shifts are the beginning of trends (and more recent figures suggest that they may well be), they at least have the merit of being reasonable. In the early postwar years it was reasonable that the dollar area should be called upon to supply many goods which the Western Europe of that epoch was unable to supply in quantity, if at all. It is equally reasonable that, as tropical African countries come to do some of their own manufacturing, they should seek to interest their continental neighbors in their wares, and to be themselves supplied with such materials as they may lack for the manufacture of those wares.

But since trends are like currents in a tidal stream — some moving one way, some another; some gaining momentum, some weakening — it is hardly to be expected that they will emerge clearly from tables that "average out" trading movements over such broad areas. To identify them, we need to narrow our territorial base of analysis. The suspicion that the percentage shifts shown in the "metropolitan country" columns of Tables 38 and 39 may be the work of new "currents" grows when we set them alongside the shifts that have been occurring in the trading relations of

4 See pp. 581ff.

specific territories. Those that have been occurring in the import trade of the Belgian Congo with West Germany and Italy are shown in Table 40. The trade returns of several other territories in tropical Africa tell

Table 40

WEST GERMAN AND ITALIAN IMPORTS INTO THE BELGIAN CONGO, BY VALUE, 1948-1957

	WEST GERMANY		ITALY	
YEAR	AMOUNT	PER CENT OF TOTAL B.C. IMPORTS	AMOUNT	PER CENT OF TOTAL B.C. IMPORTS
	(*Millions*)		(*Millions*)	
1948	Fr. 48.3	0.6	Fr. 24.4	0.3
1954	1,237.6	6.8	489.8	2.7
1955	1,305.1	7.1	460.3	2.5
1956	1,645.7	8.1	547.9	2.7
1957	1,908.0	9.0	674.8	3.2

Source: United Nations, *Yearbook of International Trade Statistics, 1957,* Volume I, New York, 1958.

a similar story — of handsome gains in the value and percentage share of business being done with these two European countries. And none can say that the Germans and Italians have not earned their gains. No effort is too great for them, and no order too small. Their salesmen can be found in the most unlikely places, always speaking the language of the country. The quality of their goods is excellent, and they have the reputation of honoring their delivery dates. In the circumstances, it is not so surprising that some of the biggest contracts for the biggest undertaking in the whole of tropical Africa — the Kariba hydroelectric scheme — should have gone to Italian firms.

Though later in getting back into the field, the Japanese are also very much aware of the trading potential of tropical Africa. By 1954 they had climbed to fifth place on the list of about 30 nations doing import business in the Belgian Congo, thereby overtaking France and the Netherlands, both of which had also improved their percentage standing in the 1949-1954 period. (They have since slipped to about ninth or tenth place.)

Clearly, not every buyer and seller can go on increasing his share of a country's or a region's trade. The increases registered by such countries as West Germany, Italy and Japan have meant decreases to other nations. But the incidence of these decreases is more patchy than the incidence of the increases. In some territories it is the United States that has lost most ground. In Angola, for instance, the United States share of the import trade fell from 20 per cent in 1948 to 11.6 in 1958. (By contrast, the

United States share of the export trade increased from 8 per cent to 25 per cent over the same period.) In the Belgian Congo the value of United States imports dropped from 31 per cent of the total imports in 1948 to less than 15 per cent of the total in 1958. Even in Liberia the percentage of the import trade done with the United States dropped from 73 in 1948 to 56 in 1958. Such decreases are not unexpected, in view of the decline, already noted, in the trade contribution of the dollar area, of which the United States is the chief occupant.

In other territories it is the metropolitan share of the business that has declined most noticeably. The United Kingdom's share of Tanganyika's export trade fell from 52 per cent in 1948 to 35 per cent in the first half of 1958. Its share of Kenya and Uganda's import trade fell in the same period from 52 per cent to less than 38 per cent, and of the export trade, from 30 per cent to 22 per cent. As the "metropolitan country" columns of Tables 38 and 39 make clear, such declines were not confined to the United Kingdom. Belgium, France and Portugal all lost some ground over the 1950-1954 period in their "domestic" African markets. In most cases they have continued to do so since then. Not that it should really be regarded as loss. Growth is never loss, and there can be no question that the volume of international trade of every part of tropical Africa has been growing, and will continue to do so. Nor should the broadening of a territory's trading base be construed as loss, but rather as gain; in good times it makes for stability, and in bad times for resilience. What we are observing is a process as natural and proper as weaning; indeed, it *is* the weaning of colonial, quasi-colonial and ex-colonial territories from their dependence on the metropolis. It is all of a piece with the decline of "dollar area" dependence and the rise of inter-African trade. Both are symptoms of the ever-widening role which tropical Africa is destined to play in the world's market place.

TERMS OF TRADE

A country's ability to export the goods it produces is governed largely by two things: the ability, and willingness, of other countries to absorb those goods at prices that make export profitable, and its ability, and willingness, to deliver them at prices acceptable to those countries. The success or failure of such transactions is closely related to what economists have come to call the "terms-of-trade index." This index is obtained by dividing the "export unit value index" by the "import unit value index," and expressing the product as a percentage.[5] The movements of the index

[5] These unit value indexes, published in the *Statistical Yearbook* and the *Monthly Bulletin of Statistics* of the United Nations, show changes in the average price of a country's aggregate exports and imports. Each index number represents a measure of the change in price, if any, in the national currency, between the period to which the number refers, called the "current period," and a fixed period, called the "publication base," in which the index is represented by the percentage 100.

Table 41 (With Opposite Page)

INDEXES OF UNIT VALUE OF IMPORTS AND
EXPORTS AND TERMS OF TRADE, BY TERRITORY, 1950-1957

(*1953 = 100*)

TERRITORY	IMPORTS							EXPORTS	
	1950	1951	1952	1954	1955	1956	1957 *	1950	1951
Angola	97	101	103	94	97	99	117	80	94
Belgian Congo ª	95	107	108	97	97	98	102	98	95
Ethiopia ᵇ	113	117	126	100	117	112	116	78	98
Ghana (Gold Coast)	88	106	111	95	92	90	97	83	109
Kenya-Uganda	83	103	110	89	90	94	—	K. 91 / U. 88	121 / 132
Nigeria	86	107	112	93	92	93	94	81	111
Federation of Rhodesia and Nyasaland	80	96	102	98	102	103	106	80	93
Republic of Sudan (Anglo-Egyptian Sudan)	85	117	122	92	93	94	—	102	148
Tanganyika	83	103	110	89	90	94	—	95	145

Source: United Nations, "Economic Developments in Africa, 1954-1955" (Supplement to *World Economic Survey, 1955*), and *ibid.*, 1956-1957, New York, 1956, 1958.

so formed represent changes in a country's trading position, that is, in the purchasing power of a given unit of its products. A rise in the index represents an improvement of its trading position; a fall in the index, a deterioration. In order to facilitate comparison of one country's terms of trade with another's, the indexes are usually adjusted to a common "publication base." In Table 41 the base is the year 1953.

It will be seen that the terms of trade of a country are continually changing. During the period under review, in two cases only, Kenya in 1955-1956 and Tanganyika in 1955-1956, did they remain constant for as much as two years on end.[6] It is also clear that the *direction* in which a country's terms-of-trade index moves seldom remains constant for long. In none of the ten territories included in Table 41 did the index stay "on course" throughout the eight-year period. The amplitude of the movements made by the index differed considerably from country to country. Thus, in Kenya it fluctuated by less than 20 per cent; in Ghana, by nearly 50 per cent. These fluctuations, which are the result more of fluctuations of the export unit value index than of fluctuations of the import unit value index,[7] tend to be greatest in those territories that lean heavily for their

[6] Actually their "constancy" was more statistical than actual, for the annual average conceals sizable monthly fluctuations. In 1957, for example, the index for the Federation of Rhodesia and Nyasaland fluctuated from one quarter to the next by anything up to 16 per cent.

[7] On the average the movements of the export unit value index were more than twice as large as those of the import index.

Table 41 (Continued)

EXPORTS					TERMS OF TRADE						
1952	1954	1955	1956	1957 *	1950	1951	1952	1954	1955	1956	1957 *
92	101	87	80	82	82	93	89	107	90	81	70
89	104	116	121	97	93	102	96	107	119	123	95
99	121	105	120	119	69	84	79	133	99	115	103
105	141	121	97	92	94	103	95	148	132	101	95
111	105	103	107	—	109	117	101	118	114	114	—
129	107	95	92	—	106	128	118	120	106	98	—
115	111	98	92	92	95	104	103	116	107	99	98
96	96	123	115	91	100	97	94	100 c	123	113	86
148	116	106	117	—	120	126	121	126	114	124	—
130	99	90	94	—	114	141	118	111	100	100	—

ª Including Ruanda-Urundi.
ᵇ Beginning 1952, Ethiopia and Eritrea.
ᶜ Both 1953 and 1954 are "base" years: from 1954 the indexes are based on figures for the two Rhodesias and Nyasaland; prior to 1954, they are based on those for Southern Rhodesia.
* For updated figures see *Economic Survey of Africa Since 1950* (United Nations, 1959).

export revenues on a single commodity, and smallest in territories where no single commodity dominates the export market.

But we should not attach too much importance to fluctuations in the terms-of-trade index, and its components. Like those of the barometer, they are sometimes less important for what they are than for the state of mind they induce. Some nations, as some barometer tappers, seem inclined to show a regard for diagnostic devices that is out of all proportion to their proven value, and to assume that things can only be as good as, or as bad as, the rules of thumb associated with their behavior. Actually, the fluctuations of a terms-of-trade index can be as misleading as those of a barometer. Just as a rising barometer does not necessarily mean fair weather, so a rising index does not necessarily mean fair trading weather. It simply means that the purchasing power of the unit of exports is increasing. It may well happen that while the purchasing power increases, the volume of exports is falling; this, of course, is anything but "fair."

In order to establish whether changes in the terms of trade are in fact advantageous to a country — whether, that is to say, they increase its capacity to import — they have to be expressed in terms of the purchasing power of its aggregate exports. This calculation — terms-of-trade index multiplied by the index of volume (or "quantum") of exports — has been carried out for a number of countries in Table 42.

Table 42 (With Opposite Page)

INDEXES OF TERMS OF TRADE AND
CAPACITY TO IMPORT, BY TERRITORY, 1950-1957

(1953 = 100)

TERRITORY	TERMS OF TRADE							QUANTUM OF EXPORTS	
	1950	1951	1952	1954	1955	1956	1957 [*]	1950	1951
Angola	82	93	89	107	90	81	70	102	104
Belgian Congo [a]	93	102	96	107	119	123	95	86	88
Ethiopia [b]	69	84	79	133	99	115	103	57	75
Ghana (Gold Coast)	94	103	95	148	132	101	95	104	94
Kenya-Uganda K.	109	117	101	118	114	114	—	99	105
U.	106	128	118	120	106	98	—	97	107
Nigeria	95	104	103	116	107	99	98	88	85
Federation of Rhodesia and Nyasaland	100	97	94	100 [c]	123	113	86	91	82
Republic of Sudan (Anglo-Egyptian Sudan)	120	126	121	126	114	124	—	76	98
Tanganyika	114	141	118	111	100	100	—	73	80

Source: United Nations, "Economic Developments in Africa, 1954-1955" (Supplement to World Economic Survey, 1955), and ibid., 1956-1957, New York, 1956, 1958.

From this table we see that, whereas only six of the ten territories finished the seven-to-eight-year period with a higher terms-of-trade index than they started with, all but one finished with a higher capacity-to-import index. We also see that, whereas the average net gain for the ten territories in the terms-of-trade index was negligible, the average net gain in the capacity-to-import index amounted to over 33 per cent. In other words, the terms-of-trade index tends to underrate the trading strength of a country in a "bullish" period — as the years 1950-1957 generally were. It might be said also to underrate the trading strength of some countries in a "bearish" market, for the table provides several instances of a falling terms-of-trade index being compensated — even overcompensated — by a rising quantum-of-exports index. It is beginning to look, then, as though some parts at least of tropical Africa are acquiring enough trading strength and flexibility to enable them to cushion the shock of slump (such as occurred in the price of many raw materials after the Korean War boom had ended) either by selling more of a given commodity for less or by selling more commodities, or both.

The respective contributions made to the growth of the Belgian Congo's capacity to import by a rising volume of exports and improved terms of trade may be seen from the breakdown for the period 1950-1955 in Table 43. The substantial size of both contributions is striking. So is the growth in size of the terms-of-trade contribution in years when business has been on the upgrade (1950-1951 being the "Korean" boom years), and of the

Table 42 (Continued)

QUANTUM OF EXPORTS					CAPACITY TO IMPORT						
1952	1954	1955	1956	1957*	1950	1951	1952	1954	1955	1956	1957*
94	98	94	120	110	84	97	84	105	85	97	77
94	102	105	112	111	80	90	90	109	125	138	105
76	96	97	85	98	39	63	60	126	103	105	101
92	91	90	101	112	98	97	88	135	119	102	106
123	101	130	139	—	108	123	124	119	148	158	—
110	113	132	131	—	103	137	130	136	139	128	—
88	104	103	115	111	84	89	91	124	110	114	109
98	120	109	122	132	91	79	92	110	112	115	113
66	79	107	130	—	91	123	80	99	121	161	—
105	105	117	136	—	83	113	124	117	117	136	—

ª Including Ruanda-Urundi.
ᵇ Beginning 1952, Ethiopia and Eritrea.
ᶜ Both 1953 and 1954 are "base" years: from 1954 the indexes are based on figures for the two Rhodesias and Nyasaland; prior to 1954, they are based on those for Southern Rhodesia.
* For updated figures see *Economic Survey of Africa Since 1950* (United Nations, 1959).

volume-of-trade contribution when business has been on the downgrade. Also noteworthy is the smaller amplitude of the year-to-year fluctuations of the volume-of-trade contribution to the country's import capacity than of the terms-of-trade contribution. From this we may conclude that, while the stuff of which a growing capacity to import is made is an expanding volume of export business, the climate that governs the rate of growth is the terms of trade, accelerating the rate in boom times and checking it in times of slump.

ORGANIZATION OF TRADE

It is easier to ask questions about the organization of the import and export trade than to answer them, for marketing practice is not the same in every territory, or for every type of produce and merchandise. Certain aspects of marketing organization are, however, widely shared.[8]

Non-African Enterprise

Perhaps the most important of these is the "foreignness" of it. It was the European, along with the Levantine, who first persuaded the African

[8] The organization of internal trade will be dealt with in a later section.

Table 43

CHANGES IN THE BELGIAN CONGO'S INDEX OF CAPACITY TO IMPORT DUE TO CHANGES IN VOLUME OF TRADE AND IN TERMS OF TRADE, 1950-1955

YEAR	ANNUAL CHANGE (IN POINTS) OF INDEX OF CAPACITY TO IMPORT	POINTS CONTRIBUTED BY	
		VOLUME OF TRADE	TERMS OF TRADE
Total, 1950-1955	+ 92.8	+ 40.1	+ 52.7
1950	+ 24.6	+ 9.0	+ 15.6
1951	+ 15.1	+ 3.2	+ 11.9
1952	− 0.3	+ 7.6	− 7.9
1953	+ 16.2	+ 9.5	+ 6.7
1954	+ 12.5	+ 4.1	+ 8.4
1955	+ 24.7	+ 6.7	+ 18.0

Source: La Situation Economique du Congo Belge et du Ruanda-Urundi en 1954, and *ibid.,* 1955, Ministry of Colonies, Brussels, 1955, 1956.

farmer to grow cocoa, oilseeds, cotton, coffee and tobacco for export, and who, over the years, has supplied most of the capital (seed, tools, etc.), bought up and shipped the surpluses, and carried the risks. It was the European, the Levantine and, in east Africa, the Asian and the Arab who organized the return traffic in merchandise. The development of large-scale mining for the overseas market was likewise due to foreign enterprise. The bulk of the wholesaling trade is still in foreign hands. Even in west Africa, with its tradition of indigenous trading, the export and import business done by firms of foreign origin still amounts to probably not less than 90 per cent of the total. The largest firms are, without exception, of foreign origin. Of the 15 largest import houses in the sterling area of west Africa, six are British, one Anglo-Greek, four continental European, three American and one Asian.

At the middleman level also, most of the buying and selling is still conducted by non-Africans — mainly Levantines in west Africa and the Congo basin, and Asians in central and east Africa. Only at the retail level do Africans form important links in the chain of organization, and then only in west Africa. In east Africa even village stores, or *dukas*, are more often run by Asians than by Africans.

Size of Firm

A second widely shared aspect of market organization is its bigness. Since the state of health of tropical African trade depends mainly on the vitality of world demand for a limited range of primary products, it has long been addicted to ups and downs. As a result, trade has tended to become concentrated in the hands of those with the greatest staying power, which usually means those with the broadest base of operations and the largest financial resources. The big have therefore tended to get bigger, and the small to go under. From time to time some of the big firms have become big enough to corner the market in a given region, or have entered into cartel-type agreements with their kin to protect their share of it. Although the activities of the biggest firms now come under close government scrutiny, their scope remains impressive. In the sterling area of west Africa the United Africa Group,[9] for instance, handles on the average about one third of the entire import trade. In some years it handles more than this. In its 1956-1957 fiscal year the Group sold more than £103 million worth of merchandise in Ghana and Nigeria alone; this was equivalent to approximately 42 per cent of the total imports of these two countries in the calendar year 1957. The Group's share of the west African export trade is less, but still large. In the same fiscal year the Group purchased Ghanaian and Nigerian produce to the value of more than £35 million, a sum equal to approximately one sixth of the domestic exports of the two countries in 1957. Its purchases covered the gamut of west African produce, with the emphasis on palm oil, palm kernels, cotton, benniseed, copra, peanuts, kola, cocoa, hides, skins, rubber, wood and minerals. Its sales covered every type of imported consumer goods known to the African — the Kingsway Stores in Lagos had over 70 selling sections — along with a great range of producer and capital goods.

In the non-sterling areas of west and central Africa, most of the import and export trade is likewise in the hands of large firms of foreign origin. In the sterling areas of east and central Africa there are also some very large firms, notably Mitchell Cotts & Co. (East Africa) Ltd., and the Gailey & Roberts organization of British East Africa, a member of the United Africa Group.

But this is not to belittle the role of the small firm. The small firm may not have the expectation of life of the large corporation, but neither does it have its inertia. It may not be able to offer the same range of merchandise, but it can sometimes offer better prices. And though it probably cannot provide better service, it is able to preserve personal relationships, still much prized by the producer and the consumer, African and non-African alike. Even in west Africa, where the cult of bigness has its strongest following, the number of small importers and exporters runs into many hundreds, all of them hoping, by dint of walking cannily, to dodge the footfall of their giant-striding competitors. In British East Africa and the British sections of central Africa the role of the small man is larger still and seemingly more secure. Here the big corporations account for only a small part of the total volume of external trade. "The

[9] Consisting of the United Africa Company Limited and its associated and subsidiary companies.

typical pattern of the European trade is importation by retailers either through confirming houses or direct from manufacturers. The result of this is seen in the extremely large number of very small lots of merchandise imported through Mombasa and Dar-es-Salaam." [10]

Regulation

A third aspect of the organization of external trade, and one that is becoming more widely shared with each passing year, is the extent of its regulation. This is especially true of export produce, but it also applies in some territories to certain types of imported merchandise. In the old days the African producer — and for that matter the European and Asian producer — was left very much to his own devices. He sold what surpluses he had where, when and to whom he could, which meant that he usually sold them either too late or too soon, and too low. Sometimes he could not sell them at all. (On a few occasions he chose not to sell them, as when in 1937, cocoa growers in the then Gold Coast organized a "hold-up" rather than take the price offered by the trading companies.) Such a state of affairs was as inefficient as it was unfortunate. It hurt the consumer as much as the producer, for short supplies usually meant high retail prices; and it was as bad for a government as it was for a trader, since it depressed the taxable revenues of the one and the profits of the other.

The old disorderly days of monopolies, cartels and trade piracy have not entirely disappeared, but they are numbered in most territories, and gone in quite a few. Almost everywhere the interests of the African buyer and seller have become a major government concern. Naturally, different governments have different ideas about how best to safeguard these interests. In the territories of the French Community there are no outright prohibitions against anyone, European, Asian or African, carrying on any legitimate kind of import or export trade. In a paper prepared for this study William Moreland describes what the French practice has been. "Except in government-subsidized developments such as the Office du Niger," he says, "the producer may sell to whom he believes gives him the best price or return, and the considerable number of trading houses are competitive. In general, no one purchasing or selling house has a monopoly in any one area." Such restrictions as have been put on import trading were "based on foreign exchange availability, apportioned according to the need of the commodity; if no scarce foreign exchange was required to make the import, no control was imposed." Over considerable periods no preferential import duties were in effect, and at other times no duties at all. The present import duties are modest in scale and,

[10] W. T. Newlyn and D. C. Rowan, *Money and Banking in British Colonial Africa,* Clarendon Press, Oxford, 1954, pp. 16-17.

although giving preference to the territories of the French Community, do not prohibit imports from elsewhere. Such restrictions as there have been on produce trading have likewise been aimed at protection rather than prohibition. Thus the governments in these territories have the power — and use it — to regulate the times at which trading in the major cash crops may begin. This is done "to discourage farmers from harvesting their crops before they are marketable or ripe, and to prevent traders from making usurious loans in advance of harvest time." They also have the power to set the minimum price to be paid for certain kinds of produce as "a protection against low world prices which would place the farmer below the subsistence level to which he has been accustomed."

Where the French — and the Portuguese and the Belgians as well — have tended to rely on competitive private enterprise to serve the marketing needs of their wards, the British have tended to rely more on governmental and quasi-governmental regulation. The most notable of the regulating mechanisms devised by their colonial legislators is the produce buying and marketing board. This is a statutory body set up under the laws of the territory in which it operates, and having for its main objects the purchase (generally through licensed buyers, of which the United Africa Group is one), grading, marketing and export of the commodity concerned, the stabilization of producer prices, and the promotion of the economic and social welfare of the producing areas. In other words, it acts as both agent and trustee for the producer. To these ends, it is given legal power to fix, in advance of the sale of each season's crop, the prices to be paid to the grower of a crop of a given kind and quality. By so doing, the marketing board cuts the link between the price of its commodity in the territory in which it operates and the day-to-day price the commodity commands on the world market. In good seasons the world price is usually well above the price paid to the producers, with the result that the marketing board's books show a surplus. In bad years, the world price is usually below the price paid to the producers; on these occasions the books show a deficit which is financed out of the accrued surpluses. Because the commodities handled by the marketing boards have had more good years than bad, the surpluses have in most cases far exceeded the expectations of the legislators.

The prices paid to the producers are fixed by the marketing board. Behind its decisions lies a great deal of calculation and not a little intuition. It must, among other things, determine the marketing requirements of the producing areas, the cost of operating the board and keeping the producers persuaded of the value of its functions, and the tax yield of a crop sold at a given price; in addition it must attempt to predict the fluctuation of world demand during the forthcoming harvest season and the reaction of the producer to the fixing of the price at a level that may strike him as being more penal than protective.

While there may be room for difference of opinion about the policies followed by the boards, to say nothing of the morality of siphoning off producer money into development programs of which the producer may not be aware and over which he has very little control, there can be none about the boards' importance and power. Produce marketing boards operate throughout the sterling area of west Africa, and they command tremendous sums of money. The crops so marketed dominate the export trade of the territories concerned. A measure of the power the boards exercise over producer prices is given in Table 44, which deals with the operations of the Ghana Cocoa Marketing Board in the first decade or so of its history.

Table 44

OPERATIONS OF THE GHANA COCOA MARKETING BOARD, 1947-1957

SEASON	PRICE PER TON PAID TO SELLER	EXPENSES TO F.O.B. POINT	TOTAL COST PER TON	SALES PROCEEDS PER TON	SURPLUS PER TON	NET OPERATING SURPLUS FOR THE SEASON
						(*Thousands*)
1947-48	£ 75	£ 11	£ 86	£ 201	£ 115	£ 24,069
1948-49	121	18	140	137	— 3	— 134
1949-50	84	26	110	178	69	18,022
1950-51	131	65	196	268	73	20,109
1951-52	149	86	236	245	10	3,530
1952-53	131	82	213	231	19	6,420
1953-54	134	181	315	359	44	11,075
1954-55	134	193	328	355	27	8,058
1955-56	149	81	229	222	— 8	— 833
1956-57	149	64	213	189	— 24	— 5,193

Source: Annual reports of the Cocoa Marketing Board, Accra.

It might be supposed that African producers would resent denying themselves so much ready money. And there can be no question that many do, both because the idea of putting by for "a rainy day" is alien to them (especially the idea of somebody else doing the putting by for them) and because in most cases the marketing boards' payments are enough to arouse an appetite for consumer goods but not enough to satisfy it. It speaks well of their regard for authority and for the judgment of their leaders that the producers continue to allow the moneys accruing from such surpluses to be put into community, regional and national enterprises rather than directly into their own pockets. However, the existence of such good public works does not mean that the policy which makes them possible is necessarily good. Other questions are involved, as F. J. Pedler has pointed out:

Has the withholding of such large sums from producers prevented the stand-ard of living from rising? Is so much compulsory saving a good thing? Might it not be better to give producers a better chance to form the habit of personal saving? . . . Perhaps most serious of all is the question whether The Four Countries' [Gambia, Sierra Leone, Ghana and Nigeria] competitive position in the world for cocoa, palm products, and groundnuts is being affected. While the boards withhold part of the price from producers, the people who are growing these same crops in other countries get more. They get the full world price. Under these conditions, if the law of supply and demand means anything, growers in competing countries have more reason than growers in The Four Countries to improve the yield of their farms and to extend the acreage under crops. If this happens, The Four Countries' share of what the world will spend on cocoa and oil seeds may be expected to fall.[11]

But it must be confessed that not many governments anywhere are thinking as far ahead as Mr. Pedler. Most of them are too absorbed by the burdens of the present and the prospects of the near future to be greatly taken up with the possible long-term effects of a given marketing policy. And taking the short — even the medium-term — view, it is difficult not to believe that the gains of the marketing board system as practiced in west Africa outweigh the losses.

The elimination of day-to-day price fluctuations has been greatly welcomed by most producers. "No farmer liked being told that his cotton, which yesterday would have fetched 2d. a pound, could not be sold today for more that 1½d. Away went a quarter of his year's earnings, and he could not help feeling that the merchant had put it in his pocket." [12] And no exporter much cared for the bitterness engendered between seller and buyer by such fluctuations. Then again, no exporter, company or individual, enjoyed running the risk — very considerable in some years — of having to sell produce for less than he paid for it, because of a fall in world prices between the time of purchase and disposal. Now exporters are in a quite different position. They act merely as agents for the marketing board, receiving from the board the value of the produce bought (at the agreed beginning-of-season price), plus handling, bagging and transport costs, and something for their trouble. Further, by stabilizing disposable income in this way, the boards have done much to stabilize the merchandise market. The fixing of an export commodity price for a season, coupled with some shrewd guessing of the size of the season's crop, enables an importer to forecast with considerable accuracy the demand for his goods, and so to arrange for a supply of such goods commensurate with the supply of purchasing power.

Another important feature of the marketing board system is that it confers on the board the power to decide who may buy produce and who may not. It can, for instance, use its power to encourage indigenous merchants to become licensed buyers, or to encourage producers to set up their own marketing cooperatives, thereby ensuring them a "double

[11] F. J. Pedler, *Economic Geography of West Africa*, Longmans, Green & Co., Ltd., London, 1955, pp. 202-03.
[12] *Ibid.*, p. 203.

take," first from the sale of the produce and then from the servicing of it. On the whole this power has been employed beneficently up to now, but in monopolies, whether government or private, the dividing line between good and ill is hard to see and is therefore in constant danger of being crossed.[13]

As strong an argument as any in support of the produce marketing board system is the favor it has found elsewhere.[14] If not the precise institutional forms, at least the main ideas enshrined by it, such as the stabilization of the price paid to the seller, the lessening of waste, and the securing of fair shares for all, seller, buyer and government alike, are being widely adopted. In British East Africa the marketing of most of the predominantly African-produced crops is now regulated by law, and handled either by cooperatives (such as the Bugisu Cooperative Union of Uganda) or statutory boards that lay down fixed schedules of "seller" prices, and generally act as the African farmers' agent and trustee. Several European-produced commodities, including sisal, maize, wheat, pyrethrum and beef cattle, are also marketed by statutory boards in British East Africa. In the west African territories of the French Community, where no such statutory boards exist, there has been talk for some time of the possible gains to be had from setting up something like them.

Differences in Trading Practice

Which brings us back to the circumstances noted at the beginning of this section, namely, the wide differences in tropical African trading practice. While some of these differences tend to be "polarized" politically — French commercial policy has differed from British in more than the matter of price control, and Belgian and Portuguese policy has historically been less liberal in regard to foreign business enterprise than either British or French policy — some have arisen for no other reason, seemingly, than the need to exploit differences of environment, history, economic levels, and the nature of the goods to be bought and sold. To take a case in point: it would not be difficult to relate the characteristically greater scale and scope of the commercial organizations of west Africa compared with those of east Africa to the facts, first, that it is much easier to grow and ship exportable produce in the former than in the latter; second, that the people of west Africa have been much longer in touch with the outside world, more "sold" on its merchandise and therefore willing to increase their per capita output of salable produce; and, third,

[13] It appears to have been crossed, among other places, in Ghana, where an African-run cocoa-buying company, licensed and financed by the Cocoa Marketing Board, was charged in 1956 with mismanagement of its funds.

[14] Not everybody is in love with it, needless to say. It has been strongly attacked by P. T. Bauer in his *West African Trade* (Cambridge University Press, Cambridge, 1954), and by the authors of the *East Africa Royal Commission 1953-1955 Report* (H.M.S.O., London, 1955).

that most of west Africa's foreign traders have been Europeans and Levantines, who as a rule are more quick to perceive the advantages of cooperative and corporate enterprise than the highly individualistic Asians who run so much of east Africa's commerce. Again, it would not be difficult to show that what is a suitable marketing organization for one type of commodity is not necessarily a suitable marketing organization for another. Middlemen undoubtedly have a place where the commodity is cocoa or copra that has to be gathered at frequent intervals in small quantities over a wide area, parts of which may not be accessible to bulk transportation services. They have little or no place where the commodity is timber (that can be moved only with difficulty and at great expense), or diamonds (that are difficult enough to protect from illicit trading as it is), or gold and uranium (that only move at the behest of governments and under the strictest surveillance).

Much the same applies to cooperatives and marketing boards. They may be fine in palm kernel, coffee and kola country, where few men are "big" enough to be able to do business on their own terms and where both capital and skills are scarce, but not in the world of copper, cobalt or chrome. The areas in which these minerals are produced are highly localized and the producers of them as highly organized — often to the extent of being affiliated with overseas mining companies. They mostly operate at a level of efficiency and economy that no amount of cooperativeness could improve upon; if they didn't, they would not be operating at all. Further, any government that supposed it could ask the shareholders of a mining company earning good money to take less than the market price for the company's products would be likely to find that the company soon had no shareholders, and that it had no business. In good times, moreover, companies have no difficulty in doing their own marketing, while in bad times no amount of price support would enable them to sell what was unsalable.

Similar considerations help to explain the kinds of differences which are frequently encountered in the organization of import trading. Let us take a look at the differences that have emerged over the years in the European sector of the Federation of Rhodesia and Nyasaland's import market, a market that is among the most highly organized in tropical Africa.

Most overseas, including British, manufacturers doing business in the Federation tend to follow one or more of four forms of trading.

1. They may supply their goods direct to the importer on the basis of an order placed by mail or through the importer's buying and confirming agency in the country where the manufacture originated. As yet not a large volume of import business is done in this way.

2. More often in the case of producer goods, the manufacturer may appoint distributors who will themselves sell to the public through branches in one or more of the main towns. In the smaller centers, or where no branches exist, they may also appoint representatives or dealers.

These will buy from the distributor at a discount and rely on him for technical advice and the supply of replacements. But, as always, some distributors are more interested in sales than in service, neither carrying replacements of parts nor knowing how to service the goods they carry. The shortcomings, on these two scores, of many local distributors have been a source of frequent complaint; "and there is no doubt whatsoever that the standard of servicing provided largely determines the direction in which orders are placed." [15]

It is not difficult to see how such an unsatisfactory situation came about. With a European and Asian population of little more than 300,000 to run factories and mines, the basic services and the far-reaching development programs, to say nothing of most of the cash crop farming, there has never been enough skill available in one place at one time to ensure that "unsatisfactory situations" do not arise. The wonder is that more such situations did not arise, especially in the postwar period of rapid economic expansion. Not enough working capital has been available to most distributors to enable them to build up adequate inventories. Distributors who have had capital have rather naturally put it into lines that move fast, require little servicing, and so make more profit. Nor has there been enough business up to now in most import fields to warrant manufacturers paying the costs of having a salaried representative in the territory to supervise distribution, to see that service is adequate, and to keep in touch with all existing and potential customers.

3. Exporters to the Federation may work through indent, or commission, agents. This is the usual way of handling consumer goods.[16] The agent's job is to display his company's samples to his clients, to quote current prices, and to prepare a requisition upon his company. As can be imagined, in a country where distances are great, markets farflung, and the cost of living high, the customer pays a fancy price for the commission agent. In the course of a year an agent with a Federation-wide franchise must cover 25,000 miles or more, mostly by air or road, and spend most of his nights in hotels, if he is to give his customers service. Agents — and there are some — whose franchise also includes British East Africa would need to do upward of 50,000 miles of travel annually. This costs money — far too much in the opinion of many customers. To keep down expenses, some agents stay close to the main centers. By doing this, however, they intensify the competition for urban business, the amount of which is still quite limited in all but low-priced goods. To keep some sort of hold on the rural markets, they find it increasingly desirable to appoint local subagents, the cost of whose commissions must also be passed on to the public. Even so, few agents make much of a living by

[15] H. W. Woodruff, *The Federation of Rhodesia and Nyasaland,* Overseas Economic Surveys, H.M.S.O., London, 1955, p. 64.
[16] Some of the large urban department stores and bazaars buy through their own agents in foreign countries.

confining their interests to one or two lines of merchandise. Most of them try to do business in a wide range of goods and to represent a large number of manufacturers.

4. Foreign manufacturers may allow their indent, or commission, agents to act as wholesalers and retailers of their lines. Where they do, they are likely to limit the number of their accounts in a given territory. Such an arrangement is naturally favored by the merchants to whom sales are entrusted, and because the manufacturers who employ this method of selling are frequently the largest in business, it can be a very satisfactory procedure, ensuring stability of sales through guaranteed channels. In some cases, though, the appointed agents will merely carry what are known locally as "filling stocks" sufficient to tide their customers over an emergency. This practice is gaining favor among European exporters as a way of meeting the growing competition in many consumer lines from South African exporters, whose main advantage is that they can supply small quantities quickly.

The Federation of Rhodesia and Nyasaland may be regarded as tropical Africa's pace setter in this respect. It does one of the most diversified import businesses in the entire region. (See Figure 33.) It has one of its highest disposable incomes, and a larger reservoir of managerial skill and experience than most of the other territories. Moreover, it is energetically educating the African in the importance of earning more and spending more, and giving him increasing opportunities of doing both. In all this it has only been doing what every one of its tropical African neighbors is set on doing. As common ambitions, like common wants, tend to give rise to common means of satisfaction, it is not surprising that the trading systems of several other territories are showing signs of increasing conformity with those of the Federation.

FISCAL LEGISLATION

If as much could be said for government manipulation of trade, analysis of it would be greatly simplified. But the fact is that, while governments are generally impelled by the same ambitions, they do not always have the same wants. Accordingly, they are not all under the same pressure to protect trade here, restrain it there, and stimulate it elsewhere. And not all of them are run by businessmen. There are areas of sameness in their fiscal policies, but they are not always as noticeable as the areas of difference. And certainly the amount of fiscal legislation is getting larger all the time. Each newly sensed imbalance, maladjustment and crisis is made the occasion, more often than not, for a new regulation — a type of therapy that does not always leave the patient stronger than it found him, but that at least keeps up his spirits.

The scope of such legislation is least in countries, like Liberia, which have little to offer the world in the way of either goods or services, and whose only hope of being able to offer it more, and receive more, is by keeping their fences down and their gates open. It is almost certainly greatest in the Federation of Rhodesia and Nyasaland, which is the guardian of an exotic growth — a self-governing, multiracial state based on equal rights for all civilized men and opportunities for all men to become civilized — that needs for its nurture everything in the way of nursing, protection and controlled feeding that the best doctors of economic science can devise. The aggregate amount of trade legislation in the Federation is already massive. A recent customs and excise regulation ran to 55 closely printed octavo pages, and on its heels came a nine-page amendment. A few weeks later a 15-page trade agreement came into force between the Federation and the Union of South Africa.

The reader who is interested in the details of such legislation is referred to the trade and commerce agencies of the countries in which he is interested — with the *caveat* that he may find it necessary to replenish his interest while waiting for the information he is seeking. By way of background we shall try to indicate some of the considerations which govern the thinking of administrators and which find expression in the kind of fiscal legislation passed by them.

TARIFFS

In a part of the world where, with few exceptions, the direct tax potential is still low, it remains necessary for governments to derive the bulk of their revenues from import and export duties. The import duties have the same effect as a retail sales tax on consumers (substantially increased, however, by the markups of the distribution process), and the export duties operate as an income tax on the producers of the items exported. Control, not everywhere very effective, over the points of import and export provides the mechanism by which such taxes can be collected. The proportion of the ordinary revenue so derived tends to be lowest in the territories with the largest "settler" populations and highest in those with the smallest "settler" populations. Thus, in the Federation of Rhodesia and Nyasaland, the proportion is approximately one fifth; in Angola and Kenya, about two fifths; in the Belgian Congo, about one half. In Ghana, Nigeria, British Somaliland and Zanzibar, in none of which is the settler population considerable, the proportion is between two thirds and three quarters. Exceptions are Liberia, Mozambique and Tanganyika, where plantation production for export provides a number of people with incomes capable of heavy taxation. In Mozambique customs duties bring in only about one fifth of the total ordinary revenue; in Liberia, only about one quarter; in Tanganyika, between one quarter and two fifths.

Import Duties

In most territories import duties continue to be one of the major sources of government spending money. In Ghana and Uganda they usually account for not less than one fourth of the ordinary revenue. In Tanganyika they usually account for between one fifth and one third; in Nigeria for a slightly higher proportion; and in British Somaliland and Zanzibar, for more than one half.

On the whole, the schedule of import duties continues to follow the usual "colonial" pattern, that is, it is designed to encourage the import of producer goods needed for the economic development of a territory, to discourage the import of nonessential goods such as beverages and tobacco — albeit unsuccessfully in most cases; while in regard to necessary consumer goods it is designed to produce the maximum amount of revenue with the minimum amount of hardship.

Consider, for instance, the situation in Tanganyika, where import duties are regulated by the Customs Tariff Ordinance (No. 39 of 1954), the Excise Tariff Ordinance (No. 30 of 1952) and the Export Tax Ordinance (No. 31 of 1946), as amended from time to time. Under these ordinances the basic rate of import duty is 22 per cent *ad valorem*. This rate applies to such things as cotton textiles (piece goods and clothing), hollow ware, hardware and other necessary consumer goods. There is, however, a long free list of imports required for development purposes; included in it are industrial, mining and agricultural machinery, certain foods, packing materials, fertilizers, explosives and educational supplies. For most building materials, artisans' tools and most military materials, the rate is 10 per cent; for private motor vehicles and parts it is 15 per cent. Specific duties are charged on some items, mostly foodstuffs and tobacco. On a number of other items a minimum specific duty is provided as an alternative to the *ad valorem* rate. Provision is also made for the temporary exemption from duty of certain essential foodstuffs.

Some idea of the relative revenue-earning importance of the main classes of imports into Tanganyika can be had from Table 45. While it is not claimed that the figures are especially representative, they apply to a territory that is still very much in the "colonial" stage of economic development, and to a year — 1952 — that was not noticeably more abnormal than its immediate predecessors and successors, at least so far as the range and volume of imports was concerned.

Where the colonial stage of development is passing, and the emphasis in economic activity is shifting from production of a few commodities primarily for export to production of many commodities partly for export and partly for domestic consumption, the import duty pattern tends to be somewhat different. For instance, in Angola, which, in the view of metropolitan Portugal, has passed out of the colonial stage, existing industries have been aided since 1948 by the substantial lowering of import

Table 45

REVENUE FROM IMPORT DUTIES
ON SELECTED ITEMS, TANGANYIKA, 1952

ITEM	NET REVENUE FROM IMPORT DUTIES (AFTER ADJUSTMENTS FOR TRANSFERS)	PER CENT OF TOTAL REVENUE
	(*Thousands*)	
Total	£4,210	100.0
Wine	21	0.5
Ale, beer, etc.	25	0.6
Spirits	390	9.3
Cigarettes	24	0.6
Tobacco	369	8.8
Other food and drink	185	4.4
Chemicals and allied products	118	2.8
Rubber and manufactures	59	1.4
Paper and manufactures	55	1.3
Cotton yarns and manufactures	1,051	25.0
Other textile manufactures	214	5.1
Articles of clothing (all materials)	90	2.1
Petroleum products	441	10.5
Nonmetallic minerals and manufactures	132	3.1
Base metals and manufactures	254	6.0
Machinery, apparatus, etc.	151	3.6
Vehicles	251	6.0
Parcel post	97	2.4
Miscellaneous	283	6.8

Source: Tanganyika: A Review of Its Resources and Their Development, edited by J. P. Moffett, Government of Tanganyika, Dar-es-Salaam, 1955, p. 746.

duties on the raw materials necessary to those industries; and the development of new industries has been assisted by the lowering of duties on all kinds of instruments, apparatus, machinery, tools, boats and vehicles essential to them. Protection has been provided, by the mechanism of the preferential tariff, for products of Portuguese industry, among which woolen and cotton piece goods, alcoholic beverages, tiles, tires and inner tubes, products of asbestos cement, cork and glass, pine timber, footwear, hunting ammunition and matches are specified. Such losses of revenue as these changes produced have been more than met by the increases, provided for at the same time, in the yield of direct — including income — taxes.

The preferential tariff is not confined to former colonial territories. It is one of tropical Africa's most widely applied fiscal devices. In many cases the preference is a simple family affair. Portugal favors Angola, and *vice versa*. British East Africa favors the United Kingdom, and *vice versa*. And similarly with the French and Belgian families. But perhaps it should not be called simple. Even families can be formal at times, and prefer to have their agreements in writing. Some of the preferential tariff schedules took a lot of writing. And some of their advantages take quite a lot of winning, and keeping. For example, Portuguese African territories can enjoy the full benefit of the family tie only if the goods they import from Portugal, or from one another, are transported in Portuguese bottoms and if they do not fall below a certain quota of the goods imported from foreign countries. Indeed, they are not allowed to buy more than a stated percentage of the total import of certain classes of goods from foreign countries.[17]

Though the family comes first, friends are not excluded from the circle of preference. But not all friends sit in the same circle. The tariff schedule that came into force in the Federation of Rhodesia and Nyasaland in 1955 had four tariff circles, or, more precisely, columns. This is to say that for every article on the dutiable import list there were four possible *ad valorem* rates of duty. The rates varied considerably. For soft soap the range was from 20 per cent under Column A (applicable to goods originating in countries not entitled to most-favored-nation treatment) to 10 per cent in Column B (applicable to goods originating in countries outside the British Commonwealth that are entitled to most-favored-nation treatment) and Column C (applicable to goods originating in the British Dominions), to free entry under Column D (applicable to goods originating in the United Kingdom and British colonies). For plastic sheeting, the range was wider still: from 35 per cent (Column A) to free entry (Column D).

To complicate matters further, not all the circles were concentric; or, to put it another way, not all the preferences were coextensive territorially. Thus, of the four columns in the Federation's tariff, only Column C applied to Nyasaland and the northeastern part of Northern Rhodesia. The reason for this will become apparent shortly, when we consider the matter of trade agreements.

Export Duties

Export duties form an important source of ordinary revenue in many of the territories. In some they have, over the years, been a bigger source of revenue than import duties. Thus, in Uganda during the 1952-1957 period they contributed about one fifth as much again as import duties — approximately £38 million as against approximately £31 million (Table 46). In Ghana, too, their contribution has been very handsome,

---

[17] The import into, say, Mozambique of certain varieties of cotton textiles of foreign origin may be restricted to a maximum of 30 per cent of the value of imports from Portugal; for other varieties the figure may be 50 per cent or even 80 per cent. Bryce J. M. Nairn, *Portuguese East Africa*, Overseas Economic Surveys, H.M.S.O., London, 1955, p. 19.

Table 46

REVENUE FROM IMPORT AND EXPORT DUTIES,
UGANDA, 1952-1957

	1952	1953	1954 [a]	1955 [b]	1957 [b]
Import duties (customs, excise):					
Revenue (*millions*)	£3.9	£4.3	£2.4	£5.6	£6.4
Per cent of total ordinary revenue	23	24	23	29	26
Export duties:					
Revenue (*millions*)	£8.3	£4.0	£3.4	£6.4	£7.1
Per cent of total ordinary revenue	48	23	33	33	28

Source: Uganda (annual), H.M.S.O., London.

[a] First six months only.   [b] Year ending June 30.

far exceeding that of other imposts in a good cocoa year. In the fiscal year 1954-1955 it amounted to more than £38 million, or about half of the country's budget. In general, however, export duties run behind import duties as revenue raisers. In Nigeria they account on the average for between one quarter and two fifths of the ordinary revenue; in the west African territories of the French Community they account on the average for 15 to 20 per cent; in Kenya, for less than 5 per cent.

Further, export duties are inclined to be a much less dependable source of revenue than import duties. The latter can be and usually are imposed on a very wide range of commodities which, in the nature of things, are in pretty steady demand. But export duties can be imposed on only a few commodities, since, with possibly one or two exceptions, no country has more than a dozen exports capable of yielding enough tax to justify the expense of collecting it. The foreign demand for these products can be anything but steady. This means that, while a country may be able to apply high export taxes, and reap a fine revenue from them, in times of strong demand, it is unlikely to derive much revenue from them in times of weak demand. As Table 46 shows, in 1953, the year of the "post-Korean" recession, Uganda was able to collect less than half the sum it had collected in 1952 from export taxes (£4.0 million against £8.3 million).

Important as the export tax still is to many territories, it is unlikely to get more important. Indeed, if the general trend toward lower produce prices and more keenly competitive world markets continues, the yield of such taxes will unquestionably decline. Already, in some territories, no export duty is paid when the f.o.b. price of certain commodities falls below a given value. In Uganda in the middle 1950s no duty was paid on *robusta* coffee when the f.o.b. price at Mombasa was less than £90 a ton. And in Tanganyika the administration found it desirable to lift its export tax on copra, copra cake and coconut oil within four years of imposing it, because of the steep decline in world prices of these commodities in the early 1950s.[18] Thus, whereas the revenue from export duties in Tanganyika in 1951 was £1.4 million and in 1952 £1.35 million, in 1953 it fell to £143,000. In 1956-1957 it was less than £25,000. Several other territories, including most of those in the French franc area, have seen the yield, both relative and absolute, of their export duties decline discouragingly in the past few years.

While the dew is still on the veld, governments will doubtless go on gathering it gratefully. But as the African sun rises higher in the heavens, they will need to look to other sources of supply, notably to the rains of direct taxation — which, alas, cannot be gathered as easily or as painlessly. For in most parts of tropical Africa, as in most other places, direct taxation is regarded as an unmerciful visitation to be quietly dodged, if not openly denounced.

TRADE AGREEMENTS

The oldest and most far-reaching trade agreements affecting tropical Africa are those generally, if inappropriately, known as the Congo Basin Treaties. These treaties (dated February 26, 1885, July 2, 1890 and September 10, 1919) regulate mercantile matters over an area considerably larger than the Congo basin proper, since it extends to the shores of the Indian Ocean as far north as the fifth parallel and as far south as the mouth of the Zambezi, thus embracing the whole of Nyasaland and the northeastern part of Northern Rhodesia. The original treaty provided for completely free trade within the defined area. The 1919 revision of it (known as the Convention of St. Germain-en-Laye), still in force in 1959, requires that the signatory powers — Belgium, France, Japan, Portugal, the United States, Canada, Australia, New Zealand and the Union of South Africa — maintain between their respective nationals and those of other member states of the then League of Nations complete commercial equality within the defined area and the continued prohibition of the manufacture and distribution of spirits.

All three treaties were intended to be permanent, terminable neither by denunciation nor by notice. Unfortunately their wording is so loose that it is possible for any territory, or part of a territory, falling within the Convention area to defeat the free-trade principle and create conditions favoring trade in any given direction. At the same time, territories adjacent to the Convention area are precluded from making regional agreements with those within it.

Such treaties undoubtedly served a very useful purpose in the days of

---

[18] In this instance, though, it is only fair to say that the administration's purpose in imposing the tax in 1949 was partly to "facilitate export control by keeping the return on exports in line with the return on internal sales [of the same commodities] at controlled prices." *Tanganyika: A Review of Its Resources and Their Development*, edited by J. P. Moffett, Government of Tanganyika, Dar-es-Salaam, 1955, p. 747.

slave trading, gun running and liquor peddling, but they bear little or no relation to the present economic development of the adjacent territories, or to the regime of law and order within the territories covered by them. It is difficult to believe that they have much of a future in the world of GATT (General Agreement on Tariffs and Trade), with its exchange controls, payment agreements, bulk purchasing by governments, and import and export quotas. It is indicative that the Federal Government of Rhodesia and Nyasaland, the country most adversely affected, has already succeeded in persuading fellow members of GATT to release the parts of the Convention area falling within its jurisdiction from the provisions of the treaties. All customs tariff discriminations — and internal customs posts — were abolished on March 11, 1957. Since then Nyasaland and the northeastern part of Northern Rhodesia have enjoyed the same Commonwealth preferences as the rest of the Federation. The fact is that the advantages of an interterritorial customs union are too substantial to be long denied a country as energetic and as purposeful as the Federation — a country, furthermore, that is landlocked and so in need of every countervailing commercial boost it can devise.

The governments of Kenya, Uganda and Tanganyika long ago sensed the advantages of such a union, and took the first step toward achieving it, when, in 1922, they adopted a common tariff schedule. Revised in 1930, this schedule remained in force, with the addition of some wartime surcharges, until 1946. A further step was taken in 1949 when the work of the customs departments of the three territories came under the administrative control of a single commissioner appointed by the East Africa High Commission. However, this unification did not affect in any way the right of each territory to vary its own tariff. While import duties have remained in line, apart from a few temporary and minor divergencies, export duties continue to be imposed on a purely territorial basis. The reason for this is probably less fiscal than psychological, it being colonial nature to disagree with neighbors.

As more territories slip their colonial moorings, more trading agreements between themselves and with outside nations and groups of nations may be expected. Recently Ghana and the Federation of Rhodesia and Nyasaland have become "contracting parties" of GATT. The Federation already has trade agreements with the United Kingdom (a Southern Rhodesian legacy dating from the Ottawa Agreement of 1932), with Australia (also a Southern Rhodesian legacy) and, as mentioned earlier, with the Union of South Africa. The last had its origin partly in the customs agreement of 1930 with Northern Rhodesia and partly in the customs union agreement of 1949 between Southern Rhodesia and the Union.

OTHER TRADE CONTROLS

Controls have long been part of the incubus of international trade, and tropical Africa has had its full share of them. Even before the end of

World War II most men doing business there would have been willing to concede, in the words of a League of Nations publication of the time, that "trade had ceased or was ceasing to be the business of the merchant operating under simple and stable laws and concerned with providing the consumer he served with goods at the lowest available prices." [19] For governments were assuming more rigorous control of all trading operations by means of import restrictions and prohibitions, quotas, currency regulations and subsidies. However, it is doubtful if even the most perceptive League of Nations economist, or anybody else, could have foreseen the need to retain controls of this kind so long.

At the core of the postwar problem was the rapidly mounting demand by tropical African countries for all manner of consumer and producer goods for their economic development, and the inability of their customary European and Asiatic suppliers, struggling to get back onto their industrial feet, to do much about it. The only countries capable of supplying many of their requirements were the United States and Canada. But, with the exception of a few commodities needed for the American strategic stockpile, tropical Africa had little to offer in return. To keep the goods moving, while protecting the balance-of-payments position, has been an unremitting preoccupation with most tropical African governments and the chief reason for their continued juggling of import and export licensing and currency control systems. It is to be hoped that the jugglers can keep their act going, for there will almost certainly be need of jugglers so long as the price of gold continues to be tied to artificial paper-currency values.

Tanganyika is not untypical either of the need for such controls or of the skill acquired in the art of manipulating them. The following account of its endeavors in the early postwar years to "equilibrize" the balance of payments is taken from the government's own record of it:

The first dollar crisis came in 1947. Imports of American goods during that year were exceptionally heavy and represented 22 per cent of all imports. This was largely due to imports of American tractors for the Overseas Food Corporation [i.e., the Tanganyika Groundnut Scheme]. From 1947, with licensing restricted to essentials, the percentage of American imports declined. Initially there were similar restrictions on a number of other non-sterling countries, including Japan, but from 1949 to 1951 there was a tendency towards freer licensing except in the case of dollar goods. By 1951 Japan had got back to a 9 per cent share of the import trade, or just under half her pre-war performance. Imports from European countries also increased as war-devastated countries came back into production and as licensing restrictions were eased with the formation of the European Payments Union. By 1951 import licenses were fairly easily obtainable for goods from most sources except the dollar area, and there was a significant rise in the percentage of non-sterling imports as compared with 1949 and 1950. In 1952 with the second major balance of payments crisis, the movement towards unrestricted trading was reversed, and licensing restrictions re-inforced with the object of bringing total non-sterling

---

[19] *The Transition from War to Peace*, Geneva, 1943, p. 25.

imports down below the level of 1951. The largest deduction was obtained in Japanese textiles, which were entirely restricted during the latter part of 1952.[20]

Although things have improved much since 1952, the need for fiscal agility continues. And it will continue, because so long as the sterling area has balance-of-payments troubles "there can be no natural development of a pattern of import trade such as there was before the war." [21] Meanwhile the amount of trade which Tanganyika does with any given territory continues to depend to some extent on its licensing policy. But this much can be said of Tanganyika's external trade in recent years: it has come to depend less on licensing policy, and more on world prices and supply. There are now fewer restrictions in force than at any time in the past fifteen to twenty years. The same is true of most other tropical African territories.

Where controls are retained, it is generally for the purpose of promoting orderly marketing and maintaining, or improving, standards of quality. Moreover, most territories have lived so long with their dollar shortages that they are no longer greatly worried by them. For most "dollar" commodities there are now acceptable "non-dollar" substitutes, including automobiles that make the rough African places plain. Notwithstanding, the end of control is not in sight. This is partly because dollars are still badly needed for some things (including heavy agricultural and road-building machinery) and partly because the interest of the up-and-coming manufacturing countries of tropical Africa is deemed to demand protection from the rising winds of world competition. In Mozambique, for instance, import permits are now usually withheld from those categories of goods that compete with local industries, and for that matter, those of metropolitan Portugal.

However, to judge from the accelerating tempo of tropical Africa's external trade, it takes more than a little "control" to keep a young country down.

BALANCE OF PAYMENTS

Few tropical African territories have yet begun to issue comprehensive statements of their international transactions. The International Monetary Fund's *Balance of Payments Yearbook* for 1958-1959 lists only the following: the Belgian Congo, Ethiopia, Ghana, the Federation of Rhodesia and Nyasaland, Somalia and the Republic of Sudan; and in the case of some of these the data do not cover a long enough period and are not reliable enough to make a balance-of-payments analysis worth while. Even so, enough is known about the finances of enough territories to enable us to draw attention to certain widely shared fiscal features.

1. The volume of international business done by nearly all of the ter-

[20] *Tanganyika: A Review of Its Resources and Their Development*, p. 741.
[21] *Ibid.*

ritories is still very small by modern standards. Even for so large and comparatively well developed an entity as the Federation of Rhodesia and Nyasaland, it is rather smaller than for New Zealand, and only about one tenth as large as that done by Canada.

2. All of the territories are dependent on foreign capital. Apart from the outright gifts and interest-free loans made by governments and other bodies, this capital has to be paid for. One characteristic fiscal activity of the territories, therefore, is the regular transference abroad of a portion of their export income in the form of dividends, amortization payments and interest. The proportion varies from about one per cent of the value of total exports in the case of Ethiopia to between one third and one half in the case of Liberia. It varies with the amounts of capital invested and the terms of the investment. It varies, too, with the success of the enterprise for which the capital was raised — with such things as the efficiency and integrity of the administering agency, the acceptance of its "product" (be it copper, bananas, electricity, or urban housing for Africans), and the willingness of the people, their labor leaders and their politicians to pay the price of foreign confidence.

3. The need of foreign capital is growing in every territory, since no government can begin to undertake development programs at a rate matching the necessities of the times solely out of its revenues from customs and excise taxation and other fiscal imposts. The water in the wells of tropical Africa is deep, the pumps expensive and in need of much priming. Of the money needed for the Volta River project — estimated in 1956 to be £309 million — the government of Ghana expects to raise internally about one third. The rest must be found on foreign money markets. Of the money needed for the first stage of the Kariba project in the Federation of Rhodesia and Nyasaland, only about £34 million is being raised locally; the rest — approximately £46.6 million — is coming from the International Bank for Reconstruction and Development and the London market.

4. Because such long-term investment capital is not as abundant as it was, and because tropical Africa is not regarded by brokers as the "safest" of places on earth, the cost of such capital is increasing. This spells higher interest rates. It also spells a growing reluctance on the part of investors to put money into marginal economic enterprises, and growing difficulties in finding money for low-yield social welfare and development projects. Thus, while Southern Rhodesia was able in 1955 to attract £18 million of company capital — more than two thirds of it for new companies — its government was unable to raise overseas more than £1 million for its urgently needed African housing projects.

5. Closely related to the foregoing, the external liabilities of almost every territory are increasing. This is especially true of such liabilities as company dividends and profits and mineral royalties. It is also true of amortization payments, insurance, transportation charges and the like.

It is true, too, of pension payments, gratuities and other worker benefits. Although the Africanization of public services is well under way in many territories — almost finished in Ghana and the Republic of Sudan — the call for expatriate skills in engineering, education and business administration grows rather than declines with the growth of their economies. To attract outsiders with such skills, it is necessary as a rule to offer high salaries and costly perquisites. Even territories like Kenya and the Rhodesias suffer a sizable loss of export revenues through the departure of settlers who settled just long enough to earn what was needed to be able to spend the rest of their lives somewhere else. In some of the labor-importing territories, for example Uganda, the outward remittances of migrant workers now constitute an important net debit item on the balance sheet.

6. An increasing number of territories are now deriving revenue from "invisible" sources of this kind. Among these are the inward remittances of African workers (these are most important in labor surplus areas such as Nyasaland, Mozambique and Ruanda-Urundi), the capital of incoming settlers (chiefly important in Southern Rhodesia), the earnings of the tourist and traveler trade (probably most substantial in British East Africa), company and personal taxation, customs and excise duties, and donations of foreign mission societies, foundations and other philanthropic agencies. Certain territories — notably Southern Rhodesia, the Belgian Congo and Ghana — derive very considerable revenues from the export of nonmonetary gold. It is doubtful, however, if the sum of the revenue accruing from all these sources is, in most territories, of the same order of magnitude as the external liabilities.

In short, it would look as though the ratio between invisible and visible, between capital and current transactions is generally increasing, and that the gap in the current account between payments and receipts will get wider before it closes. What happens to the ratio, and the gap, in a given territory depends mainly on the skill of the men at the treasury helm in steering a course between easy optimism and unwarranted extravagance — between the rocks of No Confidence and the whirlpools of No Return. No course is more difficult to steer. Yet there are signs that it can be held — at least in territories blessed with the resources, skills and imagination of the Belgian Congo and the Federation of Rhodesia and Nyasaland.

It is clear from Tables 47 and 48 that the Belgian Congo and the Federation share most of the trends that have been spoken of. In both territories the volume of international transactions is increasing steadily. So, too, is the size of the capital account, and the services and income [22] items

[22] The "services" entry of the Federation table covers much the same categories as the "foreign travel" and "transport and insurance" entries of the Belgian Congo table, and the "income" entry of the one much the same as the "investment income" and "government transactions" entries of the other.

Table 47

THE BELGIAN CONGO AND RUANDA-URUNDI:
BALANCE OF PAYMENTS, 1950-1957

(*Millions of Belgian Congo Francs*)

	1950	1951	1952	1953	1954	1956	1957
Net change in reserves[a]	5,864	3,722	1,931	827	42	−294	−7,482
Current account: Balance	3,087	1,361	−1,801	−1,668	−1,978	−3,861	−7,826
Net current transactions:							
Merchandise	6,972	6,196	4,022	5,109	6,931	11,365	7,750
Nonmonetary gold	633	682	716	650	658	652	631
Foreign travel	—	−159	−229	−614	−829	−1,392	−1,526
Transport & insurance	−1,123	−2,158	−2,831	−3,596	−4,584	−6,409	−6,873
Investment income	−1,295	−1,316	−1,778	−2,212	−2,460	−4,411	−3,569
Government trans- actions	−352	−199	−68	267	231	−948	−1,131
Miscellaneous	−858	−1,147	−1,237	−706	−1,314	−1,712	−1,755
Donations (including migrant funds) and remittances	−890	−538	−396	−566	−611	−1,006	−1,353
Receipts	—	—	25,499	25,753	28,179	34,862	32,024
Payments	—	—	27,300	27,421	30,157	38,723	39,850
Movement of long-term capital	2,935	767	3,224	2,727	2,189	3,703	441
Receipts	—	—	—	4,204	4,147	7,103	4,134
Payments	—	—	—	1,477	1,958	3,400	3,693
Private	378	931	763	125	−326	−623	365
Receipts	—	1,252	1,058	1,581	1,532	2,374	3,565
Payments	—	321	295	1,456	1,858	2,998	3,200
Public	2,557	−164	2,461	2,602	2,515	4,326	76
Receipts	—	230	2,576	2,623	2,615	4,728	560
Payments	—	394	115	21	100	402	493

Source: La Situation Economique du Congo Belge et du Ruanda-Urundi (annual), Ministry of Colonies, Brussels.

[a] Including errors and omissions.

in the current account; that is, the role of foreign investment is growing in both. It is equally clear that not all territories have the same luck with their housekeeping, or the same ideas about it. Whereas the Federation of Rhodesia and Nyasaland can point to a most striking decline in the size of its current-account debit balance during the 1951-1954 period, the Belgian Congo turned a very comfortable credit balance into a rather disturbing debit balance over the same period. Whereas the Federation

Table 48

THE FEDERATION OF RHODESIA AND NYASALAND:
BALANCE OF PAYMENTS, 1950-1957

(£ *Million*)

	1950	1951	1952	1953	1954	1956	1957
Net change in reserves [a]	−15.8	−34.9	−23.2	10.9	12.9	−4.3	−46.1
Current account: Balance	−28.2	−49.1	−42.5	−23.9	−11.4	−33.6	−70.0
Net current transactions:							
Goods:							
Merchandise	}−3.0	−16.7	−10.9{	13.9	27.9	21.1	−23.3
Nonmonetary gold				6.6	6.5	6.5	6.8
Services:							
Freights and insurance on merchandise	}−3.7	−4.3	−5.7{	−12.2	−11.4	−16.4	−12.8
Foreign travel				−7.1	−7.5	−9.9	−11.4
Other services				1.3	0.1	0.6	0.7
Income:							
Government income receipts and payments	}−26.0	−33.4	−30.5{	−2.5	−2.8	−2.6	−2.3
Private income receipts and payments				−27.7	−27.0	−36.7	−30.4
Transfers: Current transfers [b]	4.6	5.3	4.6	3.7	2.8	3.8	2.8
Receipts	109.3	135.9	153.1	162.5	183.2	219.5	197.0
Payments	137.5	185.2	195.6	186.4	194.6	253.2	267.0
Movement of long-term capital	12.4	14.4	19.3	24.7	22.8	26.6	29.1
Receipts	18.1	19.4	26.3	31.0	27.0	30.1	36.3
Payments	5.6	5.0	7.0	6.3	4.3	3.4	7.3
Private	2.9	2.2	1.5	12.7	7.1	21.4	21.1
Receipts	6.1	4.3	5.5	13.3	9.7	23.1	25.6
Payments	3.2	2.1	4.0	0.6	2.6	1.7	4.5
Public	9.6	12.2	17.8	12.0	15.7	5.2	8.1
Receipts	12.0	15.1	20.8	17.7	17.3	7.0	10.8
Payments	2.4	2.9	3.0	5.7	1.6	1.8	2.7

Sources: Monthly Digest of Statistics, Central African Statistical Office, Salisbury; *Economic Report* (annual), Federation of Rhodesia and Nyasaland.

[a] Including errors and omissions.
[b] Including migrants' funds and remittances, lotteries, mission funds, pensions, etc.

has had little difficulty in holding onto both the private and public long-term capital it has been attracting, the Belgian Congo has managed to keep only the public capital it has attracted. (In both 1954 and 1956 more private long-term capital left the territory than entered it.) Further, whereas the movement of the Belgian Congo's long-term capital has fluctuated widely, and less long-term capital was available for employment in 1957 than in 1950, the amount of such capital in the Federation has grown fairly consistently and in 1957 was more than twice as large as in 1950.

But it would be wrong to infer from this that the Belgian Congo is in a weaker fiscal position than the Federation. The fact is that the economy of the Belgian Congo remains (1959) what it has long been — government-regulated. Capital is injected into it as prescribed by government economists and planners, not by financiers looking for a "good thing." The government is in an excellent position to know the optimum capital-injection rate for the country, since it has its finger on the pulse of all the largest undertakings, if indeed it does not hold them in a vise-tight grip. And, being both family physician and head of the house, it is able to specify the form which the injection shall take; whether, for instance, it shall be in the form of plowed-back profits (as it often is), in which case it is not recorded in the balance of international payments, or in the form of development money raised internally (about half the estimated 100 billion francs invested in the 1950-1959 development plan has been so raised), or in the form of loans raised on foreign money markets. Largely because of this, private foreign investment has at no time been a big factor in the financing of Belgian Congo business. While there is now no lack of warmth toward the foreign investor, he still finds that it is difficult to put his money into mining or power or the other fields where it is likely to do him the most good.

The fiscal philosophy of the Rhodesias has been based essentially on the premise that the less a government has to do with running a business for profit, the better. Not that the Rhodesian governments had, until recently, very much money in their coffers for business ventures. And perhaps there would not be much in them now but for the investment "privateers" of a generation and more ago who did not despise the day of long delays and short shrift.

INTERNAL TRADE

Low purchasing power has never prevented the mercantile-minded from trading, and clearly tropical Africa has long had its share of the mercantile-minded. Today indigenous interest in trading is keener and more widespread than ever. Plenty of Africans still know nothing about shopkeeping and little about the kinds of things to be had in shops, and see nothing odd about standing half-naked before a roadside display of underwear and overalls; but very few are without the means of regularly buying some shop goods, and of increasing their buying power.

It is true that the people with the highest buying power continue to be, with few exceptions, non-Africans. In territories like the Federation of Rhodesia and Nyasaland it is the Europeans and Asians that do most of the trading in goods and services, and that have the largest disposable incomes and the highest standards of material comfort. However, even there the amount of spending money circulated in the African sector of the market is now (1958) between £80 and £100 million a year. In some of the richer non-settler countries, it is at least twice as much.

THE AFRICAN CONSUMER

By Western standards these are small sums; they represent very small average cash incomes. In the Federation the average cash income of the employed African is (1958) about £75 (say $210) a year; but not all Africans are employed, and of those that are, not all work the year around. The figures are somewhat higher in territories with flourishing African cash crop economies, such as Ghana, Nigeria, the Republic of the Ivory Coast and Uganda, but considerably lower in some others, such as Angola, Ethiopia and the Somalilands. Taking the region as a whole, it is improbable that the average cash income of the employed African exceeds £40, or about $110, a year. Not all that is earned is expendable on shop goods, naturally; some of it must go on taxes and rents, and some on savings for "bride wealth" and so on.

To be "passing rich with forty pounds a year" is much more difficult for the African worker in Salisbury, Southern Rhodesia, or Lagos, Nigeria, today than it was for the clergy of Oliver Goldsmith's eighteenth-century England. Just because he does not have very much to spend, he is inclined to spend it carefully. Though he will sometimes make purchases which are foolish by European criteria, he is unlikely to make any purchase without giving considerable time to it. The buying of a pair of trousers may well take the better part of a day and involve a tour of the town in company with his friends. But time so spent will be judged well spent if it enables him to compare prices, qualities of cloth, stitching, seams and linings, since the difference in the length of life between a good pair of trousers and an inferior pair will more than compensate him for the time spent in choosing them. Of articles he understands, the African consumer is frequently a much more exacting purchaser than the European. Except in the deep bush, it is no longer possible to fob him off with inferior "kaffir truck." Even there, the traveling vendor of such goods is not as welcome as he used to be, for the chances are that the migrant menfolk, if not the women, know bad quality when they see it.

Because of his concern with quality, the African buyer is frequently very brand-conscious. Over many parts of Africa, such things as bicycles, soaps, perfumes, salt, kerosene and cigarettes are more widely known by brand name than by description. In some instances, however, this brand-consciousness appears to be founded more on prejudice than on demonstrable superiority. Many Nigerians, it seems, have little use for any but Norwegian and Icelandic varieties of dried fish — so little that before now they have chosen to do without rather than accept a substitute, a cheaper one at that. The women of Ghana have shown themselves to be no less strong-minded about the merits, supposed or real, of certain kinds of printed cotton cloths. The strong preferences of African consumers sometimes have the effect of producing a public outcry against the price charged for a particular brand or variety of goods. As F. J. Pedler remarks in his study of the west African market:

> It is difficult to imagine that in Europe or America there would ever be a public outcry against the charging of high prices for a particular brand of bicycle, or for cotton cloth printed by a particular process. The purchasing public would find its own solution by turning to alternative brands of bicycle, or to cloths printed by other processes.[23]

By so doing he would cause the soaring balloon of cost to explode in the rarefied atmosphere of demand.

In some other respects, too, the African buyer is far from being a slavish follower of the European. On the contrary, he remains himself, given to conservatism in this, flamboyance in that, by turns level-headed, prejudiced and impulsive. The Masai continue to prefer skins and blankets to shirts and suitings, but they have developed quite a taste for sherry. The inhabitants of Harari, an African township outside Salisbury in Southern Rhodesia, eat kippers — long a favorite English breakfast food — with their *posho*, which is a kind of porridge made of maize. Many Ghanaian and Nigerian legislators continue to dress in the style of their forebears while driving late-model Jaguars, Mercedes and Cadillacs. It is not uncommon for the African newly come to the buyer's estate to take such a fancy to a particular item of merchandise that he will stock up on it to the neglect of other possibilities. One worker of modest means recently confessed to possessing nine pairs of shoes. A study of the spending habits of mine workers in Northern Rhodesia has shown that, over a period of several months, the average expenditure on clothes amounted to 90 per cent of their disposable income. The "one-track-mindedness" is not confined to those at the lower income levels. The man with one bicycle is quite likely to be saving up for a second. At least one African head of state has had difficulty in remembering exactly how many cars he owned — though, to be fair, some American heads of business and industry have been known to have the same difficulty. Then, again, in some localities, Buganda for instance, a woman often takes such a fancy to a

[23] *Op. cit.*, p. 149.

particular style of dress that she will wear no other. The same may apply to the color or colors she wears — once approved, either by long-standing tradition or by the modern arbiters of fashion, they could no more be changed overnight than the colors of the Stars and Stripes.

OTHER CONSUMERS

Of the other groups of consumers there is no need to speak at length; first because, with the exception of three or four territories, they do not form an important segment of the consumer market, and second because the range of purchases they are interested in is much the same as it is in Europe and Asia.

Contrary to the common belief, the standard of living of most Europeans in tropical Africa is quite modest. True, many of them own cars, live in nice houses on spacious lots, have servants, belong to clubs, and run up big bills at the local store. But the chances are their cars are small and tired, their houses poorly supplied with conveniences, their gardens more utilitarian than ornamental, their servants less expensive than the gadgets which have largely replaced domestic help in some other parts of the world, the annual club dues and charges much smaller than the amount spent on entertainment by the average suburban American, and their per capita consumption of food and liquor not excessive when judged by the standards of those who practice the civilized art of dining. Nor are most Europeans conspicuous spenders on clothes, vacations, sports and hobbies. Those in government service — who form the majority in the non-settler territories — cannot afford to be, for by the time they have educated their children abroad and put something aside for the long years of retirement they have little "discretionary" money left. Those in business, industry and agriculture are often in a position to spend more money than they do, but with the memory of bad times behind them and the never-absent fear of others to come, they, too, shy away from ostentation. There are exceptions, of course: men who build themselves homes in a paler image of European palaces and employ enough servants to run a hotel; and men who, starting with no money and little education, have been unable to resist the temptation, when wealthy, of surrounding themselves with high-priced American and European cars, private airplanes, roof tennis courts, swimming pools and so on.

In general, the Levantines, Arabs, Goans, Indians and Pakistanis spend less on housing, food, drink and the accessories of life than the Europeans. This, no doubt, is partly because many of them have less to spend, but it is also partly because they tend to be more abstemious, more interested in saving their surpluses or in remitting them to relatives in the lands from which they or their parents emigrated. They mostly live in mean and overcrowded homes, work long hours and take little time off for anything but the honoring of religious and family obligations. Here, too, there are exceptions. Some of the most impressive, not to say ostentatious, badges of success to be found in tropical Africa are the property of Asians.

THE MERCHANDISE

To see the consumer market in its proper perspective it is important to remember that in no territory are the wealthy, whether European, Asian or African, in anything but a tiny minority. For every man who can afford to own a Mercedes, live in a large house complete with plumbing and piano, refrigerator and air conditioning, there are 10,000 who cannot. And of the 10,000 it is safe to say that 9,600 are not yet thinking much about anything beyond getting some more to eat, drink and wear, a better roof over their heads, and a little extra money in their hands with which to buy a little extra leisure. That is, the consumer market is still largely a poor man's market in which a limited range of goods commands most of his attention. In the ordinary village store at least 95 per cent of the merchandise will consist of low-priced cottons and apparel, "essential" foodstuffs such as sugar, tea, grain and flour, and a limited choice of cooked, canned and bottled goods, kerosene, hardware, hoes and other simple household requirements.

The "four hundred" have their place, naturally. Already on an annual wage of $100 to $200 many Africans are interested in many things besides having a tin roof, a trunkful of clothes and a storehut full of food. Those who live in the towns or on the mines, where most of the wage-earning possibilities exist, generally want to live like the non-Africans around them, to the extent at least of having a table and some chairs, a bedstead, a kitchen cupboard stocked with dishes and cutlery, along with some curtains and a floor covering. High on the purchase list of many are a radio set, a sewing machine, a kitchen range and an electric lamp or two. Higher still on the list, if not at the very top, is a bicycle, which few urbanized wage earners can afford to do without, since most African residential areas are located well away from the business district. Also near the top of many people's lists there are likely to be such things as a decent pair of trousers, a fancy shirt, perhaps a whole suit, a watch and maybe a banjo or camera, party dresses for the wife and children,[24] patent medicines (especially the quick-healing variety), toilet preparations and cosmetics, fountain pens and similar accessories to the task of living in an advertiser's world.

For the small but rapidly growing African middle class — the civil servant, the teacher, the artisan, the trader and the yeoman farmer — there will be other priorities: a motorcycle or even an automobile, a phonograph, a pressure stove, an icebox, and a house full of furniture.

[24] Formal dances, with evening dress obligatory, have become part of the social pattern on the Copperbelt mines.

DISTRIBUTION SYSTEMS

There are almost as many ways of getting goods to consumers as there are kinds of goods, and the way employed often bears a relationship to the goods involved. Thus, hawkers who cycle from village to village concentrate on articles having a comparatively high ratio of value to bulk or weight, such as medicine pills, combs, brushes, pins, needles, toiletries and, for the very poor householder, small measures of salt, tea and sugar. (It is not uncommon to find such traders selling sugar by the single lump and tea and salt by the penny "twist.") Bush storekeepers seldom stock goods which move slowly or deteriorate fast, such as sewing machines, bicycles and batteries. But, on the whole, the way employed depends much more on where the trading is done, who does it, and on what scale. Of the many points of sale, the most significant are the market place, the village or roadside store, the farm store, the cooperative store, and the town shop, bazaar and department store.

The Market

The oldest and most widespread of tropical Africa's shopping centers is the market. It is also the most liked, for it is a place of companionship, color and, frequently, gaiety, where a man may dawdle, drink, gossip or haggle as his fancy takes him. When it comes to doing business, there are few better places than a market. Its running costs are low compared with those of a shop. Its wide range of offerings, all in view, provides opportunities for examination and comparison equaled only by the large city store. It is the original supermarket, self-service and all. At least the characteristically big west African market may claim to be, and it is in west Africa that the market reaches its largest public and does its largest business.

Exactly how large a public is served and how much business is done it is impossible to say, but both are certainly substantial, as anybody can see who has visited the markets of Kano, Onitsha, Aba, Ibadan and Lagos in Nigeria, Accra and Kumasi in Ghana, or Dakar in the Republic of Senegal and Bamako in the Sudanese Republic. The Aba market usually has between 7,000 and 8,000 sellers, the Kumasi market up to twice as many. In some parts of Nigeria there are so many markets, large and small, that no village is more than a short ride by "mammy lorry" from one or more of them.

They cater to the customer's every need, and whim. There he may buy the latest in footwear, hardware and hollow ware. There he will find menders of bicycles and makers of cupboards; butchers, bakers, tinkers and tailors. There he will be able to drink a mug of tea or beer; eat braised meat, fried termites, a slice of bread, or an ice cream; find medicines for every pain, and a scholar to read the directions for him. There a woman may buy spices, sugar, salt, silks and satins — the latest

Europe and Asia have to offer — a dozen kinds of soaps, perfumes (often bought by the drop applied to the buyer's gown) and pomades, and a bewildering array of knickknacks for the home.

In most west African markets, and increasingly elsewhere, the merchandise is well organized. It is common practice for the sellers to group themselves according to the class of goods in which they specialize, and the tendency to specialize has increased noticeably in recent years. Sellers of textiles will occupy one section of the market, sellers of footwear another, and so on. Some markets have sections that do business in commodities as unlikely as empty bottles and tin cans, scrap iron and aluminum, and old coins. The Kano market has a money-changing section where the traveler may satisfy his requirements of French francs, Louis-Napoleons, silver of Alfonso XIII, and Maria Theresa dollars of varying degrees of similitude.

Perhaps the most striking feature of the west African market is the extent to which it is run by women. Men may do most of the wholesaling and transporting, the barbering, butchering, carpentry and repair work, but women do most of the retailing. In some fields, such as textiles, they do practically all of it, and very successfully. In the great markets of Ghana and Nigeria some of the market mammies — to give them their customary name — have a trading turnover of more than £5,000 a month, live in spacious homes run by servants, drive fine cars, own valuable real estate and securities, take holidays abroad, and enjoy a credit standing with their suppliers of which any European or American businessman might be proud. Such rewards have generally been hard-earned, for these women are likely to have started as child vendors of fruit, nuts and sweetmeats and for many years thereafter to have taken their place daily, from dawn till after dark, selling small items at small profit — sometimes taking a loss in one line in the expectation of later getting a customer's business in another. The profit on a sale seldom amounts to more than 5 per cent and frequently not more than 2 per cent. But they see nothing wrong with small profits, provided they can get enough of them. And for the successful ones who have built up a turnover of £5,000 a month, even a 2 per cent profit represents gross annual earnings of £1,200. With overhead costs low, it is not difficult to see how an enterprising trader might clear between £1,000 and £2,500 a year.

Although markets are to be found scattered throughout tropical Africa, those of the east and central parts do not in general compare, either as social centers or as points of sale, with those found in the lands lying immediately to the south of the Sahara. There are several reasons why this should be so, not the least of which have been the scarcity until a few years ago of regular salable surpluses of goods sufficiently different and desirable to warrant the trouble of their marketing, and the fact that not all Bantu peoples find the attractions of the trader's life irresistible. Another reason may be that the pacification of east and central Africa and the opening up of its highways and byways to friendly exchange occurred too recently for the market to have become a widely established institution. The situation is changing, however, especially in the vicinity of the great new urban, industrial and mining centers. The markets located in the African sectors of such cities as Léopoldville, Elisabethville, Brazzaville, Nairobi and Mombasa already bustle and seethe like the best west African markets, and their pace of growth exceeds all the projections made of it.

The Village Store

To designate as the village store the one-man market found all through the African bush may seem to some to be making rather free with the use of words. For the village store is often in no village but simply at a place where two roads meet; frequently it can be called a store only by courtesy; and usually it is owned and operated by a man who is not a "native." But at least it fills most of the functions of the traditional village store. It serves a wide constituency, its customers being drawn from five, ten or fifteen miles away and sometimes farther. It buys and sells a little of everything that is in common demand. It is willing to do business at all hours of the day or night, and to provide credit to those deserving of it. And it serves as a meeting place, frequently as a clearinghouse for news and gossip, and, in a very real sense, as a school where the goods are the teachers, the eye speaks more eloquently than the tongue, and the price tags supply a constant spur to the industrious.

The words of a government publication pay a deserved tribute to the village storekeeper:

He has penetrated to every corner of the country and has been largely instrumental in introducing the local inhabitants to a money economy and to the advantages of such things as cloth, knives, lamps, matches, shoes, tea. The typical *duka* [25] in the remoter areas is a small shop made of sun-dried mud bricks (or even of wattle and daub) with corrugated iron roof, in which the . . . trader often lives a life of extreme simplicity, buying the produce brought in by the local inhabitants and supplying their simple wants. These traders have been the pioneers in many areas and they have existed in places and at times when no other traders could have survived.[26]

The description is of Tanganyika, but it fits a score of territories. For whether he is Indian (as he generally is in Tanganyika) or Greek, or Cypriot or Syrian (as he is in many parts of central and west Africa), or African (as he is coming to be increasingly in territories like Ghana, Nigeria and Uganda), and whether his store is simple or substantial and its location central or remote, the village trader has been far more than a bit player in the drama of twentieth-century Africa. Some would say

[25] The Swahili name by which the village store is known throughout east Africa.
[26] *Tanganyika: A Review of Its Resources and Their Development*, p. 723.

he has been the star — not the hero necessarily, in fact more often, in the minds of his customers, the villain of the piece.

It is difficult for the best of economists to explain to the uninstructed how and why prices change with changes in the relationship of supply to demand, and the village storekeeper is not the best of economists. Even economists resent having to pay more for sugar this month than they paid last, particularly if their income happens to be less than it was last month. The African, faced with a situation of this kind, finds it easier and more satisfying to assume that it is the trader he knows rather than the "market" he never so much as sees that is responsible for his financial anxieties. Some village traders, having a virtual monopoly of the retail buying and selling in their area, undoubtedly do exploit their advantage. The credit system run by some of them, whereby a customer is supplied with food in the "hungry season" in return for a lien on the next season's crops, is also the cause of widespread resentment.

The village storekeeper also comes in for criticism from his wholesaler, whose common complaint it is that, in face of the known conservatism and poverty of the bush African, the storekeeper is reluctant to introduce new and often more expensive lines of goods. Frequently, however, the only reason the African is conservative is because the storekeeper has never been given a chance to experiment.

With the amount of money in circulation increasing year by year, the small trader's role is becoming at once smaller and more difficult. He no longer has the stage to himself, even in the country, for many of the large farms and plantations run stores of the PX type, and many cooperatives also do a retail business. In the towns he must pit his strength against the department store and bazaar, neither of which the *duka* can match when it comes to range of merchandise, price cutting, and the pleasure of browsing. Nevertheless, he can still make a good living if he tries, for nobody can take from him the advantages of propinquity and of being able to exploit the buyer's chronic need of credit.

The Farm Store

The farm store is a phenomenon of the settler and planter areas. It may be European- or Asian-owned. It may consist of only a few shelves in the farmer's kitchen stocked with everyday requirements; or it may be housed in its own building, have its own staff, and carry a highly diversified stock. Some farmers look upon their stores as a means of keeping money "in the family," reaping with one hand what they sowed with the other. Many, however, run their stores on a nonprofit basis, desiring to supply their laborers with needed merchandise at low prices and (very important in these days of labor shortage) to gain the reputation of being good employers. Where they do their buying through cooperative societies, the discounts they are able to pass on are often large enough to be an important drawing card. Since most farmers are unwilling to tie up money in slow-moving stock, the usual run of goods to be had at a farm store does not extend much beyond cigarettes, combs, khaki clothing, raincoats, belts, soap, and foodstuffs other than those grown on the farm.

The Town Store

Coming in many different sizes, serving several different clienteles and more than one function, town stores would seem to have few characteristics in common. However, one thing that sets them apart as a group from village stores is their tendency to specialize. This is particularly true of stores doing most of their business with the European market; here tropical African practice is not very different from West European or North American. It is also true, though, of many stores catering primarily to the African and Asian markets. In the larger centers it is common to find stores specializing in such things as cheap clocks and watches, imitation jewelry, bicycles and accessories, musical instruments or records.

The storekeeper tends to "shop around" for his merchandise instead of tying himself to one wholesaler. By so doing he can take advantage of good offers, and do business in a greater number of lines of a given class of goods, usually at lower prices than his rural competitor, whose turnover is slower and whose shipment costs are higher. This applies especially to the big department stores and bazaars in cities like Salisbury and Lagos. Because these stores do so much of the retail business, wholesalers are only too happy to compete for their favors, and there is hardly an agency they cannot have for the asking.

With the growth of suburban and intercity transport services, and the rising ratio of urban to total population, the town storekeeper has few anxieties, beyond keeping abreast of the demand and in step with its capricious mistress, the price level.

The Consumer Society

While there have been consumer societies, or cooperatives, in different parts of Africa for many years, it is only since about 1945 that they have become numerous, and even today they are by no means as numerous or as widespread as marketing societies.[27] In the British colonies as a whole there were fewer than 50 consumer societies in 1945; in 1957 there were 648, of which roughly 100 were in tropical Africa. The number of marketing societies in the same region increased over that period from 418 to well over 4,000, of which all but 250 or so were in tropical Africa. Table 49 shows the distribution of the consumer societies, along with that of the marketing societies for comparison, in nine African territories. There are also a number of consumer societies in several other territories.

[27] For a general discussion of the cooperative movement, see Volume II.

All but a few of the organizations exist to serve African needs and operate under government supervision.

Most consumer societies, or their sponsors at least, find the going hard. They are small and lack sufficient funds to be able to go in for bulk buying with its attendant economies; consequently they do not carry as large or attractive a range of stock as the ordinary town store. Because they are small, they are seldom able to afford the services of a qualified shopkeeper and thereby avoid irregularities in their bookkeeping. And because they tend to be inefficiently run, their life expectancy is short. In several territories the rate of formation of African consumer societies is exceeded in some years by the rate of liquidation. Between 1954 and 1957 the number of such societies fell in six out of the nine territories listed in Table 49, and increased in only one of them. Where a consumer society has

Table 49

NUMBER AND VOLUME OF TRADE
OF CONSUMER AND MARKETING SOCIETIES IN
SELECTED TERRITORIES, 1954 AND 1957

TERRITORY	NUMBER [a]		TRADE	
	1954	1957	1954	1957
			(*Thousands*)	
CONSUMER SOCIETIES				
Northern Rhodesia	24	21	£ 490	£2,020
Nyasaland	16	12	36	124
Kenya	17	17	3,787	4,510
Tanganyika	4	5	26	35
Uganda	11	5	128	53
Zanzibar	2	2	2	9
Ghana (Gold Coast)	16	6 [b]	—	27 [b]
Nigeria	50	37	41	500
Sierra Leone	2	1	—	16
MARKETING SOCIETIES				
Northern Rhodesia	80	138	£ 3,638	£ 4,578
Nyasaland	48	70	68	83
Kenya	297	425	12,264	18,491
Tanganyika	231	462	7,830	10,360
Uganda	991	1,373	2,619	4,112
Zanzibar	1	2	—	c
Ghana (Gold Coast)	363	376 [b]	6,059	7,457
Nigeria	538	1,105	2,188	4,331
Sierra Leone	133	216	138	218

Source: Cooperative Information Circular for the Colonial Territories, November 1955, January 1957, February 1958 and March 1959 (issued by the Cooperative Union Ltd., Manchester, England).

[a] At end of year.   [b] 1955.   [c] Less than £1,000.

capital and a quick turnover, and is well managed, it can usually stay in business. This is true of such European-run societies as the farmers' co-operatives of Southern Rhodesia and the East African Cooperative Trading Society, and some African-run societies — notably those on the Northern Rhodesian Copperbelt.

ADVERTISING

As the tropical African market grows in size and spending power, so does the role of the consumer goods advertiser. Up to now nearly all of the advertising has been done through the medium of the press. Where the press serves a predominantly European constituency, as do the daily papers of British territories in east and central Africa, the advertiser quite naturally concentrates on the European reader. Where it serves a predominantly African constituency, as in west Africa, he naturally concentrates on the African reader. Multiracial communities frequently have two press groups, European and African; less frequently, they have a third — Asian — group. Where these exist, it would be foolish for a merchant to suppose that by advertising in the European papers he can expect to reach the non-European market, or *vice versa*. For one thing, the readership tends to be segregated. Some Africans and Asians habitually read the "European" papers, but very few Europeans habitually read the "African" and "Asian" papers even when they are published in a European language. And for another, there is still a fairly wide difference in the kinds of things that interest Africans and non-Africans. This is not to say that Africans don't enjoy reading advertisements addressed to the non-Africans. They most certainly do; many an African's appetite for a Jaguar and a diamond ring was first whetted by advertisements in a "European" or "Asian" paper. But for the most part their interests run perforce to less expensive though not necessarily more utilitarian goods. In the Federation of Rhodesia and Nyasaland the goods most commonly offered Africans, and so presumably most salable, are bicycles and bicycle accessories, patent medicines, toilet preparations and cosmetics. Running these a close second are musical instruments, phonographs and records, clothes, cameras and films, food-stuffs and nonalcoholic drinks. In other territories the list would read somewhat differently: the utility of bicycles is considerably impaired in places like Liberia, where roads are few and often impassable; and in places like Angola, Mozambique and the Somalilands the demand for such things as cameras and phonographs still lags behind the demand for clothing and food. At the same time, an advertiser who thinks that any African able to read an advertisement is not interested in bicycles, cameras, phonographs and so on should spend some time studying the pin-up pictures with which aspiring African consumers like to cover their walls.

Point-of-sale advertising is growing in popularity in the bigger shopping centers, but has had little place so far in the typically small, dark and cluttered country stores. In some areas, notably west Africa, billboard advertising is yearly making a stronger bid for the African's patronage — including his patronage of the airlines, which shows how far some Africans, and some advertisers, have come from the old "kaffir truck" days.

In most territories the radio program is still out of bounds to the advertiser, but his trumpetings have tumbled stronger walls than Jericho's, and in time he will surely be granted entry into all the broadcasting strongholds of Africa.

Meanwhile there is plenty he can be doing, for virtually no serious study has yet been made of the advertising field, either as regards its size, fecundity or "climate." About the only rules that have been established are that subtlety doesn't pay and that flattery, alas, does.

CREDIT

It is one particular kind of credit that concerns us here: the short-term credit necessary for the conduct of wholesale and retail domestic trade. For the European or Asian trader the getting of credit presents little more difficulty than it does in most other parts of the world. He may complain that it is expensive and that there is never enough available, but credit can usually be had. Many wholesalers are more than ready to give it to a retailer of proven reliability, for it puts him in their stable — and in business, as in racing, the bigger the string, the bigger the prize money. In many cases it can be had as easily from the commercial banks or from the European- and Asian-run cooperatives, many of which offer credit facilities.

Not everybody in tropical Africa, however, has the ability, or the right, to borrow and repay money. In many areas the Africans have neither; in many others they can borrow only the smallest of sums on the most onerous of terms. There are at least three reasons why this is so.

First and foremost, the ability to borrow depends upon the existence of a negotiable security and an income out of which the loan can be serviced. Over most of the region these conditions are not found as yet. There is no negotiable security in the traditional African subsistence economy, and no surplus out of which the service of the loan can be met. Where the would-be borrower has a negotiable security in the form of land,[28] crops, cattle or merchandise, usually he does not have enough of it to do him much good.

---

[28] Only where an African holds a certificate of title, on either a freehold or a leasehold basis, can land be so used. As we saw earlier, most land in tropical Africa is still held communally. But times are changing. Thus, since the Mau Mau troubles (and partly as a result of them), many thousands of Kenya Africans have acquired an indefeasible title to their farm land, and so the ability to use it as collateral.

Second, few Africans, even those who have moved over into the money sector of the economy, have yet come to appreciate the nature of a borrower's obligations. "The material advantages which accrue to an African in his traditional society appear to him as the gifts of a bountiful providence, and it need occasion no great surprise if he frequently regards money loans in a similar light." [29] As with many of us, he finds it easier to show proof of need than of capacity to repay.

Third, where the African is able to show himself creditworthy, he is seldom able to provide enough business to warrant the setting up of the necessary credit organization. Frequently the overhead costs involved in providing local lending facilities among scattered communities and in managing small accounts are higher than those of managing large urban accounts, a fact which is daily urged by private lending agencies in extenuation of their customarily high charges.

It is easy to diagnose the cause of the African's credit troubles. It is easy also to prescribe treatment for them; to say, for instance, that there is nothing so wrong that it cannot be put right by regular injections of capital, preferably in small doses. If the prescription is right (and the doctors differ), the treatment still takes time, especially since there are so many patients and so few competent doctors to look after them.

Signs of progress may be seen, nevertheless, and none are more encouraging than those in the petty trading field. This is not to say that petty traders are everywhere being courted by creditors. Even in the Federation of Rhodesia and Nyasaland the vast majority of African traders are required to do business with their wholesalers on a cash basis. But in territories like Uganda, Ghana and Nigeria the position is very different. Here it is scarcely an exaggeration to say that most of the retail merchandising business is now run on credit. To attract custom in the face of keen competition the large wholesale firm extends credit to the middleman. The middleman extends credit to the retailer for the same reason, and also because, quite frequently, the retailer, having little or no capital of his own, would be unable to do business without it. The retailer in turn extends credit to the customer to keep him going between paydays. Sometimes market women wait outside the pay offices in order to be the first to claim their share of the workers' wages.

Each charge made by a creditor is, of course, passed on to the next in line. These charges can be high, since some of the loans cannot be quickly recovered, especially those made by itinerant traders on their year-long rounds. But at least it is arguable that if there were fewer creditors, there would be fewer retail outlets; that if there were fewer retail outlets, there would be fewer consumers; and that if there were fewer consumers there would be fewer producers. As it is, in some places — for instance, the outlying cotton-growing regions of Uganda — the producers

[29] *East Africa Royal Commission 1953-1955 Report,* p. 97.

do not pick more than a part of their crop in a good year, largely, it is said, because they lack the incentives which a well-stocked retail shop can supply.

What is really needed, in the view of many, to bring prices down, increase profits, speed up turnover, and quicken incentives is credit in the form of ready cash that will enable a trader to buy from the wholesaler offering the best terms and that will tide him over the lean weeks or months when spending money is scarce. Clearly the right place to meet this need is at the local level, since personal knowledge of the borrower is the best security. Possible sources of such credit are the cooperative society and the commercial bank.

So far very little use has been made of the former, notwithstanding the constant urgings of government officials, notably in British areas, that cooperative credit societies, deriving their funds from existing thrift or marketing societies or from both, be established. Even in territories like Uganda, where the by-laws of the agricultural producers' cooperatives allow for the making of such loans, these facilities are little used — a state of affairs which suggests incapacity on the part of the borrower.

Where commercial banks are authorized and willing to make loans to traders, the results appear to have lagged behind the hopes of both borrower and lender. On this point some of the findings of a committee appointed by the Governor of Uganda in 1954 to study the question of "the advancement of Africans in trade and commerce" seem to be in accord with those of observers in other territories.

The charging of 5 per cent [rate of interest on loans] provides no margin to cover risk and in view of the considerable default experienced by the [Uganda Credit and Savings] Bank and of the difficulty in realizing on such security as might have been given, we do not recommend any reduction in the rate of interest charged by the Bank.

We deplore the general attitude that the money of the Uganda Credit and Savings Bank is Government money and therefore fair game.

The majority of African traders have yet to prove themselves credit-worthy.[30]

Credit, it seems clear, is not the biggest, or the most basic, of the African trader's problems.

THE ADVANCEMENT OF THE AFRICAN IN TRADE

Exactly what the African trader's biggest problems are and how they can be overcome are matters on which traders, customers, wholesalers, bankers and government officials disagree among themselves and with each other. Some opinions, however, are too widely held and too well supported to be dismissed as either tendentious or inconsequential. Euro-

[30] *The Advancement of Africans in Trade*, Uganda Protectorate, Government Printer, Entebbe, 1955, pp. 35 and 38.

peans and Asians are not the only ones to hold them; in affairs of trade, as in many others, the enlightened African is his own best critic.

These opinions may be summarized as follows: (1) What the African trader needs more than more credit and capital is the ability to handle what he already has to better advantage. (2) To do this, he needs more education, and better transport and banking facilities. (3) These things alone can never be a substitute for integrity, dependability and good old-fashioned gumption — without which no businessman anywhere can hope to advance his interests.

It does not take the traveler long to see that, with some conspicuous exceptions such as the more successful of the market women, the African trader has not yet acquired the art of displaying his goods. The typical African shop is nothing more than a few boxes or a table on which the trader spreads his offerings, often in broken lots, of sugar, salt, soap, cigarettes, matches and the like. If his wares include kerosene, as is customary, he is unlikely to have proper containers for dispensing it, with consequent contamination of other goods. If he sells perishables, as also is customary, he is most unlikely to have any way of safeguarding them against spoilage. Nothing is protected from flies, fingers and the corruption of humid heat. He is unlikely to have any very effective means of preventing pilferage. Indeed, if he had, he might suffer loss of custom through being thought antisocial.[31] Individual losses from such causes may be small, but they mount up, sometimes faster than the profits. It was estimated in 1952 that in Uganda alone one in every six African traders made a loss — or at least no profit — on his year's trading, largely through "the uncomprehended mystery of overhead expenses and relative rates of turnover."[32]

This in itself testifies eloquently to the need for more education. The need is not simply for technical education in produce and merchandise dealing, display and management, salesmanship, pricing and bookkeeping; primary education is needed also, and this need is not confined to the more backward countries. In writing of Uganda in 1954 the authors of the above-quoted report had to confess that "one of the main obstacles to African advancement in trade is ignorance, not only of trading technique, but even of elementary subjects such as the three 'R's' "[33] No one who has had dealings with African traders in any territory can doubt that the authors knew what they were writing about. Often the simplest of

[31] In his little book, *Africans on Safari* (Friendship Press, New York, 1952), Leslie C. Sayre tells the story of an old Belgian Congo couple who were brought before the local administrator for repeatedly stealing small amounts of peanuts, manioc and salt from the local trading post. When asked why they stole, they replied that since their son was in charge of the store they supposed that the things he sold were his. According to the custom of their tribe, they therefore helped themselves, their son having no power to refuse.

[32] *The Advancement of Africans in Trade*, p. 33.

[33] *Ibid.*, p. 17.

over-the-counter transactions takes on the appearance of a ritual whose meaning no uninitiated customer can follow.

Unfortunately, to remove the ignorance is not always the way to get a trader. Most of the people who have the three R's think they can earn more money, have more leisure and enjoy a higher social status by going into government service or industry, and generally they are right. Yet the trading instinct is strong enough in many Africans — including many Bantus [34] — to enable them to resist the appeal of the steady job and the regular pay check. Where this instinct is coupled with competence in reading, writing and arithmetic, and a little knowledge of how to run a business, the hurdles to advancement in trade begin to lose height. Some of the most successful traders in Uganda are those who have taken the residential traders' course at the Nsamizi Training Centre, at Entebbe. In Kenya the same is true of those who have taken the traders' course offered by the Jeanes School near Nairobi. That the students who take such courses are not run-of-the-mill traders to begin with is readily granted.

No amount of training can make a trader successful unless he can get his supplies when he needs them. At present few rural communities have good transportation services, so that wholesale delivery services are seldom frequent or regular enough to enable a merchant to manage his stocks efficiently. It is especially difficult to deal efficiently with perishable goods when the interval between deliveries may be months rather than days. In many places even things like matches, sugar, salt and flour must be counted perishable. In such circumstances, it is often as difficult to keep one's customers as it is to keep one's goods, Africans being frequently fastidious about the goods they buy and reluctant to do business with a man who is periodically out of stock. Although it may be a useful expedient now and again for a trader to act as his own transporter, traveling by bus to the nearest market and returning with small lots for which he has to pay almost retail prices plus transport charges, this is obviously not the solution to his problem. Equally it is no solution to increase the frequency of rural deliveries so long as the rural market remains as small and scattered as it still is almost everywhere, for this would increase overhead costs without proportionately increasing revenues.

From this it might be concluded that there is no solution to the small trader's transport problem. The writers of the Uganda report believe otherwise, however. They hold that the problem could be solved, in their country at any rate, by mobile wholesaling, "the system by which wholesalers take their goods into the rural areas by lorry and sell to the re-

---

[34] According to Sir Andrew Cohen, onetime Governor of Uganda, there were no less than 15,000 African traders in the country at the end of 1956 ("Uganda's Progress and Problems," *African Affairs*, April 1957, p. 114).

tailer on the spot, either for cash or on credit." [35] Such a system would not only be of the greatest service to the retailer, but

a very appropriate means whereby the more energetic African retailer might enter the wholesale trade. . . . Such wholesalers should not need to carry large capital stocks, but should rather operate as the agents of primary wholesalers and carry most of their stocks on consignment. [The writers further] suggest that as a sound basis to their development, the distribution of main "bread and butter" lines such as cigarettes, matches, kerosene, tea, sugar, etc., might be decentralised to them. They would then have the assurance of such a regular income as would be likely to cover the major part of their overhead expenditure on transport. The sale of other goods in less regular demand and of a more competitive character such as clothing, piece goods, and hardware would produce the net profit required. [36]

Where the system has been tried, though seldom as yet under African auspices, it appears to have justified the hopes of its proponents.

A little more "mobility" could probably be used to good effect in the field of banking. Up to now the African trader has undoubtedly been hampered by lack of facilities for the day-to-day custody and ready transfer of money, without which no business can be conducted securely. The fact that the trader does not have much money to safeguard does nothing to lessen the call for such facilities. If anything, it increases it, for, as the biblical parable reminds us, the man who stands most in need of a banker to manage his assets is the one-talent man. The man in the parable probably exercised more self-control than the small African trader customarily does in regard to money hidden in a napkin; but since the African environment works a quicker corruption than the Palestinian, perhaps part of the African's widely advertised spendthriftiness is not so much incapacity to save as inability to keep money safe from prowlers, fire and other hazards.

While it takes time to alter a people's thinking on such subjects, there is little doubt that it can be done. Many urban Africans are already making regular use of post-office banks for savings and of commercial banks for savings and cash transactions. Rural African traders can surely be expected to make the same use of mobile branch banks (recently introduced in British East Africa), once the advantages in security and profit become clear.

It is beginning to look, therefore, as though there are ways of leaping the high hurdles. Often, however, it is not the highest but the last hurdle that causes a runner most trouble, and it may be so here. Qualities of character such as initiative, self-help, determination and trustworthiness are long aborning in the best of peoples, all too frequently undernourished by those whose job it is to tend them, and liable to collapse in moments of stress, passion and disillusionment. Yet these alone are the stuff of which a man's good name is made and sustained, and the passport to a

[35] *Op. cit.*, p. 31.
[36] *Ibid.*, pp. 31-32.

better society contrived. The authors of the Uganda report — the first of its kind — said on this point:

The development of such qualities among African traders is of the greatest importance to the evolution of a useful and progressive middle class in an emergent community . . . [If African traders] are to succeed, and if any plans to assist them are to succeed, they must establish a reputation for honesty and integrity without which commercial enterprise of any kind is doomed to failure.[37]

Not the least significant thing about this conviction is that the group expressing it consisted of Europeans, Asians and Africans.

[37] *Ibid.*, pp. 12-13.

CHAPTER 13

The Workers

THE AFRICAN LABOR POOL

THE USE OF AFRICAN LABOR

THE MIGRANT WORKER

THE PROBLEM OF AFRICAN
ADVANCEMENT

NON-AFRICAN LABOR

THE WORKER'S WAGES

DURING the course of this discussion of the land and livelihood of
tropical Africa reference has frequently been made to the labor question.
In this final chapter of Volume I we return to the question, for it is a
fundamental one. It is fundamental for two reasons: first, the supply
of almost all kinds of labor, other than unskilled, is generally less than
the demand (in some territories even unskilled labor is hard to come by
without coaxing and shoving); second, with few exceptions the quality
of the supply does not measure up to the norms found in most other
parts of the world.

Until these shortcomings have been removed, the economic and, with
it, the social and political development of the region is bound to lag, to
the continuing impoverishment of the great mass of its peoples and the
embarrassment of their rulers.

THE AFRICAN LABOR POOL

It is difficult for the casual visitor to tropical Africa to credit all the
stories he hears of labor shortage, for if there is one impression more
than another that he is likely to gather from his travels, it is of men with-

out work — or without enough work to keep them busy more than a small part of their time. Almost every roadside village has its group of able-bodied idlers with nothing better to do, seemingly, than watch the world go by. And every town and market place is crowded with men still unacquainted with the time clocks and treadmills that govern the lives of their fellows in Asia, Europe and North America. Even on the white man's plantations and around his factories, it is a common sight to see more men doing nothing than doing something.

It is true that not all of the idleness is voluntary. There are parts of Nyasaland and Ruanda-Urundi, for instance, where, with the best will in the world, a young man would be hard put to it to find steady employment. He is not needed on the land, because there are already too many cultivators for the space available to them; and alternative occupations do not exist, because of economic backwardness, physical isolation or natural poverty. But there are many more places in tropical Africa where, if we are to believe the complaints of employers, labor recruiters and headmen, there is work aplenty, but few workers.

Unfortunately it is next to impossible to obtain the dimensions of the total manpower resources of the region. Figures exist for non-African manpower, but they are so small as not to affect the total greatly. In most territories, moreover, the demand for the type of skills supplied by such people bears a reasonably close relationship to the supply; when gaps arise, they can be made good by immigration of Europeans — if no longer of Asians — from the Old World and the Union of South Africa.

The unknown in the manpower equation is the African figure. It is unknown partly because of the dearth of demographic statistics; partly because manpower is not so much a matter of numbers as it is of numbers willing and able to work; and partly because there can be no discussion of African manpower without a discussion of womanpower, and even less is known about the age group distribution of African women and other significant data than is known about African men. The best we can hope for is a first approximation based on indirect evidence.

The productivity of African agriculture is still so low that it takes anywhere from two to ten people — men, women and children — to raise enough food to supply their own needs and those of one additional — non-food-growing — adult. If we take six as the average,[1] this means that of the estimated 120 million people of working age (eight and over),[2]

---

[1] The average may well be higher. A semi-official Belgian Congo publication declared in 1955 that "at the moment it takes nine natives on the land to keep one in some non-agricultural pursuit" (*The Belgian Congo: From Wilderness to Civilization*, published as a special issue of *Les Beaux-Arts*, Brussels, 1955, p. 17). While no one territory is representative of tropical Africa, the Belgian Congo, it could be argued, is sufficiently large and diversified to warrant its not being classed among the least representative.

[2] Based on age group data assembled from various sources by Glenn T. Trewartha and Wilbur Zelinsky.

not more than 20 million are able to leave their lands at any one time, without seriously upsetting the traditional economy. Since between one half and two thirds of these are women and children who do not normally seek wage-earning jobs, we arrive at a potential wage labor force of not more than 10 million and conceivably less than 7 million — very much less, if the factor by which we should divide the working population is nearer ten than six. The labor pool from which this force can be drawn — that is, the total number of people who are able to leave their homes over a period of time — is, of course, much larger. Trewartha and Zelinsky in their paper prepared for this study put it at roughly 26.5 per cent of the total population, or approximately 44 million.

From such evidence as may be gleaned from management and labor organizations, the manpower needs of the wage economy at the present time are nothing like as large as 10 million, and are even less than 7 million.[3] Yet, with a few notable exceptions, these needs are not being met satisfactorily. Many of the larger employers, like the mining companies, find themselves compelled to resort to expensive recruitment campaigns five hundred to a thousand miles from the seat of their operations. Many others find it increasingly difficult to keep the labor they have.

Part of the trouble arises from the African's long-established work habits and attitudes, about which something was said in Chapter 1. It was one thing for an African to clear bush, build a house, hunt a rogue elephant or fight a tribal enemy. These are enterprises that were self-evidently to his own and his community's advantage, and could be done in his own way and in company with his friends and neighbors. They also gave him standing in his community and a sense of significance. It is quite another thing to get him to take a sustained interest in a lathe that turns out things he cannot use, in a loom that makes cloth he cannot afford, in the face of a copper mine that he doesn't own, and in the track of a railroad that belongs to people he never sees. True, in most of the territories he is free to choose how and where he shall work, but in few is he any longer free *not* to work, and this for him is generally the greater freedom.[4] It is no less true that in most territories the new employers of labor are teaching him how to use leisure more positively, but they have not given him more of it, and many Africans, like many Americans and Europeans, it seems, would still prefer to do a little with a lot of leisure than a lot with a little.

---

[3] Using such data as were available in 1955, Trewartha and Zelinsky obtained the figure of 3.7 million male African employees. This figure covers fourteen of the largest territories with about 70 per cent of the population of tropical Africa. Assuming that the ratio of male African employees to total population was roughly the same in the other territories, the total number of male employees would have been about 5.3 million.

[4] A recent strike in the Nigerian tin fields hinged on just this question of loss of freedom. The laborers had assumed that what they were being paid for was their willingness to surrender their idleness; what they wanted was to be paid also for working.

In part also the trouble arises from the fact that in working for the European the African is called upon to do things for which his world provides no precedents and no understanding. The writer of the following passage is referring specifically to the African of British East Africa, but the description is valid for many other parts as well:

Even where the occupation offered by Europeans resembles his native pursuits, as in agriculture and the care of cattle, its patterns are different, more detailed and more intricate than those to which he has been accustomed. The hoe was the characteristic tool of his husbandry, the patient, plodding ox the symbol, though not the instrument, of his activities. Most new occupations have to be learned. But so many lessons pressing one upon the other are more than he can learn. Not that he is inherently inferior in capacity: he is unequal to what is demanded of him. The mechanical world, with its far-reaching implications of cause and effect, is a test of his powers of comprehension and memory. The mental patterns inwoven upon the minds of the very children of our industrial civilization are for him matters to be learned with labor and by dint of much repetition. He has to see a thing done, and done many times, before its recall under every circumstance becomes easy.[5]

Then again, the African is called upon to do most of his work in a very different social environment from the one in which he has habitually lived. On the mines and plantations and in the towns — although the situation is slowly changing — he is usually unable to live en famille, or even with people of the same ethnic and linguistic background. He may be unable to eat his accustomed food, drink his accustomed beverages, or find his accustomed pleasures. All this may be to the good of his physical health, but the effect of it on his mental health is more in question. Further, he is required to learn, usually without adequate time for adjustment, the difficult lesson of handling money and of appraising himself as a producing unit in industry, and of weighing the rewards and incentives offered him. In an environment where the dominant values are still nonmonetary, and where a man's life does not yet consist in the abundance of things he possesses, these lessons are difficult indeed to learn.

Against this background the existence of a labor problem need not surprise us. What is surprising is that the problem is no greater, and that the African worker should have come as far as he has in so short a time.

THE USE OF AFRICAN LABOR

Much as we may deplore the "hewer of wood and drawer of water" concept of African labor, we must admit that it is the African's unskilled labor that has done most to change the face of his land. Without the African stone breaker, ditch digger, cement mixer, hod carrier, bushwhacker, porter, servant and general factotum things would still be very

[5] C. H. Northcott, *African Labour Efficiency Survey 1947*, Colonial Office, H.M.-S.O., London, 1949, pp. 7-8.

much as they were fifty or a hundred years ago. In a very real sense, the tropical Africa of today is the work of the African's hands; almost every railroad, highway, harbor, public and private building, mine, plantation and European farm is a monument to his physical exertions.

And the demand for the African's unskilled labor continues. Indeed, it was never stronger, for there were never so many jobs of construction and maintenance to be done, or so few non-Africans interested in doing things of this kind. At the same time it is no longer true to say that the African laborer is, anywhere in the region, regarded solely as a filler of unwanted jobs. Exactly what jobs are open to him depends much on where he lives, but taking tropical Africa as a whole, some Africans are found in practically every occupational category, and in almost every subdivision of every category. The bulk of the wage earners, nevertheless, are engaged at the unskilled or semiskilled level, whether they are employed in agriculture, mining, transport, industry, commerce or civil service.

Agriculture

Of these activities, agriculture commands the largest labor force. Even in a territory like Northern Rhodesia, which derives more than 90 per cent of its export revenues from mining, the number of African paid employees in agriculture is, on the average, only about one third less than the number engaged in mining and refining (in 1956, 34,000 as against 48,000). In Southern Rhodesia, where minerals and farm products run almost neck and neck as revenue earners, there are three male African agricultural employees for every mining employee. In most of the territories for which figures are available, between 20 and 50 per cent of all male African employees are in agriculture. Only where most of the farmers are self-employed peasants, as in Ghana and Nigeria, do the percentages fall much below 20.

In most territories the chief employer of agricultural labor is the European-owned and European-managed plantation. In a few territories, notably those, like Kenya and the Rhodesias, with a settler element, the chief employer is the European farmer. In at least one territory, Uganda, the chief employer is the well-to-do African farmer.

The hierarchy of jobs performed by African employees varies widely. On the large plantations the postwar trend has been toward the mechanization of all mechanizable operations and the "Africanization" of as many of those operations as possible. On the sisal plantations of Tanganyika, Africans drive the light trains that collect the daily "cut," run the decorticators and the packing plant. On the sugar plantations of Uganda, the Belgian Congo and the Republic of the Congo, they drive the bulldozers that clear the bush and the multiple-disc plows that prepare the ground. They do the same on many of the tea plantations of

Nyasaland and Southern Rhodesia, and the rubber and palm oil plantations of the Congo basin and west Africa.

It is less easy to generalize about the use of African labor on European farms, because these vary from the family-run small holding of the type found in the Cela district of Angola through the medium-sized dairy and mixed farms common on the outskirts of Nairobi, Salisbury, Lusaka, Bulawayo and other large European centers, to the many-thousand-acre ranches and field crop enterprises found in the more rural parts of the Rhodesias, Kenya, the Belgian Congo, Mozambique, Angola and the Republic of the Congo. On some of these farms, including some of the smaller ones, Africans have been trained to handle every piece of equipment and to supervise the tasks done by their unskilled fellow workers. On others, including some of the largest and most heavily capitalized, they continue to be employed at little else than fetching and carrying, planting and weeding. Much depends on the attitude of the employer and his view on the educability of the African. But here, too, the trend is clear. Each year sees more European farmers giving the African laborer greater responsibility.

It is on the small farms run by Africans primarily for the production of cash crops — and as we have seen there are many such — that the status of the agricultural wage worker is at its lowliest. Because of the characteristic fragmentation of the land, the poor financial standing of the farmer, and the unhandy growth habits of his crops, the tasks usually performed by the hired help are manual, unskilled and irksome. They consist of stripping cocoa trees of their pods and releasing the shell-encased beans, clambering up and down palm trees, weeding and picking cotton, hauling 50-to-100-pound hands of bananas from *shamba* to shop and market place, and so on. However, African farmers are beginning to take a leaf out of the European's book. As we shall see in Volume II (Chapter 18), cooperative buying, selling and credit organizations have made great headway since the end of the last war, with the result that many coffee and cotton growers have been able partially to mechanize their operations. More than a few growers of cocoa, coffee and other high-priced export crops have been making sufficient money to be able to farm on a large enough scale to warrant the private purchase of mechanical equipment.[6]

Mining

The use made of African labor on mines is narrower in function, and more localized. The exigent need for engineering skill and judgment and the ever-present risk of accident and attendant jeopardy of life and prop-

---

[6] Some Chagga (Mt. Kilimanjaro) growers of coffee have been grossing between £3,000 and £4,000 annually from their crop; recently one of them paid £800 for a tractor — cash down *in shillings!*

erty leave little scope, underground especially, for the unskilled worker. And so far not many Africans have had the chance to acquire the kinds of skills that would enable them to "run" mines in the sense in which many Africans now "run" farms. Because of this, mines of every type and in every territory continue to rely almost exclusively upon Europeans and other nonindigenous peoples for their technical and supervisory labor force, and very heavily upon the same peoples for their semiskilled labor. This leaves few other than manual jobs for the African. Wherever a job can be done manually by an African, the chances are that it will be so done. A union official in Northern Rhodesia has affirmed that there are jobs done by hand on African mines that are not done by human labor anywhere else in the world. All the same, the range of mechanical jobs open to African mine workers is not inconsiderable. On the Northern Rhodesian Copperbelt some Africans are now employed as drivers of electric and diesel locomotives, hoists and overhead cranes, as power hammer and ladle winch operators, and as furnace skimmers and tappers. On the copper mines of Katanga, Africans now work as fitters, turners, plumbers, carpenters, pattern makers, electricians, moulders and blacksmiths. Much the same is true on the gold, manganese and diamond mines of Ghana, the tin, coal and columbite mines of Nigeria, and the newly developed copper mines of Uganda. And the range of employment opportunities is slowly widening.

Transport

In the transport category, much heavier dependence is put on the African. For instance, the "mammy lorry" (bus) services that ply the length and breadth of west Africa and take many of the men, as well as the women, to and from their markets are almost entirely owned and operated by Africans. Most of the European-owned passenger and freight motor services employ African drivers, and in some cities Africans now drive the buses that serve the needs of non-Africans.

Water transport services, too, are run largely by Africans. As a navigator of treacherous waters the African can match the skill of any man, thanks to his long apprenticeship to the canoe and, on the larger lakes and rivers, to sailing craft. As an engineer he is still a beginner; but it is not uncommon for the smaller vessels to have an African captain as well as an African crew. On the largest river vessels, such as those that ply between Stanleyville and Léopoldville in the Belgian Congo, only the captain is likely to be a European.

The railroads have always made great use of African labor. In the early days this labor was entirely unskilled, as most of it still is. However, in recent years many semiskilled and skilled job categories have been opened up to the more experienced worker. Today, on the Kenya-Uganda Line of the East African Railways and Harbours organization, Africans work as guards, firemen and drivers (on almost all trains except the Mombasa Mail), as shunters, yard staff, station clerks, assistant station masters and station masters (of smaller stations), as well as track layers, porters, cleaners and general laborers. In several other territories the indigenous peoples do most, if not all, of the train driving and maintaining.

The least Africanized of all transportation services are the airlines. This is in the nature of things, for the kind of skill needed to fly planes and keep them airworthy is of a high order, requiring training of a sort that few Africans have had. In the whole of tropical Africa there are probably not more than two hundred Africans who can fly a Piper Cub, let alone a DC-3 or a Viscount, and even fewer who know how to service such craft beyond checking them for oil and gas consumption. Consequently, although every airport has its complement of African employees, many of whom earn good wages by African standards, no airport yet possesses an all-African supervisory staff, either technical or administrative. Those airports and airlines that are seeking to integrate Africans into their operations do not find the going easy.

So far it is the Ethiopians who are the pace setters. In 1957 Ethiopian Airlines announced that an Ethiopian pilot assisted by an Ethiopian co-pilot had flown one of its regular passenger planes (hitherto piloted by Americans) from Addis Ababa to Aden and back. More recently Ghana has begun to use its own nationals as pilots and navigators on internal and inter-west African services.

Industry

The use of African labor in industry has increased greatly in the post-war period in most territories. The Republic of Senegal, Ghana, the Belgian Congo, Kenya, Nigeria and Southern Rhodesia are among those that have shown substantial increases. In Southern Rhodesia the number of Africans employed in manufacturing rose from less than 15,000 in 1938 to more than 100,000 in the late 1950s. The trend may be expected to spread with the growth of African nationalism (which is inclined to equate dependence upon imported manufactures with colonialism), the rise of African living standards, and the related increase in the demand for a wide range of consumer goods that can be manufactured more economically locally than abroad.

Here again, although there are exceptions that may well prove much about the African's potential as a factory hand, the great majority of employees are engaged in unskilled or semiskilled jobs. At the semiskilled level, many work as welders, as in the engineering shops of Dakar, Khartoum and Nairobi; machine minders, as in the textile mills of Léopoldville and Luanda; and assemblers of parts, as in the radio, boot-and-shoe and window frame factories of Southern Rhodesia. As such they do the work of artisans' mates rather than of artisans. At the unskilled level, where most African factory hands are still employed, they do everything there is to be done, from preparing the endless cups of tea demanded in the British territories by their European bosses and tidying the factory grounds to feeding their more skilled colleagues with the stuff of which the factory product is made.

Commerce

In commerce, the African generally seems to prefer to be the "boss-boy," no matter how small, rather than an employee, no matter how big. And thousands are, especially in west Africa. However, few of these, even the big women traders of Ghana and Nigeria, employ paid labor. They prefer to keep the money "in the family," and the reckonings in their heads. Up to quite recent times, the openings for Africans in European, Asian and other non-African business houses were few. In the larger towns, and in settler country generally, they continue to be few, and rather menial; it is still not common to find Africans serving behind the counter, taking money or keeping stock. In the non-settler territories, African office and clerical workers are rapidly increasing in number and are being advanced from supernumerary to more responsible positions; but the advance is frequently painful for employer and employee alike.

Some of the most responsible business positions now open to Africans are in the cooperative societies that are mushrooming in almost every African cash crop farming area. Many of the societies do not administer big enough funds to need much in the way of staff, but others, like the Kilimanjaro (Tanganyika) Native Co-operative Union, Ltd., and the Bugisu (Uganda) Cooperative Union, Ltd., are sufficiently large to have their own administrative headquarters and branch offices, and to need a battalion of bookkeepers, cashiers and clerks.

Civil Service

Civil service has long been "big business" in tropical Africa, in the eyes of the African onlooker if not always in fact. With the spectacular post-war extension of the field of government it has become one of the largest employers of labor. As in the other main categories of employment, unskilled jobs continue to be those most accessible to Africans. In some territories, they continue to be virtually the only jobs an African can take; this is especially true of those, as, for instance, Angola and Mozambique, which have very high illiteracy rates. In other territories, notably in Ghana, Nigeria, British East Africa, the Belgian Congo and the member states of the French Community, the ratio of skilled and semiskilled to unskilled job openings is increasing yearly, though nothing like as rapidly as most educated Africans would wish. For if there is one thing more than another that looks attractive to the educated African it is a white-collar job in a government office. Apart from the money it yields — very considerable indeed in many cases — it carries great prestige. What is more, it relieves its incumbent of the necessity of doing manual work, which, wittingly or unwittingly, the European functionary has taught the African to despise.[7]

In most British and ex-British territories the range of government jobs now filled by Africans is enormous. The civil service of the Republic of Sudan had been largely "Sudanized" long before the British retired. Except for a small group of Europeans whose role is advisory, both the central and the local government is run entirely by nationals. In Ghana and Nigeria, the Africanizing process, though starting later, has moved faster; it is only in the more technical fields of administration such as agriculture, education and community development that any considerable numbers of Europeans are retained in executive positions.[8] In British East Africa, the openings for semiskilled and skilled Africans in government service are much the same as in British West Africa, but the number of Africans capable of filling them to advantage is much smaller. For instance, as of 1955 no African was employed in the central government of Uganda above the level of assistant district officer and it was said that none was available.[9] At the same time, the Kabaka's government — which has jurisdiction over the approximately 1.25 million indigenous inhabitants of the Buganda Province of Uganda, raises and administers its own funds, and does a great deal of law making — was being run almost entirely by native ministers, councilors and civil servants.

In the territories that have not been under British rule the ratio of semiskilled and skilled Africans to total government employees varies widely. Though exact figures are hard to come by, the ratio is, without doubt, lowest in the Portuguese territories. This is not because of racial prejudice on the part of the administration, for "any African," as one official put it in a recent conversation, "is eligible to climb the ladder — right to the top." It is merely because there are so few rungs. The ratio is higher in the Belgian Congo, but the general level of employment of semiskilled

[7] This attitude reveals itself in many ways. In some territories the films that get the biggest laughs are those which show Europeans working with their hands, and not the intentionally "funny" films (American or European).

[8] Around 1924, only two Africans were employed in "senior service," that is, in high executive and administrative positions, in the then Gold Coast. In 1949 there were 171; in 1954, 916. (See "A Statement on the Programme of the Africanisation of the Public Service," Government Printing Department, Accra, 1954.) On the eve of independence, December 1956, all but 1,123 of the employees (well over 100,000) in government offices were African.

[9] Among the reasons given was lack of responsibility. One provincial commissioner, with more than twenty years' experience of British East Africa, avowed that it was "impossible" to trust Africans with confidential material and that he would take care to see no African district officer posted to his province would ever handle secret despatches.

and skilled Africans in government service remained low until 1959. Few served above the clerical level, and most served below. Many higher openings existed, however, and through its greatly expanded program of secondary and university education, the government had high hopes of filling them. In the French territories and those until recently French it has long been possible for the gifted African to climb to the top. Félix Eboué was for several years Governor of Chad, and later Governor-General of French Equatorial Africa. In each of these territories there are today African policemen, teachers, doctors, lawyers, broadcasters, political advisers, cabinet ministers and premiers. Even some of the pygmies of the Sangha region of the Republic of the Congo are moving ahead; at least they have started to go to school, and to work for the local government officer.

THE MIGRANT WORKER

While it is true that until the present century many millions of Africans never had been outside their tribal borders, there have always been Africans who moved about. Some did not move by choice. Among these were the luckless victims of the slavers of the nineteenth and earlier centuries, and those, scarcely less numerous in the aggregate, who moved whenever the local diviner, sorcerer or other dealers in magic held such a move to be necessary for continued good standing in the spirit world. But many moved of their own volition, in search of better pastures, healthier homes and more room. Since the coming of the European enterpriser and administrator, the movement of Africans from place to place has greatly increased; indeed, it is now perhaps the most impressive demographic phenomenon of the continent.

The paramount reason for this modern-day movement can be given in three words: need of money — money for the payment of taxes, money for the purchase of food, clothing and shelter, and money for the satisfaction of personal whims and fancies. Since there is hardly an adult in Africa who does not need money, for taxes if for nothing else, and since few of the places where money is most easily earned are close to the places where it is most needed, all Africa, in a manner of speaking, is on the move. Needless to say, there are other reasons why men leave home. In an analysis of labor migrations from Bechuanaland to the Transvaal, I. Schapera gives no less than ten reasons, most of which (including, for instance, the desire to escape from the tedium and restraint of tribal life and to be regarded as a "man of the world," and the prevailingly low productivity of subsistence farming) have their place, at some time or other, in the thinking of young adults everywhere.[10] But none of these speak as loudly or as eloquently as an empty pocket.

[10] See I. Schapera, *Migrant Labour and Tribal Life,* Oxford University Press, London, 1947.

FORMS OF MIGRATION

These population movements assume different forms, directions and durations. Four major forms are identifiable. The oldest of these is the movement of whole tribes, clans or villages. While it is not as common as it used to be, it continues, on a mainly seasonal basis, among the cattle- and camel-owning groups that inhabit the drier fringes of tropical Africa. Examples are the Somali, the Arabic-speaking peoples of the northern and central provinces, and the Nilotic tribes of the southern provinces of the Republic of Sudan. Even among sedentary populations, such as the Fang of the Gabon Republic and the forest dwellers of the Equateur Province of the Belgian Congo, it is by no means a thing of the past. It is generally motivated by the need periodically to replace worn-out land. The need to find tax money merely makes the movement more compelling.

Most present-day migrations are not tribal so much as individual. According to D. Hobart Houghton, a contributor to this study, those who take part in them can be divided into three broad categories: bread-winners, migrant families and absconders.

The migrant breadwinners are those who move temporarily to an area with a large cash economy — such as a plantation, mine, factory or town — leaving their families behind them. They hope to meet the economic pressure which forces them to go out to work by earning enough to keep themselves and provide a surplus which they can either send back to their families in the form of periodic remittances or take home with them on their return. Where the economic pressure is great, several breadwinners may go from a single family; where it is less there may be only one. Migration of this type has its origin in family loyalty and the desire to provide financial support for the family group. The people involved in it are not making a career of wage earning, but simply trying to earn enough cash to subsidize their traditional subsistence economy and their tribal way of life. Although they are away from home only for a limited period of time — seldom more than eighteen months, frequently less than nine — they constitute in fact a continuous stream of persons, each of whom is likely to spend the greater part of his adult life circulating between membership in a modern urban, or rural, proletariat and membership in a traditional African society. They go out to work, return home, go out to work again, return home again. Some repeat the routine a dozen times, some a score of times, during the span of their working lives.

The family type of migration may involve only the breadwinner and his wife or wives, or it may also involve his children and even some members of the extended family. The migration may be temporary or permanent. If the former, it is very little different from the breadwinner type of migration, since the goal of all concerned is to return to the tribal home as soon as possible. If the latter (and permanent migration is becoming increasingly important in many sections), the whole way of life must of necessity undergo great change. Already there are many second-generation families on the mines of Katanga and the Copperbelt and in the big cities of east and central Africa who have not so much as seen the bush where their parents were born. Many of these families have in fact ceased to "belong" to tribal life; they have their roots in the bricks and mortar, the dirt and dust of a new world. But most migrant families still keep one foot in the old world, whither they return from time to time to see their people, to parade their children and their clothes, to tell of their accomplishments and, perchance, to renew their vows to the spirits of their fathers.

The absconders are those who find the economic and social obligations imposed upon them by kinship and tribal tradition so burdensome that they seek an escape from them in the new, anonymous and free and easy world of the European. In so doing they cut themselves off from their families, and become "the lost ones." There have always been absconders the world over, but the temptation for the African to abscond was never greater than it is today when almost every town, mine, factory and plantation offers excitement for the bored, opportunity for the ambitious, and asylum for the resentful. While boredom and ambition may not drive many to the length of "losing" themselves, resentment self-evidently does. The grounds for the resentment are, to the Western way of thinking, not unsubstantial. When money saved from a man's wages is taken back to the tribal home, the chances are it will have to be shared; it may be taken away. When a man is promoted, and his relatives get to hear of it, they are likely to visit him — and not merely for the purpose of a celebration; the more he earns, the longer the visit usually lasts, and the larger the household he is expected to maintain. When it comes to the time for marrying, the man is expected, if he follows the general practice of his people, to take a woman (or have one chosen for him) who is a stranger to everything he has come to regard as important, who is uneducated, fearful and, by his standards, uncouth. It is not surprising that in the more backward territories "the lost ones" are thought to number already hundreds of thousands.

PATTERNS OF MIGRATION

The distances these labor migrants travel — breadwinners, families and absconders alike — are seldom short and frequently long. A journey of 250 miles is thought nothing of. Journeys of up to a thousand miles are customary for many laborers on the mines of the Copperbelt and Katanga; for the Witwatersrand miners much longer journeys are by no means rare.

[Thither] they come on foot, on horseback, on bicycles, by dug-out canoe, by . . . steamer, in lorries, by train, and some even by air. They come from as far afield as 2,000 miles. They come from all points of the compass — from the peaceful hills of the Transkei, from the lion country of the Bechuanaland bush, down the broad reaches of the Zambesi, from the tropical shores of Lake Nyasa and the mountain fastnesses of Basutoland. They come, too, in their thousands from the hills and valleys of Portuguese East Africa, from the rocky uplands of Sekukuniland, the tangled swamp country of the Okavango delta and the green folds of Swaziland.[11]

A diagrammatic analysis of some of the main postwar labor migrations in southern and eastern Africa, where they reach their greatest extent and complexity, is shown in Figure 34. Why men should travel where

[11] "How the Native Workers Reach the Mines," *Mining Survey* (Transvaal Chamber of Mines, Johannesburg), June 1951, p. 6.

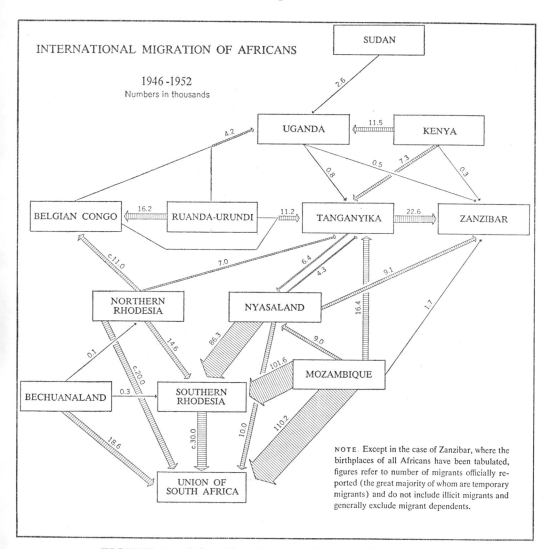

FIGURE 34 (After Glenn T. Trewartha and Wilbur Zelinsky)

they do is not always quickly apparent. Even a generalized pattern of their travels is surprisingly complex. Differential wage rates no doubt explain some of its features. Thus, the fact that wages on the Witwatersrand mines and in the towns of Southern Rhodesia are higher than on the farms and plantations of Nyasaland and Tanganyika is enough to explain why so many Mozambique Africans head south and southwest rather than north. But other things go into the making of the pattern. In many tribes, the fact that a man has worked on the mines gives him status among his fellows and favor among the women — as the killing of a lion or an elephant used to do in the old days.[12] Many Angola and Mozambique Africans prefer to work for foreign employers than for their own government, and many of the indigenous inhabitants of the lands formerly constituting French Equatorial Africa have always preferred to seek employment in Spanish Guinea or Fernando Po in order to avoid military service. Some travel with no set plan in mind; they either play their hunches, often to find that their journey was unnecessary, or drift from place to place, turning their hands to any job that comes along no matter how menial or poorly paid.

More impressive still are the great numbers involved in many of the migrations. The greatest migration of all — that to and from the Witwatersrand mines — is a "trek" more than 300,000 strong.[13] Every year some 300,000 men set off from their tribal homes and their subsistence farms for "Egoli" — the City of Gold — and every year 300,000 return bringing money, clothes, blankets, phonographs and other city things. Almost as great is the seasonal migration of workers into Ghana for domestic, farm, factory and mine employment. "Most recent estimates show that this movement is as high as 300,000 a year in each direction — more, in fact, than the total labour force employed at any one time in regular employment."[14] In Tanganyika, it has been estimated that in 1953 "the total of long-distance migrants [comprised] perhaps one-third of the number of men in paid employment — say, 120,000 workers."[15] The total number of migrant workers was even bigger, for in the same year some 21,000 men were away in the Rhodesias and South Africa, between 8,000 and 10,000 in Uganda, and over 36,000 non-Tanganyika Africans were at work in the territory.[16] Most of the immigrants were employed in

[12] Returned miners in the back areas of Mozambique wear their blast helmets long after they have done with the mines, and on the most unlikely and unnecessary occasions.

[13] Although the Rand falls outside the territorial limits of this study, it draws so heavily on labor sources north of the Limpopo River that it cannot be excluded from any study of tropical African labor.

[14] Meredyth Hyde-Clarke, "The Labour Problem: Britain's Research into Human Relations," *The Times British Colonies Review*, London, Autumn 1954, p. 8.

[15] P. H. Gulliver, *Labour Migration in a Rural Economy: A Study of the Ngoni and Ndendeuli of Southern Tanganyika* (*East African Studies*, No. 6), East African Institute of Social Research, Kampala, Uganda, 1955, p. ii.

[16] *Ibid.*

rural occupations. In Uganda, more than 100,000 laborers came across the western borders (from Ruanda-Urundi, the Belgian Congo and the Republic of Sudan) in search of work. Here, too, most of them gravitated to the more prosperous countrysides. It is probable that the migrations of farm workers in and out of the Republic of Sudan were of the same order of size.

However, taking tropical Africa as a whole, it is the towns rather than the mines, the plantations and the farms that draw the biggest crowds. In the late 1950s the "European" city of Nairobi had an African labor force of over 50,000; Léopoldville had one of over 100,000, and so did Salisbury. (In the mid-1940s the corresponding figures were roughly 15,000, 25,000 and 20,000.) All told, there are certainly not less than 2 million African workers living in tropical African towns.[17] Of this number, at least half and perhaps three quarters may be regarded as migrants — in the sense at least that they do not regard the town as "home." [18] With new factories, businesses and government agencies being opened in almost every town worthy of the name, it seems certain that the volume of labor moving in and out of the towns will go on swelling. Such a prospect is not without its anxieties, for laborer, employer and administrator alike.

STABILITY OF EMPLOYMENT

Up to now, the typical term worked by the migrant laborer has been measured in months rather than years. In many areas, mostly rural, it has been no more than six to eight months. Such a short term has many advantages from the laborer's point of view. It enables him to keep an eye on his land and to do the heavy work of felling trees and burning bush and, perhaps, the plowing. It also enables him to keep up most of his social as well as his economic obligations to his family and age group, and to have plenty of leisure. There is very little to be said for the short term from the employer's point of view, however. Skills, whether of the hand or the head, are seldom developed in a matter of months. The training of a man to do even the simplest of new things, such as pushing a wheelbarrow, frequently takes an amount of time out of all proportion to the gains to be derived by the employer.

On the mines, the labor term has generally been somewhat longer. This allowed the employer to get a better return on his investment and the employee to get more money, but it did not allow the employee to per-

[17] The number may be considerably higher. Trewartha and Zelinsky estimate that over 10 million people live in towns; not more than a million, at the most, can be non-Africans.

[18] It has been estimated that only some 20 per cent of the Africans now living in the towns of Southern Rhodesia intend *not* to go back to the bush in the long run. Much the same conclusion may be drawn from studies made in the Republic of Guinea, Northern Rhodesia, southern Nigeria, and central Africa as a whole.

form his social responsibility to his family or to ensure that his land was maintained in the best tribal tradition. And it was still not long enough, so the argument went, to warrant provision of married quarters and other desirable services by the employer. Furthermore, as there was no guarantee that the employee would come back to the same mine, the employer was not disposed to waste time teaching him intricate jobs. Of course, some migrants did, and do, come back, again and again, but it is commonly said of these that, while they are away, they lose such skills as they have come to possess. The need to teach them all over again is an additional reason for not teaching them anything very difficult or laborious.

Just how wasteful of time, effort and money the migrant system can be may be gleaned from a case history made a few years ago by Houghton. The home of this man is extra-tropical, but that is of small consequence; the man's name is legion, his habitat almost anywhere in sub-Saharan Africa.

The man was born in 1892. In 1908, at the age of 16, he took his first "migrant" job. From then until 1949 when his case history closed, he took fifteen such jobs (the average duration of which was 16 months) and thirteen rest periods (averaging 19 months in duration) at his home. Nine of the fifteen jobs were in different places. None of the fifteen was nearer than 700 miles from home; three were more than 800 miles away and one, in Southwest Africa, was 1,200 miles away.

While there is evidence that the African migrant worker is willing to work for longer periods now than he was forty or fifty years ago, it is patchy. Some employers can point to remarkable decreases in their labor turnover. On the mines of the Union Minière du Haut-Katanga, for instance, the number of workers with at least ten years of service rose from approximately 2,000 in 1941 to approximately 9,500 in 1955, representing a percentage increase from 14 to 45. And whereas in 1925 it was necessary to recruit 96 fresh laborers each year to have 100 constantly at work on the mines, in 1955 the corresponding figure was 7. Even in some of the much newer Southern Rhodesian plants the turnover is now down to 25 per cent a year, and getting lower. On the Witwatersrand mines, on the other hand, the average duration of an African's service is still less than twelve months, the turnover being more than 110 per cent a year. Turnover figures of the same order of magnitude are also being reported from the mines of Southern Rhodesia, Nigeria, Ghana and Angola, and from the plantations of west, central and east Africa.

Various reasons are advanced for these sharp differences of experience, the chief of them being the quality of management, the background and marital status of the worker, the nature of the work done, the basis of payment (e.g., by time or stint), opportunities for advancement, and the kind of accommodation provided. Possibly no two employers would agree on the order of relative importance of these factors. Some employers would be reluctant to attach much importance to any of them.

The majority, however, would probably be willing to concede that at least two of these factors, namely, marital status and accommodation, cannot be left out of their reckoning entirely.

If there is one conviction that is held by employers of labor more widely than another it is that married labor is more stable than unmarried labor. It is a conviction that many employers can back with figures. On the Wankie coal mines of Southern Rhodesia the average married worker stays more than ten times as long as the average single worker. At the Bata shoe factory in Gwelo in the same colony, the average turnover among the unmarried workers in the mid-1950s was approximately 10 per cent a month, but many of the married workers had completed ten years' service. On the Copperbelt-Katanga mines there are many married workers who have completed twenty-five years' service, and are now enjoying a well-paid retirement.

What is the explanation of this circumstance? The fact that married men have more to work for, and more need of money, is no doubt part of the explanation — but not the whole of it, for there are mines, factories and shops that can report no comparable figures. What appears to be equally important is whether or not the married worker can live with his family. Where married accommodation is available, if only a single room in a barrack-like block or a mud-and-thatch shanty, the turnover of married labor commonly proves to be lower than where such accommodation is not available. Where more ample accommodation is available, and with it a backyard in which the woman, or women, of the household can grow their customary kitchen crops, and where a family finds it possible to live among its own linguistic kin, the turnover is almost invariably lower than where such accommodation is not available. Where the worker is able to buy his home on an installment basis, or a plot of land on which to build his home, it tends to decline still further. "House ownership," a European member of the Nyasaland Legislative Council said in a recent interview, "offers the greatest hope [of increased labor stability]: an African will work harder, and longer, to own a house than for any other thing." Judging by the impressive African housing developments already complete and under way on most of the large mines and plantations and around the perimeter of most large cities, many employers share his opinion.

THE PROBLEM OF AFRICAN ADVANCEMENT

PRODUCTIVITY FACTOR

There is more to the African labor problem than the turning of migrants into "settlers." The fact that a worker may live — as many do in some areas — with his family on, or near to, his job in a three-room house complete with tap water, flush toilet, street lighting and garden may well make him a more contented worker than the man who has only a bed space in a waterless, lightless and loveless shanty. It does not necessarily mean that he is a more productive worker, and it is more productive workers that constitute Africa's biggest economic need today.

No one goes far in tropical Africa without hearing, and seeing, evidence of lethargy, shiftlessness, unreliability and incompetence. In the opinion of many employers these qualities are almost as apparent today as they were a generation ago. In the *Rhodesian Farmer Year Book* for 1953 it is contended, for example, that "in the course of the last 30 years there has been remarkably little improvement in the standard of efficiency displayed by the Native Worker." And none can say that in the interval strenuous efforts have not been made to increase the efficiency of the Rhodesian African. As the Secretary for Native Affairs in Southern Rhodesia points out in his annual report for 1953, employers have tried "better feeding, improved housing, social and recreational amenities, higher wages [and] incentive systems." The sum of all these changes, he argues, "is a demand for more and more while doing less and less." Give an unskilled African more money and you will get less work out of him, because he is simply a "target" worker. Once the target money has been earned, whether the target is a bicycle, a banjo or a wife, he will quit. (And it is true that when the bonus on tea picking in Nyasaland was increased 20 per cent some time ago, the daily intake at one of the Cholo factories went down by 10 per cent.) Give him a better house and he will sublet part of it to some of his many "brothers" and soon turn it into more of a hovel than the house he came from. Give him better tools and he will either ruin them or sell them. (Kenya householders who have bought power mowers to cut down on garden labor have been known to complain that the gasoline in them is traded for cigarettes and beer and that spare parts are turned into hoes, knives, etc.) Give him an automobile or a truck and sooner or later he will drive it to a standstill. (And it must be confessed that the ratio of "going" to "gone" — including wrecked vehicles is uncommonly low in many parts of tropical Africa.)

So runs one side of the record, the side that is most frequently played in conversations and discussions. On the other side is the stirring chorus of the employers who claim that they are already getting good work out of their African employees, that it is getting better, and that there is no reason why, in the long run, the "average African employee" should not become as productive and as versatile as the "average European employee." In British East Africa, the Belgian Congo, Southern Rhodesia, Kenya and elsewhere, manufacturers, mining officials and other employers, and officials of trade schools as well, testify to the amenability of African workers. Africans, they will frequently tell you, enjoy repetitive work; monotony doesn't bother them; they have no need for diversion in conversation, radio programs, soccer pools or parties; they learn quickly and produce as much in mills and factories as the Europeans working beside them.

Those who speak thus of their African labor hold that the productivity problem, in addition to being an accommodation problem, is a management problem. What makes for higher productivity are opportunities for advancement, helpful supervision and exemplary managerial conduct, quite as much as — perhaps more than — good wages, health checkups and nice houses. The knowledge that an African worker, if he has it in him, will be allowed to do the kind of job usually reserved for the European is, so they maintain, likely to be more of an incentive to increased effort than the knowledge that he can make good money spending his days filling tubs at the bottom of a mine. Not many Africans may readily make the grade, or want to, but the fact that some can, and do, is said to have a tonic effect on the morale of many a labor force. Likewise, those who take this view maintain that an African is more inclined to work well for a man who, in Laurens van der Post's phrase, has "the right look in his eye" than for the man who thinks of his employee only as a soulless, unfeeling "tool" to be kept in shape by mechanical care and maintenance.

Many of these satisfied employers also hold that the productivity problem is a training problem; that you get higher productivity only when you give higher education to all those who are capable of profiting by it — systematic instruction in technical and trade schools and apprenticeship programs in trades and professions. But education of this kind is expensive. It requires more elaborate accommodation and equipment than elementary or even secondary education. It also requires a high ratio of instructors to instructed, and highly skilled, well-paid instructors — mainly expatriates at that, for few Africans at present are equal to such responsibilities. At a time when most African territories are still a long way from providing universal elementary education, the rising demand for job training is more easily explained than satisfied.

In the majority of industries and areas training until recently was done, when it was done at all, on the job. And it was done haphazardly. The employee picked up his knowledge and skill by watching his supervisor, or his more experienced neighbor. While this hit-or-miss method is still pretty general, it is on the way out. As a result of the increasing complexity of most industrial operations and in conformity with the now generally accepted policy of African advancement, trade and technical training institutions are being established in nearly every territory. Some of these institutions are the result of mission initiative, some are financed by private industry, and some by government funds. Almost all of them are pint-sized, but given enough pints, even an empty reservoir can be filled eventually.

The kind of instruction offered by them varies from place to place, and from industry to industry. It may be no more than a once-over-lightly kind of briefing on the operation of a particular tool. It may, on the other hand, be a complete schooling — first in general education, then in elementary trade training, and later in the theory and practice of specific technologies.[19]

RACE FACTOR

We shall have occasion to refer frequently to the race factor when we come to deal (in Volume II) with the changing society and polity of tropical Africa. Here we are concerned solely with the extent to which "race" enters into the reckoning of a man's eligibility for a job, and his promotion to a better one. And by "race" we mean in the present context, not so much what the word means to an anthropologist, as what the everyday user of the word in Africa means, namely, skin color and culture (or its absence — judged by European criteria).

Needless to say, there are marked territorial differences in the extent to which "race" enters into such matters. While some of these differences reflect differences in the legal status of European and non-European, in most cases they reflect to a far greater extent differences of social attitude and custom. Thus, you will look almost in vain through the lawbooks of the Federation of Rhodesia and Nyasaland for signs of "racial" legislation, but whereas in Nyasaland an African will probably drive your train and serve you in the post office, in Northern Rhodesia he may serve you in the post office but will certainly not drive your train, and in Southern Rhodesia he will most probably do neither. Even within a single territory, variations commonly exist in the use made of laborers of different races. For instance, in some Southern Rhodesian industries Africans operate the cranes and the bulldozers, while in others it is the Asians and Coloreds who do this kind of work, and in still others, the Europeans.

Not all such differences are due to race, however. Some are due to the absence, or scarcity, of training facilities that would enable the African to take on "European" jobs. Thus the absence of African bank clerks in the Bank of Angola is readily explained by reference to the school enrollment figures. Some of the differences arise from the differing attitudes of Europeans toward a particular kind of work. The average Portuguese farmer in tropical Africa has not the least objection to laboring with his own hands or, for that matter, doing everything himself. The average Belgian or British settler, on the other hand, automatically assumes that Africans will do most of the manual work for him.

Where race is a factor, it does not follow that any one ingredient of race will be more potent than any other. Culture can be, and often is, as important as color. Not infrequently the thing that gives it its greatest

[19] See Volume II, Chapter 16, for a discussion of trades training.

force is neither culture nor color, but conceit. Sooner or later, each tribe, group and nation, it seems, tries to create man in the image of its own God. It is therefore not surprising that race is a factor in the African advancement equation even in some territories which, to the casual visitor at least, are composed of people of homogeneous stock. Liberia, Ghana and Nigeria are examples. Many Americo-Liberians find it difficult to conceal their disdain for the Afro-Liberians who live all around them. Until recently the Liberian government, which is virtually run by the former, made little effort to advance the economic status of the latter and still less to utilize the skills of those who had advanced. In Ghana it is possible to sense a similar attitude on the part of many of the sophisticated southerners toward their more homespun northern neighbors. In Nigeria the Yorubas and Ibos, likewise of the south, have long been inclined to feel that the government of the whole land should be upon their shoulders.

Race consciousness is even more of a factor in those countries where the indigenous peoples are derived from widely differing stocks. It is especially noticeable in the Republic of Sudan and in Ethiopia. In the Sudan the shrouded Moslemized northerners, many of whom have Negro as well as Arab blood, tend to think of themselves as superior to the still largely pagan, Nilotic southerners, most of whom go unclothed and couldn't care less. The town dwellers with "their brittle veneer of western education" — to use John Gunther's phrase — habitually dub the jungle and desert dwellers as "savages" lacking both the wit and the willingness to do a decent day's work. In Ethiopia the Amharic people of the central highland region continually let it be known that they are the elite. No matter how dark their skin, or their perceptions, they think of themselves as "white" and everybody else (except the Europeans and Americans, who rate "pink"!) as black. And, like the Americo-Liberians, they continue to do most of the ruling — at all levels.

Race probably takes on its greatest significance as a labor factor in those territories where nonindigenous peoples have been settled long enough and in large enough numbers to develop fixed assumptions about work — one of which is that some jobs are in the domain of the indigenous peoples, and some in the domain of the nonindigenous. So long as these assumptions remain unwritten and uncodified, there is a possibility they will be flouted by the employer of the bright young machinist who has asked for a chance to supervise an assembly line, or the well-informed typesetter who claims he can read proof. Indeed, many employers, if left to themselves, are only too happy to have an African demonstrate his competence since it means that they can cut labor costs by replacing high-priced with lower-priced help. The trouble starts when these assumptions get written into the laws of governments and trade unions. Then African advancement of an evolutionary kind becomes much more difficult, for the division of the labor field between Europeans and non-Europeans is clearly defined, carefully guarded by the European workers' watchdogs, and not readily amenable to "boundary" adjustment.

During the past decade or so the problem of what to do in such circumstances has exercised many minds, and nowhere more deeply than in the Rhodesias. While the principle of African advancement has found growing acceptance among all the mining companies and the members of the European labor unions there, including those of the highly influential Northern Rhodesia Mine Workers Union, the obstacles to such advancement are still formidable. The biggest obstacle is unquestionably the insistence of these unions on the principles of "equal pay for equal work" and "no fragmentation of jobs." To adhere to these principles would, in the opinion of most of the companies, be calamitous. If Africans were to be paid the same wages as Europeans, the effect, having regard to the cost-of-living levels current in African society, would be the same as if the European labor force were to be paid at the fantastic rate of £15,000 per capita per year. Furthermore, if the companies were to pay skilled Africans at the prevailing European rates, these Africans, so the argument goes, would either find themselves saddled with hordes of hangers-on, or they would push off into the bush with their easily gotten gains and quit daily or monthly paid work in favor of petty trading. If employers were required to pay a trained African the same rates and give him the same conditions as they give their European labor, very few of them would use African labor at all, since they know from experience, it is claimed, that the European is more reliable and responsible in his handling of emergencies, and more productive.[20]

Scarcely less of an obstacle is the unwillingness of those concerned, both in labor and management, to open up enough "European" job categories to give the talk of advancement more than a token value. The September 1955 agreement between the Northern Rhodesia Mine Workers Union and the mining companies carries promise for the future, for it spoke of throwing open jobs at all levels to all races on the basis of skill only, and of giving the African, when the time comes for him to assume high responsibilities, the same rates of pay and conditions of service as Europeans doing the same work. While this is in one sense a concession to the European union's fears that cheap labor policies might be behind the companies' support of African advancement, it is in another sense a step forward, being in effect an admission that it is not possible indefinitely to fly in the face of world opinion and that to refuse to relax the color bar would mean endless unrest on the Copperbelt — and elsewhere in central Africa. However, at the end of 1958 only 679 Africans

[20] The relatively small use of Africans in mining may in part reflect this line of thinking. Between 1949 and 1954, the percentage increase in African manpower on the Copperbelt was 30; in European manpower, 49.

had been promoted to "advanced" jobs on the Copperbelt mines, and only 318 were undergoing training, or had completed training, for such jobs.[21]

NON-AFRICAN LABOR

The non-African population of tropical Africa is, as we have seen, very small — less than one per cent of the total. Its occupational role, however, is anything but small. It is the Europeans who, with some help from the Asians, have designed and supervised the building of every transportation and power facility, every industrial establishment, and most of the educational, welfare and cultural institutions. It is the Europeans who, again with some help here and there from the Asians, have run them and who, for the most part, continue to do so. It is likewise the Europeans, with generally less help from the Asians, who have maintained order and trained Africans to be teachers and traders, clerks and clergy, policemen and soldiers, and, not least, politicians. It is also the Europeans who, notwithstanding their widely advertised taboo about manual labor, have tamed forests, turned intractable bush into pasture and plowland, raised most of the export crops (and many of the domestic ones), and shown the African how to make two ears of corn grow in place of one and raise a dozen crops where none grew before. And it is the Asians who, with some help from the Europeans, have handled the bulk of the retail business, and supplied most of the artisan and semiskilled labor force.

EUROPEANS

At the most, the number of Europeans gainfully employed in tropical Africa is half a million. This figure includes settlers in town and country, workers on short-term contract in mine, factory and business, soldiers and civil servants. Possibly not more than half of these think of themselves as permanent residents; the rest expect one day to "go home" to Europe, the Union of South Africa, or elsewhere. Most of them would rank as skilled workers, and, by the standard of their country of origin, most of them live well. Most of them have servants, a larder well stocked with food and drink, and a car.[22] Most of them work a five-day week and a 48-week year, or less. Many live in homes provided for them at subeconomic rents, if not free, and receive heavily subsidized or free medical, social and recreational services, and free transportation for themselves and their families when they go on long leave. Nearly all of them qualify for good pensions after twenty-five to thirty years of continuous service. It is possible that some live too well — for their own good, their employ-

[21] See *Northern Rhodesia Chamber of Mines Yearbook, 1958*, Kitwe, Northern Rhodesia, 1959, p. 12.

[22] It is possible that the highest car:population ratio in the world exists in the European sector of towns such as Léopoldville, Elisabethville, Nairobi and Salisbury.

ers' and the Africans'. Thus, it is open to question whether the copper companies in Northern Rhodesia can much longer afford to pay their European employees a wage on which savings up to £1,000 a year are possible.[23] It is equally open to question whether the things some workers do with their money are in the interest of their health, or calculated to help the African onlooker to a better understanding of his growing responsibilities.

Even so, it is not the easiest thing in the world to find Europeans willing to work in tropical Africa. Many government departments have less staff than the establishment calls for. Many farms and plantations lack adequate supervisory and managerial personnel, and the response to the periodic search for more settlers in such territories as Kenya and the Rhodesias becomes almost progressively poorer. The reason is fairly obvious: the metropolitan countries can offer the ambitious young man full employment, good if not high wages, social security benefits, a mature cultural environment in which to raise his family without hazard to their health and education, plenty of like-minded neighbors, and ready-made entertainment. While tropical Africa can match some of these drawing cards, no part can match all of them. And even if there were parts that could, they might still have their labor problems, since not many Europeans have a liking for the role of trail blazer or national publicity agent, let alone home guard or martyr. Some recent happenings in tropical Africa have done nothing to increase its appeal.

And when the European worker has been found, there is the difficulty of getting him to work well. On the whole he is a rather indifferent producer. In many cases it is easy to see why. Working days tend to be shorter, and holiday periods longer, than in most Western European and North American establishments. Climatic conditions are frequently more conducive to absenteeism than to sustained output. The toll taken by minor ailments — colds, low fevers, stomach disorders and so on — is undoubtedly higher than in middle latitudes. The reluctance of most European factory, mine and plantation workers to do manual work is also a factor, and likely to go on being one until the ordinary African has acquired much greater dexterity, and the habit of working faster. At the executive level likewise, productivity tends to sag in some areas and in many individuals. "West coast memory" is a widely invoked phenomenon to explain failure to do a job or recall a fact; and it is not confined to west Africa. Even in the highlands of east and central Africa there are many brain workers — teachers, clergymen, journalists, scientists, administrators, doctors — who insist that their energy and output decline unless they get away to the coast, or overseas, every two or three years.

[23] The average earnings per European mine employee for the year ended June 30, 1958 were £1,699; for the "boom" year ended June 30, 1956 they were £2,295. See *Northern Rhodesia Chamber of Mines Yearbook, 1958,* p. 37.

The cares white workers have are not merely physical and psychological. Many have financial ones, too. This is particularly true of those of the "French" areas, which received a large influx of European (mostly French) construction workers after World War II. L. Gray Cowan reports on their plight in his paper prepared for this study:

The booming construction industry in French Africa since 1945 has meant that jobs have been available . . . for large numbers of artisans, and as a result many more men have come to Africa than are likely to be needed permanently. Most of them have brought families and fully expect to make Africa their home with only occasional visits to France . . . The drop in the construction rate since 1953 has made jobs harder to find . . . In the larger cities such as Dakar a social class is rapidly evolving which strongly resembles the "poor whites" of the southern United States.

These workers came with very little capital and they have acquired none, for living costs are high and wages no more than adequate. Consequently, "they have not the financial means to withstand a long period of unemployment and are the more willing to accept posts which lower their living standards." In the circumstances it is not surprising that many "small whites," as the French call them, are violently anti-African.

The largest concentrations of European workers occur in the "settler" areas, and mostly in or near the larger towns and mines. More than one third of the employed Europeans of Kenya live in or near Nairobi. In Southern Rhodesia about the same percentage of employed Europeans live and work in the two towns of Salisbury and Bulawayo. In Northern Rhodesia over one fourth of the employed Europeans work on the Copperbelt. In the Belgian Congo there are heavy European concentrations in Katanga and in Léopoldville, and in Senegal in the Dakar area. Only in the Malagasy Republic, Uganda, Tanganyika and Angola is a sizable proportion of the economically active European population to be found in country areas — a fact related, in each instance, to the dominance of commercial agriculture in the European sector of the economy.

In colonial and ex-colonial British West Africa the working European population is much smaller, and because these are not settler territories, the *non*-working European population is smaller still. In the whole of Nigeria, with its more than 32 million population, there were in 1957 less than 13,000 Europeans, of whom around 10,000 were employed. In Ghana, with its approximately 4.8 million population, the corresponding figures were nearer 8,000 and 6,000. And before long they are almost certain to become less.

The other independent territories, the Republic of Guinea, Liberia, Ethiopia and the Republic of Sudan, also find it convenient — perhaps imperative — to make use of non-African manpower. In Liberia most of this manpower is American. Americans help to train the Liberian Frontier Force and run the Free Port of Monrovia and the international airport (Robertsfield). Through the agency of the International Cooperation Administration — the successor to "Point Four," the name by which most Liberians still refer to it — they help direct several phases of the country's educational, agricultural and research activities. Americans also own and manage the Firestone Plantations and the Liberia Mining Company, without which the government of the country could not operate.

Ethiopia makes even wider use of outside help. In fact, so many Europeans and Americans work there for the government that it is probably true to say that more Europeans work for Africans than *vice versa*. Certainly more nationalities are represented on the government payroll than on that of any other country in Africa. There are Americans in the Ethiopian Airlines, the Army, the ministries of Commerce, Finance and Foreign Affairs, the State Planning Board, the Imperial Ethiopian College of Agriculture, the Imperial Ethiopian Mapping and Geography Institute, and in the Royal Household itself. And, as in Liberia, many Americans are serving the country's urgent economic and social needs through agencies of the United States government. Swedes serve in the Military Air Force, in the schools, in the High Court and the Telecommunications Authority. There are British in the High Court and the police force; Norwegians in Her Majesty's Handicraft School; Canadians in the schools and in the ministries of Finance and Commerce. A score of other nations, including some from behind the Iron Curtain, are represented.

As for the Republic of Sudan, although it was pretty well "Sudanized" by the time of its independence in 1956, it, too, finds itself short of many necessary skills and the people to exercise them. It is especially short of teachers, engineers and technologists of all kinds. For this reason, the government continues to employ about half as many expatriates as in the last days of the condominium.

The same sort of thing has been happening in the Republic of Guinea and will almost certainly happen to every other African territory that becomes independent.

ASIANS

The number of employed Asians is even smaller than the number of employed Europeans. It is probably not more than 200,000. Like the Europeans, the Asians work at practically every kind of trade and profession. There are Asian farmers and planters; Asian civil servants, policemen and soldiers; Asian doctors, lawyers, teachers, judges and editors; Asian politicians; Asian merchants (wholesale and retail), building contractors, and money lenders; and Asian artisans and laborers (semiskilled or skilled for the most part).

As workers the Asians differ from the general run of Europeans in a number of respects. They are willing to work harder, and for less. Most

Asian artisans think nothing of doing a 12-hour day six or even seven days a week, 52 weeks in the year; and most shopkeepers do the same. To get started in their chosen line of business, they are willing to go anywhere, and to live in almost any kind of hovel. Many go on living in hovels even after they have made good. They are generally frugal as well, saving every cent they can for investment in loan services to Africans, in real estate and business expansion — often with spectacular results.[24]

It follows that the Asian worker is not much liked by either the European or the African worker. The European resents being unable to compete with him in a whole range of marginal jobs, and even in some which he used to consider in his domain, such as custom tailoring, hairdressing, motor maintenance and electrical work. The more ambitious African resents being unable to break the Asian's near-monopoly, which he is most reluctant to lose, in the fields of trading and artisanship.

While the governments of those territories which have a substantial Asian population — Uganda, Kenya, Zanzibar, Tanganyika, Southern Rhodesia, Northern Rhodesia and Nyasaland — are appreciative of the role of Asian labor in building up the economy, they have no desire to see it greatly extended. On the contrary, in every government there are those who would like to see it immediately curtailed. Most of the affected governments have already introduced legislation restricting the further immigration of Asians.

THE WORKER'S WAGES

All that has been said so far has a bearing on the subject of wages. For what men earn is related, among other things, to what they are worth to the economy; and what they are worth is related to productivity, which in turn is related to environment and skill, custom and attitude. Hence it is necessary to look at this subject in a social as well as in an economic context. Partly because of this complexity, the subject of wages is one that is more than usually hard to see steadily and whole. What applies to one territory, industry and category frequently does not apply to the next. Employers seldom have the same viewpoint as employees; and not all employers or all employees have the same views on what is or is not a living wage, let alone a fair wage. To compound the viewer's troubles, the objects of his interest keep changing their posture and shape.

But though the picture is still blurred and unfinished, certain features of it can easily be identified.

The first and, to a Westerner, the most striking of these is the smallness of the average African worker's cash wage. It is true that what is small

[24] A recent east African survey showed that about 75 per cent of Nairobi was Asian-owned and that in every town the majority of both land and property was in Asian hands.

in most parts of America is not small in most parts of Africa. However, even in countries like Bechuanaland and British Somaliland, where life is lived simply and where most of a man's necessities can be supplied very cheaply, a cash wage of 20 shillings a week cannot by any stretch of the mind be reckoned as riches. The same applies to a wage of between $1 and $2 a week in Liberia, and 30 to 40 shillings a week in Kenya and the Federation of Rhodesia and Nyasaland. It will cover taxes, soap, shirts, shoes, tobacco, and an occasional beer party; it does not leave much for a bicycle, a better home or the bank.

A second and scarcely less general feature is the existence of "hidden emoluments." In most places and in most occupations where unskilled and semiskilled employment is to be had, cash forms only a part of the laborer's income. Services, subsidies and rations make up the balance — in many cases a very considerable balance. On the Firestone Plantations in Liberia every one of the 25,000 to 30,000 workers is entitled to free housing and medical care, and to purchase food, kerosene, tobacco, native cloth and other essentials in the company's stores at prices very much below those in the open market.[25] For many years the Copperbelt mines provided not only free housing and free medical services but also free food rations for the great majority (about 88 per cent) of their African employees and such members of their families as resided on the mines. These rations included maize meal (the staple food of most of the mine laborers), meat, vegetables, fruit, bread, sugar, fats, salt, tea, nuts and beans. According to F. Grévisse, the Union Minière du Haut-Katanga, which provides much the same services for its employees, has been spending in recent years about 12,000 francs, or $240, annually on each unskilled mine worker, his wife and child for "maintenance" only.

The thinking behind these paternal practices is not difficult to follow. In the long run a worker is only as good as his health, and his health is unlikely to be better than his diet, hygiene and shelter. Since the family man is known to be a steadier and more responsive worker than the single man, what could be more rational than to increase the attractiveness of steady work by offering the married man family quarters, his wife maternity care, and his children the chance of a better life?

A third feature is the big gap between African and non-African wage levels — after every allowance has been made for hidden income. It is a gap that will take some closing. Consider, for instance, the position on the Copperbelt, where the African worker is as well done-by as anywhere in tropical Africa. In 1958 the average monthly earnings of the European mine worker were roughly £141. The average monthly earnings of the African mine worker in that year, including the value of food

[25] Rice, the food staple of most of the workers, was being sold at $3 per hundred-pound bag in 1954 — the price it was twenty years earlier — as against $8 to $10 in the open market.

provided, were somewhat less than £17. It is true that some African underground workers were earning over £36 a month, but this still left the average European underground worker with an almost 5:1 lead over the top African worker. And the top European underground worker had more than a 10:1 lead over the top African underground worker. But, on the whole, this type of disparity does not cause as much discontent as the disparity that all too commonly exists between the rates for the so-called "ragged edge" and transitional jobs which the African is taking over from the non-African — jobs which he believes he can do just as well. In some cases the European rate for these jobs is three times the African rate.

Comparable disparities could be cited from most of the multiracial territories. At Dakar (Senegal), for instance, the basic salary in the mid-1950s of a European clerk employed in a commercial house ranged from the equivalent of $170 a month to $300 a month, depending on his length of service in the country. The basic salary of an African clerk employed in the same kind of work ranged from the equivalent of $35 a month to $150.

Those who fix these differentials have their reasons for them, including the customarily lower productivity of the African worker, the impossibility of getting the European to work for "African" wages, and the avowed inability of their enterprises to survive the application of the "equal pay for equal work" principle. But compelling as these reasons may be, they do not often carry conviction to the heart of the African.

The even greater differentials in African wage rates than in non-African wage rates constitute a fourth feature of the picture. Not many Africans are as yet earning high salaries; but those who are, such as the African members of the legislatures and administrations, corporation officials and college instructors, commonly have the same basic income as their European associates. Thus, African and non-African members of the Legislative Council of Kenya all received in 1958 an annual salary of £500 plus a constituency allowance of £120, a subsistence allowance of £4 a day for each day they were engaged on government business, and "travelling allowances at government rates." This, though in no way princely, is big money by any African criterion. At the other end of the scale come the anonymous thousands of unskilled and semiskilled domestic workers, farm workers, road workers and so on, who earn perhaps a tithe of what the lowest-paid non-African workers earn. Whereas the spread of non-African wages and salaries is of the order of ten times the minimum, the spread of African wages and salaries is of the order of one hundred times the minimum. Such disparities may not yet deeply touch the conscience of the "haves," but they are beginning to cause a stir among the "have-nots." In their eyes it is one thing for the expatriate European to live in the manner to which he is accustomed, or even better, but quite another for the privileged African to live in the manner of the European.

What of tomorrow's wage picture? Whatever its composition, we can be reasonably sure that it will show at least three characteristics.

1. A rising wage level. It could hardly be otherwise of course — and not merely for the cynic's reason that when wages are as low as they are in tropical Africa there is only one way for them to move! They will rise because the employee will demand that they do and will be organized to give teeth to his demand.[26] And they will rise because the employer is willing to do almost anything to increase the productivity and efficiency of his labor. While not every employer believes that higher wages will bring this about, very few believe that higher productivity and efficiency can be brought about without them. Some are willing to go further and concede that one of the main causes of the African's disinclination to work harder than he does is that, characteristically, the relationship between wages and prices is such that leisure seems a better buy than almost anything else; that men will only come to work harder, better and longer when this relationship is more favorable; and that since it is inconceivable that such a change can be brought about by a depressing of the price level, their only hope is to boost the wage level.

This is being done in many places. Between 1949 and 1958 African wages on the Copperbelt increased by over 200 per cent and their purchasing power by well over 100 per cent. In Uganda in 1954 unskilled labor rates in the towns increased by 20 to 40 per cent (the cost-of-living index increasing by only two points, from 115 to 117) and in 1955 rates for skilled and semiskilled workers increased by 27 to 38 per cent. There was, over the same two years, an appreciable increase in the percentage of Africans earning higher wages. Among construction workers, for example, the number in the 61-to-80-shillings-a-month wage group rose from 6.7 per cent of the total in 1954 to 23.8 per cent in 1955, while the number in the 41-to-50-shillings-a-month group fell from 22.2 per cent of the total to 12 per cent.

To encourage this upward trend, most African administrations now have the power to pass wage-fixing bills. Some of them have not hesitated to make good use of their power. Thus, in the years preceding the "Community" era, the French divided each of the 15 territories over which they had jurisdiction into wage zones. In each territory a general minimum wage (normally an hourly rate) was established for each zone. Except in the French Cameroons and Niger, there was one minimum for agricultural workers and one for nonagricultural workers, the difference being based mainly on the fact that permissible hours of work for these two categories varied. In all 15 territories the maximum amount which might be deducted from the minimum wage for rations supplied in accordance with the law was prescribed. In most of the territories the maximum amount which an employer might legally deduct when he

---

[26] For a discussion of trade unionism, see Volume II, Chapter 18.

provided housing in accordance with the law was also laid down. The legislation also covered the rates to be paid for overtime and for work on Sundays and holidays. In several of the territories where no collective agreements between labor and management existed, the administration laid down fixed minimum wage rates for specific occupations, such as domestic service and dock work. Where collective agreements did exist these were frequently given the force of law.

It is true that the minima — and the same applies to those set by the non-French administrations — were low by almost any yardstick.[27] Moreover, in many cases they were calculated on the basis of what it cost to maintain the worker only — and not his family — in the necessities of life. But here, as in all species of infancy, it is the first step that counts. As the African comes to have a larger say in the ordering of his affairs, we can be quite sure that he will see to it that many other steps are taken along the legislative road to fair wages.

2. A growing interest, among African and non-African workers alike, in fringe benefits — the prosperity bonus, the family allowance, the paid holiday, the pension, educational and recreational amenities, medical care and in-service training. It is true that among employers there are considerable differences of opinion about the wisdom, and even the feasibility, of providing so much for so many. Take, for instance, the matter of the family allowance. Whereas most non-British administrations favor the family allowance and employ it, the British administrations are generally opposed to it on the grounds, among others, that remuneration should be related to efficiency and not fertility, and that it is so much easier for the African worker to produce a large "family" than for the administration to prove its paternity.

The employees, too, have differences of opinion. The Belgian Congo administration has found that family allowances do not sit well with many of their childless and unmarried workers. Are not they the poor ones who should be helped? The married workers at least have wives, one or more, to work for them, and in most cases able-bodied children too. Why, then, should more be given to those who already have so much? (In 1954 alone the Belgian government gave out to some 413,000 employed family heads the equivalent of nearly $16 million.)

But here also the objectors are apt to find themselves hopelessly outmatched; first, because in many parts of tropical Africa labor is already a "seller's market" and likely to go on being so and, second, because labor unions all over the Western world are obtaining more and more fringe benefits for their members and are set upon helping their African colleagues do the same. So far, most of the employers have kept well ahead of their employees' expectations of such benefits.

[27] In 1955 the highest minimum wage in any French territory was approximately 16 cents an hour. In 1958 the corresponding wage in the Belgian Congo was 39 francs, or

3. A growing insistence on equal pay for equal work. This principle is already accepted in some multiracial territories. The *Code du Travail* promulgated on December 15, 1952 as the labor code for all of France's overseas territories declares, in Article 91, that "In equal conditions as regards work, skill and output, the same wage shall be payable to all workers irrespective of origin, sex, age and status." As we saw earlier, the same principle has also been recognized by some of the European mine workers' unions.

This is not to say that as yet the practice is as good as the principle. Indeed, if we are to accept the reasoning of numerous industrialists, including mine managers, the principle is not even practicable at the present time. Not just for financial reasons, either. There are many employers, both in and out of the mining industry, who would endorse the conviction of the Belgian Congo company director, expressed in a recent conversation, that

If the equal pay for equal work principle were put into practice now, it would produce a racism worse than any the region has known. The white worker would immediately think of himself as in competition with the black, instead of, as at present, in collaboration with him.

But good principles are hardy things; it takes more than logic to wilt them and adversity to kill them. They may flower sooner in some climates than in others, but they always flower. In tropical Africa it is possible that the principle of equal pay for equal work will flower only when the European is willing to take less pay, and the African to do more work.

---

approximately 78 cents, a day. This included the estimated value of rations, lodgings, etc., with which the wage earner was provided.

Date Due

FE 22 '64			
SE 20 '65			
SEP 2			
SEP 25 '65			
SEP 30 '65			
FEB 28 '69 IN			
MAR 3 '69 IN			
MAY 6 '76			
MAY 19 '76			
SEP 7 '76			
PRINTED IN U. S. A.			